# A Global Guide to Human Resource Management

*A Global Guide to Human Resource Management* is a concise HRM introductory text offering a uniquely non-region-specific approach to people management in international business organisations.

The book presents an alternative to standard managerial approaches, reflecting the perspectives of multiple stakeholders (workers, trade unions, states and governments, NGOs) to critically evaluate HRM in practice and, in so doing, enables students to make effective decisions in their own practice, wherever their careers take them. Its accessibility and concision make it well suited to short courses for non-HRM and non-business specialists. This text covers all major introductory topics for non-specialists, introducing the concept and purpose of HRM, through recruitment, people, skills, designing work, promoting health, rewarding success, and successful and ethical people management. This edition includes a new chapter on green HRM.

Rich with pedagogical features, the book includes five case studies per chapter to connect theory with practice. It is also supported with a range of instructor materials including online guest lectures, general discussion questions, a glossary, an index, and online documentaries that explain how to manage people. It is essential reading for students interested in Human Resources and Personnel Management, Organisational Behaviour and Development and Workplace Culture.

**Thomas Klikauer** is a Senior Lecturer in Human Resource Management at the Sydney Graduate School of Management at Western Sydney University, Australia.

# A Global Guide to Human Resource Management

## Managing Across Stakeholders

## Second Edition

## Thomas Klikauer

**Routledge**
Taylor & Francis Group

LONDON AND NEW YORK

Cover image: wildpixel

Second edition published 2022
by Routledge
4 Park Square, Milton Park, Abingdon, Oxon, OX14 4RN

and by Routledge
605 Third Avenue, New York, NY 10158

*Routledge is an imprint of the Taylor & Francis Group, an informa business*

First edition published by Red Globe Press 2018

*British Library Cataloguing-in-Publication Data*
A catalogue record for this book is available from the British Library

*Library of Congress Cataloging-in-Publication Data*
Names: Klikauer, Thomas, 1962- author.
Title: A global guide to human resource management : managing across stakeholders/Thomas Klikauer.
Description: 2nd edition. | Milton Park, Abingdon, Oxon; New York, NY : Routledge, 2022. | Includes bibliographical references and index.
Identifiers: LCCN 2021059447 | ISBN 9781032276632 (hardback) | ISBN 9781032276618 (paperback) | ISBN 9781003293637 (ebook)
Subjects: LCSH: Personnel management.
Classification: LCC HF5549 .K545 2022 | DDC 658.3–dc23/eng/20211214
LC record available at https://lccn.loc.gov/2021059447

ISBN: 978-1-032-27663-2 (hbk)
ISBN: 978-1-032-27661-8 (pbk)
ISBN: 978-1-003-29363-7 (ebk)

DOI: 10.4324/9781003293637

Typeset in Baskerville
by SPi Technologies India Pvt Ltd (Straive)

Access the Support Material: www.routledge.com/9781032276618

**This book is dedicated to**

*all the birds, beetles, bees, flora and fauna, people,*
*and nature soon to be destroyed by global warming.*

# Contents

# Figures

# Tables

# Case Studies

# Acknowledgements

My first thank you goes to my wife Katja Klikauer for proofreading the first edition of this textbook comprehensively and most thoroughly and for proofreading its new edition. I also thank Meg Young for proofreading Chapter 11. I am also most obliged to many HR managers attending my class and for their assistance on the subject of Human Resource Management. I am indebted to the initial referees for their most valuable input and suggestions. The first and second edition of the book has received no administrative, technical, editorial support or funding from the Western Sydney University or any other private or public source.

I am grateful to those at WSU who shielded me from the worst excesses of university Managerialism. This allowed me to write the initial textbook and the new edition. A sincere thank you goes to Renee Kovaliskis, Louise Ingersoll, and Jayne Bye from the Sydney Graduate School of Management.

My appreciation also goes to the German trade union foundation, the Hans-Böckler-Foundation (www.boeckler.de) for supporting my transition from tool-maker to academic, graduating from Bremen University (Germany), Boston University (USA), and Warwick University (UK). Finally, I would like to express my appreciation to Routledge's commissioning and production team and, above all, its editorial group at Routledge Publishing, Amy Laurens, Alex de Brauw for their kind help to get this book off the ground and for their semi-surgical dedication to transforming my manuscript into a presentable book.

# The Author

**Thomas Klikauer** is a Senior Lecturer at the Sydney Graduate School of Management, teaching MBC (Master of Business and Commerce) and more recently MBA (Master of Business Administration) students for more than a decade as well as undergraduate students for the previous decade. Before that, Dr. Klikauer worked in the German car industry also undertaking an internship (Detroit, USA).

He accomplished a BA at the Technical University Darmstadt and an MA at Bremen University (Germany). He also received an MA from Boston University (USA) and completed a PhD in Industrial and Business Studies at Warwick Business School (UK). Thomas Klikauer has well over 650 publications including ten books and those published in the British Journal of Industrial Relations, the Industrial Relations Journal, the International Journal of HRM, Critical Sociology, Thesis Eleven, The Journal of Economic and Public Finance, the Australian University's Review, Labour History, Holocaust Studies, Capital and Class, Management Philosophy. He also is a frequent contributor to Counterpunch.org, Buzzflash, BraveNewEurope, The Barricade, Coutercurrents, ZNet, etc. Married with two children, he lives in a beachside suburb of Sydney, Australia.

His book publications include: Media Capitalism (2021), Management Education (2017), Hegel's Moral Corporation (2015), Seven Moralities of Human Resource Management (2014), Managerialism – A Critique of An Ideology (2013), Seven Management Moralities (2012), Critical Management Ethics (2010), Management Communication – Communicative Ethics and Action (2008), and Communication and Management at Work (2007).

# 1    Introducing Global HRM

## What This Book Is About and How to Use It

This textbook is written for students, general managers of companies, and business organisations. It focuses on three things: (1) how to manage people in organisations; (2) as managing people is generally associated with HRM, the book explains what HRM is;[1] and (3) it outlines what HR managers do. This book is the synthesis of more than a decade's experience of teaching how to manage people under the common heading of HRM, which is taught as part of an MBA (Master of Business Administration).[2] Candidates on these degree programmes are predominantly from one of three groups:

1. **Baby Boomers**: born between 1946 and 1964;
2. **Gen-X**: born between late 1960s and 1980s; and
3. **Gen-Y**: born between late 1980s and early 2000s, often called Millennials.

Many master's candidates come from companies[3] such as AAPT, Aldi, Allianz Insurance, Coca-Cola, Coles Supermarkets, Commonwealth Bank, David Jones, IBM, IKEA, KPMG, Macquarie Bank, OPTUS, Qantas Airlines, St. George Bank, Telstra, Volkswagen, Woolworths, etc. Having taught HRM to approximately over 500 students per year for a decade, I started to recognise some of the shortcomings of country-specific Human Resource Management textbooks, as some of these HR texts deliver country-specific knowledge that is not necessarily applicable elsewhere.

While these texts are most valuable for HR managers in one country, the same might not be the case for HR managers from another country. These textbooks deliver national – not global – perspectives. Secondly, many of these texts are written specifically for HR managers – not for more general managers such as Bachelor of Management, Master of Management, *BBAs (Bachelor of Business Administration)* and MBAs.[4] Often these HRM textbooks deliver great insights into the intimate integrities of HRM and are doing a great job on this. However, they fall short of a general overview that focuses on the core of HRM.

As a consequence, this textbook engages with HRM from the standpoint of general managers – BBAs, MBAs, etc. – not from the standpoint of HR managers, and not from the perspective of one country or one specific company. It is, therefore, not another standard HRM textbook written for HRM specialists. A great number of HRM textbooks – including many of those called "Happy HRM Books"[5] – already do a reasonably good job on this while simultaneously camouflaging HRM's numerous and rather well known "rhetoric-vs.-reality" problems,[6] which are widely known contradictions such as HRM's "customer first" rhetoric versus the reality of "market forces are supreme"; HRM's empowerment rhetoric versus its tendency to offload risks onto

DOI: 10.4324/9781003293637-1

others; or HRM's rhetoric of so-called "high performance work systems"[7] versus the reality of the global – and growing – "precariat",[8] to name but a few.

## An Analytical and Critical Approach to Global HRM

*A Global Guide to Human Resource Management: Managing Across Stakeholders* will not shy away from looking at both sides of the coin, from examining the positives and negatives, nor from highlighting inconsistencies.[9] But instead of putting yet another ordinary – or even Happy – HRM textbook on the pile of existing ones, this book's foremost differentiating element is the fact that it highlights key HR themes relevant to general managers, postgraduates, engineers, and business and management students, including BBAs and MBAs. This makes *A Global Guide to Human Resource Management* a unique textbook as it emphasises the middle ground between textbooks that are too general (e.g. HRM for Dummies) and those too specific (e.g. standard HR textbooks).[10]

*A Global Guide to Human Resource Management: Managing Across Stakeholders* does not purport to be either and avoids getting lost in the fine nuances and inner workings of HRM. Nor does it provide HR jargon or the latest managerial buzzwords.[11] Instead, the book concentrates on what is relevant to HRM. *A Global Guide to Human Resource Management* does not use the language of a fashion magazine or a hyped up theory language pretending to be scientific when common sense ideas are present. *A Global Guide to Human Resource Management* is a textbook and as such uses educational and didactic language instead of the language of theories. It is practical and easy to read.

## What Do HRM and HR-Managers Actually Do?

This is a general and practical textbook that uses observation, empirical research findings, and a realistic language to describe the field of HRM to non-HRM experts. In order to avoid a dummy's approach to HRM[12] or the "ultimate expert" version of it, *A Global Guide to Human Resource Management* explores core themes that are most significant to a general manager of a business seeking to understand how to "manage other people at work" – in companies, businesses, and corporations. The book is designed for private, public sector, and for-profit industries. As the public sector takes on elements of private management, the book will focus more on private company management while implicitly including the public sector.[13] The book is not a textbook to be used to organise non-profit institutions albeit many of the generic themes can also be very useful to these organisations.

Designed and written for the commercial business world, *A Global Guide to Human Resource Management* provides a comprehensive understanding of how to manage people, what HRM is, and how it operates. It assists general managers in managing what is easily the most important but quite often also the most complicated element in business: people. By comparison, managing numbers[14] (accounting), operations (production processes), and sales (marketing) can be relatively easy. Numbers do not need to be recruited, machines are not late for work, and marketing strategies do not get pregnant – but people do all this and more.

As a consequence, this book presents HRM in a concise but also human and even humanistic way, even though HRM sees itself quite often simply as a top-down affair – "I manage you". More officially, HRM tends to be defined as activities associated with the management of people in organisations. In fact, many would define HRM as being primarily concerned with the management of people within organisations with a focus on policies and systems. One of such systems is, for example, the ISO certification of a company. Swiss-based ISO or International Organisation for Standardisation consists of 160 countries. It develops quality standards for management (ISO 9000) including HRM (ISO 30400).[15] By 2016, roughly 1.7 million companies were ISO certified.[16]

HR managers in HR departments are responsible for employee recruitment; they often engage in labour or industrial relations; are developing programmes for training and development; participate in workplace designs and OHS; structure and organise performance management; design benefits and reward systems; are involved in the strategic outlook of a company (HR strategy); and finally, they are concerned with business ethics and corporate social responsibility. HR and general managers often assume a managerial position believing that workers or employees only exist to carry out managerial orders and directives.

In many workplace situations, HRM assumes its role as a mediator between senior management, line management, and employees for the good of the company. Rejecting such simplicities and inherent authoritarianism, the book also explains what HR managers do. Many HR managers experience something of a "role ambiguity",[17] seeking to balance at least one of their five classical roles (Table 1.1)[18]:

*Table 1.1* Five Classical HR Roles

| | Role | Description |
|---|---|---|
| 1 | Functional expert | Focuses on administrative efficiency as part of the management team |
| 2 | Human capital developer | Focuses on developing human resources as a corporate asset (HRD) |
| 3 | Employee advocate | Focuses on the needs of employees representing these to management |
| 4 | HR leader | Focuses on developing HRM into a management leadership function |
| 5 | Strategic business partner | Focuses on the contribution of HRM at the strategic business level |

Perhaps all of these roles[19] have at least one thing in common: they relate to people and indeed management as much as HRM has to deal with people. HRM likes to view itself as being dedicated to two basic dichotomies: (1) the "Harvard-vs.-Michigan" model and (2) the **hard-vs.-soft HRM** model. Briefly, the **Harvard model of HRM** combines stakeholders (shareholders, management, employees, government, community, trade unions, etc.) with situational factors (workforce profile, state and legal framework, the labour market, business strategy, etc.), with HRM's policy options (work and reward systems, employee and trade union influences, etc.), with HR outcomes (competitiveness, cost-awareness, competence, performance, etc.), and long-term planning (company and employee wellbeing, effectiveness, sustainability, etc.). The **Michigan model of HRM**, by contrast, focuses on recruitment and selection ⇒ performance ⇒ rewarding/development ⇒ appraisals (feeding back to performance via rewarding and developing). The second model of HRM – soft versus hard – focuses on engagement, trust, motivation, wellbeing, and development (**soft HRM**) or on cost-benefit calculations, direction-giving, managerial control, and overall efficiency (**hard HRM**).

The best way to understand HRM lies in the awareness that HRM – like marketing, operations management, accounting, etc. – is a function of management.[20] The former editor of the Harvard Business Review, Joan Magretta,[21] sees management in the following way:

> looked at from a distance, it's easy to think that management is only about economics and engineering but, up close, it's very much about people. Rightly understood, management is a liberal art, drawing freely from all the disciplines that help us make sense of ourselves and our world.

In other words, much of what general managers (BBA and MBA) do is "very much about people" with the emphasis on "managing people at work". This has been the case throughout the history of capitalism and its companies.

Historically, HRM (since the 1990s) – which was preceded by **factory administration** (pre-World War II) and its successor **personnel management** (post-World War II to 1990s)[22] – saw itself mostly as the supplier of an administrative function. With the personnel → HRM transition, this transformed into a development function in which HRM saw its prime role as a developer of human resources.[23] This always meant the conversion of people into human resources[24] and assets, including "human asset accounting".[25] HR's developer role (1–3) demanded a focus on people development, training, and organisational learning, a role in which HR managers view themselves as employee advocates taking on representative functions of employees *vis-à-vis* management. This challenged the traditional role of trade unions as employee advocates. In versions 4 and 5, HR managers move away from these roles (1–3) by taking on leadership[26] (4) and even strategic (5) functions (see chapter on strategic HRM in this textbook). A recent trend has been to split **C**hief **H**uman **R**esource **O**fficers – CHRO – into CHRO-A (administrative) and CHRO-LO (leadership and organisation).

### *Why A Global Guide to Human Resource Management Helps You*

This textbook, suitable for full-time as well as part-time students, intends to engage business students within a group. In particular, the second part of each chapter is somewhat less suitable for distant learning and online students. In my experience, students learn best when engaging with other students as learning is a social enterprise. Just as Benjamin Franklin once said,[27]

> Tell me and I forget,
> teach me and I may remember,
> involve me and I learn.

And indeed, we learn better with others. Take "the other" away and we will learn less or, as Benjamin Franklin said, we might forget. Survey after survey has shown this to be the case for online students, and this comes on top of the social isolation many experience. But what surveys also show is that when companies seek to employ managers, they are looking, in part, for those skills that we learn while we learn, for example, communication skills and the ability to work collaboratively.[28] While students engaging with the euphemism of "distant learning" almost by definition cannot improve these two skill sets, this book – at least the workbook part – is designed specifically to train those skills.

In addition, this book allows students to collaboratively discuss how HRM works in general – in companies, corporations, and business settings irrespective of their location. *A Global Guide to Human Resource Management* helps general management students working in India as it helps those in England, Spain, Brazil, Iceland, or Malawi. It provides a truly global perspective for international managers, transcending national and country-specific boundaries. It helps the global manager of a global corporation in the same way as it helps a manager managing a local enterprise.

*A Global Guide to Human Resource Management* does not focus on a country-specific legal framework and avoids any historically specific illumination of one country. It also does not focus on a group of counties (ALBA, ASEAN, African Union, EU, OECD, NAFTA, etc.)[29] or on a specific continent: the book is not Euro-centric nor Asia-centric or US-centric. Instead, it presents general HRM knowledge applicable to almost all companies, industries, and countries.

Being global also means that all monetary accounts and financial figures used in the book rely on today's only global currency: the US dollar ($). The use of country- and industry-specific examples and case studies has been avoided. Instead of focusing on a particular company, private sector, or country, the fifty case studies of GoHRM are generic. They illuminate key HR issues at a global generic level. These carefully selected case studies work in all industries from ice-cream manufacturing to global banking – from large multinational corporations to small and medium-size enterprises. *A Global Guide to Human Resource Management* helps general managers in small(ish) firms, medium companies, large multinational corporations, and the public sector, from your driver licence registration office or your local pizza place with twelve employees around the corner to the world's largest corporations such as Walmart with 2.2 million employees, McDonald's with 1.9 million, and Volkswagen with 600,000 employees.[30]

## The Four Core Functions of Management and HRM

The ability to manage people successfully is of ever-increasing importance to management. When all management functions work in unison, businesses succeed. The successful management of people enables other business functions such as marketing, accounting, and operations management to work towards the success of a company. After all, it is not marketing, accounting, and operations management that create corporate success but the people in these departments. When managers say "marketing is the most important part of our business", they actually do not mean "marketing" but the people who have created a successful marketing department. Without them, a marketing department is no more than an empty room. In other words, what underwrites all success stories – from the Ford Motor Company to Exxon, to Volkswagen to Apple, and Microsoft – is their people. This book is about that key part of a business. It is about people. Almost all for-profit companies (and increasingly the public sector) depend on four basic managerial functional areas that need to be covered by general management.[31] These are

1.  **marketing**: someone needs to know what your company offers – advertising;
2.  **accounting**: wages and supplies are paid, goods and services are sold, etc.;
3.  **operations**: workflows and production processes need to be managed; and
4.  **HRM**: all this demands people who, as it is believed, need to be managed.

Like marketing, accounting, and operations management, HRM is a managerial function "always located in an economic context".[32] Any company seeking the infamous "competitive advantage"[33] needs to manage all four of these areas successfully. *A Global Guide to Human Resource Management* does not argue that corporate success, shareholder-value, and profit maximisation depend on marketing nor that they depend on accounting or operations management but equally, it also does not rehearse the worn-out and rather empty HRM phrase that "people are our greatest asset".[34] Instead, it argues that all four areas are equally important for success in business. As a consequence, the key for good managers does not come from focusing overtly on one of the four areas but from skilfully combining them all. This is what makes a successful company.

## HRM as a Global Issue

*A Global Guide to Human Resource Management* focuses on the fourth managerial area outlined above: Human Resource Management. It provides hands-on advice to general managers in the area of managing people at work while focusing on what is relevant, appropriate, and significant to general managers. But how does one know what is relevant? *A Global Guide to Human Resource Management* has achieved this in three ways:

1.  key experiences are based on teaching MBAs and HRM for more than a decade, drawing on a rich volume of experience about what is relevant to general managers;
2.  by having detailed discussions with MBAs and industry experts; and
3.  by analysing well over thirty key HR textbooks from many different countries.

As a synthesis of these three elements, this book offers a lively engagement with managing people that is positioned one level above country-specific textbooks. Much of the academic research for HRM is produced by scholars in the field of management, psychology, labour economics, political science, labour history, industrial sociology, and labour and industrial relations experts. From that, a "three level hierarchy" emerges that shows the basic relationships between research, country-specific HRM textbooks, and *A Global Guide to Human Resource Management* (Figure 1.1):

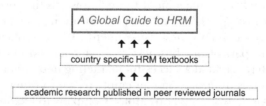

*Figure 1.1* From Research to Global Textbook.

At the bottom of the hierarchy, one finds scholarly publications in academic journals such as, for example, the International Journal of Human Resource Management, Human Resource Management, Industrial Relations Journals, Work, Employment & Society, the Harvard Business Review, the Academy of Management Review, etc. Despite being placed at the bottom, these are typically the most relevant and most important publications as they produce new knowledge – things that we did not know before. They are the knowledge base from which the rest – books, textbooks, the business press, etc. – emanates. At the next level above from academic journal writing, one often finds country-specific HRM textbooks.[35]

All of these present a rather limited array of country-specific HRM knowledge. Yet much of what we know about HRM today comes from the detailed research published in academic journals, some from newspaper and even website reporting.[36] This general and academic knowledge then flows into books and textbooks. The current book's usefulness lies in being practical and handy for the general manager in the vast field of different businesses, corporations, and industries. These managers might manage a ski resort in Aspen or St. Moritz, a holiday resort in Fiji, a government agency in Moscow, a car factory in Japan, the mayor's office in Toronto,[37] a legal firm working with the European Union, a mining company in South Africa, a motor scooter factory in India or China, a shipping company in Brazil, or an airline in Australia. *A Global Guide to Human Resource Management* helps managers by focusing on what is relevant to managing people at work in a generic understanding spanning nine key areas outlined below.

## Managing People in Ten Key Areas

Most HR managers in the English-speaking world – Australia, Canada, Great Britain, Ireland, New Zealand, South Africa, and the USA – cover ten relevant HRM issues.[38] These ten core HRM issues are:

1. recruitment and selection;
2. labour and industrial relations;
3. learning and development;
4. OHS or occupational health and safety;
5. performance management;
6. designing work;
7. compensation and rewards;
8. strategic HRM;
9. ethics at work; and finally
10. Green HRM

These ten functions remain highly significant to HRM that sees itself as operating in at least several different contexts: economical, social, political, legal, technological, organisational, moral–ethical, and the environment.[39] The ninth field – moral and ethics – becomes relevant as "all" human-to-human interaction involves morality ever since human beings left the animal kingdom and developed social forms of conscious and (more or less) rational cooperative and communal forms of social living and making things as homo faber.[40]

The tenth issue for HRM relates to **sustainability**, **corporate social responsibility**, **global warming**,[41] **climate change**,[42] **peak oil** (or any other natural resource that is harvested faster than it can be replaced), the protection of **biodiversity** (the variety of life on earth in all forms[43]), the **Anthropocene**,[44] and our global **carbon footprint**.[45] These issues impact on all life forms on our planet including human beings.[46] As a consequence, HRM has developed what became known as Green HRM (GHRM) and sustainable HRM.

During the process of making, designing, and managing things, much of what many managers do – managing other people – is covered in this book while focusing on the above nine key HR issues. The book starts with the original place and location where virtually all managers start: at the place of employment and by being recruited. HRM calls the process of employing people recruitment and selection.

There is a somewhat inherent logic to HRM suggesting that the common engagement with HR starts with becoming employed. Being employed by a company and employing people for companies remains a vital component of HRM. But with their employment, people also enter into various relationships at work – relationships to other employees, to management, and so on. As a consequence, employment may be followed up by a system and structure that sets the overall framework for employment. This is called industrial, labour, or employment relations.

Unlike relationships to fellow workers, employment relations, labour, and industrial relations reach far beyond the relationships we engage in when working for a company. In many cases, industrial relations (IR) frameworks set the general framework inside which HRM operates, i.e. IR shapes many HR issues such as employment laws, OHS laws, and general rules and regulations. In some cases, governments undertake a stakeholder approach when formulating changes to industrial relations or labour laws. These governments often set up a round table discussion involving three stakeholders: employers, trade unions, and the state itself. These discussions often inform labour law under which HRM has to operate as they can regulate working time, set up anti-discrimination legislation, and so on.

However, getting a job not only means following such labour laws and company-based HR policies, it also means learning new things. HR calls these initial learning processes "induction programmes". As a consequence, the subsequent chapter discusses learning and development. Learning about a new job also includes learning about new tasks and how work is organised and designed. HRM calls this "workplace design" whilst general management often prefers the term "operations management". Learning about a new job not only involves discovering the way a company operates, interacting with new colleagues, and so on, it can also include learning about the safety aspects of work which comes as part of OHS. In the world of HRM, OHS is a particularly important subject, not only because "there are 270 million occupational accidents and 160 million occupational diseases each year, incurring US$ 2.8 trillion in costs for lost working time and expenses for treatment, compensation and rehabilitation"[47] but, for one, OHS issues are related to HRM – not to marketing, accounting, etc. – and secondly, in some jurisdictions, HR managers can be severely punished for OHS failings and wrongdoings.

Once the initial learning process has been accomplished, the employee is ready to perform a given work task. For that, HRM has developed what many see as being the very core of HRM: performance management. How employees perform a work task is in many cases linked to the reward system of a company. HRM calls this "managing compensation" or "reward management". In many successful companies, all this is linked to the strategic plan of a business. This is the point where "The Human Side of The Enterprise" becomes strategic HRM.[48]

Since all of this involves people, finally and inevitably the aforementioned morality also enters the picture in the form of business ethics and corporate social responsibility. More recently, as the impacts of global warming become increasingly noticeable, this also involves climate change and ways to create a carbon neutral company.[49] Highlighting these new developments and HRM's contribution to sustainability, etc. is the task of the final chapter.

**How to Use This Book and Its Workbook**

*A Global Guide to Human Resource Management* contains eleven concise chapters – nine chapters and an obligatory introduction – designed to be studied during the course of ten weeks. The book is a thought-provoking and meaningful textbook on an important subject. The book refrains from following a digitally enhanced but often rather disruptive layout and style, instead prioritising relevance, substance, and content. *A Global Guide to Human Resource Management* relies on two colours: black and blue. Words highlighted in **"BOLD"** are designed to highlight key HR terms and themes while black is used for standard text. Definitions of the key terms can be found in the Glossary on the book's companion website at:

All chapters follow a uniform structure divided into two basic parts. Part one contains three elements while part two offers seven sections. The first part of each chapter presents (1) a chapter summary and (2) key learning objectives for each chapter. It also presents (3) the main body of knowledge for each chapter. The second part is the "workbook". It starts with five general discussion questions reflective of each chapter's content.

This is followed by a "five-by-five" exercise offering five real, practical, international, and generic case studies reflective of each chapter's subject at hand. These cases are each followed by five case-related questions. Many of the case studies are drawn from international students working for global corporations. The selected case studies reflect not only the given mix found in many general management classes of the roughly 12,000 internationally recognised business schools but are also tailored to a certain "international-domestic" student audiences.[50] In today's business schools, many classes consist of two rather different groups: domestic mature candidates, often with years of experience in management, and overseas international candidates, at times with but at times without such experiences and relevant degrees.[51] In some cases, students attend such classes with an English language understanding that has not been fully developed.

As a consequence, the case studies as well as the textbook as a whole, try to balance their "language use".[52] The language of the textbook is designed not to be underwhelming for degree candidates in general management with a solid language comprehension while also not being too overwhelming for students with developing language capabilities. In addition to balancing different language capabilities, the case studies used are designed to avoid being Euro- or North-American-centric and rely on truly international experiences.

Although originally based on specific companies, these case studies have been converted into general, global, and often anonymous but always generic case studies. On a few occasions, several rather company-specific case studies have provided a base from which a somewhat more "purpose built" case study was constructed. The aim of these generic case studies is not to say "oh, this is what corporation X-Y-Z does" but to engage students with practical case study knowledge that is transferable to other companies. The final three parts of the workbook are suggestions for the use of an online guest lecture to be watched in class. They also contain ideas for the use of several online documentaries on the subjects of each chapter. Taken together, this allows for the construction of seminars under the provisions of "blended learning".[53] Finally, a short-list of key readings for further study is presented. Each chapter's workbook ends with endnotes – often designed to entice further readings. The structure of each chapter looks as follows:

**Section 1: The Main Part of Each Chapter:**

1. **Executive Summary**
   provides a short synopsis of the key elements of each chapter.
2. **Key Learning Objectives**
   are designed to outline what kind of learning can be achieved by using each chapter.
3. **Content**
   of each chapter presents the largest section and the main part of each chapter.

**Section 2: The Workbook with Material, Information, and Case Studies**

4. **General Discussion Questions**
   for classroom debates and small group discussions offer in-depth debating points of each chapter's main content.
5. **The "Five-by-Five" Exercise**
   offers five generic case studies relevant to each chapter and organised as "5X5". Each case study is followed by five questions, designed to be conducted as a small group exercise. It allows students to practise face-to-face discussions, exercise, and improve inter-subjective communication and presentation skills.
6. **Online Guest Lectures**
   are suggested in each chapter for current and up-to-date thinking on the issues of the chapter (e.g. YouTube, Ted-Talks, etc.). Websites such as, for example, www.ted.com/talks offer additional material to choose from.
7. **Documentaries**
   provide a list with potentially useful online training videos that can be watched during each session and placed in the context of the respective subject, aided through questions or – alternatively – even a structured or semi-structured tutorial questionnaire.[54] This exercise can also take the form of a game using, for example, https://kahoot.it/.
8. **Documentaries**
   provide additional literature for those seeking to deepen their understanding of specific areas of HRM.
9. **Endnotes**
   list the sources used in each chapter while also focusing on short, concise, and helpful further literature. They are designed as "useful hints". Although "wikipedia.org" provides a great entry point to deepen our understanding of HRM, the endnotes at the end of each chapter are designed to reach beyond this. Nevertheless, "wikipedia.org" remains one of "the" initial starting points for further engagement with specific aspects of management, work, and HRM.

*A Global Guide to Human Resource Management* is not designed as a book simply to be read. Instead, as a textbook, it is to be studied. It encourages studying and discussing, and is designed as a comprehensive text with key readings as well as a workbook to be used and worked through individually as well as in classroom and tutorial settings. Taken as a whole, the book deepens and at the same time broadens our understanding of managing people, HRM, and its role in managing firms, companies, and corporations.

A *Global Guide to Human Resource Management* not only introduces HRM to the "non-HR expert", it also critically reflects on the role of HRM in companies and society. Above that, it engages with HRM as a managerial, academic, and, above all, "critical" subject.[55] It is not a simple "recipe book" on HRM overloaded with "official knowledge".[56] A *Global Guide to Human Resource Management* takes critical thinking beyond the stereotypical cliché all too often dutifully rehearsed in so many introductions to it.[57] Instead, it follows the moral philosopher Immanuel Kant's postulation that[58]

> our age is the age of criticism
> to which everything must submit.

Being specifically designed for postgraduate levels of critical thinking, this book does not shy away from mentioning the inevitable negatives – not just the positives – of management and HRM as these represent the two sides of the coin. This book follows a critical approach,[59] meaning, for example, that when discussing recruitment and selection and labour markets, it will also mention HRM's darker sides (for example, reports that pre-Brexit[60] in Great Britain alone, "each year, 30,000 women (were) sacked for being pregnant, and this is despite the fact that legislations exist to protect them").[61] As well as the fact that HRM[62] dismissed thousands of people – mostly those in low-wage jobs – during the 2020[63] Covid-19 or coronavirus pandemic.[64]

HRM is often no innocent bystander in these developments; it also has its own and somewhat tainted history – for example, its historical predecessors' feudalism and, before that, slavery, where human beings were bought and sold.[65] The book does not avoid mentioning the actual re-appearance of slave markets in the North African state of Libya in 2017[66] as they are more than just an historical fact of a long bygone era.[67] Today there are "estimates of the number of *slaves* ranging from around 21 million to 29 million".[68]

A *Global Guide to Human Resource Management* will also highlight company internal issues such as sexual harassment that despite the best efforts of many trade unions, government agencies, and good HR managers still remains a visible – but often rather invisible – problem.[69] At times, such issues receive substantial levels of media attention. Yet for many HR managers who engage with the running of HR in a company, some of these issues are not necessarily the most pressing daily affairs. Instead of following media reports and sensationalism, this book will strongly focus on the reality of the daily work of HR managers.

This book will neither overrate issues nor will it deny them. The aforementioned slavery, for example, cannot be seen as "a thing of the past" when people to the magnitude of the entire population of countries like Australia, Taiwan, Rumania, Chile, and the Netherlands are globally held as slaves. This remains a fact even though for most HR managers it might be a rather marginal issue. But it can become one, for example, when outsourcing to distant sweatshops is on the agenda – which can increase the likelihood of large corporations engaging in slavery by proxy.[70] Equally, A *Global Guide to Human Resource Management* will not exclude the "Boys Without Names"[71] who are confined to child labour.[72] As a consequence, virtually every chapter of A *Global Guide to Human Resource Management* features "excursions" into critical areas of global HRM, putting the searchlight onto the – often hidden but still existing – dark corners of capitalism, globalisation, and environmental degradation.

Truthful and quite often rather critical approaches to global HRM, such as a critique of globalisation, management, and HRM, always and necessarily involve taking risks – just as every educational process worth its name needs to shed light on different angles of a problem. What education is all about can be observed, for example, by taking an interest in these few documentaries:

| | |
|---|---|
| What is education: | ted.com/talks/ken_robinson_changing_education_paradigms |
| | ted.com/talks/sir_ken_robinson_bring_on_the_revolution? |
| | language=en |
| | ted.com/talks/ken_robinson_says_schools_kill_creativity? |
| | language=en |
| The human in HRM: | youtube.com/watch?v=0Mq2TiJmqCI |
| The history of HRM: | youtube.com/watch?v=RpHX03q_3UI |
| HRM – the big mistake: | youtube.com/watch?v=RR5OffXFLsg |
| The HR partner: | youtube.com/watch?v=f0URM-jQrB0 |
| Jack Welsh on HRM: | youtube.com/watch?v=rByDmC0SqtM |

While education changes things, so do the things that are being taught. For example, HRM's predecessor – personnel management – placed a different emphasis on education than its own predecessor, factory administration. The same applies to HRM. Within the general frame of HRM, new knowledge constantly emerges and, like in all other academic fields, this process changes and improves HRM. As a consequence, textbooks need to be constantly upgraded and improved to represent the "leading edge of knowledge". And as the author of this textbook, I will take your constructive critique and suggestions for improvement on board.[73] But ultimately, education as such and learning about HRM is always a somewhat formative step into the unknown – perhaps even a risky step but nevertheless one worthwhile taking. This has been expressed by one of the world's leading writers on education, Brazilian educator Paulo Freire (1921–1997)[74]:

Life in its totality taught me a great lesson
that it is impossible to embrace it without taking risks.
This is how life is.

## Notes

1  Heery, E. & Noon, M. 2017. *A Dictionary of HRM*, Oxford: Oxford University Press.
2  Ruth, D. 2016. What is your MBA for? What's the story? *Management Learning*, 48(1): 7–22.
3  Some of these companies can be found on this list: http://beta.fortune.com/global500/list.
4  Fifteen Top General Management degrees (https://www.masterstudies.com, accessed: 30th January 2018).
5  Grugulis, I. 2017. *A Very Short, Fairly Interesting and Reasonably Cheap Book about HRM*, London: Sage (p. 1).
6  Legge, K. 1995. *Human Resource Management – Rhetoric and Reality*, London: MacMillan; Watson, T. J. 1995. In search of HRM: beyond the rhetoric and reality distinction or the case of the dog that didn't bark, *Personnel Review*, 24(4): 6–16; Boxall, P. & Purcell, J. 2015. *Strategy and Human Resource Management* (4th ed.), Basingstoke: Palgrave.
7  Van De Voorde, K. & Beijer, S. 2015. The role of employee HR attributions in the relationship between high-performance work systems and employee outcomes, *Human Resource Management Journal*, 25(1): 62–78.
8  Standing, G. 2011. *The Precariat: The New Dangerous Class*, New York: Bloomsbury; Johnson, M. 2016. *Precariat: Labour, Work and Politics*, London: Routledge.
9  Klikauer, T. 2016. Selling students short: why you won't get the university education you deserve, *Management Learning*, 47(5): 629–633.
10  Messmer, M. 2012. *Human Resources Kit For Dummies*, New York: John Wiley & Sons; Pell, A. 2001. *The Complete Idiot's Guide to HRM*, New York: Penguin.

11  Abrahamson, E. 1996. Management fashion, *Academy of Management Review*, 21(1): 254–285; Cluley, R. 2013. What makes a management buzzword buzz? *Organization Studies*, 34(1): 33–43.

12  Messmer, M. 2012. *Human Resources Kit for Dummies*, New York: John Wiley & Sons; Cooper, C. L., Johnson, S. & Holdsworth, L. 2012. *Organisational Behaviour for Dummies*, Hoboken, NJ: John Wiley & Sons; Biech, E. & Bingham, T. 2015. *Training & Development for Dummies*, Hoboken, NJ: Wiley.

13  Boyne, G. A. 2002. Public and private management: what's the difference? *Journal of Management Studies*, 39(1): 97–122; Van der Wal Z., De Graaf, G. & Lasthuizen, K., 2008. What's valued most? Similarities and differences between the organizational values of the public and private sector, *Public Administration*, 86(2): 465–482.

14  Compared to HRM, accounting is a rather simple affaire. As Isaac Newton once said, *I Can Calculate the Motions of the Planets, But I Cannot Calculate the Madness of Men* (https://en.wikiquote.org/wiki/Isaac_Newton). This is not to say that HRM marks *the madness of men*. Yet, because of its human component, HRM remains inherently complicated.

15  ISO. 2018. HRM Vocabulary (https://www.iso.org/standard/66032.html, accessed: 24th April 2018).

16  ISO Survey. 2016. (https://www.iso.org/the-iso-survey.html, accessed: accessed: 26th April 2018.

17  Rizzo, J. R., House, R. J., & Lirtzman, S. I., 1970. Role conflict and ambiguity in complex organizations, *Administrative Science Quarterly*, 15(2): 150–163.

18  Ulrich, D. 1998. A new mandate for human resources, *Harvard Business Review* (76): 124–135.

19  https://study.com/academy/lesson/henry-mintzbergs-managerial-roles.html.

20  'Management…can be presented as general, abstract of technical laws as against the merely selfish desires of individuals. This has powerful ideological effects' (Holborow, M. 2012. Neoliberal Keywords, in: Block, D., Gray, J., & Holborow, M. (eds.) *Neoliberalism and Applied Linguistics*, London: Routledge, p. 37).

21  Magretta, J. 2012. *What Management Is: How It Works and Why It's Everyone's Business*, London: Profile, p. 4.

22  Walton, R. E. 1985. From control to commitment in the workplace, *Harvard Business Review*. 77–85.

23  Some have even argued that since the 2000s a fourth transition of HRM is taking place making the transition from HRM to "strategic" HRM.

24  McGaughey, E. 2018. A Human is not a resource, *King's Law Journal* (https://papers.ssrn.com/sol3/papers.cfm?abstract_id=3099470, posted: 15th January 2018, accessed: 15th May 2021).

25  Sikula, A. 2001. The five biggest HRM lies, *Public Personnel Management*, 30(3): 421.

26  Quite apart from the leader-vs.-follower problem and the inherently anti-democratic character of "leadership", certainly "leadership" is a current fashion in management. This textbook is not a fashion-catalogue following each and every fashion (cf. Abrahamson E., 1996. Management fashion, *Academy of Management Review*, 21(1): 254–285). Virtually the same goes for "talent". While most of today's companies are not exactly overflowing with Mozarts, Kandinskys, Victor Hugos, and Einsteins, it appears as if the word "talent" has simply replaced the words employee, worker, and person without adding much content to HRM (cf. Gladwell, M. 2002. *The Talent Myth*, www.newyorker.com/printables/fact/0207222fa_fact).

27  http://www.goodreads.com/quotes/21262-tell-me-and-i-forget-teach-me-and-i-may.

28  http://www.bloomberg.com/graphics/2016-job-skills-report/.

29  www.au.int/.

30  www.forbes.com/sites/liyanchen/2015/05/06/the-worlds-largest-companies/.

31  This, of course, includes the basic functions as outlined by Fayol: "forecasting, planning, organising, commanding, coordinating, and controlling" (Fayol, H. 1916. *Managerialism Industrielle et Generale* (Industrial and General Managerialism), London: Sir I. Pitman & Sons, ltd. (1930).

32  Boxall, P. & Purcell, J. 2015. *Strategy and Human Resource Management* (4th ed.), Basingstoke: Palgrave, p. 8.

33  Porter, M. E. 1985. *Competitive Advantage*, New York: Free Press.

34  Adonis, J. 2010. *Corporate Punishment – Smashing the Management Clichés for Leaders in a New World*, Milton: Wiley.

35 Kramar et al.'s, Nankervis et al.'s, and Härtel & Jujimoto's Australian HRM textbooks; Schwind et al.'s Canadian HRM textbook; Beardwell & Claydon's, Grugulis' and Wilton's UK textbooks; Gunnigle et al.'s Irish textbook; Macky's New Zealand textbook; Grobler et al.'s South African textbook; Jackson et al.'s, Snell et al.'s, Noe et al.'s, Rue et al.'s, Gomez-Mejia et al.'s, and Mello's US textbooks, and so on.

36 masters-in-human-resources.org/50-online-resources-for-hr-professionals/.

37 http://www.ctvnews.ca/canada/rob-ford-timeline-of-events.

38 Klikauer, T. 2014. *Seven Moralities of HRM*, Basingstoke: Palgrave.

39 Guest, D. E. 1987. HRM and industrial relations, *Journal of management Studies*, 24(5): 503–521; McKibben, B. 2019. *Falter – Has the Human Game Begun to Play Itself Out?*, New York: Henry Holt and Company.

40 Axelrod, R. & Hamilton, W. D. 1981. The evolution of cooperation, *Science*, 211:1390–1396; Krebs, D. 2011. *The Origins of Morality: An Evolutionary Account*, Oxford: Oxford University Press; Klikauer, T. 2012. Evolution, altruism, and human behaviour, *Organization*, 19(6): 939–940.

41 Kemper, A. 2012. Saving the planet: a tale of two strategies, *Harvard Business Review*, April 1st.

42 Bernotat, W. H. 2007. Take responsibility for climate change, *Harvard Business Review*, 85(7/8).

43 Wallace-Wells, D. 2019. *The Uninhabitable Earth: Life after Warming*, New York: Tim Duggan Books.

44 Steffen, W., Crutzen, P. J. & McNeill, J. R., 2007. The Anthropocene: are humans now overwhelming the great forces of nature, *AMBIO: A Journal of the Human Environment*, 36(8): 614–621; Young, H. S., McCauley, D. J., Galetti, M. & Dirzo, R., 2016. Patterns, causes, and consequences of anthropocene defaunation, *Annual Review of Ecology, Evolution, and Systematics*, 47(1): 333–358; Bonneuil, C. & Fressoz, J.-B. 2017. *The Shock of the Anthropocene: The Earth, History and Us*, London: Verso.

45 Frederick, H. et al. 2016. *Entrepreneurship – Theory, Process, Practice* (4th ed.), Melbourne, Cengage, p. 5.

46 Klikauer, T. 2019. Accelerating ecological genocide, *Counterpunch*, 7th June 2019 (www.counterpunch.org); Klikauer, T. & Simms, N. 2020. Falter, *Marx & Philosophy Review of Books*, 19th March 2020.

47 http://www.un.org/en/events/safeworkday/.

48 McGregor, D. 1960. *The Human Side of Enterprise*, New York: McGraw-Hill; McGregor, D. 2006. *The Human Side of Enterprise* (updated and with new commentary by Joel Cutcher-Gershenfeld), New York: McGraw-Hill.

49 Bernotat, W. H. 2007. Take responsibility for climate change, *Harvard Business Review*, 85(7/8); Kemper, A. 2012. Saving the planet: a tale of two strategies, *Harvard Business Review*, 1st April; Eleftheriadis I. M. & Anagnostopoulou, E. G. 2015. Relationship between corporate climate change disclosures and firm factors, *Business Strategy and the Environment*, 24(8): 780–789.

50 There are 12,000 business schools (www.economist.com, 8th February 2014).

51 A few years ago, The Economist Magazine noted that "business schools exist to teach the value of management" (www.economist.com, 8th February 2014).

52 Klikauer, T. 2017. Why only us: language and evolution, *The European Legacy*, 22(4): 496–497; Klikauer, T. 2017. What kind of creatures are we?, *The European Legacy*, 22(4): 494–496.

53 Turner, Y. 2015. Last orders for the lecture theatre? Exploring blended learning approaches and accessibility for full-time international students, *International Journal of Management Education*, 13(2): 163–169; Arbaugh, J. B. 2016. Where are the dedicated scholars of management learning and education?, *Management Learning*, 47(2): 230–240.

54 While feature films on work, management, and HRM (e.g. Chaplin's "Modern Times" on factory life, youtube.com/watch?v=DfGs2Y5WJ14), are useful, this textbook relies on documentaries (cf. Lafferty, G. 2016. Opening the learning process: the potential role of feature film in teaching employment relations, *Australian Journal of Adult Learning*, 56(1): 8–28).

55 Klikauer, T. 2016. Unplugged: questions a book on 'questions business schools don't ask' doesn't dare to ask, *M@n@gement*, 19(3): 228–239.

56 Apple, M. M. 2014. *Official Knowledge: Democratic Education in a Conservative Age* (3rd ed.), London: Routledge.

57  Hughes, W. 2015. *Critical Thinking: An Introduction to the Basic Skills* (7th ed.), Peterborough: Broadview Press.

58  plato.stanford.edu/entries/kant/.

59  Brookfield, S. 2015. Speaking truth to power: teaching critical thinking in the critical theory tradition, in: Davies, M. & Barnett, R. (eds.). *The Palgrave Handbook of Critical Thinking in Higher Education.* New York: Palgrave Macmillan.

60  http://www.economist.com/Brexit.

61  https://www.theguardian.com/culture/2009/nov/01/gaby-hinsliff-quits-working-motherhood.

62  Collie, A. 2020. 90% Out of Work with One Week's Notice (https://theconversation.com, 28th April 2020, accessed: 25th August 2020).

63  Klikauer, T. & Széll, G. 2020. Reflections on a pandemic, *Countercurrents* (https://countercurrents.org/, 24th June 2020, accessed: 25th August 2020).

64  Klikauer, T. 2020. COVID-19 in Germany: explaining a low death rate, *Counterpunch*, 31st March 2020; Klikauer, T. & Simms, N. 2021. Post-corona work changes in Germany, *Countercurrents*, 16th February 2021.

65  https://edition.cnn.com/world/live-news/myfreedomday-2020-intl/index.html.

66  Reuters, 2017. *Libyan Government Says Investigating Migrant 'Slave Market'* (www.reuters.com, 23rd November 2017, accessed: 18th December 2017).

67  This book does not camouflage the true history of HRM. Many standard HRM textbooks do this by quickly moving on to more recent ideas such as the "human relations" school (Mayo, E., 1945. *The Social Problems of an Industrial Civilisation*, Boston, MA: Harvard University Press and "The Myth of the Docile Worker", Bramel, C. & Friend, R., 1981. Hawthorne, the myth of the docile worker, and class bias in psychology, *American Psychologist*, 36(8): 867–878). Today, these ideas are, for example, found in the journal "human relations".

68  www.antislavery.org/english/slavery_today/what_is_modern_slavery.aspx; cf. https://www.alliance87.org/2017ge/modernslavery#!section=0.

69  On the very day I wrote the introduction to this book, for example, "fastcompany.com" reported that "60% of women in Silicon Valley have been sexually harassed" (Lydia Dishman, 13th January 2016).

70  occupywallstreet.net/story/15-major-corporations-you-never-knew-profited-slavery.

71  Sheth, K. 2010. *Boys without Names* (1st ed.), New York: Balzer + Bray.

72  Rainforestactionnetwork2016...Human_Cost_of_Conflict_Palm_Oil_RAN.pdf.

73  Please contact me via my homepage: "https://klikauer.wordpress.com/" or wikipedia.org/wiki/Thomas_Klikauer.

74  Quoted from Cruz, A. L. 2015. From practice to theory & from theory to practice – a journey with Paulo Freire, in: Porfilio, B. J. & Ford, D. R. (eds.) *Leaders in Critical Pedagogy*, Rotterdam: Sense Publishers, p. 180.

# 2 Getting the Right People

## Recruitment and Selection

### Executive Summary

Recruitment and selection is the process through which companies hire people. It is divided into two parts: (1) recruitment that establishes a pool of suitable candidates and (2) selection which is the process of selecting the right candidate from this pool. The pool of candidates should have the right number of people with the right skills who are likely to accept the position. Recruitment and selection should be underscored by a formal HR policy. This demands that recruiters engage with the labour market that is different from, for example, the commodity market. Recruiters use different strategies to advertise positions while looking for a few basic overall characteristics in future employees. The selection process starts when recruiters establish a short list of candidates and conduct interviews which are followed by reference checking and additional testing. Once this is completed, HR recruiters can offer the position to the potential candidates. The recruitment and selection process ends when a position is offered and accepted and the candidate participates in an induction programme.

### Key Learning Objectives

1. Realise the importance of recruiting talent for business success;
2. Identify the difference between "recruitment" and "selection";
3. Outline the recruitment strategies a company can use to fill job vacancies;
4. Describe the key elements of the recruitment and selection process;
5. Explain the role of recruiters in the recruitment process;
6. Understand the preferred methods used in selecting human resources;
7. Show an awareness of how culture can influence the recruitment process;
8. Ascertain key fallacies in recruiting and selecting; and
9. Develop a formal HR policy on recruitment and selection.

DOI: 10.4324/9781003293637-2

## Recruitment

For most people, working life starts with being recruited to work for a company, a firm, or a corporation. At its most basic level, a **company** is an organisational structure set up as a legal entity for the economic purpose of achieving profit maximisation. At a larger level, **corporations** are owned and controlled by shareholders and each of their shares creates ownership in the corporation.[1] Control over a corporation and its profits is determined by the portion of shares owned in the company. One of the crucial legal decisions on corporations came with "Dodge vs. Ford Motor Company"[2] when the Michigan Supreme Court decided that Henry Ford had to operate his corporation in the interests of shareholders rather than in a charitable manner for the benefit of his employees or customers, thereby setting up the "shareholder primacy" principle. Hence, corporations are legally bound to make profit or achieve shareholder value. Whether company or corporation, all firms must focus on four key tasks demanded of any business:

(a) **operations management** often organised as a flow of products and services through the business;
(b) **accounting** as wages are paid, supplies are purchased, and products and services are sold;
(c) people – now called customers – also need to know about the availability of the products and services. This is the task of marketing; and
(d) since all of the above three business functions demand people inside a business to operate it, **Human Resource Management** (HRM) concludes the fourth part of business. There is no business without people.[3] The HRM part is often seen as a business function performed inside an organisation and designed to maximise employee performance. HRM concerns the management of people. The former Harvard Business Review editor, Joan Magretta defines "managers, using the word loosely, to refer to people in positions of institutional power such as owners and overseers, [and] management [as] creating performance through others".[4] These "others" are typically employees in a managerial "top-down" function – often signified as "I manage you" – within a company, focusing on policies,[5] systems, and processes such as, for example, the process of recruitment and selection.

## Recruitment and HR Planning

The process of recruiting and selecting people converts human beings into labour, workers, employees, or human resources. Most commonly, people are hired because of their "labour-power", i.e. the power to labour or work.[6] This is also called "labour process" while HRM calls the hiring process recruitment and selection, a term that indicates two elements: recruiting and selecting. Before selecting someone from a pool of suitable candidates (part 2), the recruitment process (part 1) has to take place. HRM defines recruitment as any practice carried out by an organisation with the primary purpose of identifying and attracting potential employees. Recruitment is often part of personnel, workforce, or **HR planning** (HRP). The recruitment process (plan → source → pre-screen → select → offer[7]) balances *current* staffing positions with *desired* staffing positions. HRP involves balancing the forecast of labour demand with forecasts of labour supply. Overall, HRP helps HR managers to plan human resources as effectively as possible – where and when they are needed to accomplish organisational goals. HR managers do this in four ways:

(a) determining the human resources' impact on the organisation's objective regarding specific organisational units;
(b) defining the skills, expertise, and total number of employees needed to achieve the company's or a department's objectives;
(c) determining additional HRP requirements (downsizing, outsourcing, restructuring, etc.); and
(d) developing detailed action plans for the anticipated human resource requirements. This can, for example, take the form of the Delphi method[8] (a method of forecasting that is done by a panel of experts) or through scenario planning (using the workforce environment to develop workforce planning).[9] HRP takes into account external and internal scanning while **Strategic HRP** links HRP to the overall strategies a company pursues.[10]

Strategic HRP often informs the recruitment and selection process as it identifies current and future human resources' needs necessary for the achievement of a company's strategic goals. HRP links HRM to the strategic plan. Strategic HRP can be seen as a process that ensures the organisational HR requirements, that these are correctly identified, and that the HR implications of a strategic business plan are clarified.[11] This involves a process in which a business organisation estimates its future HR demand and calculates the expected size and composition of labour supply.[12] Strategic HRP can lead to creating recruitment and selection strategies as well as retention strategies. Strategic HRP includes four basic steps:

1.  Evaluating the existing workforce
    HR creates a skills register of current employees to clarify the skills, knowledge, and ability current staff holds.[13] Such a portfolio includes: volunteer work, certifications, degrees, training awards, employee responsibilities, etc.[14]
2.  Forecasting workforce requirements
    HR projects labour needs for the future based on a strategic business plan. Many HR managers are aware that external challenges might force an organisation to adjust its business strategy that, in turn, impacts on future staffing needs. In general, HR managers identify positions and skill sets needed for the duration of the strategic business plan (recruitment needs) and assess the external or internal labour market to supply the right people.
3.  Bridging existing staff levels to future needs
    This assures that an organisation's current staffing levels are assessed and predictions are conducted ascertaining future staffing needs. This includes a simple employee count as well as a skills and knowledge evaluation. These will have to be compared to what will be needed in the near future to achieve the company's business strategy. This might demand a review of current HR practices and HR policies. Both need to be aligned to the company's business strategy.
4.  HR strategies that support the organisation's business strategy
    Aligning HR strategies with an organisation's business strategy involves four core HR strategies: a restructuring strategy (this includes hiring/reducing staff, regrouping work tasks, re-designing jobs, and re-organising workgroups); training and development strategies (training needs of current and future staff and

organisational development opportunities); recruitment strategies (recruiting new employees with the skill sets and knowledge to support the organisation's business strategy); and potentially, an outsourcing strategy.

Strategic HRP achieves all this by focusing, for example, on short-term strategies (zero to two years), intermediate strategies (two to five years), or long-term strategies (beyond five years). To accomplish this, HRM's recruitment activities are designed to affect three key elements of the recruitment process:

1. attracting a sufficient **number of people** who apply for a job vacancy;
2. attracting **the type** of people who would apply; and finally,
3. assuring the likelihood that the candidates who apply will **accept the position** once it is offered to them.

## Formal and Informal HR Policies

The first element of the recruitment process is crucial because HR managers have to ensure that only a reasonable number of job applicants will apply for a position in order to prevent that "two million people reply to a job ad for just 300 clerical jobs".[15] Later this chapter will outline how this can be achieved but before that, most HR managers will have made sure that the company has a suitable **HR policy** on recruitment and selection.[16] Such HR policies can be **formal policies** or **informal policies**. Most informal policies relate to "the way things are done around here" such as common practices at the workplace. Good examples for an informal policy might be a dress code, casual days, breaks, etc. Formal policies can also have these clearly noted in employee handbooks or even contracts of employment that often carry, at least implicitly, a **psychological contract** with them.[17]

By contrast, formal policies are always statements of intent indicating an organisation's intention, goal, and objectives. For example, a formal HR policy of one of the most recognised global NGOs might say, "we aim to achieve a harmonious workplace and recognise the right of all people who interact with us to be treated with dignity and respect". One of the world's most elite universities, for example, might have an HR policy called **code of practice** of staff recruitment and selection. Such a policy might read,

> the university welcomes diversity amongst its staff and seeks to ensure that all candidates for employment are treated fairly, and that selection is based solely on the individual merits of candidates and on selection criteria relevant to the post.

Whether an HR policy is called "code of practice", "policy", or "recruitment policy", converting such a policy into reality means that HR managers need to engage with the market. This market is called labour market.[18] It is a market with its own particularities and specifics.

## Recruitment and the Labour Market

In the case of recruitment and selection, HR policies indicate to potential applicants the kind of workplace they are going to encounter and what the aims of the organisation are. For recruitment purposes, such formal, codified, and written HR policies are placed in advertisements and on corporate websites. Having made clear what kind of organisation one wants to be, one of the first decisions HR managers have to make when recruiting someone is the choice between internal versus **external recruiting** or internal vs. **external labour market**.[19] Management deals with two kinds of markets: firstly, the commodity market that exchanges goods and services. In the commodity market, two kinds of goods are exchanged:

1.  commercial goods (e.g. cars, hairdryers, etc.) and
2.  services which are signified by the ever-growing **service industry**.

Unlike the commercial goods market, the service industry involves the provision of services to businesses as well as consumers, such as, for example, accounting, tradesmen (e.g. mechanic or plumber services), computer services, restaurants, tourism, etc.[20] In short, a service industry is one where "no goods" are produced. The second market is the labour market[21] which is fundamentally different from the commodity market. Here we find not one labour market but **labour market segmentation** as the labour market is divided along occupational lines.[22] For example, the labour market for CEO is different from the labour market for delivery drivers.[23]

While the service industry differs from the manufacturing industry and the labour markets for each might be overlapping, the recruitment and selection process remains similar in both labour markets. In the commodity market goods change ownership (A sells X to B) or commercial entities change hands between old and new owners. The same does not happen in the labour market – ownership does not change.[24]

## HRM Does Not Buy People

HRM cannot buy a person or a worker; systems that allow this are called slavery.[25] Slavery is an economic system in which principles of property law and commodity exchanges are applied to humans.[26] Under slavery, people are treated as property. Human beings are owned, bought and sold accordingly, and cannot withdraw unilaterally from the arrangement.[27] In other words, "human capital cannot be owned or traded".[28]

Today's capitalism[29] – despite the still existing forms of slavery such as forced and **bonded labour**[30] engaging roughly 21 million people while generating "\$150bn in profits each year"[31] – does not, in general, operate with slavery.[32] Bonded labour exists when becoming a labourer is enforced through demands, such as by means of repayment for a loan, as an example. The person is then tricked or trapped into working for very little or no pay. Since this is no longer standard practice as it was during the 17th,18th, and even 19th centuries in many parts of the world, today's HRM needs to recruit labour – in fact, it is renting (for a set daily and weekly time) a person's ability to work.

Despite the free market ideology, these are not voluntary engagements. There are structural forces that compel people to work as most of us have no other means of sustaining our existence than through selling the one thing we have – our ability to work. As a matter of fact, with the end of the **welfare state** under neo-liberalism's deregulation, shrinking of welfare provisions, etc., non-participation in work regimes is increasingly punished by poverty.[33] This reinforces the **structural violence** of being unemployed.[34] All this is hardly new. It simply mirrors 19th-century affairs where welfare states were largely absent, forcing people into factories in order to avoid starvation and abject poverty.

Today, under the ideology of the free market, people are even made to believe that seeking employment – an existence inside managerial domination – is their free choice; in reality, this is rather different as French Nobel Prize winner *François-Anatole Thibault* (1844–1924) made us aware in *Le Lys Rouge*: "the law, in its majestic equality, forbids the rich and the poor alike to sleep under bridges, to beg in the streets, and to steal bread".[35] Avoiding starvation level poverty "forces" us to seek employment. After 200+ years of capitalism, it almost feels "natural" to work but – then as today – there are structural forces operating behind the scene that push us into the recruitment process.

## Internal Recruitment

Good companies will have a formal HR policy, not just for external but also for internal recruitment. Equally, some organisations might prefer to recruit internally while others select to recruit externally. Both are used to balance **labour supply**, e.g. the availability of workers with the required skills to meet a firm's **labour demand**. Labour demand is the forecasted or assumed number of workers a company will need in the near future. Often, good **labour market analyses** are used to identify the availability of required skills and current pay practices, examine market competitors and current benchmarking, and identify labour market trends. As with many things in life, there is no right or wrong way, but there are advantages and disadvantages with internal and external recruitment. On the positive side of internal recruitment, HR managers tend to note at least seven advantages:

1.  internal recruitment often works as a great motivational opportunity as it shows employees that there is career progression inside the organisation – it is promotion from within;[36]
2.  internal recruitment also supports a sense of being recognised and valued by the organisation which, in turn, might lead to improvements in productivity;
3.  most HR managers agree and value the fact that internal recruitment improves retention rates and flattens **turnover rates** because internal recruitment tends to prevent employees from leaving for better job opportunities elsewhere;[37]
4.  perhaps one of the key factors in favour of internal recruitment is the reduction of recruitment costs as – at least in most cases – no external recruitment agency will have to be engaged and costly advertising can be avoided;
5.  one of the additional reasons for internal recruitment is that it works fast which can be important if an organisation needs to fill a position quickly;
6.  internal recruitment also results in placements of employees who already have a sound understanding of the organisation, thereby possessing what is called "organisational knowledge" about the organisation's culture, policies, practices, goals and missions; in turn, this also means that the organisation (and HR) knows the candidate who is applying for a position; and finally,
7.  inevitably and quite often preferably, internal recruitment will lead to a reduction in training costs as, for example, corporate induction programmes are not required for employees already working within the organisation.

Yet internal recruitment has its disadvantages. One of the most common and perhaps strongest disincentives for internal recruitment is the fact that internal candidates do not bring fresh ideas into the organisation. Another negative set against internal recruitment is that when HR managers fill one position through internal recruitment, it immediately and inescapably opens up a vacancy that used to be filled by the person offered the new position. This can – at least potentially – create a whole chain of subsequent recruitment processes opening up to fill the internal positions. To avoid such problems, HR managers often rely on **succession planning**[38] which means the evaluation of promotional potentials of employees and making decisions on a replacement for positions that open up. This can be linked to **Career Self-Management** which is the extent to which an employee gathers information and plans for career decisions.

## External Recruitment

External recruitment is often used to bring in expertise not available inside a business and to encourage innovation seen as better supported through an external candidate. For some of these reasons, HR managers opt for external recruitment. Deciding to go **external** for recruitment means encountering what is known as the external labour market. In some organisations such as, for example, local government and public sectors, it can be mandatory to recruit externally. In other cases, external recruitment dominates when positions with a higher monetary value (e.g. CEOs and senior executives) are to be filled.

If one sees the external labour market divided into a female and a male labour market, the male labour market is defined by a beginning – recruitment and selection – and often continuous employment that ends in retirement. Female **labour market participation** – often defined as the proportion of a given population aged 15 and over that is economically active – differs from that.[39] Quite often, there is a difference in the rate or proportion of labour market participation for women compared to men. For women, the curve is shown below:

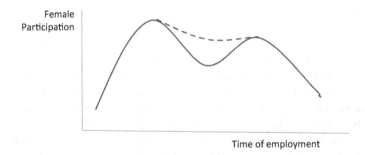

*Figure 2.1* The M-Curve – Female Labour Market Participation.

Figure 2.1 shows the so-called "M-Curve". At the horizontal "X" axis, we find ages ranging from 15+ to retirement while the vertical "Y" axis shows the rate of participation. The curve remains rather factual even if one considers that many women work part-time, are on short-term contracts or crowdworkers, etc.[40] The highest level of participation would mean that all women (100%) between the age of 15 and retirement work. Since this is never the case, rates of labour market participation globally rank roughly between 55% and 70% which means approximately half to two-thirds of a working-age population work. The key difference between men and women, however, is the M-curve and what is ideologically framed as "career choice" but is in reality more or less determined by external factors.[41] Such choices can be explained through the KCM model which is based on: authenticity (be true to yourself); balance (work–life balance[42]); and challenge (stimulating work).[43]

Typically, female working life starts with employment through HRM's recruitment and selection process. As women give birth and often remain the prime carer for children during their early years, women are given the so-called "option" of being a "stay-at-home-mum" while men, on the other hand, continue to work. This means that the labour market participation rate of women declines. Once children reach school age or leave the family home, many women re-enter the labour market and the participation rate increases until retirement. This forms the M-curve.

The key deciding factor for a woman's choice to work or stay at home is the availability of maternity leave[44] and affordable childcare. If childcare is plentiful and affordable, more women are likely to remain in the labour market and the M-curve is not as marked as in those cases where childcare is scarce and expensive. In the former scenario, the M-curve flattens (dotted line in Figure 2.1 linking the top female participation rate before childbirth and after re-entering the labour market). Progressive countries and political parties tend to work towards flattening the M-curve while conservatives tend to favour a more marked one. In any case, the M-curve applies overwhelmingly to women – not men. In addition to the external M-curve, women also face the internal **glass ceiling** where those seeking higher positions are blocked by "unseen" barriers as well as **glass walls** that prevent them from moving across functions inside an organisation. To counteract that, HRM uses **gender streaming** – actively encouraging women into such positions. Similarly, **grey ceilings** occur when such positions and appointments are blocked as a case of age discrimination.

The advantages and disadvantages of external versus internal recruitment can also be summed up through a cost versus speed matrix:

*Table 2.1* Internal/External Recruitment: Cost or Speed

|  | Cost | Speed |
| --- | --- | --- |
| External | ↑ High ↑ | ↓ Low ↓ |
| Internal | ↓ Low ↓ | ↑ High ↑ |

The disadvantage of external recruitment is that it is costly and slow while internal recruitment is a low-cost speedy option (Table 2.1). Yet despite this, much of today's recruitment takes place externally, perhaps for one single reason: external recruitment delivers new ideas, also known as "fresh blood", thereby avoiding the endless recycling of "ever-the-same" ideas.[45]

## Common Advertising Strategies

HRM's recruitment experts use a number of instruments to attract potential employees. These strategies are not to be confused with **strategic recruitment** which is when HR experts link the recruitment process to the overall strategy pursued by a company. One recruitment instrument, whether linked to company strategy or not, is called **lead market strategy** which offers higher than current market level wages and bonuses and is often applied when high-level pay is designed to make up for negative or less desirable job features.[46]

One of the more common problems with such a strategy is that potential candidates focus strongly on the monetary side of the job and consequently are often equally quick in leaving the organization for a "better deal" elsewhere. Another method used to recruit employees is **image advertising** and **branding** where companies advertise and promote themselves rather than actually looking for new recruits.[47] It is a form of deception to show that this company is a good place to work and if this leads to new recruits, HRM sees this as a welcome side-effect. Other organisations use **online recruitment strategies** such as, for example, social recruitment,[48] advertising on internet sites, job boards, and discussion forums such as, for example[49]:

- https://twitter.com;
- https://www.facebook.com;
- https://www.linkedin.com;
- https://au.indeed.com;
- https://www.indeed.co.uk.

The recruitment and selection process also deals with **direct applicants** who apply for a position without being prompted or solicited. Instead, they often express an interest in working for a specific organisation (e.g. flight attendants for an airline, etc.). In these cases, a company does not advertise such positions. As the HR director of a major airline told me once, "we do not need to advertise positions for flight attendants. We receive enough applications as it is." Other companies do not process any direct, i.e. **unsolicited applications**.

In addition, there are also **referrals**. They occur when people apply for positions encouraged by someone already working in the business. In many cases, this depends on networking. "As the president of the New York Stock Exchange Tom Farley declared in 2015 in *Fortune Magazine, When I think about my own career, I owe every job I've ever had to networking*".[50] The downside of networking is the potential occurrence of **nepotism**.[51]

### Advertising for a Position

If HRM opts for the external labour market option, usually some form of advertising is required. This leads to two fundamental questions regarding such advertising: (1) what does the advertisement need to say? and (2) to whom do we say it? This advertising has two facts attached to it: it is expensive but it also works. Typically, advertisements are placed in newspapers or job-related trade journals such as, for example, engineering journals. Increasingly, newspaper advertising is being replaced by **internet recruiting** focusing on five objectives:

1. internet recruitment is faster when compared to newspaper advertising;
2. it can be used as a marketing activity, e.g. image advertising;
3. it provides easy access for candidates as many have access to the internet;
4. potential applications/resumes can easily be directed to a corporate website; and
5. internet recruitment is relatively cheap compared to traditional advertising.

Internet recruitment tends to use **job boards** that are websites providing lists of positions to which an applicant can apply. Potential applicants can also post their **resumes** or **curriculum vitae** that provide a written overview of their experience and other qualifications, and are typically the first item that a potential employer encounters from a job seeker. Another problem is outright racism. "In one study, in which an identical set of resumes was sent out to employers, white applications with criminal records were called back more often than black applicants without criminal records".[52] However, the potential disadvantage of job boards as well as internet recruitment in general is that these forms of recruitment can lead to receiving a high number of unqualified applications – HRM calls this "dead wood".

Despite cases of actual "resume manipulation",[53] "80 per cent of resumes are rejected within eleven seconds".[54] To avoid this, HRM can rely on **e-recruitment** where recruitment experts search online for potential candidates. This is sometimes called **green recruitment** as the recruitment process is conducted paper-free with minimal environmental impact. It is organised through online mediums like e-mail, online application forms, online **job portals** and **applicant tracking systems** (ATS[55]), and, if possible, telephone and video interviews.[56] Here are ten issues to be mindful of[57]:

1. Dress the part.
2. Organize your surroundings.
3. Use appropriate lighting to look your best.
4. Use decent equipment.
5. Test your internet connection.
6. Look at the camera, not yourself.
7. Don't be checking your email.
8. First impressions count.
9. Practice.
10. Plan a video interview and test it.

Video – via Skype, Zoom,[58] etc. – interviews[59] minimise any travel-related environmental impacts and thereby lowers a company's carbon footprint.[60] In a further step, companies such as HireVU.com[61] have automated such interviews using AI[62] while other – Yobs.io[63] and Intervyo[64] – offer interview simulators for interview candidates.

In the process of recruitment, HR also uses what is euphemistically called **relationship recruitment**. This is when HR recruiters search the internet to investigate the private interests of potential candidates. This became known as **Cyber-Vetting** (which is often done ad hoc and without permission of the candidate). Cyber-vetting occurs by stealth when checking candidates on Facebook, etc., or when "employers are asking prospective employees to provide access to their social media passwords".[65] As a consequence, some decline to be on social media in order to protect their privacy from spying HRM recruitment consultants because "a fun social posting could screen you out of job".[66] In a future step, HR mangers might make computer-based personality judgements because they are more accurate than those made by humans.[67]

## Recruitment Agencies

There are cases when HRM decides not to go through the process outlined above and instead opts for **external recruitment agencies**, also called staffing agencies, recruitment firms, and the like. These come in two forms, (1) as public and (2) as private employment agencies. In not privatised **state job agencies**, the state provides this vital service to limit the potential corruption experienced with job placements. In many countries however, these independent state services have been privatised in the wake of the ideology of neo-liberalism. **Private employment agencies**, by contrast, charge a commission or fee to companies for their service of finding a suitable candidate. When selecting a recruitment agency, companies generally consider the following: what is the fee and how is it charged; what are the parameters of the search (where and when); who will do, for example, the labour market analysis; and who performs the interviews and reference checking, etc. In some industries (coalmining, waterfront, etc.), **trade unions** have been proven to be a good source of recruitment.

## Top Management Positions and International HRM

In the case of top management and executive positions (i.e. high ranking executives with titles such as chairman and chairperson, chief executive officer, managing director, president, executive director, executive vice-president, etc. with responsibilities for the entire enterprise), **head hunters** or **executive search firms** are used for recruitment.[68] These firms specialise in the top end of the labour market and often operate globally.[69] In some cases, this leads to **poaching** that takes place when a company hires an employee from a competing company – which by many is seen as a gross violation of ethics. Since head hunting often tends to go global, **international recruitment**[70] offers three options (Table 2.2) when recruiting. HRM categorises this under **International HRM** (IHRM). IHRM and business organisations in general often take one of the following approaches in their management style:

1. **ethnocentric**: key positions filled by nationals of a parent company;
2. **polycentric**: host country nationals recruited from within their own country;
3. **geocentric**: best people recruited, whatever their nationality;
4. **regiocentric**: best people recruited within region of subsidiary (EU, USA).

Disregarding the specific management approach (1–4), IHRM is concerned with the human resource issues of multinational firms in foreign subsidiaries (e.g. **expatriate management**) seen as an international process. This includes key HRM issues (global recruitment, performance management, rewards, OHS, training, trade unions, etc.) crossing national boundaries, for example, when recruiting a CEO or manager for an overseas assignment:

*Table 2.2* Expatriate Recruitment

| HCN | Host country national | A local employee from the foreign location is recruited |
|---|---|---|
| PCN | Parent country national | An expatriate who is a citizen of the country where the company is headquartered is recruited |
| TCN | Third country national | A citizen of a country different from the parent or host country is recruited. |

Each option has its own advantages and disadvantages. A HCN avoids cultural adjustment, language problems, and the possible **culture shock** that are one of the more common reasons why expatriates return early from their assignments (Table 2.2).[71] By hiring a PCN, mutual trust is usually high and company knowledge is assured while TCNs offer a more neutral position by avoiding to be seen as "the new overseas boss with no local knowledge, flown in from HQ" and the perceived lack of trust.

## University Recruitment, Skills, and Advertising Media

Another and less ethically damaging option is **university recruitment** as most universities offer a placement service for their graduates seeking employment. This occurs at undergraduate and postgraduate level and often includes **job fairs** organised by universities as **recruiting events** where employers and recruiters meet – often informally – with potential candidates.[72] Many universities offer such a service through dedicated departments.

When HR experts engage in recruitment, they quite often seek potential employees who offer **transportable skills** that show a suitable level of **employability**[73] – skills that can be used at home as well as abroad. In general, recruiters look for key selection criteria such as[74]:

1. interpersonal skills and the ability to communicate in written as well as oral language;
2. enthusiasm, knowledge of the business area, self-motivation, commitment, and a positive attitude;
3. the ability for critical reasoning;
4. the possession of analytical skills and problem-solving expertise;
5. academic qualifications such as, for example, MBA;
6. the ability to fit into an organisational culture;
7. practical work experiences in a relevant industry;
8. emotional intelligence (not just IQ) such as a mature character, etc.;[75]
9. teamwork and leadership skills, and finally,
10. intra- and extra-curricular interests and activities (hobbies, etc.)

On the downside, recruiters tend to look less favourably on the negatives of the items listed above such as the inability to communicate, the lack of passion or motivation, arrogance, selfishness, inappropriate qualifications, inflexibility, etc.[76] These down-sides do not only impact on potential employees, they also influence recruiters. Most people expect that recruiters care about the potential applicant and his or her poten-tial contribution to a business.

They should be well informed about the vacant position and aware of an inherent bias many people call **same as me bias** when establishing a suitable pool of candidates from which to select. This bias influences recruiters as they often tend to hire someone who is essentially similar to themselves.[77] Awareness of this bias, good HR policies, for-mal, somewhat rigid recruitment processes, and even the right medium of recruitment can help reducing this bias. On the recruitment tools of newspapers and magazines (declining) versus internet and networks (increasing), the advantages and disadvan-tages of each medium can be highlighted as follows:

*Table 2.3* Advantages and Disadvantages of the Recruitment Medium

| Medium | Advantages | Disadvantages |
| --- | --- | --- |
| Newspapers and magazines | Flexible ad size; tailored to geographical area; good corporate branding; accessing specific occupations; good for ongoing recruitment | Easily ignored, facing clutter of job ads; limited recruitment area, costly, slow |
| Internet and social networking | Access to local or global labour markets; can access niche markets; allows specific job searches; offers large pool; quick solution | Untidiness of sites; confusing; HRM can be flooded with inappropriate applications; potential for discrimination (no internet access) |

Table 2.3 shows that each medium of recruitment has advantages and disadvantages. To guide advertising, experienced HR recruiters often use **AIDA** which consists of

Attention, Interest, Desire, and Action. An advertisement that works must grab the **attention** of a job seeker – the target audience – whether online or in printed form. It must spark the job seeker's **interest** which is done by creating relevance of the advertised job to the person. It must also create a **desire** to apply for the job. Finally, all this should stimulate a person into **action**, it needs to move a person from a "willingness to read" towards a "willingness to act", i.e. to apply for the position advertised. Once all of the above has been taken into account and a suitable pool of candidates has been established, recruitment moves on towards the selection process.

## Selection

The selection process is designed to select the right candidate from a pool of suitable applicants. Currently, the term "talent" is used in HR literature to focus on the right applicant.[78] Talent is commonly seen as a skill or ability someone has naturally and was born with – not everyone has talent and not everyone gets a dream job that suits your talent.[79] Someone who has talent is able to do certain things without trying as hard as someone who does not have that talent. Over the years, the term "talent" has become somewhat controversial. Some even suggest there is a "Talent Myth".[80] Whether myth or not, most people who are selected for a job are hired because of their ability to do a job. In order to find the right person who can do the job, HR managers draw up a list of potential candidates.

Once this pool has been established, HR experts create a **short list**, for example, of three to seven potential candidates to be interviewed. In some cases, HR mangers like those at *Unilever* and *Hilton Worldwide* rely on companies like *HireVue*[81] and *Workday*[82] provide HR software assisting HR managers when filtering through applications. These are used by **algorithmic management** but also by **algorithmic HR**[83] when, for example, sorting through job applications opening up the option that "as many as 72% of CYVs never been seen by human eyes".[84] Workplace expert Dan Lyons writes[85]:

> The next time you look for a job, your first interview might not be with a human being – but with an AI-powered software system. Instead of talking to a recruiter from the HR department, you sit in front of a computer, or even your smartphone, and answer questions that pop up on the screen. You use your device's camera to record your responses on video. You might also be asked to solve a puzzle or play a game. The whole thing takes about ten minutes.

Unsuccessful candidates should receive a "respectful rejection" through a personalised response being sent to them. The candidates included in the short list move on to selection interviews that are seen as dialogues initiated by an HR expert with one or, commonly, more people from the company's side who form an interview panel often consisting of an HR expert, the person to whom the new recruit will report to – his or her immediate boss – and one or two other people such as, for example, a trade union representative, etc. The purpose of the selection interview is to gather information about the candidate and to evaluate suitability. This is the moment when first impressions become important, even if a video interview is conducted.[86]

HR uses **four types of interviews**:

(a) competency interviews (focusing on an applicant's skills, etc.),
(b) behaviour-based interviews (assessing job-related behaviours),

(c)  situational interviews (create critical incidents for problem-solving skills), and
(d)  telephone/video interviews.

## The Actual Interview

Before the actual job interview takes place, some HR experts elect to conduct a pre-job interview known as realistic job preview (RJP). The RJP informs candidates about the realistic aspects of the job including its desirable and undesirable facts. Today, HRM is aware that not properly conducted interviews can be rather unreliable indicators for a candidate's suitability when, for example, the aforementioned bias influences hiring decisions or when such decisions are used against a specific group of employees (e.g. ethnical background, age, gender, etc.). To validate these pitfalls, selection experts use seven basic measures:

1.  They ask standardised questions during a **structured job interview** in order to expose different candidates to the same questions.[87] This procedure also increases comparability between candidates and is better suited than unstructured interviews where the interviewer asks questions from a list of possible topics and **semi-structured questions** where only some core questions are structured;
2.  HR experts ask specific questions that are job related and likely to arise with the position to be filled. This helps determining how candidates will respond to a given situation;
3.  Interviewers also ask questions related to past experiences and potential job activities in the future. These take the form of hypothetical questions;
4.  They investigate whether a candidate has knowledge about their company (47% of interviewees are discarded because they didn't know enough about the company);
5.  They check whether a candidate is passionate about the job;
6.  They favour challenges while also looking for candidates who are not afraid to ask questions; and finally,
7.  They assess whether a candidate shows good old fashioned courtesy, adheres to employee etiquette 101 and makes a lasting impression.[88]

### *Employee Etiquette 101*

Seth Godin says catching someone's eye means being truly remarkable. For example, imagine you see a purple cow in a field of black-and-white ones – what will you remember? To make a lasting impression and land the job, you have to stand out before, during, and after the interview.

Together with the use of an interview panel and the avoidance of inappropriate or outright **discriminatory questions**[89] (race,[90] sexual orientation, political affiliations, age, potentially "over-qualification", etc.), these measures can avoid bias and lower individual subjectivities.[91] What they cannot avoid is the **power asymmetry** of recruitment.[92] This occurs because the cost of a company to recruit or not recruit candidate A over candidate B is minimal while, for example, the cost of getting or not getting a job is much larger for the candidate. Hence, candidates – not HR recruiters – are nervous during interviews (Table 2.4).

HR recruiters often use an evaluation form during their interviews. This consists, for example, of criteria such as

*Table 2.4* Evaluation During Interviews

| | First Impression | | Appearance | | Self-expression (English and Articulation) |
|---|---|---|---|---|---|
| ☐ | Very poor | ☐ | Untidy and sloppy | ☐ | Confused |
| ☐ | Good impression | ☐ | Overdressed and flashy | ☐ | Difficult to understand |
| ☐ | Very good | ☐ | Professional appearance | ☐ | Clear, fluent, logical, and persuasive |
| | **Behaviour** | | **Responsiveness** | | **Background and Experience** |
| ☐ | Overbearing and rude | ☐ | Withdrawn and dull | ☐ | Not related to position on offer |
| ☐ | Confident and tactful | ☐ | Responded directly | ☐ | Partly related to position on offer |
| ☐ | Enthusiastic | ☐ | Alert and intelligent | ☐ | Well-suited and unusually well-qualified |

While experienced HR interviewers use standard evaluation sheets like the one above, they also rely on **WASP**, answering "how do we conduct an interview"? WASP stands for: Welcome, Acquire, Supply, and Part. The **welcoming** part greets the applicant, shows hospitality, and "breaks the ice"; the **acquire** section asks questions such as: what information do you have?; what else do you need?; and what else do we need to check? The **supply** ascertains what kind of information should you offer and what will happen next while the **part** section simply farewells the candidate.[93]

Once interviews are completed, recruiters will compare the responses of interviewees and move on to the next step that consists of **references** and biographical data. This is done to collect more general background data of the candidates. Generally, HR recruiters regard reference checking as a weak predictor of a candidate's suitability for two reasons:

1. first of all, because it is the candidate who names the potential referees and
2. such reference letters tend to be positive in character.

In some cases, companies have even used police checks and private investigators to explore a candidate's past or to avoid outright fraud. Increasingly, however, HR managers move away from reference checking in favour of accessing social network sites and thereby causing privacy problems. Still, reference checking is mostly done only for the successful candidate on a shortlist. In other cases, it is conducted when an interview panel cannot reach a decision between, for example, two candidates. In these cases, reference checking can be a helpful tool.

## Testing Candidates

In addition to interviews and reference checking, some potential employees undergo a **physical ability test** that is used to analyse five common areas: (1) muscular tension, power, strength, and endurance; (2) cardiovascular endurance; (3) flexibility; (4) balance; and (5) general coordination. These tests are only relevant for a few positions, for example, in fire brigades, police service, for rescue personnel, etc., and since many countries are moving from manufacturing towards the service industry, these tests are becoming increasingly irrelevant. Virtually all countries go through something called **structural change** when moving from agriculture to manufacturing and to the service industry.[94] This is a one-way and irreversible movement often measured through the percentage of labour employed in all three sectors.[95]

It shows that, for example, the stage of economic development in Afghanistan is on the agriculture to manufacturing trajectory with 80% working in agriculture, 6% in manufacturing, and 14% in the service industry. By contrast, in Belgium, for example, the pattern is 1.3%; 18.6%, and 80.1% in the service industry. In other words, physical ability tests might be relevant for a recruiter in Afghanistan but they are less relevant in Belgium and many other of the thirty-four **OECD** and other developed countries.[96] Yet many human resources in the developed world still undergo general medical checks as a norm before employment commences. This is partly because of an emphasis on occupational health and safety (OHS) and/or workers' compensation obligations (insurance). These general medical checkups can be combined with physical ability tests. For some occupations[97] (pilots, police, fire fighters, etc.) even drug and alcohol tests[98] (urine analysis) can be conducted. For others such as police officers, security, army personnel, etc. a criminal record check is conducted.[99]

**Cognitive ability tests** (CAT), on the other hand, tend to become more relevant.[100] They usually cover three key areas: (1) verbal comprehension as the ability to understand verbal instructions and communicate; (2) quantitative abilities as the ability to deal with numbers; and (3) logical reasoning abilities seen as the ability to solve problems and find solutions to job related problems. Many recruiters are aware of the downsides (e.g. unreliability, invasion of privacy, etc.) of simple **IQ-tests** (IQ = intelligence quotient). Surprisingly, the famous Hawthorne experiment found that "the worker who ranked first in intelligence was the lowest in individual productivity while the one with the highest individual productivity ranked last in intelligence".[101] Whatever the case with IQ may be, next to IQ, there is also **EQ** or **emotional intelligence** (Table 2.5).[102]

Even though there is an increasing awareness that it is not individual ability that counts but the ability to work in teams while also sharing knowledge in a corporate "community of knowledge",[103] these tests are still used to determine the relative intelligence of people in order to compare their test scores to a standard measure.[104] Today, the most common addition to IQ is EQ/EI or emotional intelligence.[105] EI is used to describe the ability of individuals to recognise their own and other people's emotions and to use emotional information to guide thinking and behaviours. In addition to IQ and EQ we know that there are seven intelligences as shown in Table 1.3[106]:

*Table 2.5* Seven Intelligences and Job Applications

| Form of Intelligence | Jobs, Positions, and Professions | Abilities and Application in Various Jobs |
|---|---|---|
| Standard logical IQ | Scientist, systems analyst, mathematician, IT-expert | Analyse logical and numerical patterns, use logical reasoning |
| Linguistic | Public relations, corporate communications, journalism | Semiotic skills, sounds, meaning of words, language functions |
| Music and sound | Composer, marketing, corporate public relations | Ability to produce rhythm, pitch, timbre, skills in musical expressions |
| Spatial | Operations management, web-designers, etc. | Analyse and construct a visual-spatial world and perform transformation of initial perspectives |

(*Continued*)

*Table 2.5* (Continued)

| Form of Intelligence | Jobs, Positions, and Professions | Abilities and Application in Various Jobs |
|---|---|---|
| Motor-kinesthetic[107] | Team coach, athlete, presenter | Skills in controlling body movements and handling objects skilfully |
| Inter-personal | Salesperson, HRM, manager, organisational psychologist | Understanding others: appropriate responses to motivations and desires of other people |
| Intra-personal | Coordinator, team leader, general manager, MBA, CEO | Understand own and group behaviours: ability to draw on them for guidance, knowledge of strengths, weaknesses, and desires of groups, coordination skills |

In addition to these seven forms of intelligence, recruiters also conduct **personality tests**[108] while tending to simplify human emotions and behaviours by relying on key **personality inventories**.[109] These rather simplistic inventories are used to assist recruiters in assessing candidates:

(a) **extroversion**: being social, communicative, and expressive;[110]
(b) **adjustment**: being emotionally stable and secure;
(c) **agreeableness**: being courageous, trusting, and tolerant;
(d) **conscientiousness**: being dependable, organised, and thorough; and
(e) **inquisitiveness**: being curious, imaginative, and broad minded.

Others rely on the so-called "Big-Five":[111] "openness to experience, conscientiousness, extroversion, agreeableness, and neuroticism".[112] But there are also negatives associated with personality tests and candidates can be "red-lighted" by algorism based "personality tests" as US mathematician Cathy O'Niel explains.[113]

Some of the items listed above are assessed when recruiters use **psychometric testing** that is often administered online and predominantly used for managerial rather than non-managerial positions. It is a standard method that measures an individual's mental capabilities and behavioural style and assesses a candidate's suitability for managerial roles that require a certain personality, mental characteristics, and cognitive and emotional abilities.[114] Despite the prevalence of psychometric testing, however, these tests have three important downsides. They are considered to be an intrusion into privacy, to be unethical and – perhaps more importantly – they are also considered to be unreliable as, for example, the case of US-Astronaut Lisa M. Nowak showed (she was most likely put through all the psychometrical testing NASA could muster):

> Nowak gained international attention on 5 February 2007, when she was arrested in Orlando, Florida, and subsequently charged with the attempted kidnapping of U.S. Air Force Captain Colleen Shipman, who was romantically involved with astronaut William Oefelein. Nowak drove from Houston to Orlando, Florida, on 4–5 February 2007. Police reports indicated she wore space diapers during the trip in order to claim that she could have never made the trip in time and kidnap her female competitor to get the man she wanted.

The use of such standardised psychometric testing can be flawed as candidates may be able to not only cheat in the actual test but can also learn "the tricks of the trade" by repeatedly going through such tests before doing the actual one for the company. Perhaps somewhat more reliable than psychometric testing are simple **work samples** that interviewees bring to job interviews showing past achievements and skills. These are seen as valuable predictors for future achievements ranking higher than, for example, a candidate's mental ability or results from assessment centres.

**Assessment centres** are procedures, not locations. They are used when employees' performances, for example, in team situations, are formally assessed by raters who evaluate team ability, leadership skills, and the ability to coordinate teams. They are actual performances in **simulated work situations** using a multitude of techniques, actual observations by multiple observers, and separating observation from evaluation.[115] Somewhat more controversial is **drug testing** that is also considered an invasion into privacy and – because of that – only used for certain occupations where companies feel a need for it. Aligned to that are also **honesty tests** and **polygraph testing** but both are used only when sensitive positions are to be filled – despite the criticism that these tests are weak predictors of an employee's future behaviour.

## Offering Position and Induction Programmes

Once the application has been assessed, references have been checked, interviews conducted, and tests evaluated, the position was offered and the candidate has accepted the position, what follows the two stage process of recruitment → selection is the participation in an **induction programme**. The main purpose of this programme is to help new employees integrate into the organisation, ensure performance, and retain suitable staff. Induction programmes usually take two forms:

1. *general topics* of interest for new employees such as information about the organisation (corporate videos, brochures, mission statements, policies, etc.) and
2. *specific job-related issues* concerning only the job holder.

Induction programmes can be formal or informal. In formal inductions, companies provide a structured entry into the organisation, while in informal inductions, one is often simply told, "this is Lara, Lara will show you around and tell you how things work around here". Being introduced to a new job is often linked to what is known as the **honeymoon-hangover effect** whereby job satisfaction increases sharply when starting a new job, but quickly falls back to the original level.[116] Whether honeymoon-hangover or not getting a new job means going through the recruitment and selection process which contains seven steps:

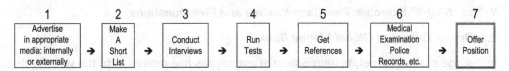

*Figure 2.2* The RS-Process – Shown as a Seven-Step Flow Chart

## Workbook

### IV  Five Discussion Questions on Recruitment and Selection

### And One Report Question on Recruitment and Selection

#### 1.  *Discussion Questions:*

1. Whenever HR experts are faced with recruitment, one of the first things on their minds is "internal versus external" recruitment. Both – internal and external – recruitment have advantages and disadvantages; discuss the pros and cons of these forms of recruitment.
2. Online or internet recruitment is often considered to be inexpensive and fast. But e-recruitment also has disadvantages. Discuss the shortcomings of e-recruitment.
3. There are several elements recruiters use during interviews to reduce the "same as me" bias and increase the comparability of responses given by interviewees during formal interviews. What are these elements?
4. Quite often HR recruiters rely on cognitive ability tests to assess the mental capabilities of candidates. These tests tend to focus on IQ but today we are aware that people have more than just one version of intelligence. Discuss how the seven forms of intelligence can assist companies.
5. HR recruiters often use psychometrical testing when assessing the suitability of a candidate, but they are also aware of the negatives associated with this form of testing. Discuss these negatives.

#### 2.  *Report Question:*

#### *Asymmetrical Power Relations in Recruitment and Selection*

When applying for a position, the recruiter often has more power than the recruited person. In an interview, for example, one is calm while the other is often nervous! For recruitment managers, the cost of employing resource (A) over resource (B) is small when both are otherwise equal (experience, professionalism, fitting-in, pay-grades, education, etc.). For the person to be recruited, on the other hand, not getting a position comes at a significant cost (job vs. no job). Develop four [4] recommendations on how this asymmetrical power relationship can be overcome?

### V  The "5-by-5" Exercise: Five Case Studies and Five Questions

#### *2.1  Online Testing at Global Money Bank*

In the age of the internet, testing potential employees has moved onto the web. With it comes the problem of cheating as a potential problem. Nicola *Sacco*, Global Money Bank's top recruitment manager says, "it (the web) remains a valuable tool for us". Being a truly multinational corporation, Global Money Bank hires literally hundreds of new staff members and managers every year in many different countries. "Before we moved onto the web for online testing, we spent thousands of dollars on testing, it was time and manpower intensive", explains Sacco.

"Moving online, allows us to be consistent across different countries while focusing on testing reduces the turnover rate for GMB. Based on a careful job analysis, Global Money Bank now follows a tailored process." Sacco notes that "we needed to identify candidates who are highly motivated, have a positive attitude towards banking, and depict numerical as well as communicative skills". The online test starts by asking candidates basic biodata information while also simulating on the job situations to be judged. Candidates successfully passing the test can – in a next step – take part in real-life work simulations and at an onsite as well as internet-based (Skype) interview during which structured and open questions are asked.

1.   Given the substantial number of new candidates, was Global Money Bank's decision to move towards online testing valid?
2.   What are the advantages and disadvantages of online testing?
3.   Are these tests a good predictor of a candidate's future behaviour at Global Money Bank?
4.   Should such tests be used to screen out unsuitable candidates before personal interviews take place?
5.   Discuss the ethical implications – intrusion in privacy, for example – of such tests.

### 2.2 Selecting Sales people for Global Food Corp.

Every day, Global Food Corp. deals with thousands of tons of perishable food products for resale to global wholesalers in twenty-seven countries. Internet and phone sales personnel take orders from major food wholesalers, write up the orders, and send them to the appropriate food producers. Nearly 950 of the company's 13,000 global employees work in Global Food Corp.'s sales department. Since these sales jobs often require unusually long hours using the internet and on the phone dealing with different accounts, the work is extremely demanding and turnover remains high. The manager of Global Food Corp.'s sales department, Beate Klarsfeld, recently formulated the following interpretation in the presence of Global Food Corp.'s HR manager, Daniel Craig:

Most of the people who work in our sales department fall into two broad groups. There are those who have been here for many years. They seem reasonably content and some are what I would call "top sellers". We are happy to hold on to them. The second group consists of people who have been here for less than a year. Global Food Corp. is still plagued by our unreasonable turnover. In fact, we have lost one in three new employees during recent months. During exit interviews, most people who are leaving mentioned that they "had no idea how much time they had to spend on the internet and on the phone". They also said that "balancing different accounts and different customer demands was stressful". While department managers were generally pleased with the quality of recruits and appreciated the work of HRM at Global Food Corp. when recruiting new employees, one department manager was still concerned, arguing that "we cannot continue with this high turnover". In addition, the department manager also argued that Global Food Corp. is spending too much time constantly training new workers, suggesting that HRM should hire employees who are more aware of what the job actually involves so that Global Food Corp. would hire more stable workers.

1. Are the concerns of Global Food Corp.'s department managers reason enough to re-evaluate the recruitment and selection process of Global Food Corp.? If so, why?
2. As an HR manager, is high turnover a problem for Global Food Corp.? Do the numbers support the department manager's assertion? If so, should the turnover rate be lower?
3. Do you think that new recruits should be made aware of what the job actually involves? At which point of the recruitment and/or selection process should this occur?
4. Do you think that work simulations are useful to raise awareness of the demands of the job?
5. Should the department manager participate in job interviews? If so, why?

### 2.3 Experienced Green Development Engineer

This is your opportunity to work for a results focused position at "Global.Mining.Com". "Global.Mining.Com" provides engineering expertise to the resource extraction industry such as mining, minerals, and energy resources. Our global client list includes large resource companies operating in several continents. We employ 22,500 people globally. "Global.Mining.Com" is looking for a "green" engineer with engineering expertise and knowledge in the following three areas: corporate social responsibility, climate change, corporate sustainability and carbon footprint reduction. You can be assured there will be no shortage of interesting and challenging projects. The position includes working at a global level with worldwide projects. "Global.Mining.Com" has regional headquarters in New York, London, Moscow, Tokyo, Sydney, and Rio de Janeiro.

We have just won a contract to work on a large-scale environmental project and are looking for a "Green Development Engineer" to help establish, assist, and oversee our Project Team. As the "Green Development Engineer" you will have the opportunity to design and implement policies and processes and be involved in our projects from start to finish in various locations.

To be considered for this position, it is essential that you have:

1. tertiary engineering qualifications
2. experience in cost and schedule management with strong logical-mathematical skills (MS Project and Excel)
3. proven ability to identify potential environmental impacts and take appropriate preventative actions.

Your responsibilities will include:

* providing leadership, developing guidelines,[117] as well as planning
* develop environment plans for budgets, cost trends, forecasts, and cost analysis
* management of environmental impact and detailed design phases

- revision of planning and scheduling documentation to identify risk issues
- liaison with engineering staff and external "stakeholders" to obtain accurate information on environmental issues for our project and provide project management support
- creation and on-going management of environmental programmes in our four key environmental areas:

1. corporate social responsibility,
2. addressing climate change,
3. corporate sustainability, and
4. carbon footprint reduction

Send your resume and cover letter to Mr Sean Connery, email to sean.connery@global.mining.com

1. Develop a "formal recruitment policy" for the above case.
2. Discuss the advantages and disadvantages of the internal and external labour market for the position advertised.
3. Write a cover letter addressing the selection criteria.
4. Should the filling of this position involve psychometric testing? What are the advantages and problems of psychometric testing?
5. Would you expect candidates to bring work samples? If so, which ones?

### 2.4 Internal Recruitment at Online.Store.Com

Online.Store.Com promotes career opportunities on our dedicated careers website. When recruiting, we aim to attract new colleagues with the best fit for our organisational culture.[118] Part of the attraction comes from offering above market salaries and benefits such as our corporate "Share.Owner" scheme and colleague discounts. In 2016, Online.Store.Com's "Share.Owner" scheme had record payouts where 29,850 employees shared $129 million.

Our exclusive online recruitment website has improved the swiftness and effectiveness of our recruitment process, making job applications straightforward for potential candidates and resulting in prompt selection outcomes for HR management. We advertise around 1,100 new positions per year globally. Our specifically created "careers site" handles well above over half a million applications for positions at Online.Store.Com annually. We also use social media channels such as LinkedIn as well as recruitment firms such as "I Look For You", accessing the widest range of potential recruits when advertising job vacancies at Online.Store.Com.[119]

**Roles and Responsibilities**

As one of the largest employers, Online.Store.Com offers a wide scope of opportunities. These range from positions for university students seeking part-time work experience to full-scale apprenticeships and specialised graduate training in a variety of management areas. Our policy "Living Online.Store.Com" means that the company and working colleagues pledge that everyone is treated fairly and respectfully. It gives all employees equal opportunity to progress their career. Regardless of what point of entry a candidate chooses, Online.Store.Com has the same goal for recruitment: recruiting new employees who share our beliefs and outlook as our company continues to grow. What makes Online.Store.Com stand out is our ability to offer a wide variety of managerial roles because of our unique business formats. These range from roles in Online.Store.Com's "superstores" (physical locations) to online supermarkets. Managerial positions range from Shift Leaders and Department Managers to logistics roles within Distribution. In addition, Online.Store.Com offers managerial roles within our Home Office including key functions such as accounting, supply chain management, marketing, and HRM. Online.Store.Com offers global career possibilities.

Ms Cathy Middleton began her career as a checkout operator in one of Online.Store.Com's upmarket stores and from there has undertaken roles as "customer care manager, corporate people manager, Online.Store.Com's living store supervisor, and store manager. Ms Middleton is currently our "Living Store Manager" in Beijing. Cathy states: "For me, moving around in Online.Store.Com in very different roles – service, people and trading – has really helped in what I'm doing now because I've seen the business from so many angles – Online.Store.Com's internal recruitment process works for me".

1.  What are the reasons for Online.Store.Com to focus on internal recruitment?
2.  What was HRM's experience with internal promotion through the ranks of Online.Store.Com? Give examples.
3.  What are the – unmentioned – negatives of internal recruitment? Mention at least three.
4.  Has Online.Store.Com – potentially – been able to avoid these negatives?
5.  Write a formal selection policy for Online.Store.Com.

### 2.5 Job Opportunities with Global Care

Position: Senior Research Associate (GC-INT.2016)
Added: 22 November 2016
Region: Asia, Division: International
Job Type: Fixed Term in Nepal
Job: Global Care is looking for two dynamic team players. This is a temporary fixed-term national position. The contract duration of this position is fifteen months initially (Nepalese nationals are eligible to apply).
Location: London and Kathmandu with frequent field visits to Nepal (on an average 80%).
No. of posts: TWO

You will report to the Senior Program Officer (Public Health Promoter), and will work in close coordination with a number of partners, NGOs, state representatives and project teams in Nepal. The purpose of these positions is to support and conduct surveys related to the hazard prone districts of Nepal. The task also includes organising and managing local programmes and engage with cultural, social, and business communities as well as those groups affected by potential disasters. This may include local community and local governments.

**Roles and Responsibilities:**

- Conduct surveys using Emergency Market Mapping Analysis (EMMA) and Market Mapping Analysis (MMA) tools for market assessment.
- Carry out household, community, market, and private sector surveys.
- Facilitate local projects closely linked to government institutions and the private sector.
- Organise meetings and events with government departments and the private sector.
- Recordkeeping and data completion of field survey and meeting/event minutes.
- Draft report preparation for all events as well as sharing these with local stakeholders.
- Work closely with the development team and support the application of market mapping tools.

Skills and Competencies:

- Graduate studies in a relevant field (Social Science/Marketing/Civil Diploma);
- experience in both qualitative and quantitative research;
- minimum three (3) years of experience in supporting role, working or investing in small and medium enterprises;
- understanding mobile-based survey systems;
- strategic thinking and analytical skills; understanding of economic development and market-based programming;
- willingness to understand the socio-economic context of the country;
- knowledge of market, value chain systems and role of private sectors in development, especially growing importance of micro and small enterprise and entrepreneurship;
- knowledge and understanding of emergency management;
- good verbal and written communications skills (English), ability to convey ideas clearly and succinctly;
- being a confident speaker able to represent these ideas to local organisations.
  1. Write a cover letter addressing Global Care's selection criteria for this position.
  2. Develop a formal recruitment policy for Global.Care.
  3. Construct a semi-structured interview questionnaire with at least five questions for the job interviews.
  4. Do you suggest searching for these two positions internally or externally? Why?
  5. If you opt for external recruitment, what is the best medium?

### VI  A Suggestion for an Online Guest Lecture

Economist Andrew McAfee talks about the
*"Jobs of the Future" (2013)*
https://www.ted.com/talks/andrew_mcafee_what_will_future_jobs_look_like
[the online guest lecture above is merely a suggestion – www.ted.com/talks offers additional material to choose from]

## VII List of Suggested Documentaries on Recruitment and Selection

The carefully selected documentary videos below are mere suggestions to be used during tutorials. Documentaries have been selected to achieve two things: (1) to explain key HRM themes and (2) to provide an insight into the reality of HRM. Typically, these short documentaries should be viewed in class followed by a class discussion on the content of the video. Alternatively, questions on documentaries can be prepared beforehand and small group discussions can follow up the video after viewing is concluded. Should any of the web links no longer function, please conduct an internet search for other – alternative – documentaries related to your tutorial topic (e.g. filmsforaction.org):

> HR-Basics Recruitment & Selection: youtube.com/watch?v=7TNxZclJPr4
> Randstad Recruitment & Selection: youtube.com/watch?v=RlnuBNwjeOQ
> Samsung Recruitment Process: youtube.com/watch?v=RvuHolRTQig
> The New Boss: youtube.com/watch?v=f9OT0HTauKU

## Notes

1  www.thecorporation.com/.
2  https://www.law.illinois.edu/aviram/Dodge.pdf.
3  Armstrong, S. J. & Fukami, C. V. 2009. Past, present and future perspectives of management learning, education, and development, in: Armstrong, S. J. & Fukami, C. V. (eds.) *Handbook of Management Learning, Education and Development*, London: Sage, p. 5.
4  Magretta, J. 2012. *What Management Is: How It Works and Why It's Everyone's Business*, London: Profile, pp. 4 & 196.
5  HR policies are formulated as "statements of intent" while their formulation often excludes those "for" whom these policies are written. CEO John Calder of the Remington Typewriter Company in 1912 [noted], "the last thing a good manager would think of doing would be to make his policies of shop management the subject of a referendum" (Montgomery, D. 1979. *Workers' Control in America*, Cambridge: Cambridge University Press, p. 1).
6  Boxall, P. & Purcell, J. 2015. *Strategy and Human Resource Management* (4th ed.), Basingstoke: Palgrave, p. 4; cf. Smith, C. 2006. The double indeterminacy of labour power, labour effort and labour mobility, *Work, Employment & Society*, 20(2): 389–402.
7  Dessain, N. 2016. Human resource marketing and recruiting, in: Zeuch, M. (eds.) *Handbook of HRM*, Heidelberg: Springer, p. 24.
8  http://www.rand.org/topics/delphi-method.html.
9  http://www.mckinsey.com/business-functions/strategy-and-corporate-finance/our-insights/the-use-and-abuse-of-scenarios.
10  Ulrich, D. et al. 1995. Human resource competencies: an empirical assessment, *Human Resource Management*, 34(4): 473–495.
11  Cunningham, J. B. 2016. *Strategic Human Resource Management in the Public and Non-profit Sectors*, New York: Palgrave Macmillan.
12  Sparkman, R. 2018. *Strategic Workforce Planning*, New York: Kogan Page.
13  Edwards, M. R. 2016. *Predictive HR Analytics: Mastering the HR Metric*, London: Kogan Page.
14  Valeva, S. et al. 2017. Balancing flexibility and inventory in workforce planning with learning, *International Journal of Production Economics*, (183): 194–207.
15  http://www.bbc.com/news/world-asia-india-34276253.
16  A good example is:

> Deutsche Bank AG Recruitment is designed to identify and hire the very best people available in the fairest manner possible. Known by its brand promise of Passion to Perform, the bank solely recognises the capabilities and experiences of an individual and promotes the value of equal opportunities.

17  Employment contracts always include what is known as "psychological contracts" (a set of unwritten but often reciprocal expectations between employees and companies); Robinson, S. L., 1996. Trust and breach of the psychological contract, *Administrative Science Quarterly*, 41(4):574–599.

18  Berg, J. 2015. *Labour Markets, Institutions and Inequality*, Cheltenham: Edward Elgar.

19  Many are aware that 'external hires are paid nearly 20 percent more than company veterans at the same level, despite receiving lower performance evolutions and still being more likely to quit' (Galloway, S. 2018. *The Four: The Hidden DNA of Amazon, Apple, Facebook, and Google*, (eBook) New York: Portfolio, p. 427).

20  Nieves, J. & Quintana, A. 2018. Human resource practices and innovation in the hotel industry: the mediating role of human capital, *Tourism and Hospitality Research*, 18(1): 72–83.

21  ILO. 2020. Labour Market and Covid-19 (https://www.ilo.org/wcmsp5/groups/public/@dgreports/@dcomm/documents/briefingnote/wcms_749399.pdf, accessed: 25th August 2020).

22  Williams, M. et al. 2020. *Mapping Good Work – The Quality of Working Life across the Occupational Structure*, Bristol: Bristol University Press, p. 6.

23  Loach, K. 2019. *Sorry We Missed You* (movie, 100 min), London: Entertainment One (https://www.youtube.com/watch?v=ysjwg-MnZao).

24  Even though a worker 'sells himself to an exploiter [while] the life of the poor is valued as nothing by the rich...women are cheaper than men [and] child flesh is the cheapest', wrote Johann Most in 1884 (https://theanarchistlibrary.org/library/johann-most-the-beast-of-property.pdf). More than 100 years later, the world still has poverty, workers still need to sell themselves to employers, child labour is still not eliminated, and many women still earn less than men.

25  15 major corporations you never knew profited from slavery (atlantablackstar.com, August 26, 2013): Lehman Brothers, Aetna, JPMorgan, New York Life, Wachovia Corporation, N M Rothschild & Sons Bank, Norfolk Southern, FleetBoston, CSX, Canadian National Railway Company, Brown Brothers Harriman, Barclays, and AIG.

26  On HRM and Slavery, see: https://www.hrmonline.com.au/section/legal/hr-needs-modern-slavery-legislation/, https://www.shrm.org/hr-today/news/hr-magazine/pages/0512meinert.aspx; Hodal, K. 2019. One in 200 People Is a Slave. Why? (https://www.theguardian.com, 25th February 2019, accessed: 25th August 2020).

27  Parreñas, R. S. & Silvey, R. 2016. Domestic workers refusing neo-slavery in the UAE, *Contexts*, 15(3):36–41.

28  Holborow, M. 2015. *Language and Neoliberalism*, London: Routledge, p. 16.

29  LaPierre, S. One last chance to fix capitalism, *Harvard Business Review*, 98(2): 146–147 (cf. https://www.youtube.com/watch?v=ynbgMKclWWc).

30  A kind of "bonded" labour exploitation also exists in prisons (https://www.bbc.com/news/business-53234485).

31  Dolack, P. 2017. Eight people own as much as half the world (counterpunch.org, 20th January 2017, p. 1).

32  http://slaveryfootprint.org/.

33  Wahl, A. 2011. *The Rise and Fall of the Welfare State*, London: Pluto Press.

34  Kreckel, R. 1980. Unequal opportunity structure and labour market segmentation, *Sociology*, 14(4):525–550; Vorobej, M. 2016. *The Concept of Violence*, London: Routledge.

35  Klikauer, T. 2013. *Managerialism – Critique of an Ideology*, Basingstoke: Palgrave, p. 222; Cohen G. A., 1983. The structure of proletarian unfreedom, *Philosophy & Public Affairs*, 12(1):3–33; Reiman, J. 1987. Exploitation, force, and the moral assessment of capitalism: thoughts on Roemer and Cohen, *Philosophy & Public Affairs*, 16(1):3–41; Gini A. R. & Sullivan, T. 1987. Work: the process and the person, *Journal of Business Ethics*, 6(8):649–655; Varoufakis, Y. 1998. "Labour as more than a commodity" & "wages, prices, and profits", in: *Foundations of Economics: A Beginner's Companion*, London: Routledge, pp. 170–200.

36  For an overview of "old" vs. "new" ways of career planning, see Wilton's *Introduction to HRM* (2016:325).

37  NPR 2018. Turnover in Trump's White House (https://www.npr.org, 19th January 2018, accessed: 22nd January 2018).

38  Hildebrand, U. 2016. Performance and talent: essentials of succession planning, in: Zeuch, M. (eds.) *Handbook of HRM*, Heidelberg: Springer, p. 596.

39  Overall, the 'participation rates between women and men [stays] at 26% [with] little or no improvement' (Peetz, D. 2019. *The Realities and Futures of Work*, Canberra: ANU Press, p. 86).

40  Howcroft, D. & Bergvall-Kåreborn, B. 2019. A typology of crowdwork platforms, *Work, Employment & Society*, 33(1): 21–38; cf. https://data.oecd.org/emp/part-time-employment-rate.htm.

41  Cavoulacos, A. & Minshew, K. 2017. *The New Rules of Work*, New York: Crown Business.

42  https://www.harvardbusiness.org/wp-content/uploads/2020/04/HBR-What-will-Work-Life-Balance-Look-Like-After-the-Pandemic.pdf.

43  Sullivan, S. E. & Mainiero, L. 2008. Using the kaleidoscope career model to understand the changing patterns of women's careers: designing HRD programs that attract and retain women, *Advances in Developing Human Resources*, 10(1): 32–49.

44  https://www.bbc.com/worklife/article/20210624-why-doesnt-the-us-have-mandated-paid-maternity-leave.

45  Messmer, M. 2007. *HR Kit for Dummies*, Indianapolis, IN: Wiley, p. 49.

46  Sample, I. 2017. We cannot compete: why universities are losing their best AI scientists (https://www.theguardian.com/science/2017/nov/01/cant-compete-universities-losing-best-ai-scientists, accessed 12th November 2017).

47  Lane, P. 2016. HR marketing and recruiting, in: Zeuch, M. (eds.) *Handbook of HRM*, Cham: Springer, pp. 23–52.

48  Gravili, G. & Fait, M. 2017. *Social Recruitment in HRM: A Theoretical Approach and Empirical Analysis*, Bingley: Emerald.

49  Hochschild, A. R. 2012. *The Outsourced Self: Intimate Life in Market Times*, New York: Metropolitan Books.

50  Bloom, P. & Rhodes, C. 2018. *CEO Society*, London: Zed-Books (epub version), p. 152.

51  Nepotism is the practice among those with power or influence of favouring relatives or friends, especially by giving them jobs.

52  Saini, A. 2019. *Superior – The Return of Race Science*, Boson, MA: Beacon Press, p. 192.

53  Spicer, A. 2018, *Bullshit Business*, London: Routledge, p. 42.

54  Scudamore, B. 2016. How to Gain an Edge When a Job Opportunity Arises (www.theglobeandmail.com, 22nd November 2016); cf. https://www.bbc.com/news/business-51371670.

55  https://www.bbc.com/worklife/article/20200715-the-reason-employers-love-online-job-portals.

56  Krys, K. et al. 2016. Be careful where you smile: culture shapes judgments of intelligence and honesty of smiling individuals, *Journal of Nonverbal Behavior*, 40(2):101–116.

57  Walsh, G. 2019. How To Ace A Video Interview (https://www.geraldwalsh.com/blog?c=how-to-ace-a-video-interview, accessed: 30th November 2019).

58  https://www.bbc.com/news/newsbeat-54164417.

59  Such as, for example, using Skype, FaceTime, Zoom, etc.

60  Markey, R., McIvor, J. & Wright, C. F. 2016. Employee participation and carbon emissions reduction in Australian workplaces, *International Journal of Human Resource Management*, 27(2): 173–191.

61  https://www.hirevue.com/.

62  https://edition.cnn.com/2020/01/15/tech/ai-job-interview/index.html.

63  https://yobs.io/candidate-simulator.

64  https://www.intervyo.com/en_US/.

65  Ajunwa, I., Crawford, K., & Schultz, J. 2017. Limitless worker surveillance, *California Law Review*, 105:752.

66  Gomez-Meji, L. R. 2016. *Managing HR* (11th ed.), Harlow: Pearson, p. 188.

67  Youyou, W., Kosinski, M. & Stillwell, D. 2015. Computer-based personality judgments are more accurate than those made by humans, *Proceedings of the National Academy of Sciences*, 112(4): 1036–1040.

68  Abraham, C. 2017. When hiring execs, context matters most, *Harvard Business Review*, September–October Issue; Illing, L. & Anders, F. 2016. HR-marketing and recruiting: essentials of executive search, in: Zeuch, M. (eds.) *Handbook of HRM*, Heidelberg: Springer, p. 141.

69  Vance, C. M. & Paik, Y. 2015. *Managing a Global Workforce*, London: Routledge.

70  See, for example: http://www.mercerint.com (cf. Global City Index at www.atkearney.com).

71  A culture shock is the reaction of expatriates who enter a new unpredictable and therefore uncertain environment (Kamoche, K. 1997. Knowledge creation and learning in international HRM, *International Journal of HRM*, 8(2):213–225).

72  Dessain, N. & Zeuch, M. 2016. HR marketing and recruiting: essentials of recruiting events, in: Zeuch, M. (eds.) *Handbook of HRM*, Heidelberg: Springer, p. 84.

73  Neugebauer, J. & Evans-Brain, J. 2016. *Employability – Making the Most of Your Career Development*, London: Sage.

74  World Economic Forum, 2016. *The Future of Jobs* (www3.weforum.org; p. 21); in addition to the ten skills outlined, the other skill consistently ranked high is the ability of "report writing" (Ballard, C. and Daniel, B. 2016. What skills are important? A replication, *Journal of Applied Social Science*, 10(1):71).

75  Goleman, D. & Boyatzis, R. E. 2017. Emotional intelligence has 12 elements. Which do you need to work on?, *Harvard Business Review*, 6th February.

76  Monster. 2019. Despite Recruiter Confidence, Exaggeration and Skills Gaps Plague the Hiring Process (https://www.monster.com/about/a/state-of-the-recruiter-2019, 21st October 2019, accessed: 15th December 2019).

77  In social psychology, this is called "homophily" (Kleinbaum, A. M. Stuart, T. E. & Tushman, M. L. 2013. Discretion within constraint: homophily and structure in a formal organization, *Organization Science*, 24(5): 1316–1336; cf. Hood B., 2012. *Self Illusion*, Oxford: Oxford University Press, p. 185).

78  Chamorro-Premuzic, T. 2017. How to highlight your talents in a job interview without showing off, *Harvard Business Review*, 28th December 2017; Fernandez-Araoz, C. 2017. 21st-century talent spotting, *Harvard Business Review*, 6th November 2017; HBR-Press, 2017. *Hiring and Developing Top Talent*, Cambridge: Harvard Business Publishing; Amankwah-Amoah, J., Nyuur, R. B., & Ifere, S. 2017. A question of top talent? The effects of lateral hiring in two emerging economies, *International Journal of Human Resource Management*, 28(11): 1527–1546.

79  https://theconversation.com/when-your-dream-job-is-a-nightmare-158749.

80  Gladwell, M. 2002. *The Talent Myth* (https://www.newyorker.com/magazine/2002/07/22/the-talent-myth, accessed: 30th January 2018).

81  https://www.hirevue.com.

82  https://www.workday.com.

83  Bogen, M. 2019. All the ways hiring algorithms can introduce bias, *Harvard Business Review*, 6th May 2019.

84  Warin, R. & McCann, D. 2018. Who Watches the Workers? (https://neweconomics.org, 2018, accessed: 5th May 2019), p. 8.

85  Lyons, D. 2018. *Lab Rats*, London: Atlantic Books, p. 155.

86  https://www.seek.com.au/career-advice/what-to-wear-to-an-interview-really... And one might like to remember Mark Twain who said once, "naked people have little or no influence in society" (Carstensen J., 2013. Dress for evolutionary success, *Nautilus*, 29th April 2013, p. 5).

87  Markman, A. 2019. 3 questions hiring managers want you to answer, *Harvard Business Review*, 12th July 2019.

88  Scudamore, B. 2016. How to gain an edge when a job opportunity arises, www.theglobeandmail.com (22nd November 2016).

89  Moss, P. & Till, C. 2001. *Stories Employers Tell: Race, Skill, and Hiring in America*, New York: Russell Sage Foundation.

90  Quillian, L., Pager, D., Midtboen, A., & Hexel, O. 2017. Hiring discrimination against Black Americans hasn't declined in 25 years. *Harvard Business Review*, October issue (https://hbr.org/2017/10/hiring-discrimination-against-black-americans-hasnt-declined-in-25-years).

91  One of the key unexplained areas for potential discrimination remains the rejection of a candidate based on being seen as being "overqualified" (blog.careerbuilder.co.uk/2015/07/21; Green, F. & McIntosh, S. 2007. Is there a genuine under-utilization of skills amongst the overqualified?, *Applied Economics*, 39(4):427–439; Alfes, K., Shantz, A., & van Baalen, S., 2016. Reducing perceptions of overqualification and its impact on job satisfaction: the dual roles of interpersonal relationships at work, *Human Resource Management Journal*, 26(1):85–101).

92  Sutton, G. 2019. The dark triad in personnel selection: an exploration of narcissism, psychopathy, and machiavellianism in candidates involved in an organisational selection process (PhD Thesis), Christchurch: University of Canterbury (free download: http://hdl.handle.net/10092/16621).

93  Dooley, E. 2016. Why you should follow an interview with a simple 'thank you', *The Globe and Mail*, Wednesday, 28th September 2016.

94    'Between 1970 and 2013, manufacturing jobs share of the total employment fell from 24.3% to 11.9% across the OECD' (Peetz, D. 2019. *The Realities and Futures of Work*, Canberra: ANU Press, p. 87).

95    https://www.cia.gov/library/publications/the-world-factbook/fields/2048.html.

96    www.oecd.org.

97    for example: https://www.onetonline.org/, https://www.bls.gov/soc/.

98    https://www.youtube.com/watch?v=XOVOn3K0vlM.

99    Thite, M. 2019. *e-HRM: Digital Approaches, Directions & Applications*, London: Routledge; Aamodt, M. G. 2015. Using background checks in the employee selection process, in: Hanvey, C. et al. (eds.) *Practitioner's Guide to Legal Issues in Organizations*, New York: Springer, pp. 85–110); Hickox, S. A. & Roehling, M. V. 2013. Negative credentials: fair and effective consideration of criminal records, *American Business Law Journal*, 50(2): 201–279; Fletcher, D. R. 2003. Employers, recruitment and offenders: underlining the limits of work-focused welfare?, *Policy & Politics*, 31(4): 497–510.

100   O'Neil, C. 2016. Ineligible to server: getting a job, Chapter 6, in: *Weapons of Math Destruction: How Big Data Increases Inequality and Threatens Democracy*, London: Penguin.

101   Gantman, E. R. 2005. *Capitalism, Social Privilege, and Managerial Ideologies*, Aldershot: Ashgate, p. 61.

102   Muncer, S. J. & Ling, J. 2006. Psychometric analysis of the empathy quotient (EQ) scale, *Personality and Individual differences*, 40(6): 1111–1119.

103   Sloman, S. & Fernbach, P. 2017. *The Knowledge Illusion – Why We Never Think Alone*, New York, Macmillan.

104   Price, L. 2016. *Psychometric Methods: Theory into Practice*, London: Guilford Press.

105   McKee, A. 2016. How to hire for emotional intelligence, *Harvard Business Review*, 5th February 2016.

106   Gardner, H. 1983. *Frames of Mind: The Theory of Multiple Intelligences*, New York: Basic Books.

107   Moyer, M. & Savino, D. M. 2015. The role of the kinesthetic learning style and prompted responses in teaching management courses, *Global Education Journal*, 1(1):85–104.

108   Harrell, E. 2017. A brief history of personality tests, *Harvard Business Review*, 95(2): 63.

109   Beard, A. 2017. If you understand how the brain works, you can reach anyone, *Harvard Business Review*, March–April Issue.

110   https://www.bbc.com/reel/video/p09hg3dd/why-extroverts-have-their-own-extreme-language.

111   15 Minute Online Free Self-Testing (https://www.truity.com/test/big-five-personality-test).

112   Harrell, E. 2017. A brief history of personality tests, *Harvard Business Review*, 95(2): 63.

113   O'Neil, C. 2016. *Weapons of Math Destruction*, New York: Crown, p. 182ff.

114   It appears as if HRM and organizational psychology are 'build on individualism [but] fail to speak directly to the individual' (Holborow, M. 2012. Neoliberal keywords, in: Block, D., Gray, J., & Holborow, M. (eds.) *Neoliberalism and applied linguistics*, London: Routledge, p. 50).

115   Baudrillard, J. 1994. *Simulacra and Simulation*, Ann Arbor: University of Michigan Press.

116   Williams, M. et al. 2020. *Mapping Good Work – The Quality of Working Life across the Occupational Structure*, Bristol: Bristol University Press, p. 46.

117   Mackin, N. J. 2016. HR governance and compliance: essentials of policies and guidelines, in: Zeuch, M. (eds.) *Handbook of HRM*, Heidelberg: Springer, p. 1119f.

118   Even though it should not be as Sullivan writes about Silicon Valley 'where the HR-friendly term "cultural fit" masks sexism, elitism or racism' (*The Guardian Weekly*, 2nd September 2016, p. 35).

119   McDonald, P. & Thompson, P. 2016. Social media (tion) and the reshaping of public/private boundaries in employment relations, *International Journal of Management Reviews*, 18(1): 69–84.

## Further Readings

Bateson, J. et al. 2013. *When Hiring, First Test, and Then Interview*, Harvard Business Review.

Bowles, D. 2013. Social Stratification, *American Journal of Economics & Sociology*, 72(1):32–58.

Brass, T. 2015. Free Markets, Unfree Labour, *Journal of Contemporary Asia*, 45(3):531–540.

Calderón-Valencia, I. et al. 2021. *Promotion, Recruitment and Retention of Members in Nonprofit Organizations*, Bingley: Emerald.

Chen, V. T. 2015. *Cut Loose – Jobless and Hopeless in an Unfair Economy*, Berkeley: University of California Press.

CIPD. 2020. *Recruitment and Workforce Development Challenges in Low-Status Sectors with High Labour Demand*, London: Chartered Institute of Personnel and Development.

Coffey, D. & Thornley, C. 2013. *Industrial & Labour Market Policy & Performance*, London: Routledge.

DeMars, N. 2012. *You've Got to Be Kidding!: How to Keep Your job*, Hoboken, NJ: Wiley.

Fluhr, J. 2013. Finding Employees Who Fit, *New York Times*, 10th October 2013.

Gatewood, R. D., Field, H. S. & Barrick, M. 2011. *Human Resource Selection*, Mason: South-Western

Gerard, J. G. 2012. Linking in with LinkedIn® Three Exercises That Enhance Professional Social Networking and Career Building, *Journal of Management Education*, 36(6):866–897.

Groysberg, B. 2012. *Chasing Stars: The Myth of Talent*, Princeton, NJ: Princeton University Press.

Harvey, D. 2014. Contradiction 5 [Use- & Exchange Value], in: *17 Contradictions & the End of Capitalism*, New York: Oxford University Press.

HBR. 2015. Why Job Postings Don't Equal Jobs, *Harvard Business Review*, May, 93:5.

Heneman, H. 2021. *Staffing Organizations* (10th ed.), Dubuque, IA: McGraw-Hill Education.

ISER. 2020. *Methods for Recruitment and Retention*, Colchester: Institute for Social and Economic Research (University of Essex).

Lees, K. 2015. *Stop Fantasizing about the Perfect Job* (hbr.org/2015/04).

Kramer, M. S. 2010. *Organizational Socialization – Joining and Leaving Organizations*, Oxford: Polity.

Lin, K.-H. 2015. The Financial Premium in the US Labor Market, *Social Forces*, 94(1):1–30.

Pavlopoulos, D. 2013. Starting Your Career with a Fixed-Term Job: Stepping-Stone or "Dead End"?, *Review of Social Economy*, 71(4):474–501.

Rees W. & Porter C. 2015. *Skills of Management*, London: Palgrave, Chapter 9, Recruitment & Selection.

Rehmann, J. 2015. Surplus Population, *Rethinking Marxism*, 27(2):303–311.

Savitz, A. W. 2013. *Talent, Transformation, and the Triple Bottom Line: How Companies Can Leverage Human Resources to Achieve Sustainable Growth*, New York: John Wiley & Sons.

Taylor-Gooby, P. 2015. Paid Work Is Never Enough (blogs.lse.ac.uk).

Wentland, D. M. 2015. *Is Your Organization a Great Place to Work?*, Charlotte: Information Age Pub.

Wilton, N. 2016. *Introduction to HRM* (3rd ed.), London: Sage.

Yong, E. 2015. How Reliable Are Psychology Studies?, *The Atlantic*, 27th August (www.theatlantic.com).

# 3 People in Working Relationships

## The Three Actors at Work

### Executive Summary

Virtually all economically developed and many developing countries have some sort of industrial and labour relations arrangements. These include the classical three actors: trade unions, employer federations, and the state. While modern Industrial Relations establishes institutions of conflict resolution, different countries took different pathways towards modernity and well-developed industrial relations systems. Five different pathways and outcomes towards modern industrial relations systems have been identified: dynastic/paternalistic industrial relations; middle class industrial relations; state industrial relations, colonial industrial relations, and nationalistic industrial relations. But whatever the pathway towards a modern industrial relations system is, ultimately all of these systems share a few basic similarities. Much of industrial relations operates on three levels: (a) workplace, plant, and company level; (b) the industry level; and (c) the national/international level. These levels and their actors and relationships can be seen from three different political-ideological perspectives: the utilitarian view, the pluralist view, and the radical perspective. Ultimately they all provide the institutions with a mechanism to solve problems that occur in the world of work.

### Key Learning Objectives

1. Realise the importance of good industrial relations for business success;
2. Understand the basic principles of industrial and labour relations;
3. Outline the difference between HRM and industrial relations;
4. Discuss the relationship between the three actors (state, employers, trade unions);
5. Conceptualise how industrial relations sets the framework for HRM;
6. Provide a description of different IR approaches (unitarist, pluralist, radical);
7. Explain arbitration and conciliation as problem-solving instruments;
8. Understand how different societal cultures shape industrial relations;
9. Develop a formal IR policy on good working relationships with trade unions.

### Labour and Industrial Relations

This chapter is concerned with **labour relations** (the preferred term in the USA) and IR or **industrial relations** (Great Britain, etc.).[1] Historically, the origins of labour and IR date back to a time when the first, predominantly agrarian, societies moved towards industrial

DOI: 10.4324/9781003293637-3

capitalism by establishing manufacturing workshops. It moved the feudalist subsistence economy towards "money, goods, and service" based economies, commonly known as market economies or capitalism. This occurred first in Great Britain and is perhaps best signified in Newcomen's atmospheric engine pumping water out of a coalmine, a development that not just increased productivity but also heralded a new age: the age of capitalism.[2] This new age not only needed machinery, it also needed people.

## 1. The Historical Differences Between HRM and Industrial Relations

How people in work situations relate to each other under capitalism is the subject of IR. The term "industrial relations" is commonly used to describe a multidisciplinary field that studies the employment relationship. Increasingly, these workplace relations are called **industrial relations** (IR) as well as **employee or employment relations** (ER), largely because of the rising importance of non-industrial forms of employment such as those found in the service and knowledge economies. The IR to ER move is sometimes seen as a broadening of ER to include elements of HRM. One of the "IR-vs.-HRM" differences is that IR has always been a more academic discipline originating in sociology, political science, legal studies, and labour economics. HRM meanwhile carries administrative and managerial connotations dating back to early factory administration which was later converted into personnel management to become today's HRM. Fundamentally, both are also different in their relationship approaches. HRM takes the top-down managerial "I manage you" approach while IR has a more horizontal approach and relationship-oriented perspective:

| HRM = vertical ↕ | ||| | Industrial Relations = horizontal ↔ | | |
|---|---|---|---|---|
| HR-manager | ||| | management | trade | the |
| ↓ | ||| | employers ↔ | unions ↔ | state |
| employees | ||| | companies | workers | government |

*Figure 3.1* Industrial Relations and Human Resource Management.

IR is shaped by employers, trade unions,[3] and the state (Figure 3.1) quite often taking a national or societal perspective.[4] By contrast, and to a large extent, HRM exists within such IR frameworks while focusing on the company. Employment or **labour law** that determines terms of employment, minimum wage, working hours,[5] OHS, discrimination, dismissal, trade unions, workplace participation, information and consultation, collective bargaining, etc. may serve as a classical example for the existence of HRM within IR.[6] Within the human rights framework of the United Nations and the ILO[7] (see below),[8] labour laws are enacted by states with prior consultation of employers and trade unions.[9] The outcomes of these consultations may well be changes in labour law setting binding rules for HRM. Unlike the broader framework of IR, HRM remains strongly company focused (e.g. recruitment and selection, performance management, etc.). Whether HRM, IR, labour relations, labour process theory,[10] or employment relations, the origins of all date back to a time when feudalism moved towards modern capitalism.

This "Great Transition" from feudalism to capitalism is defined by the conversion of agrarian societies into manufacturing and industrial societies.[11] It is a process known as industrialisation. While the birthplace of capitalism is England, today this process has reached virtually all countries establishing the economic system called capitalism.

**Capitalism** can be seen as an economic system based on private ownership of the means of production allowing the creation of goods and services for profit with the profit motive remaining the single most important driving force of capitalism.

Just about 200 years ago somewhere in the English Midlands, society began to cross the great divide on the road toward the **industrial society**.[12] Today, in the 21st century, almost all of the world's entire population lives in countries which are at least partially industrialised – or industrialising – and under an economic system that reflects capitalism.[13] The few remaining non-capitalist tribes rather than entire societies still depict rising aspirations to become industrialised and to live under capitalism. In many cases, this pathway has already been initiated and will lead towards the establishment of capitalism.[14] In all probability around the end of the 21st century, the inevitable triage of:

agriculture/feudalism → manufacturing/industrialisation → service/knowledge capitalism

will have swept away almost all feudalist forms of society, except possibly for a few odd backwaters that might remain untouched by the forces of capitalism.[15] This process signifies one of the great transformations in human history that will eventually encompass the entire planet. But capitalism's **creative destruction** will – rapidly and globally – also alter anything that was ever done before.[16] Capitalism knew no national boundaries long before the word **globalisation** had replaced **imperialism** and imperialism had replaced colonialism as new stages in capitalism's development. Capitalism's final stage may indeed be a worldwide society defined by the global rule of the capitalist system. There are common characteristics and certain imperatives that are inherently found in virtually all capitalist societies. These common characteristics of capitalism may be defined through five key elements:

## 2. Knowledge as Investment

Virtually all capitalist societies are associated with high levels of technological development, far in advance of earlier societies such as feudalism and, before that, the slavery society. As a consequence, science and technology take on an increased level of relevance under capitalism. As such, capitalism is based on significant investment research organisations such as, for example, universities, research institutions, laboratories, and specialised corporate "research and development" (R&D) departments. In a capitalist society, it remains axiomatic that the frontiers of knowledge are limitless. Technological progress never stands still. As a consequence, capitalism is characterised by substantial investments in production plants, manufacturing facilities, technical equipment, and machinery. This demands the accumulation of capital on a massive scale leading to investment and ROI – the return of investment.

## 3. Functional Training

In order to make all this possible, capitalism demands a **labour force** with a wide range of professions and skills. Indeed, the creation of suitable levels and useable human resources remains one of the major challenges encountered not just during the process of the "feudalism → capitalism" transition but also beyond that. Yet because science, knowledge, and technological progress constantly generate uninterrupted demands for change, new skills and occupations are constantly replacing the old. Progress in technologies, operative systems, new processes, and forms of work will render older skills and jobs obsolete (e.g. from blacksmith to software engineer). Consequently, capitalism requires a **vocational training** system that is functionally related to the skills and professions demanded by the system (e.g. Chapter 4). These skills, responsibilities, and general employment conditions as found in many workplaces constantly create a new order while they also restructure the education regime found in many societies.

## 4. Industrial Relations at Work

Inside companies, the **worker-vs.-management** relationship remains defined by a hierarchical structure with successive levels of authority assigned to managers and – below that – the managed (e.g. the image of the pyramid as organisational chart of business organisations).[17] This is paralleled by an extensive specialisation of work functions found at various levels within a company's hierarchy (e.g. Chapter 5). As part of this hierarchical and functional structuring process, capitalism's working force is governed by a **web of rules** that prescribe things like recruitment and selection; rewards, wages, and compensation; dismissals and layoffs,[18] promotions, workers transferring within an organisation, retirement, and even what HRM calls "disciplinary action" which is designed to punish workers.

## 5. Capitalism as Organised Industrial Relations

Modern capitalism is always associated with sizeable organisations as well as urban societies. **Urbanisation** – moving from the countryside to cities – has become a global movement.[19] It is necessarily supported by substantial governmental organisations including IR institutions. Meanwhile, the production of goods and services becomes ever more concentrated in the hands of large multinational corporations (MNCs).[20] Increased urbanisation, governmental agencies, voluntary associations, the power of global advertising and marking, and multinational corporations will continue to create structures that organise societies.

## 6. The Global Ideology of Industrial Relations

Virtually all IR systems establish order that is legitimised through a near global consensus consisting of a few basic ideologies. Such **ideology** can be seen as a belief system that camouflages capitalism's inherent contradictions but it also sustains domination and prevents emancipation. Many of these ideologies relate to individuals, groups, nations, and institutions under the governance of capitalism. They are overseen by a master ideology or **hegemonic ideology** (e.g. free market, global trade, neo-liberalism,[21] monetary exchanges, etc.). A hegemonic ideology provides a common body of beliefs and values.[22] For example, it tells all IR systems and, more importantly, virtually all workers that they must be dedicated to hard work and are individually responsible for their action. Below that certain ideologies sustain managerial regimes and the performance of managerially assigned tasks. Regardless of the specific historical and cultural pathways in which this might be achieved, IR ideologically legitimises industrial peace, i.e. it prevents revolts, strikes,[23] revolutions, etc.[24]

Taken together, these five key elements of global IR outline the most common features of virtually all "feudalism → capitalism" transitions. However, each country also remains a specific case of this transition. Nobody can ever expect history to occur in an identical fashion. As a consequence, with the end of feudalism, very different pathways to modern IR appeared. There was no global one-way movement towards capitalism's IR. Instead of a **one best way**, the historical pathways that define today's IR, i.e. the relationship between workers, capitalists, and states, led, even though quite differently, to a rather common outcome: the move towards a global post-agrarian society.[25]

For the purpose of showing these IR pathways, five broad avenues can be identified. Each of them occurred under varying circumstances and was dependent on class relations shaped during a country's pre-industrial period. In different countries, different social groups were able to assume leadership of processes that eventually led to industrial capitalism. In each of the five cases, the **ruling elites** played a rather decisive role, following different strategies and thereby creating different types of social orders. This shaped their respective societies as well as their IR system. Broadly speaking, these five pathways can be identified as:

### 1. Dynastic Industrial Relations

In some countries, the "feudalism → capitalism" move was driven by a **dynastic elite** that was drawn from the old military establishment and/or feudalist landed aristocracy that simply owned vast areas of land. Land and soil were relevant to **feudalism** but became increasingly irrelevant for capitalism that focused on production, commercial goods and services with a new and fast rising commodity: money. Some parts of these dynastic elites survived the "feudalism → capitalism" transition and were held together by a common allegiance to an established **conservative order**. They treasured preserving the status quo, conservative virtues, strong institutions, the family, a powerful leader, national states, and private property.

This includes the ideology of **being born into one class** and **being born to rule**.[26] It is your class – be it working class, middle or upper class – that sets your destiny as a deterministic destination and what shapes and organises a **paternalistic society** with a paternalistic state and paternalistic IR. This is furthered by the ideology of the dependent worker showing loyalty to employers and the state. Workers remain beholden to employers for their personal welfare as they live under a strong paternalistic leadership. The paternalistic elites have been known to move rather slowly along the pathway to capitalism.

Dynastic and paternalistic IR often rely on what became known as **corporatism**. This is the socio-political organisation of IR at the top – often at the national – level by major interest groups (state, trade unions, and employers) on the basis of the ideology that there is a **common interest**. It represents the ideology of a nation as an organic body often setting national wage levels, working time arrangements, and general working conditions.[27] But these elites also organised an extremely conservative and – at times even fascist – passage from their traditional agrarian society to industrial capitalism.[28] Prominent examples of this pathway to industrial capitalism are Japan, Italy, Germany, and perhaps Singapore.

### 2. Middle-Class Industrial Relations

The second pathway to capitalism occurs when organising powers are drawn from the commercial **middle class**. Unlike the democracy enhancing section of the middle class called *citoyen*, the ideology of the commercial middle class (*bourgeois*) remains thoroughly economic with the image of *homo economicus* as the cost-benefit calculating individual that looks for a good deal.[29] While it is individualistic in economic terms yet politically **egalitarian** – "one man one vote" – this pathway tends to establish pluralist IR. It is shaped by a commercial bourgeois middle class believing in individual opportunities. Economically, it favours the **free market** and **laissez-faire** approach of minimum state intervention supported by the ideology of self-sustaining market forces. This ideology shapes IR and governmental institutions that often show a certain decentralisation of decision-making powers.

Economically, middle-class IR takes progress for granted and relies on an unhindered play of market forces. It believes in **Adam Smith**'s ideological image of an **invisible hand** where individual advancement, profit-making, and business success translates into the common good.[30] Since Adam Smith could not quite explain how individual economic greed can become a common good – the famous wealth of the common or commonwealth – he invented the metaphor of a camouflaging "invisible hand". Classical examples of this pathway to capitalism and IR are England and subsequently the United States and Australia.

### 3. State Industrial Relations

The third "feudalism → capitalism" transition was guided by revolutionary intellectuals. Their power is linked to revolutionary peasants and workers removing the conservative and fascist[31] elites while preventing a rising middle class' transition to capitalism. These revolutionary intellectuals are self-identified.[32] They claim superior knowledge of the "feudalism → modernity" transition, advocating not capitalism but state socialism and communism as the ultimate goal of society. For the task of leadership, they promote intellectual-revolutionary elites trained in the affairs of social change. This project is supported through a claim to be in possession of scientific and superior theory and knowledge. This pathway to modernity generally leads to a monolithic state with centralised IR institutions. Since "revolutions are the locomotives of history", they rely on rapid force and fast movements towards industrial societies. Under this project, education, art, literature, and IR are organised so that they support state socialism. The classical examples for this pathway are the Soviet Union (Lenin and Stalin), China (Mao), North Korea, and Cuba.

### 4. Colonial Industrial Relations

The fourth pathway to industrial capitalism occurs under the colonial administrator. These administrators are often from overseas. They – at least in the past – have been a decisive factor for the "feudalism → capitalism" transition. The colonial administrator simply becomes the organiser of industrial capitalism, its institutions, and IR. In some cases, this might reflect educational–cultural **imperialism**.[33] In other cases, imperialism was simply outsourced to business corporations.[34] All this occurred mostly in underdeveloped countries, often under brutal colonial regimes and "gunboat" imperialism.[35] But the concern of the colonial-imperialist powers has never been with the countries they ruled, brutalised, and exploited. Instead, they followed the interests of their home countries shaping IR institutions in their image so that these furthered colonial exploitation. To accomplish this, these administrators had a twofold task:

1. they were the promoter of a colonial, imperialist, and capitalist system of production, ruthless exploitation, and surplus extraction;
2. but they also represented an external and invading force.[36]

These colonial and imperial regimes ruled some countries for centuries. Inescapably, these regimes were dislodged peacefully or overthrown violently. One of the most striking examples of this pathway is India.

### 5. Nationalistic Industrial Relations

The fifth pathway to capitalism occurred through a new nationalist leader and his (they were mostly men) followers. This was a model of the emerging nations. The elites were drawn, for example, from the leadership of independence movements set against colonial rule. But they were also recruited from military leaders and, in some cases, even from individuals who were initially sent abroad (mostly to the UK) to be educated. Disregarding their actual background, these nationalistic leaders moved towards capitalism fast. To cement their rule, they needed to deliver economic gains as this sustained their power. They were inspired by political **nationalism**. For them, nationalism became much more than being merely a sentiment. It became a rational system of thought capable of organising social institutions such as, for example, IR. In some cases, they were democratic leaders, while in others, they were outright dictators. Quite often, they seized any opportunity showing a "will to power". In other cases, they used any means to rapidly build the political and economic structures of their country. IR served these goals.

Depending on the actual situation, these countries took different pathways while using different roads towards capitalism. Their leaders often came from the middle class, the dynastic elite, or even from revolutionary intellectuals. But as a uniting characteristic, these countries were late starters when it came to the "feudalism → capitalism" transition. Since countries such as England, France, Italy, the USA, etc. developed before them, they were able to engage in **regime picking**, using various forms of IR to further their nation. Classical examples are Egypt under Nasser and Iraq under Saddam Hussein.

Whatever the pathway to capitalism, ultimately they all triumphed over out-dated and feudal constraints, establishing modern capitalism with modern IR. The above-mentioned different approaches shaped their respective forms of IR between employers, unions, and the state as well as IR institutions. Eventually, the somewhat inherent logic of the "feudalism → capitalism" transition also led to several common features that can be identified and that became part of all IR systems.

## Common Industrial Relations Features

All IR systems around the world share some commonalities. The main similarities are outlined below:

### Managers and Managed

Much of IR have their origin in the relationship between those who manage (management) and those who are managed (workers). This was and still is a conflicting relationship giving rise to a web of rules regulating the conflicts between management and workers. These conflicts are related to domination, authoritarian managerial rule, managerial power, position, and policies of managers but they were also influenced by the development of an industrially usable workforce.[37]

The often harsh brutalities (e.g. signified in the overseer's whip) of the "feudalism → capitalism" transition created not just **Satanic Mills** and **Bleak Houses** but also widespread and abject poverty, decease, and early death. Workers responded to the inhumanity of early capitalism with revolts, rebellion, strikes, and other forms of industrial actions.[38] Many states initially reacted to the organised movement of workers with military force, legal instruments, and a well-equipped police force but eventually, managers, workers, and states found more organised solutions in establishing functioning IR systems.

## Managers

Most of today's managers manage workers, professionals, and employees. Over time, **management** became a hierarchy of functions managing administrators, engineers, and professional specialists. Some became CEOs holding top positions. But the institution of management also became crucial to the success of capitalism. Management represents a threefold institution:

1. **social resource**: management is a socio-economical human resource,
2. **social class**: management is found in the middle class (e.g. business class), and
3. **authority**: management is system of authority and domination.

With the advances of capitalism, management became even more important and managers grew in numbers. This seems to be an inevitable consequence of advanced capitalism. As companies grew into corporations developing larger structures – often, for example, through mergers and acquisitions – corporate managers engaged in managing these "company-to-corporation" processes and thereby became more important.[39] These developments were also aided by innovation, the growth of markets, and increased economic complexities. As a consequence, there is an ever-increasing demand for managerial training (e.g. MBA) and growing educational-vocational institutions (universities). These become more and more functionally oriented towards the training of managers as demanded by capitalism. As a consequence, many universities become vocational training facilities – structural appendages of capitalism.

But management also became a professional class. During the early stages of capitalism's development when workshops were rather small, the need for management was insignificant. But as companies grew into substantial organisations and **corporations**, and with the separation between owners (shareholders) and the management of such corporations, management gained in importance. Capitalist societies began to focus more strongly on the management of commercial discovery (R&D), technological innovation, and economic growth.[40] In companies and corporations, management sustains domination as a non-democratic institution dedicated to authoritarian rule. But over time, it also became somewhat less dictatorial in its approach to labour. In all capitalist societies, management retains its self-assigned and non-democratic prerogative as **rule maker**.[41] In its extreme expression, this can lead to "Macho-Management".[42] Rule-making in HRM relates to **HR policies** that are statements of intent outlining a company's intentions.

Meanwhile, having no **exit** option and rejecting the surrendering **loyalty** option, state and labour sought **voice** in the overall rule-making process of IR.[43] The outcome of the voice option is an agreement between management/employers, states, workers, and their trade unions.[44] This tends to limit and regulate the otherwise unilateral domination of management over labour. As a consequence, outright dictatorial and paternalistic management started to give some way once the rules of employment became increasingly based on state laws, decisions of governments, and **collective bargaining**. The latter is a process of negotiation between employers and a group of employees aimed at reaching an agreement. Collective bargaining is generally divided into two versions: the first version is **distributive bargaining** as "zero-sum" bargaining in an "I win, you lose" situation (e.g. higher wages equals less profit).[45] Groups of workers seek the best outcome. Collective bargaining often extends to three core issues: wages (living wage, minimum wage, etc.),[46] working time, and working conditions.[47] As for wages, trade unions often base their demands on three basics:[48]

a.   gaining a fair share of increases in productivity[49];
b.   compensations of the ills of capitalism such as, for example, rises in inflation; and
c.   a Robin Hood like transfer of wealth (taking from the rich and giving to the poor).

But collective bargaining does not only have a distributive component. Its second form is called **integrative bargaining** and entails negotiations that reconcile or integrate both parties' interests trying to yield joint benefits.[50] This is the "both win" situation or sharing an expanding pie. Both versions are often conducted as a five-step process:[51]

1.   preparing and planning for the negotiation;
2.   defining ground rules for negotiations;
3.   clarification and justification;
4.   bargaining and problem solving; and
5.   closure of negotiation (settlement) and implementation of agreement.

Workers are commonly presented by a trade union to which employees belong. The **collective agreement** reached through "employer-union" negotiations regulates, for example, wages, working hours, training, health and safety, overtime, and rights to participate in workplace and company affairs.[52]

The typically historical move from outright dictatorial to a more accommodating form of management is often related to the actual stage in the chronology of industrial development. Put simply, early IR used force and brutality while later IR relied on accommodation, inclusion, and negotiations. The dynastic elite, for example, relies on families and paternalistic IR under the "we take care of you" ideology. Middle-class IR rely on professional managers. The revolutionary intellectuals see management as political management and IR as structure that supports state socialism.

Nationalistic IR develop as the occasion demands. Whatever the pathway to capitalism, management remains important for capitalism. But management as a class has (at least) not yet become the dominant class that rules society.[53] Instead, managers remain the **agents of stockholders**. Since they are preoccupied with the internal affairs – which tend to become more complex – the managerial class consists of conformists rather than leaders in the larger affairs of society.[54]

## Labour Force Development

In all countries, capitalism has found human beings that were and are converted into human resources available for employment in companies and corporations. But in many countries there also exist different traditions, customs, habits, skills, and know-how necessary for the conversion of human beings into human resources. As a consequence, rising capitalism and company management were required to create diversified labour forces. Generally, this involved:

### 1. Recruitment

This is the first step into becoming part of a labour force. It is the process of attracting, selecting, hiring, and assigning people so that these can fill positions.

### 2. Commitment

This establishes ideological commitment, obedience, compliance, etc. to working in a company. Establishing this turns out to be a somewhat longer and more intricate process. It is achieved once workers are permanently attached to a company and accept the terms and conditions of management and employment – HRM calls this trust even though trust remains a contentious subject, especially when one party (usually management and employers) would prefer that trade unions did not exist at all.[55] Whether with or without trade unions, historically the consequence of this process was that work under capitalism began to appear as "the natural way of life".[56] Converting unsuspecting human beings into human resources carrying ideology is often paralleled by the vocational process of building skills, work habits, and the incentives for employment.

### 3. Training

Work in a company also involves training of the workforce to update knowledge in an ever-changing environment. Typically, this is not conducted in-house but is offloaded to state institutions such as schools, colleges, and universities.

### 4. Employment Security

In many ways, working under capitalism also provides – at least – some level of general security. This includes various institutions and IR facilities capable of providing some level of worker security both at work (employment security) and in the reproductive sphere (state welfare provisions).

All this creates human resources ready to be employed in companies. However, these human resources and forms of employment have never been the product of a particular culture, inheritance, and ancestry. The conversion of human beings into human resources rather came with a persistent effort and investment being applied by capitalism. With or without resistance to capitalism, eventually most human beings were made to accept their new existence as human resources, rendering them as auxiliaries and appendages to the functioning of capitalism.[57]

The feudalism → capitalism transition was never a smooth process. It often created **surplus labour** resulting in mass unemployment as a rather common problem in most, if not all, developing countries. This led to a "Planet of Slums"[58] and it remains a feature of the early and later stages of capitalism.[59] Surplus labour, for example, is created when a working population keeps expanding – by converting peasants into workers, etc. – more rapidly than employment can absorb. As a consequence, urban areas become overcrowded and slums are created. As capitalism advances, much of the underemployment also persists in rural areas. Given these problems, workers have responded in various ways to the rise of capitalism.

### Workers' Response to Capitalism

Capitalism totally restructured human life, converting it into human material whatever the source or the place. As a consequence, the creation of industrial work and the conversion of human beings into human resources involved the near-total destruction of many of the old ways of life. It forced people into accepting the imperatives of capitalism and managerial regimes which came with many forms of protest against capitalism.

In some cases, resistance against capitalism and managerial regimes was expressed through forms of protest such as excessive absenteeism, high turnover, theft, sabotage,[60] spontaneous and sporadic work stoppages, and more organised **strikes**.[61] Strikes are commonly seen as a withdrawal from work by a group of employees, or a refusal by an employer or a number of employers to permit some or all of their employees to work, each withdrawal or refusal being made to enforce a demand, to resist a demand, or to express a grievance.[62] With capitalism came labour[63] and with labour came organised labour which still remains the foundation to organise industry-wide strikes and political activities to improve wages, working time, and working conditions. Meanwhile smaller day-to-day **grievances** (steps taken by workers against management, e.g. management violates collective agreements, unjust treatment, outright mistreatment, etc.) no longer escalate into **boss-napping**, for example, but are presented through institutions solving organisational disputes such as, for example, labour courts.[64] In many cases, these grievances do no longer lead to large stoppages.

German philosopher and economist **Karl Marx** (1818–1883)[65] saw the intensity of protest increasing in the course of capitalist development as poverty and misery became widespread. He predicted that the growing poverty would inevitably lead to revolts turning into revolutions that would eventually end capitalism. Capitalism then would be replaced with socialism which in turn would ultimately lead to communism.[66] But **Henry Ford** (1863–1947) ended Marx's prediction dramatically when spectacularly reshaping capitalism forever. **Fordism** not only introduced **mass production** through the mechanised assembly line turning out massive amounts of cars to a much-reduced price, it also needed to sell these cars.[67] This led to mass **consumerism** and petit-bourgeois middle-class affluence.[68] Instead of Marx's revolution based on the mass poverty of workers, the latter were merged into a mass-consuming middle class carrying middle-class values. As a consequence, in all societies that go through the feudalism → capitalism transformation, workers' protest tends to reach its peak relatively early in the process. It tends to decline as capitalism reaches its Fordist mass consumerist stage. **Protest** becomes moderated, channelled, organised, and redirected as it moves from being "about" capitalism to protest from "within" capitalism.

For quite some time, the organising elites of capitalism were forced to deal with workers' protest. They adopted different policies towards the formation of labour's trade unions that at least potentially threatened capitalism through their initial rising economic and political power. During the early stage of capitalism, each society saw emerging labour organisations, but they adapted themselves rather distinctively to their given environment. Most labour organisations and trade unions, and particularly those in developing countries, posed serious problems for capitalism, mainly in four ways:

1. Workers and trade unions claimed higher wages while capitalism remained preoccupied with capital formation;
2. Workers went on strike against inhuman working conditions and long working hours, often at times when management saw such stoppages as detrimental to profit-making;
3. Workers often forced management to address worker grievances and complaints while management sought to create workplace discipline – often through brutalities – to achieve a faster rate of work for increased surplus extraction, profits, and more output; and finally,
4. Labour organisations and trade unions often sought independence and freedom as democratic institutions while capitalism and management wanted them to be subservient or – alternatively – wanted trade unions to remain politically neutral or, ideally, powerless.

The conditions and treatment of labour organisations, trade unions, and IR remain essentially reflections of any society in which they develop but the universal responses of workers to capitalism, their initial protests, strikes, and revolts increasingly weakened as many employees were successfully made to accept the rules of management. In some cases, they contributed to the perceived imperatives of capitalism's development. As a consequence, leaders of labour seldom rise to dominating positions in societies while conservatives act as the ruling party in government and labour parties often remain as their loyal opposition.[69] This is flanked by corporate mass media in a frequently rehearsed mass spectacle called elections. Managerial regimes meanwhile remain largely unaffected by such elections as workplaces are ruled by management and without democracy.[70]

### Rule Makers and Rules

In all counties affected, capitalism creates workers, managers, and government agencies – the triage of IR.[71] All three are necessarily involved in IR. But as capitalism carries variations into its economic setup, it also brings variations into its actual IR setups.[72] Yet despite individual country differences, virtually all versions of IR accomplish at least seven purposes. IR...

1. defines the rights and responsibilities of workers, managers, and states;
2. establishes a relationship among these three IR actors;
3. channels and controls the responses of workers to capitalism[73]; but also
4. deals with frustrations and insecurities inherent in the capitalist process;
5. establishes the network of rules in a substantive and procedural way;
6. assists in governing workplaces and working communities; and
7. reflects an overall uniformity as well as some institutional diversity.

Every system of IR supplies a structured and functional relationship between the managers and the managed (workers) in any capitalist society. But IR also remains related to individual economies (e.g. coordinated or liberal market economies), distinct political systems, distinctive historical contingencies, idiosyncratic cultures, and distinctive legal frameworks with which IR operate. As such, it can be analysed and compared.[74] Overall, IR is not unique as there is no local institutional arrangement with highly exceptional significance only to one particular country. Instead, IR fulfils the aforementioned seven tasks in almost all countries that operate as a capitalist system.

### Industrial Relations Today

As global capitalism spreads, global economic and political forces increase global uniformity among different societies and different countries. These forces are stronger than those perpetuating diversity. As globalisation extends, nations move further away from their feudalist specifics. Yet these newcomers in the realm of modern global capitalism will also bring new recruits from different social strata into their companies. With that, previously rather varying elites will become more uniform, adopting the image of management. Simultaneously, cultural and ideological differences tend to fade away in favour of the uniformity of company management. Through technically advanced and global media, cultural patterns intermingle and increasingly move towards a global society. The once vast ideological and cultural differences between many countries, nations, regions, and cultures give way to the pragmatism of management.

This global trend toward greater uniformity comes due to a variety of forces: perhaps developments, not just in information technology (IT), act strongly as a global unifying force but there is also a global thrust in economic and human progress serving global uniformity. Gradually the world will also see a less marked difference between various categories of workers in each country. In addition, global advances in mass education will bring the global elimination of illiteracy while universal management training (MBA), for example, will develop the universal skills of management and perhaps even Managerialism.[75]

Yet despite the ideology of neo-liberalism, the state will not wither away.[76] Larger-scale multinational enterprises remain common hallmarks of all advanced societies. Finally, the pressures of economic, human, and environmental progress and the human participation in economic orders are enhanced by the global character of international trade, through the availability of global travel, and through modern means of communication enhancing the global exchange not just of scientific knowledge and ideas. All this will lead to **pluralist industrial relations** in which conflict remains an inevitable feature between management and workers as well as capitalism. But IR will also produce structures and institutions capable of dealing with what has been identified as the three main forms of contradictions[77]:

*Table 3.1* Contradictions Between Management and Workers

|  |  | *Management's Interest* | *Workers' Interest* |
| --- | --- | --- | --- |
| Wages and income | $ | Cost factor to be reduced | Livelihood, family, existence, life |
| Working time | ☺ | Long – to be extended | Short – to be reduced |
| Working conditions | ✍ | Impediment on the right to manage | Participation and democracy |

Table 3.1 shows that there are roughly three classical contradictions between management and workers. While management seeks to reduce wages as they are seen as a cost, wages and salaries are the basic means of livelihood for workers.[78] They sustain their existence and that of their families but they also provide spending power and **disposable income** needed to sustain consumer capitalism.[79] The contradiction arises from the system of consumer capitalism's need for disposable income so that workers can spend it on goods and services whilst individual companies see wages as a cost to be reduced. So far nobody – not Adam Smith, not Karl Marx, not John Maynard Keynes – has been able to solve this inherent and severe contradiction plaguing capitalism.[80] In contrast to this, however, IR can solve conflicts over working time.

Management tends to seek extended working time while for workers the reduction of daily, weekly, annual, and life working (e.g. early retirement) time remains essential. There are also contradictory views on general working conditions as management sees investment in improved working conditions as a cost while workers see good working conditions as part of their working life. Equally, industrial democracy remains viewed by management as an intrusion into their self-assigned **right to manage**, also known as managerial prerogative or even as **macho-management**[81] while for workers participation in the affairs of a company remains an essential part of good working conditions. All this shows that IR, for the foreseeable future, will continue to play a decisive role in managing these conflicts.

In all capitalist societies with developed IR, conflict (Table 3.1) will persist. However, conflicts over work issues will increasingly take the form of organised encounters between management, workers, trade unions, and states rather than existing as a form of class war.[82] IR actors will seek to enforce their positions over the setting of labour jurisdictions, the ability to make workplace-related decisions, the forming of trade unions alliances and cooperation with other NGOs, and the granting or withdrawal of support for a prevailing IR structure, and so on. But overall, the great battles of conflicting parties – e.g. **general strikes**[83] – are replaced through minor contests over comparative details solved within standard institutional arrangements of IR. Today, most labour organisations and trade unions are no longer part of class movements urging the end of capitalism.[84] Instead, trade unions are pressure groups representing the occupational interests of their members.[85] As such, they serve a very useful purpose just as President Roosevelt…once publicly declared…if I were a worker, I would certainly join the union.[86]

Yet in global capitalism, human beings still remain subject to immense pressures directed towards conformity. These are often imposed by global multinational corporations (MNC) and corporate mass media. For most people confined to managerial regimes any true autonomy, self-determination and self-actualisation will remain missing. Instead, managerial regimes continue to be locations of **alienation**.[87] Meanwhile, outside of these regimes, many people enjoy more individual, economic, and political freedom than in almost all earlier and some present societies – with some noticeable exceptions.[88] Through modern IR, many workers will have some form of political influence. Many will also have somewhat higher living standards, greater leisure, and more education – albeit not necessarily greater happiness.[89]

### *The Industrial Relations Matrix*

The first bloc in the IR matrix is that of trade unions. Perhaps the most common definition of a **trade union** is "a continuous association of wage earners for the purpose of maintaining or improving the conditions of their employment"; a second definition sees trade unions as institutional representatives of workers' interests both within the labour market and in the wider society, and they accentuate the collective rather than the individual power-resource of employees. Meanwhile a third definition views them as the unionised working class that, intimidated by the scale and complexity of capitalist production, and weakened in its original revolutionary impetus by the gains afforded by the rapid increase of productivity, increasingly lost the will and ambition to wrest control of production from capitalist hands and turned ever more to bargaining over labour's share in the product.[90] Whatever the definition of trade unions is, the key difference and defining issue of trade unions is that they – unlike management – are democratic institutions with members electing someone to represent them.[91] As a consequence, trade unions share three common features:

1.  **unity is strength**: workers find strength in size when facing management, often signified in the maxim: together we bargain – individually we beg;
2.  **commonality of interests**: the rationale is that individual employees share the same interests (e.g. Table 3.1) in, for example, higher wages, shorter working time, and better working conditions but do not have sufficient power relative to single employers (management) and so workers need to collectivise.[92]
3.  **workplace democracy**: more often than not trade unions provide the only opportunity for workers to influence workplace affairs through their elected representatives in a place where many spend eight hours per day (or more), five days a week, and roughly forty years of their working lives.[93]

The awareness that unity is strength and there is a commonality of interest shared among workers leads the latter to create and organise[94] in trade unions.[95] In other cases, workers experience that their economic needs (Table 3.1) are not the same as management's needs. They are also quite often dissatisfied with management[96] and their inhumane treatment of being merely a resource, a tool, an asset, a human resource, and underling, and a subordinate.

Trade unions also offer protection against potentially wrongful managerial **disciplinary action** – when management merges the civil and criminal system's police and sentencing judge into one. Disciplinary action occurs when, for example, workers violate *unilateral* managerial rules (corporate policies) leading to a sequence of managerial actions under the infamous "three-strike rule": (1) verbal warning, (2) written warning, and (3) suspension/dismissal. In other cases, workers might view the introduction of democracy – democratically elected local union representatives – as a counterbalance against non-democratic and authoritarian management rule. These and more – such as the ability of trade unions to safeguard state regulations and labour laws – are some of the reasons for the existence of trade unions.

The second building bloc of the IR matrix is the **employer federation**. Employer federations have three basic forms:

1.  **professional associations**: (internal) that encourage communication, often working as political pressure organisations lobbying politicians, etc.;
2.  **trade associations**: (external) that are predominately engaged in public relations, but also undertake political lobbying. These are often internally organised focusing on being information providers while also encouraging research, etc. while
3.  **employers' associations**: (IR) engage more strongly with and remain rather central to the development of IR.

Their membership is often primarily open to organisations (companies, firms, corporations) rather than individuals. These associations are involved in collective bargaining through advice, and are influential in government policy. They have three main functions:

a. counterbalance trade unions' strength
b. collective bargaining
c. political pressure group

The final building bloc of the IR matrix is the state.[97] States operate with horizontal and vertical divisions of power.[98] At the horizontal level – and this dates back to French philosopher Montesquieu[99] (1689–1755) – we find the *trias politica* principle of legislative (making labour law), executive (administering labour law), and judiciary (assuring that labour laws are obeyed). At the vertical level, we often find federalist states with local, regional/state, and national/federal levels. While all three of the *trias politica* are involved in IR, in some states, only specific vertical levels are involved as IR may be governed at state/regional level or – alternatively – at national/federal level. Other states are more monolithically organised – France, Sweden, China, the UK, etc. – organising IR at the national level. Whatever the level, the general role of the state in IR is fourfold as the state:

1. sets ground rules for employers, workers (trade unions), and the relations between them
2. provides basic protection for people at work,
3. is a major employer in its own right, and
4. provides assistance to IR parties in cases of industrial conflicts.

In many cases, states provide dispute settlement mechanisms. These are third-party peace-keeping procedures to avoid industrial action. Most often they relate to two kinds of conflicts: (1) **rights disputes**: these relate to the interpretation of the existing collective agreement; and (2) **interest disputes**: these relate to matters ungoverned by law or contracts, such as the negotiation for a new agreement or the renewal of an existing one. Most commonly, these mechanisms take two forms:

I. judicial settlement via courts such as, for example, labour courts; and
II. state sponsored conciliation, mediation or voluntary arbitration.[100]

Crucial is the distinction between **conciliation** and arbitration. The former describes a process through which a third party, mostly the state or a state institution as a quasi-independent empire attempts to resolve a dispute – mostly between management and workers (e.g. trade unions) – through discussions and negotiations leading to a voluntary outcome or agreement. In the case of **arbitration**, a more structured form of negotiations takes place – usually between employers/management and workers/unions – when a third party (often a judge) hears evidence in a court like procedure resulting in the IR judge making "binding determinations". Although formal, arbitration procedures are not labour courts.

To complete the IR matrix, all three actors – employers/management, workers and trade unions, and the state[101] – also operate at – at least – three levels: the company, plant, and workplace level; the industry level; and the national level.[102] In some cases, the industry level may be substituted by a regional level while the national/state level might also include supra-national forms[103] (e.g. the European Union) and even international levels.[104] The prime institution for IR at the international level is the **International Labour Organization** (ILO) which is a United Nations agency dealing with labour issues, particularly international labour standards, social protection, and work opportunities for all. The ILO has 186 member states out of the 193 UN member states. Unlike other United Nations specialised agencies, the International Labour Organization has a **tripartite governing structure** – representing governments, employers, and workers (usually with a ratio of 2:1:1). The rationale behind the tripartite structure is the creation of free and open debate among governments and social partners. Seen from plant to international level, the following IR matrix emerges (Table 3.2)[105]:

*Table 3.2* Three Levels and Three Actors

| Levels/Actors | Employers | Trade Unions | States |
| --- | --- | --- | --- |
| Company | Supervisory role | Worker participation | Individual rights |
| Industry | Industry policies and collective bargaining | Industry collective bargaining | Industry policies labour law |
| National | Strategy, lobbying, and collective bargaining | Organising strategies collective bargaining | Macro-economic social policies |

As is often the case, these are rough boxes and the emphasis of country-specific IR may vary between individual states. Collective bargaining is one case in point as in some countries states get heavily involved in collective bargaining while in others the state refrains from direct and indirect involvement in this process. In some cases, collective bargaining may take place at workplace or company level (**enterprise bargaining**), while in other states, it may happen at industry or national level. But the three dimensional IR matrix does not end with these three levels; IR scholars have added an additional perspective. This is a rather ideological level as – in some cases – ideologies can shape the behaviour and strategies of individual IR actors: employers/management, workers/union, and states. IR experts call these three added perspectives: unitarism, pluralism, and radical. The following table will explain this[106]:

*Table 3.3* The Three Ideological Perspectives

| | Ideology | Conflict | Trade Unions |
| --- | --- | --- | --- |
| Unitarism | Management and capitalism are accepted as legitimate | Conflict is irrational as bosses and workers seek the same | Trade unions are irrelevant and a disturbance; they are unnecessary |
| Pluralism | Management and workers represent different interests | Conflict is inherent but can be managed through negotiations | Trade unions play a legitimate part in a pluralist democratic society |
| Radical | Management is a force of domination and is to be eliminated | Class conflict is inevitable; workers should fight managers | Trade unions are agents of class war designed to overthrow capitalism |

Table 3.3 shows that the entire IR system can be influenced by overarching political and ideological perspectives. Perhaps the unitarist ideology is most closely associated with HRM as it legitimises capitalism while seeing itself as being part of management. For HRM, conflict is alien as both workers and management seek the same organisational outcomes. Trade unions are viewed as a hindrance and are not needed for the successful operation of companies. The pluralist ideology is associated with democratic rule and acknowledges that people in society and workplaces have different interests. Just like in society through democracy, these interests can be negotiated in the world of work where IR provide the best mechanism. For pluralists, management, HRM, and trade unions are legitimate while a well-crafted IR system assists the solving of conflicts between management/employers and workers/unions.

The radical and "Labour Process"[107] approach on the other hand sees management as an instrument of domination that needs to be replaced with **workers cooperatives**[108] leading to the end of capitalism.[109] The radical approach views trade unions as an instrument of class war waged against capitalism and its agents, i.e. management, with the ultimate goal of creating a socialist (nationalisation) or an **anarchist** (collectivisation) society. The word anarchy comes from the Greek ἀναρχία (anarchia) combining "not or without" with "ruler, leader, authority". It refers to a society "without rulers and leaders" where companies become self-organising cooperatives that are no longer managed but organised by workers themselves.[110] This would end the need for IR.

## Workbook

### III.   Five Discussion Questions on Industrial Relations

*And One Report Question on Industrial Relations*

*1.  Discussion Question:*

1.  Discuss the role of the three actors in a pluralist industrial relationship.
2.  Discuss the three contradictions outlined in Table 3.1 under the radical approach to IR.
3.  Find five more country examples for the five different pathways to IR and explain the specifics that supported your choice.
4.  Imagine you are an HR manager with the task of writing an HR policy for IR that incorporates pluralistic IR. Write a formal policy.
5.  Discuss the role and task of the state in IR.

*2.  Report Question:*

*On Industrial Relations, HR Managers and the Global South*

IR include three core actors. These are: (1) state and government; (2) employer federations and management; and (3) workers and trade unions. In an essay on "The Coming of the Global Working Class",[111] Klikauer describes the plight of workers and IR in the Global South. Develop four [4] recommendations on how HR managers can eliminate this plight while working towards "decent work"[112] arrangements for the workers of the Global South.[113]

### IV.   The "5-by-5" Exercise: Five Case Studies and Five Questions

### 3.1   *Your $5.–T-Shirt and Ships of Shame*

Under the ideology of globalisation, world trade is increasing. Among that are many cheap consumer goods shipped from overseas to your local shopping mall. Many consumer goods – such as your next $5-shirt – are transported by sea travelling in a container ship. Much of this is possible because of cheap diesel fuel and very low wages for seafarers. These ships with low wages and bad working conditions are called "Ships of Shame". Since 1948, the "international transport federation" trade union or ITF (www.itfglobal.org) has been organising an international campaign to end such ships of shame (maritimeaccident.org/tags/ships-of-shame). ITF seeks to protect workers who are at severe physical risk and being exploited under poor working conditions and starvation wages. The ITF's fight has been targeting commercial ships flying "Flags of Convenience".[114]

Flag of convenience is the business practice of registering a merchant ship in a sovereign state different from that of the ship's owners and flying that state's civil ensign on the ship. Ships are registered under flags of convenience to reduce operating costs or avoid the regulations of the owner's country. FOCs began in the 1920s in the United States, when ship owners cut labour costs by beginning to register their ships in Panama. FOCs steadily increased, and in 1968, Liberia grew to surpass the UK as the world's largest shipping register. As of 2009, more than half of the world's merchant ships were FOC registered with countries such as Panama, Liberia, and the Marshall Islands accounting for almost 40% of the entire world fleet, in terms of deadweight tonnage.

According to the ITF, FOCs provide a means of avoiding labour regulation in the countries of ownership, becoming a vehicle for paying low wages, and enforcing long working hours and unsafe working conditions. Often crews are signed onto the FOC for contracted periods of time and are not allowed on shore during the life of the contract. Seafarers are almost kept as prisoners on the ship. FOC ships have no real nationality and are therefore beyond the reach of any single national seafarers' trade union. FOCs are often poorly maintained older vessels, increasing their risk of sinking during transit. They pose a risk to the life of the crew as well as the environment, as their cargo often includes chemicals and industrial waste products.

ITF's fight combines a political and an industrial approach: a political strategy seeks to establish international governmental agreements providing a genuine link between the flag a ship flies and the nationality or residence of its owners, managers, and sea-farers. This would eliminate FOCs; ITF's industrial strategy is designed to protect sea-farers on FOC ships, irrespective of their nationality, from exploitation by shipowners.

Despite the ITF's decade long fight, it was not successful in preventing the growth of FOCs. But its industrial fight was partially successful in enforcing somewhat more decent minimum wages and basic working conditions on board of nearly 5,000 FOC ships. The ITF has become the main institution fighting against the exploitation and mistreatment of seafarers independent of their nationality or trade union affiliations. This has been a global success. The ITF recovers millions of dollars annually in wages back pay and compensation for death and working injuries on behalf of seafarers.

1. What advantage might a trade union in your country have from joining the ITF?
2. Imagine you are an HR manager of a shipping company. What steps can you undertake to end "ships of shame"?
3. Imagine you are a trade unions delegate seeking to forge an alliance with your government to end FOCs. What would you do?
4. Can you find reasons for why the ITF's political fight has not been successful dur-ing the last decades? How can this be changed?
5. Imagine you are an ITF official. Should the ITF follow their political or industrial strategy? What are the advantages and disadvantages of both approaches?

## 3.2   *Flipping Burger Tells Employees Whopping Lies*

Brad Pitty has been working for "Flipping Burgers" at their city restaurant for three years and four months before it closed its doors last month. It appears that "Flipping Burger" did not pay his wages in full while also neglecting his entitlements. John Clooney was employed for six years. Both started working for "Flipping Burger" when they were teen-agers. Both were also expected to obtain their "training qualifications" as part of their employment. Mr John Clooney did not receive this while Mr Pitty's training never started.

In a statement in the local newspaper, the "Flipping Burger" chain said, "it takes its employment responsibilities as well as its customer relations and its corporate social responsibility toward the local community very seriously". However, in a corporate email, "Flipping Burger" has stated that it believes that it has no further responsibilities to attend to. It also alleges that the failed store was an independent business operating under a franchise agreement until the store went bankrupt.

As a consequence, Flipping Burger's head office has no obligation to seek to have the debtor company wound up and will consider whether the cost of initiating the process is likely to be money well spent. The training arrangements concerning Mr Pitty are a matter between (franchise owner) Mr Alex Frankenstein's company (city store), Mr Pitty (the employee), and the government as training provider – not Flipping Burger's head office.

Attempts to contact Mr. Frankenstein were unsuccessful. However, the office of the state training authority is ensuring that an alternative training organisation will contact Mr Pitty. The state's IR office notified "Flipping Burger" employees that it has started to investigate the "Flipping Burger" case.

1. How can a working IR system that includes employers, trade unions, and the state solve the problems at "Flipping Burger"?
2. Imagine you are an HR manager at "Flipping Burger's" head office. What would you do to solve the problems of unpaid wages and entitlements and the failure to conduct training?
3. Imagine you are a trade union officer. What would you do to help the workers at "Flipping Burgers"?
4. Describe all IR parties involved and decide which IR levels have also been involved in the case (tab. 3.2).
5. Discuss the role of the employer (e.g. local shop and head office) and decide which IR ideology (Table 3.3) these actors (locally and at corporate level) have been following and why.

### 3.3  *Negotiations at Quick WINGS Airlines*

In 2016, Quick WINGS Airlines and its trade unions were attempting to negotiate a new collective agreement. After many negotiations between Quick WINGS Airlines and the Airline Engineers Union (AEU), the Transport Workers' Union (TWU), and the Pilot Union (PU), each trade union asked its members to vote on industrial action. They were putting forward mild forms of industrial action such as sanctions, some work bans, and a few work stoppages. All of these actions were entirely lawful forms of "protected collective bargaining".

For the trade unions, the issues at question differed somewhat in each case but all negotiations included the levels of pay, aspects of outsourcing, and job security (Table 3.1). Later in the year, pilots flying on international routes for Quick WINGS Airlines began their first industrial action in thirty-three years. It started with unauthorised in-flight announcements telling flying customers about the pilot's disputes with Quick WINGS Airlines. But trade union actions also included rolling one-hour stoppages by aircraft engineers beginning to delay thousands of customers.

All pilots flying on Quick WINGS Airlines' code sharing with other members of the airline network "Earth One" were paid the same wages. PU stated that its aim was to stop current Quick WINGS Airlines pilots from being outsourced and offered offshore alternatives. PU wanted a 2.5% increase in wages each year for the next three years. Current inflation rates at Quick WINGS Airlines' home country were at 2%.

AEU was extremely concerned about jobs being outsourced and relocated overseas. The trade union insisted that Quick WINGS Airlines was trying to base new entities offshore as a means of side stepping local labour laws and aircraft maintenance policies and procedures that were currently in place to secure Quick WINGS Airlines' global safety record. AEU wanted to increase wages and allowances by 3% over two years and for the pay system to move to an annualised salary rather than wages plus shift allowances. This was a demand that Quick WINGS Airlines had already agreed to during 2001 pay negotiations. In 2001, Quick WINGS Airlines agreed to this because of efficiency gains but never implemented the move.

Meanwhile TWU wanted job security including protection for existing employees' terms and conditions as well as earnings. At the time these wages included a base rate of $45.000 although overtime, night work, and weekend allowances were slowly eroded through Quick WINGS Airlines' use of subcontractors during the last two years. TWU demanded wage increases of 5% per year, but this was negotiable. It sought improvements for health and safety, training, and general working conditions to apply to all employees of Quick WINGS Airlines as well as subcontracted workers. Against that, Quick WINGS Airlines offered a 3% wage increase per year and 1% additional increments at top tier. Quick WINGS Airlines also announced that no workers would be made redundant as a result of the use of subcontracting and it would require any contracted company to use the collective agreement with the TWU.

Since collective bargaining rounds with trade unions made no progress, Quick WINGS Airlines started to lockout workers of all relevant unions: PU, AEU, and TWU. It sought trade unions to drop their "fanatical demands" which would render Quick WINGS Airlines uncompetitive. Under local labour laws, lockouts were legitimate bargaining strategies for employers. Trade unions and Quick WINGS Airlines were at an impasse.

1. Imagine you are a union official at Quick WINGS Airlines' Pilot Union (PU). Discuss whether your demands are "fanatical". Can these demands be amended (inclusion of other issues) in negotiations with the management of Quick WINGS Airlines? Develop three alternative demands that you can present at the bargaining table.
2. Do the negotiations at Quick WINGS Airlines represent "integrative" or "distributive" bargaining or a mixture of both? Support your answer with four arguments.
3. Imagine you are the Labour Relations Minister of the home country of Quick WINGS Airlines. What measures could you undertake to stop the lockout of Quick WINGS Airlines?
4. Imagine you are the head of Quick WINGS Airlines' negotiating team. What can you offer all three unions to solve the collective bargaining impasse (deadlock or stalemate)? Develop three suggestions for each union addressing the specifics of their membership.
5. Discuss the enduring problem of choosing between "wage increase" and "job security". Find three arguments in favour of wage increases and three arguments in favour of job security.

### 3.4    *Diversity at Spy.Net*

Together with its trade union – the Public Service Workers' Union (PSWU) – government Secret Service "Spy.Net" was one of the supporters of the United Nations' 2016 International Day of Global Diversity. Events and ceremonies were held at the Paris Hilton Hotel on 21st October 2016, hosted by well-known socialite Donald Trumpsy and gay TV presenter Sarah Palinsy. Other event sponsors joining Spy.Net and the continuing headline sponsor Computer.Ware include the "City Transport Authority" that runs local transport, KPMG, and HSBC, as well as television station "Wacky-News", several local retail outlets, and a food cooperative.

The awards presented at the International Day of Global Diversity recognised positive role models and community organisations and businesses from the lesbian, gay, bisexual, and transgender (LGBT), ethnic minorities, age, religion, and disability communities. The awards are aimed at building a more inclusive country as well as business employment portfolio. They seek to promote equality and diversity; creating role models from all sections of society working in companies; eliminating discrimination on the grounds of race, gender identity, disability, sexual orientation, religion, and age; celebrate the achievements of people, communities, charity organisations, and companies; highlighting how diverse companies have contributed to the economy.

Yet despite the public support for these initiatives, the PSWU claims that the event supporter Spy.Net has not measured up to these goals as a public organisation. Its research – conducted by a secret source in Spy.Net's Human Resource Management department – showed that despite having a strong workforce of 15,000, employed mostly in the capital city but also in various global and undisclosed locations, the staff profile of Spy.Net workforce can be described as white middle-aged, heterosexual middle-class men. The trade union also found that the higher the hierarchical level, the more homogenous management becomes. Despite many meetings with Spy.Net's top management, the latter has consistently refused to take steps towards creating a diverse workforce, saying that Spy.Net's workforce is recruited on the basis of certain needs mirroring its tasks.

1.  Can the job of gathering intelligence justify the exclusion of LGBT people?
2.  What can the trade union do to encourage Spy.Net to diversify their workforce?
3.  Would a public "naming and shaming" campaign be a useful strategy? Discuss the pros and cons.
4.  Since Spy.Net is a governmental institution, should the trade union take the political route? What are the advantages and disadvantages of such a move?
5.  Imagine you are Spy.Net's HR manager. What would you recommend to accommodate the demands of the trade union? Formulate four policy recommendations.

### 3.5    *Social Media and Trade Unions*

Despite the many problems, social media like Facebook remain part of everyday life for many. This applies to workers but also to their representative bodies, the trade unions. Many unions have discovered that social media can assist them in organising and recruiting new members. Using social media like Facebook relieves trade unions from the need to go from door to door and from workplace to workplace. Recruiting new members in industries where workers do not regularly congregate at a specific workplace (e.g. flight attendants, delivery drivers, etc.) has always been problematic for trade unions. In these cases, trade unions have started using Email, Facebook, Union Newsletters, Twitter, Blogs (https://www.etui.org/Blog, https://blog.unionproof.com), and other forms of social media engagement.

The new forms of communication allow employees to communicate with their trade unions on a more frequent basis. In many countries, these forms of communication are protected under "free speech" legislation. Beyond that, free speech and the ability to join a trade union and engage in collective bargaining is a United Nations-supported human right. However, there are still companies that have sought to prevent communication between trade unions and workers. In other cases, companies have even resorted to corporate policies to undermine worker-union communication. Employers have even sought to prohibit the use of social media. Against that is the fact that in the USA, for example, trade unions are specifically granted permission to use Email when communicating with its members. Finally, it should be noted that there are cases in which employers monitor such communications as well as the use of email and social media.

1. Develop five arguments "in favour" of trade unions using social media (Facebook, blogs, Twitter, etc.) when recruiting new members and when communicating with its members.
2. Develop five arguments "against" trade unions using social media (Facebook, blogs, Twitter, etc.) when recruiting new members and when communicating with its members. Reflect on the argument that this eliminates personal contact between trade unions and its members.
3. Since "free speech" is a human right and protected in many countries (e.g. constitution), should the classical three actors in IR seek to develop uniform guidelines (e.g. laws) that support the communication between members and trade unions? Develop five arguments in favour of such a regulation.
4. Since employers often provide the technical equipment (hardware and software), does this override the human right of free communication? In other words, should employers be able to prevent trade unions and their members from communicating?
5. Imagine you are a trade union officer in the airline industry. What kind of way of communicating via social networks would you suggest to use and why? Explain and justify your choice.

## V. *A Suggestion for an Online Guest Lecture*

Auret van Heerden talks about:
"Making Global Labour Fair"
https://www.ted.com/talks/auret_van_heerden_making_global_labor_fair
[the online guest lecture above is merely a suggestion – www.ted.com/talks offers additional material to choose from]

## VI. *List of Suggested Documentaries on Industrial Relations*

The carefully selected documentary videos below are mere suggestions to be used during tutorials. Documentaries have been selected to achieve two things: (1) to explain key HRM themes and (2) to provide an insight into the reality of HRM. Typically, these short documentaries should be viewed in class followed by a class discussion on the content of the video. Alternatively, questions on documentaries can be prepared beforehand and small group discussions can follow up the video after viewing is concluded. Should any of the web links no longer function, please conduct an internet search for other – alternative – documentaries related to your tutorial topic (e.g. filmsforaction.org):

General IR: youtube.com/watch?v=VKq_xfpoaX0

Conflict at Work: youtube.com/watch?v=FDWOPu9Y6oM

Bullying: youtube.com/watch?v=-bhrqQ5zNmc

Off-Shoring: youtube.com/watch?v=CChAOh1X5CA

Flexible Working: youtube.com/watch?v=faVk912qxIA

Walmart Strike: en.labournet.tv/video/6405/walmart-warehouses-strike-2012

Salt of the Earth: youtube.com/watch?v=i9oY4rmDaWw

## Notes

1  http://link.springer.com/chapter/10.1007/978-1-349-15623-8_2.
2  http://www.egr.msu.edu/~lira/supp/steam/.
3  Mundlak, G. 2020. *Organizing Matters: Two Logics of Trade Union Representation*, Northampton: Edward Elgar.
4  Rockefeller, Jr., J. D. 2016. Labor and capital, *New York Times*, 9th January 1916 (https://www.nytimes.com, accessed: 5th April 2019); Peetz, D. 2019. *The Realities and Futures of Work*, Canberra: ANU Press, p. 49.
5  ILO. 2018. *International Labour Standards on Working Time* (http://www.ilo.org/global/standards/subjects-covered-by-international-labour-standards/working-time/lang--en/index.htm, accessed: 30th January 2018).
6  Blanpain, R. & Bisom-Rapp, S. 2014. *Global Workplace: International and Comparative Employment Law Cases and Materials*, New York: Kluwer Law & Business.
7  ILO. 2020. *Guidebook on How and Why to Collect and Use Data on Industrial Relations* (https://www.ilo.org/travail/whatwedo/publications/WCMS_737733/lang--en/index.htm, accessed: 25th September 2020).
8  Smith, R. 2018. *International Human Rights Law*. Oxford: Oxford University Press.
9  Visser, J. 2019. Can unions revitalize themselves?, *International Journal of Labour Research*, 9(1/2):17–48.
10  Knights, D. & Willmott, H. 1989. *Labour Process Theory*, Basingstoke: Macmillan; Armstrong, P. 1989. Management, labour process and agency, *Work, Employment & Society*, 3(3):307–322; Smith, C. 2010. Go with the flow: labour power mobility and labour process theory, in: Thompson, P. & Smith, C. (eds.) *Working Life – Renewing Labour Process Analysis*, Houndmills: Palgrave; Elliott, E. S. & Long, G. 2016. Manufacturing rate busters: computer control and social relations in the labour process, *Work, Employment & Society*, 30(1):135–151.
11  Polanyi, K. 1944. *The Great Transformation – The Political and Economical Origins of our Time*, New York: Farrar & Rinehart.
12  Hobsbawm, E. J. 1968. *Industry and Empire: An Economic History of Britain Since 1750*, London: Weidenfeld & Nicolson (rev. ed. New York: New Press).
13  Marx, K. 1890. *Das Kapital – Kritik der politischen Ökonomie (Capital – A Critique of Political Economy)*, Hamburg: 4th edited version by F. Engels, reprinted 1986: Berlin: Dietz-Press.
14  Smith, A. 1776. *The Wealth of Nations* – Books I–III, London: Penguin Books (reprinted 1986).
15  Klikauer, T. & Morris, R. 2002. Kiribati seafarers and German container shipping, *Maritime Policy & Management*, 29(1):93–101.
16  Schumpeter, J. A. 1942. *Capitalism, Socialism, and Democracy*, New York: Harper & Brothers.
17  To avoid the word *worker*, Starbucks calls workers *partners* and Walmart *associates* (Peetz, D. 2019. *The Realities and Futures of Work*, Canberra: ANU Press, p. 50).

18  Weiss, A. 1980. Job queues and layoffs in labor markets with flexible wages, *Journal of Political Economy*, 88(3):526–538; cf. Brown, J. 2011. Hotel Workers Turn Up Heat on Stubborn Hyatt (http://labornotes.org/, 22nd July 2011, accessed: 15th December 2018).

19  Herod, A. 2018. *Labor*, London: Polity Press.

20  Mikler, J. 2018. *The Political Power of Global Corporations*, London: Polity Press.

21  Baines, D. & Cunningham, I. (eds.) 2020. *Working in the Context of Austerity – Challenges and Struggles*, Bristol: Bristol University Press.

22  Rehmann, J. 2013. *Theories of Ideology: The Powers of Alienation and Subjection*, Leiden: Brill.

23  https://www.transnational-strike.info/.

24  Hyman, R. 1972. *Strikes*, London: Fontana; Hyman, R. 1989. *The Political Economy of Industrial Relations: Theory and Practice in a Cold Climate*, Houndmills: Macmillan.

25  Moore, B. 1966. *Social Origins of Dictatorship and Democracy – Lord and Peasant in the Making of the Modern World*, Boston, MA: Beacon Press.

26  Dahrendorf, R. 1959. *Class and Class Conflict in Industrial Society*. Stanford, CA: Stanford University Press.

27  Lehmbruch, G. & Schmitter, P. C. 1982. *Patterns of Corporatist Policy-Making*, London: Sage Publications; Schmitter, P. C. & Lehmbruch, G. 1979 (eds.) *Trends toward Corporatist Intermediation*, London: Sage.

28  Bauman, Z. 1989. *Modernity and the Holocaust*, Oxford: Blackwell.

29  Rosenow, E. 1992. Bourgeois or citoyen? The democratic concept of man, *Educational Philosophy and Theory*, 24(1):44–50.

30  Pack, S. J. 2010. *Aristotle, Adam Smith, and Karl Marx – On Some Fundamental Issues of 21st Century Political Economy*, Cheltenham: Edward Elgar.

31  For example, the move from fascism in Poland and Hungary to the soviet model of socialism when the Red Army ended fascist rule in many Eastern European Countries.

32  Schmermund, E. 2016. *Vladimir Lenin and the Russian Revolution*, New York: Enslow Publishing; Lukacs, G. 2009. *Lenin: A Study on the Unity of His Thought*, London: Verso; Krausz, T. 2015. *Reconstructing Lenin: An Intellectual Biography*, New York: Monthly Review Press; Badiou, A. 2015. *What Is to Be Done? A Dialogue on Communism, Capitalism, and the Future of Democracy*, Malden, MA: Polity Press.

33  Said, E. W. 1978. *Orientalism*, New York: Vintage Books; Said, E. W. 1994. *Culture & Imperialism*, New York: Knopf; Smith, J. 2016. *Imperialism in the Twenty-First Century*, New York: NYU Press; Lowrie, C. 2016. *Masters and Servants – Cultures of Empire and Tropics*, Manchester: Manchester University Press.

34  Dalrymple, W. 2015. The East India Company: the original corporate raiders, Wednesday 4th March 2015 (www.theguardian.com); Lawson, P. 2014. *The East India Company: A History*, London: Routledge; Klikauer, T. 2017. Southern insurgency – the coming of the global working class, *Employee Relations*, 39(4):582–590.

35  Magoc, C. J. & Bernstein, C. D. 2016. *Imperialism and Expansionism in American History: A Social, Political, and Cultural Encyclopaedia and Document Collection*, Santa Barbara, CA: ABC-CLIO; Headley, J. M. 2016. *The Europeanization of the World: On the Origins of Human Rights and Democracy*, Princeton, NJ: Princeton University Press.

36  Petras, J. F. & Veltmeyer, H. 2002. *Globalization Unmasked: Imperialism in the 21st Century* (2nd reprint), London: Zed Books.

37  Garfinkle, J. 2017. How to have difficult conversations when you don't like conflict, *Harvard Business Review*, 24th May 2017.

38  Blake, W. 1804. *Jerusalem – The Emanation of the Giant Albion* (edited with an introduction and notes by Morton D. Paley), London & Princeton, NJ: William Blake Trust/Princeton University Press (1991); Dickens, C. 1853. *Bleak House*, published monthly: March 1852–September 1853, London: Bradbury & Evans (London Penguin Classics, 2003); Dow, G. 1979. *Dark Satanic Mills*, Nottingham: Shaftesbury Project; Gillies, A. 1981. *Those Dark Satanic Mills: An Illustrated Record of the Industrial Revolution in South Lancashire*, Leigh: Wigan Record Office.

39  Risberg, A. et al (eds.). *The Routledge Companion to Mergers and Acquisitions*, London: Routledge.

40  Gardner, D. 2011. *GrowthBusters – Hooked on Growth* (DVD/video), Colorado Springs: Citizen-Powered Media (www.growthbusters.org/).

41 Fayol, H. 1916. *Managerialism Industrielle et Generale* (Industrial and General Managerialism), London: Sir I. Pitman & Sons, ltd. (1930).

42 Purcell, J. 1982. Macho managers and the new industrial relations, *Employee Relations*, 4(1):3–5.

43 Hirschman, A. 1970. *Exit, Voice, and Loyalty: Responses to Decline in Firms, Organizations, and States*, Cambridge: Harvard University Press; Johnstone, S & Ackers, P. 2015. *Finding a Voice at Work?: New Perspectives on Employment Relations*, Oxford: Oxford University Press.

44 EPI. 2020. Why Unions Are Good for Workers—Especially in a Crisis Like COVID-19 (https://files.epi.org/pdf/204014.pdf, 25th August 2020, accessed: 15th September 2020).

45 Despite the common idea of a "trickle down" effect, by 2016 we were made painfully aware that 'far from trickling down, income and wealth are instead being sucked upwards at an alarming rate" (Oxfam 2016:3).

46 Stabile, D. 2016. *The Political Economy of a Living Wage*, New York: Nature America Inc.; Grover, C. 2016. *Social Security and Wage Poverty*, Houndmills: Palgrave Macmillan; Levin-Waldman, O. M. 2016. *The Minimum Wage*, Santa Barbara, CA: ABC-CLIO; Standing, G. 2016. *The Precariat* (revised edition), London: Bloomsbury Academic.

47 Richardson-Price, A. 2016. The Fight for a Six Hour Workday (www.counterpunch.org, 19th August).

48 Donado, A. & Walde, K. 2012. How trade unions increase welfare, *Economic Journal*, 122(563):990–1009.

49 Bivens, J. 2019. The Fed shouldn't give up on restoring labor's share of income—and measure it correctly, Washington, DC: Economic Policy Institute (https://www.epi.org, 30th January 2019, accessed: 5th April 2019).

50 Johnstone, S. & Wilkinson, A. 2016. *Developing Positive Employment Relations*, Basingstoke: Palgrave; see also Wilton's "the management of workplace conflict" in his textbook: "Introduction to HRM" (2016:352–380).

51 Robbins. S. P. & Judge, T. 2016. *Essentials of Organizational Behaviour* (13th ed.), Boston, MA: Pearson.

52 Appelbaum, R. P. & Lichtenstein, N. (eds.) 2016. *Achieving Workers' Rights*, New York: Columbia University Press; Getman, J. G. 2016. *The Supreme Court on Unions*, New York: Columbia University Press; HRW. 2017. *Human Rights Watch's World Report 2017*, New York: Seven Stories Press.

53 Klikauer, T. 2013. *Managerialism – Critique of an Ideology*, Basingstoke: Palgrave.

54 Mabey, C. & Mayrhofer, W. 2015. *Developing Leadership: Questions Business Schools Don't Ask*, Los Angles, CA: Sage.

55 Vachon, T.E., Wallace, M. & Hyde, A. 2016. Union decline in a neoliberal age globalization, financialization, European integration, and union density in 18 affluent democracies, *Socius: Sociological Research for a Dynamic World*, 2.

56 Marcuse, H. 1966. *One-Dimensional Man: Studies in the Ideology of Advanced Industrial Societies*, Boston, MA: Beacon Press.

57 Angie, T. N. 2016. *Class, and Law in Vietnam's Labor Resistance*, New York: Columbia University Press.

58 Davis, M. 2007. *Planet of Slums*, London: Verso.

59 "Credit Suisse recently revealed that the richest 1% have now accumulated more wealth than the rest of the world put together. This occurred a year earlier than Oxfam's much publicized prediction ahead of last year's World Economic Forum. Meanwhile, the wealth owned by the bottom half of humanity has fallen by a trillion dollars in the past five years" (Oxfam 2016:2).

60 CIA. 1944. *Simple Sabotage Field Manual – Strategic Service*, Washington, DC: Office of Strategic Services (www.cia.gov, 17th January 1944).

61 www.labornotes.org/.

62 Nowak. J. et al. 2018. *Workers' Movements and Strikes in the Twenty-First Century: A Global Perspective*, Lanham: Rowman & Littlefield.

63 Luce, S. 2019, Contribution to GTI Roundtable Planetizing the Labor Movement - An Exchange on the Essay Workers of the World Unite (At Last) (https://greattransition.org/roundtable/workers-world-stephanie-luce, accessed: 15th January 2021).

64 In situations where a refined industrial relations system is not in existence, conflict is likely to be expressed in radical and even militant actions as the examples of "bossnapping" have shown (Hayes, G. 2012. Bossnapping: situating repertoires of industrial action in national and global contexts, *Modern & Contemporary France*, 20(2):185–201).

65 http://plato.stanford.edu/entries/marx/.
66 https://www.marxists.org/archive/marx/works/download/pdf/Manifesto.pdf.
67 Tolliday, S. & Zeitlin, J. (eds.) 1986. *The Automobile Industry and Its Workers: Between Fordism and Flexibility*, Cambridge: Polity & Blackwell; https://www.marxists.org/glossary/terms/f/o. htm.
68 Galbraith, J. K. 1958. *The Affluent Society*, Boston, MA: Houghton Mifflin; Goldthorpe, J. H., Lockwood, D., Bechhofer, F. & Platt, J. 1969. *The Affluent Worker in the Class Structure*, Cambridge: Cambridge University Press; Marcuse, H. 1968. Liberation from the affluent society, in: Cooper, D. (eds.), *The Dialectics of Liberation*, Harmondsworth: Penguin.
69 The same might not always be said for employers and management: Pearson, C. 2016. *Reform or Repression: Organizing America's Anti-union Movement*, Philadelphia: University of Pennsylvania Press.
70 Hyman, R. 2015. The very idea of democracy at work, *Transfer* (published online before print: December 14, 2015, https://doi.org/10.1177/1024258915619283).
71 Dunlop, J. 1958. *Industrial Relations Systems*, New York: Holt; Abbott, K., Mackinnon, B. H. & Fallon, P. 2016. *Understanding Employment Relations*, Oxford: Oxford University Press.
72 Hall, P. A. & Soskice, D. 2001. *Varieties of Capitalism: The Institutional Foundations of Comparative Advantage*, Oxford: Oxford University Press; Klikauer, T. 2012. A General Motors works council's response to the capitalist global financial crisis – a case study from Germany, *Capital & Class*, 36(2):303–322.
73 Ramsay, H. 1977. Cycle of control: worker participation in sociological and historical perspective, *Sociology*, 11(3):441–506.
74 Gall, G. 2012. Richard Hyman: an assessment of his industrial relations: a Marxist introduction, *Capital & Class*, 36(1):135–149.
75 Locke, R. R. & Spender, J. C. 2011. *Confronting Managerialism: How the Business Elite and Their Schools Threw Our Lives Out of Balance*, London: Zed Books.
76 Harvey, D. 2005. *A Brief History of Neoliberalism*, Oxford: Oxford University Press; Crouch, C. 2011. *The Strange Non-death of Neoliberalism*, Cambridge: Polity; Davies, W. 2014. *The Limits of Neoliberalism – Authority, Sovereignty and the Logic of Competition*, London: Sage.
77 Offe, C. & Wiesenthal, H. 1980. Two logics of collective action: theoretical notes on social class and organisational form, in: Zeitlin, M. (eds.), *Political Power and Social Theory - A Research Annual*, vol. 1, Greenwich: JAI Press.
78 Oxfam. 2018. Reward Work, Not Wealth (PFD download from: https://www.oxfam.org/sites/www.oxfam.org/files/file_attachments/bp-reward-work-not-wealth-220118-summ-en. pdf, January 2018, accessed: 6th February 2018).
79 http://www.investopedia.com/terms/d/disposableincome.asp.
80 Harvey, D. 2014. *Seventeen Contradictions and the End of Capitalism*, New York: Oxford University Press; Bell, D. 1976. *The Cultural Contradictions of Capitalism*, New York: Basic Books.
81 Horstman, B. 1988. Labour flexibility strategies and management style, *Journal of Industrial Relations*, 30(3):412–431.
82 Gorz, A. 1982. *Farewell to the Working Class – An Essay on Post-Industrial Socialism*, London: South End Press.
83 http://www.bbc.com/news/uk-13828537.
84 Freeman, R. B. 1984. *What Do Unions Do?*, New York: Basic Books.
85 Doerflinger, N. & Pulignano, V. 2015. Temporary agency work and trade unions in comparative perspective, *SAGE Open*, 5(2):2158244015575633.
86 Marens, R. 2013. What comes around: the early 20th century American roots of legitimating corporate social responsibility, *Organization*, 20(3):460.
87 Blauner, R. 1964. *Alienation and Freedom – The Factory Worker and His Industry*, Chicago, IL: Chicago University Press; Klikauer, T. 2013. Marx & alienation – essays on Hegelian themes, *Labour & Industry*, 23(3):182–186.
88 https://cpj.org/2015/04/10-most-censored-countries.php (Committee to Protect Journalists: Press Freedom Online); e.g. Internet censorship (freedomhouse.org).
89 Layard, T. 2005. *Happiness – Lessons from a New Science*, London: Allan Lane.
90 Braverman, H. 1974. *Labor and Monopoly Capital – The Degradation of Work in the Twentieth Century*, New York: Monthly Review Press.
91 McCluskey, L. 2020. *Why You Should Be a Trade Unionist*, London: Verso Books.
92 Olson, M. 1971. *The Logics of Collective Action*, Cambridge: Harvard University Press.

93    Johnstone, S. & Ackers, P. 2015. *Finding a Voice at Work? New Perspectives on Employment Relations*, Oxford: Oxford University Press; Morschett, D., Schramm-Klein, H. & Zentes, J. 2015. *Strategic International Management* (3rd ed.), Heidelberg: Springer, p. 517.

94    Cf. https://home.coworker.org/; https://www.fixmyjob.com/.

95    Common reasons for joining trade unions are, for example: health and safety, compulsion (closed shop), protection, social pressure, voice, legal protection, political convictions, solidarity, tradition, pay, conditions, etc.

96    http://www.reuters.com/article/us-tyco-curtain-idUSBRE85D1M620120615.

97    Jessop, B. 2007, *State Power*, Oxford: Polity Press.

98    Möllers, C. 2013. *The Three Branches: A Comparative Model of Separation of Powers*, Oxford: Oxford University Press.

99    Montesquieu, C. d. S. 1752, *The Spirit of Laws* (transl. Nugent, T. 1914), London: G. Bell & Sons, Ltd.

100   Goldberg, S. B. 2017. *How Mediation Works: Theory, Research, and Practice*, Bingley: Emerald Publishing.

101   Dunlop, J. T. 1958. *Industrial Relations Systems*, New York: Holt.

102   Kochan, T. A., Katz, H. & McKersie, R. B. 1986. *The Transformation of American Industrial Relations*, New York: Basic Books.

103   Hyman, R. 2018. What future for industrial relations in Europe?, *Employee Relations*, 40(4):569–579.

104   Hyman, R. 2015. Three scenarios for industrial relations in Europe, *International Labour Review*, 154(1):5–14; cf. Waddington, J. & Conchon, A. 2015. *Board Level Employee Representation in Europe: Priorities, Power and Articulation*, London: Routledge.

105   Kochan, T., Katz, H. & McKersie, R. 1986. *The Transformation of American Industrial Relations*, New York: Basic Books.

106   Wilton, N. 2013. *An Introduction to HRM*, London: Sage, p. 276.

107   http://www.ilpc.org.uk/Portals/56/ilpc-docs/ILPC-Background.pdf.

108   Williams, R. C. 2016. *The Cooperative Movement: Globalization from Below*, London: Routledge.

109   Gibson-Graham, J. K., Cameron, J. & Healy, S. 2013. *Take Back the Economy: An Ethical Guide for Transforming Our Communities*, Minneapolis: University of Minnesota Press; Klikauer, T. 2015. The actuality of 'a better world is possible', *Organization*, 22(6):942–944.

110   Ridley-Duff, R. 2010. Communitarian governance in social enterprises: case evidence from the Mondragon Cooperative Corporation and School Trends Ltd., *Social Enterprise Journal*, 6(2):125–145.

111   Klikauer, T. 2017. The coming of the global working class, *Employee Relations*, 39(4):582–590.

112   Bescond, D., Chataignier, A. & Mehran, F. 2003. Seven indicators to measure decent work: an international comparison, *International Labour Review*, 142(2):179–211.

113   Heereden's TED talk. 2010. Can be useful to answer the report question! (https://www.ted.com/talks/auret_van_heerden_making_global_labor_fair).

114   Klikauer, T. & Donn, C. 2004. Varieties of industrial relations in the shipping industry: a comparison of two Anglo-Saxon liberal market economies and two European coordinated market economies, *New Zealand Journal of Employment Relations*, 29(1):39–61; Klikauer, T. 2002. Into murky waters: globalisation and deregulation in Germany's shipping employee relations, *Employee Relations*, 24(1):12–28 [with Richard Morris]; Klikauer, T. 2002. Kiribati seafarers and German container shipping, *Maritime Policy Journal*, 29(1):93–101 [with Richard Morris]; Klikauer, T. 2001. Responses to globalisation: employee relations in the German and Australian shipping Industries, *Employee Relations Review*, (19):9–14 [with Richard Morris].

## Further Readings

Balfour, C. 2020. *Industrial Relations in the Common Market*, London: Routledge.

Bamber, G. J. et al. 2021. *International and Comparative Employment Relations*, London: Sage.

Bendix, R. 1956. *Work & Authority in Industry – Ideologies of Management*, New York: Wiley.

Berg, J. 2015. *Labour Markets, Institutions and Inequality: Building Just Societies in the 21st Century*, Cheltenham: Edward Elgar.

Beynon, H. 1973. *Working for Ford*, London: Allen Lane.

Boxall, P. et al. 2014. The Future of ER from the Perspective of HRM, *Journal of Industrial Relations*, 56(4):578–593.

Braverman, H. 1974. *Labor & Monopoly Capital*, New York: Monthly Review Press.

Brenner, A., Day, B. & Ness, I. 2015. *The Encyclopedia of Strikes in American History*, New York: Routledge.

Burawoy, M. 1979. *Manufacturing Consent*, Chicago, IL: University of Chicago Press.

Edwards, R. 1979. *Contested Terrain*, London: Heinemann.

EU. 2020. *Industrial Relations: Developments 2015-2019*, Luxembourg: Publications Office of the European Union.

Gapper, J. 2015. *The Ghost Shift*, New York: Ballantine Books.

Gall, G. (eds.). 2016. *The Future of Union Organising: Building for Tomorrow*, Heidelberg: Springer.

Geary, I. & Pabst, A. 2015. *Blue Labour: Forging a New Politics*, London: I.B. Tauris Publishers.

Goulston, M. 2015. How People Communicate During Conflict, *Harvard Business Review*, June, 93:6.

Halimi, S. 2015. Post-union Inequality, *Le Monde Diplomatique* (engl. edition), no. 1504, April.

Hipp, L. & Givan, R. K. 2015. What Do Unions Do?, *Social Forces*, 94(1):349–377.

Hyman, R. 1972. *Strikes*, London: Fontana.

Hyman, R. 1979. *Industrial Relations*, London: MacMillan.

Hyman, R. 1989. *The Political Economy of Industrial Relations*, London: MacMillan.

Hyman, R. & Price, R. 2016. *The New Working Class?: White-Collar Workers and Their Organizations - A Reader*, Heidelberg: Springer.

Jaumotte, F. & Buitron, C. O. 2015. *Power from the People*, Washington, DC: International Monetary Fund.

Johnstone, S. 2015. *Finding a Voice at Work? New Perspectives on Employment Relations*, New York: Oxford University Press.

Katz, H. C. et al. 2015. *Labor Relations in a Globalizing World*, Ithaca, NY: ILR Press.

Knights, D., & Willmott, H. 1989. *Labour Process Theory*, Basingstoke: Macmillan.

Lansbury, R. 2020. *Crossing Boundaries: Work and Industrial Relations in Perspective*, London: Routledge.

Liu, M. & Smith, C. 2016. *China at Work*, London: Palgrave Macmillan.

Lynd, S. 2015. *Solidarity Unionism: Rebuilding the Labor Movement from Below*, Chicago, IL: PM Press.

Marcuse, H. 1966. *One-Dimensional Man*, Boston, MA: Beacon Press, Chapter 4.

Marglin, S. 1974. What Do Bosses Do?, *Review of Radical Political Economy*, 6(2).

Ness, I. 2015. *Southern Insurgency: The Coming of the Global Working Class*, London: Pluto Press.

Newsome, K. et al. 2015. *Putting Labour in Its Place*, London: Palgrave.

Oxfam. 2016. *An Economy for the 1%*, Oxford: Oxfam Briefing Paper 210 (18th January).

Pijl, K. (eds.). 2015. *Handbook of the International Political Economy of Production*, Northampton: Edward Elgar.

Suffield, L. & Cannon, G. L. 2016. *Labour Relations*, Toronto: Pearson Canada.

Tapia, M. et al. 2015. Theory in IR, *Socio-Economic Review*, 13(1):157–184.

Weller, C. E. (eds.) 2015. *Inequality, Uncertainty & Opportunity*, Ithaca, NY: Cornell University Press.

White, A. 2016. *The Last Great Strike*, Berkeley: University of California Press.

Williams, S. 2020. *Introducing Employment Relations: A Critical Approach*, Oxford: Oxford University Press.

Yeoman, Y. 2014. *Meaningful Work and Workplace Democracy*, Basingstoke: Palgrave.

# 4 Training People

## Learning and Human Resource Development

### Executive Summary

Learning in work situations – also called management learning and human resource development (HRD) – relates to training for skill development. It is often technical whilst education is generally seen as a broader concept. At work as in business schools, learning focuses on the vocational training of professionals (e.g. MBAs). Prior to engaging in organisational learning, HR managers often conduct a needs assessment focusing on organisational needs, personal needs, and task needs. When making decisions for organisational learning, HR managers also discuss the pros and cons of training as organisational training has many positives for a company but also for employees. In an ever changing business environment the transferability of new skills, knowledge, and behaviours remains important to companies as up-to-date knowledge supports the competitive advantage of a business. To achieve that, the right training method (training on the job, blended learning, etc.) remains relevant. This is just as important as, for example, group building methods (e.g. forming, storming, norming, and performing). At the end of organisational learning, HR managers conduct an evaluation of cognitive, skill-based, and motivational outcomes as well as ROI, the return of investment.

### Key Learning Objectives

1. Realise the importance of knowledge and employee learning for business;
2. Conceptualise the role of HRM in education and training;
3. Outline the key elements of a "needs assessment";
4. Explain what an HR policy on learning can achieve;
5. List the core elements that result in an effective training session;
6. Recognise the link between culture and organisational learning;
7. Appreciate the critical approach to learning; and
8. Develop a formal HR policy on employee training and development.

### Learning, Development, and Professionalism

People – whether at work or not – constantly learn new things. But learning can also take a more structured form of acquiring new knowledge. In work situations, this is called organisational or **management learning**[1] while HRM uses the terms **human resource**

DOI: 10.4324/9781003293637-4

**development** (HRD) and employee training and development (EDT).[2] Overall, one might distinguish between education[3] and training. **Training** is seen as a rather narrow form of instruction often directed towards the improvement of skills and knowledge while **education** is broader and often described as a process that facilitates **learning**. Learning, in turn, is seen as the act of acquiring new or modifying existing knowledge, behaviours, or values. Learning is viewed as a process, not the pure accumulation of factual knowledge. It produces changes which are relatively permanent. Learning is a continuous process which means improving your job-related knowledge, known as **lifelong learning**, has become imperative.[4] This may indicate a shift from "lifetime employment" to "life-long employability".[5] For lifelong employability, ongoing training remains essential. It can be said that one can train a dog but there hardly ever will be an educated dog and certainly not one with an MBA that discusses the pros and cons of organisational learning.[6]

Perhaps HRD is more akin to **vocational training** than to holistic education because organisational training as well as the education in business schools is designed to prepare people for a profession – the profession of being a manager (MBA). Such vocational training programmes are often directed towards developing expertise and specific techniques related to all aspects of management. Already in 1835, the Scottish noticed the importance of training for industrial capitalism when noting "the training of human beings to renounce their desultory habits of work, and to identify themselves with the unvarying regularity of the complex automation".[7] Ure's *complex automation* might no longer be *Spinning Jenny*[8] but today are advanced computer programmes. Yet the basics of training remains.

Training is often conducted in skill-focused vocational schools such as, for example, business schools.[9] In the area of HRM, much of vocational training takes place inside business organisations, whilst inside business schools, for example, vocational training also prepares for positions in careers such as marketing, accounting, HRM, operations management, and so forth. As such, it is related to a professional career. What distinguishes a **profession** from other forms of occupation (such as, for example, bricklaying) is shown below:

1. **Formal**: a profession is linked to formal rather than informal training;
2. **Theoretical**: the training is theoretical rather than practical;
3. **University**: professionals (lawyers, medical doctors, etc.) receive university training;
4. **Associations**: there is a professional body or association for a profession; and finally,
5. **Accreditation**: these associations certify and accredit professional training.

Given this definition, HRM can be seen as a profession. There are many professional bodies in many countries for HRM (e.g. AHRI in Australia, SHRM in the USA, CIPD in the UK, etc.) that – among other things – certify what is being taught in HRM programmes. These bodies assure that the degrees are certified and that the graduates (HR managers or general managers) are aware of the basics of HRM such as recruitment and selection, OHS, HRD, performance management, OHS, industrial relations, etc. Training occurs at several educational levels. Professional education occurs at roughly five different ranks:

*Table 4.1* The Ranking of Professional Training Achievements

| Rank 1 | Rank 2 | Rank 3 | Rank 4 | Rank 5 |
|---|---|---|---|---|
| Graduates have a general knowledge of HRM – often at entry level – with the aim of further learning | Basic university degree with coherent understanding of HRM gained at university | Graduates have a specialised understanding of HRM gained through post-graduate training | Graduates have specialised knowledge of HRM gained through research and thesis writing – not course work (above level 3) | Graduates have a systematic, critical, and theoretical knowledge of HRM gained through scientific research resulting in a "thesis" (publications) |
| **Diploma** | **Bachelor Degree** | **Master degree** | **Master degree** | **Doctoral degree (PhD)** |

Table 4.1 shows the ascendancy in knowledge from learning new knowledge (rank 1–3) to creating knowledge (rank 4 and 5). Among the many concepts of **knowledge creation**, Nonaka's dynamic theory of organisational knowledge creation has risen to prominence.[10] Organisational knowledge is inventive when shaped through four patterns[11]: **socialisation** (observing, discussing, analysing, spending time together in an organisation); **combination** (organising and integrating knowledge as well as combining different types of explicit knowledge, for example, building prototypes); **internalisation** (knowledge receiving and application by an individual and learning by doing); and **externalisation** (publishing, articulating knowledge, enabling communication, and sharing with others).[12]

Much of this links to organisational innovation often understood as the implementation of new organisational methods innovating current business practices, workplace organisation and the external relations of a company. This involves the implementation of new organisational working methods to re-shape, for example, the distribution of managerial responsibilities and organisational decision-making processes. This may change relationships between employees, divisions, departments, and organisational units and the way knowledge is managed.

**Knowledge management** has come to be known as the process of creating, sharing, using, and managing organisational knowledge and information seen as a multi-dimensional approach directed towards the efficient use of organisational knowledge.[13] To realise this, HR managers engage in knowledge management towards strategic objectives such as improved performance, cultivating a firm's competitive advantage, business and organisational innovation, and the sharing of new knowledge. The broader focus of knowledge management often interfaces with the more specific focus of organisational learning. What ultimately drives learning is the specific interest people have in acquiring and creating new knowledge.

> Knowledge management is a clear example of rational control. It tries to codify or formalise every piece of information considered relevant for organisational purposes, not only the information routinely gathered and not exploited, but also the workers' tacit or personal knowledge.[14]

Generally, there are three basic **types of knowledge** interest[15]:

1.  The first is the technical or empirical-analytic interest focusing on testable general explanations and sciences, often linked to rational choice and formal modelling and deduction with an interest in control.
2.  The second knowledge interest is found in historical-interpretive and cultural-hermeneutic sciences. It seeks understanding within socio-cultural forms of life. Human societies have always interpreted the natural world to understand it. But it is also used to understand features of everyday interaction at work and beyond.
3.  Finally, the emancipatory interest seeks to overcome dogmatism, compulsion, and domination. It combines the Frankfurt School of critical theory with **critical pedagogy**.[16] It seeks to unmask cases of self-deception, mass-deception, and social-political ideologies.[17] It is directed towards liberation and emancipation, using critical pedagogy to point out, for example, how power asymmetries and domination between instructors and students can prevent inter-subjectivity and human emancipation.[18]

Many forms of knowledge and education remain inevitably linked to the status of a profession. They are based on **competency-based training** where candidates are educated to meet the specific competencies of a profession as defined by occupation (e.g. marketing for MBAs and recruitment and selection for HR managers). Below this level, one might find the **apprenticeship**, originally associated with feudal guilds (stonemasons, etc.) and organised in the form of years of practical training under a master to acquire the trade. Training in modern organisations, however, is very different from these ancient and medieval traditions.

## Stages of Organisational Training

Organisational training, HRD, and employee training and development are names that indicate training at the workplace level. Whilst HR managers remain involved in the process or organisation of training, they are not necessarily delivering it themselves. In order to evaluate a specific organisational training need, assess gaps in the skill level of employees, and design a training regime for them, HR managers often analyse training requirements by focusing on a "gap" in training. To fill such training gaps, in accordance with line management, HR managers rely on a six stage process:

*Table 4.2* Closing the Training Gap

| At | HR Managers |
| --- | --- |
| Stage 1 | Conduct a "needs assessment"; |
| Stage 2 | Assess whether an employee has the necessary motivation for training; |
| Stage 3 | Make sure that a positive learning environment is in place; |
| Stage 4 | Check that what is learned can be applied to a job; |
| Stage 5 | Select the correct training method[19]; and finally, |
| Stage 6 | Evaluate whether or not the desired learning has taken place |

Before HR managers enter into stage one of the training process (Table 4.2), they use several **pressure points** that are capable of indicating that there is a need for organisational training. Among the many pressure points, key indicators for a need for organisational training are performance problems, the introduction of new technology (e.g. IT), changes in internal or external customer requests for training, job redesign and restructuring processes (e.g. Chapter 5), changes in consumer preferences, new lines of products, new legislations, or new regulations coming from the sphere of industrial relations (e.g. Chapter 3). Once HR managers have identified a training need, the first step is the needs assessment or **needs analysis** which includes three elements:

a.   an organisational analysis,
b.   a personal analysis, and
c.   a task analysis.

### 1. Organisational Analysis

The organisational analysis assesses the appropriateness of training. It evaluates whether there is a need for training that could benefit the organisation. Under this test, organisational training is not analysed and designed for the benefit of a person but for the benefit of the company. The organisational analysis evaluates and assesses seven key elements:

1.   the support of immediate managers, supervisors, and peers;
2.   a positive attitude among peers and managers directed towards training;
3.   the availability of the employee to engage in a training programme;
4.   the ability to utilise the training (outcomes) on the job;
5.   the link between training and the company's business strategies;
6.   the budgeting (finances, time invested, and expertise) of the training; and
7.   the level, depth, and scope of training.

### 2. Personal Analysis

The tasks of the personal analysis is designed to answer questions such as: "who needs training?" to determine whether (1) performance deficiencies and problems result from inadequate or inappropriate levels of training, the lack of knowledge and skills; and (2) this process helps determining an employee's readiness for training, i.e. whether the general skill level is sufficient to engage in further training (e.g. logical comprehension might be a necessary precursor for training in computer programming). In addition, HR managers assess whether training is seen as important by the trainee, whether it helps performing more effectively, whether it leads to improved behaviours, removes obstacles to better performance, and finally, if other – non-training – solutions can be found to a given organisational problem.[20]

### 3. Task Analysis

The task analysis determines the organisational relevance of a task as well as the skills, knowledge, and behaviours needed to accomplish the given work task. This process also assesses what kind of training is appropriate for the completion of the work task. A task analysis is a four-way process in which HR managers

1. select the position or job to be analysed;
2. compose a list of those tasks that are performed in the job;
3. determine the four basic elements of these tasks:
   (a) the frequency a task is performed,
   (b) the time spent on a specific task,
   (c) the relevance of the work task for the job,
   (d) the degree of difficulty associated with the task; and finally,
4. HR managers assess the knowledge, skills, abilities, and behaviours needed to carry out these tasks.

Once HR managers have completed the three-fold needs assessment (organisational analysis, personal analysis, and task analysis), companies can engage employees in organisational learning – a process that has, throughout recent history, become increasingly important for companies seeking a strategic competitive advantage (Chapter 9).

## Organisational Learning

As human societies have moved from feudal and agriculture-based economies to manufacturing capitalism (19th and 20th century) eventually reaching today's **knowledge economy** (21st century), knowledge, individual skill levels, and organisational learning have gained importance. Organisational learning is increasingly linked to a corporate business strategy, but despite the importance of organisational learning, not all learning, teaching, training, and education take place inside companies (e.g. MBAs).[21] Even though much of today's external training is rather vocational in character and associated with business, many companies do not invest enough in organisational learning.[22] Placed in the "exit, voice, and loyalty" model,[23] organisational learning would generally increase loyalty and the voice option.

Simultaneously, organisational learning can also increase the exit option – an employee leaving the company. That way a company not only loses its theory investment but the particular employee/manager might also start working for a competitor. As a consequence and because of the fear a trained employee or manager might leave for an external position, reaping the rewards of the training, much of the organisational learning is not conducted in-house (inside a company).[24]

Companies typically see training – as economists call it – an **externality**.[25] This means that the cost of training is offloaded onto someone else (e.g. society) rather than the company bearing the cost.[26] This happens even though many forms of vocational training – MBA, etc. – are to a high degree predominantly useful to companies and not individuals. For a long time, companies have offloaded the cost of training onto the state and individuals.[27] States remain significant providers of vocational training from apprenticeships to technical colleges to universities.[28] But under neo-liberalism, the burden is increasingly shifting towards individuals who are asked to pay for their training under the "user-pay" ideology. As a consequence, there are high costs associated with MBA degrees. In addition to the above-mentioned "exit" option, companies state mainly five reasons for not training:

1. training is only for large enterprises;
2. training takes a lot of time;
3. training is expensive;
4. employees do not want to study; and
5. training is now freely available on the internet (e.g. YouTube, MOOC, etc.).[29]

But there are good reasons companies should engage in organisational learning:

1. **competition**: it allows a company to stay ahead of competitors;
2. **change**: it assists in keeping up-to-date with industry changes;
3. **technology**: it helps to remain aligned with the latest technologies;
4. **skill gap**: it helps to ascertain and identify organisational weaknesses and skill gaps;
5. **knowledge**: it assists in maintaining knowledge and skill levels;
6. **advancing**: it assists in developing organisation skill portfolios (skill management)[30];
7. **satisfaction**: it increases job satisfaction and organisational wellbeing;
8. **promotion**: it enhances internal promotion while maintaining retention[31];
9. **talent**: it helps attract new talent; and
10. **learning**: it provides strong incentives to learn more.

These are some of the reasons why companies engage in organisation learning. In many ways, training companies adhere to the basics of organisational learning and education. Perhaps the two names most associated with learning and education are Jean Piaget (1896–1980) and Lev Vygotsky (1896–1934).[32] The scientific work of both has led to four key principles that govern all learning: (1) knowledge is never passively accumulated but an active and cognitive (rational, understanding) engagement by an individual[33]; (2) organisational learning is an adaptive activity assisting individuals in engaging with their social (organisational) environment; (3) organisational learning assists employees in organisation sense-making[34] and understanding of work; and (4) organisational learning is associated with our biological and neurological existence (Piaget) and remains inextricably linked to our social environment, class,[35] culture[36] (e.g. HRM's **diversity training**[37]), work,[38] and language (Vygotsky).[39]

Often learning assists **social mobility**,[40] i.e. the upward movement of individuals and people between the social strata and classes of a society (worker → manager (MBA) → CEO).[41] In general, this means a movement between social classes while class immobility denotes the asphyxiation in one's class with little or no mobility.[42] Essentially, there are two theories about social classes:

1. **the sociological class**: it is defined by income, status, and education creating a lower, middle, and upper class[43] (e.g. education leads to a "lower to middle class" movement)[44]; and
2. **the Marxist class**: capitalism creates workers (those who sell their labour) and capitalists (those who extract surplus value while owning the means of production: firms, companies, corporations, shareholders).[45] In this theory, the two classes are totally opposed, tending to struggle against each other – the infamous **class war**. This idea has been brought to the fore by none other than Berkshire Hathaway investor **Warren Buffett** (owning $66.7 billion): "there's class warfare, all right… but it's my class, the rich class, that's making war, and we're winning."[46] In this version of class, education will lead to an upward movement within a class – the working class.[47]

In the first (non-class war) version, MBAs, for example, might belong to the middle class given their income, status, and educational level. In the second version, MBAs rather belong to the working class as they generally sell their labour for an income – MBAs tend to work in a company. The MBA degree is a work-related degree that is only useful to someone in employment. It increases the exchange value of labour – you can sell "yourself" (e.g. your ability to work) for a higher wage. All of these factors can shape learning – whether organisational learning or external education (e.g. university). When HR managers design or select modules for successful organisational learning, they include the following twelve key elements. As such organisational learning should…

1. …take place in an authentic place reflecting the real world;
2. …involve social negotiations and mediations;
3. …be made relevant;
4. …link new knowledge to prior knowledge;
5. …be assessed formally;
6. …enable and assist future learning;
7. …encourage self-regulation and self-management;
8. …promote critical reflective self-awareness[48];
9. …further entrepreneurial skills[49] and critical-analytical skills;
10. …present a multitude of perspectives using a variety of presentation formats;
11. …encourage communities of practices and social learning; and finally,
12. …trainers are guides and facilitators – not top-down instructors.

## Creating a Positive Learning Experience

In contrast to the ideology of individualism, we – as human beings – remain social beings.[50] People learn best in social settings – kindergarten, schools,[51] colleges, universities (group work), etc. – rather than in individual settings (**e-learning**).[52] Knowledge often relies on some form of participation in these social settings. This creates a positive social environment for organisational learning. HR managers are also aware that employees learn better when they understand "why" they engage in organisational learning. It has been shown that clear and good **learning objectives** help the process of organisational learning by giving directions. Secondly, when employees can link learning to their own **experience** – whether work or private experience – they get a better understanding. Thirdly, organisational learning is assisted through providing opportunities to practise what has been learned. This reflects on four key learning principles[53]:

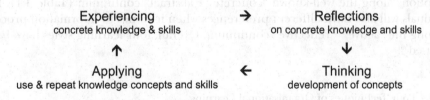

Experiencing → Reflections
concrete knowledge & skills — on concrete knowledge and skills
↑ ↓
Applying ← Thinking
use & repeat knowledge concepts and skills — development of concepts

*Figure 4.1* Principles of Organisational Learning.

The four-stage model shown in Figure 4.1 helps individuals in organisations decide what kinds of learning experiences are most satisfying while also improving an individual's learning achievements.[54] These individuals are often grouped into four basic learners: (1) the activist; (2) the reflector; (3) the pragmatist; and (4) the theorist.[55] The circular model of Figure 4.1 provides generic qualities that can also be applied beyond organisational learning. The four-stage learning process is explained in the following.

*Table 4.3* The Four-Stage Learning Process

| Stages | Learning Activity and Examples |
| --- | --- |
| Stage 1 Experience | Organisational learning often begins with an individual's experience – doing – and the acquisition of a concrete experience. This is the actual experience of learning when, for example, a management trainer carries out a team-building exercise involving "adventure learning" (see below). |
| Stage 2 Observation and Reflection | The goal of this stage is to engage with "reflective observation". This is the ability to critically reflect and observe (watching rather than doing). This can occur when, for example, a management trainer reflects on the above-noted example of an adventure learning session "after" the session has concluded. Critical reflections often focus on questions such as: how did the training go? Were participants engaged in the session? Were participants interested in the team building activity? Were the objectives of the training session achieved? |
| Stage 3 Thinking | This is the stage that focuses on "abstract conceptualisation" – thinking. Here, abstract concepts about training are formulated while simultaneously generalisation – converting a specific learning experience into general knowledge – takes place. For example, a management trainer analyses a team-building exercise in the light of the "forming → storming → norming → performing" model (see below) to formulate general knowledge about the process of team-building exercises for management training. This may lead to questions such as: do these methods achieve the desired goals? Did participants move through the stages as the model would predict? And: has the model led to the outcomes predicted (e.g. performance)? |
| Stage 4 Applying | This is the stage of "active experimentation" and planning. It relies on actively planning training sessions based on stage 3 (abstract conceptualisation) and links actual training experiences to educational models. This is also the stage where management trainers assess learning experiences with the view to improve training sessions. Such an assessment may lead to improvements and alternatives to, for example, the aforementioned team-building exercise using adventure learning. |

Linking Figure 4.1 to Table 4.3 may also lead to an awareness that most participants in organisational learning will – inevitably – vary in their preference for information perceptions along the well-known "concrete → abstract" continuum (Table 4.1). But individuals will also have different preferences when it comes to information processing along the "active → reflective" continuum. Overall, four learning styles have been identified[56]:

*Table 4.4* Four Techniques of Organisational Learning

| Technique | Description |
| --- | --- |
| Converger | The greatest advantage of convergers is their ability to apply knowledge in practical situations. They tend to accelerate when they are given the opportunity to analyse problems in order to find the single most appropriate and often right answer. Convergers tend to deal with such tasks by relatively emotionlessly focusing on the logic of the problem. Their strength lies in their ability to focus on a relatively narrow bandwidth often found in a specific managerial task. |

*Table 4.4* (Continued)

| Technique | Description |
|---|---|
| Diverger | Compared to the converger, the diverger offers the opposite ability. Divergers tend to focus on the complete picture based on their ability to view a given managerial problem from a variety of standpoints. Rather than focusing on a narrow managerial problem, they tend to take a broad approach. They also rely more on emotions compared to the converger. Finally, they are able to utilise general – e.g. non-managerial – cultural, sociological, economical, political, pedagogical, etc. knowledge when faced with problems to be solved. |
| Assimilator | Unlike convergers and divergers, assimilators' real strength lies in their ability to understand and, even more so, to create abstract, conceptual, and even theoretical models. Assimilators are mostly concerned with conceptual-theoretical models often based on logical, systematic, and precise thinking. They create systematic models that explain and solve management problems. |
| Accommodator | Unlike the systematic-analytical and model-creating assimilator, accommodators tend not to focus on theoretical issues. Instead, their strengths are in "doing things". Accommodators prefer to be involved in groups and teams. They prefer new and challenging situations using their accommodating skills to adapt to changing environments while engaging teams in managerial problem-solving. |

While the above-noted "principles of organisational learning" (Figure 4.1), the "four stage learning processes" (Table 4.3), and the "four techniques of organisational learning" (Table 4.4) are not without critique,[57] like any model, they still provide a useful guide for organisational learning. In many ways, reflective organisational learning can lead to a more tailored approach supportive of a positive learning experience that in turn includes feedback given to the participants of organisational learning.

Beyond organisational learning techniques (Table 4.4) and the principles of organisational learning (Figure 4.1), HR managers also focus on **giving feedback**. Giving feedback remains a vital process of organisational learning as it does of any form of learning. It brings closure to a vital feedback loop that allows HR managers to complete organisational learning (Figure 4.1). Crucially, feedback provides information about how well employees are meeting the objectives of organisational learning. It can focus on an employee's behaviour but also on the three key skill developments: (1) personal skills (vocational training); (2) job skills (job demands, limitations, task allocation, and control); and (3) social-situational skills (cooperation, communication, and teamwork ability).[58]

Successful educators provide good, structured, positive, constructive, and ongoing feedback to reinforce positive behaviours. Employees – as adult learners – often adhere to the six principles of adult learning[59]:

1. Adults are internally motivated and self-directed;
2. Adults bring life experiences and knowledge to learning experiences;
3. Adults are goal oriented;
4. Adults are relevancy oriented;
5. Adults are practical;
6. Adult learners like to be respected.

As mature adults, employees also learn by observing and interacting with others inside work situations – known as **on the job training**.[60] Organisational learning should be properly coordinated, arranged, and delivered.[61] Finally, organisational educators ensure the **transferability** of learned knowledge, skills, and behaviours. Such transferability can be divided into two elements:

1. **use-value** transferability: indicates the usefulness of learned skills, knowledge, and behaviours within a company[62];
2. **exchange-value** transferability: carries connotations to the exchange of new knowledge for money and higher wages – either internal or external to a company.

The importance of use-value can be best explained through the element human beings are most in need of – air. While air has the highest use-value to us – without air we will cease to exist in about three minutes – so far, it is relatively cheap; in fact, it is still free of charge. On the other side of the coin, the element with perhaps the highest exchange value globally is money ($). Money can be exchanged for virtually anything, anytime, anywhere. Yet it has a very limited use-value as we cannot eat it, it is unsuitable to heat houses, we can hardly write anything on it, and so on. As it turns out, money has actually no use- but great exchange value while air is very useful but can hardly be exchanged. Similarly, as an MBA candidate, you can increase your use-value because you are of some "use" to a company but this fact also increases the exchange value of an MBA degree. It increases the price of the only thing you have for sale – your labour.

Crucial to the success of organisational learning is **management support** emphasising the importance of training and the application of what has been learned. In some cases, management provides trainees with a mentor.[63] **Coaching**[64] and **mentoring** describe an employee relationship[65] which can also take place in the form of **reverse mentoring**.[66] Mentoring occurs when a more experienced and knowledgeable senior manager guides a less experienced and less knowledgeable junior manager or employee. Mentoring is organisational learning based on a partnership between someone with considerable organisational experience and someone seeking to learn. Such a mentorship extends to psychosocial support, career guidance, and often includes role modelling.[67] Organisational mentoring can be:

1. **informal mentoring**: that often takes place spontaneously without the direct involvement of HR;
2. **formal mentoring**: that occurs through a specific HR programme based on established rules and structures and is based on codified HR policies).

A mentor's role usually includes acting for an employee who usually, but not necessarily, reports to the mentor. Mentors are advocates for employees.[68] Mentoring is not about any particular behaviour. Instead, it is about learning opportunities for a junior manager or employee. Similar to mentoring is peer support. It is a strong indicator for positive learning outcomes just as being given the opportunity to practise new skills and new knowledge. But before all this can occur, HR managers first need to plan the organisational training.

## Selecting the Right Training Methods

Once HR managers have completed the aforementioned threefold "needs assessment", the next step is to select an appropriate training method. This relates to three elements: the presentation methods used in the training; so-called "hands-on" methods; and "group-building" methods.[69] **Presentation methods** are methods used in classroom settings. They might include lecturing a group of students but can also include Socratic **question and answer** methods. Under this method a subject is discussed by asking questions while also outlining the pros and cons. It is a truth-finding exercise.[70] This and other learning processes can be supported through the use of audio-visual devices such as PowerPoint, DVDs, videos, online files, (www.youtube.com), and the like. When educators use, mix, and blend these methods, the term **blended learning** is used. It describes a multitude of presentation methods used within the same training programme.

During **hands-on methods**, educators and students are actively involved in the learning, with **on-the-job training** (OJT) perhaps being the classic form of an example for the hands-on method used in organisational learning. When designing OJT, HR managers focus on six elements for the training programme:

1.  HR managers develop a clear OJT policy;
2.  They have clear specifications about who delivers and is accountable for OJT;
3.  HR managers provide the OJT assessment (content, jobs, tasks, length, cost, etc.);
4.  They assess peer and managerial support for OJT;
5.  They assess the availability of lesson plans, procedure manuals, contracts, etc.; and
6.  They evaluate skills, knowledge, and motivation of employees "before" engaging in OJT.

**Simulations** are another important and highly useful part of organisational training as they simulate "real life" working situations.[71] One version of this method is the use of business games and case studies that simulate learning. Business schools and management training often rely heavily on case study methods. They are seen as useful tools for the development of intellectual, analytical, and problem-solving skills. Their downside is the narrowness and non-theoretical character (limited transferability) of many case studies. Finally, presentation methods also include e-learning that has, however, been linked to social isolation.[72] One of the methods that achieve the very opposite of social isolation are group building methods.

## Group Building Methods

Perhaps one of the most recognised forms of group behaviour is Tuckman's forming → storming → norming → performing model.[73] At the **forming** stage, a team of managers often meets for the first time and learns about the opportunities and challenges, then agrees on goals and begins to tackle the work or team building tasks ahead of them. The key activity at this stage is to "get to know one another" and exchange some personal information. At the **storming** stage, management participants form opinions about the character and integrity of other managers. Key to the second state is that disagreements and personality clashes must be resolved before the team can progress from this stage. The task is to solve intra-group conflicts while establishing tolerance for each team member. Differences are overcome through tolerance and patience. Normally tensions, struggles and sometimes arguments occur.

Once the forming and storming stages have been resolved, the **norming** occurs. At this stage, the spirit of co-operation emerges when the team of managers becomes aware of sharing a common goal. All team members take on this responsibility with the ambition to work for the success of the team. Once collectivism and cooperation are established, the management team moves to the final level: **performing**. All members of the managerial team are now competent and engaging in decision making without direct supervision. Dissent remains expected and allowed and is channelled through means acceptable to the team. The team starts to perform either as a face-to-face or virtual team.[74]

Forming → storming → norming → performing will occur when, for example, a group building exercise is based on **adventure learning** seen as an outdoor activity to develop team spirit and cooperation. Such team training often involves coordination and the performance of individuals inside a group – working together. One way of achieving this can be **action learning** that involves real-life training situations of work groups using actual management problems.

## Evaluation of Training

Even though education does not end with a simple training session as there is **lifelong learning**,[75] at the end of an organisational learning session, after learning has occurred, HR managers evaluate the training programme. For this assessment they focus on five elements: (1) **cognitive outcomes**, asking questions such as: has the trainee acquired new knowledge, skills, and behaviours?; (2) **skill-based outcomes** are assessed when focusing on technical skills.[76] (3) **motivational outcomes** are assessed when attitudes and motivations have changed; (4) **result-based outcomes** assess whether a training programme has benefited the company; and lastly, (5) **ROI**: is there a **return of investment** in terms of direct cost (wages, cost of instructors, etc.) of the training and indirect costs (design of training, office supplies, facilities, etc.)?[77]

# Workbook

## III. Five Discussion Questions on Organisational Learning

### *And One Report Question on Organisational Learning*

### *1. Discussion Questions*

1. Discuss the difference between "education" and "training". Is an MBA degree more akin to training or education? Why is this so?
2. When HR managers design organisational learning, they often focus on a needs assessment. Describe the three key elements of a needs assessment and outline which is the most relevant and why?
3. Discuss the pros and cons of organisational learning. Should companies invest in training? Find, at least, five reasons for such an investment in organisational learning and five against.
4. Explain the use-value and exchange-value of an MBA degree?
5. Using the distinction between empirical, interpretive, and critical knowledge, discuss whether management and organisational learning can move towards inter-subjectivity for human emancipation from domination? How could this be achieved?

### *2. Report Question:*

### *On Company Training: From a Functional to a Critical Approach*

Company-based employee training and development (ETD) and human resource development (HRD) often follow a rather functional approach to training and education as outlined in this chapter. The chapter advocates avoiding a one-sided view [such as functionalism] through examining "both" sides (for-&-against). Following the outlined "for-&-against" approach, an educational approach dedicated towards "critical pedagogy"[78] (critical self-awareness, critically reflective, self-determining human beings, etc.)[79] would argue for a substantially different way of developing EDT/HRD programmes at company level. Develop four [4] recommendation on how EDT/HRD can move towards a more critical approach to EDT.

## IV. The "5-by-5" Exercise: Five Case Studies and Five Questions

### *4.1 After Hours Training at MoneyBank*

Recently, MoneyBank has suffered heavy losses and is undergoing a major restructuring programme. The new board of directors and top management are aggressively engaged in cost cutting. They are under extreme pressure to turn MoneyBank around before it collapses under the weight of excessive dept. MoneyBank's top management, however, has remained committed to employee training and development. After completing a comprehensive training needs assessment, Ms Money Penny – MoneyBank's HR manager – has introduced a training programme on product marketing. MoneyBank's management has also announced a policy change that requires training to be done in the company but mostly during employee time. Consequently, the twelve 2½ hour training sessions for bank managers are scheduled to start at 4:30 pm and finish at 7 pm. Ms Money Penny is enthusiastic about her new training programme because it is job related (OJT) and, after her initial evaluation of the training, has demonstrated a positive impact on MoneyBank's real bottom line. But her thoughts are interrupted by the ringing of her mobile phone. It is Mrs Anna Jolie, the local trade union representative at MoneyBank. Anna says, "Ms Money Penny I am deeply shocked!" Ms Jolie continues,

> I can't believe that you, as a woman, can allow this bank to conduct a training programme outside of normal working hours. It is simply ridiculous. We have many female employees, as you know. Apart from the unsolved question of overtime payments, the proposal is discriminatory and is an abusive intrusion on personal time. As the HR manager you should be ashamed of yourself. You must be aware that women as partners and primary caregivers have limited time to attend such training programmes outside of normal working hours. On top of that, it collides with our "work life balance" policy. Your thinking is so archaic. It is incredible!

Ms Money Penny shifts her chair, looks out of her window at a local park with playground, park benches, and trees, and thinks about what was said.

1. Describe the main stakeholders in the MoneyBank case. Discuss what Ms Money Penny might reply to the bank's trade union officer Anna Jolie.
2. Given the financial pressure the bank is exposed to and the commitment of top management to organisational learning, was the decision to locate parts of the training outside of office hours correct? Can this decision be justified? Support your assessment with four arguments.
3. Do you think the HR manager's decision is discriminatory? Should her decision attract overtime payments? Is her idea to move the training outside of normal office hours archaic and out of date? If so, why? Alternatively, why not?
4. The new training programme seems to conflict with MoneyBank's policy on the "work life balance". Can this be reconciled? Which policy should be given priority and why?
5. Imagine you are Anna Jolie, what would you do as the bank's trade union officer to stop HR from going ahead with the training session? Develop four strategy recommendations.

### 4.2 The Training Passport at Ashley Matison Hotels

With increased global competition in the marketplace of the high-end luxurious hotel industry, global hotel chain "Ashley Matison" has embarked on a complete re-branding programme starting in late 2016. Its task is to re-position Ashley Matison hotels as an exclusive hotel globally offering VIP guests a unique hotel experience. To facilitate Ashley Matison's marketing programme, an extensive organisational learning and employee training programme has been developed by HRM. The organisational learning programme was rolled out in over forty global locations in which Ashley Matison Hotels are in operation. The training concept will make every one of Ashley Matison's 15,000 global employees a "good will ambassador". Every employee – from newly employed workers to the most senior employees – will receive one-day on-site training at individual hotel locations.

The internal training is provided by Ashley Matison's own corporate training team travelling to all locations where training is conducted. The training focuses on how to create a sense of exclusiveness for the hotel's VIP guests, empowering employees at all levels of the hotel with the freedom to make unique and personalised experiences for any guest on the spot. This has been part of the hotel's "Customer is King" strategy. All employees participating and completing the training graduate by being issued a "good will ambassador passport" that certifies the completion of the training. As the company also experienced a somewhat high turnover rate, the passport is seen as a training passport in which new training accomplishments are noted and certified. Employees are offered ongoing training in a chosen area of the hotel business. Upon completion, the passport is stamped. So far, the training programme has resulted in significant improvements, enhanced customer care, and aiding a higher retention rate.

1. Using the above-noted pressure points that indicate the need for new training, which of these pressure points are evident in Ashley Matison's new programme and why? Support your answer with three arguments.
2. Is the training programme designed to increase the responsibilities of individual employees? If so, how and why? Support your answer with three arguments.
3. Develop four recommendations for a formal HR policy for Ashley Matison's training programme.
4. Given the experience of Ashley Matison's training programme, should organisational learning be an ongoing programme? If so, develop four recommendations for a training programme that supports the ongoing training needs of Ashley Matison Hotel.
5. Imagine you are Ashley Matison's HR manager given the task of organising a "team building" training programme. Make four suggestions on what kind of training methods you think are useful for such a programme and why.

### 4.3 *Corporate Success and Organisational Training*

The Global Power Tool Corporation (GPT) manufactures power tools including drills, saws, air blowers, hedge trimmers, sledgehammers, etc. Manufactured mostly in South East Asia, these power tools are distributed to GPT's global network of 35,000 dealerships situated in 125 countries. The tools are used by professionals (blue line) and DIY home users (yellow line). Tom Mix is the CEO of GPT. Mr Mix has long recognised that employee training and development (EDT) is essential for the global success of the business. As a consequence, he has involved key stakeholders in the development of EDT. These are foremost the workers of GPT, but also trade unions, wholesale distributors, retailers, and customers. Tom Mix is convinced that a good training programme will not only lead to higher workplace satisfaction (including low turnover rates) but also to better OHS (occupational health and safety) as well as increased productivity.

One part of GPT's training programme is designed to assist retailers in understanding how to sell the products of GPT. For this, GPT runs on-site training programmes as well as offering an online training programme which it calls "The Online Academy". Both include sales-related topics such as understanding customers, in-store marketing, communication skills, customer service, and troubleshooting. GPT employees can attend "The Online Academy" to develop technical skills. The academy also offers management courses for supervisors and line managers. GPT has developed a "YouTube" style facility that allows workers to access knowledge related to their position. In addition, successful candidates are supported when attending external courses (technical colleges and universities).

Tom Mix is convinced that "well trained employees are the key to success". Furthermore, Mr Mix believes that the training programmes at GPT are not just providing entertainment. GPT's educational programme is meaningful as it leads to outcomes and results. He acknowledges that decades of experience in EDT have been a contributor to the company's annual sales increase of between 8% and 10% (on average).

1. Does the multinational corporation GPT value organisational learning and why? Support your answer with four arguments.
2. Imagine you are an HR manager responsible for EDT at GPT. Given the company's successful record, what can be possible strategies for the future of organisational learning at GPT?
3. Is organisational learning at GPT designed to support a low retention rate? Are workers in favour of GPT's training programme?
4. Has GPT involved key stakeholders in their plans for organisational learning? What are the benefits for a corporation to involve employee representatives (trade unions) in training? Name five reasons for such an involvement.
5. Imagine you are the HR manager responsible for organisational learning at GPT and have been asked to develop GPT's "academy" programme further. Develop four recommendations on how this programme could be extended?

### 4.4 Turnover and Training at Great Taste Winery

When workers' attitudes and a higher turnover of casual labour increasingly became a problem, Great Taste Winery decided to invest more into training and development. Starting as a small boutique winery in 1739, today Great Taste Winery is still located at Grape Hills. But it is now owned by a large multinational food and beverage corporation. While the business was expanding during the last years, Great Taste Winery's HR managers found it increasingly challenging to recruit good employees. To the dissatisfaction of HR managers, the business was experiencing high turnovers within casual labour employed in its vineyards. The company's director wanted consistency in its labour force. He sought to establish a reliable group of workers that he could depend upon. Many of the average vineyard workers had left school early and were often from disadvantaged socio-economic backgrounds with limited opportunities. At the time of the changes there was a government traineeship programme that offered state assistance to employers who invested in their employee's education. The company director was

> so excited about the whole concept that we made it a provision of putting someone on permanently in order to further education.

Various outcomes were seen as a result of investing in their staff's education. They saw people from very diverse backgrounds achieving certificates and diplomas in viticulture-accredited trade qualifications. They had a range of people who started with level 1 certification progressing through to level 4 and were then undertaking a degree. They had also linked these educational achievements to pay increases.

Great Taste Winery now invests thousands of dollars a year in staff education and has a number of employees on the traineeship programme. Both management and employees saw positive outcomes as a result of the fact that they now have a large vineyard of enthusiastic and happy employees (both skilled and semi-skilled). For employees, the additional knowledge and the skills they gained from the training programmes have enhanced their mental wellbeing and given them the determination and hunger to continue to increase their knowledge. Finally, employee turnover is lower, people are not leaving and if they are leaving it is because the person is not right for the environment.

1. What are the advantages of the training programme for Great Taste Winery? Find five advantages.
2. What are the advantages of the training programme for employees? Find five advantages.
3. What are the advantages of the training programme for the state? Find five advantages.
4. Despite the neo-liberal ideology of "less state", should the state be involved in organisational learning and if so, why? Find five reasons.
5. Imagine you are the HR manager at Great Taste Winery. How can the positive experience of the training programme for casual labour in the vineyard be extended to other areas of the company?

### 4.5 *Training at Ozzy Osbourne Printing*

Ozzy Osbourne Printing is a medium-size graphic design studio operating downtown with its office near the river. Generally, Ozzy Osbourne Printing runs smoothly and its design work has been highly commended in the industry and beyond. It has received several national and international awards. Danny Kay has been the production manager at Ozzy Osbourne Printing for 6½ years and he takes his role and its responsibilities very seriously. As such, he has undertaken several "in house" management training courses to complement his print and production skills. During Danny Kay's in house management training he was introduced to HR's concept of organisational learning. He is very keen to explore experiential learning processes and learning style models. Since Danny Kay became the manager, he has been extremely focused on employee empowerment and motivation. Danny currently supervises 135 employees at Ozzy Osbourne Printing. Many are graphic designers and printers. Most have been employed by Ozzy Osbourne Printing for well over ten years.

Up until now, most of the training that the printers and graphic designers have received has been informal in the form of OJT mentoring and job rotation. Danny now wants to formalise, expand, and capture the full range of current organisational learning. For many years, the design and print industry has undergone some of the most significant changes seen in any industry, from analogue to digital and ultimately online design and printing, changing printing fundamentally during the last decade. Virtually all printers and designers had to adjust to these changes. They had to learn new skills as their work changed. This has often included horizontal job enrichment (e.g. rotations) and vertical job enlargement (more managerial responsibilities).[80] It has also resulted in an increase in complexities. To sustain the competitive edge of Ozzy Osbourne Printing, Danny has realised that it remains imperative for Ozzy Osbourne Printing and its staff to develop organisational and individual capabilities for the future.

In the future, organisational learning needs to be closely aligned to the business strategy of Ozzy Osbourne Printing. To secure this, Danny needs to align Ozzy Osbourne Printing's business strategy with future skill sets needed by employees. Danny is aware that Ozzy Osbourne Printing needs to constantly re-align itself – organisational learning, organisational structure, and individual employee skills and knowledge – to these changing circumstances.

1.  Imagine you are the HR manager of Ozzy Osbourne Printing assisting Danny in his quest to move towards continuous organisational learning. What would you recommend to be changed? Develop four recommendations to move to continuous learning.
2.  Imagine you are the HR manager of Ozzy Osbourne Printing assisting Danny in his quest to move towards improved organisational learning. Conduct a needs assessment focusing on the "organisational needs". Develop four recommendations.
3.  Imagine you are the HR manager of Ozzy Osbourne Printing assisting Danny in his quest to move towards improved organisational learning. Conduct a needs assessment focusing on "tasks" and "personal needs". Develop three recommendations for each.
4.  Imagine you are the HR manager of Ozzy Osbourne Printing assisting Danny in his quest to move towards improved organisational responsibilities. Danny seeks to transfer responsibilities towards job enlargement and job enrichment to workers. Would a team approach facilitate this? Why? And if so, what kind of organisational training – group building methods – would you suggest and why?
5.  Imagine you are the HR manager of Ozzy Osbourne Printing assisting Danny in his quest to move towards improved organisational responsibilities. Develop four HR policy recommendations for: (1) a general organisational learning policy for Ozzy Osbourne Printing; (2) a policy for selecting people to engage in training; (3) a policy for job enlargement and finally, (4) a policy for job enrichment.

## V. Online Guest Lecture

Sir Ken Robinson
**"Three Principles Crucial for the Human Mind to Flourish"**
www.ted.com/talks/ken_robinson_how_to_escape_education_s_death_valley

## VI. List of Suggested Documentaries on Learning and HRD

The carefully selected documentary videos below are mere suggestions to be used during tutorials. Documentaries have been selected to achieve two things: (1) to explain key HRM themes and (2) to provide an insight into the reality of HRM. Typically, these short documentaries should be viewed in class followed by a class discussion on the content of the video. Alternatively, questions on documentaries can be prepared beforehand and small group discussions can follow up the video after viewing is concluded. Should any of the web links no longer function, please conduct an internet search for other – alternative – documentaries related to your tutorial topic (e.g. filmsforaction.org):

Woolworth's Education: www.youtube.com/watch?v=yYEd2BRUWsk
HRD & Learning: www.youtube.com/watch?v=OA3HxvYPzbU
Higher Education: youtube.com/watch?v=eLdU7uts4ws

## Notes

1  http://mlq.sagepub.com/.
2  www.oecd.org/skills/.
3  Ryan, H. 2016. *Educational Justice: Teaching and Organizing against the Corporate Juggernaut*, New York: Monthly Review Press.
4  Bohlinger, S. et al. 2015. *Working and Learning in Times of Uncertainty: Challenges to Adult, Professional and Vocational Education*, Heidelberg: Springer; Wingard, J. & LaPointe, M. 2016. *Learning for Life*, New York: AMACOM.
5  Micklethwait, J. & Wooldridge, A. 1996. *The Witch Doctors: Making Sense of the Management Gurus*, New York: Times Books, p. 209.
6  Prasad, R. K. 2015. Is leadership training the same as management training?, *Training & Development*, 42(6):22.
7  Quoted in: Lozonick, W. H. 1990. *Competitive Advantage on the Shop Floor*, Cambridge: Harvard University Press, p. 40; cf. Ure, A. 1835. *The Philosophy of Manufactures*, London: C. Knight Press.
8  Allen, R. C. 2009. The industrial revolution in miniature: the spinning jenny in Britain, France, and India, *Journal of Economic History*, 69(4):901–927.
9  OECD. 2017. *Skills Outlook*, PDF-download, 4th May 2017, from: www.oecd-ilibrary.org (https://doi.org/10.1787/9789264273351-en).
10  Nonaka, I. 1994. A dynamic theory of organizational knowledge creation, *Organization Science*, 5(1):14–37; Edwards, J. S. (eds.) 2016. *The Essentials of Knowledge Management*, London: Palgrave.
11  The Process of Knowledge Creation (http://www.allkm.com/km-basics/knowledge-process.php, accessed: 30th January 2018).
12  Nonaka, I. & Konno, N. 1998. The concept of "ba": building a foundation for knowledge creation, *California Management Review*, 40(3):40–54.
13  Gold, A. H., Malhotra, A. & Segars, A. H. 2001. Knowledge management: an organizational capabilities perspective, *Journal of Management Information Systems*, 18(1):185–214; Morabito, J. et al. 2018. *Designing Knowledge Organizations*, Hoboken, NJ: John Wiley; Jones, N. 2018. *Knowledge Transfer and Innovation*, New York: Routledge.

14  Gantman, E. R. 2005. *Capitalism, Social Privilege, and Managerial Ideologies*, Aldershot: Ashgate, p. 95.

15  http://plato.stanford.edu/entries/habermas/; Habermas, J. 1987. *Knowledge and Human Interests*, Cambridge: Polity Press.

16  Generally, pedagogy is seen as the discipline, theory, and practice of education. It is the study of teaching aimed at the general and full development of human beings via liberal education rather than the narrower specifics of vocational education (acquisition of specific skills). For the Frankfurt School of critical theory see: plato.stanford.edu/entries/critical-theory/; Horkheimer, M. 1937. Traditional and critical theory [pp. 188–244], in: Horkheimer, M. (eds.) *Critical Theory - Selected Essays*, translated by O'Connell, M. J. et al. 1972, New York: Herder; Klikauer, T. 2016. Critical pedagogy in adult education – unfit to be a Slave, *Australian Universities Review*, 58(1):89–92; Klikauer, T. 2016. Reflections on critical pedagogy, *Australian Universities Review*, 58(2):74–77.

17  Therborn, G. 1988. *The Ideology of Power and the Power of Ideology*, London: Verso; Rehmann, J. 2013. *Theories of Ideology: The Powers of Alienation and Subjection*, Leiden: Brill; Klikauer, T. 2015. Ideology, anarchy & society – a review essay, *Capital & Class*, 39(3):550–554.

18  Freire, P. 1970. *Pedagogy of the Oppressed* (transl. by Myra Bergman Ramos), New York: Continuum; Giroux, H. A. 2011. *On Critical Pedagogy*, New York: Continuum.

19  Scholl. H. & Baldus, A. 2016. Training and qualification: essentials in new learning, in: Zeuch, M. (eds.) *Handbook of HRM*, Heidelberg: Springer, pp. 307–314.

20  In recent years, 'many employers have abandoned their role in training workers' (Lewchuck, W. 2021. The age of increased precarious employment: origins and implications, in: Baines, D. & Cunningham, I. (eds.) *Working in the Context of Austerity*, Bristol: Bristol University Press, p. 30).

21  Grey, C. & Mitev, N. 1995. Management education: a polemic, *Management Learning*, 26(1):73–90.

22  http://www.bloomberg.com/bw/articles/2014-08-22/is-on-the-job-training-still-worth-it-for-companies.

23  Hirschman, A. 1970. *Exit, Voice, and Loyalty: Responses to Decline in Firms, Organizations, and States*, Cambridge: Harvard University Press.

24  In fact 'American companies spend the equivalent of only about 1.4% of their payroll on educating their workers' (Micklethwait, J. & Wooldridge, A. 1996. *The Witch Doctors: Making Sense of the Management Gurus*, New York: Times Books, p. 212).

25  Cornes, R. & Sandler, T. 1986. *The Theory of Externalities, Public Goods, and Club Goods*, Cambridge: Cambridge University Press.

26  The OECD's report on "Cost and Benefits in Vocational Education and Training" by Kathrin Hoeckel (p. 4) offers a good comparison on cost (oecd-ilibrary.org); Klikauer, T. 2015. The ghost of education, *Australian University Review*, 57(1):93–95.

27  'Overall, the average U.S. firm today invests less than 2 percent of its payroll budget on training' (Markovits, D. 2019. *The Meritocracy Trap*, New York: Penguin Press, eBook, p. 360).

28  Stanford, J. 2018. The future of work, and the future of skills, *Australian TAFE Teacher*, 52(1):20.

29  Terras, M. M. & Ramsay, J. 2015. Massive open online courses (MOOCs): insights and challenges from a psychological perspective, *British Journal of Educational Technology*, 46(3):472–487.

30  Chen, A. 2016. Training and qualification: essentials of skill management, in: Zeuch, M. (eds.) *Handbook of HRM*, Heidelberg: Springer, p. 214.

31  Siby, B. 2016. Engagement and retention: essentials of retention tools, in: Zeuch, M. (eds.) *Handbook of HRM*, Heidelberg: Springer, p. 666f.

32  Pass, S. 2004. *Parallel Paths to Constructivism: Jean Piaget and Lev Vygotsky*, Greenwich: Information Age Pub.

33  Tomasello, M. 2009. *The Cultural Origins of Human Cognition*, Cambridge: Harvard University Press.

34  Weick, K. E. 1995. *Sensemaking in Organisations*, London: Sage; Maclean, M. 2014. Living up to the past? Ideological sensemaking in organizational transition, *Organization*, 21(4):543–567; Maitlis, S. & Christianson, M. 2014. Sensemaking in organizations: taking stock and moving forward, *Academy of Management Annals*, 8(1):57–125.

35  Standing, G. 2017. *What is the Precariat* (https://www.youtube.com, 16th February 2017, accessed: 28th January 2018).

36 Szkudlarek, B. et al. (eds.) 2020. *The SAGE Handbook of Contemporary Cross-Cultural Management*, London: Sage.
37 Stephens, N. M., Rivera, L. A. & Townsend, S. S. 2020. What works to increase diversity? A multi-level approach, *Research in Organizational Behavior* (free download: https://www.nicolemstephens.com/uploads/3/9/5/9/39596235/stephensriveratownsend_robsubmission_8-28.pdf; https://www.bbc.com/worklife/article/20210614-why-ineffective-diversity-training-wont-go-away).
38 HBR. 2020. Can knowledge work be "gigified"? *Harvard Business Review*, 98(5):27.
39 Klikauer, T. 2015. The triumph of emptiness, *Journal of Organizational Change Management*, 28(6):1129–1132.
40 Klikauer T. & Simms, N. 2020. The class ceiling, *Marx & Philosophy Review of Books* (https://marxandphilosophy.org.uk, 11th March 2020).
41 Isenberg, N. 2016. *White Trash: The 400-Year Untold History of Class in America*, New York: Penguin; Klikauer, T. 2016. Bread and roses: voices of Australian academics from the working class, *Journal of Higher Education Policy and Management*, 38(1):102–106.
42 Stephens, N. & Townsend, S. 2017. How you feel about individualism is influenced by your social class, *Harvard Business Review*, 22nd May 2017; Curtis, J. 2016. Social mobility and class identity: the role of economic conditions in 33 societies, 1999–2009, *European Sociological Review*, 32(1):108–121.
43 For seven classes, see: https://en.wikipedia.org/wiki/Great_British_Class_Survey.
44 Recently, based on "The Great British Class Survey" (asking 161,000 people), it has been argued that there are seven classes: (1) the elite; (2) the established middle class; (3) the technical middle class; (4) the new affluent worker; (5) the emergent service worker; (6) the traditional working class; and (7) the precariat (c.f. Savage, M. 2015. *Social Class in the 21st Century*, London: Penguin Press).
45 www.bbc.com/news/magazine-22000973.
46 Stein, B. 2006. In Class Warfare, Guess Which Class Is Winning (www.nytimes.com, 26th November 2016).
47 Next to the proletariat and capitalists (bourgeoisie), there might also be class of *petit-bourgeois* and the *Lumpenproletariat* as well as class based on 'wealth, place of residence, occupation, education, social network, consumptive patterns and symbolic behaviour' (Block, D. 2012. Economising globalisation and identity, in: Block, D., Gray, J. & Holborow, M. (eds.) *Neoliberalism and Applied Linguistics*, London: Routledge, pp. 75 & 80f.).
48 Klikauer, T. 2016. Critical management research: reflections from the field, *Capital & Class*, 40(1):201–204.
49 Klikauer, T. 2014. Emancipatory education – a review essay, *Australian University Review*, 56(1):91–96.
50 Mead, G. H. 1934. *Mind, Self, and Society*, Chicago, IL: University of Chicago Press; Argyris, C. 1964. *Integrating the Individual and the Organization*, New York: Wiley; Crawdford, C. & Krebs, D. 2012. *Foundations of Evolutionary Psychology*, New York: Psychology Press.
51 Ball, S. J. 2004. *Education For Sale! – The Commodification of Everything?*, King's Annual Education Lecture 2004, University of London 17th June 2004 (http://nepc.colorado.edu/files/CERU-0410-253-OWI.pdf).
52 Nowak, M. & Highfield, R. 2011. *Super Cooperators: Evolution, Altruism and Human Behaviour (Or Why We Need Each Other to Succeed)*, London: Penguin Press; Klikauer, T. 2012. Evolution, altruism, and human behaviour, *Organization*, 19(6):939–940.
53 Kolb, D. A. & Fry, R. 1975. Toward an applied theory of experiential learning [pp. 33-57], in: Cooper, C. (eds.) *Theories of Group Process*, London: John Wiley; Mainemelis, C., Boyatzis, R. E. & Kolb, D. A. 2002. Learning styles and adaptive flexibility testing experiential learning theory, *Management learning*, 33(1):5–33; Peterson, K., DeCato, L. & Kolb, D. A. 2015. Moving and learning expanding style and increasing flexibility, *Journal of Experiential Education*, 38(3):228–244.
54 Kolb, D. A., Boyatzis, R. E. & Mainemelis, C. 2001. Experiential learning theory: previous research and new directions [pp. 227–247], in: Sternberg, R. J. & Zhang, L.-F. (eds.) *Perspectives on Thinking, Learning, and Cognitive Styles*, London: Routledge; Kolb, A. Y. & Kolb, D. A. 2005. Learning styles and learning spaces: enhancing experiential learning in higher education, *Academy of management learning & education*, 4(2):193–212; Kolb, D. A. 2014. *Experiential Learning: Experience as the Source of Learning and Development*, London: FT Press.

55  Allinson, C. W. & Hayes, J. 1988. The learning styles questionnaire: an alternative to Kolb's inventory?, *Journal of Management studies*, 25(3): 269–281; Furnham, A., Jackson, C. J. & Miller, T. 1999. Personality, learning style and work performance, *Personality and Individual Differences*, 27(6):1113–1122.

56  Kolb, D. A. 1976. Management and the learning process, *California Management Review*, 18(3):21–31.

57  De Ciantis, S. M. & Kirton, M. J. 1996. A psychometric re-examination of Kolb's experiential learning cycle construct: a separation of level, style, and process, *Educational and Psychological Measurement*, 56(5):809–820.

58  Tavares, M. A. 2017. Worker, the Market is the Worst Boss, *Critique*, 45(1–2):60.

59  Knowles, M. 1984. The adult learner: a neglected species (3rd ed.), Houston, TX: Gulf Publishing; Knowles, M. 1984. *Andragogy in Action*, San Francisco, CA: Jossey-Bass.

60  Mincer, J. 1962. On-the-job training: costs, returns, and some implications, *Journal of Political Economy*, 70(5): 50–79; Gomersall, E. R. & Myers, M. S. 1966. Breakthrough in on-the-job training, *Harvard Business Review*, July Issue, Tan, R. 2016. A new mix – learning in and from workplaces in Singapore today, *International Journal of Humanities and Social Science*, 6(7): 225–231.

61  Scholz, C. 2016. Training and qualification: social workplace learning, in: Zeuch, M. (eds.) *Handbook of HRM*, Heidelberg: Springer, p. 345.

62  Klikauer, T. 2015. Schooling with use-value-learning from the USA, *Australian Universities' Review*, 57(2):128–130.

63  Clutterbuck, D. a. et al. 2017. *SAGE Handbook of Mentoring*, London: Sage; Meister, J. C. & Willyerd, K. 2010. Mentoring millennials, *Harvard Business Review*, 88(5):68–72; Marcinkus Murphy, W. 2012. Reverse mentoring at work: fostering cross-generational learning and developing millennial leaders, *Human Resource Management*, 51(4):549–573; cf. www.mentoring.org.

64  Thompson, B. 2020. *How to Coach: First Steps and Beyond*, London: Sage.

65  Segal, G. Z. 2015. *Getting There – A Book of Mentors*, New York: Abrams; Johnson, W. B. & Ridley, C. R. 2015. *The Elements of Mentoring*, London: St. Martin's Press.

66  Marcinkus Murphy, W. 2012. Reverse mentoring at work: fostering cross-generational learning and developing millennial leaders, *Human Resource Management*, 51(4):549–573; Garg, N., Murphy, W. & Singh, P. 2021. Reverse mentoring, job crafting and work-outcomes: the mediating role of work engagement, *Career Development International*, 26(2):290–308.

67  Caligiuri, P. 2014. Many moving parts: factors influencing the effectiveness of HRM practices designed to improve knowledge transfer within MNCs, *Journal of International Business Studies*, 45(1):63–72.

68  Cullingford, C. (eds.) 2016. *Mentoring in Education: An International Perspective*, London: Routledge.

69  Levi, D. 2016. *Group Dynamics for Teams* (5th ed.), Thousand Oaks, CA: Sage.

70  Ferreira, S. & Ferreira, R. 2015. Teaching social work values by means of Socratic questioning, *Social Work*, 51(4):500–514; Paul, R. & Elder, L. 2007. Critical thinking: the art of Socratic questioning, *Journal of Developmental Education*, 31(1):36–37.

71  http://store.steampowered.com/video/314160/; Sherrin, D. 2016. *Judging for Themselves: Using Mock Trials to Bring Social Studies and English to Life*, London: Routledge.

72  Al-Samarraie, H., Selim, H., Teo, T. & Zaqout, F. 2016. Isolation and distinctiveness in the design of e-learning systems influence user preferences, *Interactive Learning Environments* (published online: 17th February 2016).

73  Tuckman, B. W. 1965. Developmental sequence in small groups, *Ppsychological Bulletin*, 63(6):384–399.

74  Griesinger, A. & Schmitt, T. 2016. Training and qualification: recommendations for virtual team development, in: Zeuch, M. (eds.) *Handbook of HRM*, Heidelberg: Springer, p. 399.

75  Regmi, K. D. 2015. Lifelong learning: foundational models, underlying assumptions and critiques, *International Review of Education*, 61(2):133–151.

76  "What is technical education? It is one which condemns all but the extraordinary individual to a minor part in life" (quoted from Stanley, J. 2015. *How Propaganda Works*, Princeton, NJ: Princeton University Press, p. 278).

77  HBR. 2017. Investing in employees pays off, *Harvard Business Review*, July–August Issue.

78  Giroux, H. A. 2020. *On Critical Pedagogy*, New York: Bloomsbury Publishing.

79 Robinson, K. 2010. *Educational Revolution* (https://www.ted.com/talks); Robinson, K. 2013. *Education's Death Valley* (https://www.ted.com/talks).

80 The difference between job enrichment and job enlargement is quality and quantity. Job enrichment means improvement or an increase with the help of upgrading and development. Job enlargement means to add more duties, and an increased workload. By job enrichment, an employee finds satisfaction in respect to their position and personal growth potential, whereas job enlargement refers to having additional duties and responsibilities in a current job description. Job enlargement is a vehicle that employers use to put additional workloads on employees, perhaps in economical downtime. Due to downsizing, an employee might feel lucky to have a job at all, despite the fact that his duties and responsibilities have increased. Another approach is that by adding more variety and enlarging, the responsibilities will provide the chance of enhancement and more productivity. Job enrichment involves organising and planning in order to gain more control over their duties and work as a manager. The execution of plans and evaluation of results motivates workers and relieves boredom. Job enlargement and job enrichment are both useful for motivating workers to perform their tasks enthusiastically. Although job enlargement and enrichment have a relationship with each other, they also possess some distinct features that differentiate them, such as area of expansion, mutual reliance, allocation of duties and responsibilities, motivation and profundity. Job enrichment is largely dependent on job enlargement, whereas job enlargement has no such dependency. Job enlargement expands horizontally when compared to job enrichment, which expands vertically. Vertical growth of job or augmentation is helpful to obtain managerial rights. In spite of mutual dependency, managerial duties are sanctioned, as in the case of enhancement. The employee focuses more on job depth, which does not happen in job enlargement. Job enrichment has a greater motivational impact than job enlargement. The job enlargement theory involving horizontal expansion to increase job satisfaction and productivity is relatively simple, and applied in numerous situations. Job enrichment, when compared to job enlargement, not only includes more duties and responsibilities, but also gives the right of decision making and control.

## Further Readings

Al-Daraweesh, D. & Snauwaert, D. 2015. *Human Rights Education*, London: Palgrave.

Biech, E. 2016. *Change Management Training*, Alexandria: Association for Talent Development.

Bolton, R. & Bolton D. G. 2016. *What Great Trainers Do*, New York: American Management Association.

Bowles, S. & Gintis, H. 1976. *Schooling in Capitalist America*, New York: Basic Books.

Bratton, J. & Gold, J. 2015. Towards Critical HRM Education, *Work, Employment & Society*, 29(3):496–507.

Carbery, R. & Cross, C. 2015. *Human Resource Development*, Basingstoke: Palgrave.

Cooney, R. & Stuart, M. 2013. *Trade Unions and Workplace Training*, London: Routledge.

de Pablos, P. O. & Tennyson, R. D. (eds.) 2016. *Impact of Economic Crisis on Education and the Next-Generation Workforce*, Hershey, PA: Information Science.

Dowson, P. 2015. *Personal and Professional Development for Business Students*, London: Sage.

Evans, R. W. 2015. *Schooling Corporate Citizens*, New York: Routledge.

Farnelli, C. 2015. *Neoliberalism and Education*, Toronto: Alternative Routes Press.

Freire, P. 2000. *Pedagogy of the Oppressed*, New York: Continuum.

Giroux, H. A. 2011. *On Critical Pedagogy*, New York: Continuum.

Godwin, W. 1791. *The Enquirer – Reflections on Education*, London: G.G. & J. Robinson.

Hunt, J. M. & Weintraub, J. R. 2017. *The Coaching Manager* (3rd ed.), Los Angeles, CA: Sage.

Illich, I. 1971. *Deschooling Society*, New York: Harper & Row.

Klikauer, T. 2020. Resisting Neoliberal Education, *Australian Universities' Review*, 62(1):67–69.

Knowles, M. S. 2020. *The Adult Learner: The Definitive Classic in Adult Education and Human Resource Development*, London: Routledge.

Lancaster, S. & Di Milia, L. 2015. Developing a Supportive Learning Environment, *Journal of Workplace Learning*, 27(6): 442–465.

Lee, C. J. G. 2014. Systemic Colonization of the Educational Lifeworld, *Educational Philosophy & Theory*, 46(1):87–99.

Lines, D. & Evans, C. 2020. *Global Business Coaching*, London: Routledge.

Lussier, R. N. & Hendon, R. 2021. *HRM: Functions, Applications, and Skill Development*, Los Angeles, CA: Sage.

Lynd, R. S. 1939. *Knowledge for What?* Princeton, NJ: Princeton University Press.

Malloch, M. et al. 2013. *Sage Handbook of Workplace Learning*, London: Sage.

McCarthy, G. 2014. *Coaching and Mentoring for Business*, London: Sage.

Merriam, S. B. & Bierema, L. L. 2013. *Adult Learning: Linking Theory & Practice*, New York: Wiley.

Nohl, A. M. 2015. Typical Phases of Transformative Learning, *Adult Education Quarterly*, 65(1), 35–49.

Rees, W. & Porter, C. 2015. *Skills of Management*, London: Palgrave, Chapter 11, Training & Development.

Sinclair, U. 1923. *The Goose-Step: A Study of American Education*, Pasadena, CA: The Author.

Slater, R. E. 2020. *The Professionalisation of Human Resource Management*, New York: Routledge.

Smith, C. 2010. Go with the Flow – Labour Power Mobility and Labour Process Theory [pp. 269–296], in: Thompson, P. & Smith, C. (eds.) *Working Life – Renewing Labour Process Analysis*, Houndmills: Palgrave.

Spring, J. 1975. *A Primer of Libertarian Education*, New York: Free Life Editions.

Stirner, M. 1842. *The False Principles of Our Education* (available online: https://theanarchistlibrary.org/library/max-stirner-the-false-principle-of-our-education).

Thompson, N. 2015. *People Skills* (4th ed.), London: Palgrave.

Tolstoy, L. 1852. The Path to Education (www.ibe.unesco.org/publications).

Turner, K. J. & Sheckels, T. F. 2015. *Communication Centers, Training & Management*, Lanham: Lexington.

Wills, P. 1977. *Learning to Labor*, New York: Columbia University Press.

# 5   Working with People
## Crafting Productive Work Systems

## Executive Summary

HR managers routinely analyse and are involved in designing how work is done. This relates to work analysis and work design. Work analysis is important for recruitment and selection, performance management, rewarding people and developing organisational learning. Work design involves four basic instruments: designing work so that it is motivational; so that work is efficient; so that work fits human beings (ergonomics); and so that it does not overload the mental capacity of people. But historical changes in work also brought changes in control, moving from simple control to technical and later to bureaucratic control. Eventually new forms of work such as, for example, knowledge and emotional work, entered the workplace. The future of work may move towards three different types of work: some jobs will be analytical; others will remain routine production jobs; while one of the biggest growths is predicted in the area of in-person jobs.

## Key Learning Objectives

1.   Realise the importance of work design for business success;
2.   Explain workflow processes;
3.   Analyse the relationship between operations management and HRM;
4.   Discuss the relevance of the job analysis for HRM;
5.   Describe key terms such as Fordism, Taylorism, McDonaldisation;
6.   Critically evaluate the different approaches to job design;
7.   Discuss the pros-&-cons of work design;
8.   Examine the concept of work in relation to work design; and
9.   Develop a formal HR policy on humanistic design of work.

## Work, Corporate Structures and Companies

Many people are accustomed to the idea of "working smarter, not harder". Both can relate to **work intensification**, particularly when people are working harder while working longer hours – which might not necessarily be an indicator for working harder and it certainly isn't working smarter. Working harder and work intensification are often features of flexible work arrangements.[1] Inside HRM, flexibility can take on the following form described by a worker:

DOI: 10.4324/9781003293637-5

we have an intranet that HR was told to make into a kind of internal "community," like Facebook. They set it up; nobody used it. So they then started to try and bully everyone into using it, which made us hate it even more. Then they tried to entice people in by having HR post a load of touchy-feely crap or people writing "internal blogs" that nobody cared about. Still nobody comes.[2]

In HRM, flexible work comes in two versions: **numerical flexibility** is when HR managers deal with fluctuating numbers of employees in industries such as tourism, retail (festive seasons), agriculture (harvesting time), etc. But HR managers also work with **functional flexibility** which is often divided into horizontal **job enlargement** (e.g. rotation under horizontal loading) and vertical **job enrichment** (vertical loading) that relates to additional responsibilities – often managerial in character.[3] The former tends more towards multi-tasking while the latter more towards multi-skilling. On the negative side of flexibility lies **flexible despotism** established when managers use time flexibility of scheduling infrequent work to establish a regime of despotism over workers.[4]

During the 1990s, flexibility promised **teleworking**,[5] home-office work,[6] and **working from home**.[7] Largely, these had failed to materialise for many[8] until the **Coronavirus**[9] or **Covid-19**[10] appeared in 2020.[11] One study[12] showed a 13% productivity increase when working from home.[13] For many, working from home[14] has increased. The following also has occurred:

- According to the *Institute of Directors*,[15] 74% of company directors said, "they would be keeping increased home-working after coronavirus";[16]
- "whereas we once used to compartmentalize out lives into the working day and time with family, the Web has destroyed those boundaries forever";[17]
- 82% of Gen Z workers said they feel "less connected";[18]
- working from home can mean that "soft skills are weakened because workers are not getting human contact".[19]

Yet there has, however, been a trend towards **McJobs**.[20] These are low-paying, low-prestige, and somewhat dead-end jobs requiring few skills while offering little advancement. The term McJob comes from the name of the fast-food chain McDonald's but is used to describe any low-status job in general where very little training is required, turnover is high, and workers' activities are tightly regulated by managers.[21] Whether flexible work arrangements or McJobs, most jobs and work in general are linked to operations management and **job analysis** defined as receiving detailed information about a job. Job analysis is a seven-step process: (1) involve employees; (2) investigate "job ↔ organisation" relationship; (3) determine reasons for job analysis; (4) select job to be analysed; (5) determine method of data collection; (6) collect data; (7) convert job data into job description. In general, there are four key reasons for conducting a job analysis:

1. HR managers analyse jobs for recruitment and selection purposes;
2. HR managers analyse jobs for performance management;
3. HR managers analyse jobs for compensation and rewards; and
4. HR managers analyse jobs for employee training and development.

Whatever the jobs are that HR managers analyse, these jobs are part of a **company structure** (e.g. pyramid). Key ideas of **organisational development** and **organisational**

**design** often expressed as an organisational chart seen as a stable, formal, and hierarchical network of vertical more than horizontal interconnections among formal positions constitutive of a company.[22] Despite the recent fashion of "flattening hierarchies",[23] the key metaphor used for company structures remains the pyramid.[24] The typical organisational pyramid starts with the CEO (chief executive officer (USA)) or managing director (UK), followed by a CFO (chief financial officer), a COO (chief operating officer) with general middle management[25] down the line reaching downward to line managers and supervisors, and finally workers.[26]

Company structures are not tension free. For one, there are pressures of **centralisation vs. decentralisation** and departmental structures. Centralised company structures locate the main decision making at the top of the hierarchy while at the decentralised structure these reside inside departments and work units. It even centralises management's right to manage, the so-called **managerial prerogative**.[27] One such structure is the **functional structure** where functional levels – marketing, operations management, accounting, and HRM – have a high degree of decision making powers compared to the top.

Next to functional structures, HR plays a specific role during **mergers and acquisitions**.[28] Whenever these result in **divisional structures**, they show a low level of centralised decision-making powers. One form of such a divisional structure is the M-company or **multi-divisional company**.[29] A good example is the virgin group with virgin records as the starting point expanding into virgin trains, virgin mobile, virgin airlines, virgin credit cards, etc. Often many HR functions in M-form, decentralised, departmental companies are located at the divisional level. At the M-Form company, "P&O" HR policies for its container shipping line are different from P&O's cruise shipping as one needs policies on customer service while container shipping carries no customers at all. In addition to these structures, companies can also have a **geographical structure** (European, Asian, American, etc.) or can have a **client-based structure**.

### Job Analysis

Common to all company structures is that most interaction between workers and management takes place at the supervisory or line management level even though there has been a noted lack of management training for such line managers. HR managers and line management are those who conduct job analyses to identify the tasks performed as well as the knowledge, skills, and attitudes required. Both – line managers and HR managers – are involved in recruitment and selection processes, and finally also in performance management. HR managers develop detailed **job descriptions** that are lists of the tasks, duties, and responsibilities that a job entails. Job specifications meanwhile list the knowledge, skills, abilities, and other characteristics that an employee needs in order to perform a job. To develop job descriptions and specifications, HR managers often conduct a position or job analysis focusing on seven key aspects:

1. the scope of the job (number and variety of tasks) and job depth (level of personal autonomy);
2. the input tells HR managers from where an employee receives information to conduct the job;
3. mental processes tell HR managers the level of reasoning and logical thinking that is required;
4. work output tells HR managers the physical activities needed and the tools used;

5. the liaison aspect tells HR managers the necessary level of cooperation with other people;
6. job context tells HR managers the social, physical, and organisational context of a job; and
7. there are other aspects such as work conditions, legal requirements, etc. relevant to the job.

In addition, **Fleischman's Job Analysis** Survey lists cognitive, psychomotor, physical, sensory, perception, social, and interpersonal skills and abilities.[30] Among these are, for example: written and oral comprehension and expression, fluency of ideas and originality, memorisation, problem-solving skills, deductive and inductive reasoning, information ordering, selective attention, time management, dynamic flexibility, stamina, night vision, speech recognition, and clarity. All of these can inform **job design** and **job redesign**.[31] The former is a process of identifying the way work is performed and the tasks that are required. The latter occurs when jobs change or an already existing job is altered.

## Four Basic Approaches to Job Design

HR managers have identified four basic ways in which most forms of work are organised. These are the behavioural-motivational approach to designing work, the industrial-engineering approach, the ergonomic-biological approach, and finally the perceptual-motor approach.

### 1. The Behavioural-Motivational Approach

The fundamental idea of the behavioural-motivational approach is to design work so that it is motivational and employees are stimulated to do the job. This approach has its origins in organisational psychology that itself is influenced by **behaviourism**.[32] The psychological theory of behaviourism dates back to Russian physiologist Ivan Pavlov (1849–1936) and American behaviourist BF Skinner (1904–1990). Pavlov discovered the conditioning reflex. He had come to learn this concept of conditioned reflex when examining the rates of salivations among dogs. Skinner also undertook extensive experiments with the "skinner box"[33] using rats. Behaviourism developed classical (Pavlov) conditioning first and operant conditioning later (Skinner).[34] In a somewhat seamless transition from rat to human being, behaviourism believes that not just animals but also people can be conditioned. This has principally replaced the "carrot and stick" approach with the more scientific three-way model of positive and negative reinforcement and punishment[35]:

1. Positive Reinforcement
   Skinner showed how positive reinforcement worked by placing a hungry rat in his Skinner box. The box contained a lever on the side and as the rat moved about the box, it would accidentally knock the lever. Immediately, a food pellet would drop into a container next to the lever. The rat quickly learned to go straight to the lever after a few times of being put in the box. The consequence of receiving food if they pressed the lever ensured that they would repeat the action again and again. Positive reinforcement strengthens a behaviour by providing a consequence an individual finds rewarding. For example, if your teacher gives you $5 – each time you

complete a work task (i.e. a reward) you will be more likely to repeat this behaviour in the future, thus strengthening the behaviour of completing your work task.

2. Negative Reinforcement

The removal of an unpleasant "reinforcer" can also strengthen positive behaviour. Known as negative reinforcement, the removal of an adverse stimulus strengthens behaviour as it stops or removes an unwanted experience. An example of negative reinforcement might be nagging. Being continuously prompted to be more productive can engineer negative work relations and appear as nagging to a worker even though it might be applied unintentionally. It also means that when the worker fulfils a set productivity, the nagging stops. This reinforces the desired behaviour and might force a worker to improve. On the downside, this technique does not encourage people to endeavour reaching beyond minimum levels in order to stop the negative situation. It just strengthens the behaviour to complete the work task. Skinner showed how negative reinforcement worked by placing a rat in the Skinner box and then subjecting it to an unpleasant electric current which caused it some discomfort. As the rat moved about the box, it would accidentally knock the lever. Immediately, the electric current would be switched off. The rat quickly learned to go straight to the lever after a few times of being put into the box. The consequence of escaping the electric current ensured that the rat would repeat the action again and again. In fact, Skinner even taught rats to avoid the impending electric current altogether signalling with a light that switched on just before the current would start. The rats soon learned to press the lever when the light came on because they knew that this would stop the electric current from being switched on.

3. Punishment

Punishment is defined as the opposite of reinforcement since it is designed to weaken or eliminate a response rather than increase it. It is an aversive event that decreases the behaviour it follows. Like reinforcement, punishment can work either by directly applying an unpleasant stimulus like a shock after a response or by removing a potentially rewarding stimulus, for instance, deducting someone's pocket money, to punish undesirable behaviour.

What behaviourism learnt from starving and electrocuting rats and other animals is transferred to human beings, arriving – via organisational psychology – at management and HRM. The rat holding a sign "will lever for food" transfers to the worker holding a sign "will work for money".[36] The application of behaviourism to human beings has been criticised as being inhuman by the world's most influential intellectual, Noam Chomsky.[37] But despite this, behaviourism has entered virtually every textbook on organisational psychology, HRM, and even standard management textbooks.

In HRM, behaviourism became prominent through **Herzberg**'s two-factor model of **intrinsic and extrinsic motivation**.[38] The former refers to, for example, the meaningfulness of a job while the latter relates to pay, bonus, etc. Intrinsic and extrinsic rewards often occur in the managerial tension between control[39] and **empowerment** consisting of:

1. the meaningfulness of a job;
2. the level of autonomy granted by management;
3. the impact of a job (does it make a difference); and
4. competencies, i.e. the skills, knowledge, and competencies needed for a job.

These four (1–4) might well have created the "myth of the happy worker".[40] HRM's move towards intrinsic and extrinsic rewards signified a general shift from stick to carrot under what became known as theory X (punishment) and theory Y (rewards), emphasising the "Human Side of the Enterprise".[41]

## 2. The Industrial-Engineering Approach

Long before mechanised mass manufacturing became the domineering feature of the industry, American engineer Frederick Taylor (1856–1915[42]) made the fragmentation of work tasks in manufacturing popular. By the time Taylor and what later became known as Taylorism appeared, separating work into minute tasks wasn't anything new. Already Scottish philosopher and economist Adam Smith (1723–1790) had described this kind of organisation of work and its impacts on individuals. Two sections from Adam Smith's *An Inquiry into the Nature and Causes of the Wealth of Nations* (1776) will show this[43]:

One man draws out the wire, another straights it, a third cuts it, a fourth points it, a fifth grinds it at the top for receiving the head, to make the head requires two or three distinct operations, to put it on is a peculiar business, to whiten the pins is another, it is even a trade by itself to put them into the paper, and the important business of making a pin, is in this manner, divided into about eighteen distinct operations, which in some manufactories, are all performed by distinct hands, though in others the same man will sometimes perform two or three of them...The man whose whole life is spent in performing a few simple operations, of which the effects too are, perhaps always the same, or very nearly the same, has no occasion to exert his understanding, or to exercise his mind in finding out expedients for removing difficulties which never occur. He naturally loses, therefore, the habit of such exertion, and generally becomes as stupid and ignorant as it is possible for a human creature to become. The torpor of his mind renders him, not only incapable of relishing or bearing a part in any rational conversation, but of conceiving any generous, noble, or tender sentiment, and consequently of forming any just judgement concerning many even of the ordinary duties of private life.

While Taylor's updating of Adam Smith made things worse for workers, it made things better for management. Under Taylor, craftsmen's knowledge moved into management that now organised the work flow while workers became little more than appendages to machines – a form of "machine enslavement".[44] While he was fragmenting work, deskilling workers, and calling employees "gorilla and ox",[45] Taylor legitimised management's "one-best-way" by extracting the organisation of work away from workers and locating it in management. Taylorism has entered workplaces like Amazon.[46] One of the outcomes has been described in the following way[47]:

In Ohio, seven hundred Amazon workers are so poorly paid that they are receiving food stamps...[Amazon boss] Bezos is not just frugal, or cheap, or a tightwad. He runs what many have called modern-day sweatshops,[48] where human beings are pushed beyond their limits in ways that make Frederick Taylor and his stopwatch seem like Mother Teresa.

The second major change in manufacturing came with American "carmaker" – actually, he did not "make" cars, his workers did – **Henry Ford** (1863–1947).[49] Ford not only shifted capitalism towards consumer capitalism with mass production,[50] he also brought the assembly line[51] from the meat-packing industry into the car industry.[52] Today, many forms of industrial engineering rely increasingly on **robotics**.[53]

Henry Ford's distaste for workers shows when he famously bemoaned: "why is it every time I ask for a pair of hands, they come with a brain attached".[54] Apart from an anti-worker attitude, Ford also pushed **standardisation** so that every wheel fits onto every car. Later, we saw the standardisation of the human body: t-shirt sizes S, M, L, XL, bra sizes, etc.[55] and the mass synchronisation of taste lead to a loss of subjectivity and identity on a planetary scale. Ford also legitimised management further through the horizontal and vertical division of labour[56]:

**Horizontal**: The horizontal division of labour enshrines the fragmentation of skills and knowledge previously owned by craftsmen. It divides work into an endless amount of little tasks. This creates a further level of alienation as the producer [worker] of a product is increasingly disconnected from the product of his work as he never completes the whole product – only a little part of it.[57] It also enhances domination of labour at work as management organises the work process while workers only complete a little part of it.[58]

**Vertical**: At the *vertical* level, the second division of labour allows the social re-organisation of work, dividing production in a managerial top-down fashion where the *top* designs tasks and the *down* operates them.

Perhaps the latest stage in the developments of the industrial engineering approach is **McDonaldisation**,[59] working for *Uber*,[60] as well as facing **automation**.[61] On the latter, an "Amazon warehouse [worker commented], *you're sort of like a robot, but in human form*".[62] The former has led to **Uberization**, which allows on-demand labour to be contracted by the task via online platforms threatening to turn jobs into tasks.[63] In Uber as in Deliveroo, workers are managed through **algorithmic management**.[64] Under this, rafts of management decisions are handed over to mathematical formulas.[65] It is a managerial technique to remotely manage a workforce[66] by relying on the data collection and surveillance of workers to enable automated or semi-automated decision-making.

This is called **gig economy**[67] which has three parts[68]: (1) app-work (Uber, Deliveroo, etc.); (2) capital platform work (Airbnb, Etsy, etc.); and (3) Crowdwork (Amazon's Mechanical Turk). The gig economy is not really filled with gig workers[69] as it covers roughly 0.5% of an economy.[70] A gig worker is an independent contractor using an online platform having a contract with a firm who is an on-call and/or temporary worker. In the USA, this has led to the fact that "adjunct (sessional) academic staff living in relative's basement or homeless shelters".[71]

According to the EU, "between 1% and 5% of the adult working population has earned some income" that way.[72] Uberization and automation included "disappearing routine jobs").[73] The risk of job loss in the future because of automation is 97% for file clerks, payroll and timekeeping clerks, grinding and polishing workers, and 99% for date entry keyers, tax preparers, and telemarketers. Relative secure jobs are, for example, first-line supervisors (0.3%), occupational therapists (0.4%), counsellors (0.5%) HR managers (0.6%), social and community service managers (0.7%), secondary school teachers (0.8%).[74] Part of future work is the internet of things (IoT),[75] AI (artificial intelligence),[76] and Industry 4.0.[77] All of these signify a

Taylor → Fordism → Neo/Post-Fordism[78] → McDonaldization → Industry 4.0

trajectory.[79] According to the ILO, there are six drivers of this: (1) the internet of things; (2) big data[80]; (3) cloud computing; (4) robotics; (5) 3D printers, and (6) machine learning.[81] In addition, there is also **outsourcing**,[82] **off-shoring**, **crowd working**,[83] and crowd fleecing.[84] What crowd working means has been expressed by *CrowdFlower*[85] CEO Lukas Biewald[86]:

> In 2010, speaking to young tech entrepreneurs, CEO of CrowdFlower Lukas Biewald, shared that "[b]efore the Internet, it would be really difficult to find someone, sit them down for ten minutes and get them to work for you, and then fire them after those ten minutes. But with technology, you can actually find them, pay them the tiny amount of money, and then get rid of them after you don't need them anymore."

Crowd working or crowd labour[87] is commonly defined as

> the act of taking a job once performed by a designated agent (an employee, freelancer or a separate firm) and outsourcing it to an undefined, generally large group of people through the form of an open call, which usually takes place over the Internet.[88]

These are low-wage arrangements paying US$4.43 per hour with low protection, no health cover, no retirement fund, no OHS. Beyond that nine out of ten workers have had their pay refused based on one-sided ratings with next to no appeal resulting in unpredictable income. Crowd labour companies in the online labour market[89] are, for example:

- Amazon's Mechanical Turk (www.mturk.com),
- Microworkers (www.microworkers.com),
- CrowdFlower (www.crowdflower.com),
- Clickworker (www.clickworker.com),
- InnoCentive (www.innocentive.com) and
- Jovoto (www.jovoto.com).

Next to that, there are arrangements that split an existing workforce into three groups, (1) those to be retrenched;[90] (2) the core workforce, and (3) periphery employees. The latter is often pushed into atypical[91] and precarious forms of employment.[92] These are pushed even further by neoliberalism and austerity.[93] They create the **Precariat**.[94] The precariat is also created through McDonaldization which is defined through four basic regimes:

> **Efficiency**: finding the optimal method for accomplishing a task for which efficiency[95] is the ultimate objective. For McDonald's, it is the fastest way, meaning that the entire organisation is geared toward the minimisation of time.[96]
>
> **Calculability**: every objective is to be made quantifiable (sales) rather than subjective (taste) under the idea that "quantity equals quality" and that a large amount of products delivered to a huge number of customers in a very short time equals quality. Workers are judged by how fast they are instead of by the quality of the work they do.[97]

**Predictability**: Ford's standardisation reappears as uniform service with the maxim: no matter where a customer is, the same service will be received, the same products will be served every time. Meanwhile, work tasks are highly repetitive, very routinely, and extremely predictable.

**Control**: standardised and uniform employees work under increased managerial control.

These four principles of the fast-food industry have meanwhile been adopted by other industries and spread to other parts of society. The issue of control has been an inherent feature of this approach to work. Control has changed historically when workers were employed in small workshops at the beginning of industrialism moving towards Taylorist/Fordist mass manufacturing and finally to the service industry[98] creating **service work** that is defined through three interactions:

1. service work is primarily human-to-human interaction;[99]
2. the output of service work is often intangible; and
3. service work highlights the role of the customer.

At this stage, managerial control shifts from direct → technical[100] → bureaucratic control:

### Simple Control

Simple control requires the direct intervention of an authority figure. A supervisor provides the direction to workers, evaluating their performance and administering disciplinary action (reward/punishment).[101] This control strategy relies upon the strength of the relationship between the supervisor and the subordinate even when – as in the case of Deliveroo, etc. – the app on your phone effectively becomes your new boss.[102]

It is also a fairly obtrusive management strategy; the worker is not required to internalise or actively participate in the control process. This can be a powerful management strategy because the supervisor is directly involved with the entire process (e.g. managers see and hear everything). However, this system can become compromised if the organisation becomes too large or complex to control through the line of sight management. As a result, simple control systems tend to be found in small organisations as workers try to outwit systems of direct control.

### Algorithmic Control

Rather more difficult is to outwit algorithmic control which is defined by the "6 Rs" of restricting (forms of work, output, etc.), recommending (prompting worker to select options "choice architects" want), recording (computational processes that monitor workers), rating (calculating and measuring performance of workers); replacing (firing underperforming workers); and rewarding (remunerating high and punishing low performing workers).[103]

### Technical Control

Technical control relies on the intervention of some physical devices (e.g., machines, computer software, including the move "from face-to-face interaction to terminal-to-terminal interaction"[104]) to substitute for the presence of a supervisor. Technical control strategies became particularly popular during the later stage of industrialism when technological innovations and the mass production of goods encouraged organisations to grow. Now the machine (e.g. conveyor belts and assembly lines with pace rates) exercise control. Workers receive disciplinary information from an inanimate device rather than from a supervisor (e.g. automated e-mail warnings sent to employees/academics when they fail to submit reports and final examination marks on time).[105] Today's "management-by-algorithm" can create "the boss from hell" in the form of a machine.[106] Technical control enables managerial control to be mediated through external devices, limiting the ability of workers to question or resist these directives.

Technical control can be an effective management strategy when the work performance is relatively repetitive and the supervisor's span of control is too broad to monitor all subordinates through direct observation. In recent years, technical control as advanced through the use of surveillance techniques linked to IT. The impact of that is shown in two examples[107]:

1.  In Leipzig, Germany, a worker in an Amazon *fulfillment center* who was accused of having been inactive on two occasions was informed five minutes after his second digression that he was being fired.
2.  Following the logic of digital piecemeal work[108] (an electronic panopticon[109]) and surpassing the cruelty of Walmart,[110] laborers are issued *inactivity protocols*: Colleague…was inactive 07:27 am to 07:36 am (nine minutes). Worker… and worker…were seen standing in between shelves 05–06 and 05–07. Already on….2014…was seen inactive from 8:15 am–8:17 am (two minutes). Also on…2014…was inactive from 07:13 to 07:14 (one minute).[111]

### Bureaucratic Control

Bureaucratic control uses rule systems (e.g. HR policies) to shape and manipulate employees' behaviours. Managers direct the behaviour of their workers through the creation of rules, carefully defining how to perform specific tasks and make decisions (e.g. handbooks, training programmes, policies, performance management, etc.). Such policies can discipline employees (e.g. bonuses determined by a pre-determined formula rather than left to managerial discretion). Although supervisors may still be physically present within the work environment, bureaucratic control strategies reduce the time and effort they need to spend managing their subordinates. Even when there is no supervisor present, the impersonal force of a carefully designed rule system extends to all corners of the organisation and provides a consistent and rational basis for managerial control.

### 3. The Ergonomic-Biological Approach

Perhaps as a reaction to the industrial engineering approach, many sought to reduce the alienation[112] that was enhanced under this approach.[113] **Alienation** often manifests itself in four forms[114]:

1.  Alienation of employees from the product of their labour: The product does not belong to the employee.
2.  Alienation from the activity of producing: the activity of production is external and separate from the employee, such that the employee no longer controls the activity of production (Taylorism & Fordism), but rather is controlled by it.

3. Alienation from humanity: since workers are separated from the product of labour and the labour process itself, they are separated from humanity, alienated from the characteristic activity of the human species and human evolution. Human beings are no longer "tool making animals" as "homo faber", Man the Maker.[115]

4. Alienation from being human: human beings are treated as things, as human resources, not as human beings. Workers become a function, a tool of the production process, a thing that can be exchanged.

Set against alienation is the **biomechanical approach** seen as the study of body movements, work physiology, and occupational medicine. Rather than inventing a production system and adjusting human beings to it, this approach places the human at the centre and creates systems and technologies that match the human being. The second approach is that of ergonomics.[116] The goal of **ergonomics** is to reduce and eventually eliminate the physical strains of work processes, creating an environment that supports the way the human body works.[117] It changes, for example, the outdated computer keyboard originating in the mechanics of the typewriter with an ergonomic keyboard.[118] This reduces RSI: **repetitive strain injuries**.[119]

One method that can reduce RSI is rotation within **self-managed teams** even though the term self-managed is somewhat of a euphemism because these teams are often managed semi-autonomously with limited self-organisation powers.[120] In fact, they are very rarely autonomous teams with serious co-determination powers via management.[121] Unlike short-term teams like problem-solving and **project teams**, they are permanent teams with some internal self-governing powers most commonly relating to task rotation, working together, and using the assistance of other team members. Many companies prefer a team structure rather than the typical worker-supervisor structure because teamwork improves workers' attitudes, improves quality, lowers absenteeism[122] and turnover, eases covering for absent workers, and reduces the number of supervisors. Many have argued that the future of work may well be defined by teamwork and working in projects.[123]

In today's businesses, working on a project and inside a team refers to an individual and more often collaborative enterprise involving careful planning.[124] Project work usually consists of a work team with the task to achieve a particular organisational goal. Such project teams may also involve a set of interrelated tasks to be executed over a fixed period and within certain costs or other limitations. In some cases, project teams may be temporary rather than permanent and often, a work project may be a part of a wider organisational programme or strategic business plan.

Originating in the Latin word *projectum* (before an action), project work is used for a plan or performance in accordance with a work project carried out in a concrete and organised effort. Each work project and work team has a beginning and an end. Work teams and projects are considered dynamic systems often based on the 4 P's of project management:

1. people,
2. plan,
3. processes, and
4. project

Many project teams are restricted by calendar (deadlines), costs, and quality. Management can measure project work effectively and objectively along its lifecycle. Project teams ensure a good level of formal documentation. In many cases, teamwork and teams are seen as a vital part of **Quality of Working Life** (QWL)[125] programmes seeking to increase individual power, enhance employee participation in the management, secure fairness and equality at work, create social support mechanisms, use people's present skills, provide space for self-development, create a meaningful future at work, ensure social relevance of the work or product, positively effect on extra work activities, ensure adequate compensation, a safe and healthy work environment, develop human capabilities,[126] increase social integration, produce dignity and respect for employees, generate social relevance and self-esteem, and a sensible work–family interface.

Finally, there are two further features associated with this approach. One is the **work–life balance** – also known as *work–life interference*[127] – that seems to remain an organisational myth rather than reality for many, hence the multitude of publications like "The Myth of the Work-Life Balance"; "Off Balance"; and "The Balance Myth: Rethinking Work-Life Success".[128] Beyond that, GE CEO Jack Welch once – perhaps correctly-claimed, "there's no such thing as work-life balance".[129]

### 4. The Perceptual-Motor Approach

The perceptual-motor approach focuses on the mental capacities of employees and – most importantly – their limitations and restrictions.[130] The key idea of this approach is to design work that does not overload an individual's mental capacity. This is particularly relevant for the work of air traffic controllers, oil refinery operators, atomic power station operators, etc. Some have argued that this impacts people differently when viewed from, for example, the standpoint of mono-chronic and poly-chronic people:

### Mono-chronic People

do one thing at a time; concentrate on the job; take time commitments seriously; are low in context and need information; are committed to the job; adhere religiously to plans; are concerned about not disturbing others; follow rules of privacy and consideration; show great respect for private property; seldom borrow or lend; emphasise promptness; are accustomed to short-term relationships.

### Poly-chronic People

do many things at once; can be easily distracted and manage interruptions well; consider an objective to be achieved, if possible; are high in context and already have information; are committed to people and human relationships; change plans often and easily; are more concerned with those who are closely related than with privacy; borrow and lend things often and easily; base promptness on the relationship; have a strong tendency to build lifetime relationships.

The difference between mono- and poly-chronic people might become even more exposed when industries move from manufacturing to service and eventually towards **knowledge work** putting a higher premium on research and development (R&D).[131] The knowledge industry demands knowledge workers who are highly skilled – often professionals – whose work relies more on analytical, logical, and theoretical knowledge than on individual capabilities.[132]

There is also a growth in **emotional labour**[133] defined as the management of feelings to create a publicly observable facial and bodily display of affection: "can you smile at three o'clock in the morning", as an advertisement for flight attendants once said.[134] While traditional manufacturing work has been associated with blue collar and office work with white collar,[135] emotional labour has been associated with pink collar.

Commonly, blue- and white-collar jobs are associated with manufacturing and office work. Many look at future jobs[136] in three broad areas: (1) agricultural jobs (a global decline of –13% between 1991 and 2019); (2) manufacturing jobs (+43%); and (3) service industry jobs (+137%).[137] Yet, job growth might be different for different jobs. The former *Secretary of Labor* under President Bill Clinton (1993–1997), for example, has outlined three future jobs[138]:

1. **Symbolic Analytical Jobs**: The first group are **symbolic analytical jobs** as conducted by engineers, attorneys, scientists, professors, executives, journalists, consultants, etc.;

2. **Routine Production Jobs**: the second group are **routine production jobs** carried out by assembly line workers, data processing workers, foremen, etc.; and

3. **In-Person Jobs**: the final group are **in-person jobs** carried out by supervisors, waitresses, hospital attendants, child care workers, etc. Several of these jobs of the future will have a high degree of involvement demanding significant levels of cooperation among "Super Cooperators".[139]

## Workbook

### III. Five Discussion Questions on the Design of Work

*And One Report Question on the Design of Work*

*1. Discussion Questions:*

1. The organisational structure of most companies shows the image of a pyramid organised as a top-down hierarchy. What organisational structure do you think is the least authoritarian? Can a non-authoritarian and empowering organisational structure ever be achieved? Develop four recommendations towards such a goal.
2. Imagine you are the HR manager of a new "green field" site asked to participate in a project group on work design. Which of the four approaches to work do you think you might suggest as the most humane approach and why? Develop four reasons.
3. Alienation has been an inherent problem of nearly all forms of work. Is there a way of eliminating alienation? Develop four recommendations.
4. Imagine you have designed a work system that edges on the danger of overloading people. What are the advantages and disadvantages of mono- and poly-chronic people? What kind of jobs would you suggest for each category? Develop four possible jobs most suitable for each category.
5. Forms of managerial control have changed over time from simple or direct control to technical and eventually to bureaucratic control. Can control ever be eliminated from companies? Develop four recommendations towards this goal.

*2. Report Question:*

*On Work Design and Alienation:*

Many (if not all) approaches to job design will lead to alienation.[140] The article "Alienation – essays on Hegelian themes"[141] outlines four versions of alienation. Develop four [4] recommendations on how to avoid these four forms of alienation.

### IV. The "5-by-5" Exercise: Five Case Studies and Five Questions

*5.1 Participatory Ergonomics at Super.Good.Auto*

Participatory Ergonomics can be cost-effective for a firm. Just ask the automotive parts plant "Super.Good.Auto" that set up a PE programme as a process that brings workers, supervisors, and other key workplace employees together to identify and solve problems to reduce the risk of musculoskeletal disorders (MSDs). Through an economic evaluation by the local university's Institute for Work & Health (WH) the company discovered that it can save about ten times more than it spent on the programme, to the tune of almost $785,000.

"It indicates that Participatory Ergonomics can play a key role in both primary and secondary injury prevention in the workplace," says WH scientist Dr. Harrison Fordy, who led the economic evaluation. His process looked at the costs and consequences of an improved occupational health and safety programme. "In short, Participatory Ergonomics can be effective in not only reducing injuries, but also in reducing the severity of injuries when they do occur."

Super.Good.Auto's journey began in 2010. The 1,300 employee company which manufactures foam parts for vehicle interiors, took part in a Participatory Ergonomics intervention study led by WH Adjunct Scientist Dr. Orson Wells, director of the Centre for Research Expertise for the Prevention of Musculoskeletal Disorders (CRE-MSD) at the University of Ergonomic Science. An ergonomics change team was set up to implement the program at the worksite. The team included worker representatives from all shifts, a union and a corporate health and safety representative, a mechanical engineer, the production manager, the tooling supervisor, human resources representatives, and a person from the research team. The team identified and prioritised potential ergonomic changes based on departmental injury rates, worker suggestions, worker pain reports, and production and quality issues.

Over the next year, the project team introduced ten physical changes to the production plant of Super.Good.Auto. They included five easy to implement "fast track" ergonomic changes such as installing anti-fatigue matting to reduce leg and back fatigue and fabricating a 45-degree angle on a tool to reduce wrist flexion. They also included five more "full process" projects such as installing platforms to reduce lower-back stressors and changing a packing protocol to reduce above-shoulder work. Orson Wells' research team concluded that the Participatory Ergonomics programme reduced exposures to MSD risk factors. But what about the cost-effectiveness of the Participatory Ergonomics programme? How did the company fare on that front?

That's where Clint Westwood's team came in with the economic evaluation of the programme. They calculated programme costs of $255,000 including the time and money spent on training, meetings, change implementation, ergonomics expertise, and equipment. They then looked at the number and duration of workers' compensation claims, modified work cases, first-aid-only injuries, short- and long-term disability (STD/LTD) claims, and casual absences before and after the Participatory Ergonomics programme was introduced. They found significant reductions were seen in only one measure – the length of time workers spent on STD/LTD benefits. That figure went down by 52%, representing savings of about $569,420 over a two-year period.

All in all, the findings indicate how important it is for companies to look beyond workers' compensation costs when determining the economic benefits of prevention programmes. "The benefits of a Participatory Ergonomics programme can surface in many places within a company," Mr Westwood points out. This is especially the case with MSDs which often arise from the interplay of personal, workplace, and non-workplace risk factors.

1.  Describe who the project team of Participatory Ergonomics involved and find the reason why each of the persons on the team was important to the success of the programme?
2.  From the four approaches outlined in the main chapter, which approach was used at Super.Good.Auto? Or was there a mixture of two approaches? Support your answer with five key arguments.

3.  Imagine you are the HR manager at Super.Good.Auto. How would you support the project team of Participatory Ergonomics? Develop three HR policy recommendations to support the project team.

4.  Imagine you are the trade union representative representing the workers of Super. Good.Auto on the Participatory Ergonomics project team. What are your concerns for the welfare of the workers at Super.Good.Auto? Develop three to four key trade union concerns and think about extending the programme to non-factory work.

5.  Imagine you are the HR manager at Super.Good.Auto. After the evaluation of the programme, would you agree that the Participatory Ergonomics programme was a success in terms of finances? If so, how can you convince general management to introduce such a programme for office workers? Develop four recommendations.

### 5.2 Ten Office Ergonomics Tips

Follow these ten office ergonomics tips to help avoid fatigue:

1)  Make sure that the weight of your arms is supported at all times. If your arms are not supported, the muscles of your neck and shoulders will be crying by the end of the day.

2)  Watch your head position and try to keep the weight of your head directly above its base of support (neck). Don't "crane" your head and neck forward.

3)  Don't be a slouch! Slouching puts more pressure on the discs and vertebrae of your back. Use the lumbar support of your chair and avoid sitting in a way that places body weight more on one than on the other side. Move your chair as close to your work as possible to avoid leaning and reaching. Make sure to "scoot" your chair in every time you sit down.

4)  The monitor should be placed directly in front of you, with the top no higher than eye level. The keyboard should be directly in front of the monitor so you don't have to frequently turn your head and neck.

5)  Talking on the phone with the phone receiver jammed between the neck and ear is really bad practice. You know that's true, so don't do it!

6)  The keyboard and the mouse should be close enough to prevent excessive reaching which strains the shoulders and arms.

7)  Avoid eye strain by making sure that your monitor is not too close, it should be at least an arm's length away.

8)  Take steps to control screen glare, and make sure that the monitor is not placed in front of a window or a bright background.

9)  You can rest your eyes periodically for several seconds by looking at objects at a distance to give your eyes a break.

10) The feet should not be dangling when you are seated. If your feet don't comfortably reach the floor or there is pressure on the backs of your legs, use a footrest or lower the keyboard and chair.

1.  Imagine you are the HR manager of an insurance company with many people working at office desks. Are the first five tips useful? Develop two reasons and one example for each of the first five (no. 1–5) tips on why this is the case.

2. Imagine you are the HR manager of a corporate HQ with many people working at office desks for extended periods of time. Are the second five (no. 6–10) tips useful? Develop two reasons and one example for each of the second five (no. 6–10) tips on why this is the case.

3. Imagine you are a trade union officer in a company with a large workforce spending long hours at the office desk. Given that the company has so far refused to adhere to the ten suggestions outlined above, what strategies could you employ to get the company to take ergonomics at your workplace into account? Develop four strategies.

4. Discuss the "positives" of the ergonomics recommendations outlined above. Develop five arguments in favour of these recommendations to make office work better.

5. Discuss the "negatives" of the ergonomics recommendations outlined above. Aren't these just suggestions to make work that is intolerable more tolerable? Aren't these just suggestions to make capitalism work better while appearing to be nice to workers? Develop five arguments against ergonomics.

### 5.3 *Your Cup of Coffee and a Child's Schooling*

Since they were young children, Claudio and Angelina have been working on local corn and coffee farms in Western Honduras helping their family earn a small income. At the end of a 4 am to 6 pm workday, threatened by poisonous snakes, rats, and unkind adult supervisors, they come home, tired and hungry, to their large family in their one-room house made of plastic, clay, and timber.

Claudio and Angelina support their family, armed with baskets, machetes, and their bare hands to pluck coffee beans from trees or break up land, plant, and harvest corn. Both suffer from respiratory sickness, poor nutrition, and the at times freezing temperatures of early mornings labouring in the field that compromise their health.

The work is hard and exhausting. It can take Claudio and Angelina days to travel through the coffee forests to harvest the beans required for a 50 kg bag of coffee. They then carry the bag alone, all 50 kg, to a farmer's scale where they will earn only $8.00 to $10.00 for this work. These beans are then sold to the processor, the broker, and on through the supply chain until it gets to us – those who drink coffee. We – the end consumer – will pay $20.00 or more for just one kilo of Claudio and Angelina's coffee.

Claudio and Angelina are quite proud of what they contribute to their family while dreaming of one day becoming a lawyer (Claudio) and a doctor (Angelina). During corn season, both often lapse in attending their local school even though their work ethic is excellent. Unfortunately, the work–school inconsistency threatens to compromise their dreams. Often both are behind in school and are in desperate need to be given the opportunity to catch up in their studies. Both are currently in grade 8 when they should be in grade 9 and according to the school they attend, Claudio and Angelina are only at a grade 6 level in certain subjects.

Sadly, not only are Claudio and Angelina risking their health to help their family, but both are also risking their future by not being able to focus properly on school. Better prices for farmers would result in better pay for adults working on the farms and would give children the opportunity to go to school regularly.

1. The chapter mentions three forms of control – simple or direct, mechanical, and finally bureaucratic control. Discuss which form of control is applied in the case of child labour. Develop four reasons that support your answer.
2. Imagine you are the HR manager of a large supermarket chain willing to change the situation of children like Claudio and Angelina. What four recommendations would you suggest to alter their lives?
3. The chapter discusses four types of how work is organised. Which of the four is used in the case of child labour? Support your choice with four arguments.
4. Imagine you are the local buyer of the coffee the siblings are harvesting, seeking to change their working conditions for the better. What "six" short-term and immediate changes would you introduce to change their working conditions in terms of (1) harvesting (three recommendations) and (2) transportation (three recommendations) of the coffee to the place of sale?
5. Imagine you are the local representative of the coffee harvester trade union invited to an international conference on the elimination of child labour where representatives of the entire supply chain meet. What "four" proposals would you recommend to end child labour of coffee harvesting children?

### 5.4 Global Cardboard in Malaysia

Global Cardboard Inc. employs 12,000 people and is a division of a global paper giant located in the European Union. It has substantial manufacturing facilities throughout Asia, mostly in Malaysia and Indonesia. It also operates joint ventures in Japan and China. Global Cardboard Inc.'s strongest sales products are basic paper and cardboard. It also manufactures "rough" paper used for paper bags, packaging, boxes, packing materials, cardboard cartons, one-way boxes, etc.

Until the early 2000s, Global Cardboard Inc. was part of a large corporation but eventually it was sold to a hedge fund and operates now as an independent company. Global Cardboard Inc. is a low-cost manufacturer offering low prices. Its headquarter is based in Singapore where "research and development" as well as marketing are also located. Inside its main production facilities in Malaysia and Indonesia, older production workers were often transferred away from large machinery. They were employed in adjacent divisions that require semi-skilled and largely routine work. This arrangement was set to change.

In 2017, all this changed when a new management team was appointed by Global Cardboard Inc.'s Singapore headquarter to operate its Malaysian manufacturing plant employing 720 workers. The new management team was set to increase Global Cardboard Inc.'s market share, moving rapidly into "fine" paper. Moving from "rough" to "fine" paper meant using smaller but more sophisticated machinery such as, for example, electronic guillotines, and trimming and computerised machines (CNC). This is designed to produce higher product quality and greater product consistency. It also sets forth new demands to Global Cardboard Inc.'s workers. It demanded from workers to change their work attitude from standard mass production focusing on output towards a more sophisticated production focusing increasingly on specific customer needs.

As a consequence, Global Cardboard Inc.'s new Malaysian management started to hire increasingly more sophisticated and skilled employees. In some cases, exiting workers were re-trained building on their existing expertise in paper manufacturing. The increase of skilled workers and the changes in Global Cardboard Inc.'s technology resulted in severe "demarcation" disputes. The conflict occurred between newly hired skilled workers and re-trained workers on the one side and older workers working in established roles on the site. Many of Global Cardboard Inc.'s traditional demarcations had developed historically. They were common in many paper operations in Malaysia and Indonesia. At Global Cardboard Inc.'s Malaysian operation, these demarcations divided the workforce into un-skilled machine operators and its newly hired skilled workforce. This led to conflicts between management, skilled and unskilled workers.

As these conflicts increased, quality declined while workflow disruptions occurred. There were also cases of restrictions of output and even sabotage. The fact that Global Cardboard Inc.'s Malaysian operation contained two groups – older and traditional workers and younger more skilled workers – did not help the situation. Traditionally, the Malaysian plant operated with good relations between supervisors and line managers on the one side and manufacturing workers on the other. Often these well-functioning relationships had existed for decades – at least until 2015 when the new management team arrived.

In addition, many older workers started to fear many of the new management changes as their functions where increasingly taken over by computerised equipment. Work stress also increased through increased linkages between customers and manufacturing. Finally, Global Cardboard Inc.'s management was gradually challenged by external factors such as, for example, increased paper imports from overseas.

1. Was Global Cardboard Inc.'s Singapore headquarter right in appointing a new management team for its Malaysian operation that moved the company from "rough" to "fine" paper? Develop five arguments in favour of this move.
2. Was Global Cardboard Inc.'s Singapore headquarter right in appointing a new management team in Malaysia that moved the company from "rough" to "fine" paper? Develop five arguments against this move.
3. The introduction of new technology is often accompanied by increased training. Do you think increased up-skilling of the existing workforce would have avoided the "demarcation" dispute? Develop five answers that focus on re-training.
4. How could Global Cardboard Inc.'s Singapore headquarter and its local management at the Malaysian facility have avoided the "demarcation" dispute? Make five suggestions on how Global Cardboard Inc. could have achieved this.
5. Imagine you are the HR manager at Global Cardboard Inc.'s Malaysian plant seeking to involve other stakeholders to solve the "demarcation" dispute. Develop five arguments for the inclusion of, for example, local educational and training providers, the state and local authorities, trade unions, etc.

### 5.5 Open-Plan Offices can be Bad for Your Health

The "Fresh Lemonade" management team at its Chicago office might have been one of the first to develop what has become known as an "open plan office". That was back in the 1960s. After almost sixty years of experience with open plan offices, hardly any worker will tell you that this is an ideal setup. Yet for many decades, it has been management's solution when it comes to office design. According to a recent study of 30,000 employees in hundreds of office buildings, the answer to the question on the pros and cons of open-plan offices is that they are problematic to say the least. Despite this, the open-plan office lives on. If management at your workplace seeks to introduce an open plan office, there are potentially disastrous mistakes that can be made.

#### OHS (Occupational Health and Safety)

Open-plan offices are often designed with partitions and work cubicles between workers. However, an open-plan office has no walls – everyone is breathing the same air. Illness (cold and flu) can, and indeed does, spread easily and quickly. One study found the following: when there are more than six employees in an open plan office, these are 62% more likely to become ill when compared to an enclosed office.

#### No Personal Space

Every employee has different preferences. Some workers find open-plan offices beneficial to their preferences. Others are unhappy in a large open space and prefer a quiet space. One survey found that open-plan office workers take more than two days off annually, largely because they felt uncomfortable. Another study found that the more personal control workers were given over their environment, the more satisfied they were with their work.

#### Personal Privacy Remains Important

Many managers like the fact that they can stand in an open-plan office and observe what every single person in this office is doing. However, most employees loathe feelings of surveillance, being watched and even judged. A call centre worker even described himself as a *call-centre drone*.[142] The absence of personal privacy harms the managerially claimed collaboration that open-plan offices should bring. And there are workers who are nervous about being in a public place. A recent study found that personal privacy remains central to almost all workers. Having a high level of autonomy increases not just job satisfaction but also performance. This is despite the fact that "Victor Vroom [has argued that] a clear correlation between job satisfaction and job performance does not exist".[143]

#### The Three "I's": Interruptions, Intrusions, and Interferences

In an open-plan office, employees are often barraged with external stimuli. They literally come from all sides. For example, when a work team works together in one space, almost anything becomes an intrusion. There are visual impacts and noise. These remain major problems. Research found that the more effective you are at screening out distractions, the more effectively you work in an open office.

*High Cost and Low Productivity The High Cost of Low Productivity?*

Open-plan offices are known to be less productive. For management and HRM, this means managers need to work with employees to circumvent the negatives of open-plan offices, for example, project teams should re-design these offices. These re-designs should combine "open" and "closed" offices to lower the negatives of open-plan offices. The truth is that individual and quiet offices and even private corners and partitions will increase productivity.

*No Security and More Mistrust*

In any open-plan office, employees talk and even walk in close proximity of your desk. But it is not just the office co-workers but often also managers, suppliers, customers, delivery workers, cleaning staff, copy machine repairers, etc. And worse, many don't even know who is walking past. In an open-plan office, it is simply impossible to be absolutely certain that your belongings are safe. Some may just "borrow" your stapler and forget to return it! If your mobile phone, your wallet, or something else is "borrowed" or goes missing, many will have suspicions about probable wrongdoers. Slowly, this can create an environment of mistrust.

*Office Noise Versus Collaboration*

The more employees are crammed into an open-plan office, the noisier the office becomes. Often, there are work- and non-work-related talks occurring all around your desk. These include face-to-face and phone conversations. Research suggests that overhearing even pieces of conversation can be very annoying and distractive. Management believes that collaboration increases in an open-plan office. But when the noise gets so bad that employees cannot hear others during, for example, an important phone call, disaster is programmed.

*Interpersonal Conflicts and Quarrels*

Management believes that in an open-plan office, every employee is completely equal. This is how the open-plan office is, at least hypothetically, designed to work. More often than not, top management typically has their own special offices. Even when these offices are not really "private" offices, there is always this special place, a special desk, a special space. In some cases, there can be conflicts and quarrels over these spaces.

*Work Stress*

Finally, it has become clear that noise is part of the daily working life in an open-plan office. But longitudinal research shows that just three hours of office noise increase the level of stress. In the long run, this can lead to heart conditions, high blood pressure, insomnia, and a weakened immune system.

1. The case study mentions many employees are dissatisfied with their working environment. Find ten more reasons why workers are dissatisfied with open-plan offices.
2. The case study mentions that employees who work in open-plan offices take more sick days than those working in a closed office. Explain why this might be

the case. Develop three reasons for this and three recommendations about how this could be improved.

3. The case study mentions that employers and managers are putting employees' safety at risk and damage their health due to the open-plan workplace environment. Imagine you are an HR manager, what kind of reports might come your way? Develop three possible complaints and create possible solutions for these requests.

4. Develop four arguments in favour of open plan offices and four arguments against them.

5. Imagine you are the HR manager in a company that operates open-plan offices. Over time employees report their dissatisfaction with the open-plan office. You have decided to move back into the initial offices. Develop four recommendations on how such a move could be achieved.

### V. A Suggestion for an Online Guest Lecture

Brazilian CEO Ricardo Semler talks about
*"How to Run a Company" (2014)*
www.ted.com/talks/ricardo_semler_radical_wisdom_for_a_company_a_school_a_
  life
[the online guest lecture above is merely a suggestion – www.ted.com/talks offers
  additional material to choose from]

### VI. List of Suggested Documentaries on Work

The carefully selected documentary videos below are mere suggestions to be used during tutorials. Documentaries have been selected to achieve two things: (1) to explain key HRM themes and (2) to provide an insight into the reality of HRM. Typically, these short documentaries should be viewed in class followed by a class discussion on the content of the video. Alternatively, questions on documentaries can be prepared beforehand and small group discussions can follow up the video after viewing is concluded. Should any of the web links no longer function, please conduct an internet search for other – alternative – documentaries related to your tutorial topic (e.g. filmsforaction.org):

Fordism: www.youtube.com/watch?v=zmHwkWOZI58
Taylorism: https://study.com/academy/lesson/fredrick-taylor-management-
  maximizing-productivity-efficiency.html
Why we work: www.artthesystem.com/2013/11/the-best-short-movie-has-ever-
  made-102.html
Motivation: www.crmlearning.com/fish-video & www.crmlearning.com/fish-video
Work Design: youtube.com/watch?v=M6vBo_uTGIY&list=WL8xrPWmgcM7ap-
  UKBUT9Tv-YSJc9I2dIG
Knowledge: www.youtube.com/watch?v=WFflr54f7H8
Process: www.youtube.com/watch?v=WFflr54f7H8

Telework:   www.npr.org/2014/02/27/283507813/telework-not-just-for-moms-and-millennials

McDonalds: www.youtube.com/watch?v=Fdy1AgO6Fp4

Work at Pixar: www.youtube.com/watch?v=CXtsEhUwTmc

Motivation: www.youtube.com/watch?v=u6XAPnuFjJc

## Notes

1 Quite often "flexibility means you better work extra hours, without knowing whether you have a job tomorrow, or else. There are no contracts and no rights. That's flexibility" (Noam Chomsky, Loyola University Chicago lecture, 19th October 1994, Noam Chomsky "Democracy and Education" (Chapter 2) in: Chomsky, N. 2004. *Mis-Education*, Lanham: Roman & Littlefield, p. 51).

2 Graeber, D. 2019, *Bullshit Jobs*, London: Penguin books, p. 169; Klikauer, T. 2020. Bullshit jobs, *Australian Universities' Review*, 61(1):70–73.

3 Gantman, E. R. 2005. *Capitalism, Social Privilege, and Managerial Ideologies*, Aldershot: Ashgate, p. 60; Williams, M. et al. 2020. *Mapping Good Work - The Quality of Working Life across the Occupational Structure*, Bristol: Bristol University Press, p. 55 (Klikauer, T. & Simms, N. 2020. Mapping good work, *Marx & Philosophy Review of Books*, 23rd October 2020).

4 Chun, J. 2001. Flexible despotism: the intensification of insecurity and uncertainty in the lives of Silicon Valley's high-tech assembly workers, In: Baldoz, R. et al. (eds.) *The Critical Study of Work: Labor, Technology, and Global Production*, Philadelphia, PA: Temple University Press, pp. 127–154; Wood, A. J. 2015. Networks of injustice and worker mobilisation at Walmart, *Industrial Relations Journal*, 46(4):259–274; Wood, A. J. 2016. Flexible scheduling, degradation of job quality and barriers to collective voice, *Human Relations*, 69(10):1989–2010; Wood, A. J., Graham, M., Lehdonvirta, V. & Hjorth, I. 2019. Good gig, bad gig: autonomy and algorithmic control in the global gig economy, *Work, Employment and Society*, 33(1):56–75; Klikauer, T. & Campbell, N. 2021. The Despotism of Workplace Flexibility, *ZNet* (https://zcomm.org/znetarticle/the-despotism-of-workplace-flexibility/, 27th May 2021).

5 https://www.youtube.com/watch?v=A7C4knUrs0U.

6 https://www.bbc.com/worklife/article/20210713-why-introverts-excelled-at-working-from-home; https://bigthink.com/coronavirus/work-from-home-burnout.

7 https://www.bbc.com/worklife/article/20200409-how-to-work-remotely-what-the-past-50-years-teaches-us; https://www.iod.com/news-campaigns/press-office/details/Home-working-here-to-stay-new-IoD-figures-suggest.

8 Knight, R. 2017. How to convince your boss to let you work from home, *Harvard Business Review*, 5th March 2017; Dowling, D. W. 2017. How to work from home when you have kids, *Harvard Business Review*, 14th September 2017.

9 https://www.bbc.com/news/resources/idt-dc2d6e2d-3ab4-42de-8d03-bb7eda5fff8e; https://www.ilo.org/wcmsp5/groups/public/@dgreports/@dcomm/documents/briefingnote/wcms_755910.pdf; cf. Klikauer, T. & Simms, N. 2021. Post-corona work changes in Germany, *Countercurrents*, 16th February 2021.

10 Klikauer, T. & Széll, G. 2020. Reflections on a pandemic, *Countercurrents* (https://countercurrents.org/, 24th June 2020, accessed: 25th July 2020).

11 McCarthy, H. 2020. Working from home has a troubled history. Coronavirus is exposing its flaws again (https://www.theguardian.com/commentisfree/2020/apr/12/working-from-home-history-coronavirus-uk-lockdown, accessed: 15th June 2020).

12 https://www.bbc.com/worklife/article/20200710-the-remote-work-experiment-that-made-staff-more-productive.

13 cf. Choudhury, P. 2020. Our work-from-anywhere future, *Harvard Business Review*, November–December Issue.

14 https://www.marketscreener.com/SIEMENS-AG-56358595/news/Siemens-to-let-staff-spend-less-time-in-the-office-permanently-30933937/.

15 https://www.iod.com/about.

16 https://www.iod.com/news-campaigns/press-office/details/Home-working-here-to-stay-new-IoD-figures-suggest.

17 Hood, B. 2012. *Self Illusion*, Oxford: Oxford University Press, p. 205.

18  https://www.bbc.com/worklife/article/20201023-can-young-people-thrive-in-a-remote-work-world.

19  https://www.bbc.com/worklife/article/20201023-can-young-people-thrive-in-a-remote-work-world.

20  Gould, A. M. 2010. Working at McDonalds: some redeeming features of McJobs, *Work, Employment & Society*, 24(4):780–802.

21  Ford, R. 1994. The McDonaldization of society: an investigation into the changing character of contemporary social life, *Clinical Sociology Review*, 12(1):25.

22  Nagel, R. 2016. HR strategy and change: essentials of organisational change, in: Zeuch, M. (eds.) *Handbook of HRM*, Heidelberg: Springer, p. 1267.

23  Abrahamson, E. 1996. Management fashion, *Academy of Management Review*, 21(1):254–285.

24  Diefenbach, T. 2013. *Hierarchy and Organization*, London: Routledge; Lise Bjørnstad, A. & MJ Lichacz, F. 2013. Organizational flexibility from a network organizational perspective: a study of central predictors and moderating factors in military contexts, *Leadership & Organization Development Journal*, 34(8):763–783; Lemons, J. F. 2015. Issue: Flat Management (businessresearcher.sagepub.com).

25  Hassard, J. & Morris, J. 2021. The extensification of managerial work in the digital age, *Human Relations* (first published: 25th April 2021, https://doi.org/10.1177/00187267211003123).

26  Chadwick, C., Super, J. F. & Kwon, K. 2015. Resource orchestration in practice: CEO emphasis on SHRM, commitment-based HR systems, and firm performance, *Strategic Management Journal*, 36(3):360–376.

27  Storey, J. 1983. *Managerial Prerogative and the Question of Control*, London: Routledge; McKinlay, A. & Zeitlin, J. 1989. The meanings of managerial prerogative: industrial relations and the organisation of work in British engineering, 1880–1939, *Business History*, 31(2):32–47.

28  Schuster, L. & Hunter, M. 2016. HR strategy and change: essentials of mergers, acquisitions, and joint ventures; in: Zeuch, M. (eds.) *Handbook of HRM*, Heidelberg: Springer, p. 1375ff.

29  https://he.palgrave.com/companion/Bratton-And-Gold-Human-Resource-Management/student-zone/Chapter-summaries/; Purcell, J. & Ahlstrand, B. W. 1995. *HRM in the Multi-Divisional Company*, Oxford: Oxford University Press.

30  https://www.eurocontrol.int/ehp/?q=node/1560; Fleishman, E. A. & Mumford, M. D. 1991. Evaluating classifications of job behavior: a construct validation of the ability requirement scales, *Personnel Psychology*, 44(3):523–575.

31  AI. 2017. Time to Recharge (https://www.amnestyusa.org/wp-content/uploads/2017/11/Time-to-recharge-online-1411.pdf, accessed: 21st November 2017).

32  Block, N. 1981. Psychologism and behaviourism, *The Philosophical Review*, 90(1):5–43.

33  Operant conditioning chamber: youtube.com/watch?v=SUwCgFSb6Nk.

34  http://www.simplypsychology.org/operant-conditioning.html.

35  HR. 2010. *Human Resource Social Engineering* (1:59 min video: www.filmsforaction.org).

36  http://funderstanding.com/wp-content/uploads/2011/04/behaviorism.jpg.

37  Chomsky, N. 1971. The case against B. F. Skinner, *The New York Review of Books*, 30th December (internet download).

38  Herzberg, F. 1966. *Work and the Nature of Man*, Cleveland, OH: World Publishing; Herzberg, F. 2011. One more time: how do you motivate employees?, in: HBR (eds.) *HBR's 10 Must Reads – On Managing People*, Cambridge: Harvard Business School Press; Locke, E. A. 1969. What is job satisfaction?, *Organizational Behavior and Human Performance*, 4(4):309–336; Gantman, E. R. 2005. *Capitalism, Social Privilege, and Managerial Ideologies*, Aldershot: Ashgate, p. 59.

39  Vidal, M. 2019. Contradictions of the labour process, worker empowerment and capitalist inefficiency, *Historical Materialism*, 28(2):170–204.

40  Gantman, E. R. 2005. *Capitalism, Social Privilege, and Managerial Ideologies*, Aldershot: Ashgate, p. 60.

41  McGregor, D. 1960. *The Human Side of Enterprise*, New York: McGraw-Hill; McGregor, D. 2006. *The Human Side of Enterprise* (updated and with new commentary by Joel Cutcher-Gershenfeld), New York: McGraw-Hill; cf. Gantman, E. R. 2005. *Capitalism, Social Privilege, and Managerial Ideologies*, Aldershot: Ashgate, p. 60.

42  Wren, D. A., Bedeian, A. G. & Breeze, J. D. 2002. The foundations of Henri Fayol's administrative theory, *Management Decision*, 40(9):906–918.

43  Smith, A. 1776. *An Inquiry into the Nature and Causes of the Wealth of Nations*, Dublin: Whitestone, pp. 603 & 609.

44 Moore, P. & Robinson, A. 2016. The quantified self: what counts in the neoliberal workplace, *New Media & Society*, 18(11):2783.

45 Taylor, F. W. 1911. *The Principle of Scientific Management*, New York: Norton Press (reprinted in Handel, M. (eds.) 2003. *The Sociology of Organizations – Classic, Contemporary and Critical Readings*, London: Sage); Schachter, H. L. 1989. *Frederick Taylor and the Public Administration Community: A Reevaluation*, New York: Suny Press, p. 40.

46 https://notesfrombelow.org/article/amazon-inquiry.

47 Lyons, D. 2018. *Lab Rats*, London: Atlantic Books, p. 102.

48 Kumar, A. 2020. *Monopsony Capitalism: Power and Production in the Twilight of the Sweatshop Age*, Cambridge: Cambridge University Press.

49 Henry Ford may not have really wanted human workers. After all, he once said "how come when I ask for a pair of hands, I get a human being as well" (from: Bruce, A. & Montanez, S. M. 2012. *Leaders Start to Finish: A Road Map for Developing Top Performers*, Alexandria: American Society for Training and Development Press, p. 12).

50 One might keep in mind that "capitalist production is not merely the production of commodities, it is essentially the production of surplus-value" (Marx) and therefore profits with the euphemism "shareholder value" attached to it.

51 https://m.youtube.com/watch?v=NkQ58I53mjk.

52 Beynon, H. 1973. *Working for Ford*, London: Allen Lane; Lynch, C. & Chamberlain, W. 2015. Reflections from a life on the line, in: Gershon, I (eds.) *A World of Work*, Ithaca, NY: ILR Press.

53 Bernstein, A. 2016. Globalization, robots, and the future of work: an interview with Jeffrey Joerres, *Harvard Business Review*, October 2016 (https://www.youtube.com/watch?v=Jky9I1ihAkg).

54 Holborow, M. 2015. *Language and Neoliberalism*, London: Routledge, p. 23.

55 Rothstein, J. S. 2016. Contextualizing work: the influence of workplace history and perceptions of the future on lean production at three GM plants, *Critical Sociology*, 42(7–8):1143–1161.

56 Klikauer, T. 2007. *Communication and Management at Work*, Basingstoke: Palgrave, p. 153.

57 Berardi, F. 2009. *The Soul at Work: From Alienation to Autonomy*, Cambridge: MIT Press; Musto, M. 2010. Revisiting Marx's concept of alienation, *Socialism and Democracy*, 24(3):79–101.

58 Christ, O. 2015. The concept of alienation in the early works of Karl Marx, *European Scientific Journal*, 11(7):551–563.

59 Ritzer, G. 2014. *The McDonaldization of Society* (8th ed.), London: Sage.

60 Rosenblat, A. *Uberland: How Algorithms Are Rewriting the Rules of Work*, Oakland: University of California Press.

61 Dellot, B. 2017. *8 Key Takeaways from Our New Report on AI, Robotics and Automation* (https://www.thersa.org, 20th September 2017; accessed: 17th January 2018).

62 Peetz, D. 2019. *The Realities and Futures of Work*, Canberra: ANU Press, p. 9.

63 Davis, G. F. 2015. What might replace the modern corporation: uberization and the web page enterprise, *Seattle University Law Review*, (39):505.

64 Wood, A. J., Graham, M., Lehdonvirta, V. & Hjorth, I. 2019. Good gig, bad gig: autonomy and algorithmic control in the global gig economy, *Work, Employment and Society*, 33(1):56–75; Duggan, J., Sherman, U., Carbery, R. & McDonnell, A. 2020. Algorithmic management and app-work in the gig economy: a research agenda for employment relations and HRM, *Human Resource Management Journal*, 30(1):114–132 (https://www.bbc.com/worklife/article/20200826-how-algorithms-keep-workers-in-the-dark); Bucher, E. L., Schou, P. K. & Waldkirch, M. 2021. Pacifying the algorithm–anticipatory compliance in the face of algorithmic management in the gig economy, *Organization*, 28(1):44–67.

65 Lee, M. K. 2018. Understanding perception of algorithmic decisions: fairness, trust, and emotion in response to algorithmic management, *Big Data & Society*, 5(1); Gal, U., Jensen, T. B. & Stein, M. K. 2020. Breaking the vicious cycle of algorithmic management: a virtue ethics approach to people analytics, *Information and Organization*, 30(2).

66 Another version of "remote work" occurs when workers control machines remotely (Baraniuk, C. 2020. The Forklift Truck Drivers Who Never Leave Their Desks, https://www.bbc.com/news/business-54431056, accessed: 25th October 2020).

67 Wood, A. J. et al. 2019. Good gig, bad gig: autonomy and algorithmic control in the global gig economy, *Work, Employment and Society*, 33(1):56–75; Fuller, J. et al. 2020. Rethinking the on-demand workforce, *Harvard Business Review*, 98(6):96–103; Gandini, A. 2019. Labour process theory and the gig economy, *Human Relations*, 72(6):1039–1056.

68  Duggan, J., Sherman, U., Carbery, R. & McDonnell, A. 2020. Algorithmic management and app-work in the gig economy: a research agenda for employment relations and HRM, *Human Resource Management Journal*, 30(1):1157.

69  Crouch, C. 2019. *Will the Gig Economy Prevail?* Cambridge: Polity Press.

70  Duggan, J., Sherman, U., Carbery, R. & McDonnell, A. 2020. Algorithmic management and app-work in the gig economy: a research agenda for employment relations and HRM, *Human Resource Management Journal*, 30(1):115.

71  Peetz, D. 2019. *The Realities and Futures of Work*, Canberra: ANU Press, p. 11.

72  Forde, C. et al. 2017. The Social Protection of Workers in the Platform Economy (http://www.europarl.europa.eu/RegData/etudes/STUD/2017/614184/IPOL_STU(2017)614184_EN.pdf, accessed: 5th April 2019).

73  Damm, D. 2017. As machines take jobs, companies need to get creative about making, *Harvard Business Review*, 24th May 2017; Word Bank. 2016. *Digital Dividends – World Development Report 2016*, Washington, DC: World Bank, p. 23; Cortes, G. M., Jaimovich, N. & Siu, H. E. 2016. *Disappearing Routine Jobs: Who, How, and Why?* Washington, DC: National Bureau of Economic Research (No. w22918).

74  Peetz, D. 2019. *The Realities and Futures of Work*, Canberra: ANU Press, p. 101f.

75  Xia, F., Yang, L. T., Wang, L. & Vinel, A. 2012. Internet of things, *International Journal of Communication Systems*, 25(9):1101; Shah, P. A. A., Habib, M., Sajjad, T., Umar, M. & Babar, M. 2016, Applications and challenges faced by internet of things-a survey, in: Ferreira J. & Alam M. (eds.) *International Conference on Future Intelligent Vehicular Technologies*, Cham: Springer, pp. 182–188.

76  Frank, M. R. et al. 2019. Toward understanding the impact of artificial intelligence on labor, *Proceedings of the National Academy of Sciences*, 116(14):6531–6539.

77  Lee, J., Bagheri, B. & Kao, H. A. 2015. A cyber-physical systems architecture for industry 4.0-based manufacturing systems, *Manufacturing Letters*, (3):18–23; cf. Brygo, J. 2018. Big rigs with no one aboard, *LeMonde Diplomatique*, August 2018 Edition, p. 8; Korinek, A. & Stiglitz, J. E. 2017. Artificial intelligence, worker-replacing technological progress and income distribution, *NBER Working Paper*, no. 24174.

78  Gottfried, H. 1995. Developing neo-fordism: a comparative perspective, *Critical Sociology*, 21(3):39–70; Rothstein, J. S. 2015. Contextualizing work: the influence of workplace history and perceptions of the future on lean production at three GM plants, *Critical Sociology*, 42(7–8):1143–1161; Amin, A. 2011. *Post-Fordism: A Reader*, Oxford: Blackwell/Wiley.

79  Klikauer, T., Cybernetics, labor and capitalism rise of the machines, *Journal of Labor and Society*, 21(2):271–275.

80  O'Neil, C. 2016. *Weapons of Math Destruction: How Big Data Increases Inequality and Threatens Democracy*, London: Penguin.

81  Peetz, D. 2019. *The Realities and Futures of Work*, Canberra: ANU Press, p. 93.

82  Hartrath, H. 2016. Administration and payroll: essentials of shared services and outsourcing, in: Zeuch, M. (eds.) *Handbook of HRM*, Heidelberg: Springer, p. 1012.

83  Howcroft, D. & Bergvall-Kåreborn, B. 2019. A typology of crowdwork platforms, *Work, Employment & Society*, 33(1):21–38.

84  Belleflamme, P., Lambert, T. & Schwienbacher, A. 2014. Crowdfunding: tapping the right crowd, *Journal of Business Venturing*, 29(5):585–609.

85  That later became: https://www.figure-eight.com/.

86  Marvit, M. Z. 2014. How Crowdworkers Became the Ghosts in the Digital Machine (https://www.thenation.com/article/how-crowdworkers-became-ghosts-digital-machine/, 5th February 2014, accessed: 5th April 2019).

87  http://faircrowd.work/.

88  Berg, J. et al. 2018. *Digital Labour Platforms and the Future of Work*, Geneva: ILO, p. 3.

89  Cf. Schmidt, F. A. 2017. *Digital Labour Markets*, Bonn: Friedrich Ebert Stiftung, 28 pages.

90  Advocates of the *Internet of Things*, *Industry 4.0*, etc. expect huge changes in the workforce. 'A pair of economists recently predicted that by 2033, there was a 99 percent chance that insurance underwriters would lose their jobs to computer programs. Sports referees faced a 98 percent risk of obsolescence, waiters a 94 percent chance, and so on. (Archaeologists were the safest, "because the job requires highly sophisticated types of pattern recognition, and doesn't produce huge profits' (McKibben, B. 2019. *Falter – Has the Human Game Begun to Play Itself Out?*, New York: Henry Holt and Company, ebook, p. 235).

91  https://www.bbc.com/worklife/article/20200317-the-evolution-of-the-modern-workday.

92  https://www.youtube.com/watch?v=QdMhdFVBeew.

93  Baines, D. & Cunningham, I. (eds.) 2021. *Working in the Context of Austerity: Challenges and Struggles*, Bristol: Bristol University Press.

94  Johnson, M. 2016. *Precariat: Labour, Work and Politics*, London: Routledge; the splitting of the workforce into core and periphery has been known as "neo-bondage [that] polarises the labour force into a small stable core enjoying many benefits and a very large periphery stripped of any stability"; Youssef K. W. F. 2016. Anti-capital & workers and labour in a globalised capitalism, *Work, Employment & Society*, online before printing, p. 3; Antunes, R. 2016. The new morphology of labour and its main trends: informalisation, precarisation, (im) materiality and value 1, *Critique*, 44(1–2):13–30; Crain, M. et al. 2016. *Invisible Labor: Hidden Work in the Contemporary World*, Berkeley: University of California Press; Vij, R. et al. (eds.) 2020. *Precarity and International Relations*, London: Palgrave Macmillan.

95  Kanigel, R. 1997. *The One Best Way: Frederick Winslow Taylor and the Enigma of Efficiency*, New York: Viking.

96  Jenkins, J. & Blyton, P. 2016. In debt to the time-bank: the manipulation of working time in Indian garment factories and "working dead horse", *Work, employment and society*, published before pint, https://doi.org/10.1177/0950017016664679.

97  https://www.youtube.com/watch?v=paaen3b44XY.

98  Edwards, R. 1979. *Contested Terrain*, London: Heinemann; Fleming, P. & Sturdy, A. 2009. *Just Be Yourself!: Towards Neo-Normative Control in Organisations?*, Employee Relations, 31(6);569–583.

99  https://www.youtube.com/watch?v=6cLf0i-kYio;  https://www.bbc.com/worklife/article/20201023-can-young-people-thrive-in-a-remote-work-world.

100  Kellogg, K. C., Valentine, M. A. & Christin, A. 2020. Algorithms at work: the new contested terrain of control, *Academy of Management Annals*, 14(1):366–410; Hatch, P. 2018. In Amazon's "hellscape" (https://www.smh.com.au/, 7th September 2018, accessed: 15th December 2018).

101  This might well be part of what management guru Tom Peters will later call MBWA "Management by walking around" (fortune.com, 23rd August 2012); cf. Mumby, D. K. 2019. Work: what is it good for? (Absolutely nothing) – a critical theorist's perspective, *Industrial and Organizational Psychology*, 1–15 (https://doi-org.ezproxy.uws.edu.au/10.1017/iop.2019.69, accessed: 15th January 2020).

102  Bloodworth, J. 2018. *Hired: Six Months Undercover in Low-Wage Britain*, London: Atlantic Books.

103  Kellogg, K. C., Valentine, M. A. & Christin, A. 2020. Algorithms at work: the new contested terrain of control, *Academy of Management Annals*, 14(1):366–410.

104  Hood, B. 2012. *Self Illusion*, Oxford: Oxford University Press, p. 205.

105  Duggan, J., Sherman, U., Carbery, R. & McDonnell, A. 2020. Algorithmic management and app-work in the gig economy: a research agenda for employment relations and HRM, *Human Resource Management Journal*, 30(1):126.

106  Duggan, J., Sherman, U., Carbery, R. & McDonnell, A. 2020. Algorithmic management and app-work in the gig economy: a research agenda for employment relations and HRM, *Human Resource Management Journal*, 30(1):119f.

107  Die Welt. 2015. Amazon schüchtert mit „Inaktivitätsprotokollen" ein (https://www.welt.de/wirtschaft/article138353783/Amazon-schuechtert-mit-Inaktivitaetsprotokollen-ein.html, 13th March 2015, accessed: 5th April 2019).

108  Smith, Z. 2019. Blame the boss, not the robot, *New Labor Forum*, 28(2):66–69);

109  Woodcock, J. 2021. Towards a digital workerism: workers' inquiry, methods, and technologies, *NanoEthics*, 15(1):87–98 (cf. https://www.jamiewoodcock.net/blog/digital-workerism/).

110  https://www.youtube.com/watch?app=desktop&v=jf-Sr3SjBzk.

111  Klikauer, T. & Campbell, N. 2020. The People's Republic of Walmart, *Countercurrents*, 22nd July 2020.

112  https://plato.stanford.edu/entries/alienation/.

113  Seeman, M. 1959. On the meaning of alienation, *American Sociological Review*, 24(6):783–791; Pearlin, L. I. 1962. Alienation from work: a study of nursing personnel, *American Sociological Review*, 27(3):314–326; Seeman, M. 1967. On the personal consequences of alienation in work, *American Sociological Review*, 32(2):273–285; Greaves, M. D. 2016. Cycles of alienation, *New Proposals*, 9(1):49–63.

114    Padgett, B. L. 2007. *Marx and Alienation in Contemporary Society*, London: Continuum Press, pp. 7–9; Klikauer, T. 2013. Marx & alienation – essays on Hegelian themes, *Labour & Industry*, 23(3):182–186.

115    https://study.com/academy/lesson/the-hawthorne-effect-the-study-of-employee-productivity.html.

116    Bagnara, S. et al. 2018. *Proceedings of the 20th Congress of the International Ergonomics Association (IEA 2018): Healthcare Ergonomics*, Heidelberg: Springer; Dul, J. et al. 2012. A strategy for human factors/ergonomics: developing the discipline and profession, *Ergonomics*, 55(4):377–395; Danielsson, C. B. et al. 2014. Office design's impact on sick leave rates, *Ergonomics*, 57(2):139–147; Guastello, S. J. 2013. *Human Factors Engineering and Ergonomics: A Systems Approach* (2nd ed.), Boca Raton, FL: CRC Press/Taylor & Francis Group.

117    Deml, B., Stock, P., Bruder, R. & Schlick, C. M. (eds.) 2016. *Advances in Ergonomic Design of Systems, Products and Processes*, Heidelberg: Springer.

118    Salvendy, G. & Karwowski, W. 2016. *Advances in Cognitive Ergonomics*, Boca Raton, FL: CRC Press, p. 156.

119    Yassi, A. 1997. Repetitive strain injuries, *The Lancet*, 349(9056):943–947.

120    Barker, J. R. 1993. Tightening the iron cage: concertive control in self-managing teams, *Administrative Science Quarterly*, 38(3):408–437; cf. Blauner, R. 1964. *Alienation and Freedom – The Factory Worker and His Industry*, Chicago, IL: Chicago University Press.

121    Brockling, U. 2016. *Entrepreneurial Self: Fabricating a New Type of Subject*, London: Sage.

122    On "presenteeism" (Dietz, C. et al. 2020. Leaders as role models: effects of leader presenteeism on employee presenteeism and sick leave, *Work & Stress*, 34(3):300–322); https://www.bbc.com/worklife/article/20210604-why-presenteeism-always-wins-out-over-productivity; https://www.bbc.com/news/business-47911210.

123    Kerzner, H. 2017. *Project Management* (12th ed.), Hoboken, NJ: Wiley; Too, E. G. & Weaver, P., 2014. The management of project management: a conceptual framework for project governance, *International Journal of Project Management*, 32(8):1382–1394.

124    Belout, A. & Gauvreau, C. 2004. Factors influencing project success: the impact of human resource management, *International Journal of Project Management*, 22(1):1–11.

125    Grote, G. & Guest, D. 2016. The case for reinvigorating quality of working life research, *Human Relations*, 70(2):149–167; Stefana, E. et al. 2021. Composite indicators to measure quality of working life in Europe, *Social Indicators Research* (https://link.springer.com/article/10.1007/s11205-021-02688-6; https://www.bbc.com/news/business-57724779).

126    Saito, M. 2003. Amartya Sen's capability approach to education: a critical exploration, *Journal of Philosophy of Education*, 37(1):17–33.

127    Peetz, D. 2019. *The Realities and Futures of Work*, Canberra: ANU Press, p. 63; cf. https://www.harvardbusiness.org/wp-content/uploads/2020/04/HBR-What-will-Work-Life-Balance-Look-Like-After-the-Pandemic.pdf.

128    Gambles, R., Lewis, S. & Rapoport, R. 2006. *The Myth of Work-Life Balance*, Chichester: John Wiley & Sons; Kelly, M. 2011. *Off Balance: Getting Beyond the Work-Life Balance Myth*, New York: Penguin; Taylor, T. A. 2013. *The Balance Myth: Rethinking Work-Life Success*, Austin, TX: Greenleaf Books; cf. Munkejord, M. C. 2016. His or her work–life balance? Experiences of self-employed immigrant parents, *Work Employment & Society*, October 26, 2016, https://doi.org/0950017016667041.

129    Dunn, K. 2010. *The Five Biggest Lies in HR* (http://www.workforce.com/2010/03/04/the-five-biggest-lies-in-hr/).

130    Jex, S. M. & Britt, T. W. 2014. *Organizational Psychology: A Scientist-Practitioner Approach*, New York: John Wiley, p. 360.

131    In the knowledge economy...people work by communicating (Holborow, M. 2012. What is neoliberalism?, in: Block, D., Gray, J. & Holborow, M. (eds.) *Neoliberalism and Applied Linguistics*, London: Routledge, p. 21).

132    Sloman, S. & Fernbach, P. 2017. *The Knowledge Illusion – Why We Never Think Alone*, New York: Macmillan.

133    Hochschild, A. R. 1983. *The Managed Heart: Commercialization of Human Feeling*, Berkeley: University of California Press.

134    Bolton, S. C. & Boyd, C. 2003. Trolley dolly or skilled emotion manager? Moving on from Hochschild's managed heart, *Work, Employment & Society*, 17(2):289–308.

135    Perhaps the difference is between jobs where you take a shower before you go to work and jobs where you take a shower once you get home.

136 https://bigthink.com/politics-current-affairs/jobs-of-the-future.
137 Fuchs, C. 2020. *Communication and Capitalism – A Critical Theory*, London: University of Westminster Press, p. 187.
138 Reich, R. 1992. *The Work of Nations – Preparing Ourselves for 21st Century Capitalism*, New York: Vintage Books; cf. https://countercurrents.org/2021/07/the-future-of-work/.
139 Nowak, M. & Highfield, R. 2011. *Super Cooperators: Evolution, Altruism and Human Behaviour (Or Why We Need Each Other to Succeed)*, London: Penguin Press; Klikauer, T. 2012. Evolution, altruism, and human behaviour, *Organization*, 19(6):939–940.
140 https://www.youtube.com/watch?v=PZ4VzhIuKCQ.
141 Klikauer, T. 2013. Marx & alienation – essays on Hegelian themes, *Labour & Industry*, 23(3):182–186.
142 Holborow, M. 2015. *Language and Neoliberalism*, London: Routledge, p. 22.
143 Gantman, E. R. 2005. *Capitalism, Social Privilege, and Managerial Ideologies*, Aldershot: Ashgate, p. 60.

## Further Readings

Bateson, J. et al. 2013. When Hiring, First Test, and Then Interview, *Harvard Business Review*.
Bowles, D. 2013. Social Stratification, *American Journl of Economics & Sociology*, 72(1):32–58.
Brass, T. 2015. Free Markets, Unfree Labour, *Journal of Contemporary Asia*, 45(3):531–540.
Chen, V. T. 2015. *Cut Loose – Jobless and Hopeless in an Unfair Economy*, Berkeley: University of California Press.
Coffey, D. & Thornley, C. 2013. *Industrial & Labour Market Policy & Performance*, London: Routledge.
DeMars, N. 2012. *You've Got to Be Kidding! How to Keep Your Job*, Hoboken, NJ: Wiley.
Fluhr, J. 2013. Finding Employees Who Fit, *New York Times*, 10th October 2013.
Gatewood, R. D., Field, H. S. & Barrick, M. 2011. *Human Resource Selection*, Mason: South-Western.
Gerard, J. G. 2012. Linking in with LinkedIn® Three Exercises That Enhance Professional Social Networking and Career Building, *Journal of Management Education*, 36(6):866–897.
Groysberg, B. 2012. *Chasing Stars: The Myth of Talent*, Princeton, NJ: Princeton University Press.
Harvey, D. 2014. Contradiction 5 [Use- & Exchange Value], in: *17 Contradictions & the End of Capitalism*, New York: Oxford University Press.
HBR. 2015. Why Job Postings Don't Equal Jobs, *Harvard Business Review*, May, 93:5.
Kramer, M. S. 2010. *Organizational Socialization – Joining and Leaving Organizations*, Oxford: Polity.
Lees, K. 2015. *Stop Fantasizing about the Perfect Job* (hbr.org/2015/04).
Lin, K.-H. 2015. The Financial Premium in the US Labor Market, *Social Forces*, 94(1):1–30.
Pavlopoulos, D. 2013. Starting Your Career with a Fixed-Term Job: Stepping-Stone or "Dead End"?, *Review of Social Economy*, 71(4):474–501.
Ritzer, G. 2020. *The McDonaldization of Society: Into the Digital Age*, Thousand Oaks, CA: Sage.
Rees W. & Porter C. 2015. *Skills of Management*, London: Palgrave, Chapter 9, Recruitment & Selection.
Rehmann, J. 2015. Surplus Population, *Rethinking Marxism*, 27(2):303–311.
Savitz, A. W. 2013. *Talent, Transformation, and the Triple Bottom Line: How Companies Can Leverage Human Resources to Achieve Sustainable Growth*, New York: John Wiley & Sons.
Taylor-Gooby, P. 2015. Paid Work Is Never Enough (blogs.lse.ac.uk).
Wentland, D. M. 2015. *Is Your Organization a Great Place to Work?*, Charlotte: Information Age Pub.
Wood, A. J. 2020. *Despotism on Demand – How Power Operates in the Flexible Workplace*, Ithaca, NY: Cornell University Press.
Yong, E. 2015. How Reliable Are Psychology Studies?, *The Atlantic*, 27th August (www.theatlantic.com).

# 6 Keeping People Healthy

## Occupational Health and Safety

### Executive Summary

At times, being at work can mean being exposed to danger, risks, injuries, and even death. Occupational Health and Safety (OHS) is the subject dealing with these issues. The key to OHS remains its drive towards preventing accidents at work. OHS is preventative by seeking to preserve the health of employees. On that, HR managers and employees have rights and responsibilities. Together they seek to prevent accidents by, for example, assessing risks such as physical, biological, chemical, or psychological hazards. But there are also cases when prevention fails, often leading to severe costs to employees and companies. To prevent this, HR managers have a duty of care but they also oversee an organisational safety culture as well as an OHS management system and specific OHS policies. As many industries move towards a knowledge economy, psychological hazards such as occupational stress, burnout, harassment, and bullying are on the rise. HR managers raise awareness of these issues in order to prevent them.

### Key Learning Objectives

1. Realise the importance of a positive OHS environment for business;
2. Understand the significance of OHS for HRM;
3. Define physical, mental, and social wellbeing;
4. Realise the magnitude of prevention for workplace safety;
5. Appreciate the "Duty of Care" concept;
6. Identify the main elements of a Positive Safety Culture;
7. Realise the barriers to a "Positive Safety Culture";
8. Learn how to develop a comprehensive OHS policy;
9. Describe the main features of a successful OHS system.

### Making Work Safe – Promotion and Prevention

Without a doubt, Occupational Health and Safety (OHS) is the single most important issue of HR managers and this is not just because OHS responsibilities fall within HRM – not marketing, not accounting, and usually not with operations management – but also because failures in OHS can have the direst consequences for employees, HR managers, companies, families, and societies. A wrong performance review can be changed, a wrongly hired employee can be asked to leave, and the wrong training can have negative or no outcomes. All this can be amended but a dead employee cannot be brought back to life. And yet, despite a wealth of knowledge, a long history, and

DOI: 10.4324/9781003293637-6

the best efforts of many foresighted HR managers, industrial, occupational, and work-place illnesses, injuries, and deaths[1] are still part of work.[2] And the statistics remain staggering:

> every 15 seconds, a worker dies from a work-related accident or disease; every 15 seconds, 153 workers have a work-related accident; every day, 6,300 people die as a result of occupational accidents or work-related diseases – more than 2.3 million deaths per year. 317 million accidents occur on the job annually; many of these resulting in extended absences from work. The human cost of this daily adversity is vast and the economic burden of poor occupational health and safety practices is estimated at 4 per cent of the global Gross Domestic Product each year.[3]

When seen by occupation, the ten most dangerous jobs in the world in recent years were: at number 10: farmers, ranchers, agricultural managers; 9: heavy transport drivers; 8: line installers and repairers; 7: hand labourers and material movers; 6: structural iron and steel workers; 5: roofers; 4: hazardous material workers; 3: pilots and flight engineers; 2: fishers and fishing workers, and finally as the number one most dangerous job in the world: 1: logging workers who cut down the trees from forests. The job includes high risks and dangers following deaths due to falling trees and equipment. The job has topped the list of dangerous jobs in the world because the fatality rate is approximately 128 people (mostly men) in 100,000.[4]

Commonly, **Occupational Health and Safety** is seen as the promotion and maintenance of the highest degree of physical, mental, and social **wellbeing**[5] of workers in all occupations. Wellbeing might be understood as the quality of experiences of an employee in their workplace. Wellbeing can be seen as *hedonia* (perusing pleasure and comfort) or *eudaimonia* (εὐδαιμονία: striving towards individual betterment). Both cases of wellbeing include physical wellbeing, psychological wellbeing, and social wellbeing.

The United Nations' World Health Organisation (WHO) sees OHS as being concerned "with all aspects of health and safety in the workplace and has a strong focus on primary prevention of hazards". In this context, **health** is seen as a state of complete physical, mental, and social wellbeing[6] and not merely the absence of illness and disease. The WHO defines the global health of employees as a human rights issue;[7] the UN's International Labour Organisation (ILO) also defines OHS through ILO conventions.[8] In a joint WHO/ILO statement, both UN agencies define OHS as:

> The main focus in occupational health is on three different objectives:
>
> i.   the maintenance and promotion of workers' health and working capacity;
> ii.  the improvement of working environment and work to become conducive to safety and health; and
> iii. development of work organisations and working cultures in a direction which supports health and safety at work and in doing so also promotes a positive social climate and smooth operation and may enhance productivity of the undertakings."[9]

Unlike police, laws, judges, and courts who enter the picture "after" the fact, OHS places a strong emphasis on what happens "before" it is too late. The general character of OHS is preventative as OHS seeks to prevent industrial injuries and accidents. Perhaps

OHS' **preventative concept** can best be summed up as "prevention is better than compensation". But OHS has never been a one-dimensional affair. Instead, it has developed a multi-perspective position. This tells us that OHS' three key goals outlined above can be reached in six different ways: biological and medical, occupational and epidemiological,[10] behaviourism and psychology, technical and engineering, industrial sociology, and legal and economical.[11] Whatever the perspective, many OHS regulations[12] lay out the rights and responsibilities of management[13] and employees (Table 6.1):

*Table 6.1* OHS Rights and Responsibilities

|  | *Management* | *Employees* |
|---|---|---|
| Rights | Develop OHS policies | Work in safe conditions |
|  | Enforce OHS policies | Protect one's health and safety |
|  | Introduce OHS training | Non-exposure to hazards |
|  | Allow OHS inspections | Raise OHS issues |
|  | Accompany OHS inspectors | Refuse to work in unsafe conditions |
| Responsibilities | Duty of care | Follow OHS policies, rules, laws |
|  | Apply OHS measures | Comply with supervisory OHS directives |
|  | Enforce training programmes | Wear protective gear |
|  | Enforce OHS rules and laws | Report hazards to supervisors[14] |
|  | Keep OHS records | Complete in OHS training programmes |
|  | Participate in OHS meetings | Participate in OHS meetings |

## OHS Hazards

The multi-disciplinary perspective tells HR managers that most **workplace hazards** are related to four key elements: (1) the physical, (2) psychological, (3) social, and (4) environmental aspects of work. **Physical hazards** include a range of issues such as, for example, excessive noise and heat.[15] Noise hazards can range from heavy machinery to open-plan office noise[16]: approximately 30–40 decibels = soft whisper, 60 dBs = conversation, 75 dBs = vacuum cleaner, 95 dBs = jackhammer, 125 dBs = jet take-off; 140 dBs = threshold to pain. Next to office noise in open-plan offices,[17] many of today's workplace activities – even for MBAs and HR managers – include computer work that potentially creates three hazards that can be prevented through the right office **ergonomics**[18]:

1. visual difficulties (light, reflections, etc.) causing blurred vision, sore eyes, burning and itching eyes, etc.;
2. muscular aches, pain, and cumulative trauma disorders, **repetitive strain injuries** (RSI),[19] and carpal tunnel syndrome[20] caused by wrong positioning;[21] and
3. job stress[22] caused by posture problems,[23] monotonous work, etc.[24]

Some of these problems can be avoided, for example, by placing computers 10 cm to 23 cm below the eye level; keeping monitors directly in front of the person; sitting in an adjustable chair; using shades or blinds; keeping the elbows close to the body; and placing wrist and hands in line with forearms. Physical hazards as much as biological and chemical hazards and even unforeseen external factors can lead to a **workplace emergency**.[25] To engage with often unforeseen and unforeseeable events (floods, fires, gas leaks, chemical spills, explosions, civil disturbances, hurricanes, tornados, etc.), HR managers develop an **emergency action plan** with dedicated fire or emergency wardens.

But physical hazards also include bodily exhaustion, fatigue, and, for example, vibration causing the known "dead finger" disease that damages the joints in hands caused by excessive chainsaw usage. Health damaging is also exposure to electro-physical hazards and radiation such as ultrasound, laser, microwaves, infrared radiation, and X-rays. So can exposure to just 5 rem lead to changes in blood chemistry, 75 rem = hair loss, 400 rem = possible death, 2000 rem loss of consciousness and death.[26] Next to physical hazards and **biological hazards** (rabies, parasites, anthrax, fungal diseases, food poisoning, tuberculosis, HIV, occupational cancer,[27] etc.), there are also **chemical hazards** in a world that contains more than seven million chemicals, for example:

> toxic gases (carbon monoxide, hydrogen sulphide, phosphine gas, ozone, chlorine gas), industrial solvents, heavy metals (beryllium, cadmium, mercury), rubber, petroleum, fossil fuel-based products (sooth, tars, mineral oils), persistent organic pollutants, pesticides, and other chemicals such as arsenic, flavourings, and pharmaceuticals.

Relatively minor chemical hazards, for example, are coughing from direct and indirect smoking or skin irritations caused by exposure to chemicals. These can, for example, cause asthma, but there are also chemical burns and fatal diseases. One of the most recognised chemical catastrophes is that of US company Union Carbide's Bhopal[28] plant:

> The Bhopal (India) gas tragedy occurred when a chemical gas – methyl isocyanate – leaked on the night of 2–3 December 1984. It is considered the world's worst industrial disaster. It occurred at the Union Carbide pesticide plant in Bhopal, Madhya Pradesh. Over 500,000 people were exposed to gas and other chemicals. The toxic substance made its way into and around the shanty towns located near the plant. Estimates vary on the death toll. The official immediate death toll was 2,259. The government of Madhya Pradesh confirmed a total of 3,787 deaths related to the gas release. A government affidavit in 2006 stated that the leak caused 558,125 injuries, including 38,478 temporary partial injuries and approximately 3,900 severely and permanently disabling injuries. Others estimate that 8,000 died within two weeks, and another 8,000 or more have since died from gas-related diseases.[29]

Perhaps an even more devastating chemical is **asbestos** being "responsible for 194,000 deaths in 2013" alone.[30] While companies like Monsanto and James Hardie have denied responsibility for decades, today we know the devastating impact of asbestos exposure. The WHO estimates that more than 107,000 people die each year from asbestos-related lung cancer, mesothelioma, and asbestosis resulting from occupational exposures.[31] Classified as chemical hazards are also substances from procedures such as nanotechnology – the engineered manipulation of matter on an atomic scale. While many facts about asbestos are known, nanotechnology is still a developing field. Very much in line with OHS' general concept of prevention, the European Trade Union Confederation has suggested the introduction of a **no data – no exposure principle** as a precautionary measure.[32] In many cases, limiting exposure "before" sufficient data is available would have saved the lives of many as the asbestos case shows.

Much harder to detect than physical and chemical hazards are **psychological hazards** that prevent the wellbeing of employees while obstructing healthy social relations at work. Psychosocial hazards emerge in companies with employees that experience: (1) no organisation support; (2) poor interpersonal relationships; high workloads; (3) a lack of autonomy; (4) poor rewards; and (5) lack of job security.[33] They can be caused in numerous ways ranging from spreading rumours and gossiping to corporate, supervisory, and workplace **bullying**,[34] **mobbing**, and **psycho-terror**. Bullying is the use of force, threat, coercion, abuse, and intimidation[35] of others to aggressively dominate them.[36] It is often repeated and habitual.[37] HR mangers assess abuse and bullying by asking four questions:

1. **Target**: against whom is the abuse and bullying aimed?
2. **Source**: where is the abuse and bullying coming from?
3. **Perception**: do targets perceive it as abuse and bullying?
4. **Work-Related**: does the abuse or bullying occur while undertaking work related duties?

In the same category, we also find **micro-aggression**[38] which are verbal, behavioural, or environmental humiliations – intentional or unintentional[39] – communicating hostile, derogatory, or negative prejudicial insults toward a person or group – particularly culturally marginalised groups.[40] Set against this is **resilience** which is understood when an individual recovers swiftly and effortlessly from obstructions that may occur at work. The following character trades have been associated with resilience: self-assurance, self-confidence, optimism, flexibility, and a positive outlook.

Bullying is typically carried out downward as "more than 80% of bullying cases involve a superior".[41] The *Harvard Business Review* talks of *kissing up, kicking down*.[42] Bullying is linked to power asymmetries: from manager to worker and from professor to student. One study found that 44% of nurses experienced bullying.[43]

Next to direct bullying, there is also online bullying[44] in the form of:

**Sexting**: The sending of sexually suggestive photos, messages, and videos. While sharing suggestive images and text messages may seem like innocent flirting or be considered funny, *sexting* can have serious OHS consequences;[45] and

**Doxxing**: This is publishing private information about a particular work colleague on the Internet (e.g. Facebook, Twitter, etc.) typically with cruel intentions.[46]

While bullying has mutated into "smart bullying",[47] there are more extreme forms of bullying such as **sexual harassment**[48] and **sexism**.[49]

Sexism and gender discrimination are prejudices or discrimination based on a person's sex or gender. Sexism can affect anyone, but it is particularly documented as affecting women. It is linked to stereotypes and gender roles and may include the belief that one sex or gender is intrinsically superior to another. Extreme sexism may foster sexual harassment, rape, and other forms of sexual violence. Sexual harassment is a form of bullying and coercion that is sexual in character and unwelcome or inappropriate behaviour as well as the promise of rewards in exchange for sexual favours. It can be physical, verbal, or written and is often repetitive. In most modern legal contexts, sexual harassment is illegal.

Psychological hazards can also extend to setting inappropriate work tasks that restrict higher levels of control over work, to organisational injustices and unfairness, and even to structural violence.[50] Next to structural violence, there is also **psycho-social violence** at work created through "isolating people, manipulating reputations, withholding information, assigning tasks that do not match capabilities and assigning impossible goals and deadlines".[51]

The preventative approach of OHS tells HR managers that employee care[52] needs to include a **wellness programme** – a company-sponsored plan to encourage "a healthy balance of the mind, body and spirit that results in an overall feeling of wellbeing".[53] On the downside, such programmes can also be "concerned with conditioning workers to frame personal choices in an economising manner, one that is always attentive to the employer's bottom line".[54] This may also lead to "the datafication of health". i.e. "the commodification and exploitation of health data".[55]

Unsurprisingly, many existing employer wellness programmes have been found to provide modest if any benefits to either workers or employers in terms of decreased health expenditure, improved health behaviours, or increased productivity.[56] Sill, these programmes remain popular and can even lead to a discriminatory context when employers make them mandatory. In some cases, employers have (mis-)used wellness programmes to collect "more than 30 GB of data per week"[57] through employer-driven **wearables**.[58] Such WSTTs – wearable and other self-tracking devices[59] – remain the property of the employer but record – often without the permission from employees – health data from employees. This constitutes an invasion of privacy[60] as well as "non-self-determined insecurity".[61]

Similarly, an EAP or **employee assistance programme** (a company-sponsored programme helping employees with a variety of psychological issues, often organised through an external provider) can enhance the physical and mental health of employees and prevent many potential OHS problems.[62] On the downside, such wellness programmes might potentially also be used as "surveillance on a large scale into workers".[63] It can give workers the feeling of "someone is always looking over your shoulder"[64] while simultaneously "shifting responsibility for health onto the worker"[65] and away from those holding the *duty of care*, i.e. management.

### Electronic Surveillance and Privacy

With Internet-based panoptical surveillance techniques – to see all[66] inside an **electronic panopticon**[67] – many workers have entered *The Age of The Electronic Sweatshop*[68] in which management "depicts people as techno-visuals".[69] Still **workers' privacy** are civil and human rights issues. Despite this, some companies have developed "employee ID badges fitted with a microphone, location sensor, accelerometer"[70] and "workplace nanosensors".[71] This is the **digital economy**'s corporate surveillance architecture.[72] The concept of "digital biocapital"[73] promises management to cut payroll expenses by 25% [and] increase sales by 36%.[74]

*Digital Taylorism* uses **workplace surveillance**.[75] This refers to management's ability to monitor, record, and track employee performance, behaviours, and person characteristics in real time.[76] For example, "swipe cards tell warehouse bosses[77] just how long their workers are taking to move a pallet of cans from shelf to truck…how many seconds customer service representatives where pausing between calls or taking to go to the toilet".[78] It uses "biometric tracking".[79] In some cases, it intrudes upon workers' privacy both inside and outside the workplace.[80] To assure workers' privacy, employees and managers can do ten things[81]:

1. Workers must have the right of access to data collected on them;
2. Inform workers clearly and fully before the introduction of information systems;
3. Collect data and only the right data for the right purpose;

4. Data processing must be transparent;
5. Local privacy laws and fundamental human rights must be respected;[82]
6. Workers must have full rights of explanation when data is used;
7. Biometric data and personally identifiable information must be exempt;[83]
8. Equipment revealing workers location can only be introduced if necessary;
9. An inter-company data governance body should be established; and
10. The above-outlined principle should be enforced through collective bargaining.

These principles will ensure that unnecessary conflicts will be avoided. It will also make sure that negative publicity (UPS case) can be avoided. HR managers might liaison with corporate PR. In 2009, UPS delivery trucks, for example, were fitted with 200 sensors tracking everything from driving speeds to stopping times. Amazon forces its employees to carry electronic tablets, so-called wearables (Fitbit and Jawbone)[84] while others rely on telematics which are technologies that wirelessly transmit data from remote sensors and GPS devices to computers for analysis.[85]

In office, "most employees should expect employers to monitor their work email [while] instant message, phone calls, line of written code and mouse-click leave a digital signal"[86] that can be used to monitor workers. Monitoring can become so severe that "going to the bathroom or to get a cup of coffee [can lead to] getting an inactivity alert".[87] In a more severe case of panoptical surveillance, a woman was fired because she carried a "gene linked to breast cancer"[88] – a case of "genetic testing".[89] To avoid these negatives, HR managers can do five things[90]:

1.  introduce such programmes on a non-mandatory but voluntary and participative base;
2.  guarantee a transparent use of collected data;
3.  use validated technologies;
4.  assure that data collection is limited to the workplace; and
5.  provide secure storage for the data that have been collected.[91]

On the other side of the coin are good HR policies (e.g. statements of intent) and structural support for positive OHS policies in addition to a positive workplace culture can prevent many of the psychological and social hazards at work. As much as today's workplaces vary significantly in character, as much do exposures and the danger of workplace accidents.[92] To assess the risk[93] – the likelihood, potentiality, and seriousness – of different workplace hazards, HR managers undertake a **risk assessment** focusing on a three-step procedure:

a.  the identification of hazards;
b.  the likelihood that these hazards occur; and
c.  formulating and implementing strategies that avoid and/or reduce hazards.

Such risk assessments are never "one-offs". Instead, they are ongoing, especially when work tasks change, new technologies are introduced, or operations management processes such as restructuring, etc. are undertaken. In addition, HR managers need to keep their awareness of current OHS laws and regulations up to date. In many countries, OHS legislation demands that all companies, irrespective of size, location, form of ownership, corporate structure (holdings, franchises, etc.), and industry must conduct risk assessments. In many cases, OHS is strongly overseen by state agencies such as, for example, osha.gov (USA); hse.gov.uk (UK), safeworkaustralia.gov.au (Australia), canoshweb.org (Canada), etc. In some countries, state inspectors have strong legal authorities over workplace affairs, while in other countries, trade unions play a decisive role in OHS. Some countries prefer a **consultative approach to OHS** setting up union-management committees that oversee OHS and introduce preventative measures.

## After Prevention Fails I: The Costs of OHS

Consultative approaches like those favoured by the ILO,[94] for example, prevent traditional conflicts such as those between two opposing ideologies found in the "blame the victim" versus "blame the system" idea.[95] Others who have looked beyond such a dichotomy and dug deeper have convincingly established a link between capitalism, neo-liberal ideology, managerialism, work pressure, and OHS incidents.[96] Perhaps many of today's HR managers are aware that neither one is fruitful, opting instead to no longer blame the victim but focusing on the introduction of a positive safety culture at work while overcoming the outdated idea that **OHS is a cost** to the company that is to be reduced. This – hopefully – outdated approach to OHS is still widely signified in the infamous "Ford Pinto" case[97]:

> In the 1970s, the Ford Pinto case taught the nation the basics of cost-benefit analysis. The car had a design flaw in the gas tank that caused at least fifty-nine deaths. Rubber liners would have fixed the problem at a cost of $137 million. But careful calculations of the benefits – all the costs associated with those burned and killed, down to the flowers at the funeral – only added up to $ 49.5 million. *Cost-benefit* analysis said it just didn't pay to redesign the Pinto.

Somewhat similar to the Ford Pinto case is the case of BP's Deepwater Horizon Oil Rig explosion in the Gulf of Mexico in 2010.[98] While the media interest of the explosion focused on the environmental impact, eleven workers were killed at the oil rig. BP[99] was fined US$ 4 billion dollars while the US department of justice commended, "the explosion of the rig was a disaster that resulted from BP's culture of privileging **profits over prudence**"[100] – a case of "Profit over People" as the world's most influential intellectual – Noam Chomsky – would say.[101]

Despite Ford Pinto, BP's "privileging profits over prudence", and many other cases, most HR managers are aware that preventative OHS strategies are the most cost effective way for companies when seeking to save human lives, reduce cost, and secure good corporate PR. Set against that and the idea of corporate social responsibility (CSR) are the many continuous facts about the global use of **sweatshops** with all the known OHS implications. In the living museum of human exploitation, there is nothing in the catalogue of Victorian misery, as narrated by Dickens, Zola, or Gorky, that does not exist somewhere in a Third World city today.[102]

In the continuing saga of "profit over people" more recent cases are to be found such as, for example, the 2013 Rana Plaza collapse – a structural failure and fire (2013) in Dhaka, Bangladesh where an eight-storey commercial building collapsed leading to a death toll of 1,129 and approximately 2,515 injured people being rescued from the building alive.[103] The sweatshop made clothing for Benetton, the Children's Place, Walmart, and others. The seemingly endless string of lack of OHS in sweatshops appears to conflict not only with the much-trumped PR exercise of CSR of most – if not all – western corporations but also with consumers seeking to buy a $5 shirt, raising questions such as "should you really by a \$7.- jeans?"[104] But there are also other OHS costs that come with consumers conditioned to shop cheap.

At the global level, the ILO estimates that the economic costs of work-related illness and injury would be equivalent to a range from 1.8% to 6% of GDP in 2012.[105] But the true human, social, and financial costs of work-related illnesses and deaths are not equally distributed.[106] Overall, the true combined costs of work-related accidents, injuries, illnesses, and deaths seems to follow a roughly distributed figure between company, society, and employees of an approximately "5-20-75" split: 5% of the costs fall onto the company in the form of sick leave, labour turn-over, and legal costs; 20% fall onto society in the form of government health insurance, hospitals, etc.; and 75% onto the employee in the form of lost income, medical payments, etc.[107]

While employers largely escape costs, there are also cases when employers bene-fit from the death of an employee in a very direct way. This occurs when HR sets up **corporate-owned life insurance** (COLI) also known as *janitors insurance* and *death peanuts insurance*.[108] COLI is life insurance on employees' lives that is owned by the employer, with benefits payable either to the employer.[109] Some have argued that COLI is detrimental to OHS as companies under budget pressures with substantial money due upon the death of their workers might have a financial incentive to save on health and safety measures.[110]

## After Prevention Fails II: What to Do

Despite the best efforts of many HR managers, "things still do go wrong", i.e. OHS incidents still occur. While OHS puts high premiums on prevention, OHS incidents are generally followed up by three essential mechanisms (help, compensation, and injury management): (1) immediate response to help and assist injured employees; to inform management, HRM, and regulative authorities, and to record injuries and investigate the incident (exposure to hazards, etc.); (2) OHS **compensation** that is, in many cases, regulated by state law. During this process, HR managers focus on notifying the insurer of the incident; assist with claim submission by employees; complete and forward claims with medical certificates, assess days of work, and maintain regular contact with employees, treatment doctors, and healthcare workers (rehabilitation etc.); (3) **injury management**: on this HR managers deal with questions such as "will an employee need rehabilitation to return to normal duties?" If so, HR managers will refer such employ-ees to appropriate rehabilitation providers in consultation with treating doctors (e.g. diagnosis) and other healthcare providers (trauma counselling, EAPs, etc.); discuss suitable pathways to rehabilitation; develop a "return-to-work plan" (RTW), and coordi-nate progress and implementation of the RTW plan (e.g. restrictions, job transfer, etc.).

In cases where a return to work is not possible, HR managers monitor medical progress and claims, settle issues of no return to work, and close claims. Good HR managers adhering to the "duty of care" are not only aware but also coordinate all stakeholders of injury management such as: employees, OHS officers, trade unions, insurers, doctors, heathcare providers, rehabilitation providers, as well as immediate supervisors, line management, co-workers, and families.

## The Duty of Care and OHS Culture

Perhaps because of a greater general awareness of these issues, many legal systems and jurisdictions have introduced what might be summed up as a "duty of care". The duty of care in general falls onto the employer, the company, and in its finality onto

HR managers. A "duty of care holder" is the employer and those managers who are in control of a business or undertaking. The duty of care also covers students – like those undertaking an MBA degree – while being at university. Similarly, companies have a duty of care towards employees which sometimes includes the setting up of consultative institutions such as the aforementioned employee-management committee. In some countries, the failure to consult can result in substantial corporate fines issued by local regulators. OHS and HR managers ensure the corporate adherence .to the duty of care by setting up such committees, introducing HR policies on OHS, and by fostering a positive OHS culture.

A **positive OHS culture** focuses on a comprehensive body of organisational values, mission statements, HR policies, and patterns of workplace behaviours depicted by managers and employees and directed towards a healthy workplace. Above that, it includes a strong focus on the reduction of workplace hazards, conducting risk assessments throughout the organisation and showing a general awareness and recognition of OHS issues in the daily work practices of a company. A positive OHS culture also includes an OHS **reporting culture** encouraging employees and managers to report OHS incidences, near misses (compulsory in the airline industry), unsafe work practices, inappropriate behaviours and procedures, etc. Many HR managers link good, well-formulated, and codified HR policies on OHS to an overall OHS culture that always includes a strong reporting culture. For that, three elements have been shown to be effective:

1.  the commitment of upper, middle, and line management to OHS;
2.  the involvement and participation of employees in OHS; and
3.  the functioning of a comprehensive OHS management system.

## The OHS Management System

An **OHS management system** is seen as a structured combination of an OHS culture, an OHS reporting culture, strong OHS policies, the existence of a consultative OHS committee, and an integrated approach to performance management that sharpens managers' focus on OHS. While in many cases the overall responsibility of OHS is shared between HRM, executive and senior management as well as line management and employees, the responsibilities for an OHS management system often falls with HR managers. It is HRM that, for example, sets up corporate policies on OHS management systems. In the case of one of the largest insurance corporations operating in over 70 countries with 147,000 employees, its OHS management system (OHSMS) policy states,

> OHSMS is a proactive system designed with the aim of preventing incidents occurring. This is achieved through comprehending workplace hazards and actively managing associated risks.

While OHS in large corporations is usually well organised, the same cannot be said for many, often smaller, organisations. In general, there are three key elements that often prevent a successful OHSMS. The most common five **OHSMS road-blocks** are:

1.  **management**: weak senior management that elects not to focus on OHS and a general lack of commitment to OHS;

2.  **consultation**: the imposition of OHS without sufficient consultation with employees and trade unions;
3.  **outsourcing**: when OHS is used to serve other management agendas such as outsourcing, downsizing, restructuring, internal power plays;
4.  **company size**: the application of OHS in small companies;
5.  **precarious work**: all forms of precarious and a-typical work arrangements (e.g. everything outside of permanent 9-to-5 work such as seasonal work, labour hire,[111] sub-contracting, temporary agencies, irregular working time,[112] being on-call, part-time work, casualisation,[113] etc.)[114] but also younger workers and recent employees.[115]

While these are the most common problems that prevent a successful OHSMS, it remains the case that many of these road-blocks (no. 2–5) are caused by the lack of a genuine commitment of senior management to OHS. Increasingly, the lack of management commitment manifests itself not only in industrial accidents but also in the psychological and social relations at work. As most OECD economies have passed the global trajectory from being:

feudal/agricultural → manufacturing → service/knowledge economy,

non-physical issues such as workplace, occupational, and organisational stress, harassment, bullying, etc. are on the rise. Bullying remains one form of an inappropriate organisational practice that causes stress for the victims. Perhaps more common than bullying is organisational stress. Stress in itself might not be dangerous as a modest level of stress can actually be beneficial to some people. It can encourage some to perform better, especially when working towards a deadline. Many people are relatively unaware that there is positive stress (eustress) and negative stress (distress).[116] Distress can have very serious negative impacts on employees.

### Workplace Stress

Today, occupational, organisational, and **workplace stress** is viewed as an adverse reaction of employees caused by excessive pressures and other unreasonable demands placed on workers by management (restructuring, lack of career progress, organisational change, interpersonal relationships at work, job insecurity, organisational culture, role ambiguity, etc.). In some cases, up to 35% of OHS complaints are caused by pressure placed on employees by management; 25% of stress is caused by harassment, and a staggering 20% of stress is the result of "violence" (e.g. taxi robberies, violence of managers and co-workers, healthcare settings, etc.).[117] Looking at compensation claims, a 2.35 ratio of stress-related claims versus other claims emerge, showing the volume of stress caused by managerial pressure placed on employees. Overall:

*   40% of employees report that their job is very or extremely stressful;
*   25% view their job as a number one stress factor in their lives;
*   75% of today's employees are exposed to more stress than ever before;
*   29% feel quite a bit or extremely stressed at work; and
*   26% of employees feel often or very often *burned out*[118] or *stressed* out at work.[119]

Overall, work stress is often caused by management enforcing HRM's traditional "I manage you" power relationship. In addition, companies in which work stress is more common are often organisations with low staff morale, high absenteeism, or high presenteeism,[120] i.e. "attending work in spite of heath problems",[121] high turnover, poor industrial/labour relations, low quality work, a high rate of accidents and illnesses, and high customer complaints. At Amazon's warehouse outside Fife, Scotland, which uses **wearable trackers**[122] for its 1,500 floor staff, an ambulance visits the warehouse on average once a week to attend to staff in need of medical help.[123] Wearable trackers are one of the lasted gadgets in **micromanagement**. Micromanagement is defined as "the negative controlling behaviors of managers or people with power and authority toward others. Front-line managers/supervisors, team leaders,[124] middle managers, directors, and executives are typically those seen as inflicting micromanagement on the people who report to them". There are questions to be asked to identify micromanagement[125]:

1. Dominance, control, or disruption of your time?
2. Attempts to impose their will by use of raw power or authority?
3. Consistently having to "win"?
4. Complete control over "how" things must be done?
5. Requiring excessive, unnecessary approvals of tasks or decisions?
6. Intense monitoring of your activities?
7. Excessive, unnecessary, redundant reporting requirements?
8. Refusal to delegate?
9. Refusal to accept collaboration?
10. Incomplete, unclear, or distorted information?

Other stress-causing factors are associated with Karasek's four-way "job-demand-control" model:[126]

1. high strain jobs: low decision-making power with high demands;
2. low strain jobs: low demands paired with high decision-making powers;
3. passive jobs: low demands paired with low decision-making powers; and
4. active jobs: high demand with high decision-making powers.

Additional stress factors are a general lack of opportunity for growth and advancement, too heavy workloads, uncertain and undefined job expectations, and too long working hours.[127] There are six known effects of long and irregular working hours:

1. sleep deprivation and disrupted sleeping patterns;[128]
2. increase prevalence of drug abuse;
3. long working hours are stressful;
4. excessive work hours exacerbate work-family conflict;
5. long time spent at work[129] can lead to bullying; and
6. long hours lead to hypertension – high blood pressure.

Many of these effects are less likely to occur in agriculture, forestry, fishing, mining, construction, and manufacturing but more prevalent in transportation, wholesale trade, retail trade, finance, insurance, real estate, and services. In these industries, where workers experience **Workaholism**.[130] It occurs, for example, when employees "are overloaded with duties and assignments experiencing stressful work situations and when taking their work home on weekends and holidays" – they becoming "willing slaves to their careers".[131] In many cases, "people tend to work more hours at home than when they're in the office".[132] Employees can become susceptible to **Chronic Fatigue Syndrome**.[133]

Other stress factors include organisational change and restructuring, poorly designed performance management systems and/or failures in implementation, excessive **work intensification**, reduced job security through outsourcing, off-shoring, and downsizing. Seventy global studies have shown that negative OHS impacts are linked to downsizing, **the survivor syndrome**,[134] and job insecurity.[135] Symptoms of workplace stress can range from alcoholism and depression to suicide,[136] violence, obesity,[137] etc. However, as Oliver James has convincingly demonstrated in his book "The Selfish Capitalist", there is also a close connection "between rising rates of mental stress and the neo-liberal mode of capitalism".[138] To counter mental stress and burnout (see below), forward looking HR managers are aware of the link between wellbeing and higher levels of workplace satisfaction and productivity.[139] They understand that:

- poor mental health is strongly linked to lost productivity;
- higher level of mental health is linked positively to higher productivity;
- stress and burnout impacts negatively on labour productivity;
- workplace wellness programmes deliver tangible benefits for productivity and wellbeing;
- workplace environmental factors impact on mental wellbeing;
- information and communication technology (ICT) can support wellbeing;
- the pursuit of productivity at all cost impacts negatively on wellbeing;
- blurring work/home-life[140] borders reduce wellbeing while reinforcing burnout;

## Burnout

This link not only causes work stress but also what became known as **burnout**,[141] i.e. when work is no longer meaningful to a person.[142] It results from work stress as well as a variety of other work-related factors such as being overworked but also from patterns of over-commitment and total exhaustion of physical and mental resources as a result of excessive striving to reach unrealistic organisational goals.[143] This is by no means a side issue as the increased frequency has been widely noted.[144] It manifests itself in largely four ways:

1. **behavioural**: inflexibility, substance abuse, withdrawal, blaming, making mistakes;
2. **emotional**: irritability, frustration, depression, anger, apathy, etc.;[145]
3. **mental**: lack of concentration, suspicion, self-doubt, memory loss, etc.; and
4. **physical**: exhaustion, digestive problems, muscle tensions, headaches, etc.

While burnout may appear to be a recent issue, it has been around for a long time. Today, it is related to work that includes significant levels of frustration, conflict, and pressure.[146] Burnout often encroaches rather slowly and secretly when employees fail to realise it until it has reached severe levels. HR managers are increasingly recognising this and identify those jobs with higher potentials for burnout such as, for example: air traffic controllers and certain IT-related jobs; job redesign, changes in expectations, altering work schedules, lowing stress levels, improving working conditions, and training can take place to prevent burnout.

## Organisational Suicide and Bullying

One of the more extreme forms of organisational/managerial stress can lead to what is termed organisational or **workplace suicide**. In the USA, there is an "upward trend of suicides in the workplace".[147] In Japan, this has become so common that it is identified using a special term – **karoshi** – literally meaning: death from overworking.[148] In neighbouring China, meanwhile, the infamous case is that of Apple-Foxconn where a large number of employees committed suicide between 2010 and 2013,[149] while in France, three Renault employees took their lives in 2007 and nineteen workers committed suicide (with another twelve attempted suicide) at France's telecom company *Orange*[150] because of **psychological harassment**.[151] These cases, however, only mark the renowned "tip of the iceberg".[152] A different form of workplace pathologies easily leading to bullying and organisational suicide can be found in what Kets de Vries and Miller call *organisational neurotics*.[153] They have identified five neurotic organisations:

*Table 6.2* Five Types of Organisational Neurotics

| No. | Form | Description |
| --- | --- | --- |
| 1 | The paranoid organisation | Defined by suspicion, doubt, and mistrust |
| 2 | The compulsive organisation | Obsessed with tiny details – perfectionism |
| 3 | The dramatic organization | Excessive show of emotions – narcissism |
| 4 | The depressive organisation | Engineers feelings of guilt and inadequacy |
| 5 | The schizoid organization | Detachment, withdrawal, and estrangement |

Whatever the form of an organisational pathologies may be (Table 6.2), organisational suicide is caused by what is known as a hidden problem, namely managerial or organisational bullying that is commonly identified as repeated, unreasonable behaviour directed towards a person or group of persons at the workplace and which creates a risk to health and safety. Bullying is usually directed downward, i.e. from management to employees, from professor to student, from prison warden to inmate, and the like.[154] Many experts have emphasised that organisational bullying is repeated behaviour – these are not "one-off" behaviours. Bullying can also take the form of **Cyberbullying**.[155]

What bullying is can be shown on the following case where a local court fined a company and its managers for bullying a 19-year-old waitress to a point that led to her suicide.[156] The employer was fined $250,000 and three of its employees a total of $85,000 for verbal and physical bullying including relentlessly insulting her, criticising, licking and spitting on the victim, throwing food at her, placing rat killer in her handbag, as well as restraining and pouring sauce over her.

One blogger noted that the restaurant in the above case had a Gordon Ramsay style culture. At the time of the above-noted bullying case, the blogger also noted that local "media were in a frenzy over the bombast of chef Gordon Ramsay and the lack of respect he showed on his promotional trip".[157] While the aforementioned case is certainly a drastic case, overall, organisational bullying is related to an organisational culture that allows, and in some cases, even engineers organisational bullying. Commonly, such organisational culture consists of:

1.  a strong sense of organisational conformity under an authoritarian top-down corporate culture (e.g. boys club) that denies cultural diversity,[158] pluralism, mutual cooperation, and employee participation; [159]
2.  work tasks are poorly designed leaving role ambiguities and uncertainties;[160]
3.  there is either a very low level of control over work tasks under a "do it your way" laissez-faire management style;[161] or,
4.  more commonly, however, is an excessive level of control paired with an overall lack of involvement of employees;
5.  insufficient training of supervisors and line management.

To prevent bullying and improve the general level of such OHS incidents, HR managers tend to introduce the following elements:

*   develop a codified corporate anti-bullying policy;
*   introduce clear job descriptions and specific work tasks;
*   assure that jobs and work tasks are interesting;
*   establish a committee overseeing OHS and bullying;
*   have a clearly outlined "no tolerance" approach to organisational bullying;
*   work towards a comprehensive anti-bulling organisational culture;
*   introduce such an approach to performance management plans;
*   raise bullying awareness among management and staff;
*   have a clear structure for handling of complaints;
*   nominate specific people within the organisation that can be approached in cases of bullying;
*   provide anti-bullying training for management and employees;
*   collect and publicise OHS incidents and successful prevention of bullying;
*   use corporate information systems (emails, bulletins, boards, etc.) to inform employees on OHS and anti-bullying policies and strategies;
*   create a comprehensive disciplinary action programme with clear structures and procedures; and
*   provide access to external investigation agencies and mediation facilities.

The implementation of these steps, together with a plan to ensure that bullying is part of a comprehensive OHS policy portfolio, that risk assessments are conducted, that there is a general recognition on the negative corporate impacts of bullying, and that bullying is part of an OHS management system, can prevent bullying in companies. In addition, HR managers keep records on OHS issues such as organisational injuries, deaths, and illnesses that occurred within the organisation and collect information on risk assessments undertaken, recommendations made to management, external and internal OHS inspections that have taken place, and the like.

In order to fundamentally prevent such OHS issues, HR managers focus on the four essential elements of a successful OHS structure: (1) first and foremost, there must be a commitment from management (duty of care) but also from the employees to OHS; (2) there needs to be system support in the form of state regulation, OHS laws but also internal regulations and rules and a developed body of codified OHS policies; (3) OHS is a participative issue and the more management involves employees, perhaps the more successful OHS will be; and finally, (4) OHS often boils down to an appropriate organisational OHS culture – a culture that values OHS.

# Workbook

## III. Five Discussion Questions on OHS

### And One Report Question on OHS

#### 1. Discussion Questions

1. At times, OHS is seen from three different angles. These are "blame the victim", "blame the system", and the "capitalism/neo-liberalism relationship to OHS". Develop three to four arguments in favour of each approach to OHS.
2. Assuming that forms of precarious work arrangements are indeed enhancing the risk of OHS incidents while simultaneously preventing the introduction of a successful OHS management system, which three recommendations would you – as an HR manager – suggest to eliminate the potential problems caused by precarious work arrangements? Support your answer with two arguments per recommendation.
3. Is OHS (e.g. Ford Pinto) simply a cost to be avoided? Discuss: what are the pros and cons of the "OHS versus cost" issue?
4. Name all stakeholders of OHS and discuss their relationship with one another.
5. OHS can be viewed from six different perspectives (biological-medical, occupational-epidemiological, behaviourist-psychologic, technical-engineering, industrial-sociological; and legal-economic). Find two arguments in favour of each approach to OHS.

#### 2. Report Question:

### On Working with the Corporate Psychopath

Imagine you are an HR manager in a large organisation. You have detected that a manager in your organisation fulfils the criteria of a corporate psychopath.[162] Your CEO has asked you to solve the issue. To discuss possible solutions about the corporate psychopath.[163] Develop four [4] recommendations on how to remedy such an unsustainable situation in your organisation?

## IV. The "5-by-5" Exercise: Five Case Studies and Five Questions

### 6.1 Warehouse and Retail OHS at Super Cheap Friggy

An international retail company called "Super Cheap Friggy" operates across the country specialising in imported white goods (refrigerators, stoves, etc.) but also computers (laptops, iPads, iWatches, etc.) and other consumer electronics (TVs, etc.), mostly from China, Korea, and Japan. The corporation has its headquarter in the capital and geographically distributed administrative management centres in all states. These manage the 154 stores throughout the country. Most of its stores are located in shopping malls and shopping centres. In addition, there are four warehouses (north, south, east, and west). There are independent contractors for transportation. The general working times are 8 am to 6 pm but the four warehouses operate 24/7. Workplaces are organised by a trade union to which most – but not all – employees belong. Union density is higher in the warehouses compared to the company's retail outlets. Super Cheap Friggy employs a culturally mixed workforce ranging from long-term employees to recent migrants and university students. The medium age of the workforce is 31 and the turnover is high. Super Cheap Friggy employs many female workers who work part-time to care for their children. Super Cheap Friggy has outsourced cleaning, maintenance, and security. These services often come as part of the lease agreement with shopping malls. In all warehouses, cleaning, maintenance, and security is conducted through sub-contracting.

1. Develop two OHS policies for staff at Super Cheap Friggy retail outlets and two for its warehouse staff.
2. Seek to reach an agreement with Super Cheap Friggy's trade unions covering OHS issues. Develop five strategies covering policies, training, participation, etc.
3. Imagine you are the HR manager seeking to involve employees in an in-house OHS committee at all levels. How many OHS committees do you propose and why? Name at least two reasons for your choice.
4. Imagine conducting a risk assessment. What kind of OHS risks would you – as the HR manager – reasonably expect (physical, biological, chemical, psychological, etc.)? Name at least four potential OHS risks.
5. When seeking to introduce a comprehensive OHS management system, HR managers often face "road blocks". What are the potential road-blocks at Super Cheap Friggy to establish a successful OHS management system? Name at least four.

### 6.2 Fatigue and Stress at "Fly Away Airport"

Job fatigue and work stress are significant problems faced by many employees and their managers today. These problems can lead to depression – a state of low mood and aversion to activity that can affect a person's thoughts, behaviour, feelings, and sense of well-being; people with depressed mood can feel sad, anxious, empty, hopeless, helpless, worthless, guilty, irritable, ashamed, and restless; they may lose interest in activities that were once pleasurable, experience loss of appetite or overeating, have problems concentrating, remembering details or making decisions, and may contemplate, attempt, or commit suicide. When cases of depression arise as a result of work stress, it may be difficult for HR managers to resolve the problem. In some cases, these problems can lead to situations like the following.

Charlie Shebeen was an air traffic controller supervisor at Fly Away Airport, a regional airport serving several major domestic destinations as well as some overseas locations. Charlie began to experience depression-related problems largely due to severe work stress and mental fatigue on his job. A few months later, he requested and was granted disability leave for the treatment of his mental illness. After eight months, his personal physician (Ms Jenny Fonda) – a recognised expert in depression treatment as well as a licensed consulting psychologist – agreed with Charlie Shebeen that he had sufficiently improved to return to his former position at Fly Away Airport.

Fly Away Airport then sent Charlie Shebeen to the company's physician. After an extensive evaluation, the doctor – Alice Cooper – concluded that while Charlie Shebeen had made considerable strides in overcoming his depression, he should not immediately return to his former supervisory role because the conditions of the job had not changed and Charlie Shebeen was apt to find the stress too overwhelming. Instead, Alice Cooper recommended that Charlie Shebeen be returned to a non-supervisory position on a six months trial basis. The case was to be reviewed at the end of the proposed period. Following the doctor's recommendation only partially, Fly Away Airport decided that Charlie would not return to his former supervisory job on a "permanent basis". Angered by the management decision to remove him "permanently", Charlie Shebeen filed a grievance through Fly Away Airport's dispute resolution procedure leading – potentially – to binding arbitration.

During several conversations between Charlie Shebeen and HR managers, HR maintained that it had the right to rely on the medical opinion of a recognised expert giving a fair and impartial recommendation. The doctor had determined that Charlie Shebeen should not be returned to the supervisor role as it was the cause of his original stress-related problems. HR managers pointed out that Fly Away Airport's disability leave provision states that it "may require appropriate medical documentation if it believes an employee is not fit to return to his or her former position" and that it was their right to consult the company's physician for an opinion. The company's doctor had recommended a six months non-supervisory trial.

Charlie Shebeen responded – through his lawyer, Erin Brockovich – that Fly Away Airport's disability leave provisions were clear but, nevertheless, biased against him as an employee because they completely disregarded the opinion of his own physician and psychologist. According to Charlie Shebeen, "why bother to get expert medical advice if this is dismissed by HR management?". Charlie Shebeen also noted, "I have never felt better. I'm really ready to get back to my old job". Finally, Charlie Shebeen's lawyer – Erin Brockovich – argued that Charlie was the victim of discrimination based on his former state of depression: "what happened to Charlie Shebeen would not have happened if his illness had been a more conventional physical injury".

1. Imagine you are Fly Away Airport's HR manager. What would you suggest to solve the problem outlined above? Develop three recommendations.
2. Imagine you are Fly Away Airport's HR manager. When conflicting medical evidence of two medical experts is presented (i.e. between Mr Shebeen's doctor Jenny Fonda and the company's recommended doctor Alice Cooper), how should an HR manager respond? Support your answer with three arguments.
3. Is there a reasonable ground for the lawyer's claim that the action of HRM amounts to discrimination? Support your answer with three arguments.
4. Imagine you are Fly Away Airport's HR manager seeing beyond the immediate problems of Charlie Shebeen's depression. What organisational changes would you recommend to avoid fatigue, stress, and potential depression of air traffic controllers? Develop four recommendations and support each of them with three arguments.
5. Which approach did Fly Away Airport take: "blame the victim" or "blame the system"? Rather than focusing on Charlie Shebeen, should Fly Away Airport focus

on OHS's core concept of prevention, introducing workplace changes rather than coming to terms with problems "when things go wrong"? Develop four arguments that support your choice.

### 6.3 Sexism at Forcebrook Ltd.

Too many companies are not free of sexism (discrimination based on sex or gender). Many companies and even large corporations in Silicon Valley have a bad reputation when it comes to sexism and sexual harassment. All too often this is based on a culture of masculinity in which men dominate. How these men treat women has been a contentious issue for many years. Beyond that, only about 6% of all venture capital firms are run by women. The case of sexism at Forcebrook Ltd. illustrates this. In the year 2018, Jane Fisher filed a five million dollar lawsuit against her employer, Forcebrook Ltd. The case was about alleged sexual harassment as well as retaliation. Ms Fisher alleged that the firm's top management failed to promote her and provide her with reasonable work tasks following an affair she had with a member of the firm's top management team, Mr Aldo Moro. Ms Fisher said that after the affair ended, Mr Moro made life difficult for her, alleging, "he would cut me out of email conversations, take me off email and even threatened me. Mr Moro stopped inviting me to team meetings as he tried to isolate me". In addition, Forcebrook Ltd.'s top management allegedly tried to portray Ms Fisher as vengeful and resentful. Management made her look like a scorned woman.

Eventually, Forcebrook Ltd. recruited an HR lawyer representing the firm. The lawyer stated that Ms Fisher has not been truthful about the relationship with Mr Aldo Moro. Ms Fisher had a consensual affair with Mr Moro. She wanted a serious commitment from him. During the court trial, one of Ms Fisher's co-workers – Ms Jane Fuller – testified that another manager at Forcebrook Ltd. had given Ms Fisher an erotic thriller ("Lady Chatterley's Lover" by D. H. Lawrence). Ms Fuller also suggested that the firm would benefit from improved HR, corporate policies and effective training of staff.

1. How could sexism and sexual harassment impact on the overall organisational culture at Forcebrook Ltd.? Develop five arguments.
2. In many cases of sexism and sexual harassment, there are often two sides of the story. Outline three arguments that support Mr Aldo Moro's position and three arguments that support Ms Fisher's position.
3. Discuss the following question: has Forcebrook Ltd. failed in its duty of care towards Ms Fisher or Mr Aldo Moro? Find five arguments for your choice.
4. Imagine you are the HR manager of Forcebrook Ltd. seeking to prevent sexual harassment in the future. Develop a detailed "HR policy" that safeguards Mr Aldo Moro as well as Ms Fisher.
5. Since men and women often work in close proximity and relationships between both cannot simply be outlawed, should companies have a policy on "office romance" (consensual relationships between employees)? Find three arguments in favour of such a proposition.

### 6.4 Bullying at "Call-Me" Call Centre

Georgina Bush is the manager of a Call Centre employing 220 female and male staff, half of whom are either temporary or casual employees. The Call Centre operates during normal office hours. Georgina Bush was always very pleased with the call rate the call centre was able to record and believed that her personally monitoring calls on a regular basis kept all staff on their toes. She also appeared to take great pleasure in publicly abusing staff members who she believed did not meet the Call Centre's standards in relation to call rates and customer satisfaction. Georgina Bush also tended to target the temporary and casual staff more than the permanent staff. Most of the staff believed that this tactic was to increase the general work rate.

This behaviour had been going on for some time, sufficient to cause several staff members to seek medical treatment for depression and anxiety. All this information was revealed at an after-hours meeting of trade union members to which also non-union members were invited, arranged by the trade union organiser (Sean Penn), after receiving a call from a concerned member. Sean Penn, the local union organiser, suggested that he would confront Georgina Bush with the complaints concerning her behaviour or raise the issue with senior HR management. Staff was initially reluctant to take this course of action as they were fearful of the consequences for casual staff in particular.

However, they agreed in the first instance that the union members elect a delegate for the workplace. Jennifer Aniston was successfully elected to this position, as other staff members perceived her as a person who Georgina Bush left alone. She had attempted to abuse Jennifer publicly on one occasion, but Jennifer had stood up for herself. She had also warned Georgina Bush that she would report her to senior HR management if she attempted such behaviour again.

Jennifer suggested to the organiser that, before the union take any action, she and the staff would develop a strategy to deal with Georgina Bush. The organiser agreed to this proposal, emphasising that whatever was done would need to involve everybody. Within two weeks, the staff was ready to deal with Georgina Bush. Early after lunch on a Thursday, Georgina Bush came out of her office and in her usual loud voice started to abuse Liz for allegedly giving poor information to clients. Liz ignored her behaviour, and started to tap a pencil very loudly on the edge of her desk. This was the signal for all staff to commence tapping pencils on the edge of their desks.

Georgina Bush was immediately taken aback and confused, and stopped abusing Liz. She said to Liz, "what's going on?" but was ignored. Georgina then turned on her high heels and went back to her office. The staff stopped tapping. The next day, Georgina Bush again started to abuse another staff member. The response was the same. However, this time she asked no questions and went back to her office. On the Monday, Jennifer and two other union members met with Georgina Bush and told her that call centre staff would no longer tolerate her abusive behaviour, and what had happened on Thursday and Friday the previous week was only the beginning of the action they planned to take, unless she was prepared to cease this behaviour. Jennifer also told her that any further discussions on the performance of the call centre would involve all staff – not individuals and that she had 24 hours to agree to this request, otherwise the union would be taking further action against her and the department under current occupational health and safety laws. The next day, Georgina Bush agreed to the request. In the following week, everyone at the call centre joined the union. Later on, Jennifer was also elected the OH&S representative for the workgroup.

1. Imagine you are the HR manager of the company of which the "Call Me" call centre is part. Develop two anti-bullying policies (worker to worker and worker to customer) that ensure that bullying is prevented in the future. Furthermore, develop a training programme relying on the "needs assessment" as outlined in the previous chapter of organisational learning.
2. Outline how bullying is linked to work stress and what the potential consequences for employees, the company, and management are.
3. Bullying had developed to a severe state at "Call Me" call centre while HRM seemed to have been unaware of it. What four steps would you – as the HR manager – undertake to introduce measures that monitor and prevent supervisors from bullying staff?
4. Imagine you are the new OHS representative at the call centre. What potential hazards do you think exist in a call centre working environment? Name at least five potential hazards.
5. Imagine you are a trade union organiser being made aware that bullying was a problem at the company's call centre. How would you go about checking whether bullying is or is not a systemic issue throughout the company? Develop four strategies.

### 6.5 OHS at North Sea Oil Ltd.

As the Hollywood blockbuster "Deep Water Horizon" made headlines, a broader discussion on occupational health and safety (OHS) on off-shore oil rigs took place. As many consumers are busy filling up at their local petrol station, very few think about where the petrol came from. The Hollywood movie demystifies the physical and environmental challenges of real-life oil rig workers. These workers face harsh working conditions. They work exhausting jobs. Oil rig workers also face emotional stress due to being away from their families for twenty-one days at a time. It is dangerous work that resulted in the loss of eleven lives in the case of BP's Deep Water Horizon company.

The reality is that extracting oil is about more than just these eleven BP employees. The industry often employs contractors while these contractors employ subcontractors. In fact, more than 90% of all oil and gas workers are contractors. The Hollywood movie oversimplified the reasons for the incident. It wasn't about the "hero-versus-villain" theme. In the real life, the business case of North Sea Oil Ltd. highlights the real and growing risk in the world of oil extraction.

The oil business is moving more and more towards a contractor model and outsourcing, not necessarily off-shoring. Using contractors might make great business sense. It allows for specialisation. It is assumed to deliver higher quality at reduced costs. Simultaneously, risks are externalised to people outside of the company. In such a fragmented business structure, organisational culture can simply never be controlled by the parent company. There are too many levels.

In today's oil business, contractor vetting hasn't become a standard process. Nonetheless, the industry is moving in this direction. Roughly 20% of suppliers are vetted for multinational industrial companies. For the other 80%, one might suggest the following five elements:

1. A rigorous check of qualifications before external contractors can come on oil rigs;
2. On-going monitoring of potential changes in requirements and contractors' proper industry standings;
3. An annual update of accident records;
4. Trade unions and employee involvement; and
5. Greater state involvement (e.g. regulation by individual countries and the EU).

In many companies, such data have all been kept under lock and key. Overworked general managers and HR managers have buried them in piles of Excel spread sheets. But new technologies solutions can enhance the process of systematisation across an organisation. This is what North Sea Oil Ltd. has successfully implemented. It provides a single source and location for vetting and managing external contractors.

James Dean – co-founder of North Sea Oil Ltd. – has helped to transform the way North Sea Oil Ltd. source suppliers, mitigate supply chain risks, implement sustainable business practices, and improve OHS. Mr Dean held many leadership roles within the company since the early days of North Sea Oil Ltd. Today, North Sea Oil Ltd. is a brand that not only extracts oil but also produces an industry qualification and auditing standard. Mr Dean is driven to educate suppliers and global corporations. Such standards, Mr Dean believes, have positively impacted on North Sea Oil Ltd.'s employees and OHS. It has strengthened the business of North Sea Oil Ltd. and has helped to prevent industrial accidents and save workers' lives.

1. Develop five arguments why OHS is problematic in companies – like North Sea Oil Ltd. – with a high degree of sub-contracting and outsourcing?
2. How can the five suggestions (above) improve OHS? Develop one argument for each of the five aspects.
3. How can trade unions and employee involvement improve OHS? Develop four arguments for trade unions and employee participation in OHS.
4. The case of North Sea Oil Ltd. suggests that a rigorous vetting system of sub-contractors can improve OHS. Explain why this is the case by developing four arguments in favour of such a systematic vetting system.
5. Imagine you are the HR manager at North Sea Oil Ltd. Develop two policies on OHS. One policy should be directed towards trade unions and employee involvement while the second policy should focus on the vetting of sub-contractors.

## V. A Suggestion for an Online Guest Lecture

Former Buddhist monk, *Huffington Post* and *Guardian* author Andy Puddicombe explains the significance of "All it takes is 10 mindful minutes" (2012)

www.ted.com/talks/andy_puddicombe_all_it_takes_is_10_mindful_minutes
[the online guest lecture above is merely a suggestion – www.ted.com/talks offers
additional material to choose from]

## VI. List of Suggested Documentaries on OHS

The carefully selected documentary videos below are mere suggestions to be used during tutorials. Documentaries have been selected to achieve two things: (1) to explain key HRM themes and (2) to provide an insight into the reality of HRM. Typically, these short documentaries should be viewed in class followed by a class discussion on the content of the video. Alternatively, questions on documentaries can be prepared beforehand and small group discussions can follow up the video after viewing is concluded. Should any of the web links no longer function, please conduct an internet search for other – alternative – documentaries related to your tutorial topic (e.g. filmsforaction.org):

Inside Amazon: www.youtube.com/watch?v=Xaw-yCbB3QQ

Asbestos: www.youtube.com/watch?v=OTiF3xGXFTI

Factory Fire in NY: www.youtube.com/watch?v=noL8nFSzsDc#t=14

Workplace Stress: www.youtube.com/watch?v=D-7kdUHFg9E

The New Boss: www.youtube.com/watch?v=f9OT0HTauKU

OHS Office Space: www.youtube.com/watch?v=zyISNOd7TGU

Wellness: www.youtube.com/watch?v=GOYbeW1UE_k

Oil Tank Drivers: www.youtube.com/watch?v=AZidpiFbnTI&feature=youtu.be

Fashion Industry: www.youtube.com/watch?v=VdLf4fihP78&noredirect=1

OHS-Europe: https://osha.europa.eu/en

OHS-Australia: www.safeworkaustralia.gov.au/sites/swa/pages/default

## Notes

1 With an 8% vs. 92% female to male ratio.
2 For a short history on OHS, see: Friis, R. H. 2016. *OHS for the 21st Century*, Burlington: Jones & Bartlett Learning, pp. 7–20.
3 www.ilo.org/global/topics/safety-and-health-at-work/lang–en/index.htm.
4 http://www.abcnewspoint.com/top-10-most-dangerous-jobs-in-the-world/.
5 Cederström, C. & Spicer, A. 2015. *The Wellness Syndrome*, Malden: Polity Press; Guest, D. 2002. HRM, corporate performance and employee wellbeing: building the worker into HRM, *Journal of Industrial relations*, 44(3):335–358; Renee Baptiste, N. 2008. Tightening the link between employee wellbeing at work and performance: a new dimension for HRM, *Management Decision*, 46(2):284–309; Pawar, B. S. 2016. Workplace spirituality and employee well-being: an empirical examination, *Employee Relations*, 38(6) (online before print).
6 Bal, P. M. 2020. Why we should stop measuring performance and well-being, *Zeitschrift für Arbeits-und Organisationspsychologie*, 64(3):196–215.
7 https://www.who.int/news-room/fact-sheets/detail/human-rights-and-health.
8 https://www.ilo.org/global/standards/subjects-covered-by-international-labour-standards/occupational-safety-and-health/lang–en/index.htm.
9 www.who.int/occupational_health/publications/newsletter/en/gohnet5e.pdf.
10 Epidemiology is the study of the patterns, causes, and effects of health and disease conditions in defined populations. It is the cornerstone of public health, and shapes policy decisions and evidence-based practice by identifying risk factors for disease and targets for preventive healthcare.

11 Bohle, P. & Quinlan, M. 2010. *Managing Occupational Health and Safety: A Multidisciplinary Approach* (3rd ed.), Melbourne: Macmillan.

12 Lloyd's Register Foundation World Risk Poll (2020) noted that worldwide, nine out of ten people, say governments should require business to adopts safety procedures. In other words, there is support for regulation that would reduce risks and improve safety, especially in the workplace (https://wrp.lrfoundation.org.uk/, accessed: 25th January 2021).

13 Bruyère, S. M. (eds.) 2016. *Disability and Employer Practices*, New York: Columbia University Press.

14 Kessler, S. R. et al. 2020. "Walking the talk": the role of frontline supervisors in preventing workplace accidents, *European Journal of Work and Organizational Psychology*, 29(3):450–461.

15 https://www.youtube.com/watch?v=Hdg4lfQrwC8&t=16s.

16 Baldry, C. & Barnes, A. 2012. The open-plan academy: space, control and the undermining of professional identity, *Work Employment & Society*, 26(2):228–245.

17 https://www.zdnet.com/article/coronavirus-open-offices-have-americans-worried/.

18 ergonomics.com.au/how-to-sit-at-a-computer/.

19 Van Tulder, M., Malmivaara, A. & Koes, B. 2007. Repetitive strain injury, *The Lancet*, 369(9575):1815–1822.

20 Konz, S. A. & Mital, A. 1990. Carpal tunnel syndrome, *International Journal of Industrial Ergonomics*, 5(2):175–180.

21 https://www.osha.gov/SLTC/etools/computerworkstations/positions.html.

22 Fisher, M. 2011. The privatisation of stress, *Soundings*, 48(48):127.

23 https://www.bbc.com/worklife/article/20200508-how-to-work-from-home-comfortably-ergonomic-tips-covid-19; https://osha.europa.eu/en/highlights/supporting-musculoskeletal-health-workplace-find-out-all-you-need-know.

24 Weinberg, A. et al. 2015. *Organizational Stress Management: A Strategic Approach*, Berlin/London: Springer; Parker, M. 2017. Management by stress, *Catalyst*, 1(20): catalyst-journal.com.

25 Aljazeera. 2016. Samsung Endangered Workers Health in S Korea (aljazeera.com, 10th August 2016).

26 ebooklibrary.org/articles/eng/lists_of_nuclear_disasters_and_radioactive....

27 http://www.cdc.gov/niosh/topics/cancer/.

28 https://www.youtube.com/watch?v=_zXFxwYao2Y.

29 Mukherjee, S. 2010. *Surviving Bhopal*, Basingstoke: Palgrave Macmillan.

30 http://www.asbestosdiseaseawareness.org/archives/35292.

31 http://www.who.int/occupational_health/topics/asbestos_documents/en/; http://nochrysotileban.com/archives/261; Haigh, G. 2006. *Asbestos House: The Secret History of James Hardie Industries*, Melbourne: Scribe; Teugels, M. 2007. The dirty legacy of asbestos, *Le Monde Dimplomatique*, modediplo.com, 15th January 2007, 4 pages; http://www.ibasecretariat.org/.

32 http://www.technologylawsource.com/files/2009/04/ETUC-Resolution-on-Nanotechnologies-and-Nanomateri.pdf.

33 WHO. 2010. Health Impact of the Psychosocial Hazards of Work: An Overview (https://www.who.int/occupational_health/publications/hazardpsychosocial/en/, accessed: 15th April 2021).

34 Reitz, M. & Higgins, J. 2019. Managers, You're More Intimidating Than You Think, *Harvard Business Review*, 18th July 2019; Akella, D. 2020. *Understanding Workplace Bullying*, London: Palgrave-Macmillan.

35 Taylor, S. G. 2019. Why people get away with being rude at work, *Harvard Business Review*, 10th July 2019.

36 Klikauer, T. 2018. Hannibal Lector goes to work: the psychopath factory – how capitalism organises empathy, *Organization*, 25(3):448–451.

37 Liang, L. H. et al. 2016. Why are abusive supervisors abusive?, *Academy of Management Journal*, 59(4):1385–1406.

38 https://www.youtube.com/watch?v=BJL2P0JsAS4&t=4s.

39 Yuan, Z. et al. 2020. Put you down versus tune you out: further understanding active and passive e-mail incivility, *Journal of Occupational Health Psychology*, 25(5):33–344.

40 McClure, E. & Rini, R. 2020. Microaggression: conceptual and scientific issues, *Philosophy Compass*, 15(4):e12659.

41 Kurtulmus, B. E. 2018. *The Dark Side of Leadership*, New York: Macmillan Publisher, p. 15.

42 Su, A. J. 2016. How to handle a colleague who's a jerk, *Harvard Business Review*, 22nd November 2016, p. 2; cf. https://hbr.org/product/hbr-guide-to-office-politics/13989-PBK-ENG.

43 Quine, L. 2001. Workplace bullying in nurses, *Journal of Health Psychology*, 6(1):73–84.

44 https://hbr.org/2020/06/youre-not-powerless-in-the-face-of-online-harassment.

45 Bhat, C. S. 2018. Proactive cyberbullying and sexting prevention in Australia and the USA, *Journal of Psychologists and Counsellors in Schools*, 28(1):120–130; Drouin, M., Hernandez, E. & Wehle, S. M. 2018. "Tell me lies, tell me sweet little lies:" sexting deception among adults, *Sexuality & Culture*, 22(3):865–880.

46 Binder, N. V. 2018. From the message board to the front door: addressing the offline consequences of race-and gender-based doxxing and swatting. *Suffolk University Law Review*, 51:55; Pittman, J. 2018. Privacy in the age of doxxing, *Southern Journal of Business and Ethics*, 10:53–58.

47 Patty, A. 2021. Smart bullies' emerge in universities in new workplace trend (https://www.smh.com.au/business/workplace/smart-bullies-emerge-in-universities-in-new-workplace-trend-20210418-p57k57.html, 19th April 2021, accessed: 25th April 2021).

48 Burn, S. M. 2019. The psychology of sexual harassment, *Teaching of Psychology*, 46(1):96–103.

49 Johnson, S. K. 2019. Has sexual harassment at work decreased since #MeToo?, *Harvard Business Review*, 18th July 2019.

50 DeMaio, F. 2015. Paul Farmer: structural violence and the embodiment of inequality, in: Collyer, F. (eds.) *Handbook of Social Theory for Health and Medicine*, Basingstoke: Palgrave; Cohen, A. 2015. *Fairness in the Workplace: A Global Perspective*, New York: Palgrave; Rawls, J. 2001. *Justice as Fairness: A Restatement* (edited by Erin Kelly), London: Belknap Press.

51 Doorn, N. 2021. Stepping stone or dead end, in: Baines, D. & Cunningham, I. (eds.) *Working in the Context of Austerity*, Bristol: Bristol University Press, p. 49.

52 Peisert, J. 2016. Engagement and retention: essentials of employee care; in: Zeuch, M. (eds.) *Handbook of HRM*, Heidelberg: Springer, p. 709.

53 Ajunwa, I., Crawford, K. & Schultz, J. 2017. Limitless worker surveillance. *California Law Review*, 105:764.

54 Hull, G. & Pasquale, F. 2017. Towards a critical theory of corporate wellness, *BioSocieties*, 13(1):191.

55 Ruckenstein, M. & Schüll, N. D. 2017. The datafication of health, *Annual Review of Anthropology*, (46):263.

56 Marchant, G. E. 2019. What are best practices for ethical use of nanosensors for worker surveillance?, *AMA Journal of Ethics*, 21(4):357.

57 Moore, P. & Robinson, A. 2016. The quantified self: what counts in the neoliberal workplace, *New Media & Society*, 18(11):2776.

58 https://www.bbc.com/news/business-55637328.

59 Moore, P. & Robinson, A. 2016. The quantified self: what counts in the neoliberal workplace, *New Media & Society*, 18(11):2775.

60 Miller, J. 2018. *Augmenting Workplace Wellness Programes with Biometric Monitoring*, Eugene: University of Oregon, p. 32 (https://scholarsbank.uoregon.edu/xmlui/bitstream/handle/1794/24349/Miller_2018.pdf, accessed: 5th April 2019).

61 Moore, P. & Robinson, A. 2016. The quantified self: what counts in the neoliberal workplace, *New Media & Society*, 18(11):2777.

62 fortune.com/2015/04/13/corporate-wellness.

63 O'Neil, C. 2016. *Weapons of Math Destruction*, New York: Crown, p. 303; cf. Ball, K. 2010. Workplace surveillance: an overview, *Labor History*, 51(1):87–106; Clawson, D. & Clawson, M. A. 2017. IT Is watching: workplace surveillance and worker resistance, *New Labor Forum*, 26(2):62–69; Holborow, M. 2012. What is neoliberalism?, in: Block, D., Gray, J. & Holborow, M. (eds.) *Neoliberalism and Applied Linguistics*, London: Routledge, p. 22.

64 Kaplan, E. 2015. The spy who fired me: the human costs of workplace monitoring, *Harper's Magazine*, 330(1978):10.

65 Miller, J. 2018. *Augmenting Workplace Wellness Programes with Biometric Monitoring*, Eugene: University of Oregon, p. 50 (https://scholarsbank.uoregon.edu/xmlui/bitstream/handle/1794/24349/Miller_2018.pdf, accessed: 5th April 2019).

66 Gill, S. 1995. The global panopticon?, *Alternatives*, 20(1):11.

67 Wookcock, J. 2020. The algorithmic panopticon at Deliveroo: measurement, precarity, and the illusion of control (http://www.ephemerajournal.org/contribution/algorithmic-panopticon-deliveroo-measurement-precarity-and-illusion-control, accessed: 25th October 2020).

68 Lee, L. T. 1994. Watch your e-mail-employee e-mail monitoring and privacy law in the age of the electronic sweatshop, *Journal of Marshall Law Review*, 28:139.

69 Miller, J. 2018. *Augmenting Workplace Wellness Programes with Biometric Monitoring*, Eugene: University of Oregon, p. 43 (https://scholarsbank.uoregon.edu/xmlui/bitstream/handle/1794/24349/Miller_2018.pdf, accessed: 5th April 2019).

70 Ajunwa, I., Crawford, K. & Schultz, J. 2017. Limitless worker surveillance, *California Law Review*, 105:743.

71 Marchant, G. E. 2019. What are best practices for ethical use of nanosensors for worker surveillance?, *AMA Journal of Ethics*, 21(4):356.

72 https://neweconomics.org/uploads/files/Data_and_work_FINAL.pdf.

73 Miller, J. 2018. *Augmenting Workplace Wellness Programes with Biometric Monitoring*, Eugene: University of Oregon, p. 37 (https://scholarsbank.uoregon.edu/xmlui/bitstream/handle/1794/24349/Miller_2018.pdf, accessed: 5th April 2019).

74 Kaplan, E. 2015. The spy who fired me: the human costs of workplace monitoring, *Harper's Magazine*, 330(1978):2.

75 Smith, Z. 2019. Blame the boss, not the robot, *New Labor Forum*, 28(2):67.

76 Warin, R. & McCann, D. 2018. Who Watches the Workers?, p. 7 (https://neweconomics.org, 2018, accessed: 5th May 2019).

77 https://www.youtube.com/watch?v=Xaw-yCbB3QQ.

78 Peetz, D. 2019. *The Realities and Futures of Work*, Canberra: ANU Press, p. 7.

79 Miller, J. 2018. *Augmenting Workplace Wellness Programes with Biometric Monitoring*, Eugene: University of Oregon, p. 46 (https://scholarsbank.uoregon.edu/xmlui/bitstream/handle/1794/24349/Miller_2018.pdf, accessed: 5th April 2019).

80 Marchant, G. E. 2019. What are best practices for ethical use of nanosensors for worker surveillance?, *AMA Journal of Ethics*, 21(4):357.

81 UNI. 2019. *Top 10 Principles* (http://www.thefutureworldofwork.org, accessed: 5th April 2019).

82 https://www.ilo.org/safework/info/standards-and-instruments/codes/WCMS_107797/lang--en/index.htm.

83 Miller, J. 2018. *Augmenting Workplace Wellness Programes with Biometric Monitoring*, Eugene: University of Oregon, p. 8 (https://scholarsbank.uoregon.edu/xmlui/bitstream/handle/1794/24349/Miller_2018.pdf, accessed: 5th April 2019).

84 https://neweconomics.org/uploads/files/Data_and_work_FINAL.pdf.

85 Kaplan, E. 2015. The spy who fired me: the human costs of workplace monitoring, *Harper's Magazine*, 330(1978):2.

86 Ajunwa, I., Crawford, K. & Schultz, J. 2017. Limitless worker surveillance, *California Law Review*, 105:748 & 771.

87 Kaplan, E. 2015. The spy who fired me: the human costs of workplace monitoring, *Harper's Magazine*, 330(1978):10.

88 Ajunwa, I., Crawford, K. & Schultz, J. 2017. Limitless worker surveillance, *California Law Review*, 105:755.

89 Ruckenstein, M. & Schüll, N. D. 2017. The datafication of health, *Annual Review of Anthropology*, (46):266.

90 Marchant, G. E. 2019. What are best practices for ethical use of nanosensors for worker surveillance?, *AMA Journal of Ethics*, 21(4):358f.

91 http://www.thefutureworldofwork.org/media/35421/uni_workers_data_protection.pdf.

92 https://www.entrepreneur.com/article/313483.

93 https://zcomm.org/znetarticle/the-risk-of-capitalism/.

94 ILO. 2012. Decent Work Agenda (http://www.ilo.org/wcmsp5/groups/public/--dgreports/--integration/documents/publication/wcms_229374.pdf).

95 Smith, Z. 2019. Blame the boss, not the robot, *New Labor Forum*, 28(2):66–69.

96 McQueen, H. 2009. *Framework of Flesh – Builders' Labourers Battle for Health & Safety*, Canberra: Ginninderra Press; Barnetson, B. 2011. Making capitalism safe: work safety and health regulation in America, 1880–1940, *Labour/Le Travail*, 67(1):261–263; Bittle, S. 2015. Rational corporation meets disciplined worker: the (re) production of class subjects in corporate crime law reform, *Capital & Class* (online before print).

97 motherjones.com/politics/1977/09; Magretta, J. 2012. *What Management Is – How It Works and why It's Everyone's Business*, New York: Free Press; cf. https://www.youtube.com/watch?v=2qjM0CQTBn4.

98  https://www.theguardian.com/environment/bp-oil-spill; cf. for Royal Dutch/Shell's Bent Spar see: Micklethwait, J. & Wooldridge, A. 1996. *The Witch Doctors: Making Sense of the Management Gurus*, New York: Times Books, p. 178.

99  Bakan, J. 2020. *The New Corporation*, New York: Vintage Books, pp. 36–40.

100 http://www.justice.gov/opa/pr/bp-exploration-and-production-inc-agrees-plead-guilty-felony-manslaughter-environmental.

101 Chomsky, N. 1999, *Profit over People: Neoliberalism and Global Order*, New York: Seven Stories Press.

102 Davis, M. 2007. *Planet of Slums*, London: Verso, p. 186.

103 www.bbc.com/news/world-asia-22476774.

104 http://www.smh.com.au/national/education/target-and-kmart-sell-2-school-uniforms-but-at-what-cost-20160112-gm4n1y.html;    http://www.news.com.au/lifestyle/fashion/kmart-target-and-big-w-how-do-australias-retail-giants-make-their-jeans-so-cheap/news-story/93e6bf02d566270849193384fd719c9d; Yangzom, D. 2016. Clothing & social movements, *Social Movement Studies*, 15(6):622–633.

105 http://www.ilo.org/wcmsp5/groups/public/—ed_protect/—protrav/—safework/documents/publication/wcms_207690.pdf.

106 http://www.ilo.org/wcmsp5/groups/public/—ed_protect/—protrav/—safework/documents/publication/wcms_207690.pdf;    https://www.osha.gov/dcsp/products/topics/businesscase/costs.html; Friis, R. H. 2016. *OHS for the 21st Century*, Burlington: Jones & Bartlett Learning.

107 www.ilo.org/safework/info/publications/WCMS_207690/.../index.htm.

108 Sandel, M. J. 2012. *What Money Can't Buy: The Moral Limits of Markets*, London: Penguin.

109 Veldhuizen, M. 2019. Corporate life insurance - opportunities to die for (https://www2.deloitte.com/ca/en/pages/tax/articles/corporate-life-insurance.html, accessed: 15th October 2019).

110 Ralph, M. 2017. The price of life: from slavery to corporate life insurance, *Dissent*, 64(2):63–67.

111 The first recorded employment agency was established by Théophraste Renaudot in France in 1630 (Lewchuck, W. 2021. The age of increased precarious employment: origins and implications, in: Baines, D. & Cunningham, I. (eds.) *Working in the Context of Austerity*, Bristol: Bristol University Press, p. 31).

112 https://edition.cnn.com/videos/business/2021/07/09/iceland-shorter-working-week-vpx.cnnbusiness/video/playlists/top-news-videos/.

113 The ILO noted tin its 2015 World Employment and Social Outlook report that three-quarters of the world's workforce were on temporary or short-term contracts (Tourish, D. 2020. *Management studies – Fraud, Deceptions & Meaning Research*, Cambridge, Cambridge University Press, p. 214).

114 Dekker, F. & van der Veen, R. 2015. Modern working life: a blurring of the boundaries between secondary and primary labour markets?, *Economic and Industrial Democracy* (published online before print, January 21, 2015, https://doi.org/10.1177/0143831X14563946); Bohle, P., Pitts, C., & Quinlan, M. 2010. Time to call it quits? The safety and health of older workers, *International Journal of Health Services*, 40(1):23–41.

115 Cioni, M. & Savioli, M. 2015. Safety at the workplace: accidents and illnesses, *Work, Employment & Society*, 30(5):858–875.

116 www.brocku.ca/health-services/health-education/stress/eustress-distress; Le Fevre, M., Matheny, J. & Kolt, G. S. 2003. Eustress, distress, and interpretation in occupational stress, *Journal of Managerial Psychology*, 18(7):726–744; Kozusznik, M. W., Rodríguez, I. & Peiró, J. M. 2015. Eustress and distress climates in teams: patterns and outcomes, *International Journal of Stress Management*, 22(1):1–23.

117 Guay, S., Goncalves, J. & Jarvis, J. 2015. A systematic review of exposure to physical violence across occupational domains according to victims' sex, *Aggression and Violent Behavior*, 25:133–141; Ward, J. & McMurray, R. 2015. *The Dark Side of Emotional Labour*, London: Routledge; Gill, M. et al. 2013. *Violence at Work*, London: Routledge.

118 Saunders, E. G. 2019. 6 causes of burnout, and how to avoid them, *Harvard Business Review*, 5th July 2019; Rajendran, N., Watt, H. M. & Richardson, P. W. 2020. Teacher burnout and turnover intent, *Australian Educational Researcher*, 47:477–500; cf. https://www.wired.co.uk/article/burnout-workplace-coronavirus.

119  http://www.cdc.gov/niosh/docs/99-101/.

120  "Presenteeism" is the term given when sick workers come to work, work at levels that are less than optimal, and risk infecting others (https://www.ohsrep.org.au/presenteeism; https://www.bbc.com/worklife/article/20210604-why-presenteeism-always-wins-out-over-productivity).

121  Lohaus, D. & Habermann, W. 2019. Presenteeism, *Human Resource Management Review*, 29(1):43.

122  Vidal, M., Turner, J., Bulling, A. & Gellersen, H. 2012. Wearable eye tracking for mental health monitoring, *Computer Communications*, 35(11):1306–1311; cf. Shin, G., Jarrahi, M. H., Fei, Y., Karami, A., Gafinowitz, N., Byun, A. & Lu, X. 2019. Wearable Activity trackers, accuracy, adoption, acceptance and health impact: a systematic literature review, *Journal of Biomedical Informatics*, (93):103–153.

123  Warin, R. & McCann, D. 2018. Who Watches the Workers? (https://neweconomics.org, 2018, accessed: 5th May 2019), p. 11.

124  https://hbr.org/2018/04/how-humble-leadership-really-works?utm_medium=social&utm_campaign=hbr&utm_source=facebook&tpcc=orgsocial_edit.

125  Chambers, H. E. 2014. *My Way Or the Highway: The Micromanagement Survival Guide*, San Francisco, CA: Berrett-Koehler Publishers, pp. 4–8.

126  Karasek Jr, R. A. 1979. Job demands, job decision latitude, and mental strain: implications for job redesign, *Administrative Science Quarterly*, 24(2):285–308.

127  McChesney, R. W. 2013. *Digital Disconnect*, New York: The New Press, p. 218; cf. Micklethwait, J. & Wooldridge, A. 1996. *The Witch Doctors: Making Sense of the Management Gurus*, New York: Times Books, p. 207.

128  Crary, J. 2013. *24/7: Late Capitalism and the Ends of Sleep*, London: Verso.

129  For Goldman Sachs' "inhumane workplace of 95-hours per week" see: https://edition.cnn.com/2021/03/22/business/goldman-sachs-saturday-rule-workplace-survey/index.html.

130  Bakker, A. B., Demerouti, E. & Burke, R. 2009. Workaholism and relationship quality: a spillover-crossover perspective, *Journal of Occupational Health Psychology*, 14(1):23.

131  Samuel, Y. 2010. *Organizational Pathology*, New Brunswick: Transaction Publishers, p. 43f.

132  Kaplan, E. 2015. The spy who fired me: the human costs of workplace monitoring, *Harper's Magazine*, 330(1978):9.

133  Holmes, G. P. et al. 1988. Chronic fatigue syndrome: a working case definition, *Annals of internal medicine*, 108(3):387–389; cf. Schneiderman, N. et al. 2018. *Stress and Disease Processes*, New York: Psychology Press.

134  Peetz, D. 2019. *The Realities and Futures of Work*, Canberra: ANU Press, p. 10.

135  Quinlan, M. & Bohle, P. 2009. Overstretched and unreciprocated commitment: reviewing research on the occupational health and safety effects of downsizing and job insecurity, *International Journal of Health Services*, 39(1):1–44.

136  https://edition.cnn.com/2019/05/06/business/france-telecom-orange-suicides-trial/index.html.

137  Obesity is seen as a medical condition characterised by the excessive accumulation of body fat generously supported by global junk-food corporations and its advertising agencies. Obesity can be assessed through the "body mass index": ≤30 kg/m$^2$.

138  Quoted from: Fisher, M. 2009. *Capitalist Realism: Is There No Alternative?*, Winchester: Zero Books, p. 19.

139  Isham, A. et al. 2019. Wellbeing and Productivity, Guildford: Centre for the Understanding of Sustainable Prosperity (free download: https://www.cusp.ac.uk/themes/s1/wp22/, accessed: 15th January 2020).

140  https://www.abc.net.au/news/2020-03-16/coronavirus-working-from-home-legal-liability-employment-law/12056942.

141  Maslach, C. & Goldberg, J. 1998. Prevention of burnout: new perspectives, *Applied and preventive psychology*, 7(1):63–74.

142  HBR. 2017. Beating burnout, *Harvard Business Review*, 95(1):19.

143  Han, B.-C. 2015. *The Burnout Society*, Stanford, CA: Stanford University Press.

144  It led to the introduction of an academic journal exclusively dedicated to burnout: Burnout Research (sciencedirect.com/science/journal/22130586/2/1).

145  Bugdol, M. & Nagody-Mrozowicz, K. 2021. *Management, Organization and Fear*, New York: Routledge.

146    Garton, E. 2017. Employee burnout is a problem with the company, not the person, *Harvard Business Review*, 6th April 2017.

147    Tiesman, H. M. et al. 2015. Suicide in US workplaces, 2003–2010: a comparison with non-workplace suicides, *American Journal of Preventive Medicine*, 48(6):674.

148    O'Reilly, L. 2016. The Boss of Japan's Biggest Ad Company Dentsu Is Stepping Down after an Overworked Employee Committed Suicide (www.businessinsider.com.au: 29th December 2016); cf. www.japantimes.co.jp/tag/karoshi/; www.economist.com/node/10329261.

149    Chan, J. 2013. A suicide survivor: the life of a Chinese worker, *New Technology, Work and Employment*, 28(2):84–99 (http://www.cbsnews.com/news/what-happened-after-the-foxconn-suicides).

150    Kottasová, I. & Vandoorne, S. 2019. French Telecom Company and Former CEO Face Trial over Wave of Suicides (https://edition.cnn.com, 6th May 2019, accessed: 15th May 2019).

151    Crawshaw, L. 2009. Workplace bullying? Mobbing? Harassment? Distraction by a thousand definitions, *Consulting Psychology Journal*, 61(3):263.

152    Tiesman, H. M., Konda, S., Hartley, D., Menéndez, C. C., Ridenour, M. & Hendricks, S. 2015. Suicide in US workplaces, 2003–2010: a comparison with non-workplace suicides, *American Journal of Preventive Medicine*, 48(6):674–682.

153    Kets de Vries, M. F. & Miller, D. 1984. Neurotic style and organizational pathology, *Strategic Management Journal*, 5(1):35–55.

154    Blass, T. 2002. The man who shocked the world. *Psychology Today*, March/April, pp. 68–74; Blass, T. 1999. The milgram paradigm after 35 years: some things we now know about obedience to authority, *Journal of Applied Social Psychology*, 29(5):955–978.

155    Cyberbullying…is bullying perpetrated with digital technology. Unique features of cyberbullying have been identified: Perpetrators can conceal their identities; they have constant access to targets; the potential audience is huge; the perpetrator does not see the target's immediate reaction; there are no nonverbal clues to the meaning of a message; the power imbalance is altered (the perpetrator may have little power in the real world but superior technological skills), and content that is posted online is permanent (Bauman, S. 2013. Cyberbullying: what does research tell us?, *Theory Into Practice*, 52(4):249–256).

156    http://safetyatworkblog.com/2010/02/09/ohs-and-the-death-of-brodie-panluck-from-bullying/.

157    www.parliament.vic.gov.au/publications/research-papers/…/download;    http://www.smh.com.au/national/workers-fined-115000-over-bullying-of-cafe-waitress-20100208-nlrj.html; http://www.heraldsun.com.au/news/opinion/no-justice-for-young-brodie/story-e6frfhqo-1225828034597; http://safetyatworkblog.com/2010/02/09/ohs-and-the-death-of-brodie-panluck-from-bullying/.

158    Parry, E. & McCarthy, J. (eds.) 2017. *The Palgrave Handbook of Age Diversity and Work*, Basingstoke: Palgrave.

159    Whyte, W. H. 1961. *The Organization Man*, Harmondsworth: Penguin.

160    Postle, K. 2002. Working "between the idea and the reality": ambiguities and tensions in care managers' work, *British Journal of Social Work*, 32(3):335–351.

161    Fleming, P. & Sturdy, A. 2009. *Just Be Yourself!: Towards Neo-normative Control in Organisations?*, *Employee Relations*, 31(6):569–583.

162    http://www.abc.net.au/science/articles/2015/02/06/4174047.htm;    https://www.youtube.com/watch?v=GaeJCA4nRPI.

163    Klikauer, T. 2018. Hannibal Lector goes to work: the psychopath factory – how capitalism organises empathy, *Organization*, 25(3):448–451.

## Further Readings

Adams, L. V. 2015. *Diseases of Poverty*, Hanover: Dartmouth College Press.

Alam, J. 2013. Bangladesh Factory Collapse: Death Toll Climbs Past 1,000 (www.huffingtonpost.com).

Alidina, S. & Adams, J. 2014. *Mindfulness at Work for Dummies*, New York: John Wiley & Sons.

Almond, P. 2013. *Corporate Manslaughter and Regulatory Reform*, New York: Palgrave Macmillan.

Archer, R. et al. 2015. *Work Health & Safety* (4th ed.), London: Cengage.

Berinato, S. 2015. Corporate Wellness Programs Make Us Unwell, *Harvard Business Review*, May, 93:5.

Bridger, E. 2014. *Employee Engagement*, London: Kogan Page.

Bullyboys. beatingthebullyboss.wordpress.com/2012/05/25/working-with-monsters/.

Cederström, C. & Spicer, A. 2015. *The Wellness Syndrome*, Malden: Polity Press.

Cheang, H. S. & Appelbaum, S. H. 2015. Corporate Psychopath: Deviant Workplace Behaviour and Toxic Leaders, *Industrial and Commercial Training*, 47(4).

Freudenberg, N. 2014. *Lethal But Legal: Corporations…*, *Oxford*: Oxford Uni. Press.

Giacalone, R. A. & Promislo, M. D. (ed.) 2013. *Handbook of Unethical Work Behavior*, Armonk: Sharpe.

Giddens, A. & Sutton, P. W. 2014. Health, Illness & Body, in: *Essentials of Sociology*, Oxford: Polity.

Gilbert, S. 2015. http://www.toxipedia.org.

Grady, R. K. et al. 2014. Social Position and Stress, *Teaching Sociology*, 42(1): 5–16.

Harms, P. D. & Spain, S. M. 2015. Beyond the Bright Side, *Applied Psychology*, 64(1):15–24.

Harrington, S. et al. 2015. HRM…Workplace Bullying, *Organization*, 22(3):368–389.

HBR. 2015. How Power-Hungry Bosses Keep Their Power, *Harvard Business Review*, May, 93:5.

Heino, B. 2013. The State, Class and OHS, *Labour & Industry*, 23(3):150–167.

Keegan, S. 2015. *The Psychology of Fear in Organizations*, London: Kogan Page.

Kelly, P. 2013. *The Self as Enterprise: Foucault & the Spirit of 21st Century Capitalism*, Farnh: Gower.

Leijon, O. et al. 2014. First-Time Decisions Regarding Work Injury Annuity Due to Occupational Disease: A Gender Perspective, *Occupational and Environmental Medicine*, 71(2):147–153.

Leiter, M. P. et al. 2014. *Burnout at Work: A Psychological Perspective*, New York: Psychology Press.

Lester, J. 2013. *Workplace Bullying in Higher Education*, London: Routledge.

Lockett, K. 2012. *Work / Life Balance for Dummies*, Hoboken, NJ: John Wiley & Sons.

Lopez, P. & Gillespie, K. A. 2015. *Economies of Death*, London: Routledge.

McKinnon, R. C. 2014. *Changing the Workplace Safety Culture*, Boca Raton, FL: CRC Press.

McQueen, H. 2009. *Framework of Flesh – Builders' Labourers Battle for OHS*, Canberra: Ginninderra Press.

Melhorn, M. et al. (eds.) 2014. *Guides to the Evaluation of Disease and Injury Causation – AMA Guides to the Evaluation of Disease and Injury Causation* (2nd ed.), Chicago, IL: American Medical Association.

Mercat-Bruns, M. 2015. *Discrimination at Work*, Berkeley: University of California Press.

Mogensen, V. 2015. *Worker Safety under Siege*, London: Routledge.

Nearkasen, C. et al. 2014. Roles of Age, Length of Service & Job in Work-Related Injury: A Prospective Study of 63,620 Person-Years in Female Workers, *American Journal of Industrial Medicine*, 57(2):172–183.

Otfinoski, S. 2014. *The Triangle Shirtwaist Factory Fire*, North Mankato, MN: Capstone Press.

Packard, T. G. & Nguyen, T. V. 2014. *East Asia Pacific at Work*, Washington, DC: World Bank.

Parveen, S. 2014. *Rana Plaza Factory Collapse Survivors Struggle One Year On* (bbc.com/news).

Quick, J. C. & Tetrick, L. E. (eds.) 2011. *Handbook of Occupational Health Psychology*, Washington, DC: American Psychological Association.

Quinlan, M. 2015. *Ten Pathways to Death and Disaster – Learning from Fatal Incidents in Mines and Other High Hazard Workplaces*, Sydney: Federation Press.

Rees W. & Porter C. 2015. *Skills of Management*, London: Palgrave, Chapter 6, Motivation & Stress.

Rose, E. 2014. Who's Controlling Who?, *Sociology Compass*, 8(8):1004–1017.

Sanddres Dominguez, E. 2013. Work Stressors and Creativity, *M@n@gement*, 16(4):479–504.

Sassen, S. 2014. *Expulsions: Brutality & Complexity in the Global Economy*, Harvard University Press.

Slaughter, J. 2015. Workplace Violence, April 21 (solidarity-us.org/site/node/4407).

Thaler, R. H. 2015. *Misbehaving*, London: Penguin Press.

Timming, A. R. & Johnstone, S. 2015. Employee Silence, *International Journal of Organizational Analysis*, 23(1):154–171

# 7   Performing People

## Performance Management

**Executive Summary**

Performance management is a method used to assure the performance of managers and employees. It is widely used for white- as well as blue-collar workers and relates to the power management has over their workforce. It also links the past to the present and to the future as performance management becomes a strategic tool. Performance management is predominantly designed to improve performance. As such it is not just linked to strategy but is also part of organisational culture. HRM uses a number of performance methods to assess employee performance. Crucial to the success of performance management remains its link to organisational objectives that set clear goals for performance. To improve on performance, management collects performance information for performance appraisals that remain vital. Performance appraisals allow management to feed back performance information to employees. Key to a successful performance management system remains the removal of barriers that prevent employees from performing. These can be established in feedback sessions designed as "problem solving" discussions that avoid many of the pitfalls of traditional performance management systems.

**Key Learning Objectives**

1. Realise the importance of performance management (PM);
2. Examine the general purpose of PM;
3. Discuss the role of PM in relation to business performance;
4. Detect the chief determinants of individual performance;
5. Select an appropriate PM method for a given situation;
6. Delineate the cultural influence of PM;
7. Describe what performance management is "not" designed to do;
8. List the most common problems of PM; and
9. Develop a formal performance management policy.

**Managing People and Their Performance**

Performance management is one of the most used, useful, and controversial tools of Human Resource Management (HRM) performed daily in many companies. At the very basis of performance management lies the idea to make people in organisations perform their assigned duties.[1] Performance management is even linked to one of the more classical definitions of management. This is a description delivered by the former

DOI: 10.4324/9781003293637-7

Harvard Business Review editor – Joan Magretta – who noted, "managers, using the word loosely, to refer to people in positions of **institutional power**".[2] Power is a rather interesting and highly prevalent concept in HRM and performance management.[3]

Power enters performance management with institutional top-down management exercising power and domination over employees – I manage your performance.[4] The classical definition of **power** is that "A has power over B to the extent that he can get B to do something that B would not otherwise do".[5] In other words, HR managers get employees to work. This is something they otherwise would not do. Given the choice between "a bad day at the beach" or "a good day at work"[6] HRM assumes – perhaps correctly – that many people might take the former rather than the latter.[7] To avoid this, performance management systems are applied.[8]

For management meanwhile, performance management links to Porter's "competitive advantage".[9] As a consequence, many HR managers have introduced performance management during the 1990s so that roughly 90% of clerical and managerial staff and around 60% of manual employees experience performance management.[10] Together with the infamous and much defamed KPIs – **key performance indicators** – performance management has been associated with many negatives.[11] Many HR managers, supervisors, and general managers view performance management as an annual ritual, as being deficient and flawed. They see it as being negative, often expressing their dislike for it.[12] Only 13% of employees and manager and 6% of executive officers thought their PM system is useful.[13] And indeed, it has become relatively easy to list the potential inadequacies and problems of performance management that

- uses inconsistent tools and criteria when measuring employees[14];
- is often used to further nepotism and favouritism;
- has no impact on performance[15];
- performance management forms are too complex and too long;
- measuring individual performance destroys teamwork and collegiality;
- it focuses on the top performers and on those who perform below expectations;
- it encourages short-termism damaging strategic goals;
- it can lead to unnecessary conflicts between employees and supervisors;
- it can be destructive to organisational culture;
- the process is too complicated;
- it is often exposed to subjectivity and bias;
- it violates moral standards, privacy,[16] and leads to lower employee morale; and
- it often results in emotional anguish.

Recently, Tamra Chandler (2016) and Thomas Klikauer (2017) have argued that there are no less than eight fatal flaws of performance management.[17] These are: (1) performance management is a theory without evidence. It is just a bad theory. There is no evidence that traditional performance management leads to improved performance; (2) nobody opens up with the person who pokes them in the eye. Traditional performance management impedes the reception of feedback and limits honest dialogue; (3) nobody remembers the good work. Performance reviews generally emphasise on the negatives, rather than focusing on strengths; (4) no man (or woman) is an island. The focus is on the individual, even though systems or organisational challenges often have significant influences on individual performance; (5) we are not machines. Fairness and standardisation in ratings and the judgement of performance simply cannot be achieved; (6) reviewing only output is unreliable for making talent decisions; (7)

comparing people against one another erodes efforts to create a collaborative culture – 'let me introduce you to your competition – now play nicely together!'; and finally, (8) we are not Pavlov's dog. Pay for performance does not deliver improved performance.

To avoid cases where "Performance Management Is Killing Performance" (Tamra Chandler 2016),[18] HR managers have also developed useful tools that counteract the negatives associated with performance management.[19] One option that HR managers take is to move beyond individual measurements, instead favouring collaborative criteria when employees are evaluated. Another and more classical tool of HRM is better organisational training for middle management in order to avoid the pitfalls of performance management. When HR managers apply appropriate measuring tools, performance management is capable of highlighting precisely what employees need to improve. This makes performance management a tool linking past, present, and future (Figure 7.1):

| past | → | present | → | future |
|---|---|---|---|---|
| data relating to past performance | → | assessments, appraisals & feedback | → | directed towards achieving performance goals |

*Figure 7.1* Performance Management's Past-Present-Future Linkage.

When HR managers link "past-present-future", seeking to overcome short-termism[20] and moving towards the future, performance management is applied strategically.[21] This means performance management is directed into the future. On the downside is what 'one boss at AT&T [said], *in the past we said to employees, do as you're told and you have a job for life. Then we betrayed them*'.[22] On their own level, management itself can be appraised for how it – in turn – appraises employees. Finally and most importantly, HR managers focus on issues, facts, and behaviours, not on the person. They concentrate on the task and the organisation while avoiding criticising the person.[23] Keeping this in mind can assure that performance management is a productive tool – a tool that is defined as a process through which managers ensure that the work of employees and their outputs are aligned with the strategies a company pursues.

## The Top Five Elements of Performance Management

There are five key elements of performance management on which many HR managers focus when designing and operating a performance management system.[24] These elements are measuring, promoting, removing, appraising, and communicating.

1. Measuring what is relevant
   Most performance management is designed to measure what is relevant to the organisation while establishing measurable standards against which employees can be assessed. This, for example, also includes the flexibility to measure teamwork when people work in self-managed teams.
2. Promoting organisational performance
   The key to performance management is actually not individual performance but organisational performance even though individual performance can lead to organisational performance and even to an HPO (high-performance organisation).[25] This is also known as HPWS (high-performance work systems), HCWS (**high commitment work systems**), HUM (high involvement management), and HPP (high-performance practice). The idea behind these is that 'the only

worker who is productive is one who produces surplus value for the capitalist'.[26] Ultimately and whatever the label, most of these practices include roughly seven key ingredients:

1. strategic recruitment and selection
2. attention on employees' learning
3. work in teams and flattening of hierarchies
4. open internal communication[27]
5. cooperative employment relations
6. significant (e.g. high) rewards
7. high job security

Overall, successful HPO/HPWS/HCWS/HUM/HPP managers combine these seven ingredients by providing sufficient incentives to individuals in order to translate individual performance into organisational performance. To achieve that, HR managers link performance management to organisational culture, thereby establishing a performance-driven company culture[28] while assuring that assessments are fair and legitimate.[29]

3. Removing barriers to performance management

   Many HR managers see this as the core of performance management as performance management is not a tool to be used to reward and punish – disciplinary action,[30] warnings, dismissals,[31] etc. – but remains a tool that manages performance – nothing more and nothing less. In many cases, such barriers can be found in insufficient training, out-dated equipment and machinery, and in preventative and uncreative work practices. All these (and more) can be barriers to the successful performance of employees.

4. Appraising employee performance

   The key part of performance management is the **performance appraisal**, seen as a process that allows HR managers to assess the progress an employee makes towards achieving organisational goals as outlined in key performance indicators.[32] Often conducted in three, six, or annual intervals, performance appraisals focus on the task of identifying and removing barriers to performance that are often brought up during "feedback" sessions.[33] Such sessions are typically seen as being part of a four-fold feedback loop consisting of observation → plan → act and support → review and rate → and returning to observation.[34]

5. Communicating feedback

   The most essential part of performance management is giving feedback to employees on their performance. These are conversations between managers and employees directed towards assuring maximum performance. They are two-way communications with the aim of altering an employee's behaviour and changing an organisation (work processes, etc.) so that individual performance can be converted into maximum organisational performance.

On the part of employees, performance management can focus, for example, on individual characteristics such as traits, skills, attitudes, behaviours, and abilities. These are trait appraisal instruments as they ask managers and supervisors to judge employees on their traits – in the case of a sales position, for example, this means foremost interpersonal communication skills but also product knowledge. Many HR managers are aware that success in sales, for example, never only depends on a skillful combination of interpersonal communication and product knowledge. Success – quite equally – also depends on organisational culture that HR managers in particular can shape through HR policies setting clear standards, by learning and development, and by having developed a coherent organisational strategy with clear goals.

## Strategic Performance Management

One of the key imperatives of performance management (PM) is its link to the overall business strategy. This works in the following way: strategic plan → detailed business plan → department goals → team targets → individual performance objectives. HR managers see five key elements of such an overall linkage:

1. PM needs to be aligned to the business strategy;
2. PM needs to encourage a positive organisational culture;
3. PM needs to be specific on how such goals are to be achieved;
4. PM needs to allow "discretionary effort"[35] balancing control with autonomy;
5. PM needs to be based on clear policies and documentation.

However, 'many Fortune 500 companies have ditched formal reviews.'[36] By 2015, "already 10% of Fortune 500 companies had done away with the annual performance review".[37] Accenture was one of them.[38] Still, those companies that still use performance management often link it to organisational learning and HR development (HRD).[39] This views performance management under the maxim: when employees are incapable of performing as efficient as their performance management plan (KPIs) indicates, performance management is set to improve employee performance by removing barriers that prevent employees from achieving it. HR managers in these organisations seek to improve organisational performance by focusing on HRD.

By focusing on HRD and the removal of barriers to a successful performance, HR managers avoid the many pitfalls of performance management. All too often they fall into the trap of "making performance management personal". They focus on the person rather than the issue. Getting this wrong can lead to significant problems such as, for example, absenteeism. Insufficient performance management can also lead to conflicts over not being properly recognised or rewarded. Not surprisingly, in a 2016 list of the "9 Things That Make Good Employees Quit" number two notes: "they don't recognise contributions or reward good work".[40] This becomes evident when the **CEO performance-rewards link** is examined.[41] On the other hand, there seems to be a serious disconnection between the performance of some CEOs and their handsome rewards even in the face of serious corporate loss making.[42]

Some employees and even managers feel that they are too stressed to go to work, employees avoid facing their boss, some feel too pushed to work to the deadlines of performance management, others fear failure and lack of competence, or work towards performance goals rather than being interested in the job, etc.[43] An UPS worker called Rose testifies to this. She said about the system of control at UPS, 'people get intimidated and they work faster…it's like when they whip animals. But this is a mental whip'.[44]

HR managers seek to balance this – in some cases, they may eliminate performance management (Accenture) or provide more organisational autonomy and flexibility to employees. Yet despite all this and the fact that 'most companies would rather work their existing workforce to the bone',[45] some HR and line managers[46] still use – or perhaps misuse – performance management as an administrative tool, moving away from the very idea of performance management, namely managing performance.[47]

## From Administration to Organisational Culture

Performance management can rather wrongfully become misappropriated when it is turned into a tool for salary administration, becoming linked to pay rises and bonuses. In other cases, performance management is used for promotions[48] and demotions and even retentions and terminations. The latter often means that 'successful managers are measured by their advancement within their companies [these are not necessarily those deemed to be] efficient managers'.[49] It could also mean a failure to measure up to a prevailing "workaholic long-hours" culture. It is "9am to 5pm but if you want promotion you've got to be at work from 5pm to 9pm as well and seven days a week".[50]

Perhaps the most common administrative use of performance management is when it is linked to salaries. The appropriation of performance management is equally prob-lematic when it is misaligned with organisational culture. This becomes even more arduous when it occurs in an organisational culture that favours teamwork, collec-tivism, and cooperation while valuing organisational harmony. In other words, per-formance management and organisational culture can be on a collision path when performance management tools do not support organisational culture. The classic research into organisational culture has been delivered by Hofstede's multi-country IBM study. It has shown that organisational culture has, at least, five dimensions[51]:

1. **Power distance:**
   is defined as the extent to which the less powerful members of organisations ac-cept and expect that power is distributed unequally.
2. **Individualism-vs.-collectivism:**
   explores the degree to which people in an organisation are integrated into groups. Individualistic organisations have loose ties emphasising the "I" versus the "we" while in collectivist organisations employees depict loyalty and support each other.
3. **Uncertainty avoidance:**
   is defined as an organisation's tolerance for ambiguity in which employees em-brace or avert an event of something unexpected, unknown, or away from the status quo.
4. **Masculinity-vs.-femininity:**
   Masculinity is defined as a preference for achievement, heroism, assertiveness, and material rewards for success while femininity represents a preference for coopera-tion, modesty, caring for the weak, and quality of life.[52]
5. **Long- vs.-short-term:**
   associates the connection of the past with the current and future actions/challeng-es. Organisations with a high long-term vision view adaptation and circumstantial, pragmatic problem-solving – 'discussing performance in an open review' – as a necessity.[53]

Whatever the organisational culture may be, performance management is rather inev-itably linked to "long-vs.-short term" cultures as well as individualism as a rather indi-vidualistic tool. Both – short-&-long-termism and individualism – are typically based on an organisational culture in which performance management (PM) operates. Such organisational culture is, in turn, influenced by a national culture (Table 7.1)[54]:

*Table 7.1* Individualism and Culture

| Group | Countries | Individualism |
|---|---|---|
| Anglo | Australia, Canada, Ireland, New Zealand, the UK, the USA | High |
| Germanic | Austria, Germany, Italy, Israel, South Africa, Switzerland | Medium |
| Nordic | Denmark, Finland, the Netherlands, Norway, Sweden | Medium |
| More Developed Asia | Japan | Medium |
| Less Developed Asia | India, Pakistan, Singapore, Taiwan, Thailand | Low |
| Southern EU and Middle East | Greece, Turkey, Iran | Medium |
| More Developed Latin | Argentina, Brazil, Belgium, France, Spain | Medium |
| Less Developed Latin | Chile, Colombia, Mexico, Peru, Portugal, Venezuela | Low |

Since performance management is about a long term plan to develop human resources, the issue of short-termism versus long-termism has a significant impact on the work of HR-managers. In countries where an organisational culture is influenced by a national culture that supports long-term – and strategic – performance management, HR managers can build on this. In countries where short-term thinking is part of the culture, HR managers need to establish long-term planning before they can successfully run performance management programmes. The way performance management is shaped is not only influenced by how a national culture influences organisational culture; it is also influenced by how the actual corporation is run. On the cultural side of this, three different ways have emerged. In multi-national corporations, for example, these cultural imperatives can take three routes:

1.  **ethnocentric PM**: reflects the practices of the home country in the case of multinational corporations;
2.  **polycentric PM**: reflects local practices of host countries while corporate headquarter grants significant local autonomy to HRM; and
3.  **geocentric PM**: occurs when 1 and 2 cooperate to find a common way to organise the philosophical approach, resulting in a mixture of policies and rules.

Whatever the philosophical approach, the outcome almost always is a reflection of an "eastern-vs.-western" culture as global-culture expert Edward Said has shown conclusively.[55] Said argues that management culture – which includes performance management – is an instrument of cultural imperialism, saying that

> although the "age of empire" has largely ended after World War II when most colonies gained independence, imperialism continues to exert considerable cultural influence in the present. To be aware of this fact, it is necessary to look at how colonialists and imperialists employed cultureto control distant lands and peoples".[56]

Perhaps performance management is used to control people but it can also become successful when applied strategically, thereby becoming an integrated part of strategic management that supplies information for strategic management decisions while also establishing **strategic congruence**, i.e. the degree of a successful "PM⇆SM" link (performance management and strategic management). This links four elements: performance management, strategy, organisational goals, and organisational culture.

Whether applied strategically (correct) or administratively (wrongful), performance management needs to show a sufficient level of validity. This is the level at which performance management, or better, performance appraisals assess relevant aspects of performance. Failing that, performance management can become deficient. Deficient performance measures occur when performance management fails to measure the relevant aspects of performance. Performance management is also exposed to the danger of producing contaminated data. **Contaminated performance management** occurs when irrelevant aspects of a performance are included into the assessment. A further task of performance management is to produce reliable data. **Reliability** refers to the level of consistency of performance measures when, for example, performance is measured over time (quarterly, annually, etc.).

It is also essential for performance management to show a sufficient level of accountability. HR managers establish **performance accountability** when employees and managers accept the way performances are measured. For this, HR managers conduct feedback sessions and **employee surveys**.[57] Commonly, accountability is seen as being linked to fairness. HR managers create **performance fairness** when adhering to three basic forms of fairness: procedural, interpersonal/communicative, and substantive fairness.

1.  **Procedural fairness:**
    is the level at which the procedure of performance management is fair and includes the availability of employees and managers to be involved in the performance management process as well as options to remedy unwanted and unwarranted performance management decisions;
2.  **Interpersonal/communicative fairness:**
    relates to the equal treatment of all employees exposed to performance management and appraisals but it also means that performance management is communicated to all employees and managers to the same degree; finally,
3.  **Substantive fairness:**
    also called outcome fairness – describes the level to which the outcome, i.e. decisions and assessments of performance management, are justified. This does not mean that every employee and manager receives the same outcome. Instead, it means that performance management decisions need to be justifiable and legitimate.

## Performance Assessment Methods

Over the years, HRM has developed sophisticated techniques and methods in conducting performance management. HR managers use **ratings** (appraisers specify on a scale to what degree relevant characteristics are appraised) and **rankings** (appraisers rank workers from best to worst establishing so-called league tables) when appraising performance.[58] One of the most striking approaches to performance management has been the use of the **comparative performance** management method. As the name indicates, this method compares employees and managers with or against one another. It is also called **relative rating system** as it relates employees and managers to each other. One version of this method is used when HR managers and line managers rank employees within their section of department from high performers to poor performers (underperformance). In some cases, this method has been extended into **forced distributions** with the former CEO of General Electric (GE) being one of the more striking examples. Jack Welch's approach to performance management was to divide GE managers and employees into three groups:

| | | | | | |
|---|---|---|---|---|---|
| 1. | Group 1 | A players | The top performers | = | 20% of the workforce |
| 2. | Group 2 | B players | The middle performers | = | 70% of the workforce |
| 3. | Group 3 | C players | The low performers | = | 10% of the workforce |

Needless to say that putting people against each other weakens social ties among employees and reduces the social support that produces healthier workplaces. Undeterred, Jack Welch had a "my way or the highway" policy for low performers. They were eliminated or, as Welsh would see it, "they are likely to enervate rather than energise".[59] In some cases, Welsh's approach was surely a reminiscence of "blaming the victim". Similarly, Microsoft grates employee productivity twice a year. It uses four grates. As a Microsoftie said, "four means exceptional; one means you're out".[60] If terminating an employee is the goal, HR managers conduct an **exit interview**.[61] This can be done via Zoom.[62] Currently, the website *Glassdoor*[63] holds about 40 million employees interviews of about 700,000 business organisations. However, today's HR managers try to avoid dismissals and firings by removing the barriers to performance, encouraging organisational learning, changes to jobs, and even changing a person's position.

The comparative method also includes **paired comparison** where every employee in a team, for example, is compared with every other team member. This comparison method is quite different from **attribute methods** that are used to assess an employee's attributes that are seen as relevant to organisational success such as, for example, knowledge, communicative skills, judgment, managerial skills, teamwork ability, interpersonal skills, initiative, creativity,[64] and problem-solving abilities. While attribute methods have become popular among HR managers, they have, however, two potential problems: (a) they often show very little strategic congruence (see above); and (b) they are open to the danger of different subjective and biased interpretations.[65]

One performance method seeking to avoid these shortfalls is the **behavioural approach** based on the psychology of behaviourism.[66] Based on laboratory testing using "white lab rats" and the implicit assumption that humans behave like rats (human-equals-rat), **organisational behaviour manipulation** (OBM) manages employees through behavioural feedback. This takes the known threefold form of (a) punishment, (b) positive, and (c) negative reinforcement. Under performance management, the OBM method operates as a four-step process:

Step 1:  HR managers, line managers, supervisors, etc. in conjunction with employees develop key performance indicators (KPIs) needed to conduct a specific job and assess whether these are linked to organisational performance and the overall business strategy[67];

Step 2:  HR managers, line managers, supervisors, etc. select an appropriate performance method (outlined above) to assess whether an employee or manager depicts these behaviours and attitudes;

Step 3:  HR managers, line managers, supervisors, etc. assess whether respective employees or managers depict expected behaviours and attributes (measuring). In addition, new goals and objectives can be developed enhancing the overall performance management system; and finally,

Step 4:  HR managers, supervisors, line managers, etc. provide feedback to employees and managers on how to improve performance, remove barriers, etc. focusing on the task rather than the person. This is the part of positive reinforcement.

These steps are often used towards **MBO – management by objectives** – a tool that continues to remain popular in private industry. Generally, MBO systems have three components: (a) MBO requires specific goals linked to the business strategy; (b) these goals can be set unilaterally by management but they can also be set in consultation with employees; and (c) managers provide unbiased feedback to employees throughout a rating period assessing progress towards these goals.[68]

Similar to MBO, productivity measurements and evaluation systems are also designed to measure and increase the performance and productivity of employees. There have been cases when employers use so-called **productivity apps** which are 'electronic programmes that can tirelessly monitor an employs, twenty-four hours a day, seven days a week – an impossible feat for a human supervisor'.[69] Also used is **physiolytics** which 'is a way to extract information from wearables data to improve performance'.[70] Workers who are 'more closely monitored [experience] greater stress [while] electronic performance monitoring is associated with'[71]:

- Anxiety;
- Depression;
- Anger;
- Severe fatigue;
- Headaches; and
- Musculoskeletal injuries.

Like MBO, they start with identifying work tasks and organisational activities. This is followed by an assessment on how well the products and organisational activities are generated within an organisation. In addition, **critical incidents** can become useful when supervisors record those occurrences that are capable of highlighting good or bad performances. Lastly, a system of feedback provides room to improve the performance system geared towards productivity.

Unlike many other performance management methods, MBO and productivity measurement systems provide objective ways of minimising bias and subjectivity. There are, however, several disadvantages. These include, for example: measuring things that are not under the direct control of employees; being a narrow tool as these systems measure only some but hardly ever all elements of an employee's performance; in addition, they hardly ever assist organisational learning; and finally, these methods are open to the danger of encouraging employees to find inventive ways to make their performance appear better than it actually is.

## Performance Management Information

Disregarding which performance management methods are used, all of these methods need to have some source of information about an employee's performance. Perhaps one of the most used methods to gather such information remains a manager. In some cases, employees' performance is linked to the manager's performance (bonus), thereby encouraging managers towards positive outcomes. In other cases, supervisors or managers fail to understand what employees are doing because the employees' work takes place in remote locations distant from the manager. Even in close proximity, employees do express their dissatisfaction with bad supervision. A Boeing employee stated in 2020 that the *737 Max* was "designed by clowns [while employees were] supervised by monkeys".[72]

In other cases, work may be very complex[73] and/or work tasks vary to a substantial degree. In addition, some supervisors and managers may be biased in favour of or against a particular employee. Such **favouritism** and **nepotism** – 'the unjustified appointment of friends or relatives to office or according them favoured treatment'[74] – occurs as **relationship effect** when personal relations influence performance assessment as seen in BBC's "The Office".[75] To prevent this, HR managers often favour performance management systems that minimise bias, subjectivity, favouritism, and nepotism.

Next to managers and supervisors, a valuable source of performance management information is also peers and co-workers. These horizontal rather than vertical (top-down) sources of information are extremely valid as they deliver a different perspective. **Peer performance information** is also able to prevent favouritism and nepotism better as peer information relies on groups of workers rather than individual managers. Somewhat below this, **subordinates performance information** provides comprehensive data on the performance of managers.[76] But the sociology of asymmetric power relationships indicates that managers receive more positive upward feedback when this is supplied from subordinates who are identified.[77] Rather unsurprisingly, subordinates prefer to give upward feedback about their managers and supervisors anonymously. When employees are identified, they tend to inflate the ratings of their immediate managers.

One way of delivering additional performance data is simply by **self-rating**. Self-rating raises the problem of the **above-average effect** which means that self-raters tend to rate themselves above average.[78] Although not widely used as the only source of performance information, it remains a source even though it is somewhat exposed to the danger of an inflating self-assessment. Self-rating eliminates nepotism and top-down power relationships, but it cannot totally eliminate the three dimensions of power[79]:

**dimension 1:**   management's self-assumed right to manage over employees;

**dimension 2:**   the power of management to set the agenda, i.e. to decide what is and what is not measured during a performance review[80]; and

**dimension 3:**   management's ability to secure the ideological dependency of employees on management, the creation of corporate allegiance and compliance to management so that employees accept performance management as self-evident, natural, normal, unchangeable, and even beneficial.[81]

On the other hand, self-rating is also a method that tends to make managers blame poor performance and **underperformance** on external factors: other managers, the market, trade unions, regulations, inadequate training, destructive competition, toxic corporate politics, substandard equipment, insufficient resources, outdated production and technological systems, incompetent top-HRM, discrimination, low performance culture, no punishment for poor performers, no financial incentives, no promotional prospects, low decision-making, etc. To avoid this, external performance data are gathered from customers in situations where this applies. Today, many organisations have moved towards **customer performance information** to evaluate employees and managers. This method operates under two conditions: (a) there must be sufficient interfaces with customers and (b) it is often conducted when companies also seek to collect general information on products and services.

With increased popularity and combining many of the above-noted methods, the **360-degree appraisal** is used. 360-degree performance information relies on a multitude of sources such as, for example, self-rating, managers, peers, subordinates, and customers. This method remains one of the preferred methods when HR managers seek to reduce favouritism and nepotism. On the other hand, there are also negatives associated with the 360-degree appraisal such as, for example, it intimidates people, it raises conflicting opinions on performance, feedback is personalised and not accurate, it lacks credibility and reliability, produces untruthful feedback, feedback is not anonymous and confidential, it uses inappropriate measures not delivered by experts, it is time-consuming, demands complex administration, and raters have not received training on this performance management method. Driven to its extreme, 360-degree appraisals can – when applied constantly – produce **workplace surveillance**.[82] Employers also use electronic means as 'worker tracking' devises[83] as a many-eyed Argus Panoptes that sees everything, every minor detour, every stopping for a sandwich, every lunch and toilet break. This is the new electronic supervisor that ends privacy using means like 'nanosensors for worker surveillance'.[84]

## Assessors and Performance Management

The process of performance management is not only exposed to favouritism, nepotism, and inflated self-assessments, it can also be challenged by those who perform the assessment, evaluation, and rating. This includes, firstly, the inherent subjectivity of human beings as we are not machines but human beings with feelings and emotions, likes, and dislikes.[85] Secondly, some assessors and raters also display deliberate bias, stereotyping, and even **negative and positive prejudices**. One of the more common pitfalls for performance raters is the **similar-to-me** problem. This indicates the mistake that raters make when assessing those who are similar (ethnicity, age, culture, gender, etc.) to themselves: they receive a higher rating. This can even occur when **contrast faults** occur. More often than not, some managers fall into the trap of focusing on the person rather than the task at hand (removing performance barriers, for example). Instead of measuring managers and employees against objective criteria, they contrast them against others in a "person-vs.-person" comparison.

But there are also **distributional mistakes**. These occur when assessors and raters use only part of a rating scale against which managers and employees are to be assessed. On top of this, there is a somewhat human **central tendency** to prefer the middle box in the **Likert scale** of "strongly disagree, disagree, neither agree nor disagree, agree, and strongly agree".[86] The opposite – rating individuals higher or lower than their performance actually warrants – occurs under negative and positive skewing. Working similar to Likert's scale are the behaviour observation scale (BOS)[87] and the behaviourally anchored rating scale (BARS) featuring:

1. superior performance: highest professional standard displayed at all times
2. very good performance: excellent knowledge and application of knowledge
3. good performance: informed about company and products

4.  acceptable performance: works within parameters of job and position
5.  marginal performance: displays little interest in job and performance
6.  poor performance: performs below average, needs improvement
7.  unsatisfactory performance: performs at the bottom of the scale, urgent action
    required.

In addition, HR managers are aware of **halo and horns**.[88] Halo mistakes occur when
one positive rating influences raters to rate all other employees as positive as well.
When the opposite occurs, horn mistakes are happening: one negative result can influence assessors to rate all others also as negative. When either one – holo or horn –
appears consistently, raters call this leniency or strictness bias.

Above that, performance management is exposed to **appraisal politics** where pol-
iticking enters the scene.[89] When this happens, HR managers know that assessors
deliberately distort and even fake assessments for personal goals. In particularly severe
cases, this can lead to organisational **bullying** when employees are exposed to excessive
performance monitoring under what HR managers loosely label, "we will performance
management him out of here". This is not only immoral, counterproductive, and illegal behaviour but performance increases camouflaged as 'optimising the workforce'[90]
can lead to **work stress** as outlined in the chapter on OHS.[91] HR managers avoid all
this by providing training and development on performance management as well as
sensible feedback sessions with managers and employees.

## Performance Feedback

Perhaps the key part of any performance management system is when managers provide **performance feedback** to other managers and employees. This is a process during which defined, agreed upon, and expected performance information as well as
measured performance information is discussed with managers and employees. Performance feedback is designed to raise awareness of deficiencies as well as progress
that has been made over a given time frame. There can be many examples of wrong
performance feedback[92]:

1.  Since my last report, this employee has reached rock bottom and has started to
    dig,
2.  I would not allow this employee to breed,
3.  This associate is really not so much of a has-been, but more of a definitely won't be,
4.  He would be out of his depth in a parking lot puddle,
5.  This young lady has delusions of adequacy,
6.  This employee is depriving a village somewhere of an idiot,
7.  This employee should go far – and the sooner he starts the better,
8.  Not the sharpest knife in the drawer,
9.  A room temperature IQ,
10. Got a full six-pack, but lacks the plastic thingy to hold it all together;
11. A photographic memory but with the lens cover glued on,
12. A prime candidate for natural de-selection,
13. Bright as Alaska in December,
14. If he were any more stupid, he'd have to be watered twice a week.
15. Takes him 1 1/2 hours to watch 60 minutes.[93]

These are feedbacks that play the man rather than the ball. They are abusive and unhelpful when seeking to identify **barriers to performance** and eliminating them. Such barriers or **situational factors** can be, for example:

1. poor coordination of work processes
2. inadequate instruction and job descriptions
3. materials and tools of insufficient quality
4. lack of materials, tools, machinery, computers, software, etc.
5. inability to source needed materials and equipment
6. insufficient or non-existing supervision
7. deficient coordination among team members and workers
8. inadequate training and skills development
9. unsuitable time management (short deadlines, etc.)
10. poor work environment and working conditions (noise, heat, interruptions, etc.)

These are important situational factors impacting on performance. But wrongfully used performance instruments tend to eliminate the person – not the problems noted above. Given some of the aforementioned, ill-intended, and wrongfully personalised responses, many managers tend to avoid performance management, often seeking to delay performance assessments as long as they can. To counter that, they focus on the triage of employee ability, employee effort, and work situation. Many managers know that performance appraisals should not only focus on this triage but performance feedback should be given frequently – not annually or twice per year. Frequent feedback has two advantages: (a) it gives employees and managers ample time to correct mistakes and improve performance; and (b) managers and employees are never surprised when discussing their contribution to an organisation's overall performance.

## The Problem Solving Approach to Performance Feedback

The inevitable key to successful performance feedback is not the frequency but the way "how" feedback is given. HR managers see three options for feedback sessions:

**Tell and Sell:**
When using the "tell and sell" approach to performance feedback, managers tend to simply tell employees how they have been rated and assessed. They do not provide options for two way communication. Employees are not given the opportunity to respond to their performance assessment. This sort of performance feedback is authoritarian and highly unhelpful. Managers simply sell their decision as best as they can.

**Tell and Listen:**
Unlike the one-dimensional "tell and sell" approach, the "tell and listen" approach is a two-way form of communication. Here, managers tell employees or other managers how they have been rated but give the latter an option to reply so that they can present their perspective on a performance assessment.

**Problem Solving:**
Unlike the two vertical "top-down" approaches above, the problem-solving approach follows a rather different and more horizontal route.[94] It is designed as a thoroughly communicative effort geared towards solving problems together.[95] In this approach, managers and employees are part of the solution – not the problem. Both work in

conjunction towards common goals: removing barriers to performance and increase performance – even when video conferencing.[96] Performance feedback is discussed in a collegial setting depicting mutual respect. Employees should not be "phubbed", i.e. ignoring employees in favour of a phone.[97] The problem-solving approach to performance management should be seen as instrument of continuous improvement, establishing a feedback loop between management and employees. This approach includes the following steps:

1. **measurement**: performance is measured against goals, targets, and objectives;
2. **feedback**: information on individual performance is discussed (with the focus on being precise, giving examples, being supportive and aware of impact, encouraging reflection, turning it into an ongoing dialogue, etc.);
3. **positive reinforcement**: constructive discussion aimed at improvements linked to rewards;
4. **exchange of ideas**: this discussion includes the exchange of ideas on, for example, barriers to be removed to allow superior performance to take place; and finally,
5. **agreement**: reaching a joint understanding on future progress towards improved performance.

Yet despite an overwhelming body of research favouring the problem-solving approach, too many managers still conduct performance feedback in the "tell and sell" mode of authoritarianism. When adding some of the negative examples outlined above and mixing unhelpful feedback with personal attacks and negatives, performance management is set to fail. One of the key failures committed is the fact that the very opposite works best, namely positive feedback and **positive reinforcement** encourages positive attitudes and strengthens performance.

The second problem with approaches one and two is that these tend to focus on people rather than on the problem. Most performance problems cannot be eliminated through punishing poor performers. Instead of outdated punishing regimes, some HR managers focus on **performance coaching**[98] and **performance counselling** with the former involving employee training, providing encouragement and support and the latter focusing on giving advice to employees that can involve EAPs (employee assistance programmes) in cases of, for example:

> work-family imbalances, relationship breakdown, child care, mental illness, unethical behaviour, alcohol and/or drug abuse, racial, religious, sexual, and other forms of discrimination, physical, sexual, verbal, and psychological harassment, bullying, etc.).[99]

Overall, punishing or dismissing **poor performers** are avoidance strategies that hardly ever eliminate performance problems. Instead, when faced with "nothing else works" as performance gets worse, performance changes too little, behaviours remain unchanged, things change but do not last, etc., HR managers predominantly take three options: (a) *transfer* of employees to another position; (b) *neutralise* the situation by job restructuring so that poor performance has little impact; and (c) termination of employment as a last resort.

Good HR managers tend to minimise criticism while focusing on the task at hand. They also work with managers and employees towards setting commonly agreed goals and set dates for the achievements of these goals. These managers avoid what is known as "imposition without consultation". Instead, they establish common ownership of the performance management process focusing on performance improvement through **performance goal setting**. HR managers call this developing a **performance improve-ment plan** (PIP).[100] An inclusive approach to problem-solving and, above all, goal set-ting not only assists the so-called poor performers but also those who are identified as **marginal managers**. These are managers and employees who perform at the bare min-imum level, often because of a lack of ability, opportunity, and motivation to perform better.[101] To change this, the AMO model (ability motivation and opportunity) explains the link between performance and HRM.[102] The problem-solving approach is better suited to assist these managers and employees to move beyond **marginal performance**.

## The Administration of Performance Management

HR managers are aware that there are some key elements that remain essential when administering performance management. These are roughly six key administrative tasks:

1. HR managers maintain sufficient levels of documentation for performance management;
2. they safeguard potential legal challenges to poor performance;
3. they outline the responsibilities of managers and employees (e.g. HR policies);
4. when termination of employment appears as an option, HRM provides sufficient warnings;
5. HR managers adhere to the legal requirements of EEO (equal employment opportunity);
6. HRM assures that termination of employment is conducted within the legal framework.

Overall, however, these are safeguards "when things go wrong". These six administra-tive tasks safeguard a company against legal challenges "after the fact". The key to per-formance management is not the administration of termination but the management of performance. It is a system designed to improve performance, to identify barriers to performance, and to remove these. But it also is a system that values organisational performance and to which individual performance needs to contribute. Strong and successful organisational performance never depends on an individual instrument like performance management alone. One method of linking organisational performance to individual performance is found in the **balanced scorecard** approach.[103] Its objective is that all areas are important to organisational performance linking (a) people, (b) internal operations, (c) customer satisfaction,[104] and (d) financial goals.

HR managers aware of the performance management ⇆ organisational perfor-mance interface have long realised the overall set of HR initiatives that underwrite organisational performance. These HR managers are embedding performance man-agement into six core elements that achieve organisational performance[105]:

1. the development of employee knowledge, skills, and abilities;
2. employees' relations, coordination, and problem-solving;
3. employees' wellbeing at the organisational level;
4. a positive organisational culture that encourages performance; and
5. a reward system that links extrinsic and intrinsic rewards to performance;
6. a performance management system that supports organisational performance whilst being linked to the overall corporate strategy the company pursues.

## Workbook

### III.   Five Discussion Questions on Performance Management

*And One Report Question on Performance Management*

*1. Discussion Question*

1. Discuss the relationship between performance management and power. How does power impact performance management?
2. Discuss the pros and cons of linking performance management to a company's strategic business plan.
3. Have the negatives of performance management (betterworks.com, 15th December 2015) become so overwhelming that HR managers should follow Accenture (www.accenture.com) and eliminate performance management altogether (washingtonpost.com, 2015/07/21)?
4. Which performance method is best suited to move away from "blaming the person" and moving towards measuring relevant factors capable of overcoming barriers to performance?
5. One essential component of performance management is performance feedback. The chapter argues this is done in three ways. Discuss the pros and cons of the "tell-&-sell", the "tell-&-listen", and the "problem-solving" approach.

*2. Report Question*

*On The Fatal Flaws of Performance Management*

Chandler, in his book (2016[106]) on "Performance Management",[107] outlines eight [8] "fatal flaws" of performance management (#1: bad theory; #2: no eye poking; #3: no good work; #4: no island; #5 & 6: no machines; #7: competition; and #8: Pavlov's dog. Develop four [4] recommendations on how HRM/CPM can overcome these eight flaws of performance management?

### IV.   The "5-by-5" Exercise: Five Case Studies and Five Questions

*7.1 Performance Management at "Going Up" Elevators*

Going Up Elevators is one of the world's largest manufacturers, installers, and servicers of indoor and outdoor elevators producing and offering its products and services in over 200 countries. Going Up Elevators employs 75,000 employees globally. For many years, the company suffered problems with an inadequate performance management system. In overcoming this, Going Up Elevators' HRM moved forward to a refined performance feedback system based on "critical strategic competencies" relating these to the company's overall business strategy and to its newly created work teams. These team members are now required to display specific competencies such as team leadership, project management skills and are responsible for financial and operating results.

HRM became aware quickly that performance feedback could no longer be drawn from direct supervisors. Instead, HRM redesigned Going Up Elevators' feedback system by moving towards a custom-designed 360-degree feedback system providing management with performance data from those directly affected by the performance of its teams. This feedback system focuses on three groups:

a.   team leaders and supervisors
b.   team members and co-workers
c.   direct customers

Going Up Elevators' new performance management structure is capable of providing employees' performance ratings on several critical competencies. The new system is administered via Going Up Elevators' internal "intranet". The new online system is very practical allowing performance ratings/feedback to be completed within half an hour. The performance management system also allows Going Up Elevators to provide feedback that is linked to the company's strategic business plan. After implementation of the new system, it showed to be more sufficient than the old paper-based system. Above that, the new performance system interlinks employees better with Going Up Elevators' core business goals.

1.   Develop five core competencies elevator engineers should have and explain why you have selected these five.
2.   What is the advantage of linking Going Up Elevators' performance management system to its strategic business plan? Find at least five reasons for such a link.
3.   What are the advantages of the 360-degree feedback system for Going Up Elevators and what are the disadvantages of this system? Develop at least three advantages and three disadvantages.
4.   Imagine you are the HR manager of Going Up Elevators seeking to move beyond a feedback system based on the tell-&-sell and tell-&-listen approach. What elements are to be included in constructing a feedback system based on the "problem-solving" approach to feedback? Name at least five elements.
5.   Making, installing, and servicing elevators can depend on external factors that exist independent of Going Up Elevators. These external factors can influence the performance of employees. Name five such external factors.

### 7.2 Russell Clow's Pool Performance

Russell Clow is a tax accountant who for twenty-five years has been working in a multinational accounting company called "Numbers Matter". Liam Leeson is his manager who has joined the company only recently. In previous months, Liam Leeson has been receiving complaints from Russell Clow's work colleagues that Russell is not pulling his weight and that he is not finishing tax claims effectively. Often his workmates help out to work through backlogs of unfinished claims that have piled up. Because of this, Liam Leeson has arranged a meeting with the HR manager of Numbers Matter, Ms. Kate Wisletti.

Liam tells Kate that other employees had advised him about Russell Clow's performance being a problem for a while and that his previous managers never addressed the issue. There is also no documentation on Russell's performance. Liam Leeson believes that Russell's lack of performance is impacting negatively on the entire work team and says that "something needs to be done". On Kate Wisletti's suggestion, Liam gathers some evidence and arranges to meet with Russell. During the meeting, Russell states that his performance is the same as that of other team members and says, "there have been no complaints from customers".

Liam shows Russell Clow that his case closure rate is the lowest in his team and that some customers have indeed complained about him. Russell explains that he has been struggling with claims. The problems have escalated with new computer software that was installed last year. Although Russell has received some training on the new programme, he says that "it covered only part of the programme – I have no idea how the whole thing operates and what it can do".

During the meeting, Liam Leeson establishes that Russell's low performance is not an issue of behaviour or attitude but is related to insufficient training. As a consequence, Liam arranges with an external training provider to offer more training on the new programme for Russell. Liam also tells Russell that if he fails to take up the company's offer for training, it will lead to a formal warning. Russell agrees to the training and furthermore discusses his performance targets with Liam and the HR manager of Numbers Matter, Ms. Kate Wisletti who suggests assessing Russell's performance after a three months period. After three months, Russell Clow's performance has improved markedly.

1. What performance methods has Liam Leeson used to assess the performance of Russell Clow? Did these methods deliver the expected outcomes?
2. Was the involvement of the HR manager, Kate Wisletti, beneficial to the performance process? Describe her input.
3. When providing performance feedback, which of the three approaches – tell-&-sell, tell-&-listen, or problem-solving – did Liam Leeson use? Discuss which approach delivered the best outcome in this case and why it is superior compared to the other two approaches.
4. Develop one codified HR policy on the performance management system of Numbers Matter. Develop one HR policy on the performance methods used to assess individual work group members. Explain both policies by outlining their purpose and justify your decision.
5. Together with the HR manager Kate, Liam identified the problem that prevented Russell Clow from performing. Describe the barrier and outline what was used to overcome this barrier and assess whether it has been successful. Finally, develop two recommendations on how the performance management system of Numbers Matter can be improved.

### 7.3 Performance Management at Rollexi

The Rollexi Corp. employs 38,000 people throughout the world supplying staff in the retail industry. Rollexi Corp. offers strategic career planning to help employees reach outstanding goals. Last year, Rollexi Corp. appointed 250 new managers – 80% of whom were sourced through the internal labour market. In addition to an annual career discussion with every employee, Rollexi Corp. emphasises the development of the "whole" person. It has successfully implemented a 360-degree performance management system. Rollexi Corp. views this as a personal development tool providing feedback for its internal recruitment and selection process. All employees of Rollexi Corp. have a personal development plan that is based on the 360-degree feedback method.

During the 360-degree process, employees give and receive performance feedback not only from their managers but also from their peers, work colleagues, and – in some cases – subordinates. Annual salary increases are linked to the performance reviews. Rollexi Corp. offers performance reviews as an anonymous process. However, many of Rollexi Corp.'s employees can link performance feedback to the source of the information. The corporation also uses the 360 degree method to assist each individual employee in understanding their specific roles and duties within Rollexi Corp. Through 360-degree feedback, employees can assess not only their weaknesses and strengths but also their contribution to the overall success of Rollexi Corp. The corporation is convinced that a personalised approach to performance management based on 360-degree feedback gives its employees learning and development opportunities. Above that, it makes employees aware of how to take personal responsibility for their own development and careers. Rollexi Corp. is proud of its integrative approach to performance management.

1.  Explain why the 360 degree approach to performance management works at Rollexi Corp. Find at least five reasons.
2.  Imagine you are the HR manager at Rollexi Corp. and a group of employees has decided to jointly agree that they will all review each other and give each other the highest marks available on Rollexi Corp.'s performance measurement scale. How would you respond to this initiative?
3.  Imagine you are the HR manager at Rollexi Corp. seeking to provide feedback to an employee using the "problem-solving" approach to feedback giving. How would you plan your discussion with the employee and what points would you include in the discussion?
4.  While Rollexi Corp.'s 360-degree feedback on performance includes peers, co-workers, managers, and subordinates, is there any other additional performance information that could further improve its performance management system? Name at least three and explain them.
5.  The 360 degree method of performance measuring relies heavily on person-to-person relationships. These are inherently exposed to bias, subjectivity, nepotism, and favouritism. Imagine you are the HR manager at Rollexi Corp. How would you source additional performance information that is NOT based on personal relationships? Find at least three additional "non-personal" based sources of performance information and justify their use.

### 7.4 The End of Performance Management at Demeter Foods Ltd.

At Demeter Foods Ltd. it is time for the annual performance management review. This includes feedback to employees by their managers. HR managers are working hard at this time. They are busy writing reports, assessing, rating employees, and planning review discussions. On the other side, Demeter Foods Ltd.'s employees are starting to worry about what HR has for or against them. Performance reviews are a bit like marking at university. Employees are often assigned rankings and grades. Line managers and supervisors tell employees where they were right and what they have done wrong.

At Demeter Foods Ltd., HR mangers thought it was time to do a review of the performance review. The company questioned its workforce of 2,400 employees working in various offices in the European Union. HR asked about what these employees thought about the common practice of performance management and performance feedback. HR was truly flabbergasted by the feedback of its employees. HR had already heard comparable criticism earlier on when Demeter Foods Ltd. started its performance management system. Demeter Foods Ltd.'s 2015 review had these five key results:

1. Performance reviews were considered to be a time waste. Employees thought that performance management offered little benefits. Most managers were spending 17 hours per employee, per review. Despite this, well above 50% reported that performance management reviews have next to no impact on how employees do their jobs. An overwhelming majority thought that performance management assessments were a pointless requirement set up by the HR department.
2. The majority of employees also thought that ratings done by line managers, feedback, and reviews were causing stress. This was considered an unnecessary infringement. Almost 60% of all employees asked reported that annual performance reviews were stressful to them. Many issued deep concerns regarding OHS. One of the more common results was that employees thought that performance rankings against peers (other employees) was upsetting. In some cases, this bordered on nepotism. Some employees reported that several line managers played the system by favouring certain employees.
3. Several employees said they even wept (22%) while 37% considered looking for another job elsewhere. 20% even thought of quitting their position at Demeter Foods Ltd.
4. These results are even stronger in the case of "Generation Y" (born between the early 1980s and early 2000s) (see also: generation Z, born after 2000[108]). Generation Y employees were much more likely to look for another job. A whopping 47% reported this while 30% thought of quitting. Almost two-thirds of all generation Y employees at Demeter Foods Ltd. said they wanted to move to a company that didn't have performance management reviews even if pay and job levels were the same.
5. Finally, well above 50% of office workers and 66% of line managers at Demeter Foods Ltd. wished that the firm would eliminate performance management reviews. They said that at least serious structural changes to the current performance review process should be undertaken. When it came to performance feedback, most employees at Demeter Foods Ltd. wanted qualitative feedback.

Based on these findings, Demeter Foods Ltd. eventually eliminated its annual performance review process in early 2017. According to the HR director at Demeter Foods Ltd., Stephanie Clifford, "our employees were truly surprised". "Yes", she says, "it was a risk, but it was one I was willing to take". The elimination of annual performance reviews provided the employees with a far better experience to improve the company performance. Ms Clifford says, "we dropped the heavily formalised HR process. The firm now focuses on getting line managers, supervisors, and employees to communicate more often about what matters to Demeter Foods Ltd." There are clear work expectations, defined organisational goals, consistent and frequent performance feedback, and career growth for employees. HR at Demeter Foods Ltd. calls its new system "logging@in". Ms Clifford concluded, 'since putting "logging@in" in place at Demeter Foods Ltd., we haven't looked back'.

1. Outline the old performance management review system at Demeter Foods Ltd. Was it a reflection of some of the eight flaws of performance management as outlined by Tamra Chandler (2016) and Thomas Klikauer (2017)?
2. Was HR at Demeter Foods Ltd. correct in running a survey of employees on their attitudes about performance management? Outline four positives on asking employees directly about HR issues.
3. Discuss the first section of the results of the survey (no. 1). Why do you think that employees reported that performance reviews are a "waste of time"? Why did employees mention that performance management had virtually no impact on how they did their job? Find two reasons for each statement made by employees.
4. Discuss the survey results no. 2 and 3 on OHS. What did employees mention on the stress performance management causes them? Name four sources of potentials for workplace stress that are associated with performance management.
5. Examine Demeter Foods Ltd.'s new system called "logging@in". What are the benefits of the new way in which Demeter Foods Ltd. conducts "performance"? Name four positives of Demeter Foods Ltd.'s new "logging@in" system.

## 7.5 CEO Performance and Rewards

While most CEOs own shares in corporations, most workers don't own such shares. Still, the month of April is a peak time for shareholders. In 2018, many employees started to pay extra attention. There are several new reports on the substantially enlarged rewards CEOs receive. This includes information on companies disclosing CEO's pays in comparison to the median employee salary range. In many leading corporations (e.g. Pepsi, the makers of Cheetos and Doritos), the ratio stood at "650-to-1". Its CEO's payout of $31,082,648 compares to the median salary of $47,801. To its defence, Pepsi's corporate PR (public relations) says that about 50% of its employees are employed overseas. In developing countries, the corporation says, *the low cost of labour impacts on employee compensation*.

Meanwhile, Del Monte's CEO is paid a whopping $8.5 million. At the same time, the average worker salary was just $5,833 annually. This is a CEO–worker ratio of an unbelievable "1,465-to-1". In other words, if a worker buys one pizza, the CEO can buy almost 1,500 pizzas. Needless to say, 80% of the corporation's workforce is located in developing countries (e.g. Costa Rica, Kenya, Guatemala and the Philippines). CEO compensation includes bonuses, cash and pension boosts, share options, etc.). Commonly, these are listed in annual reports on CEO payments.

Ms Temple McDowell is the spokesperson of an NGO that monitors CEO payments. Ms McDowell said that "high CEO payouts are over-emphasising the impact a single individual has on a corporation". Rather than rewarding "one man" (usually CEOs are male), "corporations should reward the work of the many company employees", says Ms McDowell. These kinds of wage inequalities have already led to severe economic inequality.[109] Today, inequalities are already at such a high level that this system becomes increasingly incompatible with the wellbeing of our social and economic arrangements. In many cases, the stratospheric pay scales do not even correlate to CEO performance. Higher returns for investors and shareholder values are often disconnected from CEO payments.

Today, CEO payments are sortable by company name and total compensation (e.g. www.asyousow.org). Still, Ms Temple McDowell said, *this is fairly new*. Ms McDowell emphasises that eventually investors will pressure corporations in the direction of great pay equality. She also adds that, *one of the things people and investors can do is to move money to a social investment fund*. Social and ethical investment is, however, not yet a mass movement.

1.  The case above notes that there are discrepancies between the rewards CEOs receive and the wages workers receive. This has reached previously unimaginable levels. Why has this occurred? Find five arguments that explain the growing difference between the income of CEOs and that of workers.
2.  Is performance management able to explain the performance of CEOs? The case notes that high CEO payouts are "over emphasising the impact a single individual has on a corporation". Discuss this statement by finding three arguments in favour of the statement and three arguments against it.
3.  Should HR managers in such corporations work towards reducing the wage gap between CEOs and workers? Find two arguments in favour of this proposal and two arguments against such a proposal.
4.  The two corporations named in the case study employ many workers in overseas locations. Imagine you are an HR manager in such a corporation, assigned the task to re-evaluate the performance of those workers and their contribution to the corporation. What would you suggest to increase the wages of overseas workers so that these reflect their true performance? Name three possible scenarios.
5.  Imagine you are the HR manager at one of the corporations named above. You have been assigned the task of limiting the exorbitant reward of the CEO. What kind of stakeholders would you include in such a project and why? Name at least four stakeholders and explain why these should be included.

## V. A Suggestion for an Online Guest Lecture

Corporate PR Guru and IT expert David Grady explains the significance of *"Management Meetings"* (2015)

http://www.ted.com/talks/david_grady_how_to_save_the_world_or_at_least_ yourself_from_bad_meetings

[the online guest lecture above is merely a suggestion – www.ted.com/talks offers additional material to choose from]

## VI.  List of Suggested Documentaries on Performance Management

The carefully selected documentary videos below are mere suggestions to be used during tutorials. Documentaries have been selected to achieve two things: (a) to explain key HRM themes and (b) to provide an insight into the reality of HRM. Typically, these short documentaries should be viewed in class followed by a class discussion on the content of the video. Alternatively, questions on documentaries can be prepared beforehand and small group discussions can follow up the video after viewing is concluded. Should any of the web links no longer function, please conduct an internet search for other – alternative – documentaries related to your tutorial topic (e.g. filmsforaction.org):

PM Essentials: www.youtube.com/watch?v=_1oCjW_gFcg
The Office (BBC-UK): youtube.com/watch?v=IkYUDQCYGHA
Penny's Performance Review: youtube.com/watch?v=_7CEmBZyGF8
The Performance Review: youtube.com/watch?v=gdp4sPviV74
Scrubs Performance: www.youtube.com/watch?v=09bp__4Muh8
PM & Responsibility: youtube.com/watch?v=N8XsBFLZB7s
PM Instructions: youtube.com/watch?v=ZT2I2EQngN4

## Notes

1  A good overview of the "performance management-HRM" link is provided in Wilton's *"Introduction to HRM"* (2016), pp. 74–75.
2  Magretta, J. 2012. *What Management Is: How It Works and Why It's Everyone's Business*, London: Profile, p. 4.
3  Clegg, S. 1989. *Frameworks of Power*, London: Sage.
4  Zettler, I. & Solga, M. 2013. Not enough of a 'dark'trait? Linking Machiavellianism to job performance, *European Journal of Personality*, 27(6):545–554.
5  Dahl, R. A. 1957. The Concept of Power, *Behavioural Science*, 2:202f; Peetz, D. 2019. *The Realities and Futures of Work*, Canberra: ANU Press, p. 31.
6  http://www.wildtimecaribbean.com/product-p/667.htm.
7  Lafargue, P. 1883. *The Right to be Lazy*, written in Saint Pelagie Prison, translated by Charles Kerr and first published by Charles Kerr Cooperative, download: www.marxist.org/archive/lafargue/1883/lazy.
8  Schleicher, D. J., Baumann, H. M., Sullivan, D. W. & Yim, J. 2019. Evaluating the effectiveness of performance management: a 30-year integrative conceptual review, *Journal of Applied Psychology*, 104(7), 851–887.
9  Porter, M. E. 1985. *Competitive Advantage*, New York: Free Press.
10  Pulakos, E. D. & Battista, M. (eds.) 2020. *Performance Management Transformation: Lessons Learned and Next Steps*, Oxford: Oxford University Press.
11  Key performance indicators are types of performance measurement evaluating the success of employees in an organisation. Often an employee's achievement is periodically assessed at some levels of operational goals (e.g. zero defects, 10/10 customer satisfaction, etc.). But success can also be defined in terms of making progress toward strategic organisational goals. Accordingly, choosing the right KPIs relies upon a good understanding of what is important to the organisation. In turn, what is important often depends on the department measuring the performance – KPIs are particularly useful to finance but will differ from KPIs applied in sales, for example.
12  Culbert, S. A. 2010. *Get Rid of the Performance Review*, New York & London: Hachette Book Group.
13  Tweedie, D., Wild, D., Rhodes, C. & Martinov-Bennie, N. 2019. How does performance management affect workers? Beyond human resource management and its critique, *International Journal of Management Reviews*, 21(1):80.

14  Bal, P. M. 2020. Why we should stop measuring performance and well-being, *Zeitschrift für Arbeits-und Organisationspsychologie*, 64(3):196–215.

15  While employing 65,000 people, "in a public survey Deloitte conducted recently, more than half the executives questioned (58%) believe that their current performance management approach drives neither employee engagement nor high performance" (Buckingham, M. & Goodall, A. 2015. Reinventing performance management, *Harvard Business Review*, 93(4):4).

16  Moussa, M. 2015. Monitoring employee behavior through the use of technology and issues of employee privacy in America, *SAGE Open*, 5(2):2158244015580168.

17  Chandler, T. M. 2016. *How Performance Management Is Killing Performance – And What to Do About It: Rethink, Redesign, Reboot*, San Francisco, CA: Berrett-Koehler Publishers; Buckingham, M. & Klikauer, T. 2017. Eight fatal flaws of performance management: how performance management is killing performance – and what to do about it: rethink, redesign, reboot, *Management Learning*, 48(4):492–497.

18  Goodall, A. 2015. Reinventing performance management, *Harvard Business Review*, 93(4):40–50.

19  Galang, M. C. & Osman, I. 2015. HR managers in five countries: what do they do and why does it matter?, *International Journal of Human Resource Management*, 27(13), 1341-1372.

20  Pinto, J. 2019. Key to effective organisational performance management, *International Journal of Management Reviews*, 21(2):185–208.

21  Vanderstraeten, A. 2018. *Strategic HRM and Performance – A Conceptual Framework*, London: Red Globe Press.

22  Micklethwait, J. & Wooldrige, A. 1996. *The Witch Doctors: Making Sense of the Management Gurus*, New York: Times Books, p. 36.

23  McAllister, V. et al. 2019. Why likable leaders seem more effective, *Harvard Business Review*, 29th October 2019.

24  Varma, A. & Budhwar, P. 2019. *Performance Management Systems*, London: Sage.

25  Holbeche, L. 2012. *The High Performance Organization*, London: Routledge.

26  Chandra, N. 2019. The Surplus University, in: Bhattacharya, D. (eds.) *The Idea of the University*, London: Routledge, p. 63.

27  Klikauer, T. 2007. *Communication and Management at Work*, Basingstoke: Palgrave; Klikauer, T. 2008. *Management and Communication – Communicative Ethics and Action*, Basingstoke: Palgrave.

28  Stack, L. 2016. *Doing the Right Things Right: How the Effective Executive Spends Time*, San Francisco, CA: Berrett-Koehler Publishers, p. 129.

29  Rawls, J. 2001. *Justice as Fairness: A Restatement* (edited by Erin Kelly), London: Belknap Press.

30  HRM's disciplinary action is called upon when the general production discipline that requires the voluntary discipline of employees concerning the logic and purpose of production fails.

31  One CEO doing this was Linda Wachner who Fortune magazine called the 'toughest boss in the US. She had a brutal attitude towards people. On one occasion, she order a colleague to fire people at random to show that he was serious about improving performance' (Tourish, D. 2020. *Management Studies – Fraud, Deceptions & Meaning Research*, Cambridge: Cambridge University Press, p. 171).

32  Goler, L., Gale, J. & Grant, A. 2016. Let's not kill performance evaluations yet, *Harvard Business Review*, November 2016.

33  Grote, D. 2016. HBR tools: performance reviews, *Harvard Business Review*, 28th January 2016; Cappelli, P. & Tavis, A. 2016. The performance management revolution, *Harvard Business Review*, October 2016 issue.

34  Rodsevich, M. 2016. This is How Google Redefines Performance Management (https://talentculture.com, 6th January 2016, accessed: 17th January 2018); cf. https://hbr.org/2016/10/the-performance-management-revolution.

35  Williams, M. et al. 2020. *Mapping Good Work – The Quality of Working Life across the Occupational Structure*, Bristol: Bristol University Press, p. 49.

36  Langness, F., Schultz, N. DaPra, G. & Bersin, J. 2017. Why Facebook is keeping performance reviews, *Harvard Business Review*, 95(1):18.

37  blog.betterworks.com/2015-state-of-performance-management.

38  https://www.washingtonpost.com/news/on-leadership/wp/2015/07/21/in-big-move-accenture-will-get-rid-of-annual-performance-reviews-and-rankings/; http://www.hcamag.com/hr-news/why-accenture-is-ditching-performance-reviews-203052.aspx.

39 However, Duggan (*state of performance management*, blog.betterworks.com, 15th December 2015) argues that 'companies spend a significant amount of time on evaluation but very little on development.' (p. 4).

40 Bradberry, T. 2016. http://www.huffingtonpost.com (03/01/2016 06:02 AEST; updated: 05/01/2016 09:59 AEST).

41 https://www.cipd.co.uk/binaries/The-view-from-below_2015-what-employees-think-CEO-pay-packet%20.pdf; hrreporter.com from 2nd February 2016.

42 Australian airline CEO (Qantas) Mr. Joyce, for example, received A$22.2 million while Qantas made a loss of $2.8 billion with a newspaper reporting that "Qantas shares today are worth 40% less than when Joyce took over" (www.smh.com, 27th August 2014); Bratton, J. 2015. *Introduction to Work and Organizational Behaviour* (3rd ed.), London: Palgrave, p. 253.

43 In one of the more severe cases of being "performance managed into death", biology professor Stefan Grimm (1963–2014) at Imperial College London was put under stress by HRM's performance management system contributing to his suicide (Parr, C. 2014. Imperial College professor Stefan Grimm 'was given grant income target' (timeshighereducation.com, 3rd December 2014); Gove, J. 2015. Stefan Grimm Inquest: New Policies May Not Have Prevented Suicide (timeshighereducation.com, 9th April 2015); Death in Academia and the Mis-measurement of Science (euroscientist.com, 9th February 2015).

44 Kaplan, E. 2015. The spy who fired me: the human costs of workplace monitoring, *Harper's Magazine*, 330(1978):5.

45 Micklethwait, J. & Wooldridge, A. 1996. *The Witch Doctors: Making Sense of the Management Gurus*, New York: Times Books, p. 207.

46 Tyskbo, D. 2020. Line management involvement in performance appraisal work: toward a practice-based understanding, *Employee Relations*, ahead-of-print, https://doi.org/10.1108/ER-06-2019-0236.

47 Buckingham, M. & Goodall. A. 2015. Reinventing performance management, *Harvard Business Review*, 93(4):40–50.

48 An empirical study on the UK class system found that, 'those from working-class backgrounds are getting paid less for doing the same work (that is, for doing jobs at the same level, same company and same department)' (Friedman, S. & Laurison, D. 2019. *The Class Ceiling – Why It Pays to Be Privileged*, Bristol: Policy Press, p. 71; BBC. 2020. How to Get Promoted When Working from Home (https://www.bbc.com/news/business-54432760).

49 Gantman, E. R. 2005. *Capitalism, Social Privilege, and Managerial Ideologies*, Aldershot: Ashgate, p. 78.

50 Bloom, P. & Rhodes, C. 2018. *CEO Society*, London: Zed-Books (epub version), p. 167.

51 Hofstede, G. 1980. *Culture's Consequences: International Differences in Work-Related Values*, Beverly Hills: Sage Publications.

52 HBR. 2020. The wellness factors employees actually value, *Harvard Business Review*, 98(1):30.

53 Langness, F., Schultz, N., DaPra, G. & Bersin, J. 2017. Why Facebook is keeping performance reviews, *Harvard Business Review*, 95(1):18.

54 For more information on Hofstede's perspective on organisational culture, see: Wilton's "*Introduction to HRM*" (2016:117).

55 Said, E. W. 1978. *Orientalism*, New York: Vintage Books; Said, E. W. 1994. *Culture & Imperialism*, New York: Knopf.

56 Fanon, F. 1963. *The Wretched of the Earth* (pref. by Jean-Paul Sartre; trans. by Constance Farrington), New York: Grove Press; Fanon, F. 2008. *Black Skin, White Masks* (translated from the French by Richard Philcox), New York: Grove Press.

57 Schönebeck, J. & Schönebeck, M. 2016. Engagement and retention: essentials in employee surveys, in: Zeuch, M. (eds.) *Handbook of HRM*, Heidelberg: Springer, p. 633ff.

58 Adler, S. et al. 2016. Getting rid of performance ratings: genius or folly? A debate, *Industrial and Organizational Psychology*, 9(02):219–252.

59 http://www.economist.com/news/business/21589866-firms-keep-grading-their-staff-ruthlessly-may-not-get-best-them-ranked-and-yanked.

60 Micklethwait, J. & Wooldridge, A. 1996. *The Witch Doctors: Making Sense of the Management Gurus*, New York: Times Books, p. 135.

61 Hannon, K. 2015. Exit Interview Do's And Don'ts (forbes.com, 4th June 2015); Kulik, C. T., Treuren, G. & Bordia, P. 2012. Shocks and final straws: using exit-interview data to examine the unfolding model's decision paths, *Human Resource Management*, 51(1):25–46; Peterson, J. 2020. Firing with compassion, *Harvard Business Review*, 98(2):135–139.

62  https://www.bbc.com/news/business-52830257.

63  https://www.glassdoor.com.au.

64  As a Honda executive once said "I believe creativity is born by pushing people against the wall and pressuring them almost to the extreme" (Micklethwait, J. & Wooldridge, A. 1996. *The Witch Doctors: Making Sense of the Management Gurus*, New York: Times Books, p. 135).

65  Employing 65,000 people, Deloitte noticed in 2015 that "ratings reveal more about the rater than they do about the ratee" (Buckingham, M. & Goodall, A. 2015. Reinventing performance management, *Harvard Business Review*, 93(4):6).

66  Chomsky, N. 1971. The case against B. F. Skinner, *The New York Review of Books*, 30th December (internet download).

67  Allinger, R. et al. 2016. Performance and talent: essentials of performance and potential management, in: Zeuch, M. (eds.) *Handbook of HRM*, Heidelberg: Springer, p. 443.

68  Kislik, L. 2017. Being the boss's favorite is great, until it's not, *Harvard Business Review*, 19th May 2017.

69  Ajunwa, I., Crawford, K. & Schultz, J. 2017. Limitless worker surveillance, *California Law Review*, 105:769.

70  Moore, P. & Robinson, A. 2016. The quantified self: what counts in the neoliberal workplace, *New Media & Society*, 18(11):2781.

71  Kaplan, E. 2015. The spy who fired me: the human costs of workplace monitoring, *Harper's Magazine*, 330(1978):9.

72  https://fortune.com/2020/01/10/designed-clowns-supervised-monkeys-internal-boeing-messages-slam-737-max/.

73  Rumour has it that US TV comedy "MASH 4077" star Maxwell Klinger coined the memorable phrase, "management is when those who can't manage those who can"; http://www.forbes.com/sites/stevecooper/2012/11/15/nearly-half-of-all-managers-cant-manage/#3f4071 431549.

74  Samuel, Y. 2010. *Organizational Pathology*, New Brunswick: Transaction Publishers, p. 92.

75  http://www.bbc.co.uk/programmes/b00jd68z/episodes/guide; Schrijvers, J. 2004. *The Way of the Rat – A Survival Guide to Office Politics*, London: Cyan Books.

76  Tweedie, D., Wild, D., Rhodes, C. & Martinov-Bennie, N. 2019. How does performance management affect workers? Beyond human resource management and its critique, *International Journal of Management Reviews*, 21(1):80.

77  Parker, I. 2015, *Handbook of Critical Psychology*, London: Routledge, p. 137.

78  Beer, J. S. & Hughes, B. L. 2010. Neural systems of social comparison and the "above-average" effect, *Neuroimage*, 49(3):2671–2679.

79  Lukes, S. 1974. *Power: A Radical View*, London: Macmillan.

80  Rissell, M. 2017. Performance Reviews Suck, Here's What We Do Instead (https://www.forbes.com, 26th May 2017, accessed: 5th April 2019).

81  Bourdieu, P. 1991. *Language and Symbolic Power*, Cambridge: Harvard University Press; Nussbaum, M. C. & Glover, J. 1995. *Women, Culture, and Development: A Study of Human Capabilities*, Oxford: Clarendon Press.

82  Ball, K. 2010. Workplace surveillance: an overview, *Labor History*, 51(1):87–106; Ball, K. S. 2001. Situating workplace surveillance: ethics and computer based performance monitoring, *Ethics and Information Technology*, 3(3):209–221; Holland, P. J., Cooper, B. & Hecker, R. 2015. Electronic monitoring and surveillance in the workplace: the effects on trust in management, and the moderating role of occupational type, *Personnel Review*, 44(1):161–175; McDonald, P. & Thompson, P. 2016. Social media(tion) and the reshaping of public/private boundaries in employment relations, *International Journal of Management Reviews*, 18(1):69–84.

83  Ajunwa, I., Crawford, K. & Schultz, J. 2017. Limitless worker surveillance, *California Law Review*, 105:735–776.

84  Marchant, G. E. 2019. What are best practices for ethical use of nanosensors for worker surveillance?, *AMA Journal of Ethics*, 21(4):356–362.

85  https://www.workhuman.com/company/.

86  Matell, M. S. & Jacoby, J. 1972. Is there an optimal number of alternatives for Likert-scale items? Effects of testing time and scale properties, *Journal of Applied Psychology*, 56(6):506.

87  Latham, G. P., Fay, C. H. & Saari, L. M. 1979. The development of behavioral observation scales for appraising the performance of foremen, *Personnel Psychology*, 32(2):299–311.

88  Rowley, C. & Ramasamy, N. 2016. Horns effect, in: *Encyclopedia of Human Resource Management*, London: Edward Elgar Publishing, p. 182-83.

89   Dillon, K. 2014. *HBR Guide to Office Politics,* Boston, MA: Harvard Business Review Press; Godwin, J. 2013. *The Office Politics Handbook: Winning the Game of Power and Politics at Work / Jack Godwin,* Pompton Plains: Career Press; James, O. 2013. *Office Politics: How to Thrive in a World of Lying, Backstabbing and Dirty Tricks,* New York: Random House.

90   Kaplan, E. 2015. The spy who fired me: the human costs of workplace monitoring, *Harper's Magazine,* 330(1978):6.

91   Scholz, T. 2016. *Ueberworked and Underpaid,* Oxford: Polity Press.

92   http://meyerweb.com/other/humor/reviews.html.

93   See also Darden, Q. 2020. 90 Sample Phrases for Negative Performance Reviews (https://www.businessmanagementdaily.com/52482/90-sample-phrases-for-negative-performance-reviews/, updated 6/30/20, accessed: 15th July 2020).

94   Gruman, J. A. & Saks, A. M. 2011. Performance management and employee engagement, *Human Resource Management Review,* 21(2):123–136.

95   Mercer. 2013. *What's Working – Global Performance Management Study* (www.mercer.com).

96   https://edition.cnn.com/2020/03/16/success/video-conference-work-from-home/index.html.

97   https://www.bbc.com/worklife/article/20200316-how-your-phone-damages-trust-with-your-colleagues.

98   Mollaret, C. & Chaudepierre, C. 2016. Performance and talent: essentials of coaching, in: Zeuch, M. (eds.) *Handbook of HRM,* Heidelberg: Springer, p. 545.

99   Wilkinson, A. & Johnstone, S. 2015. *Encyclopedia of HRM,* Northampton: Edward Elgar. p. 113.

100  Carleton, R. 2010. *Implementation and Management of Performance Improvement Plans: Emphasizing Group and Organizational Interventions,* Amherst: HRD Press; SHRM. 2015. *How to Establish a Performance Improvement Plan* (www.shrm.org, 16th September 2015); Ryan, L. 2016. The Truth about 'Performance Improvement Plans' (forbes.com, 8th April 2016).

101  Heller, M. 2017. 6 Effective Performance Review Examples from the Best Companies (https://irevu.me/blog/6-effective-performance-review-examples-best-companies/ posted on 15th may 2017, accessed: 6th February 2018); cf. Adonis, J. 2018. *The Motivation Hoax,* Carlton: Schwartz Publishing.

102  Appelbaum, E. et al. 2000. *Manufacturing Advantage: Why High-Performance Work Systems Pay Off,* Ithaca, NY: Cornell University Press; Van Waeyenberg, T. & Adelien, D. 2018. Line managers' AMO to manage employees' performance: the route to effective and satisfying performance management, *International Journal of Human Resource Management,* 29(22):3093–3114.

103  Kaplan, R. S. & Norton, D. P. 1992. The balanced scorecard: measures that drive performance, *Harvard Business Review,* Januaty–Febrauary, pp. 71–80; Kaplan, R. S. & Norton, D. P. 1993. Putting the balanced scorecard to work, *Harvard Business Review,* September–October, pp. 2–16; Campbell, D., Datar, S. M., Kulp, S. L. & Narayanan, V. G. 2015. Testing strategy with multiple performance measures: evidence from a balanced scorecard at Store24, *Journal of Management Accounting Research,* 27(2):39–65.

104  https://www.qualtrics.com/lp/what-is-xm-video/.

105  Paauwe, J., Guest, D. E. & Wright, P. (eds.) 2013. *HRM and Performance: Achievements and Challenges,* Chichester Wiley.

106  Chandler, T. M. 2016. *How Performance Management Is Killing Performance – And What to Do About It: Rethink, Redesign, Reboot,* San Francisco, CA: Berrett-Koehler Publishers.

107  Klikauer, T. 2017. Eight fatal flaws of performance management: how performance management is killing performance, *Management Learning,* 48(4):492–497.

108  https://www.bbc.com/worklife/article/20201204-how-young-workers-are-changing-the-rules-of-business-speak.

109  https://inequality.org/.

## Further Readings

Adams, C. A., Muir, S. & Hoque, Z. 2014. Measurement of Sustainability Performance in the Public Sector, *Sustainability Accounting, Management and Policy Journal,* 5(1):46–67.

Adi, I. 2015. Time to Kill Forced Rankings?, *Harvard Business Review,* April, 93:4.

Andreassi, J. K., Lawter, L., Brockerhoff, M. & Rutigliano, P. J. 2014. Cultural Impact of HR Practices on Job Satisfaction: A Global Study across 48 Countries. *Cross Cultural Management,* 21(1):4.

Armstrong, M. 2014 *Armstrong's Handbook of Performance Management: An Evidence-Based Guide to Delivering High Performance* (5th ed.), London: Kogan Page.

Buckingham, M. & Goodall, A. 2015. Reinventing Performance Management, *Harvard Business Review*, 93:4.

Clark, J. & Clark, R. et al. 2014. When Do Leaders Matter…Firm Performance, *Leadership Quarterly*, 25(2), 358–372.

Decramer, A.,Smolders, C. & Vanderstraeten, A. 2013. Employee Performance Management Culture and System Features in Higher Education: Relationship with Employee Performance Management Satisfaction, *International Journal of Human Resource Management*, 24(4):352–371.

Dubois, D. et al. 2015. Social Class…Selfishness, *Journal of Personality & Social Psychology*, 108(3):436–449.

Dusterhoff, C., Cunningham, J. B. & MacGregor, J. N. 2014. The Effects of Performance Rating, Leader–Member Exchange, Perceived Utility, and Organizational Justice on Performance Appraisal Satisfaction: Applying a Moral Judgment Perspective, *Journal of Business Ethics*, 119(2):265–273.

Gabler, C. B., Nagy, K. R. & Hill, R. P. 2014. Causes and Consequences of Abusive Supervision in Sales Management: A Tale of Two Perspectives, *Psychology & Marketing*, 31(4):278–293.

Goldsmith, M. 2015. A 6-Part Structure for Giving Clear & Actionable Feedback, *Harvard Business Review*, 7th August.

Gupta, N. & Shaw, J. D. 2014. Employee Compensation, *HRM Review*, 24(1):1–4.

Hammermann, A. & Mohnen, A. 2014. The Pric(z)e of Hard Work: Different Incentive Effects of Non-monetary and Monetary Prizes, *Journal of Economic Psychology*, 43(1):1–15.

Hansen, M. T. et al. 2013. The Best-Performing CEOs in the World, *Harvard Business Review*, January.

Heavey, A. L., Beijer, S., Federman, J., Hermans, M., Klein, F., McClean, E. & Gerhart, B. 2013. Measurement of HR Practices: Issues Regarding Scale, Sources, and Substantive Content, [pp. 129–148], in: Paauwe, J., Guest, D. E. & Wright, P. (eds.) *HRM & Performance*, Chichester: Wiley.

Herzberg, F. 2011. One More Time: How Do You Motivate Employees?, https://hbr.org/2003/01/one-more-time-how-do-you-motivate-employees

Jacobsen, D. 2014. *Are Rewards Demotivating?* (www.globoforce.com/gfblog/2014).

Ma, Q. et al. 2014. The Dark Side of Monetary Incentive, *Neuroreport*, 25(3):194–198.

Martocchio, J. J. 2015. *Strategic Compensation: HRM* (8th ed.), Upper Saddle River: Pearson.

McMahan, G. C. & Harris, C. M. 2013. Measuring Human Capital: A Strategic HRM Perspective, *The Negotiated Character of Performance Appraisal, International Journal of HRM*, 24(4):853–870.

Mohan, B. et al. 2015. Paying Up for Fair Pay: Consumers Prefer Firms with Lower CEO-to-Worker Pay Ratios, *Harvard Business School Marketing Unit Working Paper* (15-091).

Paauwe, J. et al. 2013. Reconceptualising Fit in Strategic HRM [pp. 61–78], in: Paauwe, J., Guest, D. E. & Wright, P. (eds.) *HRM & Performance – Achievements & Challenges*, Chichester: Wiley.

Paladino, B. 2013. *Corporate Performance Management Best Practices*, Hoboken, NJ: Wiley

Parry, E. & Tyson, S. 2014. *Managing People in a Contemporary Context*, London: Routledge.

Rees W. & Porter C. 2015. *Skills of Management*, London: Palgrave, Chapter 10, Appraisal.

Rose, M. 2014. *Reward Management*, London: Kogan Page.

Scandura, T. A. 2015. *Essentials of Organizational Behavior*, London: Sage.

Shields, J. et al. 2015. *Managing Employee Performance*, Cambridge: Cambridge University Press.

Smith, C. & Chan, J. 2015. Working for Two Bosses, *Human Relations*, 68(2):305–326.

Srivastava, S. B. 2015. Network Intervention…Mentoring on Workplace, *Social Forces*, 94(1):427–452.

White, M. D. 2013. Can We & Should We-Measure Well-Being?, *Review of Social Economy*, 71(4): pp. 526–533.

Williams, L. S. & Bemiller, M. 2010. *Women at Work*, Boulder, CO: Lynne Rienner Press.

# 8 Rewarding People
## Managing Compensation and Rewards

## Executive Summary

Rewarding people remains a key task for HR managers. A fair and equitable remuneration (reward fairness) remains imperative for the success of a business organisation. Reward management distinguishes between wages and salaries. Six basic forms of rewards have been highlighted: time- and result-based systems, enterprise-based systems, performance-related, skill-based, and knowledge-based systems and flexible benefit plans as well as the link between rewards and motivation (e.g. positive and negative reinforcement and punishment). Inevitably, rewards are also linked to job structures and they are related to motivation. This is known as monetary reward system. An ongoing debate on rewards and motivation has been the remuneration of CEOs; on the other end of the reward spectrum are debates on the minimum wage. One way to avoid drifting towards the minimum wage has been collective bargaining between trade unions and management or employers. As a consequence, key elements of wage negotiations are explained in this chapter. This includes a five-step bargaining and negotiation process that assists HR managers in achieving positive organisational outcomes for both workers and employers.

## Key Learning Objectives

1. Understand the key imperatives of reward management;
2. Acknowledge the relevance of rewarding for business success;
3. Outline the elements of a reward system;
4. Conceptualise the link between motivation and rewarding;
5. Realise the core aspects of pay and benefit schemes;
6. Recognise the basic parameters of a pay structure;
7. Comprehend the link between a business strategy and reward management;
8. Explain the difference between financial and non-financial rewards;
9. Describe the link between equity theory, rewards, and compensation.

## The Basics of Reward Management and Compensation

Compensation and reward management is a process by which companies distribute financial and non-financial rewards to their employees.[1] Non-monetary rewards include, for example, recognition, awards, empowerment,[2] more authority and responsibility, status, great span of control, praise, etc. Compensation and reward management usually include four basic systems: (1) base pay,[3] wages,[4] and salaries[5]; (2) salary add-ons; (3) incentive pay; and (4) general benefits (e.g. company car, child care,

DOI: 10.4324/9781003293637-8

medical insurance, mobile phone, study/tuition, etc.). **Base pay** is often a flat rate paid either as an hourly rate or as a salary (weekly, monthly, or annually). Most companies see this as the core of their reward management while for many employees, it is the sole reason for "Why We Work".[6] The key difference between wages and salaries is that the former is paid on an hourly basis while the latter on a given time period regardless of the number of hours worked. Most commonly, wages are paid to blue-collar workers (manual labour) while salaries are paid to white collar labour (office work, administration, management, etc.).

Both wages and salaries can have so-called **wages and salary add-ons** often found as overtime payments or shift, overtime, weekend, holiday, etc. allowances. Thirdly, there is also **incentive and variable pay**. "The whole system of incentive pay is geared towards persuading staff to worker ever harder".[7] This is the downside for workers. For HRM and for middle managers, the administration of such incentive systems can be time-consuming and complicated. For a start and as with any pay systems based on controlling workers, coherent standards have to be created and launched. Furthermore, results and outcomes have to be measured. Yet such standards and measurements are highly dependent on the work they measure and control. Often, such standards and measurements have been found to by imprecise and very costly to develop. As a consequence, some incentive systems produce inconsistencies and inequities. Another problem is that such system can lead to the outcome that workers earn more money than their supervisors who are often salaried managers. Finally, it is not uncommon that employees fail to achieve pre-set standards because of uncontrollable fats such as, for example, delays, missing tools, supplier problems, equipment malfunctions, etc.

Incentive pay can take the form of **performance-related pay**[8] and **commissions**[9] linked to sales targets.[10] Even more common are forms such as incentive wages for **piece work** in production and manufacturing but it can also take the form of short-term pay for specific achievements and projects. In any case, "economics shows that firms hire workers as long as they generate revenue greater than their cost".[11]

Finally, there are mandatory (regulated by law) and non-mandatory or voluntary **benefits** (regulated through **HR policies**). These are indirect forms of rewards providing additional value to employees. Such benefits can include a bonus, private health insurance, retirement and pension benefits, unemployment insurance, workers' compensation (OHS), housing subsidies, free clothing, company car, notebooks, computers, iPads, profit sharing schemes,[12] and even payments for cafeteria services, gyms, tuition reimbursements, or contributions for an MBA degree, to name a few.

To govern a rewards system, HR managers put codified **reward policies** in place expressing the clear intention of a company on how compensation and rewards are administered. Such reward policies relate to the basic aspects of reward management: the **reward fairness**[13] and consistency of the reward management system; its strategic ability to strengthen the company's competitiveness; its links with employee performance; and finally, its ability to attract and retain employees; its ability to motivate and engage employees; and the system's communicative aspects (employees understand the policy, their rewards levels, the company's intentions, etc.). These policies are not only designed to inform employees, they also guide companies when making pay decisions.

When HR managers reach pay decisions, these usually concern three main areas of reward management: rewards structure, rewards levels, and rewards systems. **Rewards structures** are designed to outline the relative pay of a job within an organisation while **pay levels** indicate the average wage, salary, bonus, etc. **Rewards systems** can include[14]:

1.  **Time-based systems:**
    such as hourly rates, weekly, monthly, and annual salaries. This rewards method is straightforward, understood well by employees, and relatively trouble-free in its administration.

2.  **Result-based systems:**
    Under result-based reward systems, the output (e.g. productivity) of an employee is rewarded (cf. Taylorist piece rates).[15] Here, workers are paid more as an incentive to produce more. Albeit the OECD has recently acknowledged the rapidly declining "productivity-wage" link.[16] The OECD calls this a decoupling of wages from productivity while noting that this decoupling sets up a "winner-takes-most" dynamic that disadvantages workers (1995 = 100; by 2013, productivity dad risen to 130 while wages were only at 115).[17] Yet there still is a positive "trade union → productivity → wage" link.[18] In any case, another version of linking productivity to wages is to be paid a commission, commonly used in sales, real estate, etc.

3.  **Enterprise-based reward systems:**
    In this system, the reward of employees is linked to the overall performance of an organisation. This includes an organisation-wide bonus system.[19] Some companies reward not only organisational success at the company level but also at the department and team level.[20]

4.  **Performance-related pay:**
    Under performance-related pay (PRP) individual performance is rewarded that is linked to objectives and standards such as, for example, customer satisfaction and sales targets. PRP may include an individual bonus and pay increases based on merit (merit pay), length of service, etc. However, on PRP many HR managers have noted the credibility gap occurring when employees do not see rewards for performance as fair.[21]

5.  **Skill- and knowledge-based systems:**
    These reward systems compensate employees for acquiring new skills and new knowledge that is actionable at company level. This encourages the acquisition of new information and keeping up to date with technological (IT) and legal changes (HRM), etc. A skill-/knowledge-based reward system will encourage skill development, leading to increased productivity and performance.[22]

6.  **Flexible benefit plans:**
    These plans (FBPs) can include a variety of monetary and non-monetary incentives. FBPs are offered to employees based on organisational resources. These plans often allow employees the flexibility to select specific benefit plans best suited to individual lifestyles (e.g. parental leave, company car, mobile phone, etc.).

## Rewards and Motivation

Ever since Pavlov and Skinner's behaviourist theories linked animal behaviour (rat) to human behaviour under the seamless equation of "rat-equals-human" – incentives given to rats under laboratory conditions where they pushed a button to be rewarded (food pill and water) – these theories have been applied to human beings under the heading of organisational psychology.[23] As a consequence, most HR managers believe that rewarding employees makes them productive whilst motivating them to work.[24] In this approach, not only behaviourism but also motivation (previously called "manipulation") is linked to rewards. The "rat → food" equation is moved to "person → money".[25] This classic theory of behaviourism sees three ways of motivating rats/employees:

1. **Positive reinforcement**
   Positive reinforcement gives rats (food and water) and employees (wages and sala-ries) what they like.[26] It is designed to stimulate and motivate employees to repeat positive behaviour. When employees show such positive behaviour (being produc-tive), they are positively rewarded.

   > From roughly 1945 to 1975, there was what is sometimes referred to as a "Keynesian bargain" between workers, employers, and government—and part of the tacit understanding was that increases in worker productivity would indeed be matched by increases in worker compensation.[27]

   However, the productivity ⇔ reward link appears to be broken as "labour shares of national income are falling in many countries".[28] In Australia, for example, "labour's share has been falling for decades [and] more dramatically than in most other OECD nations: from 68% in 1960 to 52% in 2017 – despite the coun-try's much-publicised record of consistent economic growth".[29] There are three explanations[30]:

   1. corporate dominance and the spread of labour-displacing technology;
   2. financialisation and demands for "shareholder value"; and
   3. the erosion of labour laws and bargaining institutions.

2. **Negative reinforcement**
   Negative reinforcement attempts to reduce undesirable behaviours in rats (elec-tric shock) and employees (bad performance and unwarranted behaviour is elimi-nated through withholding something positive, e.g. bonus).

3. **Punishment**
   Punishment for unwarranted behaviours and poor performance can include de-motion, transferral to undesirable work situations (bad jobs), and dismissal.

Motivation models often operate on need (employee needs money and/or an interesting job); drive (employee must have a drive to change things); search (searching for ways how to change things); engage (develop goal driven behaviours); achieve (working towards achieving goals); and finally remedies (alternative pathways when goals are not achieved). This may vary depending on individual employees as the example of **Generation Y** has shown.[31] Non-pay-related elements are important as people consistently placed "I like doing it" (ranked at no. 1) over "pay" (ranked at no. 7) when asked about what is important.[32]

Historically, many of these ideas date back to Taylor's Scientific Management (1911) but have been further developed under the human relations theory.[33] By the early 1940s, the "rat → human" idea received a further boost under "Maslow, Monkeys, and Motiva-tional Theory"[34] with Maslow's infamous and never empirically tested needs hierarchy of physiological needs (working conditions), safety and security needs (job security, OHS), belonging needs (work group, solidarity, organisational culture), self-esteem needs (status, recognition, respect), and finally, self-actualisation needs (self-determination, autonomy).[35]

## Motivational Reward Models

Similarly, achievement/power/affiliation or **APA motivation** focuses on the need for achievement (business success), the need for power (CEO[36]), and the need for affil-iation (team player) while existing/relationship/growth or ERG motivation includes existing needs, relationship needs, and growth needs. Specifically designed for HRM is McGregor's **theory X and theory Y**[37]:

> **Theory X**: assumes that employees do not like to work and need to be controlled to increase productivity (e.g. Taylorism).
>
> **Theory Y**: assumes that employees are self-directed, responsible, determined, and want to do well.

As a consequence, Theory X focuses on punishment while Theory Y is based on rewards. One of the most commonly applied models of motivation is **Herzberg's two factor theme**.[38] One factor of this scheme focuses on

1.  **extrinsic rewards**: they avoid dissatisfaction and relate to work conditions such as salaries, supervision, policies and procedures, work relationships, and job security while the second factor of the scheme focuses on
2.  **intrinsic rewards**: that focus on achievement, recognition, training, responsibility, advancement, and growth.[39]

One might even combine extrinsic and intrinsic rewards and other reward system to create a **total reward system**.[40] A total reward system includes virtually everything employees value in their work: wages, commissions, bonuses, vacations, health insurance, stable, consistency in rewards, etc.

## Equity Reward Models

Both factors can be achieved, for example, through Locke's goal setting theory of **SMART-C**: specific, measurable, attainable, relevant, time bound, and challenging.[41] Similarly, **Adam's equity theory** suggests that inputs need to equal outputs for individuals to be motivated.[42] This includes *internal equity* – all employees working in similar positions with an organisation should be paid the same rate – and *external equity*: comparable rewards should be paid to employees working at similar levels in competitor organisations (benchmarking[43]). Meanwhile **Vroom's expectancy theory** suggests that individuals will be motivated if they receive a desired outcome for their input, effort,[44] and performance[45]:

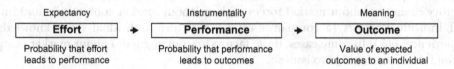

| Expectancy | | Instrumentality | | Meaning |
| --- | --- | --- | --- | --- |
| **Effort** | → | **Performance** | → | **Outcome** |
| Probability that effort leads to performance | | Probability that performance leads to outcomes | | Value of expected outcomes to an individual |

*Figure 8.1* Effort-Outcome Model.

Expectancy models suggest a link [→] between effort, performance, and outcomes, for example, a sales manager prepares a thorough and high-quality sales report that should lead to some form of reward (e.g. a bonus). In general, one might say: if the input (effort) is greater (>) than the outcome (reward) → employees might feel under-rewarded; is the input lower (<) than the outcome (reward) → employees might feel over-rewarded; but when the input equals (=) the outcome (reward) → employees experience equity (fairly rewarded).

As mentioned above, managers and employees not only expect outcomes in exchange for efforts and performance (Figure 8.1), they also compare one another. Equity theories suggest that such managers and employees also evaluate the fairness – justice as fairness[46] – of their work output in comparison to other people. It also means that they compare their own ratio of outcomes (pay, benefits, bonus, working conditions, etc.) to their inputs (effort, ability, skill, experience, etc.). When organisations violate fairness, managers and employees might (1) reduce their effort (Figure 8.1), (2) increase their outcome (white collar crime)[47], or (3) refuse to work or leave the company. For fairness, external and internal equity remains important:

**External equity**: (e.g. comparing oneself to people in other companies) can lead to problems when HR managers believe – often mistakenly – that people inside their organisation are paid well compared to those in other companies. Employees may have different information and/or make different comparisons than management.

**Internal equity**: compares the fairness of pay inside a company, often including comparison to employees at lower, higher, and "at-the-same" levels.

In general, one might coin the hypothesis: the greater the unfairness of a reward, the less likely is compliance with performance demands.

But **reward unfairness**[48] does not only result from internal and external comparisons, it can also be the outcome of the structurally imbedded **gender pay gap**[49] and failures in HR policies and/or their application in regard to distributive, procedural, and communicative fairness:

1. **communicative fairness** denotes that rewards are communicated to employees in a fair manner – somewhat contradicting the much exercised pay secrecy[50];
2. **distributive fairness** demands that rewards are distributed fairly in regard to effort and outcomes (Figure 8.1); and
3. **procedural fairness** stipulates that the procedural methods in distributing rewards are fair.

## Reward Levels

In deciding on reward levels, HR managers tend to focus on two, often rather contradictory elements: labour market forces such as labour market competition and internal/individual factors (a company's reward structure, individual skills, knowledge, experience, etc.). In some cases, these factors are not aligned. **Labour market competition** relates to roughly two issues[51]:

1. if a company is not competitive in its reward levels in the labour market, it will fail to attract and retain employees in sufficient numbers and quality;
2. if employees are not competitive in their reward demands, they will simply fail to find employment.

Obviously, there is a structural power asymmetry[52] – **labour market inequality**[53] – between companies and individual workers.

While many companies see rewards only as a "cost per employee" that needs to be reduced, others view them as a method to attract the best employees. Under globalisation,[54] it has become fashionable to simply compare the labour cost of individual countries ranking them from high to **low labour cost nations**.[55] These rankings often suggest that labour costs in OECD countries, for example, are too high – and therefore need to be reduced – and that companies like to move production to low labour cost countries under headings such as outsourcing and off-shoring.[56] But in many cases, hiring people is a bit like buying a car. One hardly ever buys the cheapest car on the market.

For many HR managers, rather than simply buying the cheapest car or looking at the location with the cheapest labour and lowest wages, they do a "best-buy" comparison asking questions such as "how much value (car) do I get for my money?" In terms of labour markets, this means how much productivity (output) do I get for my wages?

Economists call this: **unit labour costs**.[57] ULC measures the average cost of labour per unit of output. It is calculated as the ratio of total labour costs to real output. It reaches beyond the traditional world table of high- to low-wage countries[58] with the top ten "high wage"[59] but often also "low unemployment and high wealth" countries being: Luxembourg, Switzerland, Ireland, the USA, Australia, Norway, the Netherlands, and the UK. The top ten "low wage" but also quite often "high unemployment and low wealth" countries are: Armenia, Dominican Republic, Moldova, Mongolia, Syria, Kyrgyzstan, India, the Philippines, Peru, and Pakistan.

When conducting a global comparison, HR managers avoid simply looking at comparing wages. They examine the output-vs.-wage level, i.e. the unit labour cost. Such international comparison also involves exchange rates. One of the preferred tools when comparing exchange rates (also using unit labour cost) has become the Economist magazine's **Big Mac Index**.[60] It is a rather informal way of measuring the purchasing power parity (PPP[61]) between two currencies and provides a test of the extent to which market exchange rates result in goods costing the same in different countries. It seeks to make exchange-rate theory a bit more digestible.

So with $10. – in your hand, the most value for money (Big Macs) is in: Venezuela, Russia, Ukraine, and South Africa. Burgers are overpriced in Switzerland, Sweden, Norway, and the USA. Seen as "work for a burger", it means that you could buy ¼ of a burger for one hour's work in India, about ½ a burger in Russia and Brazil, about one burger in Taiwan and Singapore, but 2.7 burgers in France and three in Japan.[62]

Such global comparisons are also influenced by labour cost as a share of the total cost. This especially applies to labour cost intensive industries (e.g. textile) as compared to industries where the share of labour cost on the total cost is relatively low (e.g. automobile, aerospace, etc.). Hence textile is more likely to move to low labour cost countries while aerospace and car manufacturing are less likely to do so. Much of this leads to global inequality[63] shown in global income disparities: 11% of the global workforce earns less than $2 a day (these are the poor), 55% between $2 and $10 (low income), 13% between $10 and $20 (middle income), 9% between $20 and $50 (upper-middle income), and 7% earn above $50 per day (high income).[64]

A second reason for inequality comes from low union density: the lower union density, the higher inequality.[65] In other words, HR and other managers in multinational corporations, for example, belong to a very tiny "high-income" minority, if one takes a global outlook. In addition, HR managers also examine key jobs and non-key jobs. Key positions have a fairly stable content and are considered to be relatively important to the company while non-key jobs are often seen as positions that do not directly contribute to company profits.[66]

## Reward and Job Structures

For reward purposes, job evaluation often includes job-ranking methods that compare each job within a company.[67] These methods rank the positions in a hierarchy of importance to the company (CEO → general manager → HR manager, etc. → supervisors → sales representatives, crane drivers, etc. → machine operators, clerks, etc. → cleaners and security). The purpose and advantage of job-ranking rests on the fact that it is easy to administer and has a good cost-benefit ratio (inexpensive). On the downside, it can lead to rather arbitrary outcomes that are more practical for horizontal than vertical evaluations. To avoid these pitfalls, HR managers tend to utilise **factor comparisons** that include four key elements:

1. the mental requirements of a position;
2. the skill requirements;
3. the physical requirements;
4. the overall responsibilities of the position; and
5. the general working conditions.

These elements can be used to develop a pay structure which, in turn, includes **pay grades** that group jobs into a smaller number of pay classes. They contain jobs of similar worth or content, often grouped together for pay administration. One potential problem of pay grades can be **wage compression** that occurs when new employees require higher starting wages than the norm. This can cause a narrowing of the pay gap between experienced and new employees. Apart from such potential problems, pay grades often include a minimum, middle, and maximum pay grade. As an example, a pay grade structure based on minimum, middle, and maximum monthly pay ($) can be shown as follows (Table 8.1):

*Table 8.1* Pay Structure and Grades

| Grade | Minimum | Middle Level | Maximum |
|---|---|---|---|
| 1 | 1,755 | 2,165 | 2,705 |
| 2 | 2,545 | 3,240 | 4,050 |
| 3 | 3,564 | 4,505 | 5,453 |
| 4 | 4,501 | 5,496 | 6,710 |
| 5 | 5,295 | 6,650 | 7,995 |

Developing a comprehensive pay structure is vital for many companies as a fair reward system reflects positive on an organisation's work culture and values (Table 8.1). It is for this reason that companies also value **skill-based pay** structures that pay employees based on their skills and their capability of applying these skills. One positive of skill-based pay is that it motivates to improve skills and knowledge (organisational learning) as well as encourages flexibility directed towards horizontal job enlargement and vertical job enrichment (higher responsibilities). The acquisition of new knowledge and skills can be supported through proper reward structuring:

$40,000 \rightarrow \quad $60,000 \rightarrow \quad $80,000 \rightarrow \quad $120,000$

Learning $\rightarrow$ \qquad Applying $\rightarrow$ \qquad shaping

*Figure 8.2* Reward Structure and Competency Based Pay.

Figure 8.2 shows how reward structures can support the gaining of new skills and knowledge, their application in a job, and finally, a manager's ability to shape new knowledge and skills at work. But such skill-, knowledge-, and **competency-based pay systems** also have disadvantages, for example:

1. some companies may find it difficult to utilise new skills;
2. some employees achieve all prescribed skills with no options for further development;
3. such pay systems might be complicated to administer;
4. skills and knowledge based systems can challenge market based rates.

The last disadvantage becomes apparent when, for example, a strongly marketing driven corporation such as Coca Cola or McDonalds seeks to pay an outstanding marketing manager more than other comparable managers or when a relatively unknown technology company pays its technology manager more than its marketing manager or even its CEO. These strategies can pull against one another.

The author of "Punished by Rewards"[68] reports even more problems with rewarding, arguing that not a single controlled study has shown a long-term improvement in the quality of work as a result of any reward system. That in itself would be an astonishing fact, were it not for the existence of scores of studies – conducted with adults as well as children, in real workplaces and other venues – that have demonstrated how rewards tend to be not merely ineffective but powerfully counterproductive. "Punished by Rewards" lists fourteen key deficiencies on "why incentives fail" (Table 8.2)[69]:

*Table 8.2* Why Incentives Fail

| | Elements of Failure | Description and Explanation |
|---|---|---|
| 1 | Lack of necessity | Many employees are already doing a fine job; |
| 2 | Secrecy | People tend to overestimate the earnings, bonus pay, etc. of others; |
| 3 | Pay does not match | Pay does not correspond to performance (subjectivity, bias, etc.); |
| 4 | Expensive | Some incentive plans are too expensive to administer; |
| 5 | Too big vs. too small | If too small, they have little impact; if they are big, very few receive them; |
| 6 | Short vs. long term | Many incentives favour short-termism damaging a long-term perspective; |
| 7 | Lack of objectivity | If performance measures are too rigid they defy fixation of important elements that cannot be put in a strict protocol; |
| 8 | Subjectivity | If too subjective they lead to bias and subjectivity, if not organisational politics of the rater (self-serving motives); |
| 9 | Evaluation is futile | Assessments and evaluations are far less accurate than we are made to believe; |
| 10 | Pay is not a Motivator | Many employees are not motivated by money (but, e.g. meaningful work, working in charities, making a difference, etc.)[70]; |

(*Continued*)

*Table 8.2* (Continued)

|    | Elements of Failure | Description and Explanation |
|----|---------------------|----------------------------|
| 11 | Punished by rewards | Punishment (administrative use of performance management for demotion, pay cuts, no bonus, etc.) destroys motivation (fear is not a good motivator to work or perform better); |
| 12 | Raptures relationships | Horizontal relationships (work groups, teams, co-workers, colleagues, etc.) can be damaged through individualistic incentive schemes; |
| 13 | Ignores reasons | Performance management systems can ignore reasons for work and performance problems – "do better and here is what you will get" – is a pseudo-solution; |
| 14 | Discourages risk and initiative | People will do precisely what they are asked to do if the reward is significant; they are less inclined to go beyond, to take risks, many simply do what is necessary to receive a high score to secure a bonus. |

When examining the pros and cons of reward management and its links to performance management, many of the points raised by "Punished by Rewards" appear to make very good arguments. In fact, they suggest to follow the multinational management consulting services company "Accenture"[71] – a Fortune 500 company with $31bn net revenue (2015) and more than 373,000 employees serving clients in more than 200 cities in 120 countries – in "ditching" performance reviews altogether.[72] And indeed, there seems to be one group in management that has disconnected itself from the reward-performance link.

## Rewarding CEOs

CEO[73] do not suffer from rampant **wage stagnation**[74] lamented even by the *Wall Street Journal*.[75] Here is what wage stagnation means, "after correction for inflation, the media wages of American men have been stagnate for half a century; for white men without a four-year degree, media earnings lost 13% of their purchasing power between 1979 and 2017", write Anne Case and her Nobel Prize-winning colleague Angus Deaton.[76]

Most CEOs are rather distant to such facts.[77] One of the single most challenging issues for HR managers when it comes to rewards is the pay of executives as many headlines in the daily press suggest: "flaws in executive pay", "CEOs paid obscene levels",[78] "Here's How Outrageous The Pay Gap Between CEOs And Workers Is",[79] perks, what Citigroup calls "the plutonomists of the uber-rich",[80] and the infamous "golden parachute", etc.[81]

Some have argued that

> quite a few people [hedge fund CEOs] now make over $1 billion per year, every year [but] what is a billion dollars? If you earn the medium income in the US (2012) of about $50,000…it will take you 20,000 years to save a billion dollars.[82]

According to the UK High Pay Centre, it will take the average worker 160 years to earn what FTSE CEOs receive.[83] In historical terms, according to the *Economic Policy Institute* (EPI), this developed in the following way[84]:

**1978 → 2013**: CEO pay at American firms rose a stunning 937 per cent, compared with a mere 10.2 per cent growth in worker compensation over the same period, all adjusted for inflation.

**In 2013**: the average CEO pay at the top 350 US companies was $15.2 million.[85]

In 2008, "top UK companies lost almost a third of their value while the bosses of these companies enjoyed a 10 per cent leap in their basic salaries".[86] At times, CEO rewards are driven to pathological levels when this includes, for example, a $6,000 shower curtain, a $15,000 umbrella stand, a $17,100 travelling toilette box, and a $2,200 waste-basket.[87] Even university "CEOs" follow suite with spending $210,000 on renovating an on-campus residence and $63,000 on landscaping for a "Himalayan Garden".[88]

CEOs are often rewarded with **stock-based programmes** such as: stock options, stock purchase plans, restricted stock plans, awarded stock, formula-based stocks, junior stock, discount stock options, and tracking stock options as well as combined rewards such as: stock appreciations rights, performance plan units, performance share plans, and phantom stocks.[89] All these have quite often contributed to a widening gap between CEO and average worker pay.[90] Since 1978, CEO pay in the USA, for example – that stood at $16.3 million in 2014[91] – has increased by 937% compared to a paltry 10.2% for the average employee.[92] From 2000 to 2010, the median income in the United States declined 7% when adjusted for inflation.[93] A 2016 Oxfam Briefing Paper (2016) showed this:

The increasing pay gap between CEOs (997.2% increase) of major US firms and workers (10.9% increase) has become massive.[94] By May 2018, the CEO-workers ration was as follows for: [95]

1. Mattel's CEO: 4,987:1
2. McDonald's CEO: 3,101:1
3. Gap's CEO: 2,900:1
4. Manpower's CEO: 2,483:1

Top *earning* slots were reported for Chipotle boss Steve Ells, who earned $28.9 million, or 1,522 times the median salary of $19,000; CVS Health CEO Larry Merlo, whose $32.4 million pay was nearly 1,192 times that of the median worker's $27,139; and Walmart chief Doug McMillon, who made $25.6 million last year, about 1,133 times the median employee's $22,591. A *Wall Street Journal* report (2015[96]) – not particularly known for being overtly critical towards CEOs – pointed out the discrepancy between some CEO's performance (i.e. bad) and their rewards (i.e. good):

1. Leslie Moonves, CEO of CBS received $37.3 Million for a 12.4% decline in shareholder return;
2. Jeffrey R. Immelt, CEO of General Electric also received $37.3 Million but for a 6.7% decline;
3. W. James McNerney, CEO of Boeing received $28.9 Million for a 2.5% decline;
4. John S. Watson, CEO of Chevron received $26.0 Million for a 7.0% decline; and
5. Mark Fields, CEO Ford, received a $54 million pay-out for a 37% fall in share prices[97];
6. Howard Schultz, CEO of Starbucks received $21.5 Million for a 1.4% decline.

While there are stark differences between countries (e.g. Poland: small; USA: high[98]), HRM does not seem to have anything to offer in order to stop not only the disconnection between the pay of average workers and CEOs, but also the performance gap between CEO rewards and shareholder value as well as the gap between the fast increases in CEO rewards and the slow increases of the stock market value of their corporations.[99] According to renowned management guru **Peter Drucker**, the proper ratio between a chief executive's pay and that of the average worker should be around 20-to-1.[100] Others have suggested "that the more a CEO gets paid, the worse his (or her) company is likely to do in the coming years".[101] On the other end of the reward spectrum are those who do not even earn the average wage of a worker. They are the workers on minimum wages.[102]

## The Minimum Wage

Often regulated by national law and ranging below a **decent wage** (two-third of the average wage),[103] **minimum wage**[104] prohibits employers from hiring employees or workers for less than a given hourly, daily, or monthly minimum wage.[105] More than 90% of all countries have some kind of minimum wage legislation.[106] Until recently, minimum wage laws were usually very tightly focused to avoid becoming the norm, thereby forcing employers to pay decent wages.[107]

Minimum wage legislation is also designed to prevent underpayment and **wage theft** committed by companies and management.[108] Together with: (1) fraud, (2) crimes against consumer and the environmental (3), wage theft is one of four crimes committed by companies and corporations.[109] Wage theft is the illegal withholding of wages or the denial of benefits that are rightfully owed to an employee. Wage theft can be conducted through eight common means:

1. failure to pay overtime or forcing employees to work off the books,
2. minimum wage violations,
3. employee misclassification,
4. tips are stolen,
5. illegal deductions in pay,
6. being forced to work off the clock and/or to clock out while continuing to work,
7. no meal and rest breaks, and also
8. not being paid at all.[110]

Wage theft, particularly from low wage legal or illegal immigrant workers, is common in the United States[111]; in Australia where the state of Victoria has made it a criminal offense,[112] recently; and many other countries.[113] Still, it appears that "if you rob someone's house, you will probably go to jail. If you rob someone's wages, you might have to repay the wages. Or maybe not".[114] The USA's Economic Policy Institute, for example, reported in 2014 that survey evidence suggests wage theft costs US workers billions of dollars a year.[115] Like any other property or white collar crime, wage theft remains a crime.[116] It occurs when employers do not pay workers according to the law. So what can employees, HR managers, and trade union officers do?

1. know your rights and exercise them[117];
2. file a wage claim to recover unpaid wages with a local institution;
3. file a report of labour law violation to a trade union or lawyer;
4. file a retaliation complaint with the local EEO office, state labour office, etc. if you were fired, demoted or punished for reporting labour law violations;
5. explain your case on the website: http://www.wagetheftisacrime.com.

In the USA and the UK, for example, minimum wage laws and regulations used to apply only to women and children. Only after the Great Depression did many industrialised economies extend them to the general work force. Even then, the laws were often specific to certain industries. In France, for example, they were extensions of existing trade union legislation. In the USA, industry-specific wage restrictions were held to be unconstitutional. The country's Fair Labor Standards Act of 1938 established a uniform national minimum wage for non-farm, non-supervisory workers. Coverage was later extended to most of the labour force. The first moves to legislate wages did not set minimum wages but instead the laws created arbitration boards and councils to resolve labour conflicts before the recourse to strikes:

1. in 1894, New Zealand established an arbitration boards (Industrial Conciliation and Arbitration Act);
2. in 1907, the Harvester decision (Australia) established a "living wage"[118] for a man, his wife, and two children to live in frugal comfort[119];
3. in 1909, the Trade Boards Act was enacted in the UK establishing four such boards;
4. in 1912, the state of Massachusetts (USA) set minimum wages for women and children;
5. in the USA, statutory minimum wages were first introduced nationally in 1938;
6. in the 1960s, minimum wage laws were introduced into Latin America as part of the Alliance for Progress; however these minimum wages were, and are, low;
7. in 2015, Germany introduced a minimum wage of 8.50 Euro (by 2020 it was €10.45[120]);
8. In 2020, minimum wages in EU member states ranged from €312 to €2,142 per month.[121]

These are provisions for lower paid workers. Many workers, however, are paid above these levels. In those cases where workers are organised in trade unions, wages, and salaries are set through collective bargaining.[122] Collective bargaining moves eliminate the **monopsony power** – the power of employers to set wages unilaterally.[123]

## Wage Setting through Bargaining

Particularly in industries that are unionised, rewards, pay, salaries, and wages are not negotiated through individual claims[124] but through **collective bargaining**, a process of negotiations[125] between employers and/or management and employees and/or trade unions defining scope, depth, and coverage.[126] The interests of the employees are commonly presented by representatives of a **trade union** to which the employees belong. These highly protected rights of employees are enshrined, for example, in:

- Article 23 of "The **Universal Declaration of Human Rights**" of the United Nations stating, "everyone who works has the right to just and favourable remuneration ensuring for himself and his family an existence worthy of human dignity" and "everyone has the right to form and to join trade unions for the protection of his interests".[127] This is further detailed in the
- International Labour Organisation's **Collective Bargaining Convention**[128] (ILO 1949, no. 98) – to which many countries are members – stating, "workers shall

enjoy adequate protection against acts of anti-union discrimination in respect of their employment" and this protection includes "negotiation between employers or employers' organisations and workers' organisations with a view [of creating] collective agreements".

These highly protected collective agreements that are reached through negotiations usually set out wage scales, working hours, training, health and safety, overtime, grievance mechanisms, and rights to participate in workplace or company affairs. At the most fundamental level, management and workers have diverging interests that can be shown in a matrix table:

*Table 8.3* Wage and Salary Interests

| *Bargaining Issues* | *Employer Interest* | | *Employee Interest* |
|---|---|---|---|
| Wages and income | Low (wage = cost) | → ← | High (wage = decent living standard |
| Working time | Long (time = money) | → ← | Short (time for family and leisure) |
| General conditions | Minimum (costly) | → ← | Good (humanisation of work) |

Table 8.3 shows the different interests between employers and management on the one side and employees and trade unions on the other.[129] The single most common issue over which collective bargaining takes place are wages and salaries.[130] For many employers and managers, wages and salaries are simply seen as a cost that makes the product or service more expensive while reducing company and corporate profits[131] (shareholder-value) in a "zero-sum" game.

Some think this falls under "½-by-2-by-3 rule of corporate fitness: half as many people will be paid twice as much for doing three times as much work".[132] For employees, wages represent decent living standards and disposable income for consumerism.[133] The "zero-sum" ("I win, you lose" theme) or **distributive bargaining**[134] denotes that higher wages equal lower profits and lower wages go along with higher profits. Most commonly, trade unions start such wage negotiations by putting forward a **wage claim** that often consists of three core elements (examples given in percentage)[135]:

1. **Inflation**: compensation for inflation (not caused by employees): 2.0%
2. **Productivity**: compensation for productivity increases (e.g. higher profits): 1.5%
3. **Rich-to-Poor**: Robin Hood (taking from the rich to give to the poor)[136]: 0.5%

Adding up all three, for example, results in a 2% + 1.5% + 0.5% = 4% wage claim. Being aware and having accepted the conflict of interest between management and workers, most modern industrial relations systems include **wage negotiations** for collective bargaining. A trade union may negotiate with a single employer (who is typically representing a company's shareholders) or with a group of businesses, depending on the country, to reach an **industry wide agreement**. A collective agreement functions as a **labour contract** between an employer and one or more unions. Collective bargaining consists of the process of negotiation between representatives of a union and employers (generally represented by management, or, in some countries such as Austria, Sweden, the Netherlands, etc. by an **employers' organisation**) in respect of the terms and conditions of employment such as wages, hours of work, working conditions, grievance procedures, and about the rights and responsibilities of trade unions.

The parties often refer to the result of the negotiation as a **collective bargaining agreement** or collective employment agreement.

Such wage negotiations (see below) are part of a pluralist industrial relations system that recognises the conflict of interest between management and employees (Table 8.1) and has instruments to solve these conflicts. Overseen but the state, collective bargaining is seen as a process in which two parties – management/employers vs. employees/unions – seek to reach an agreement through exploring options and exchanging offers. Such "give-and-take" negotiations are very common in everyday life. For example, children negotiating TV time with their parents, two drivers negotiating their way around an obstacle, two lovers negotiating a Valentine's Day outing. In work-related and more formal settings such as the aforementioned collective bargaining, however, management-vs.-union negotiations take on different forms when these, for example, concern wage and salary negotiation.

## Wage and Salary Negotiations

One form of wage negotiation is the above-mentioned distributive bargaining while there is also **integrative bargaining** which are not "win-lose" but "win-win" situations (e.g. working together, sharing information, etc.). In **principled negotiations**, both parties see each other as problem solvers in order to determine an acceptable solution with a mutually beneficial outcome. Such negotiations often involve **tactical decisions** and/or an awareness of the **mutual dependence** of both parties. They are also related to power struggles (e.g. coercive power, reward power, legitimate power, expert power, information power, referent power, etc.). In addition, many negotiations take on different negotiation styles such as, for example, competition, avoidable behaviours, compromising, accommodating, collaborating, etc.). While there are many approaches to negotiations, a common way of negotiating is through a five-step process[137]:

1.  **Preparing and Planning**
    Evaluates the benefits and risks of negotiations, asking questions such as: what is the relationship between the parties and is it ongoing?; are the parties representing themselves?; which negotiation style will we choose?; what is the other side's style?; is there an audience and what impact will the negotiations have?; what are the underlying interests and the bargaining range of the other party?
2.  **Defining the Ground Rules**
    This defines the boundaries of collective bargaining by asking questions such as: where will the negotiations take place?; who will be represented?; what timeline will be followed?; how will the parties conduct themselves during the negotiations?; what are the terms of references?
3.  **Clarification and Justification**
    It is important for both parties to be clear, share information, and clarify any questions arising with the other party early. Preparation and good communication skills are essential and extremely helpful in assisting negotiations and when responding to the other party.
4.  **Bargaining and Problem Solving**
    This stage discusses options while working towards solutions that will result in an agreement. It demands flexibility and skills as well as the ability to present solutions and alternatives. It also requires the ability to consider advantages and disadvantages for each party involved.

5. **Closure and Implementation**

   This is the settlement stage of negotiations. Settlement means that an agreement has been reached but it also demands that such an agreement be implemented. It remains imperative for both parties to evaluate their targets to ensure that a negotiated settlement is consistent with the initial goals and objectives of the negotiation. At this stage, "win-win" issues are highlighted.

Successful negotiators are serious about these stages; they prepare well for negotiations and manage negotiations including themselves and the emotions of each party. They have good communication and **negotiation skills**. They look forward towards solutions rather than backward. Most importantly, however, successful negotiators separate people from the problems to be solved. They focus on problem solving by assuming the best in people rather than the worst; they avoid **blame-games** and criticising negotiators; they are innovative offering attractive alternatives; they recognise feelings and their origins while limiting their own emotional responses; they also offer apologies to move negotiations along; they always show attention to the concerns of the other party; they negotiate directly and have a clear focus; and finally, they see negotiations not as a conflict but as a **problem solving** discussion. With this, the process of negotiating wages and salaries ends. Still, many negotiators are aware of the "Ten Myths of Pay and Value":[138]

1. Low paid jobs create a ladder for people to work their way up;
2. Financial services and banking are essential for an economy;
3. Pay differentials do not matter as long as poverty is eradicated;
4. Companies must pay high salaries to attract talented CEOs;
5. Workers in highly paid jobs work harder
6. The private sector is more efficient than the public sector;
7. If a government taxes the rich,[139] they will take their money and run
8. The rich contribute more to society;
9. Some jobs are more satisfying and therefore require less pay
10. Pay always rewards underlying profitability.

# Workbook

## III. Five Discussion Questions on Reward Management

### And One Report Question on Reward Management

### 1. Discussions Questions

1. Discuss the pros and cons of (1) time-based, (2) reward-based, and (3) performance-based rewards systems.
2. Compare intrinsic with extrinsic rewards. What are the advantages and disadvantages of each reward method?
3. Your textbook states, "the greater the unfairness of a reward, the less likely is compliance with performance demands". How can HR managers avoid this from ever happening? How can HR managers assure that rewards comply with standard equity theories?
4. Discuss the advantages of collective bargaining and wage negotiations for (1) management and (2) employees.
5. According to http://www.wagetheftisacrime.com/, "if you steal form a store, you go to jail but employers who cheat their workers of wages get away with it – (83% of workers who win their wage theft case never see a dime)". Discuss this statement and find three reasons on why you go to jail for stealing but employers get away with it and three recommendations on how to eliminate wage theft.

### 2. Report Question

### On Management and Wage Theft

According to the US website "Wage Theft is a Crime",[140] "if you steal from a store, you go to jail but employers who cheat their workers of wages get away with it – (83% of workers who win their wage theft case never see a dime)". Discuss this why you go to jail for stealing in a shop but employers get away with it. Discuss possible solutions to the problem of wage theft and develop four [4] recommendations on how to remedy such an unsustainable situation?

## IV. The "5-by-5" Exercise: Five Case Studies and Five Questions

### 8.1 Hamburgers That Didn't Pay

The local employment relations office that is run by the state has recently investigated four restaurant operators in World City. The state's investigation found that 124 mostly teenage employees had been underpaid by a total of $321,000 between the years 2015 and 2017. Employees were being "compensated" with free hamburgers and soft drinks instead of the contractually agreed wages. Meanwhile, bonuses were also withheld by the employer. The case was referred to the state labour court where the sitting judge, Alfred Neuhauser, said that such a practice "belongs into the dark ages of satanic mills" that once dominated England's early rise to industrialism. The four hamburger operators were fined $405,000 each for breaching the country's minimum wage legislations and for violating contractual arrangements.

The court case centred on reward management, legal requirements, as well as the ethics of rewards. The case also included the withholding of bonuses not paid to employees. Bonuses have become a controversial subject. Many salaried employees expect bonus payments as a normal addition to their salary and do not see how it connects to performance. As industry expert and HR manager Lisa Boyne explains, "many have come to see bonuses as a sort of entitlement that comes with employment". This sort of entitlement mentality works against bonuses as a motivational tool. In a recent survey of 125 employers, researchers found that around 25% give performance based bonuses to employees who do not meet expectations. According to an online HR blog, the survey found that many line managers rate employees that underperform as "meeting or exceeding" expectations.

The CEO of a local IT corporation, for example, received a base salary of $2.86 million in 2017. When leaving the Telco, the CEO received a "golden parachute" in the form of a cash bonus of a further $3.7 million as well as long-term bonuses totalling $8.3 million that were linked to the corporation's share price. This amounted to roughly 169 times the average wage at the IT corporation.

1.  Imagine you are a newly appointed HR manager at one of the five hamburger restaurants assigned the task to assure that your company's store managers avoid violating the country's minimum wage legislation. Name three ways in which you intend to achieve this goal. Justify your selection.
2.  "A bonus should be part of the normal reward system in a restaurant". Discuss this statement by finding three arguments in favour of bonus payments and three arguments against bonus payments.
3.  Imagine you are an HR manager in a company where line managers have handed out unjustified bonuses to their employees. What four steps would you take to assure that the company's bonus policy is correctly implemented? Name three ways to achieve this.
4.  Imagine you are an HR manager assigned the task to assure that bonuses are no longer seen as a normal part of an employee's reward but instead are linked to the actual performance. Identify four ways in which this can be achieved. Justify your answer.
5.  Discuss the morality or immorality of different bonus payments to employees in a hamburger restaurant and the bonus payment to the IT corporation CEO (as outlined in the case). Can such a discrepancy be ethically justified? Find five arguments.

## 8.2 Rewards and Workforce Diversity

Many HR managers are convinced that there is need to individualise incentives and rewards. This is often designed to avoid dishonesties. To assure that employees do not by-pass incentive programmes or play the system, HR has introduced partnering, personal goal setting, individual performance management, etc. Simultaneously,

HR managers offer incentives, rewards, and bonuses to employees. This is done to encourage employees to do what management tells them – the so-called organisational goals. Research has shown that many workers prefer non-cash rewards. This remains true. On the other side, it is only true to a certain point. When researchers asked employees which sort of incentive they liked most, many selected something other than monetary rewards, however, they also found that such answers could depend on how the question was framed.

A large number of workplace studies have also shown that when people are asked what is most important to them about work, the most common answers are "interesting work" and "interesting co-workers". Other opted for involvement and participation in company and workplace affairs. Remarkably, all of these answers do not relate to incentives, bonuses, and rewards. What this seems to indicate is that the "carrot-and-stick" belief is not all there is. It still remains intriguing to talk to employees who have worked in business organisations that do not use reward systems at all. These organisations pay people a decent salary and typically assist employees in creating interesting work tasks, a sense of organisational community, and options to participate in making work-related decisions. In those organisations, employees seek to be paid a decent wage; they do not want to be incentivised. Instead, employees want to be encouraged – not praised. They want to receive respect – not reinforcement through some behaviourist plan. HR managers in such companies adhere to the three C's of choice (participation and involvement), collaboration (e.g. teamwork), and content (work organisation, workplace relations, work conditions, etc.).

Needless to say, some HR strategies can also pull against one another. This is the case when one strategy focuses on managers handing out work tasks "to" employees in a top-down vertical approach. Simultaneously, another HR strategy focuses on working "with" employees in a collaborative and horizontal mode. Some HR managers are also committed to the fallacy of taking away with one hand what they have given with the other. This contradicts individualistic rewards set against collective teamwork.

1.  What is outlined above argues that rewards can punish people. Find five arguments on how rewards can negatively work against employees.
2.  The above-outlined case places individual rewards set against workers wishing to work collaboratively as well as management's interest in fostering teamwork. Discuss the pros and cons of individual rewards versus collective work efforts. Find two arguments in favour of individual rewards and two arguments in favour of collective work systems (e.g. teamwork).
3.  The case states that employees want "to be paid – not incentivised", "encouraged, not praised", and "offered respect, not be reinforced". Find two supportive arguments for each of the claims.
4.  What are the positives of the "3Cs" (choice, collaboration, and content)? Find two supportive arguments for (1) choice, (2) collaboration, and (3) content.
5.  Finally, the case maintains that "reward systems are highly unpopular". Find five arguments why this might be the case.

### 8.3 Teamwork and Rewards at Singapore's Maternity Clinic

Singapore's main Maternity Clinic experienced several problems resulting in high staff turnover and low morale. Much of it stemmed from an ineffective and unsuccessful wage system. To eliminate low morale and high staff turnover, the clinic's HR managers developed a teamwork system that included a new wage structure. In that way, they believed, employees would be able to see a clear link between their performance and their wages. The HR team at Singapore's Maternity Clinic offered a team based bonus of $1,000, $2,000 and $3,000 for each team depending on clear benchmarks for team performance. Employee meetings were set up with HR managers. During these meetings HR managers were able to explain the new system while also obtaining employee input on the new proposal.

Upon the successful implementation of the team-based reward system, employees suddenly began to feel important, empowered, and revitalised in participating in their work as well as the affairs of Singapore's Maternity Clinic. Weekly reports compiled by teams allowed employees to self-monitor their performance. It also gave HR managers the opportunity to observe the team concept. During the first year in operation, staff morale increased why employee satisfaction reached new levels. As a result, the clinic's traditionally high staff turnover began to decline. Eventually, it reached acceptable limits when measured against the Singaporean average. Currently, other hospitals in Singapore are seeking to adopt the model developed by the Maternity Clinic.

1.  Discuss the link between a badly designed reward system, staff morale, and high turnover. Find five reasons why such an insufficient system can lead to low morale and high turnover.
2.  Given the case of Singapore's Maternity Clinic and the successful implementation of a team system, outline the advantages of team performance in a hospital compared to individual performance. Outline three arguments for the team work system and three against it.
3.  What are the advantages of team-based reward systems compared to individual reward arrangements? Find four advantages.
4.  Did the HR team's introduction of a team-based bonus ($1,000 to $3,000) work out? Find four arguments in favour of such a system.
5.  Imagine you are an HR manager in another hospital in Singapore seeking to introduce a similar team-based bonus system. Develop five criteria (e.g. KPIs) upon which your hospital would pay out a team bonus to nurses.

### 8.4 Salary inequities at Avatar Manufacturing

Eddie J. Marphy was trying to figure out what to do about a problematic salary situation he had in his plant. Mr Marphy recently took over as president of Avatar Manufacturing. The founder and former president, George Michael, had been president for 35 years. The company was family owned and with approximately 2,800 employees was the largest employer in the community. *Marphy* was a member of the family who owned Avatar Manufacturing, but he had never worked for the company prior to becoming the president. He had an MBA plus five years of management experience with a large manufacturing organisation where he was senior vice president for human resources before making his move to Avatar Manufacturing.

A short time after joining Avatar Manufacturing, Eddie J. Marphy started to notice that there was considerable inequity in the pay structure for salaried employees. A discussion with the human resources director, Ms Michelle Pfeiffy, led him to believe that salaried employees' pay was very much a matter of individual bargaining with the past president. Hourly paid factory employees were not part of this problem because they were unionised and their wages were set by collective bargaining. An examination of the salaried payroll showed that there were thirty-eight employees, ranging in pay from that of the president to that of the receptionist. A closer examination showed that eighteen of the salaried employees were female. Five of them were front-line factory supervisors and one was the human resources director. All other were non-management.

This examination also showed that Ms Michelle Pfeiffy, the human resources director, appeared to be underpaid, and that the three female supervisors were paid somewhat less than any of the male supervisors. However, there were no similar supervisory jobs in which there were both male and female job incumbents. When asked, the HR director said she thought the female supervisors may have been paid at a lower rate mainly because they were women, and perhaps George Michael, the former president, did not think that women needed as much money because they had working husbands. However, she added she personally thought that they were paid less because they supervised less-skilled employees than did the male supervisors. Eddie J. Marphy was not sure that this was true.

The company from which Eddie J. Marphy had moved had a good job evaluation system. Although he was thoroughly familiar with and capable in this compensation tool, Eddie J. Marphy did not have time to make a job evaluation study at Avatar Manufacturing. Therefore, he decided to hire a compensation consultant from a nearby university to help him. Together, they decided that all thirty-eight salaried jobs should be in the same job evaluation cluster, that a modified ranking method of job evaluation should be used, and that the job descriptions recently completed by the HR director were current, accurate, and usable in the study. The job evaluation showed that the HR director and the female supervisors were being underpaid relative to comparable male salaried employees.

Eddie J. Marphy was not sure what to do. He knew that if the underpaid female supervisors took the case to the local EEO office, the company could be found guilty of sex discrimination and then have to pay considerable back wages. He was afraid that if he gave these women an immediate salary increase large enough to bring them up to where they should be, the male supervisors would be upset and the female supervisors might comprehend the total situation and want back pay. The HR director told Eddie J. Marphy that the female supervisors had never complained about pay differences.

Ms Michelle Pfeiffy, the HR director agreed to take a sizable salary increase with no back pay, so this part of the problem was solved. But Eddie J. Marphy believed he had four choices for the female supervisors: (1) to do nothing; (2) to gradually increase the female supervisors' salaries; (3) to increase their salaries immediately; (4) to call the three supervisors into his office, discuss the situation with them, and jointly decide what to do.

1. Ms Michelle Pfeiffy (HRM), Eddie J. Marphy (CEO), the local EEO office, and the female staff members might all agree that underpaying female workers is unfair. Which of the above outlined equity models (SMART-C, Adam's equity theory, Vroom's expectancy theory) are violated and why?
2. Imagine you are Eddie J. Marphy. What would you do to solve the issue and why? Discuss the pros and cons of each of the four options of the case study by naming at least one argument in favour and one argument against each option.
3. Why did female wage discrimination occur in the area of management in the first place and not in the area of hourly paid employees? Why do trade unions fight for wage equality between men and women? Develop three reasons.
4. Could you – as the HR manager – suggest that Eddie J. Marphy pursue alternatives to the four options he has in mind? Develop three alternative solutions.
5. The case states that "hourly paid factory employees were not part of this problem because they were unionised and their wages were set by collective bargaining". As collective bargaining does not discriminate between male and female workers at Avatar Manufacturing, would extending union and collective bargaining coverage to the female staff members in question solve the problem? If yes, why (name three reasons)? If no, why not (name three reasons)?

### 8.5 *No Reward but Overworked and Underpaid*

Daryl Christine Hannasi is a personal assistant to Mr Daniel Graig, the CEO of Global WebMarketing, a company specialising in web marketing, web design, web copy writing, intellectual property law, and the development of marketing-specific web search engines for many multinational corporations such as, for example, Coca Cola, Toyota, and Nike. In addition to these corporations, WebMarketing also works for a raft of smaller, often local companies. Due to a seemingly never-ending cycle of short-term marketing projects, Daryl Hannasi has been working very hard, almost around the clock over the last one and half years, often finishing projects on the train from and to work and during lunch hours. Being a personal assistant at WebMarketing is a very demanding and time intensive position. Despite this, Daryl enjoys her work but is unsatisfied with the demanding time schedules of her work situation. Even though Daryl has been employed for some time now, her employment contract still classifies her as a casual staff member and restricts her working hours to the standard eight hours per day. But contractual statements and the reality of work as a personal assistant at WebMarkeing are worlds apart. Although Daryl's effective work days are much longer than the eight hours noted in her contract – sometimes up to ten hours per day – she has been claiming only the specified eight hours per day as her employment contract stipulates.

Her excessive and highly demanding workload is causing her a lot of work related stress. This is impacting on her health but Daryl is somewhat afraid to tell Daniel about the actual hours she spends every day finishing all the work tasks she is being given.

She is a bit worried that he might be disappointed with her and that it might affect her overall productivity levels. After having taken sick leave quite a number of times, Daryl has decided to approach the HR manager of Global WebMarketing, Ms Maggie Robbie, to ask for her help and advice. In her first meeting with Ms Robbie, Daryl tells her HR manager that she is beginning to suffer from mild depression and high blood pressure. Daryl's local doctor has recommended taking more time off work because it exposes her to the danger of increasing her chance of suffering from circulatory diseases. This might lead to heart disease as the cause of her excessive work schedules.

1. Imagine you are the HR manager of WebMarketing. What three recommendations can you develop to solve the problem of Daryl's "overwork and underpaid" problem?

2. Imagine you are the HR manager of WebMarketing. You have decided to approach the CEO – Daniel – about the problem. Taking the perspective of the CEO, what three recommendations can you develop to assist Daniel in solving the problem?

3. Imagine you are the HR manager of WebMarketing. Should HRM follow the recommendation given by Daryl's doctor? Find three arguments in favour of following Daryl's doctor's recommendations.

4. Imagine you are the HR manager of WebMarketing seeking to move beyond the specifics of Daryl's case. What four formal and codified HR policy recommendations would you develop to assure that cases like Daryl's will not be occurring again?

5. Most HR managers understand the link between reward and motivation. Would offering Daryl higher rewards solve the problem? Is this a problem of Vroom's expectancy theory (effort → performance → outcomes)? If "yes", why – develop three arguments why you think this is the case. If "no", why not – develop three arguments why you think this is not the case.

## V. A Suggestion for an Online Guest Lecture

Career Analyst Dan Pink
talks about rewards and motivations
http://www.ted.com/talks/dan_pink_on_motivation?language=en
[the online guest lecture above is merely a suggestion – www.ted.com/talks offers additional material to choose from]

## VI. List of Suggested Documentaries on Reward Management

The carefully selected documentary videos below are mere suggestions to be used during tutorials. Documentaries have been selected to achieve two things: (1) to explain key HRM themes and (2) to provide an insight into the reality of HRM. Typically, these short documentaries should be viewed in class followed by a class discussion on the content of the video. Alternatively, questions on documentaries can be prepared beforehand and small group discussions can follow up the video after viewing is concluded. Should any of the web-links no longer function, please conduct an internet search for other – alternative – documentaries related to your tutorial topic (e.g. filmsforaction.org):

Motivation & Reward: youtube.com/watch?v=u6XAPnuFjJc

Reward Management I: youtube.com/watch?v=XPQt4ekb8Tc

Reward Management II: youtube.com/watch?v=tXcOcMOdwrl

International Reward M: www.youtube.com/watch?v=A8BJqlzXZ-A

Total Reward Management: www.youtube.com/watch?v=OuH2oWCrxmU

Equity & Reward: study.com/academy/lesson/equity-theory-of-motivation-reward-effort.html

Rewarding Talent: youtube.com/watch?v=mNuFqc-vpTw

HRM-TV on Benefits: hrmonline.ca/tv/benefits-administration-made-easy-201448.aspx

Administering Rewards: hrmonline.ca/tv/benefits-administration-made-easy-201448

CEO-Rewards (USA): www.youtube.com/watch?v=IUTcuB5TZdY

## Notes

1 http://www.cipd.co.uk/hr-topics/reward-management.aspx; Hambrick, D. C., Humphrey, S. E. & Gupta, A. 2015. Structural interdependence within top management teams: a key moderator of upper echelons predictions, *Strategic Management Journal*, 36(3):449–461.

2 https://www.ted.com/talks/eric_liu_why_ordinary_people_need_to_understand_power.

3 Hofmann, A. 2016. Compensation and benefits: essentials of base salary, in: Zeuch, M. (eds.) *Handbook of HRM*, Heidelberg: Springer, p. 862.

4 Chomsky, N. 2017. Chomsky on Work and Wages (https://www.youtube.com; accessed: 17th January 2018).

5 http://www.entrepreneur.com/article/159438.

6 Schwartz, B. 2015. *Why We Work*, New York: Simon and Schuster; Oxfam. 2018. *Reward Work* (https://www.oxfam.org; accessed: 23rd January 2018).

7 Micklethwait, J. & Wooldridge, A. 1996. *The Witch Doctors: Making Sense of the Management Gurus*, New York: Times Books, p. 207.

8 Gittleman, M. & Pierce, B. 2015. Pay for performance and compensation inequality: evidence from the ECEC, *ILR Review*, 68(1):28–52.

9 Dickinson, A. M. & Gillette, K. L. 1994. A comparison of the effects of two individual monetary incentive systems on productivity: piece rate pay versus base pay plus incentives, *Journal of Organizational Behavior Management*, 14(1):3–82; Kuvaas, B., Shore, L. M., Buch, R. & Dysvik, A. 2020. Social and economic exchange relationships and performance contingency: differential effects of variable pay and base pay, *International Journal of Human Resource Management*, 31(3):408–431.

10 It has been noted (Sikula, A. 2001. The five biggest HRM lies, *Public Personnel Management*, 30(3):424) that 'linking pay and performance has always been a problem' contradicting, for example, the fact that much of our work is "team" based while PRP is an individualistic tool.

11 McChesney, R. W. 2013. *Digital Disconnect*, New York: The New Press, p. 29.

12 http://www.investopedia.com/terms/e/esop.asp.

13 Scientific testing (De Waal, F. 2017. *Are We Smart Enough to Know How Smart Animals Are?*, New York: W.W. Norton & Company) has shown that humans are inextricably linked to fairness and have an 'inequality aversion. All human societies, no matter how unequal in reality, have the same moral basis. As any parent knows, children are acutely averse to inequality – not just when it affects them negatively but also displaying generosity towards the have-nots' (Cobb, M. 2016. Intelligent relations, *The Guardian Weekly*, 195(21):36, 28th October 2016; de Waal, F. 2011. Ted-Talk (https://www.ted.com/talks/frans_de_waal_do_animals_have_morals?language=en).

14 https://www.youtube.com/watch?v=f7E0mTJQ2KM.

15 However, a recent Oxfam study (as reported in: Dolack, P. 2017. "Eight People Own" (coun-terpunch.org, 20th January 2017) has shown that the link between productivity and wage has been broken: 'the average Canadian and US household would earn hundreds of dollars per week more if wages had kept up with rising productivity'.

16 Sharpe, A. & Uguccioni, J. 2017. Decomposing the productivity-wage nexus in selected OECD countries, 1986-2013, *International Productivity Monitor*, 32(spring):42.

17 OECD. 2018. *The Decoupling of Wages*, Paris: OECD Economic Outlook, vol. 2018, no. 2, pp. 55 & 57, Chapter 2 (https://www.oecd.org/economy/outlook/Decoupling-of-wages-from-productivity-november-2018-OECD-economic-outlook-chapter.pdf, accessed: 15th May 2021).

18 Barth, E., Bryson, A. & Dale-Olsen, H. 2017. Union density, productivity and wages, *IZA Discussion Paper*, no. 11111 (https://papers.ssrn.com, 17th November 2017, accessed: 22nd January 2018).

19 Haussmann, T. 2016. Compensation and benefits: essentials of bonus plans, in: Zeuch, M. (eds.) *Handbook of HRM*, Heidelberg: Springer, p. 879.

20 Heneman, R. L. & Von Hippel, C. 1995. Balancing group and individual rewards rewarding individual contributions to the team, *Compensation & Benefits Review*, 27(4):63–68; Prooijen, A. M. & Ellemers, N. 2015. Does it pay to be moral? How indicators of morality and compe-tence enhance organizational and work team attractiveness, *British Journal of Management*, 26(2):225–236.

21 Gomez-Mejia, L. R., Balkin, D. B. & Cardy, L. R. 2016. *HRM – Global Edition*, Harlow: Pearson, p. 357.

22 But recently, the NGO Oxfam (2016:12) stated that "wages are not keeping up with the pro-ductivity of workers" and that this "removes the link between productivity and prosperity" (Oxfam 2016:13).

23 plato.stanford.edu/entries/behaviorism/; Geller, E. S. 2015. Seven life lessons from human-istic behaviorism: how to bring the best out of yourself and others, *Journal of Organizational Behavior Management*, 35(1–2):151–170; Spurgeon, P., Davies, R. & Chapman, A. (eds.) 2015. *Elements of Applied Psychology*, London: Routledge, Chapter 10.

24 The link between both has recently been questioned by Oxfam's "Figure 6: Worker pro-ductivity in developed countries has increased but wages have failed to keep up" (Oxfam 2016:17).

25 Garton, E. 2017. What if companies managed people as carefully as they manage money?, *Harvard Business Review*, 24th May 2017.

26 See for example, "Nike to raise wages for thousands of employees" (https://www.reuters.com, 24th July 2018, accessed: 5th August 2018).

27 Graeber, D. 2019, *Bullshit Jobs*, London: Penguin Books, p. 179.

28 Word Bank. 2016. *Digital Dividends – World Development Report 2016*, Washington, DC: World Bank, p. 21.

29 See also: Genuine Progress Indicator (GPI, https://en.wikipedia.org); cf. Meadows, D. H. 1972. *The Limits to Growth*, New York: Universe Books; https://www.youtube.com/watch?v=ynbgMKclWWc.

30 Lafferty, G. 2019. The Wages Crisis in Australia: What It Is and What to Do about It *ELRR Online* (20th March 2019, https://doi.org/10.1177/1035304619837434, accessed: 5th April 2019).

31 Martin, C. A. 2005. From high maintenance to high productivity: what managers need to know about Generation Y, *Industrial and Commercial Training*, 37(1):39–44; Hewlett, S. A., Sherbin, L. & Sumberg, K. 2009. How Gen Y & Boomers will reshape your agenda, *Harvard Business Review*, 87(7/8):71–76; Laird, M. D., Harvey, P. & Lancaster, J. 2015. Accountability, entitlement, tenure, and satisfaction in Generation Y, *Journal of Managerial Psychology*, 30(1):87–100.

32 Williams, M. et al. 2020. *Mapping Good Work - The Quality of Working Life across the Occupational Structure*, Bristol: Bristol University Press, p. 33.

33 Shafritz, J. M., Ott, J. S. & Jang, Y. S. 2015. *Classics of Organization Theory* (8th ed.), Stamford, CA: Cengage Learning; Henderson, G. & Long, W. C. 2016. *Introduction to Human Relations Studies: Academic Foundations and Selected Social Justice*, Springfield: Charles C Thomas Press.

34 Cullen, D. 1997. Maslow, monkeys, and motivational theory, *Organization*, 4(3):355–373.

35 Kiel, J. M. 1999. Reshaping Maslow's hierarchy of needs to reflect today's educational and managerial philosophies, *Journal of Instructional Psychology*, 26(3):167–167.

36  In July 2020, the Chesapeake Energy company filed for bankruptcy with $9bn work of death. 'It also made McClendon…the highest-aid US boss when he took home $100m in 2008' (Guardian Weekly, 10th July 2020, p. 33).

37  McGregor, D. 1960. *The Human Side of Enterprise*, New York: McGraw-Hill; McGregor, D. 2006. *The Human Side of Enterprise* (updated and with new commentary by Joel Cutcher-Gershenfeld), New York: McGraw-Hill.

38  Herzberg, F. 1966. *Work and the Nature of Man*, Cleveland, OH: World Publishing; Herzberg, F. 2011. One more time: how do you motivate employees? (online: https://hbr.org/2003/01/one-more-time-how-do-you-motivate-employees).

39  McCord, P. 2016. Meaningful work beats over-the-top perks every time, *Harvard Business Review*, HBR.ORG, 18th February 2016.

40  Chen, H. M. & Hsieh, Y. H. 2006. Key trends of the total reward system in the 21st century, *Compensation & Benefits Review*, 38(6):64–70.

41  http://guides.wsj.com/management/strategy/how-to-set-goals/.

42  Neck, C. et al. 2016. *Organizational Behavior: A Critical-Thinking Approach*, Los Angeles, CA: Sage.

43  Gruhle, T. 2016. Compensation and benefits: essentials of benchmarking, in: Zeuch, M. (eds.) *Handbook of HRM*, Heidelberg: Springer, p. 843.

44  This is what Siegrist calls *effort-reward imbalance*, i.e. a 'mismatch between high workload (high demand) and low control over long-terms rewards (Siegrist, J. & Morten, J. (eds.) 2016. *Work Stress and Health in a Globalized Economy: The Model of Effort-Reward Imbalance*, Cham: Springer; Siegrist, J. et al. 2009. A short generic measure of work stress in the era of globalization: effort–reward imbalance, *International Archives of Occupational and Environmental Health*, 82(8):1005–1013.).

45  http://www.quickmba.com/mgmt/expectancy-theory/.

46  http://plato.stanford.edu/entries/rawls/.

47  Van Slyke, S. & Cullen, F. T. (eds.) 2016. *Oxford Handbook of White-Collar Crime*, Oxford: Oxford University Press.

48  Schneider, F. H. et al. 2020. Sorting and Wage Premiums in Immoral Work, University of Zürich Working Paper #353 (http://www.econ.uzh.ch/static/wp/econwp353.pdf).

49  Blau, F. D. & Kahn, L. M. 2006. The US gender pay gap in the 1990s: slowing convergence, *Industrial & Labor Relations Review*, 60(1):45–66; Bishu, S. G. & Alkadry, M. G. 2016. A systematic review of the gender pay gap and factors that predict it, *Administration & Society* (online before printing): https://doi.org/0095399716636928; Bryson, A. 2016. Pay equity after the Equality Act 2010: does sexual orientation still matter?, *Work Employment & Society*, 31(3):483–500.

50  Colella, A., Paetzold, R. L., Zardkoohi, A. & Wesson, M. J. 2007. Exposing pay secrecy, *Academy of Management Review*, 32(1):55–71; Lussier, R. N. & Hendon, J. R. 2016. *HRM: Functions, Applications, and Skill Development* (2nd ed.). London: Sage, p. 411; Mello, J. A. 2015. *Strategic MRM* (4th ed.), Mason: South-Western/Cengage Learning, pp. 507–518).

51  Cohen, G. A. 1983. The structure of proletarian unfreedom, *Philosophy & Public Affairs*, 12(1):3–33; Varoufakis, Y. 1998. "Labour as more than a commodity" & "wages, prices, and profits, in Varoufakis, Y. (eds.) *Foundations of Economics: A Beginner's Companion*, London: Routledge, pp. 170–200.

52  Peetz, D. 2019. *The Realities and Futures of Work*, Canberra: ANU Press, p. 25.

53  Berg, J. 2015. *Labour Markets, Institutions and Inequality: Building Just Societies in the 21st Century*, Cheltenham: Edward Elgar; Zimmerman, D. 1981. Coercive wage offers, *Philosophy and Public Affairs*, 10:121–145; Zimmerman, D. 2002. Taking liberties: the perils of 'moralizing' freedom and coercion in social theory and practice, *Social Theory and Practice*, 28:577–609; Liao, T. F. 2016. Evaluating distributional differences in income inequality, *Socius* (http://srd.sagepub.com); Gantz, G. 2017. *The Age of Inequality: Corporate America's War on Working People*, London: Verso.

54  Peetz, D. 2019. *The Realities and Futures of Work*, Canberra: ANU Press, p. 16.

55  ILO. 2016. Global Wage Report (http://www.ilo.org/global/research/global-reports/global-wage-report/2016/lang–en/index.htm; accessed: 17th January 2018).

56  Sharpe, A. & Uguccioni, J. 2017. Decomposing the productivity-wage nexus in selected OECD countries, 1986-2013, *International Productivity Monitor*, 1st April, 32(spring):25–43.

57   https://data.oecd.org/lprdty/unit-labour-costs.htm.

58   https://stats.oecd.org/Index.aspx?DataSetCode=AV_AN_WAGE.

59   https://www.theguardian.com/technology/2019/nov/13/tesla-cites-brexit-as-germany-chosen-over-uk-for-european-plant-elon-musk.

60   economist.com/content/big-mac-index; cnbc.com/id/100972130; cf. Reiche, B. S., Harzing, A.-W. & Tenzer, H. 2019. *International HRM*, p. 508f.; https://www.statista.com/statistics/274326/big-mac-index-global-prices-for-a-big-mac/.

61   https://data.oecd.org/conversion/purchasing-power-parities-ppp.htm.

62   Ashenfelter, O. & Jurajda, S. 2001. Cross-country Comparisons of Wage Rates: The Big Mac Index, Princeton University/CERGE-EI/Charles University (https://economics.princeton.edu/working-papers/cross-country-comparisons-of-wage-rates-the-big-mac-index/.); Ashenfelter, O. 2012. Comparing real wage rates, *American Economic Review*, 102(2):617–642 (629).

63   https://inequality.org/.

64   Oxfam. 2018. Reward Work, Not Wealth (PFD download from: https://www.oxfam.org/sites/www.oxfam.org/files/file_attachments/bp-reward-work-not-wealth-220118-summ-en.pdf, January 2018, accessed: 6th February 2018).

65   Fung, A. 2017. It's The Gap, Stupid! (http://bostonreview.net/class-inequality/archon-fung-its-gap-stupid); Barth, E., Bryson, A. & Dale-Olsen, H. 2020. Union density effects on productivity and wages, *The Economic Journal*, 130(631):1898–1936.

66   'General Motors created economic value of approximately $232,00 per employee...Facebook has created an enterprise worth $20.5 million per employee' (Galloway, S. 2018. *The Four: The Hidden DNA of Amazon, Apple, Facebook, and Google*, (eBook) New York: Portfolio, p. 16).

67   Reiher, K. 2016. Compensation and benefits: job evaluation, in: Zeuch, M. (eds.) *Handbook of HRM*, Heidelberg: Springer, p. 829.

68   Kohn, A. 1999. *Punished By Rewards: The Trouble with Gold Stars, Incentive Plans, A's, Praise, and Other Bribes*, Boston, MA: Houghton-Mifflin.

69   Kohn, A. 1999. *Punished By Rewards: The Trouble with Gold Stars, Incentive Plans, A's, Praise, and Other Bribes*, Boston, MA: Houghton-Mifflin, pp. 126–130.

70   McCord, P. 2016. Meaningful work beats over-the-top perks every time, *Harvard Business Review*, HBR.ORG, 18th February 2016).

71   www.accenture.com.

72   http://www.hcamag.com/hr-news/why-accenture-is-ditching-performance-reviews-203052.aspx; Chandler, T. M. 2016. *How Performance Management Is Killing Performance – And What to Do About It: Rethink, Redesign, Reboot*, San Francisco, CA: Berrett-Koehler Publishers.

73   https://www.bbc.com/worklife/article/20210125-why-ceos-make-so-much-money.

74   Mishel, L., Gould, E. & Bivens, J. 2015. Wage stagnation in nine charts, *Economic Policy Institute*, 6:2–13 (https://termadiary.org/wp-content/uploads/2017/05/wage-stagnation-in-nine-charts.pdf).

75   Galston, W. A. 2018. Wage stagnation is everyone's problem, *Wall Street Journal* (https://www.wsj.com/, 14th August 2018, accessed: 15th December 2018); Peetz, D. 2019. *The Realities and Futures of Work*, Canberra: ANU Press, p. 98.

76   Case, A. & Deaton, A. 2020. *Deaths of Despair and the Future of Capitalism*, Princeton, NJ: Princeton University Press, p. 7.

77   HBR. 2020. Consider personality when structuring CEO pay, *Harvard Business Review*, 98(6):26–28.

78   Clifford, S. 2017. *The CEO Pay Machine*, New York: Blue Rider Press.

79   CIPD. 2015. Pulse Survey 2015 (*Chartered Institute of Personnel and Development*, www.cipd.co.uk, December 2015); McGregor, J. 2015. Among star CEOs, those with MBAs tend to be more self-serving (washingtonpost.com, 6th October 2015).

80   Peetz, D. 2019. *The Realities and Futures of Work*, Canberra: ANU Press, p. 99.

81   HBR. 2017. The rapid rise of golden parachutes, *Harvard Business Review*, 95(1):28; Gregersen, H. 2017. Bursting the CEO bubble, *Harvard Business Review*, 95(2):76–83; http://www.businessinsider.com/ceos-with-the-biggest-golden-parachutes-2016-8/?r=AU&IR=T.

82   Mander, J. 2012. *The Capitalism Papers*, Berkeley, CA: Counter Point Press, p. 184.

83   HighPayCentre.2017.ExecutivePay–ReviewofFTSE100ExecutivePayPackages(http://high-paycentre.org/files/2016_CEO_pay_in_the_FTSE100_report_%28WEB%29_%281%29.pdf; accessed: 17th January 2018).

84  Holmberg, S. & Schmitt, M. 2016. *The Milton Friedman Doctrine Is Wrong*, evonomics.com, 9th June 2016; cf. Mizruchi, M. S. & Marshall, L. J. 2016. Corporate CEOs, 1890–2015: titans, bureaucrats, and saviours, *Annual Review of Sociology*, 42:143–163; Mishel, L. & Wolfe, J. 2019. CEO Compensation (https://www.epi.org/publication/ceo-compensation-2018/, 14th August 2019, accessed: 5th April 2021).

85  See also: https://files.epi.org/pdf/171191.pdf.

86  NEF. 2019. *A Bit Rich: Calculating the Real Value to Society of Different Professions*, p. 5 (https://neweconomics.org/uploads/files/8c16eabdbadf83ca79_ojm6b0fzh.pdf, 44 pages, free download, accessed: 15th December 2019).

87  http://www.reuters.com/article/us-tyco-curtain-idUSBRE85D1M620120615.

88  To be seen at the University of Sterling (timeshighereducation.com, 2nd April 2015).

89  Gomez-Mejia, L. R., Balkin, D. B. & Cardy, L. R. 2016. *HRM – Global Edition*, Harlow: Pearson, p. 376; Morgenson, G. 2016. BlackRock Wields Its Big Stick Like a Wet Noodle on C.E.O. Pay (nytimes.com, 17th April, 2016).

90  "CEOs at the top US firms have seen their salaries increase by more than half (by 54.3%) since 2009, while ordinary wages have barely moved" (Oxfam 2016:4).

91  "The average salary (plus bonuses) of a CEO at one of the top 350 US firms in 2014 was $16.3m, up 3.9 percent since 2013 and by 54.3 percent since the economic recovery began in 2009" (Oxfam 2016:14).

92  Dolack, P. 2017. Eight People Own as Much as Half the World (www.counterpunch.org, 20th January 2017, 2 pages); www.cheatsheet.com/business/why-skyrocketing-ceo-pay-hurts-everyone.

93  Nadeau, E. G. 2012. *The Cooperative Solution: How the United States Can Tame Recessions, Reduce Inequality, and Protect the Environment*, Madison, WI: Createspace Independent, p. 23.

94  www.glassdoor.com.au/Salaries/ceo-salary…

95  Ellison, K. 2018. Rewarding or Hoarding? (https://ellison.house.gov, May 2018, accessed: 20th August 2018) cf. https://www.youtube.com/watch?v=IUTcuB5TZdY.

96  http://graphics.wsj.com/ceopay-2015/.

97  Bloom, P. & Rhodes, C. 2018. *CEO Society*, London: Zed-Books (epub version), p. 277.

98  Reiche, B. S., Harzing, A.-W. & Tenzer, H. 2019. *International HRM*, p. 220.

99  Gopalan, R., Horn, J. & Milbourn, T. 2017. Comp targets that work, *Harvard Business Review*, September–October Issue.

100  https://www.forbes.com/sites/shelliekarabell/2018/02/14/executive-compensation-is-out-of-control-what-now/#60cf6bf7431f.

101  http://www.thefiscaltimes.com/Columns/2015/05/01/Time-Make-CEO-Pay-Match-Shareholder-Performance.

102  https://www.epi.org/research/minimum-wage/; https://edition.cnn.com/2020/12/31/business/uk-minimum-wage-companies-list-scli-gbr-intl/index.html.

103  One measure of decent wages was the "Social Charter of the European Council" (pre-2004) defining the decency threshold in the 1960s as 68% of average earnings within a national economy. The definition was lowered to that of 60% of net earnings (as of July 2004; perhaps so that the precariat looks decent!); Standing, G. 2016. *The Precariat* (revised edition), London: Bloomsbury Academic.

104  On *starvation wages*, see: https://www.bbc.com/news/business-51604345 (Stiglitz, J. E. 1976. The efficiency wage hypothesis, surplus labour, and the distribution of income in LDCs, *Oxford Economic Papers*, 28(2):185–207); https://www.youtube.com/watch?v=JyjuQy2vrC4.

105  https://zcomm.org/znetarticle/the-coronavirus-pandemic-and-global-wages/.

106  "In the garment sector, firms are consistently using their dominant position to insist on poverty wages. Between 2001 and 2011, wages for garment workers in most of the world's 15 leading apparel-exporting countries fell in real terms" (Oxfam 2016:6).

107  People 'said that eliminating the minimum wage would help businesses grow [just as] advocating slavery again, which might help businesses grow even more' (Mander, J. 2012. *The Capitalism Papers*, Berkeley, CA: Counter Point Press, p. 73).

108  www.wagetheftisacrime.com/; https://www.actu.org.au/media/1449199/d11-actu-submission-to-senate-economics-committee-inquiry-into-the-unlawful-underpayment-of-employee-remuneration-20200306.pdf.

109  Tombs, S. & Whyte, D. 2020. The shifting imaginaries of corporate crime, *Journal of White Collar and Corporate Crime*, 1(1):18f.; Klikauer, T. & Campbell, N. 2020. The criminology

of global warming, *Counterpunch* (https://www.counterpunch.org/2020/08/14/the-criminology-of-global-warming/, 15th August, accessed: 15th May 2021).

110   https://edition.cnn.com/2020/12/15/tech/apple-iphone-india-wistron-intl-hnk/index.html.

111   In November 2011, Warehouse Workers helped Wal-Mart warehouse employees file their fourth class action lawsuit against the warehouse companies. Without Wal-Mart being a direct defendant, the argument was made that Wal-Mart has created a particular negative culture amongst the companies it works with. The first lawsuit filed was in 2009. The workers argued that poor record keeping and broken promises have led to workers receiving less than minimum wage. Walmart denied its workers the payment of vacation entitlements. These were promised by Walmart upon contracting (Lydersen, K. 2011. Wage Theft at Wal-Mart Warehouses? Fourth Lawsuit in Two Years Filed on Behalf of Underpaid Workers, AlterNet (4th March 2012); cf. https://www.brookings.edu/research/meet-the-low-wage-workforce/.

112   Victoria Government. 2021. *Victoria's Wage Theft Laws* (https://www.vic.gov.au/victorias-wage-theft-laws; accessed: 15th July 2021).

113   www.nytimes.com/2014/09/01/business/more-workers-are-claiming-wage-theft.html?_r=0.

114   Kuttner, R. 2013. The Task Rabbit Economy (https://prospect.org/article/task-rabbit-economy, 10th October 2013, accessed: 5th April 2019).

115   Meixell, B. & Eisenbrey, R. 2014. An Epidemic of Wage Theft Is Costing Workers Hundreds of Millions of Dollars a Year, Economic Policy Institute (8th June 2015).

116   http://www.wagetheftisacrime.com/.

117   http://www.labor.ucla.edu/wp-content/uploads/2015/03/WageTheftEnglishIV.jpg.

118   Pizzigati, S. 2018. *The Case for a Maximum Wage*, London: Polity Press.

119   "No business which demands for existence on paying less than living wages to its workers has any right to continue in this country" – President F. D. Roosevelt, 1933 (Parker, J., Arrowsmith, J., Fells, R. & Prowse, P. 2016. The living wage: concepts, contexts and future concerns, *Labour & Industry*, 26(1):1).

120   https://www.dw.com/en/germany-to-raise-minimum-wage-despite-pandemic/a-54005192.

121   https://ec.europa.eu/eurostat/statistics-explained/index.php/Minimum_wage_statistics.

122   Klaveren, V. M., Gregory, D. & Schulten, T. 2015. *Minimum Wages, Collective Bargaining and Economic Development in Asia and Europe: A Labour Perspective*, London: Palgrave Macmillan.

123   Ashenfelter, O. C., Farber, H. & Ransom, M. R. 2010. Labor market monopsony, *Journal of Labor Economics*, 28(2):203–210; cf.

124   Young, J. 2011. *5 Salary Negotiation Tips That Work!* (www.forbes.com, 11th May).

125   Rockmann, K. W. et al. 2019. *Negotiation: Moving From Conflict to Agreement*, London: Sage; Donaldson, M. C. 2007. *Negotiating for Dummies* (2nd ed.), Hoboken, NJ: Wiley.

126   Reiche, B. S., Harzing, A.-W. & Tenzer, H. 2019. *International HRM*, p. 217.

127   http://www.un.org/en/universal-declaration-human-rights/.

128   https://www.ilo.org/dyn/normlex/en/f?p=NORMLEXPUB:12100:0::NO::P12100_ILO_CODE:C098.

129   "Between 1988 and 2011, 46 percent of overall income growth accrued to the top 10 percent, while the bottom 10 percent received only 0.6 percent" (Oxfam 2016:9).

130   https://www.youtube.com/watch?v=1K4fO98KOKo.

131   Klikauer, T. & Link, C. 2021. Capital, profits and wages in 2021, *Counterpunch* (https://www.counterpunch.org/2021/06/24/capital-profits-and-wages-in-2021/; 24th June 2021).

132   Micklethwait, J. & Wooldridge, A. 1996. *The Witch Doctors: Making Sense of the Management Gurus*, New York: Times Books, p. 190.

133   https://www.imercer.com/content/mobility/cost-of-living-city-rankings.html?WT.mc_id=A000519#list.

134   McKersie, R. B. & Walton, R. E. 1965. *A Behavioral Theory of Labor Negotiations: An Analysis of a Social Interaction System*, Ithaca, NY: ILR Press.

135   www.socialsecurity.gov/news/cola/;   https://www.fastcompany.com/3051540/secrets-of-the-most-productive-people/15-habits-that-will-totally-transform-your-productivit;   http://www.history.com/topics/british-history/robin-hood.

136   Ton, Z. 2019. Raising wages is the right thing to do, and doesn't have to be bad for your bottom line, *Harvard Business Review*, 18th April 2019.

137   Robbins, S. P. & Judge, T. A. 2013. *Essentials of Organizational Behavior* (12th ed.), Boston, MA: Pearson.

138   NEF. 2019. *A Bit Rich: Calculating the Real Value to Society of Different Professions*, pp. 4–5 (https://neweconomics.org/uploads/files/8c16eabdbadf83ca79_ojm6b0fzh.pdf, 44 pages, free download, accessed: 15th December 2019).
139   https://www.youtube.com/watch?v=0yzeOqV7eKI.
140   http://www.wagetheftisacrime.com/.

## Further Readings

Armstrong, M. 2007. *A Handbook of Employee Reward Management and Practice* (2nd ed.), London: Kogan Page.

Armstrong, M. 2015. *Armstrong's Handbook of Reward Management Practice: Improving Performance through Reward* (5th ed.), London: Kogan Page.

Armstrong, M. 2016. *Armstrong's Handbook of Strategic HRM* (6th ed.), Philadelphia, PA: Kogan Page.

Armstrong, M., Brown, D. & Reilly, P. 2010. *Evidence-Based Reward Management: Creating Measurable Business Impact from Your Pay and Reward Practices*, London: Kogan Page.

Arnold, K. A., Connelly, C. E., Walsh, M. M. & Ginis, K. A. 2015. Leadership Styles, Emotion Regulation, and Burnout, *Journal of Occupational Health Psychology*, 20(4):481.

Bartram, T., Boyle, B., Stanton, P., Sablok, G. & Burgess, G. 2015. Performance and Reward Practices of Multinational Corporations Operating in Australia, *Journal of Industrial Relations*, 57(2):210–231.

Beck, V. & Williams, G. 2015. The (Performance) Management of Retirement and the Limits of Individual Choice, *Work, Employment & Society*, 29(2):267–277.

Fisher, J. G. 2015. *Strategic Reward and Recognition: Improving Employee Performance through Non-monetary Incentives*, Philadelphia, PA: Kogan Page.

Kohn, A. 1999. *Punished By Rewards: The Trouble with Gold Stars, Incentive Plans, A's, Praise, and Other Bribes*, Boston, MA: Houghton-Mifflin.

Kreamer, A. 2015. *Risk/Reward: Why Intelligent Leaps and Daring Choices Are the Best Career Moves You Can Make*, New York: Random House.

Malik, M. A. R., Butt, A. N. & Choi, J. N. 2015. Rewards and Employee Creative Performance: Moderating Effects of Creative Self-efficacy, Reward Importance, and Locus of Control, *Journal of Organizational Behavior*, 36(1):59–74.

Martocchio, J. J. 2016. *Strategic Compensation: A HRM Approach*, Harlow: Pearson.

Oxfam. 2016. *An Economy for the 1%*, Oxford: Oxfam Briefing Paper 210 (18th January).

Riasi, A. & Asadzadeh, N., 2015. The Relationship between Principals' Reward Power and Their Conflict Management Styles Based on Thomas Kilmann's Conflict Mode Instrument, *Management Science Letters*, 5(6):611–618.

Rose, M. 2014. *Reward Management*, London: Kogan Page.

Shaw, J. D. & Gupta, N. 2015. Let the Evidence Speak Again! Financial Incentives Are More Effective Than We Thought, *Human Resource Management Journal*, 25(3):281–293.

Shields, J., Brown, M., Kaine, S., Dolle-Samuel, C., North-Samardzic, A., McLean, P., Johns, R., Robinson, J., O'Leary, P. & Plimmer, G., 2015. *Managing Employee Performance & Reward: Concepts, Practices, Strategies*, Cambridge: Cambridge University Press.

Tulgan, B. 2014. *The 27 Challenges Managers Face: Step-By-Step Solutions to (Nearly) All of Your Management Problems*, San Francisco, CA: Jossey-Bass.

# 9 Strategies for People
## Strategic Human Resource Management

## Executive Summary

Many large companies take a strategic approach to business planning. But whatever the strategy, they all involve people and, in particular, the management of people (HRM). In strategic planning and strategy making, HRM becomes a vital actor. The strategy a company adopts – for example, Porter's cost leader vs. differentiator – also impacts on HRM so this is taken into consideration when strategies are developed, for example using a SWOT analysis or when a strategy is formulated as a prospector strategy, defender strategy, analyser strategy, or reactor strategy. Above that, four overall strategies have been identified: classical strategy, crafting strategy, an evolutionary approach to strategy, and a systemic approach to strategy. When companies develop a strategy, HRM is often faced with four levels of incorporation, the purely administrative level, the one-way, the two-way level, and a fully integrated way of strategy making. Strategy always and necessarily leads to some form of organisational change. As a consequence, change management – at the level of HRM – operates with four distinct models of change: top-down, piecemeal, bargaining, and systemic-jointism.

## Key Learning Objectives

1. Realise the importance of strategic HRM for strategic business planning;
2. Describe the characteristics of strategic people management;
3. Understand the four ways in which HRM is linked to strategic management;
4. Link strategic management to strategic people management;
5. Outline the difference between strategy formulation and implementation;
6. Ascertain the influence of culture on strategic HRM;
7. Comprehend the strategic partners in HRM strategy formulation;
8. Describe "change management" and its links to strategic HRM; and
9. Develop a formal HR policy on strategic HRM.

## Managing People Strategically

This chapter describes the role of HRM as a strategic partner in formulating a corporate business strategy. In the field of HRM, managing people[1] strategically is generally called **Strategic HRM** (SHRM). SHRM is often defined as linking human resources with an organisation's business strategy. The objectives of SHRM are the long-term improvement of business performance for the next three to five years and possibly beyond. In such a project, the strategic goals of an organisation and SHRM activities are aligned.

DOI: 10.4324/9781003293637-9

To support a business strategy, SHRM develops an organisational culture fostering strategic, i.e. long-term innovation and flexibilities, the goal to improve the long-term competitive advantage of an organisation. Inside a business organisation, general management focuses on involving core HR functions. This involvement takes on the form of a **strategic partnership**.[2] Strategic HR works with general management on the formulation and implementation of a company's strategies involving key HR activities such as recruitment and selection, performance management, reward management, etc.

By comparison, tactical and administratively focused HRM (non-SHRM) concentrates on internal HR issues such as, for example, addressing and solving problems that affect people management programs in the long run and often globally. SHRM's primary goal is not just to increase employee productivity but to focus on the strategic orientation of a business. SHRM identifies key HR areas and aligns these to the strategies the company pursues.[3] SHRM always demands communication between HR managers and top management.[4] Only with active communication SHRM becomes possible and the competitive advantage of an organisation can be improved.

Ever since Michael Porter coined the term "competitive advantage", strategy has moved even more into the centre of management.[5] But the idea of using strategy is much older than the idea of management that entered the modern era some time between **Taylor** (1911) and **Fayol** (1916) who formulated a scientific approach to management (Taylor) and fourteen tasks of management (Fayol).[6] Strategy is a much older idea. Its origins date back to ancient Greek society with **strategos στρατηγός** being the army leader. Strategy – a plan for action – became the pre-planning of war with the objective to win over the enemy. A very similar idea was developed by Chinese militarist **Sun Tzu** (500 BC) in his rather poetic "The Art of War".[7] Whether in Greece or in China, strategy has the same objective – to kill the enemy.

The man who converted the ancient idea of strategy into modernity was Prussian aristocrat and militarist **Carl von Clausewitz** (1780–1831). Clausewitz gave Prussian-Germanic armies the illusion of an always winnable war – an idea that later failed miserably twice (World War I and II). Clausewitz is mostly remembered for his statement that "war is the continuation of politics by other means". While many strategies may be no more than militaristic illusions, Clausewitz' militarism entered politics, and only a few years after WWII, strategic planning also entered the world of business often as a "military threats [equal] business threats" equation.[8] It was the post-war era in the USA, a period defined by rising multinational corporations beginning to develop ever more sophisticated organisational structures.

These new business structures were all based on the image of the **business pyramid** with a CEO at the top, top management just below, functional departments below that, and workers at the bottom.[9] Soon these rapidly growing corporations demanded a new **organisational chart** with new structures such as functional structures, divisional structures (M-form[10]), geographical structures, customer- or client-based structures, etc.[11] While all of these – more or less – mirror the pyramid, many of these new organisational forms became necessary as large business enterprises could no longer follow the neo-liberal romanticism of making something, then carrying it down to the local village market in the hope of selling it for a profit. These large business organisations needed planning – and not just planning but strategic planning. In the conflict between relying on rigid organisational structure that enforces traditional command and control strategies and the fluency, liquidity, and rapid changes of a company's business strategy, the evolution of organisational structures has not ended as the following brief history of organisations shows[12]:

| Form | Key identifier | Leadership | Organisational innovations | Examples |
|------|----------------|------------|----------------------------|----------|
| Impulsive | Power & fear, keeping people in line, reactive, short-termism, thrives in unstable environment | Predatory (wolf pack) | Division of labour Commanding authority | Mafia, street gangs, Tribal groups, militias |
| Conformist | Formal roles, hierarchical pyramid, top-down, command and control, stable, rigid processes | Paternalistic-Authoritarian | Formal roles and organisational processes | Military, Catholic Church, government, schools |
| Achiever | Strategy to win over competitors, staying ahead, innovative, MBO, long-term strategies | Goal oriented (the machine) | Innovation, accountability, meritocracy | Large corporations, some schools |
| Pluralistic | Pluralism within pyramidal structure, some empowerment, motivational | Consensus Participatory | Empowerment, participation, value culture, stakeholders | Southwest Airlines Ben & Jerry's |
| Evolutionary | Self-management replaces hierarchies, organic organisation, living entity, creative, evolutionary | Distributive Motivator | Self-management, wholeness, organic, holistic | Patagonia, FAVI, Buurtzorg, Semler[i] |

[i] Semler, R. 1989. Managing without Managers, *Harvard Businss Review*, September 1989; Semler, R. 1993. Maverick: the success story behind the world's most unusual workplace, New York: Warner Books; buurtzorgusa.org/about.html; www.favi.com/; www.mondragon-corporation.com/eng/.

*Figure 9.1* The Evolution of the Business Organisation.

In the brief history of the evolution of human organisations (Figure 9.1) ranging from early human tribes hunting in packs with a strong leader to conformist organisations such as the military and many government agencies and schools, to achievement-oriented organisations such as classical corporations as well as to more pluralistic organisations such as those seriously empowering employees, organisational structures and business organisations have covered a long historical period. Since such organisational structures are not once and for all given, they continue to evolve and develop with the evolutionary organisation being the latest development.

The evolutionary organisation sees itself as a living organism where the organisation is no longer seen as having a life of its own guided by an invisible hand. Instead of trying to predict and control its business environment, members of such organisations are invited to listen in and understand what the organisation wants to become, reflecting on its purpose and whom it wants to serve.[13] Such a more liquid organisation can operate more effectively as it has disposed of rigid hierarchical structures that prevent rapid strategic change. Instead of having an inflexible top-down structure, it operates a **flat organisational structure**[14] based on teamwork and empowerment that eliminate the need for hierarchies.[15] The new structure radically simplifies project management and strategising – the making of strategies – and their implementation. HR managers oversee strategy teams using a **strategy metrics**.[16]

A strategy metrics can be used to improve the focus of a strategy team as it measures a team on a continuous basis against its strategic objectives.[17] Ongoing measurement includes regular reporting reinforcing the organisational drive to achieve strategic objectives and track progress towards the company's strategic goals. In establishing a strategy metrics, HR managers consider that metrics includes measurements against an organisational target or strategic business goal. This assists in clarifying desired outcomes while establishing a common sense directed towards goal achievement. A strategy metrics can also include benchmarks to make the goal achievable over a set timeframe. HR managers section such goals to assess achievable milestones. A strategy metrics is particularly useful in guiding and assisting strategy teams in organisations with a flatter hierarchy. In these organisational structures, HRM gains in importance as it merges with the new setup, thereby overcoming many of the long held views of "business strategy and HRM".

## Business Strategies and HRM

The increased demand for business planning was the moment when the godfather of strategic management – **Alfred Chandler**[18] – published his seminal work "Strategy and Structure" (1962).[19] With this book, the idea of winning over the military enemy entered business as an idea of a winnable business battle for market share – with the right strategy, one can win the war (Greece, Tzu, Clausewitz) as well as the war of business (Chandler, Mintzberg, Porter, etc.).[20] Not surprisingly, Clausewitz as well as Chandler favoured a general's headquarter (CEO and top-management doing strategic planning) and field units (line managers and employees doing the tactics, i.e. the actual operation of the business war). Since the days of Alfred Chandler, many new methods of strategic planning and strategic management have entered management.

Somewhat pushed by management consultants, **strategic management** is often defined as the formulation and implementation of major goals and initiatives taken by a company's top management on behalf of its owners.[21] It is based on consideration of managerial resources (e.g. marketing, operations management, accounting, and HRM) and an internal (organisational culture, workforce, etc.) as well as external assessment (the external environment and market in which a business competes against other companies).[22] This can follow four different forms:

1. **ethnocentric approach**: decisions are taken by the headquarter,
2. **regiocentric approach**: regional focus on local stakeholders,
3. **polycentric approach**: a corporation's subsidiaries are seen as distinct entities, and
4. **geocentric approach**: world orientation.

Strategic management is seen as working towards the long-term health of a company – a timeframe often seen as roughly three to seven years. The most simplistic idea of strategy is Porter's **leadership strategy** of competing companies. Overall Porter saw two kinds of companies being exposed to his **five forces** (bargaining power of customers, bargaining power of suppliers, competitive companies, threats of new entrance, and threat of substitute products):

1. there are **cost leaders** → we have the same than the others, just cheaper
2. there are **differentiators** → we have something different (niche market).

In Porter's model, a cost leadership strategy is seen as a marketing strategy ascertaining the position of a business in a marketplace – the **positioning school** – where product price or the price of a service is the single most defining element of a company's strategic toolbox.[23] The strategic goal is to simply become the lowest cost producer in an industry or marketplace. Competition or competitive advantage is achieved through the lowering of costs. This means not just managing costs but being a relentless cost-cutting machine. Such strategic cost leadership requires

1. being aggressive in driving efficiency,
2. a vigorous pursuit of cost reductions,

3.  tightening cost and strict overhead control,
4.  and relentless cost minimisation in areas like service, HRM, sales, advertising, etc.

It essentially means "we offer the same as you, just cheaper" (budget airlines, etc.). By comparison, a **differential strategy** is applied when companies offer different products or services that are unlike those from the competitor's products or services (e.g. the product form, the brand image, features, technology, customer service, pricing, and distribution channels).[24] A differentiator company, for example, can increase margins and avoid the need to compete in the low cost section of the market. Its message is simple – "we have something different" (e.g. Porsche, Bugatti Venron, etc.).

When companies adopt Porter's cost leadership strategy or the differentiator strategy, this has implications for HRM. A cost leader often views employees simply as cost to be reduced ("work = commodity") while a differentiator is more likely to value employees ("employee = asset"). Porter's competitive models can be supported through HRM's soft versus hard model.[25] **Hard HRM** (instrumental) and **Soft HRM** (humanistic) are two distinctive ways of operating HRM.

## Hard HRM Strategies

Hard HRM sees employees as a commodity or resource – like a machine, buildings, money, etc. It has a strong link to strategy and business planning defining the human commodities that a business needs in order to be competitive and asks three essential questions:

1.  how do we get the resources;
2.  how much will they cost; and
3.  what is the cost-benefit analysis.

HRM identifies the level of workforce needed to carry out the business strategy. HR managers focus on hiring, moving, and firing. Hard HRM concentrates on numbers (cost, recruitment numbers, redundancy numbers, etc.). It is an authoritarian top-down approach with minimal communication (need to know base). Wages and salaries are kept at the lowest level – just enough to recruit human resources and retain enough staff to carry the business strategy forward. If anything, the company relies on the minimum wage. In operational terms, hard HRM works with as little empowerment as possible. Its performance management system is simply about making judgements (e.g. GE Jack Welch's 20/70/10: top 20% is rewarded; 70% work adequately; bottom 10% is fired).

## Soft HRM Strategies

Soft HRM sees employees as people, not as human resources. They are considered the most important part of the business. Well-trained people who are motivated and satisfied contribute to the company's competitive advantage. Employees are not mistreated as a commodity but seen as individuals. HRM incorporates individual needs in their system and HR managers focus on combining the needs of employees with the strategy of the business, converting employees' roles, rewards, motivation, etc. into a strategic asset for the business. Rather than short-termism, soft HRM has a strategic perspective that trains and rewards people within a longer-term view of workforce planning.[26]

Instead of authoritarianism, soft HRM values cooperation, involvement, participation, and communication. It sees employees as strategic partners, offering them a competitive pay structure with suitable performance-related rewards (i.e. profit sharing). Instead of strict hierarchies, soft HRM encourages flat structures where employees take responsibility. Finally, soft HRM encourages organisational training.

In addition to Porter's strategy and soft-vs.-hard HRM, **Miles and Snow**[27] have developed a four-fold strategy that defines a company through the strategic orientation. It consists of a prospector strategy, a defender strategy, an analyser strategy, and a reactor strategy.

### The Prospector Strategy and Soft HRM

The prospector strategy involves conquering new markets and stimulating new opportunities just like the **Blue Ocean Strategy**.[28] For new product development which is forcefully pursued, HRM relies on very well-trained people. To obtain additional market share and respond quickly to new market opportunity, an inquisitive workforce is demanded that is aware of market changes and trends because a relatively large proportion of the company's revenue comes from new products and new markets. Prospector strategists utilise the first mover advantage that allows them to exploit premium pricing opportunities and high margins. Since the strategic business offers considerable autonomy to employees, the prospector strategy is supported by soft HRM.

### The Defender Strategy and HRM's Soft-Hard Combination

Defender strategists focus on finding and maintaining stable markets. They insulate their company against market changes and changes from competitors wherever possible and stabilise their already conquered market by keeping prices and costs low, offering better quality products and superior customer service. Defender companies are slow in making decisions with the goal of efficiency. They operate in mature and well-defined industries. Sales are often repeat sales and replacement purchases. The internal business structure offers relatively low levels of autonomy. HR managers working under such a strategy rely on traditional forms of HRM and are less innovative while offering a skilful combination of hard and soft HRM.[29]

### The Analyser Strategy and Soft HRM

The analyser strategy demands taking less risk and making fewer mistakes than other strategies. In fact, the vast number of companies are analysers as they are rarely "first movers" in an industry. They tend to expand into areas close to their existing core competency. These companies are reluctant to develop new products and services. Their business strategy focuses on incremental improvements in existing products and services. These firms hardly ever expand into new markets. Instead, they prefer to expand existing markets and watch the developments in their industry closely, but do not act until they are sure that the time is right. As a consequence, HRM focuses on recruitment and selection to employ the right people with the right skill sets. The second component of HRM is the application of well-executed employee training and development regimes and organisational learning allowing its managers to analyse shifts in markets.

## The Reactor Strategy and HRM's Core Activities

The reactor strategy demands conservatism. Reactor companies do not rely on active strategy. These companies tend to react to market events as they happen, just as the name "reactor" indicates. Their strategy is underscored by Charles Darwin's evolutionary theory. Often misquoted, for Darwin it was never the strong that survive but those who can adapt to changes in the environment.[30] Reactor companies simply respond when environmental pressures force them to do so. This is the least effective of the four strategies. It follows the market without having a clear strategy. Businesses that follow this way have never articulated a strategy while management focuses on maintaining the business despite changes in the business environment. In such a non-strategy environment, HRM's function is to focus on the core activities of HRM as outlined in this book (recruitment and selection, industrial relations, organisational learning, work design, OHS, performance management, rewards, and ethics).

## Strategy Formulation and Implementation

Irrespective of which strategy is used – Porter's strategy, Miles and Snow, or any other strategy – most strategic processes focus on two distinct elements: (1) **strategy formulation and crafting**,[31] and **strategising**; (2) **strategy implementation**. For the former, a strategy planning group – usually consisting of top managers – meet to define the company's strategy. Once this process is complete, the company moves towards strategy implementation, i.e. carrying out its strategy. For both – formulation and implementation – Chandler's dictum: **structure follows strategy** remains imperative.

Based on his study of DuPont, General Motors, Standard Oil, and Sears Roebuck, Chandler showed that with any strategy arises the need to restructure. This demands that companies need to have at least four structures in place to carry out a strategy: marketing, accounting, operations management, and HRM. Without people, for example, a new strategy cannot become reality. If the Virgin Group[32] wants to not only offer banking, books, commercial aviation, commercial spaceflight, consumer electronics, films, health care, internet, jewellery, mobile phones, music, radio, retail, and travel but also a Virgin Electric Car, it will need to develop a structure that supports its "Electric Car" strategy and this necessarily involves people such as motor-car engineers, mechanics, etc.

Before moving towards such as structure and restructuring, strategy managers engage in strategy formulation often involving a **five force analysis**[33] – (1) threat of new entrants, (2) threat of substitute products or services; (3) bargaining power of customers (buyers); (4) bargaining power of suppliers; and (5) intensity of competitive rivalry or – alternatively – they will be conducting a **SWOT analysis**[34]: strengths, weaknesses, opportunities, and threats. At its most basic level, the HRM SWOT analysis focuses on internal (strength and weaknesses) and external factors (opportunities and threats):

1. **strengths**: characteristics of employees (skills, knowledge, capabilities, etc.) that give a business a strategic advantage over others;
2. **weaknesses**: characteristics of employees (insufficient training, stifling hierarchies, inappropriate performance management systems and reward structures, etc.) that create a strategic disadvantage for a business to achieve its strategic objectives;
3. **opportunities**: defining the key workforce elements (e.g. internal labour market, training, skill and knowledge levels, etc.) HRM can use to advantage a given strategy;

4. **threats**: identifies the key environmental factors (e.g. higher external wage and salary levels) causing potential problems for a business strategy (e.g. high turnover rates that often indicate significant HR problems,[35] retaining employees, labour shortage, etc.).

On the other hand, employees can cause a threat to HRM and the overall business strategy when considering **Hirschman's exit-loyalty-voice options**.[36] In the above-mentioned case of a threat (insufficient reward), employees can:

1. exit: leave the company because the wage or salary is being too low;
2. loyalty: remain devoted and stay with the company despite a low wage and salary; and
3. voice: take the voice option, i.e. negotiate higher wages.

There are many strategies (corporate strategy, business strategy, enterprise strategy, concentration strategy, internal growth strategy, external growth strategy, etc.) and no one best strategy that fits all businesses. Instead, four overall ways of strategy making have emerged since the advent of strategic management during the 1960s.[37]

### 1. The Classical Strategy (1960s)

The classical strategy relies on a very formal process with strict separation between strategy making and strategy implementation. The classical approach to strategy evolved from military thinking that was converted into **shareholder value**[38] and profit maximisation. It is rational and analytical focusing on internal affairs under the maxim "planning can do no wrong". It is associated with Chandler, Ansoff, and Porter. It tends to treat HRM as an administrative issue that is needed in the implementation part of a strategy.

### 2. The Procedural Strategy (1970s)

The key idea of the procedural approach to strategy making is Mintzberg's "crafting strategy"[39] putting emphasis on the making of strategy. The emphasis shifts from analysis towards strategising. The procedural approach to strategy making remains rational but includes internal organisational politics[40] while relying more on group dynamics, bargaining, learning processes, and **organisational psychology**. With this approach, the strict separation (e.g. no. 1) between strategy making and strategy implementation starts to vanish (e.g. no. 2–4). This approach is linked to Cyert & March, Mintzberg, and Pettigrew. It is also related to the "soft HRM" approach to people management as people and the way they make strategy moves into the centre.

### 3. The Evolutionary Strategy (1980s)

The evolutionary strategy originates in the writings of **Charles Darwin** and focuses on adaptation to market forces. It has strong biological roots assessing a company's position in external markets with the task to developing a business strategy that follows the market.[41] In the evolutionary perspective on strategy, it is capitalism and the market that determine what a business does. It is essentially a "follow the market strategy" confining managers to analysing and adopting. One might argue that this is actually no strategy at all as managers simply follow markets. The idea of strategy management is simply used to legitimise management.[42] This approach is associated with Hannan & Freeman as well as Williamson. As an example, when HRM adopts the evolutionary approach to strategy, it conducts a labour market analysis for recruitment and selection as well as for compensation and rewards to ascertain the actual salary levels in order to, for example, develop a "lead the market strategy" (as mentioned earlier).

### 4. Systematic Strategy (1990s and Onwards)

Unlike the former strategies, the systematic strategy avoids the pitfalls of "A" (active strategy making) looking at "B" (the object of strategy) but taking a more embedded approach. It does not see itself as superior and hierarchical but instead sees strategy making as developing a strategy that remains part of a more organic whole. This relies on locality and its external focus is much more geared towards markets but also includes society and the social environment. Unlike the militarist (1), the psychological (2), and the biological (3) strategies, the systematic approach is sociological and includes external **stakeholders** in strategy making (customers, competitors, governments, suppliers, employees, trade unions, technology, society, shareholders, etc.). Its inclusive approach to strategy making demands that external stakeholders such as NGOs and the environment are included.[43] It views the environment not purely as a business environment but as the natural environment[44] and sustainability[45] not just as being sustainable in a market but having an ecological carbon footprint that is sustainable.[46]

Under the latest and most current approach to strategy making, HRM is not only an institution that manages people but an institution that safeguards a company's strategy with regard to the natural environment. This is a movement towards the **ecological business strategy**.[47] But in whatever way strategy is formulated (1–4), it can never be done without involving people and HRM as any strategic reorientation of a business demands a reorientation of its people management function. As a consequence, HRM has identified four ways in which not only Chandler's "structure follows strategy" dictum but also a general business strategy can be linked to HRM.

### The Four Business Strategy and HRM Strategy Interfaces

The role of HRM in supporting strategy management can vary substantially from being simply an administrative expert to being a change agent and employees champion or a strategy partner. Common to all of these is a four step relationship between the business strategy and HRM: (1) business strategy $\Rightarrow$ HR strategy $\Rightarrow$ HR policy $\Rightarrow$ HR practice (implementation of a strategy).[48] In general, there are four forms of linking a business strategy to HRM. At the interface between those who craft a strategy (often top management) and the business function of HRM there are four ways in which strategy making involves HRM: (1) no link at all ($\rightarrow\leftarrow$); (2) the one-way link ($\rightarrow$); (3) the two-way link ($\leftrightarrows$); and (4) the integrated link ($\leftrightarrow$).

### 1. Non-Strategic and Administrative HRM

At this level of strategy making, HRM is not included in any way in the making of strategy. There is no link and almost no interface between strategy and HRM. Instead, management sees HRM as a purely functional and administrative entity with HR managers as functional managers. HRM is not viewed as a strategic partner but as a tactical and administrative issue engaging with the day-to-day running of the "Human Side of the Enterprise".[49] The role of HRM is to deal with recruitment and selection, industrial relations, organisational learning, work design, OHS, performance management, rewards, and ethics. Management sees HRM as short-term administration (fire-fighting and solving problems as they occur), not as being engaged in the long-term planning of the business.[50]

### 2. The One-Way Strategy Interface

In the **one-way strategy** interface, a strategic planning working group or committee meets, perhaps consisting of marketing, operations management, accounting, the CEO, etc. without HR managers. This group develops a strategic plan for the business. After the plan is developed, HRM is presented with it. HRM is then required to set up HR structures that enable the strategy to be carried out. At the one-way strategy interface, HRM is excluded from crafting a strategy (strategising) but is included in the implementation process and seen as providing administration and structure (Chandler). In short, a developed business strategy dictates certain HR needs (restructuring, organisational training, new workplace designs, new performance management, etc.).

### 3. The Two-Way Strategy Interface

Unlike being totally excluded (no. 1) and being included only in the implementation process of a strategy (no. 2), at the **two-way strategy** interface, HRM is not only informed about a business strategy but is also asked for feedback. With the inclusion of HR considerations, HRM then moves into the implementation process and begins to be recognised as a strategic partner. The two-way process follows a rather rigid three-phase process:

**Phase 1:** The strategic planning committee or working group informs the HR department about the strategy, involving it to some extent;

**Phase 2:** HRM – usually HR executives – analyse the strategy assessing the implications for HRM with regard to HR issues such as recruitment and selection, industrial relations, organisational learning, work design, OHS, performance management, rewards, and ethics;

**Phase 3:** After being made aware of the HR implications of a strategy, the strategy committee reshapes its plan by adhering to HR issues.

The strategy committee then finalises the business strategy with the inclusion of the HR issues as outlined by the HR department. This completes the strategy formulation process. Once the business strategy is formulated, HRM – in conjunction with others – works towards the implementation of the strategy.

### 4. The Integrative Strategy

Rather than following the rigidity and formality of the three-phase process under the two-way approach to strategy, the **integrative strategy** towards strategy making involves HRM as a fully developed strategic partner. In this approach, all four key business functions are represented: marketing, operations management, accounting, and HRM.

This is the most comprehensive and fruitful approach to strategy making as it avoids the pitfalls of excluding those who finally implement the business strategy – people. With the inclusion of HRM their input in strategy making can immediately assess the implications of a business strategy for recruitment and selection, organisational training, and so on. This makes the integrative approach far more superior compared to the other approaches to strategy making.

## Strategy and Change Management

Most inevitably any strategy, in whatever way established, demands some form of organisational change.[51] To change the strategic direction of a rather large business organisation, organisational change needs to be managed in a process that reaches beyond recalibrating the **mission statement**.[52] This remains the task of change management. **Change Management** is a management approach utilised to transition individuals, teams, and business organisations using methods intended to re-direct the use of resources, business processes, budget allocations, and other modes of operation that significantly reshape a company or organisation. Change management is influenced by many different disciplines such as behaviourism, organisational psychology, and social sciences that are used to change organisations.[53] It often involves project management as a controlled change process.[54]

At its basic level, change management consists of several stages[55]: establishing a sense of urgency; creating the guiding coalition; developing a vision and strategy; communicating the change vision; empowering employees; generating short-term wins; consolidating gains; and anchoring a new approach into the organisational culture. Another way of conducting change management is by focusing on four stages: determine the need for change; prepare and plan for the change; implement the change; and finally, sustain the change. From a Human Resource Management perspective, HR expert Storey's "managed change process" has proven to be useful.[56] This model of change operates with four processes (top-down, piecemeal, bargaining, and systemic-jointism):

### 1. The Top-Down Approach to Change Management

In the top-down approach to change management, a given business strategy is implemented by simply directing subordinates to carry out the necessary organisational change. It relies on an out-dated "I tell you – you do" approach. It is hierarchical and relies on authoritarian means directing the implementation of a strategy downwards. The undeniable strength of this approach is that it works fast and delivers quick results.

### 2. The Piecemeal Approach to Change Management

The piecemeal way of changing an organisation involves a step-by-step approach usually conducted through teamwork. This approach to change management is somewhat of a "behind your back" approach as employees are engaged in a slow and **successive change** process without being told about the strategic direction of the change. While including employee participation, it can erode the authority of management as it operates by stealth. While management retains the initiative, there are cases in which there is no strategic master plan that provides direction. Change management is introduced as a process.[57]

### 3. Bargaining for Change

Bargaining for change occurs in unionised settings where management bargains with trade unions at a collective level. It involves productivity bargaining and collective bargaining over organisational change. This is the **"with the union everything works –** without them nothing works" approach. It involves skilful negotiation between trade unions and management on how to change an organisation as well as the role of employees in the change. Unlike the former approach, this does not occur by stealth. Both sides are fully aware of the change and are working under what became known as "integrative bargaining" (a win–win situation).[58]

### 4. Systemic-Jointism

The last approach to change management offers the full integration of all relevant parties with the fullest participation; it is often conducted in project teams specifically set up for organisational change processes. While this remains the rarest form of change management, it is also the most fruitful one as it relies on full participation. It also has the capacity to establish **ownership of the change process**, thereby avoiding the pitfalls, for example, of the top-down approach. The downside of this process is that systemic-jointism is a rather slow process not suited for quick changes. This approach is carried out in two ways: (1) a project team is set up that introduces organisational change from which HR managers can learn and then improve the process of change and once the team has successfully changed, it is rolled out to the entire organisation; (2) the entire organisation changes at once in a wide-ranging process moving the entire organisation upwards and towards the desired goals of the business strategy.

# Workbook

## III. Five Discussion Questions on Strategic HRM

### And One Report Question on Strategic HRM

### 1. Discussion Questions

1. Strategic thinking – *strategos* – originated in the military. From there it moved into management where the task is not to kill the enemy but to win over competitors. Is waging a business war with strategic means unethical? Find five arguments in favour of this thesis and five arguments against it.

2. Porter's strategy divides companies into either being cost leaders or being differentiators. Describe both and discuss where such a clear cut strategy is possible at all? Find three arguments in favour of such strict separation and three arguments against it.

3. SWOT the SWOT: The SWOT analysis focuses on four key issues (strengths, weaknesses, opportunities, and threats). Is the SWOT analysis a useful tool? Can the business world be simply put in four boxes? Does it contradict Porter's five force analysis? Apply SWOT to SWOT by discussing the strengths, weaknesses, opportunities, and threats of the SWOT analysis.

4. Your textbook outlines four HRM strategic management interfaces (administration, one-way, two-way, and integrative approach). Which of the four approaches is the best suited when developing a comprehensive business strategy and why? Develop five arguments for your selection.

5. Inevitably strategy demands some sort of change management. Your textbook outlines four ways in which organisations can change (top-down, piecemeal, bargaining for change, and systemic change management). Which is the best approach to change management and why? Find five arguments in favour of your selection.

### 2. Report Question:

### On CPM's & HRM's Strategic Choices Versus Market Structures

Strategic management often demands that people management or HRM is aligned with its strategies turning HRM into a "structural" support function (e.g. Chandler's "structure follows strategy", in: *Strategy and Structure*).[59] Develop four [4] recommendations on how HRM can align itself with strategic management by reflecting on HRM's administrative, one-way, two-way, and integrative linkage?

## IV. The "5-by-5" Exercise: Five Case Studies and Five Questions

### 9.1 Strategic Change at Global Airlines

When Global Airlines was founded in 1962, it was an anomaly in the global aviation industry. Born as an original discount airline, Global Airlines quickly developed a rather successful strategy and business model resonating strongly with the new market segments of the market of leisure as well as vocational travellers. This distinguished

Global Airlines from its competitors in the aviation industry. Global Airlines was able to offer lower fares utilising short-haul flights and minimum service on board. Instead of targeting major hubs and capital cities, Global Airlines frequented smaller, local airports at reduced departing fees.

However, in recent years, the global aviation market has changed considerably. Large US carriers such as United, Delta, Northwest, Continental, US Airways, and American Airlines have faced bankruptcy. Global Airlines significantly restructured their business to re-rise with new strategies and new operations management foundations. Not only traditional carriers but also new entries such as Ryanair have increased competitive pressures on Global Airlines. Some of these large carriers have entered into code sharing arrangements while others have merged altogether (e.g. Air Canada merged with Canadian Airlines, Continental with United Airlines, Delta with Northwest, KLM with Air France, Lufthansa with Germanwings, etc.).

This allowed many airlines to compete with much improved operating systems focusing on economics of scale and also offering seamless and global transportation networks. While facing these new business strategies from their competitors, Global Airlines has remained an independent airline. Even more challenging to Global Airlines has been the fact that many new entries and established airlines have copied their strategies. Many new airlines operate as low-cost carriers (Ryanair, Eurowings, EasyJet, JetStar, LionAir, TigerAir, etc.). Based on these business strategies, Global Airlines can no longer benefit from its original strategy offering significantly cheaper fares and a lower cost structure. These industry developments warrant a re-thinking of strategy at Global Airlines.

1. Given Porter's model of cost-leader vs. niche market or differentiator which of the two strategies is Global Airlines seeking to develop? Is the airline planning to change? Would this mean a move from one to the other? Find five arguments for the above questions.
2. If an airline moves from being a differentiator towards being a cost leader (budget airline) what are the HR implications for such a strategy? Develop five such structural demands on HRM.
3. Imagine you are the HR manager at Global Airlines faced with a strategic change towards becoming a cost leader airline. Develop three HR policies (statements of intent) for: (1) airline pilots, (2) airline flight attendants; and (3) mechanics and engineers.
4. Imagine you are the HR manager at Global Airlines faced with a strategic change towards becoming a differentiator airline focusing on CEO business travel and high-end private customers. Develop three HR policies (statements of intent) for: (1) airline pilots, (2) airline flight attendants; and (3) mechanics and engineers.
5. Imagine you are the HR manager at Global Airlines asked to organise the change management process towards becoming a high-end customer airline. In your organization, there are three groups of employees: (1) airline pilots, (2) airline flight attendants; and (3) mechanics and engineers. All three groups are organised in trade unions. You have decided to follow the "bargaining for change" (no. 3) approach to change management. Develop five recommendations on how to

proceed in these negotiations (cf. see also the five steps of integrative bargaining in the chapter on labour relations in your textbook).

### 9.2 *HR Strategy at Cash-In Bank*

"Cash-In Bank" operates about 255 local branches throughout the country with its headquarter being located in the capital city. It employs 266,000 people with well over $26 billion in market capitalisation. The bank operates in 35 countries and has well over 80 million customers per year. For many years and despite being a substantial global business operation, HRM was mostly responsible for administration (recruitment and selection, industrial relations, organisational learning, work design, OHS, performance management, rewards, payroll, etc.). Faced with increased competition from banks such as HSBC, JPMorgan, BNP Paribas, Bank of America, Credit Agricole, Deutsche Bank, Barclays and Citigroup, etc.) the bank has moved towards a more strategic approach to HRM.

Cash-In Bank became increasingly aware that many of its line managers needed more specific and tailored HR solutions assisting them in improving operations and the overall bottom line. In past years, HRM has been unable to deliver this because of its confinement to traditional administration. Within the bank, HRM was traditionally highly centralised in the Cash-In Bank's headquarter. Most HR managers were assigned to HR-related divisions but remained located in the headquarter. Cash-In Bank sought to change this by creating a new structure for HRM. It reassigned many HR managers to local areas and branches in order to integrate HRM with operations management.

To facilitate this change, external consultants and experts on organisational learning were brought into Cash-In Bank. As a result, HR managers refocused their responsibilities, skills, and knowledge base. Under the new strategy, HR managers were trained in facilitation, negotiation skills, and consultation including technical skills, strategising, and, above all, moving HRM to becoming a strategic partner. HRM is now involved in setting up work agreements through negotiations, strategic problem solving, market data analysis, and the implementation of strategy as well as organisational change. As a consequence, Cash-In Bank's turnover rate was reduced by 15% while most of the part pay, rewards, and salary problems disappeared freeing up valuable time to engage in strategic planning. This led to substantial cost savings and a smooth operation of Cash-In Bank. After the changes in HRM, it now works close with top management in a strategic capacity.

1.  Porter's model includes a cost-leader vs. differentiator strategy. Which of the two strategies did Cash-In Bank develop and why? Does the bank have elements of both? Did it move from one to the other? Find five arguments for your answer.
2.  Run a SWOT analysis on the change of HRM at Cash-In Bank. What are the (1) strengths, (2) weaknesses, (3) opportunities, and (3) threats for HRM? Find at least two arguments for each of the four.
3.  The strategic approach taken by Cash-In Bank for its HRM division involved considerable change. Which of the four models of management change (outlined above)

has Cash-In Bank applied and why? Find four arguments in favour of this model of change management and four arguments against it.

4.  The textbook describes four ways in which HRM is connected to strategic management (administrative, one-way, two-way, and integrative). Which of the four models did Cash-In Bank use originally for HRM? To which model has Cash-In Bank moved? Support your answer with three arguments for each: (1) the traditional approach and (2) the new approach for HRM.

5.  As Cash-In Bank itself became more strategic in its focus, which of the four strategies (classical, procedural, evolutionary, and systemic) has the bank applied and why? Find five arguments that support your selection.

### 9.3 A New Strategy for Asian Trade Unions

In 2017, more than 350 Asian trade unionists met in Bangkok at a conference organised by the ITUC's (International Trade Union Confederation) Regional Organisation for Asia and Pacific (ITUC-PA). Leading trade unionists from 28 Asian countries representing roughly 30 million workers worked out new strategies for trade unions in the Asia Pacific region. ITUC-AP was aware of the danger of losing relevance because of the many challenges trade unions face in Asia. The meeting was initiated by ITUC's headquarter in Brussels, Belgium. The summit was in response to 2017 union membership figures showing union participation in the Asia Pacific region being at an historic low.

Many of the ITUC-PA union leaders agreed that simply working as usual and working with a compassion for workers is no longer enough to sustain trade unions in the Asia Pacific region. Neoliberalism, globalisation, new technologies, and many economic shifts (e.g. from manufacturing to the service industry, etc.) have hit industries with high numbers of union members. Overwhelmingly, many new jobs are either not in unionised industries, not in permanent employment, outsourced, or sub-contracted. Faced with this, trade unionists developed proposals for a new trade union strategy focused on three forms of unionism: (1) community unionism, (2) professional identity, and (3) digital recruiting:

#### Strategy I: Community Unionism

This strategy has often been associated with the Service Employees International Union (SEIU) in the USA. SEIU's strategy is to focus on changes inside and outside of workplaces. This includes the strategic approach to non-union stakeholders. Community unionism works in solidarity with local community groups (NGOs, etc.) that are close to trade unions. SEIU's strategy was successful. It resulted in a US$15 minimum wage. This assured a US$62 billion in wage increases.

#### Strategy II: Professional Identity Unionism

This strategy focuses on "professional identity". It is also called "professional identity unionism". Adopting this strategy means that trade unions work very close in maintaining their relevance for a specific occupation. Professional identity unionism focuses on professions, representing these in industrial tribunals and industry forums.

Professional identity unionism also engages in training on skill developments required by a specific profession. This is a strategy that has been adopted, for example, by Nursing Unions converting some nursing unions into very largest trade unions.

*Strategy III: Online Recruiting*

This strategy is called "digital unionism". Digital unionism recruits members online. These unions also maintain contact between trade unions and their members through online media (Facebook, Twitter, etc.). One of the clear advantages of "digital unionism" is that new union members can be recruited without union officers having to gaining access to business organisations, factories, etc. This by-passes anti-union employers. Digital unionism can also convert workers who sympathise with trade unions into paying members. Digital unions have been successful in recruiting union members and representing these members in negotiation with, for example, the transport/taxi company "Uber".

1.  Find three arguments in favour and three arguments against strategy I (community unionism). What are the strengths and weaknesses of community unionism?
2.  Find three arguments in favour and three arguments against strategy II (professional identity unionism). What are the strengths and weaknesses of professional identity unionism?
3.  Find three arguments in favour and three arguments against strategy III (online recruiting). What are the strengths and weaknesses of online recruiting?
4.  Imagine you are an elected trade union official in a Cambodian garment and clothing factory. Which of the three strategies would you adopt and why? Develop five arguments that support your strategy.
5.  Imagine you are an elected trade union official in a newly setup discount airline called "Cheap Thai Wings". As an official, you represent flight attendants of your trade union TAFAU. The new workforce is highly flexible. Flight attendants often work different hours and in different locations. Which of the three strategies would you adopt and why? Develop five arguments that support your strategy.

## 9.4 Cathy Heller's Labour Relations Strategy

At Cathy Heller Dairy, we have a well-established employee relations policy that provides the frame of reference for collective relationships with trade unions and employee representatives. Cathy Heller Dairy has built a culture based on the values of trust, mutual respect, and dialogue. Cathy Heller Dairy management and employees work daily to create and maintain positive individual and collective relationships, and are expected to do so as a core part of their job. As a large global company, we operate in a wide range of countries, each with their own laws, rules, and culture. This can sometimes prove challenging when it comes to developing good labour relations, which we see as imperative to the growth of the company. It is inevitable that some disputes will occur. We pro-actively seek to prevent labour disputes through a mixture of open dialogue, training, and local and regional initiatives, which helps to strengthen the relationships between managers, employees, and trade unions.

*Working Conditions*

It is our goal that no one working at Cathy Heller Dairy should be subjected to dif-ferences in employment conditions as a result of their employment status. When it comes to outsourcing work to service providers, our Policy on Conditions of Work and Employment and our Supplier Code clearly sets out the minimum standards relating to labour standards and the safety and health of employees, which we expect all our service providers to meet.

*Total Rewards Policy*

This policy was developed to clarify for our employees what they should expect as part of their employment package, when progressing through the business. It broadly covers: pay, benefits, work–life environment, and personal growth and development. It offers a common framework and in 2017, we launched a Total Rewards toolkit por-tal, designed to help local business operations ensure that their rewards programmes are competitive, compelling, cost-effective, and well understood. The toolkit has been piloted in three local contexts, and in June 2017, we trained all our Compensation & Benefits Managers on how to use it. We will follow up and support our markets with the implementation of the toolkit during 2018.

*Fostering Positive Relations with Trade Unions*

We promote positive relationships throughout our policies, principles, and values, seeking to ensure that disputes are settled openly and transparently. It has proven to be an effective approach, and in 2014, twenty-nine industrial actions took place around the world. All labour disputes are resolved according to our principles and values.

We have continued to work closely with the International Union of Food Workers (IUF), developing a more open relationship and a willingness to work together to tackle labour-related issues around the world. The relationship is based around the new Joint Operating Principles, launched in 2013, which include a commitment to bi-annual meetings between leadership teams from both Cathy Heller Dairy and the IUF leadership, as well as trade union representatives. The relationship is also supported by two working groups: one that focuses on gender equality for non-managerial posi-tions; and the second, which focuses on working conditions. We respect the right of our employees to engage in union activities. The percentage of working time lost due to labour disputes, strikes and/or lockouts is close to zero.

1.  Applying the prospector strategy, defender strategy, analyser strategy, and a reac-tor strategy, which of the above-mentioned strategies is followed by Cathy Heller Dairy in its approach to industrial relations/labour relations and why? Select one or more and argue why Cathy Heller Dairy follows this strategy. Present at least five arguments supporting your choice(s).
2.  Run a SWOT analysis on Cathy Heller Dairy's strategic approach to trade unions relations. What are the (1) strengths, (2) weaknesses, (3) opportunities, and (4) threats of Cathy Heller's strategy? Develop four arguments.

3. Imagine you are the HR manager at Cathy Heller Dairy relying on labour relations as outlined in the case above. Cathy Heller Dairy set on a fundamental organisational change programme. Which of the four change management strategies (top-down, piecemeal, bargaining for change, and systemic change management) would you use and why? Develop four arguments that support your choice.

4. Is Cathy Heller Dairy a cost leader corporation or a differentiator or a bit of both? Support your answer with five arguments in favour of your choice.

5. Which strategy (prospector strategy, defender strategy, analyser strategy, and a reactor strategy) reflects best Cathy Heller Dairy strategy towards trade unions and industrial relations? Select one and find five arguments that support your selection.

### 9.5 Child Labour Strategies – SWOT

The International Labour Organisation's (ILO) 2015 "World Child Labour Report"[60] notes that some 168 million children remain trapped in child labour. At the same time there were 75 million young persons aged 15 to 24 who are unemployed. Meanwhile, there are many more who must settle for jobs that fail to offer a fair income, security in the workplace, social protection, or other basic decent work attributes. The ILO's report contains two main issues: (1) child labour defines children as being of the age 0 to 18; youth is defined as being from the age of 15 to 24 (p. 41). The second issue (2) is that 15- to 24-year-olds cannot find adequate employment while others experience problems in what the ILO calls a successful "school-to-work transition". Child labour is not only an issue of employment; it is also an Occupational Health and Safety issue. The report states that

children are not little adults (p. 50): children have thinner skin, so toxics are more easily absorbed; children breathe faster and more deeply, so can inhale more airborne pathogens and dusts; children dehydrate more easily due to their larger skin surface and because of their faster breathing; children absorb and retain heavy metals (lead, mercury) in the brain more easily; children's endocrine system (which plays a key role in growth and development) can be disrupted by chemicals; children's enzyme systems are still developing so are less able detoxify hazardous substances; children use more energy when growing and so are at higher risk from metabolised toxins; children require more sleep for proper development; and finally, children have less-developed thermoregulatory systems making them more sensitive to heat and cold.

1. Imagine you are employed by the ministry of labour in your country being aware of the negative OHS aspects of child labour while also seeking to end child labour. You are conducting a SWOT (strengths, weaknesses, opportunities, and threats) analysis on child labour to develop recommendations to end it. Your task is to focus on the first half of SWOT (strengths and weaknesses). Develop four recommendations on how children can be protected by strengthening local regulation.

2. Imagine you are employed by the ministry of labour in your country being aware of the negative OHS aspects of child labour while also seeking to end child labour.

You are conducting a SWOT analysis on child labour to develop recommendations to end child labour. Your task is to focus on the second half of SWOT (opportunities and threats). Develop two recommendations on the opportunities that can
open up for children when attending school instead of working and two recommendations on the threats to children being made to work.

3.  Imagine you are the HR manager in a multinational corporation manufacturing
    soccer balls. Most soccer balls are made in Pakistan and you have become aware
    that your supply chain reaches deep into the backstreets of the major cities. As
    you found out, it also includes child labour. What strategies would you suggest to
    end the current practices while working together with key stakeholders such as
    NGOs (e.g. www.cleanclothes.org), trade unions, international trade bodies, local
    regulatory bodies, etc.? Develop two strategies and two HR policies (e.g. state-
    ments of intent) for your company.

4.  Imagine you are employed by the ministry of labour in your country being aware of
    youth unemployment while seeking to improve the "child-to-work" transition for
    15 to 17 year olds. Discuss the strengths of providing a smooth – unemployment
    free – transition into working life (develop three arguments). Once you have devel-
    oped these arguments, craft three strategies (for the long-term benefit of youth)
    to improve the situation.

5.  Despite years of negative publicity, the ILO's 2015 "World Child Labour Report"
    states that "some 168 million children remain trapped in child labour". Imagine
    you are working for an NGO. You have decided to take the stakeholder and indus-
    trial relations approach to the problem. This means including the three actors: (1)
    trade unions, (2) the state, and (3) employers and their federations. Imagine you
    are preparing a global "No Child Labour" conference. Develop three strategies on
    how to convince these three actors and how to make them work with you towards
    the "world without child labour" goal. You will need to develop one strategy for
    trade unions (1), one strategy for the state or states (2), and one strategy for the
    employers (3).

## V. A Suggestion for an Online Guest Lecture

Professor Emeritus of Social Epidemiology at the University of Nottingham and
author of "The Spirit Level", Richard Wilkinson talks about
**Strategies to Change Global Inequality**
https://www.ted.com/talks/richard_wilkinson?language=en
[the online guest lecture above is merely a suggestion – www.ted.com/talks offers
    additional material to choose from]

## VI. List of Suggested Documentaries on Strategic HRM

The carefully selected documentary videos below are mere suggestions to be used
during tutorials. Documentaries have been selected to achieve two things: (1) to
explain key HRM themes and (2) to provide an insight into the reality of HRM. Typically,
these short documentaries should be viewed in class followed by a class discussion

on the content of the video. Alternatively, questions on documentaries can be prepared beforehand and small group discussions can follow up the video after viewing is concluded. Should any of the web links no longer function, please conduct an internet search for other – alternative – documentaries related to your tutorial topic (e.g. filmsforaction.org):

Change Management Video: youtube.com/watch?v=__IlYNMdV9E

HRM & Business Strategy: education-portal.com/academy/lesson/aligning-hrm-and-organizational-strategy.html#lesson

Strategic HRM: youtube.com/watch?v=kB06Fjd-ZKY

Strategic HRM in Organisations: youtube.com/watch?v=SzX54V9nF3o

Strategic HRM & Workforce: youtube.com/watch?v=YnyPWy64li4

Strategic Growth: youtube.com/watch?v=glcprCtMoLg

Strategic Growth Busters: youtube.com/user/Growthbuster

Strategy & Markets: youtube.com/watch?v=-NQTOo2oOx8

Strategic Job Cuts at ANZ: youtube.com/watch?v=cg8cWXL8IGc

Strategic Job Loss at Qantas: youtube.com/watch?v=3BNmsw5Rm2o

Strategic Recruiting Abroad I: youtube.com/watch?v=QkmMebl08u0

Strategic Recruiting Abroad II: youtube.com/watch?v=K5QWPOt3T9I

## Notes

1  https://www.bcg.com/en-au/capabilities/people-strategy/overview.

2  Barney, J. B. & Wright, P. M. 1998. On becoming a strategic partner: the role of human resources in gaining competitive advantage, *Human Resource Management*, 37(1):31–46 (http://digitalcommons.ilr.cornell.edu, accessed: 30th January 2018); Nadiv, R., Raz, A. & Kuna, S. 2017. What a difference a role makes: occupational and organizational characteristics related to the HR strategic role among human resource managers, *Employee Relations*, 39(7):1131–1147.

3  Kuipers, B. S. & Giurge, L. M. 2017. Does alignment matter? The performance implications of HR roles connected to organizational strategy, *International Journal of Human Resource Management*, 28(22):3179–3201.

4  Martin, R. L. 2018. The board's role in strategy, *Harvard Business Review*, 28th December 2018.

5  Porter, M. E. 1998. *The Competitive Advantage of Nations*, New York: Free Press.

6  Division of work, authority, discipline, unity and chain of command, clear company direction, subordination of individual interests to the business interest, remuneration (financial and non-financial compensation), centralisation, order, equity (managers should be fair to staff at all times), stability (managers should strive to minimise employee turnover), initiative, and finally "esprit de corps" (Fayol, H. 1916. *Managerialism Industrielle et Generale* (Industrial and General Managerialism), London: Sir I. Pitman & Sons, ltd. 1930.

7  Tzu, Sun. (5th century BC) *The Art of War – The Oldest Military Treatise in the World* (translated by Giles, L., 1910), London: Luzac & Co.; online: http://classics.mit.edu/Tzu/artwar.html

8  Gregersen, H. 2017. Bursting the CEO bubble, *Harvard Business Review*, 95(2):78.

9  Diefenbach, T. 2013. *Hierarchy and Organization*, London: Routledge; Klikauer, T. 2014. Hierarchy and organization – towards a general theory of hierarchical social systems, *International Journal of Social Economics*, 41(8):714–719.

10  http://hr-organizational-structure-strategy.blogspot.com.au/2013/04/multi-divisional-structure-and-matrix.html.

11  https://www.smartdraw.com/organizational-chart/examples/.

12  Laloux, F. 2014. *Reinventing Organizations: A Guide to Creating Organizations Inspired by the Next Stage of Human Consciousness*, Brussels: Nelson Parker.

13  Gibson-Graham, J. K., Cameron, J. & Healy, S. 2013. *Take Back the Economy: An Ethical Guide for Transforming Our Communities*, Minneapolis: University of Minnesota Press.

14  Ashby, M. 2016. *Breakpoints: How to Shift Your Business to the Next Level*, Melbourne: Wiley & Sons.

15  On the other hand, there is a popular demand for 'decentralization [which] is one of the foggiest [and] most often abused concepts' in management (Gehl, R. W. 2014. *Reverse Engineering Social Media*, Philadelphia, PA: Temple University Press, p. 146).

16  Thomas, H. 2007. Business school strategy and the metrics for success, *Journal of Management Development*, 26(1):33–42.

17  Edwards, M. R. 2016. *Predictive HR Analytics: Mastering the HR Metric*, London: Kogan Page.

18  http://www.economist.com/node/13474552.

19  Chandler, A. 1962. *Strategy and Structure*, Cambridge: MIT Press.

20  Mintzberg, H. 1994. The fall and rise of strategic planning, *Harvard Business Review*, 72(1):107–114; Porter, M. E. 1996. What is strategy?, *Harvard Business Review*, November–December; Hamel, G. 1996. Strategy as revolution, *Harvard Business Review*, May–June.

21  McKenna, C. 2012. Strategy followed structure: management consulting and the creation of a market for strategy – 1950–2000 (p. 153 – 186), in: Kahl, S. J., Silverman, B. S. & Cusumano, M. A. (eds.) *History and Strategy* (vol. 29), Bingley: Emerald.

22  Rees, G. & Smith, P. 2017. *Strategic HRM: An International Perspective* (2nd ed.). London: Sage.

23  Clegg, S. et al. 2017. *Strategy: Theory and Practice* (2nd ed.), London: Sage.

24  Niche market: http://unionmadegoods.com/.

25  Truss, C. 1999. Soft and hard models of human resource management. In: Gratton, L. (eds.) *Strategic Human Resource Management: Corporate Rhetoric and Human Reality*, Oxford: Oxford University Press, pp. 40–58.

26  Marchington, M. 2015. HRM too busy looking up to see where it is going longer term?, *Human Resource Management Review*, 25(2):176–187.

27  Miles, R. E. & Snow, C. C. 1978. *Organisational Strategy, Structure & Process*, New York: McGraw-Hill.

28  Kim, W. C., & Mauborgne, R. 2015. *Blue Ocean Strategy, Expanded Edition: How to Create Uncontested Market Space and Make the Competition Irrelevant*, Cambridge: Harvard Business Review Press.

29  For a comparison between HRM and defender vs. HRM and prospector, see: Gomez-Mejia, L. R., Balkin, D. B. & Cardy, L. R. 2016. *HRM – Global Edition*, Harlow: Pearson, p. 58.

30  http://www.darwinproject.ac.uk/people/about-darwin/six-things-darwin-never-said-and-one-he-did.

31  Mintzberg, 1987. Crafting strategy, *Harvard Business Review*, July–August: 67–81.

32  https://www.virgin.com/.

33  Grundy, T. 2006. Rethinking and reinventing Michael Porter's five forces model, *Strategic Change*, 15(5):213–229.

34  https://hbr.org/product/hbr-tools-swot-analysis/TLSWOT-ZIP-ENG.

35  Brookings. 2018. *Trump's High Turnover Rate* (https://www.brookings.edu, 19th January 2018, accessed 22nd January 2018).

36  Hirschman, A. 1970. *Exit, Voice, and Loyalty: Responses to Decline in Firms, Organizations, and States*, Cambridge: Harvard University Press.

37  Whittington, R. 1993. *What Is Strategy – And Does It Matter?* (2nd ed.), London: Routledge; Beardwell, J. & Claydon, T. 2011. *HRM: A Contemporary Approach*, London: Financial Times Press, p. 42; Gray, C. S. 2015. *The Future of Strategy*, Oxford: Polity Press.

38  In 2009, Jack Welch CEO of GE from 1981 to 2001 declared that shareholder value is "the dumbest idea in the world" (https://www.forbes.com/sites/stevedenning/2017/07/17/making-sense-of-shareholder-value-the-worlds-dumbest-idea/).

39  https://www.youtube.com/watch?v=u-dDlRdLhWI; Heracleous, L. & Jacobs, C. D. 2011. *Crafting Strategy*, Cambridge: Cambridge University Press.

40  Clegg, S. 1989. *Frameworks of Power*, London: Sage.

41  Hyman, R. 1987. Strategy or structure, *Work, Employment & Society*, 1(1):25–55.

42  Barry, D. & Elmes, M. 1997. Strategy retold, *Academy of Management Review*, 22(2): 429–452; Shrivastava, P. 1986. Is strategic management ideological?, *Journal of Management*, 12(3):363–377.

43  http://www.ngo.org/ngoinfo/define.html.

44  www.carbonfootprint.com/calculator.aspx; Hawken, P. 1993. *The Ecology of Commerce – A Declaration of Sustainability*, London: Phoenix.

45  Ionannou, I. & Seafeim, G. 2019. Yes, sustainability can be a strategy, *Harvard Business Review*, 11th February 2019.

46  Ted-Talks (ted.com), Ray Anderson on Sustainability.

47  Freeman, J. & Boeker, W. 1984. The ecological analysis of business strategy, *California Management Review*, 26(3):73–86; Shrivastava, P. 1995. The role of corporations in achieving ecological sustainability, *Academy of Management Review*, 20(4):936–960; Iansiti, M. & Levien, R. 2004. Strategy as ecology, *Harvard Business Review*, 82(3):68–81; Kelly, E. 2015. *Deloitte Business Ecosystems* (dupress.com, 15th April 2015).

48  Grohmann, O. 2016. HR strategy and change: introduction and overview, in: Zeuch, M. (eds.) *Handbook of HRM*, Heidelberg: Springer, p. 1188.

49  McGregor, D. 1960. *The Human Side of Enterprise*, New York: McGraw-Hill; McGregor, D. 2006. *The Human Side of Enterprise* (updated and with new commentary by Joel Cutcher-Gershenfeld), New York: McGraw-Hill.

50  See Mello, J. A. 2015. *Strategic MRM* (4th ed.), Mason: South-Western, p. 157 for an overview on tactical and strategic HRM.

51  Waddell, D. M. et al. 2017. *Organisational Change – Development & Transition* (6th ed.), Melbourne: Cengage.

52  HR managers are often engaged in writing mission statements. These are statements used to communicate the purpose of a business organisation beyond the obvious (e.g. shareholder-value and profit-maximisation). Once formulated, such statements tend to remain for a long period. They are short and simple statements outlining about the company and the industry or market it operates in. Mission statements have two tasks: (i) separating what is important from what is not; and (ii) stating which market segment a firm operates in as well as the strategy direction of the business.

53  Stuart, R. 1996. The trauma of organizational change, *Journal of European Industrial Training*, 20(2):11–16.

54  Bovey, W. H. & Hede, A. 2001. Resistance to organisational change: the role of defence mechanisms, *Journal of Managerial Psychology*, 16(7):534–548; Diefenbach, T. 2007. The managerialistic ideology of organisational change management, *Journal of Organizational Change Management*, 20(1):126–144.

55  https://www.mindtools.com/pages/article/newPPM_82.htm.

56  Storey, J. 1992. *Developments in the Management of Human Resources – An analytical Review*, Oxford: Blackwell, pp. 118–161; Needham, D. et al. 1999. *Business for Higher Awards*, Oxford: Heinemann, p. 246; Bauer, G. F. & Hämmig, O. 2013. *Bridging Occupational, Organizational and Public Health: A Transdisciplinary Approach*, Heidelberg: Springer, p. 107.

57  Kets de Vries, M. F. & Miller, D. 1984. Neurotic style and organizational pathology, *Strategic Management Journal*, 5(1):49.

58  McKersie, R. B. & Walton, R. E. 1965. *A Behavioral Theory of Labor Negotiations: An Analysis of a Social Interaction System*, Ithaca, NY: ILR Press; Peng, A. C., Dunn, J. & Conlon, D. E. 2015. When vigilance prevails: the effect of regulatory focus and accountability on integrative negotiation outcomes, *Organizational Behavior and Human Decision Processes*, 126:77–87.

59  Chandler, A. 1962. *Strategy and Structure*, Cambridge: MIT Press.

60  http://www.ilo.org/ipec/Informationresources/WCMS_358969/lang–en/index.htm.

## Further Readings

Armstrong, M. & Taylor, S. 2014. *Handbook of HRM Practice* (13th ed.), London: Kogan Page.

Barclay, C. & Osei-Bryson, K.-M. (eds.) 2016. *Strategic Project Management: Contemporary Issues and Strategies for Developing Economies*, Boca Raton, FL: CRC Press.

Barry, D. & Elmes, M. 1997. Strategy Retold: Toward a Narrative View of Strategic Discourse Academy of Management, *Academy of Management Review*, 22(2):429–452.

Berg, J. 2015. *Labour Markets, Institutions & Inequality*, Cheltenham: Elgar.

Boxall, P. F. & Purcell, J. 2015. *Strategy & HRM* (4th ed.), New York: Palgrave.

Burke, W. W. 2013. *Organization Change: Theory and Practice* (4th ed.). London: Sage.

Coleman, J. 2015. *Unfinished Work*, Oxford: Oxford University Press.

Crawshaw, J. et al. 2014. *HRM – Strategic and International Perspectives*, London: Sage.

Dawson, P. & Andriopoulos, C. 2014. *Managing Change* (2nd ed.), London: Sage.

Day, D. (eds.) 2014. *Oxford Handbook of Leadership and Organizations*, Oxford: Oxford University Press.

Dess, G. G., McNamara, G. & Eisner, G. A. 2016. *Strategic Management: Creating Competitive Advantages* (8th ed.), New York: McGraw-Hill Education.

Fisher, J. G. 2015. *Strategic Reward and Recognition*, London: Kogan Page.

FitzRoy, P. T., Hulbert, J. M. & O'Shannassy, T. 2016. *Strategic Management: The Challenge of Creating Value*, Abingdon: Routledge.

Godfrey, R. D. 2016. *Strategic Management: A Critical Introduction*, Abingdon: Routledge.

Hall, D. 2013. *Contemporary Themes in Strategic People Management*, Basingstoke: Palgrave.

Harvey, G. & Turnbull, P. 2015. Can Labor Arrest the "Sky Pirates"? Transnational Trade Unionism in the European Civil Aviation Industry, *Labor History*, 56(3):308–326.

Hyman, R. 1987. Strategy or Structure, *Work, Employment & Society*, 1(1):25–55.

Jackson, S. E., Schuler, R. S. & Jiang, K. 2014. An Aspirational Framework for Strategic HRM, *Academy of Management Annals*, 8(1):1–56.

Jenkins, W. & Williamson, D. 2016. *Strategic Management and Business Analysis*, Abingdon: Routledge.

Johnson, G. et al. 2010. Ritualization of Strategy Workshops, *Organization Studies*, 31(12):1589ff.

Juul Andersen, T. & Minbaeva, D. 2013. The Role of HRM in Strategy Making, *Human Resource Management*, 52(5):809–827.

Kane, T. M. 2013. *Strategy – Key Thinkers*, Oxford: Polity.

Kearns, P. 2012. *HR Strategy*, London: Routledge.

Kim, W. C. & Mauborgne, R. 2015. *Blue Ocean Strategy, Expanded Edition: How to Create Uncontested Market Space and Make the Competition Irrelevant*, Cambridge: Harvard Business Review Press.

Laasch, O. & Conaway, R. N. 2015. *Principles of Responsible Management* (Chapter 11 on HRM), Stamford, CT: Cengage.

Longenecker, C. O. & Fink, L. S. 2013. Creating HRM Value in the Twenty-First Century: Seven Steps to Strategic HR, *HRM International Digest*, 21(2):29–32.

Mansell, S. F. 2013. *Capitalism, Corporations and the Social Contract: A Critique of Stakeholder Theory*, Cambridge: Cambridge University Press.

Marcus, B. R. 2015. *The Politics of Promotion*, Hoboken, NJ: Jossey-Bass.

Marler, J. H. 2012. Strategic Human Resource Management in Context: A Historical and Global Perspective, *Academy of Management Perspectives*, 26(2):6–11.

Martocchio, J. J. 2016. *Strategic Compensation: A HRM Approach*, Hoboken, NJ: Pearson.

McCabe, D. 2010. Strategy-as-Power, *Organization*, 17(2):151–175.

McKenna, C. 2012. Strategy Followed Structure: Management Consulting and the Creation of a Market for "Strategy," 1950–2000, in: Kahl, S. J., Silverman, B. S. & Cusumano, M. A. (eds.) *History and Strategy*, Bingley: Emerald Publishing, pp. 153–186.

Milkovich, G. T. & Newman, J. M. 2016. *Compensation* (12th ed.), New York: McGraw-Hill.

Mintzberg, H., Ahlstrand, B. & Lampel, J. 1998. *Strategy Safari – A Guided Tour through the Wilds of Strategic Management*, New York: The Free Press.

Noon, M. et al. 2013. Survival Strategies at Work (pp. 225–262), in: Noon, M., Blyton, P. & Morrell, K. (eds.) *The Realities of Work* (4th ed.), Basingstoke: Palgrave Macmillan.

Paauwe, J. & Boselie, P. 2003. Challenging Strategic HRM, *HRM Journal*, 13(3):56–70.

Paroutis, S. et al. 2016. *Practicing Strategy* (2nd ed.), London: Sage.

Paton, R. et al. 2016. *Change Management* (4th ed.), London: Sage.

Perelman, M. 2011. *The Invisible Handcuffs of Capitalism*, New York: Monthly Review Press.

Porter, M. E. & Kramar, M. R. 2006. Strategy and Society, *Harvard Business Review*, December.

Rothaermel, F. T. 2017. *Strategic Management* (3rd ed.), New York: McGraw-Hill.

Stacey, R. D. & Mowles, C. 2016. *Strategic Management and Organisational Dynamics*, Harlow: Pearson.

Thompson, P. 2007. Making Capital: Strategic Dilemmas for HRM (pp. 81–100, in: Bolton, S. & Houlihan, M. (eds.) *Searching for the Human in HRM*, Basingstoke: Palgrave.

Tourish, D. 2013. *The Dark Side of Transformational Leadership*, London: Routledge.

Tricke, R. I. 2015. *Corporate Governance* (3rd ed.), Oxford: Oxford University Press.

Truss, C., Kankin, D. & Kelliher, C. 2012. *Strategic HRM*, New York: Oxford University Press.

Walker, G. & Madsen, T. L. 2016. *Modern Competitive Strategy* (4th ed.), New York: McGraw-Hill.

Wentland, D. M. 2015. *Is Your Organization a Great Place to Work?*, Charlotte, NC: IAP-Information Age Publishing.

Wheelen, T. L. 1984. *Strategic Management*, Reading, MA: Addison-Wesley.

# 10  People and Morality

## Ethics at Work and in Management

### Executive Summary

Since the dawn of time, human beings have debated how to relate to one another. This not only marks the beginning of morality but also the fact that all human relations are inextricably linked to morality. Over thousands of years, humanity – in fact, those we call moral philosophers – have developed a vast and often bewildering array of moral philosophies. One ordering framework for these philosophies is Kohlberg's concept of seven moralities. Placed in this framework, HRM's moralities can be classified. This means that HR managers have to deal with, for example, issues at the lowest level of morality (1), e.g. bullying, sexual harassment, disciplinary action, etc. but also with issues of performance management and Machiavellianism (2), with organisational culture (3), law and order and HR policies (4), justice and fairness (5), human rights (6), and finally also with corporate social responsibility and sustainability (7).

### Key Learning Objectives

1. Realise the importance of ethics for HRM;
2. Comprehend key themes of moral philosophy;
3. Apply key themes of moral philosophy to HRM;
4. Understand some of the ethical issues HRM faces;
5. Develop formal HR policies for contemporary key themes (sustainability, corporate social responsibility, and carbon footprint);
6. Recognise the link between HRM and Corporate Social Responsibility;
7. Identify the role of HRM in moving towards sustainability;
8. Ascertain HRM's contribution to lowering the carbon foot print;
9. Evaluate HRM as a strategic partner in ethical decision making.

### Morality and Human Resource Management

Ever since human beings became human, leaving the animal kingdom behind, people sought of ways on how to relate to one another.[1] At the birth of morality, early humans sought out how to relate to each other and how to cooperate.[2] From that moment onward, every human to human interaction – and beyond – related to morality. Since Human Resource Management is destined to engage with human to human contact,

DOI: 10.4324/9781003293637-10

inevitably and inextricably it remains linked to morality. In this context, morality – as originating in the Latin *moralitas* – stands for manner, character, and proper behaviour. **Morality** offers a differentiation of intentions, decisions, and actions between those that are seen as proper and those that are improper.[3] Just as today, the early human beings were concerned with the right and wrong way of living, with good and evil. Over time, the ways of conducting oneself became moral conduct that developed into moral customs and habits. Overall, morality can be seen as a body of standards and principles derived from a **code of conduct** from moral philosophy. Morality is often seen as synonymous with goodness and rightness.

**Ethics** or moral philosophy, on the other hand, is the branch of **philosophy** – the love of wisdom – that involves systematising, defending, and recommending concepts of right and wrong conduct.[4] The term ethics derives from the Ancient Greek word ἠθικός *ethikos* originating from ἦθος *ethos* – habit or custom. Being part of philosophy, ethics investigates questions like "what is the best way for people to live?" and "what actions are right or wrong in particular circumstances?" In practice, ethics seeks to resolve questions of human morality by defining concepts such as good and evil, right, and wrong, as well as virtue and vice.

To define and discuss good and evil, right, and wrong, moral philosophy has developed a wide – and at times rather confusing and even contradictory – range of ethical theories such as, for example, virtue ethics (Aristotle), Kantian ethics, Utilitarianism and Consequentialism (Bentham, Mills, Moore, etc.), and justice ethics (Rawls)[5] to name a few. Combining moral philosophy and developmental psychology in his work, American psychologist and moralist **Lawrence Kohlberg** (1927–1987) has developed somewhat of an ordering framework[6] that places most, if not all moral philosophy in a clear structure.[7] Ethics is placed in an ascending scale – level one to seven[8] – that can also structure HRM and next to everything HRM does.[9] To understand the essence of Kohlberg's morality, it remains imperative to note that these stages provide a **universalistic foundation** as well as a moral structure.[10] Above that, these seven stages are irreversible and ascending.

Ranking from level 1 (obedience and punishment) to level 6 (human rights) and eventually level 7 (environmental ethics linked to plant and animal life[11]), Figure 10.1 shows the ascending level of morality that structures virtually every eventuality of human life including management and HRM.[12] It is easy to imagine that the moral philosophies of Figure 10.1 are relevant to many work situations generally covered by HRM. While Figure 10.1 focuses on the ascendancy of morality, Table 10.1 shows the content of each of the seven levels in more detail.

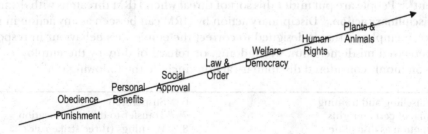

*Figure 10.1* Themes of an Ascending Morality.

*Table 10.1* Seven Moralities

| Stages | Orientation | Moral Motives |
|---|---|---|
| 0 | Impulsive and amoral | None |
| 1 | Obedience and<br>Avoidance of punishment | Irrational dread of punishment<br>Fear of those in authority |
| 2 | Personal benefits & rewards<br>Getting a good deal for oneself | How to get most pleasure and gain for oneself<br>Calculating the personal risk and payoffs of an action |
| 3 | Conforming to social expectations<br>Gaining approval | Avoiding disapproval by associates; wanting to be praised, liked & admired rather than shamed |
| 4 | Law & order: maintaining existing systems of official social arrangements | Performing formal duties, meeting official standards; working for the best interest of an institution |
| 5 | Promoting justice and welfare within a wider community as defined in open debate | Principles that serve the best interest of the great majority; being reasonable, just and purposeful in one's action. |
| 6 | Defending everyone's right to justice and welfare, universally applied | Applying well-thought principles; being ready to share and debate these openly and non-defensively with others |
| 7 | Respecting the cosmos as an integral whole reaching beyond humanity | Respecting the intrinsic value of the cosmos with its wider harmonies and paradoxes |

Table 10.1 depicts an overview of Kohlberg's model of morality. In fact, the table lists eight stages rather than seven. Kohlberg regarded the first stage ('0') as somewhat irrelevant to morality arguing that newborn babies cannot develop moral understanding because moral consciousness is not possible at this stage. It is therefore irrelevant to HRM. To assess the morality of HR subjects along these stages, each stage of morality is explained while simultaneously linked to moral philosophy and ethics as well as to cases in HRM.

### 1. The Morality of Punishment: Harassment and Bullying

Despite all the negatives, the first stage – obedience and punishment – still remains prevalent in society. Behavioural scientist Skinner[13] and linguist Chomsky[14] have noticed the use of punishment being a core element of behaviour modification and the manipulation of human beings. Chomsky writes (1971:33), "except when physically restraining, a person is the least free or dignified when he is under threat of punishment".[15] People are put under this sort of threat when HRM threatens with dismissal and **disciplinary action**.[16] Disciplinary action by HRM can be seen as any action in relation to an employee that is designed to correct the employee's behaviour in response to a perceived misdemeanour, wrongdoing, or refusal of duty by the employee. The most commonly considered disciplinary actions include the following ten[17]:

| | | | |
|---|---|---|---|
| 1 | Counselling and training | 6 | Suspension |
| 2 | Denial of certain rights | 7 | Transfer to different location |
| 3 | Demotion as discipline | 8 | Warnings (three strike rule) |
| 4 | Fines and monetary penalties | 9 | Withholding wages/salaries (theft)[18] |
| 5 | Overtime not offered | 10 | Withholding bonuses |

In all ten forms, obedience is created in order to avoid punishment. HRM takes on a rather dictatorial mode sustaining the idea that people in authority are endorsed to use punishment. In this model, the rules are set in a non-democratic way and must be obeyed. Disobedience will lead to punishment.[19] The thinking is that punishable behaviour can be minimised by creating circumstances in which the behaviour is not likely to occur.[20] Individual survival and self-preservation become important moral concepts. In this scenario, employees are preoccupied with the demands of those in power and how to avoid causing them anger.[21] Forms conveying this are **Management by Fear** and **Macho-Management**[22] (e.g. pushing too hard, arrogance and egotism, blinkered viewpoints, all-or-nothing bets; riding roughshod over others, domineering attitudes, love of a good fight, fear-based decisions, rampant office politics, inability to cooperate or share, and constant turf wars). In this model "giving orders" defines HRM; it is often underscored by panoptical suspicions expressed in extensive monitoring and **electronic surveillance**.[23] The ones who should help because they know better – HRM – turn into the ones who humiliate others through bossy privilege.[24]

HRM's authority is enshrined in what constitutes hierarchical relationships under what former Harvard Business Review editor Joan Magretta describes as "managers [who are] people in positions of institutional power".[25] Without hierarchies and authoritarian relationships, HRM is hardly possible. Each actor in this structure has a clearly defined position and even those at the bottom are still made to believe that they have subordinates – even when these are externalised (wives, husbands, children, pets, etc.). All these unequal and domineering relationships are defined through authoritarianism, asymmetry, aggressiveness, and violence.[26] In hierarchies that produce **authoritarian relationships** each level has authority over the immediate level below and over all subsequent levels below that. The structure is pyramidal and designed to generate and sustain authority.

Authoritarian relationships based on power – "I have power over you" – can lead to forms of bullying, mobbing, and harassment in which even sexual harassment can occur.[27] **Sexual harassment** is bullying and coercion of a sexual nature that is unwelcomed. It includes the inappropriate promise of rewards in exchange for sexual favours. In most modern legal contexts, sexual harassment is illegal. It is unlawful to harass a person – an applicant or employee – because of that person's sex.[28] Sexual harassment can also be defined as unwelcoming sexual advances or requests for sexual favours often including verbal and physical harassment of a sexual nature. However, precise legal definitions of sexual harassment vary between jurisdictions. This kind of workplace harassment may be considered illegal when it is so frequent and/or so severe that it creates a hostile and/or offensive work environment and/or when it results in an adverse employment decision (such as the victim being fired or demoted, or when the victim decides to quit the job).

Where laws surrounding sexual harassment exist, they generally do not prohibit simple teasing, off-hand comments, and minor isolated incidents. Having an **office romance**,[29] for example, is not sexual harassment.[30] And neither is **Sexting**.[31] Office or workplace romance exists when two members of the same organisation develop a relationship with mutual attraction.[32] According to the *Harvard Business Review*, There are perfectly good reasons why co-workers fall for one another.[33]

Something very different is Bullying. **Bullying** is the use of force, threat, or coercion to abuse, intimidate, or aggressively dominate others.[34] The behaviour is often repeated and habitual. One essential prerequisite is the perception, by the bully or by others, of an imbalance of organisational, social, and physical power, which distinguishes bullying from conflict. Behaviours used to assert such domination can include verbal harassment or threat, physical assault, or coercion, and such acts may be directed repeatedly towards particular targets. Rationalisations for such behaviour sometimes include differences of age, social class, race,[35] disabilities, religion, gender,[36] sexual orientation, appearance, behaviour, body language, personality, reputation, lineage, strength, size, and ability. If bullying is done by a group, it is called **mobbing**.[37]

Not surprisingly, bullying is linked to organisational stress, loss of productivity, high absenteeism, and high turnover rates. Bullying is no longer a hidden problem as it has become a widespread problem in many business organisations. As a consequence, many HR managers have introduced **anti-bulling policies** and preventative structures.[38] Bullying is usually downward as it is linked to asymmetrical power relations – the defining element of top-down "manager → employee" relations. These managerial structures show three commonalities:

1.  Managerial structures furthering organisational conformity are set against diversity and mutual respect, recognition, and cooperation;
2.  Work design that enhances bullying through restricting an employee's autonomy through authoritarian means while on the other hand providing very limited guidance through an overtly laissez-faire approach; and
3.  Working under job descriptions, performance management, and reward structures that create role ambiguities and role conflicts.

### 2. Benefits, Rewards, and Performance Management

At stage two in Kohlberg's seven-stage model, punishment avoidance moves towards rewarding people through pay, benefits, rewards, etc. Beyond that, HRM acts in its own when, for example, making deals with labour and trade unions that are seen as a necessity to sustain the power of HRM. If HRM deems a working relationship with employees and their representative bodies – trade unions – as unavoidable, then this is conducted through "give and take" or **zero-sum bargaining** (I win – you lose). Relationships with others become a means and only take place when they serve HRM. Information provided to employees, for example, is viewed as a loss to HRM. This is the stage of outright **Machiavellianism**.[39] The key to success is the desire to manipulate others for one's own benefit. It fosters the "me, myself, and I" view even when it means setting "all against all".[40] A fine example came in "December 2008 when President Barack Obama scolded the heads of the largest US auto firms for flying to Washington in private jets to ask for financial bailouts".[41]

Deviousness and deception[42] may be applied whenever these are required to get ahead.[43] Machiavellians and even **corporate psychopaths**[44] can be found working successfully in professional occupations, particularly in those dealing with people (e.g. HRM) as they excel in bargaining and even more so in bargaining a better deal for themselves. CEOs are particular good in this. In fact their work ethic has been described as relying "more on being opportunistic, cunning and ruthless in the pursuit of one's own" advantage.[45] As for level two, HRM is mostly engaged when it is involved in rewards and performance management (performance related pay, balanced score cards, etc.).

### 3. Organisational Culture and Ethical Climate

At stage three, HRM positions employees in a way that forces them to be supportive to management. This is done, for example, in order to prevent employees from taking on any anti-managerial attitudes. Avoiding criticism ensures that HRM's self-interests are not exposed and hurt. Employees are made to show loyalty and live up to HRM's expectations. Organisational relationships are based on obedience, seeking approval and endorsement by HRM that no longer directly punishes employees and is less self-centred. HRM operates with phrases like "you must live up to policy XYZ". Non-compliance however is punished through exclusion: "from this day on, you will be a stranger amongst us".[46] Compliance is also supported inside HRM's frame of reference constructed around the managerial use of the language of trust and the one-dimensional **shared organisational interest**.[47] To convey this image, HRM strongly enhances ideologies such as "we are all in one boat".

HRM uses an inclusive language to support compliance and engineers social exclusion when employees are non-compliant. Employees are forced to value HRM for its own sake and subscribe to a **common corporate culture**.[48] When employees enter such an organisational culture, they have already undergone years of conditioning to system compliance (e.g. parents, schools, universities,[49] etc.). System conformity is further fostered through accepting the authority of established work rules and work requirements (HR policies). Conformity is policed through a system of hierarchical structures that mirror the virtues – **virtue ethics**[50] – and structures previously adopted at home and school. When individuals are converted from human beings into human resources they tend to carry with them a tremendous amount of **conformity enhancing attitudes**.[51] As long as employees behave inside the conforming boundaries set by HRM and accept these as legitimate, the structure of authoritarian conformity lives on.

Within this structure, HR managers seek to establish a **positive ethical climate** seen as a general organisational culture that encourages ethical behaviour rather than unethical behaviours that are shown, for example, in bullying, bribery,[52] lying, white-collar crime, etc. In immoral organisational cultures management often takes a "blind eye" approach tolerating these unethical behaviours. One way of creating a positive ethical climate is when HR managers apply Berlin's **two concepts of liberty**.[53] They move from **negative liberty** – the freedom from (something) – towards **positive liberty** found in the "freedom to" (do something). They become proactive when moving forward in introducing a positive ethical climate.[54]

One way of achieving this is, for example, through **affirmative action** and employment equity creating HR policies and an organisational culture that favours members of a disadvantaged group who suffer from discrimination within an organisational culture.[55] Often, these people are disadvantaged for historical reasons, such as oppression or slavery.[56] Historically and internationally, support for affirmative action has sought to achieve goals such as bridging inequalities in employment and pay, increasing access to education, promoting diversity, and redressing apparent past wrongs, harms, or hindrances.

### 4. The Law, HR Policies, Rules, and Regulations

Under law and order, employees are seen as fulfilling their role by performing management determined duties as laid out by company law, e.g. written and codified **HR policies** and codes of conduct.[57] HR mangers assure that such a *code of conduct* meets three criteria:

1.  It explicitly states legal and ethical guidelines governing behaviour at work;
2.  Violations and transgressions of the code are reported, acknowledges, and addressed; and
3.  Outcomes are consistent with the general ethical values outlined in the code of conduct.

HR managers ensure that these HR policies do not contradict the law – they are **statutory rights**. HRM invents and enforces occupational roles and workplace duties while upholding corporate policies, formal regulations, directives, rules, laws, and procedures. All of these are means ends generalisations as they tell employees what to do and how to behave in a general sense. HRM uses a technical legalistic language that enforces **rule compliance**. Inevitably however, rules must be linked to those who are supposed to follow them, making them "follow-able". In that way, employees can be made to comply with such rules and follow rather than break them.

Secondly, rules (e.g. HR policies) are **prescriptive rules** as they direct employees' action towards organisational goals (e.g. MBO).[58] **Rule governed behaviour** must be adjustable so that non-conforming employees can be exposed to managerial rule adjustment and **behaviour modification** (e.g. manipulation).[59] Employees' **rule deviance** is evaluated negatively while conformity and compliance are appraised positively through performance management.

HR policy rules are impersonalised as this decreases the visibility of HRM's power. Rule-based patterns of behaviour that guide the relationship between HRM and employees can be portrayed as free of power and conflict simply because they are based on rules.[60] These rules are made to take on a neutral or even natural appearance to which employees must adapt. An employee's role is seen as being a compliant contributor to the goodness of the business and to make special efforts to act consistent with managerially defined official duties. Employees are asphyxiated in the ideology of **rule obedience** (law-&-order).

On the managerial side, "law-&-order" means that HR managers need to be up-to-date with their country's legal regulations that affect HRM while simultaneously adhering to the local legal regulations.[61] Broadly, law-&-order covers at least four common areas – **common law duties** – of HRM:

1. HR managers must adhere to the contractual obligations of the employment contract;
2. HR managers must ensure employees are paid lawful salaries and wages;
3. HR managers must create a safe working environment (OHS) installing a positive OHS management system; and
4. HR managers must adhere to local laws regulating work time and general working conditions as well as create a fair working environment (EEO)[62] while ensuring the cooperation between management and employees.

**Equal Employment Opportunity** (EEO) is designed to assist in the protection of employees from discrimination.[63] Country-specific labour laws protect many employees from employment discrimination based upon age, ethnicity, race, colour, religion, sex, sexual orientation[64] (**LGBTQ**),[65] political believes, national origin, etc. In the context of EEO, discrimination entails areas such as hiring, firing, promotions, transfers, and wage practices. Often, it is also illegal to discriminate in advertising, referral of job applicants, and classification. This also applies to cases resulting in an **unfair dismissal** when an employee is dismissed from their job in a harsh, unjust, or unreasonable manner.[66] A **wrongful dismissal** occurs when management breaches the terms of an employment contract. On the other hand, a **constructive discharge** occurs when an employee quits or resigns from a job because intolerable acts of management left no other choice and the employee is "forced" to resign.

## 5. *Justice, Fairness, Democracy, and Organisational Welfare*

At stage five, HRM reaches beyond law and order by engaging in democratic processes that create law and order. Kohlberg's code word for democracy is "open and reasonable debate". At level five, two fundamentally different ideas collide: one is the idea of self-government through creating one's own laws in a democratic process while the other is an authoritarian setting of laws and corporate policies. This sets up two distinctively different forms of institutions: (1) democratic institutions and (2) non-democratic institutions.[67] In workplaces, for example, we find one institution that is authoritarian (e.g. non-elected managers in management) and one that is – historically and as a collective – fundamentally democratic with elected trade union officials, workplace representatives, and shop stewards.[68] In many jurisdictions, current labour law demands democracy for elected trade union officials but not for management as managers are nowhere elected. Traditionally, democratic trade unions have sought to extend democracy into workplaces and industry.[69] This became known as **industrial democracy**.[70]

People at this level also show an interest in the betterment of social affairs, human, civil, political, and economic justice, and human welfare.[71] This version of ethics reflects on **stakeholder models**, being a good **corporate citizen** by adhering to, for example, **corporate social responsibility**.[72] These concepts carry strong connotations to **Utilitarianism** and **Consequentialism** (Bentham, Mills, Moore, etc.) as they often adhere to the utilitarian idea that the best action is the one that procures the greatest happiness for the greatest numbers[73] – and the worst is the one that causes the most misery. The former is the "greater happiness principle" while the latter refers to the "no harm principle".[74] HRM has even a list of most *happiest company* to work for.[75] Others have introduced a CHO – a **Chief Happiness Officer**.[76]

Inside companies and corporations, Utilitarianism's two forms of ethics are often reduced to a mere ethical code created as an add-on (e.g. public relations) supportive to HRM. Ethics is still seen as a surplus, as **corporate philanthropy**,[77] an add-on to managerial processes that adds value to the operation[78]:

> ...wish to demonstrate their concern for the less fortunate or the less profitable, or the community at large, they speak of addressing the triple bottom line through corporate social responsibility known as CSR...Principally...their language has been stripped of meaning. They don't have words like generous, charitable, kind, and share...welfare, wealth transfer, social service, social benefit, social policy, and social contract...[79]

Over and above HRM's organisational needs, concern for a greater good is developed. This includes democracy, the participation of employees, involvement, and collaborative "employee-HRM" relationships. A wider democratic public interest is served when the principles of basic **organisational justice**[80] are followed.[81] The moral philosophical underpinning for organisational justice remains Rawl's seminal work **Justice as Fairness**.[82] For HRM justice and fairness relates predominantly to three forms of organisational justice:

**Distributive justice**: fairness of rewards and their distribution among employees;
**Procedural justice**: methods that determine rewards offer a fair procedure allowing employees "natural justice" – the right to a fair hearing (audi alteram partem)[83]; and
**Communicative justice**: the fair and equal distribution of information to all employees.

These forms of justice as well as justice as fairness often reach far beyond present forms of HRM that is typically confined to stabilising rules, conventions, and policies. In this stage, relationships between employees and HRM start to shift away from instrumentalism that serves the instrumental purposes of HRM. Instead, they become directed towards social action, truth, mutual understanding, and democracy.

A classical case of Utilitarianism's "no harm principle", for example, is **whistle blowing** that occurs when an employee values the greater good higher than corporate profits, applying the "no harm principle" in cases of corporate harm to people and the environment.[84] US consumer advocate Ralph Nader and environmentalist Erin Brockovich are famous cases.[85] Whistle blowers expose any kind of information or activity that is illegal, unethical, and not correct within a private (business) or public organisation (government). The information of wrongdoing can be classified in the following ways:

a.   violation of company policy and corporate rules,
b.   violation of laws and regulation;
c.   threats to public interest and the natural environment's **ecosystem**[86]; and
d.   business corruption and white collar crime.[87]

Whistle blowers often bring information to surface either internally or externally. Internal whistle blowing means a whistleblower brings accusations to the attention of other people within the accused organisation (HRM). External whistle blowing means a whistle blower brings allegations to light by contacting a third party outside of an accused organisation (e.g. the media, government, law enforcement, or those who are concerned, e.g. NGOs). Whistle blowers often face stiff reprisal and retaliation from those who are accused of the wrongdoing. As a consequence, whistle blowing is often protected by law that still varies from country to country. Over a dozen countries have now adopted comprehensive **whistle blower protection** laws which create mechanisms for reporting wrongdoing and provide legal protections to the people who informed them. Over fifty countries have adopted more limited protections as part of their anti-corruption, freedom of information, or employment laws.

### 6. HRM and Human Rights

At stage six, HRM applies universal principles such as those, for example, developed by **Kantian ethics** – categorical imperatives[88] – and **deontological theory**.[89] One such Kantian imperative, for example, is: "act in such a way that you treat humanity, whether in your own person or in the person of any other, never merely as a means to an end, but always at the same time as an end". Kant's **categorical imperatives**[90] – either/or formulations of ethics – mean that either you are ethical or you are not. This means, for example, treating a person as a means, a tool, an implement, or a human resource is not ethical. You need to treat people as "ends in-themselves" and no amount of respect shown to a tool, a human resource, or a means can change that.[91]

Under this imperative, HRM–employee relations become less distorted as they move away from purely self-serving managerial goals. Respectful, non-distorted, and open discussions are no longer seen as mere instruments to meet the other side's purposes but to enable HRM to adopt a reflective and self-critical approach in ethical decision-making. It is thoroughly democratic based on an adherence to "The **Universal Declaration of Human Rights**".[92] This includes all **ILO conventions** and declarations which a country has ratified such as[93]:

1. Declaration on Social Justice for a Fair Globalisation;
2. Declaration on Fundamental Principles and Rights at Work;
3. Declaration on Gender Equality;
4. Declaration on Multinational Enterprises and Social Policy.

Beyond that the subjects covered by ILO conventions concern four basic areas:

1. individual rights at work, mainly on safety, wage standards, working time, or social security, and the rights to not be forced to work or work during childhood[94];
2. there are also collective labour rights to participation in the workplace, particularly to join a trade union, collectively bargain and take strike action, as well as direct representation within the management of organisations;
3. there are a series of rights to equal treatment that are referential to the terms and conditions of people in comparable situations, with special protections for indigenous communities and migrants; and
4. there is a set of conventions promoting job security through labour standards[95] for dismissals, protection upon an employer's insolvency, regulation of employment agencies, and requirements upon member states to promote full and fulfilling employment.

Forward-looking HR managers ensure all this by also focusing on **diversity management**[96] under well thought out HR policies that adhere to the human rights obligation of fostering a diverse workforce.[97] Diversity management is the recognition and support for individual differences.[98] The concept of diversity includes acceptance and respect. It means understanding that each individual is unique and recognises individual differences that can be along the dimensions of race, ethnicity, gender, sexual orientation, socio-economic status, age, physical abilities, religious beliefs, political beliefs, and other ideologies.

### 7. Sustainability and the Natural Environment

At stage seven, domination-free dialogues, ethics, and human rights are extended beyond issues that are immediately useful to HRM.[99] Human rights are applied to a wider context rather than being restricted to human beings alone so that ethical awareness reaches beyond fellow humans. It embraces other forms of life such as animal species and ecological systems regardless of their social utility.[100] HRM includes issues related to nature, environment, plant life, corporate social responsibility, **sustainability**,[101] **global warming**,[102] **carbon footprint**,[103] animal life, etc. reflecting an acute awareness of **environmental ethics**.[104]

Within the field of HRM, this approach is known as Sustainable or **Green HRM** (GHRM).[105] As a move from "greed to green",[106] GHRM[107] is understood as using HRM policies to promote the sustainable use of resources within organizations and, more generally promotes the causes of environment sustainability. This includes HRM areas such as: green recruitment; green performance management; green training and development; green compensation; green employee relations; green initiatives for HR, the paperless office; conservation of energy; and recycling and waste disposal.[108] Green HRM can be seen as being part of the UN's *2030 Agenda for Sustainable Development*.[109] In business organisations such as IKEA, Siemens, and Lego, Green HRM is part of their organisational strategy.

HRM develops responsiveness to the integrity of the natural environment, linking the natural environment to human society outside company confinements. By November 2019, *National Geographic* predicted eleven green jobs of the future.[110] These are:

1. urban growers
2. water quality technicians
3. clean car engineers
4. recyclers
5. natural scientists
6. green builders
7. solar cell technicians
8. green design professionals
9. wave energy producers
10. wind energy workers
11. biofuel jobs

## Corporate Social Responsibility

As sub-division of business ethics,[111] corporate social responsibility – known by its oxymoronic acronym: CSR – but also called corporate citizenship is a form of voluntary corporate self-regulation at times used to offset CSI – **Corporate Social Irresponsibility**.[112] Corporate **CSR policies** function as a mechanism whereby a business monitors and ensures its active compliance with the spirit of the law, human rights, social and ethical standards, and national and even international norms. To achieve this, HR managers assure that the implementation of CSR policies reaches beyond simple compliance. They design a system that allows for human engagement in corporate activities thereby furthering the social good (level 5) beyond the interests of the firm (level 2) and those required by law (level 4).

CSR's aim is to increase long-term profits through positive public relations, set high ethical standards to reduce business and legal risk, and increase shareholder trust by taking responsibility for corporate actions. To achieve this, companies have moved beyond "The Real Bottom Line" (shareholder value and profit maximisation) towards the **triple bottom line**[113] (also known as PPP, TBL, 3BL) used as an accounting framework based on the inclusion of three key parts:

1. People, the social, communities, and society;
2. Planet, the environmental and ecological sphere[114]; and
3. Accounting and financial, i.e. profits, shareholder value, and profit maximisation.

Today, many organisations have adopted the TBL framework to evaluate their performance in a broader perspective and create greater business value. One tool to achieve this is to conduct what is known as **environmental audit** reflecting on various types of evaluations intended to identify **environmental compliance** and management system implementation gaps, along with related corrective actions. Together with the TBL and environmental auditing, CSR strategies encourage companies to make a positive impact on the environment and stakeholders including consumers, employees, investors, communities, and others.

The benefit of CSR is that companies can increase long-term profits by operating with a CSR perspective. Critiques, on the other hand, argue that CSR distracts from the core economic role of a business.[115] CSR critiques also question the unrealistic expectations in CSR and the fact that CSR is merely window dressing, a PR exercise, and an attempt to pre-empt the role of governments as a watchdog over powerful multinational corporations. They also argue that CSR came to light in the context of neo-liberal globalisation, economic neo-liberalism, and late capitalism to give ideological legitimacy to uninhibited corporate power.

## Sustainability

**Corporate sustainability** seeks to create long-term consumer and employee value by creating an ecological corporate strategy aiming towards our natural environment while taking into consideration all four dimensions – Accounting, Human Resource Management, Marketing, Operations Management – of a business, firm, company, or corporation.[116] Sustainability focuses on the social, cultural, natural, and economic environment. It formulates corporate **sustainability policies** and strategies to build companies that encourage longevity through corporate transparency and employee development (e.g. HRD in Chapter 4).

As such, corporate sustainability is closely associated with CSR and corporate citizenship. It is more than simply an "add-on". Instead, it is an overarching approach of corporate practices built around social and environmental considerations. Corporate sustainability originates in the Brundtland Commission's Report Our Common Future.[117] The report describes **sustainable development** as development that meets the needs of the present generation without compromising the ability of future generations to meet their own. This desire to grow without damaging future generations' prospects is becoming more and more central to business. In the business/HRM realm, this is linked to TBL (see above) proposing that business goals are inseparable from societies and environments within which businesses operate.

## Global Warming and Carbon Footprint

**Global warming or climate change** has been observed in the rise of the average temperature of the earth's climate system and its related effects.[118] Multiple lines of scientific evidence show that the climate system is warming.[119] Scientific understanding of global warming is increasing. The *Intergovernmental Panel on Climate Change* reported in 2014 that scientists were more than 95% certain that global warming is mostly being caused by increasing concentrations of **greenhouse gas**[120] and other human activities[121] that have also led to **peak oil**.[122]

These human developments and research findings have been recognised by national science academies of all major industrialised nations and are not disputed by any scientific body of national or international standing. While impacts will differ from region to region around the globe, anticipated effects include a warming global temperature, rising sea levels, changing precipitation, and an expansion of deserts in the subtropics. The **Climate Change Performance Index** provides a clear picture of this.[123] Warming is expected to be greater over land than over the oceans and greatest in the Arctic, with the continuing retreat of glaciers, permafrost, and sea ice. The five key changes include:

1. more frequent extreme weather events including heat waves;
2. droughts, heavy rainfall with floods, and heavy snowfall;
3. oceanic acidification and species extinctions due to shifting temperature regimes;

4.   threat to food security from decreasing crop yields and
5.   the abandonment of populated areas due to rising sea levels.

The **carbon footprint** is defined as the total set of greenhouse gas emissions caused by an individual, event, organisation, or product. The total global carbon footprint cannot be calculated because of the large amount of data required and the fact that carbon dioxide can also be produced by natural occurrences. Another and somewhat more practicable definition is a measure of the total amount of carbon dioxide and methane emissions of a defined population, system, or activity, considering all relevant sources, sink, and storage options within the spatial and temporal boundary of the population, system, or activity of interest. Most of the carbon footprint emissions for the average US household, for example, come from:

> **indirect carbon footprint**: fuel burned to produce goods far away from the final consumer (e.g. data.worldbank.org).[124] This is distinguished from
> **direct carbon footprint**: emissions coming from burning fuel in one's car and stove.[125]

A good measurement of an individual's carbon footprint is the WWF's **carbon footprint calculator**.[126] Completing it results in a number, i.e. 1 means you are sustaining life of earth, any number below 1 means you are contributing positively to sustainability, while everything above 1 means that we simply need more than one earth to sustain a person's current lifestyle. All of this not only impacts on the environment, it also falls under ethics, hence the concept of environmental ethics.

### Environmental Ethics

While environmental ethics – or the ethics of human-environment interactions – is a wide field,[127] one of the most interesting concepts is that of shallow ecology and deep ecology.[128] **Shallow ecology** relates to utilitarianism and a human-centred – anthropocentric[129] – attitude to nature. It has a materialist and consumerist oriented outlook centred on economic growth.[130] Shallow ecology has a short-term orientation often promoting technological fixes such as recycling, increased automotive efficiency, or export-driven mono-cultural organic agriculture. It is based on traditional and outdated consumption oriented values and methods of industrial economies.

The shallow approach to ecology differs from what is called the "long-range deep ecology movement". In fact, **deep ecology** is distinctively different from the "shallow ecology movement". The word "deep" in deep ecology refers to a profound questioning of fundamental environmental issues. Deep ecology involves going to the root cause of environmental problems. Such a long-range and deep approach involves redesigning our whole systems based on values and methods that truly preserve the ecological and cultural diversity of natural systems. As a consequence, the deep ecology leads to sustainability. Deep ecology is an ecological philosophy promoting the inherent worth of living beings regardless of their instrumental utility to human needs, plus a radical restructuring of modern human societies in accordance with such ideas. Deep ecology argues that the natural world is a subtle balance (e.g. carbon footprint of 1) of complex inter-relationships in which the existence of organisms is dependent on the existence of others within the eco system. Human interference with or destruction of the natural world therefore poses a threat not only to humans but to all organisms constituting the natural order.

Deep ecology's core principle is the belief that the living environment as a whole should be respected and regarded as having certain inalienable legal rights to live and flourish, independent of its utilitarian instrumental benefits for human use. It describes itself as "deep" because it is looking more deeply into the actual reality of humanity's relationship with the natural world arriving at philosophically more profound conclusions. Deep ecology offers an eight-tier platform:

1.  The well-being and flourishing of human and nonhuman life on earth have values in themselves – these values are independent of the usefulness of the nonhuman world for human purposes;
2.  Richness and diversity of life forms contribute to the realisation of these values and are also values in themselves;
3.  Humans have no right to reduce this richness and diversity except to satisfy vital human needs;
4.  The flourishing of human life and cultures is compatible with the plateauing and eventual reduction of the human population;
5.  Present human interference with the nonhuman world is excessive, and the situation is rapidly worsening;
6.  Policies must therefore be changed while the resulting state of affairs will be deeply different from the present;
7.  Change is mainly that of appreciating life quality rather than adhering to an increasingly higher standard of living; and
8.  Those who subscribe to the foregoing points have an obligation directly or indirectly to try to implement the necessary changes.

## HRM and Practical Environmental Ethics

In many cases, today's corporations have reached beyond seeing CSR and sustainability as mere PR exercises. Some companies have embraced the concept of **ethical stewardship**.[131] Some of these companies have even placed a CSO, a **chief sustainability officer**[132] next to the CEO (see Chapter 5). While there are rather intensive links between HRM, environmental ethics, CSR, TBL, sustainability, etc.,[133] HR managers engage with creating a sustainable **carbon neutral business**[134] by achieving the following five steps:

1.  Set organisational carbon reduction targets.
2.  Audit carbon footprint.
3.  Reduce carbon emissions.
4.  Offset remaining carbon emissions.
5.  Evaluate progress.

### 1. Set Organisational Carbon Reduction Targets

Reducing a business's carbon emissions and becoming carbon neutral requires organisational leadership not just from HR managers but also at top level. There needs to be an organisational commitment. This can be achieved, for example, by the long-term strategic goal of becoming a carbon neutral business: year one: 20% reduction in baseline emissions via energy efficiency actions or carbon offsets; year two: 40% reduction, etc.

## 2. Audit Carbon Footprint

This process creates a clear picture of the organisation's carbon emissions (carbon footprint) enabling management to apply targets in real numbers (see above for measuring carbon footprint). It establishes an **emissions inventory** that contains the main sources of emissions identifying opportunities for abatement. It covers all areas of a business, i.e. energy use, operation of stationary equipment, transport, supply chain engagement, and waste generation. Direct emissions produced by the daily operational activities of a business include:

1. gas consumption;
2. other fuels consumed on-site, e.g. diesel for back-up generator and LPG, etc.
3. fugitive emissions (e.g. refrigerants: type, quantity and cost of refrigerant used to recharge heating, ventilation, and air-conditioning (HVAC) equipment);
4. fuel used and paid for by a business when staff or contractors travel in business vehicles for business purposes only;
5. electricity units in kWh.

## 3. Reduce Carbon Emissions

Resulting from carbon auditing the following actions provide options for HR managers to lowering carbon emissions (by linking these suggestions to, for example, reward structures such as intrinsic and extrinsic rewards, performance management, OHS, promotions, labour relations, recruitment and selection, workforce planning, strategic HRM, etc.):

| | | | |
|---|---|---|---|
| 1 | Reduce and offset car, air, etc. transport emissions | 5 | Encourage car-pooling; |
| 2 | Install solar hot water and electricity systems | 6 | Travel together to meetings |
| 3 | Encourage waste minimisation | 7 | Embrace energy efficiency |
| 4 | Cultivate waste reduction habits | 8 | Foster water conservation |

## 4. Offset Remaining Carbon Emissions

The above actions may not be sufficient to generate all the emissions reductions required to achieve the required strategic target. To compensate, **carbon offsets** can be used through, for example, changing conventional power sources to green power (buy renewable electricity). This is a quick, effective, and popular way to address the many tonnes of greenhouse gases a company emits. It means to pay someone to offset these emission by, for example, planting enough trees to absorb the emitted $CO_2$ of a company.

## 5. Evaluate Progress

Environmentally aware HR managers regularly evaluate the process, strategies, policies, and actions taken by a business to become carbon neutral. This aids future efforts and actions and re-calibrates emission reductions and offsets. This process will also create organisational knowledge of success. All this is important. To create a sustainable company means not just the company but also HRM must be more efficient in the daily use of energy.[135] Corporate sustainability action can eliminate significant levels of organisational energy wastage through a few steps that create an environmental organisational culture as well as changes in attitudes and behaviours.

# Workbook

## III. Five Discussion Questions on the Ethics at Work

### And One Report Question on the Ethics at Work

*1. Discussion Question:*

1. Virtue ethics carries connotations to an ethical organisational climate. How can HRM create and sustain an ethical organisational climate?
2. One Kantian categorical imperative denotes, "act in such a way that you treat humanity, whether in your own person or in the person of any other, never merely as a means to an end, but always at the same time as an end". This means treating a person as a means, a tool, an implement, or a human resource is not ethical. To be ethical means treating people as people and as "ends in-themselves". No amount of respect shown to a tool, a human resource, and a means can change that. Can HRM ever be ethical?
3. Utilitarianism denotes that a good person (HR manager) should always bring the greatest happiness to the greatest number of people (the happiness principle) and simultaneously avoid bringing harm to people (the no-harm principle). Can HRM ever achieve this?
4. At Kohlberg's level 6 of morality, one finds a demand to adhere to universal human rights. This includes collective labour rights (participation in the workplace, particularly to join a trade union, collectively bargain and take strike action, as well as direct representation within the management of organisations). What steps can HRM undertake to support these universal human rights?
5. Kohlberg's morality denotes that there are seven levels of morality. At which level would you see HRM and why?

## 2. Report Question

### On Kohlberg's Highest Stage of Morality

Kohlberg's highest stage of morality (seven) is about environmental ethics. Contemporary People Management has to be concerned with: Corporate Social Responsibility; Sustainability & Carbon Footprint and; Global Warming & Carbon Neutral Business. How can Contemporary People Management (CPM) and/or Human Resource Management (HRM) achieve a higher awareness of these issues at corporate and human resource level? Develop four [4] recommendations.

## IV. The "5-by-5" Exercise: Five Case Studies and Five Questions

### 10.1 The High Price of French Fashion at Chic-Chic

In March 2017, French fashion designer and clothing manufacturer "Chic-Chic" found itself in a major dispute. Chic-Chic is one of the leading brands in the French fashion industry. The case centred on the understanding of ethics and corporate social responsibility at Chic-Chic. The controversy began after Chic-Chic's top management announced that it would make 1390 employees in France redundant. Chic-Chic's management justified the move by stating that it was outsourcing its manufacturing division to Cambodia and Vietnam. Management claimed that labour costs were a fraction of those in France. It also emerged that in the two years leading to the management decision on outsourcing, Chic-Chic had granted a large pay increase to its CEO, Mr Pierre Ardito. In fact, the payment Mr Ardito received more than doubled. On top of that Mr Ardito received a generous bonus.

During the same two-year period, Chic-Chic had received €21 million in government assistance from the French state. The case had received widespread media coverage inside France and throughout Europe. It caused public outrage particularly over state, i.e. taxpayer support for Chic-Chic and the more than generous rewards given to Chic-Chic's glamorous CEO, Mr Ardito. The president of the *European Trade Union Federation*, Mr Luca Visentini (www.etuc.org/) stated publicly that "corporate France has lost its moral compass". Politicians from all sides of France criticised Chic-Chic and Mr Ardito. France's fashion industry trade unions, the *Fédération Française de la Couture* together with the *Trade Unions International of Transport Workers* (www.itfglobal.org) threatened to boycott the shipping of manufacturing equipment offshore. In addition, French consumer groups called on people to stop buying products of Chic-Chic.

1. What are the moral implications of Chic-Chic's move to offshore its manufacturing division to Cambodia and Vietnam? Use the Kohlberg scale to assess the level of morality. Justify your choice by finding three arguments that support your selection.
2. On what level of morality measured on Kohlberg's scale would you locate Chic-Chic's corporate behaviour given the large rewards paid to its CEO Mr Ardito and the taxpayer support it had received by the French government during the two years prior to its decision of offshore manufacturing? Use the Kohlberg scale to assess the level of morality. Justify your choice by finding three arguments that support your selection.
3. Imagine you are a trade union officer at the ITF, what additional three measures would you suggest (beyond what the ITF was already planning) to prevent Chic-Chic from moving production offshore?
4. Imagine you are the HR manager at Chic-Chic. Your CEO, Mr Ardito has asked you to justify Chic-Chic's immoral decision even though you find the corporate decision immoral. What would you do as an HR manager? Find three arguments in favour of justifying Chic-Chic's outsourcing decision (following the corporate line) and three arguments that support the moral stance of not supporting the outsourcing decision.

## 10.2 HRM and Office Romance

Today, HR managers use the term "office romance" to describe a consensual relationship between people at work. Office romance is fundamentally different from sexual harassment. It is consensual in character. Nevertheless, office romances are often judged by other employees as well as managers. A recent survey found that 40% of employees have dated someone from their workplace. And about 17% have done it twice. Today, office romances occur more than ever before. For one, more and more men and women work side by side in offices. And there are more singles in today's work-place than ever before. Beyond that, many employees spend long hours at work. Over time, this can create familiarity with co-workers as common interests are developed.

In addition to the close proximity there is also convenience. At work, there is much to talk about – work and other issues. The aforementioned survey also found that three-fourth of all employees engaging in office romance did not seek to hide their relation-ship. Earlier, around half still sought to conceal their office romance. However, an office romance among colleagues on equal levels, also if in different departments, can incur negative reactions. All too often, those engaging in an office romance are judged.

The research found that many employees have negative perceptions of office romances. Surprisingly, this also remains the case for those who have been part in an office romance. Many studies suggest that there are three motivating factors behind dating a colleague at a workplace: job advancement, ego, and love. To a large degree, the acceptance of an office romance depends on the motivations behind it.

Whether often wrongly assumed favouritism between couples is real or just per-ceived may not even matter. One of the biggest reasons HR managers like to discour-age office romances is because they generate gossip. Managers think that gossip wastes time. It can also foster distrust. This occurs particularly when employees are involved in promotions, restructuring of teams, financial bonuses, performance man-agement, etc. They become easy targets for those colleagues inclined to use office gossip as a means to undermine or get themselves ahead.

1. The case study says that office romances are increasing. It mentions a few reason for that. Discuss office romance and fine four more reason why office romance occur in today's workplace.
2. The article claims that the way office romances are judged is whether they happen for reasons of career advancement and promotion on the one hand or for love, on the other. Do you agree or disagree? Find three arguments in favour and three arguments against it.
3. Is there a difference between a "horizontal" office romance (employee to employee) and a "vertical" office romance (manager-employee)? What are the advantages and disadvantages of the former and the latter? Develop four arguments: one for and one argument against a "horizontal" romance and one argument for and one argument against a "vertical" office romance.
4. Imagine you are an HR manager being asked by your CEO to develop an HR policy for office romance. Develop four recommendations for such a policy to be shown to your CEO so that one can be approved and announced as the com-pany's official policy.
5. Having a romantic relationship is part of human nature. Some might even say "this is what makes us human" as it has done so for thousands of years. In a rushed response, some HR managers might seek to eliminate romance at work altogether thought the invention of a specific HR policy. Is prohibition of office romance an ethical approach? At what level of Kohlberg's scale of morality would you locate such a rushed response and why? Find the appropriate level and develop four arguments that support your choice.

### 10.3 Sustainability at Drink Well Brewery

Drink Well Brewery is a South East Asian beer manufacturer. In 2017, the company has issued a sustainability report for the first time. It showcased its sustainability performance in several business related areas. Drink Well Brewery has reduced its water usage to 4.2 hectolitres for every hectolitre of beer produced and achieved a general reduction in carbon emissions and electricity usage since 2015 by 23.8% and in 2016 by 18.6%. Drink Well Brewery also invested $27 million in community development projects throughout South East Asia. In addition, Drink Well Brewery developed a "party harder and drink less" PR campaign promoting responsible drinking and its new range of soft drinks. Drink Well Brewery's improved "safety is our no. 1" policy is capable of assessing employees' safety record and workplace behaviour.

Shaun Connery, Drink Well Brewery's HR director said in a recent interview with "Asia Times" that "globally about 23,000 of our employees are engaged every day in creating corporate success while also working towards global sustainability and corporate social responsibility". The brewery's strong environmental performance has also delivered strong business results. Drink Well Brewery now works on even better integrating its sustainability results into its future strategic business planning.

1. Given Kohlberg's seven levels of morality, at which level or levels of morality would you locate the management of Drink Well Brewery and why? Justify your answer with at least three arguments for the level/s you have selected.
2. Imagine you are one of the HR managers at Drink Well Brewery and your boss has asked you to focus even more on the company's carbon footprint. What initiatives would you suggest to move the company towards carbon neutrality? Develop four strategies.
3. Kohlberg's level 6 is about universal human rights. Which human rights, universal labour rights, and labour standards concern Drink Well Brewery and why? Draw up a short list and justify your answers.
4. Imagine you are an HR manager at Drink Well Brewery and your new boss has asked you to introduce an environmental education and training programme with the goal of raising increased environmental awareness among Drink Well Brewery employees. Develop four recommendations on such a training programme.
5. Imagine you are an HR manager at Drink Well Brewery with the task to run a project team on how to transfer Drink Well Brewery's environmental record from manufacturing to its office. Develop four recommendations on how office work can be made sustainable.

### 10.4 Sustainability at Africa Electrical Ltd.

Africa Electrical Ltd.'s CEO is Erol Flynn. In 2017, Mr Flynn launched Africa Electrical Ltd.'s multi-million dollar "Nature" initiative to enhance the company's financial as well as environmental performance. Simultaneously, the environmental strategy was designed to drive growth. Africa Electrical Ltd. has adopted a corporate citizenship philosophy. The idea behind this is "making money, making it ethically, and making a difference in Africa". The company's plan is to invest in clean technologies, develop environmentally friendly products while reducing Africa Electrical Ltd.'s own emissions. Every dimension of Africa Electrical Ltd.'s new initiative is driven by its employees.

To support that, Africa Electrical Ltd. sponsors employee competitions to receive ideas that reduce the use of energy. The programme also extends to the development of environmentally friendly products. As a result, the company has been able to develop energy efficient appliances tailored to the African market as well as wind turbines. Africa Electrical Ltd. has also set up an internal certification process that quantifies the environmental impacts and benefits of each new product or process on a scoreboard. This is then externally verified. Between 2015 and 2017, Africa Electrical Ltd.'s investments in green technologies have doubled from $70 million to $140 million. During the same period, its revenues from certified green technologies have doubled from around $80 million to $160 million.

1.  On Kohlberg's scale of morality, where would you locate Africa Electrical Ltd. in the year 2017 and why? Justify your answer by developing four arguments.
2.  "Africa Electrical Ltd. has made serious plans to become sustainable". Develop three arguments that support this statement and three arguments against it.
3.  Imagine you are the HR manager at Africa Electrical Ltd. and assigned the task to increase employee involvement in the company's plan to develop environmentally friendly products. What three performance management initiatives (KPIs) would you suggest to encourage employees to participate?
4.  Africa Electrical Ltd.'s statement of "making money, making it ethically, and making a difference in Africa" still places the overall emphasis of the company on "making money". As long as companies remain trapped in capitalism's "making money" (the real bottom line, i.e. profits), its environmental programmes remain purely public relations exercises designed to give the company a good image while carrying on with profit making. Develop three arguments that support this statement and three arguments against it.
5.  Can an energy producing corporation like Africa Electrical Ltd. ever be totally sustainable? Develop three arguments that support this statement and three arguments against it.

### 10.5 CSR and Community Engagement at Euro Union Bank

In the year 2016, Euro Union Bank established an educational scholarship scheme valued at € 50 million. At the 2018 European Banking Consumer Award, Euro Union Bank was named Europe's most socially responsible bank. Its corporate social responsibility (CSR) programme was named "outstanding". In 2017, Euro Union Bank gave grants to more than 150 communities inside the European Union and to not-for-profit organisations. Furthermore, the bank's HR managers encourage the employees to undertake volunteer work. It offers paid leave and flexible work arrangements for this. In general, volunteering is incorporated into employees' performance management plans. HRM has designed this inclusion as a way of fostering career prospects at Euro Union Bank.

Europe-wide, more than 75% of all employees at Euro Union Bank have been taking part in volunteer work. Participation in volunteering ranges from Euro Union Bank's CEO, Mr Philippe Martinez to its apprentices. This form of community engagement ranges from participating in "Clean Up Europe" day to fundraising activities. Beyond that, Euro Union Bank matches donations made by Euro Union Bank employees to charities on its "Euro-for-Euro" plan.

Euro Union Bank's commitment to corporate social responsibility is driven by the ideals of Generation Y employees. From the bank's HR viewpoint, supporting corporate social responsibility makes Euro Union Bank highly attractive to prospective employees. HRM has substantiated this through data on recruitment and selection throughout Europe. In addition, it also contributes to Euro Union Bank's very low turnover rate and high work satisfaction among existing employees. Euro Union Bank's initiatives support the link between corporate social responsibility and successful HRM as well as the retention of employees.

1.  Euro Union Bank's extensive corporate social responsibility programme locates the bank at level five or six of Kohlberg's scale. Select the right level and support your answer by developing three arguments.
2.  Imagine you are a HR manager at Euro Union Bank, what kind of initiative would you suggest to move the bank's corporate social responsibility from the current level of five/six towards level 7? Develop four such initiatives.
3.  The case study states that 75% of all employees participate in Euro Union Bank's corporate social responsibility programme. Imagine you are a HR manager at Euro Union Bank, what would you suggest on how to include the missing 25%? How can Human Resource Management encourage the remaining people to be part of the bank's corporate social responsibility programme? Develop four strategies.
4.  Imagine you are an HR manager at Euro Union Bank with the task of intensifying the link between performance management and corporate social responsibility. Develop three HR strategies on how this link can be strengthened.
5.  Imagine you are an HR manager at Euro Union Bank and your CEO, Mr Philippe Martinez has asked you to develop an HR policy that reflects HRM's strong link to CSR (corporate social responsibility) while also clearly stating the bank's intention. Develop a comprehensive policy on HRM, CSR, and the bank's intention.

### 10.6 The Bullying Case of Japan Motors Co.

In the year 2018, a female employee was awarded ¥2,670.000 in damages after being bullied for several months. This is the case of Sachiko Hattori vs. Japan Motors Co. based in Tokyo, Japan. It reminds many employees that self-initiative is still important in cases of corporate bullying and comes despite the fact that many HR managers, especially in large corporations, have introduced policies that manage workplace conduct and seek to prevent workplace bullying. The manager of the Osaka dealership, Ms Yuki Sato of Japan Motors Co. was found to have bullied Sachiko Hattori after Ms Hattori's return from maternity leave.

The line manager's bullying comprises excluding Ms Hattori from important business discussions, ignoring her attempts to assist management, unjustified criticism of Ms Hattori's performance, frequently speaking to Ms Hattori in a hostile and even cruel way, and attempting to isolate Ms Hattori. After weeks of distress, Ms Hattori made a bullying complaint to Japan Motors Co.'s business manager at its central office in Tokyo – Tatsuya Fuji. But instead of following HRM's codified "employee conducts, bullying and harassment policy", Mr Fuji responded by calling the store manager in Osaka to inform Ms Sato of the bullying complaint made by Ms Hattori.

This did not solve the issues. Instead, the bullying by Ms Sato continued unabated for a further three weeks. It even intensified. Eventually, Ms Hattori made a second bullying complaint. This time to Japan Motors Co.'s HR director – Ms Naomi Shiraishi. But instead of receiving support from the HR department, Ms Hattori was simply told "go and work it out yourself". Ms Hattori was subsequently diagnosed with a psychiatric disorder and filed a claim of corporate negligence and breach of contract with the local labour court.

After hearing the case, justice Nagisa Oshima found that a reasonable person in the employer's position would have realised that Japan Motors Co. had failed. The judge also found HRM's failure to address the initial complaint. The judgement noted that the conduct of Japan Motors Co.'s managers worsened the bullying. This led to the emotional distress of Ms Hattori. Justice Nagisa Oshima concluded that Japan Motors Co. and several of its managers at JMC's head office in Tokyo had been negligent in permitting the local dealership manager, Ms Sato, to bully Ms Hattori. Japan Motors Co.'s management had failed to enforce their own "employees conduct, bullying and harassment" policy as formulated by its HR department. Judge Nagisa Oshima awarded Ms Hattori ¥2,670.000 in damages.

1. Imagine you are the HR manager at Japan Motors Co. set with the task to rewrite the company's bullying policy. Make four recommendations for such a policy.
2. The company – Japan Motors Co. – has an anti-bulling policy but management did not follow these guidelines. What can HRM do to improve the situation? Develop four recommendations designed to improve the adherence of dealership managers to the given HR policies.
3. Given the standard definition of bullying provided in the textbook above, was Sachiko Hattori bullied? Is the definition workable and can it be applied to this case? Does the definition assist you in deciding whether or not Ms Hattori was bullied? Support your answers with two arguments per answer.
4. Imagine you are the HR manager at Japan Motors Co. seeking to improve the organisational culture through management training. What kind of organisational culture should be developed at Japan Motors Co. and how would you support an anti-bullying culture through organisational learning? Develop four recommendations.
5. Locate the (im)morality of bullying on Kohlberg's scale. Support your choice through two arguments. Bullying is psychologically damaging. It is also highly immoral. In your effort to provide a bullying free workplace, to which level of Kohlberg's scale should Japan Motors Co. move and why? Support your answer with two arguments.

## V. A Suggestion for an Online Guest Lecture

The late CEO Ray Anderson who has
given more than 1000 speeches talks about
*"Sustainability" (2009)*
ted.com/talks/ray_anderson_on_the_business_logic_of_sustainability?
   language=en
[the online guest lecture above is merely a suggestion – www.ted.com/talks offers
   additional material to choose from]

## VI. List of Suggested Documentaries on Ethics at Work

The carefully selected documentary videos below are mere suggestions to be used during tutorials. Documentaries have been selected to achieve two things: (1) to explain key HRM themes and (2) to provide an insight into the reality of HRM. Typically, these short documentaries should be viewed in class followed by a class discussion on the content of the video. Alternatively, questions on documentaries can be prepared beforehand and small group discussions can follow up the video after viewing is concluded. Should any of the web links no longer function, please conduct an internet search for other – alternative – documentaries related to your tutorial topic (e.g. filmsforaction.org):

3 Minutes Kant: youtube.com/watch?v=xwOCmJevigw&feature=youtu.be
3 Minutes Utilitarian: youtube.com/watch?v=wS9bey162PU
Virtue Ethics: youtube.com/watch?v=cpE6qIlLheU
Rawls on Fairness: youtube.com/watch?v=kZ2CaSl1dvM
HRM & Fairness: youtube.com/watch?v=hsH3RujWDGI
HRM/SCR: youtube.com/watch?v=Z4g6W6BtEzA
CSR: youtube.com/watch?v=Z4g6W6BtEzA
Global Warming: www.anthropocene.info/en/home
Economics of Happiness: youtube.com/watch?v=VkdnFYDbiBE
Sustainability at Citibank: youtube.com/watch?v=_GjPgD_oz_g
Workplace ethics: https://www.youtube.com/watch?v=loXqK6D6lbk

## Notes

1  Singer, P. 1994. *Ethics*, Oxford: Oxford University Press.
2  Nowak, M. & Highfield, R. 2011. *Super Cooperators: Evolution, Altruism and Human Behaviour (Or Why We Need Each Other to Succeed)*, London: Penguin Press; Klikauer, T. 2012. Evolution, Altruism, and Human Behaviour, *Organization*, 19(6):939–940.
3  plato.stanford.edu/entries/morality-definition/.
4  plato.stanford.edu/.
5  Klikauer, T. 2014. Social justice and the ethics of resistance: a review essay, *Social Justice Research*, 27(4):518–525.
6  http://www.simplypsychology.org/kohlberg.html; Klikauer, T. 2011. Ethics of the ILO: Kohlberg's universal moral development scale, *Journal of Applied Ethics*, 1(2):33–56.
7  plato.stanford.edu/entries/childhood/.
8  Klikauer, T. 2011. Ethics of the ILO: Kohlberg's universal moral development scale, *Journal of Applied Ethics*, 1(2):33–56; Klikauer, T. 2012. *Seven Management Moralities*, Basingstoke: Palgrave.

9 Klikauer, T. 2014. *Seven Moralities of HRM*, Basingstoke: Palgrave; Härtel, C. E. J. & Fujimoto, Y. 2015. *HRM* (3rd ed.), Frenches Forest: Pearson, p. 74f.

10 While there is ethical relativism (dictionary.reference.com/browse/ethical-relativism), almost all moral philosophers today agree that morality is not defined by a community and that there are universal standards for ethics (e.g. you shall not kill).

11 Dauvergne, P. 2018. *Will Big Business Destroy Our Planet?*, London: Polity Press.

12 In terms of moral philosophy, this means an ascendancy from, for example, Thrasymachus, Hobbes, Marquis de Sade, Camus, Bauman, etc. (level 1); Pittacus, Protagoras, Hume, Hutcheson, Machiavelli, etc. (level 2); Plato, Socrates, Aristotle, Pascal, etc. (level 3); Aquinas, Locke, John Finnis, Rohr, Raz, etc. (level 4); Bentham, Hume, J. S. Mill, John Stuart; Sidgwick, Rawls, Notzick, etc. (level 5); Protagoras, Kant, Marx, Searle, Nozick, Adorno, Habermas, etc. (level 6); and finally Leopold, Boochin, Regan, Singer, etc. (level 7); Klikauer, T. 2012. *Seven Management Moralities*, Basingstoke: Palgrave, p. 59f.

13 plato.stanford.edu/entries/behaviorism/; plato.stanford.edu/entries/operationalism/.

14 https://chomsky.info/.

15 Chomsky, N. 1971. The case against B. F. Skinner, *The New York Review of Books*, 30th December, p. 31 (internet download).

16 Bugdol, M. 2018. *A Different Approach to Work Discipline*, London: Palgrave.

17 workplaceinfo.com.au/resources/employment-topics-a-z/disciplinary-action.

18 Wage theft occurs when employees work off the books, being forced to clock out early while continuing to work; pay is stolen by employer; they have been denied breaks and rest periods, etc. The website www.labor.ucla.edu/wage-theft/ notes that "every week workers in Los Angeles lose $26.2 million because of wage theft".

19 Amnesty International. 2017. Abuses in the Cobalt Supply Chain, 5 November 2017, Index Number: AFR 62/7395/2017 (https://www.amnesty.org, accessed: 17th January 2018).

20 Chomsky, N. 1971. The case against B. F. Skinner, *The New York Review of Books*, 30th December, p. 33 (internet download).

21 Blass, T. 2002. The man who shocked the world, *Psychology Today*, March/April, pp. 68–74; Milgram, S. 1971. *Obedience to Authority*, London: Tavistock Institute; Klikauer, T. 2014. Milgram and obedience to organizational authority, *Organization*, 21(6):947–951; Klikauer, T. 2014. Milgram and obedience to organizational authority, *Organization*, 21(6):947–951.

22 Ryan, L. 2015. *The Five Characteristics of Fear-Based Leaders* (forbes.com, 25th November 2015).

23 Aiello, J. R. 1993. Computer-based work monitoring: electronic surveillance and its effects, *Journal of Applied Social Psychology*, 23(7):499–507; Sewell, G. 1998. The discipline of teams: the control of team-based industrial work through electronic and peer surveillance, *Administrative Science Quarterly*, 43(2):397–428; Ball, K. 2010. Workplace surveillance: an overview, *Labor History*, 51(1):87–106; Elliott, E. S. & Long, G. 2016. Manufacturing rate busters: computer control and social relations in the labour process, *Work, Employment & Society*, 30(1):135–151.

24 Adorno, T. W. 1944. *Minima Moralia – Reflections from the Damaged Life* (trans. by Redmond, D. 2005: www.efn.org/~dredmond/MinimaMoralia; transl. by Jephcott, E. F. N. 1974), London: New Left Books, p. 22.

25 Magretta, J. 2012. *What Management Is: How It Works and Why It's Everyone's Business*, London: Profile, p. 4.

26 Macklin, R. 2007. The morally decent HR manager, in: Pinnington, A. et al. (eds.) *Human Resource Management – Ethics and Employment*, Oxford: Oxford University Press.

27 https://www.bbc.com/worklife/article/20191219-workplace-bullying-is-more-harmful-than-we-realised.

28 Rothlin, S. P. & McCann, D. P. 2016. HR governance and compliance: sexual harassment policy at international monetary fund, in: Zeuch, M. (eds.) *Handbook of HRM*, Heidelberg: Springer, p. 1106.

29 Berdahl, J. L. & Aquino, K. 2009. Sexual behavior at work: fun or folly?, *Journal of Applied Psychology*, 94(1):34.

30 Pierce, C. A., Byrne, D. & Aguinis, H. 1996. Attraction in organizations: a model of workplace romance, *Journal of Organizational Behavior*, 17(1):5–32.

31 Stasko, E. C. & Geller, P. A. 2015. Reframing sexting as a positive relationship behaviour, *American Psychological Association* (APA), pp. 6–9 (www.apa.org/news/press/releases/2015/08/reframing-sexting.pdf).

32  Nicole Salvaggio, A., Hopper, J. & Packell, K. M. 2011. Coworker reactions to observing sexual behavior at work, *Journal of Managerial Psychology*, 26(7):604–622.

33  Gallo, A. 2019. How to approach an office romance (and how not to), *Harvard Business Review* (https://hbr.org, 1st February 2019, accessed: 5th April 2019).

34  Shenoy-Packer, S. 2015. Immigrant professionals, microaggressions, and critical sensemaking in the US workplace, *Management Communication Quarterly*, 29(2):257–275.

35  https://www.bbc.com/news/business-53245501.

36  Sircar, O. & Jain, D. (eds.) 2016. *New Intimacies, Old Desires (LGBTI)*, Chicago, IL: Chicago University Press for Zubaan Books; see also: the Global Gender Gap Report (http://www3.weforum.org/docs/WEF_GGGR_2017.pdf).

37  Duffy, M. P. 2014. *Overcoming Mobbing: A Recovery Guide for Workplace Aggression and Bullying*, Oxford: Oxford University Press; Balcerzak, J. G. 2015. *Workplace Bullying: Clinical and Organizational Perspectives*, Washington, DC: NASW Press.

38  www.b21pubs.com/b21downloadables/Bullying_Policy/bullypol.doc.

39  Ruiz-Palomino, P. & Bañón-Gomis, A. 2016. The negative impact of chameleon-inducing personalities on employees' ethical work intentions: the mediating role of Machiavellianism, *European Management Journal* (online before print).

40  Hobbes, T. 1651. *Leviathan*, London: Dent.

41  Bloom, P. & Rhodes, C. 2018. *CEO Society*, London: Zed-Books (epub version), p. 265.

42  McCarthy, I. P., Hannah, D., Pitt, L. F. & McCarthy, J. M. 2020. Confronting indifference toward truth: dealing with workplace bullshit, *Business Horizons* (https://www.sciencedirect.com/science/article/pii/S000768132030001X, accessed: 15th June 2020).

43  Klikauer, T. 2015. Morality, competition, and the firm: the market failure, approach to business ethics, *Philosophy of Management*, 14(2):223–228.

44  Babiak, P. & Hare, R. D. 2006. *Snakes in Suits: When Psychopaths Go to Work*, New York: Regan Books; Boddy, C., Miles, D., Sanyal, C. & Hartog, M. 2015. Extreme managers, extreme workplaces: capitalism, organizations and corporate psychopaths, *Organization*, 22(4):530–551.

45  Bloom, P. & Rhodes, C. 2018. *CEO Society*, London: Zed-Books (epub version), p. 279.

46  Asch, S. E. 1955. Opinions and social pressure, *Scientific American*, (193):31–35.

47  Klikauer, T. 2007. *Communication and Management at Work*, Basingstoke: Palgrave; Klikauer, T. 2008. *Management and Communication – Communicative Ethics and Action*, Basingstoke: Palgrave.

48  Fleming, P. & Sturdy, A. 2009. *Just Be Yourself!: Towards Neo-normative Control in Organisations?*, *Employee Relations*, 31(6):569–583.

49  Klikauer, T. 2015. The ghost of education, *Australian University Review*, 57(1):93–95.

50  www.iep.utm.edu/virtue/.

51  Bolton, S. C. & Houlian, M. (eds.) 2008. *Searching for the Human in Human Resource Management*, Basingstoke: Palgrave.

52  https://edition.cnn.com/2020/10/22/business/goldman-sachs-1mdb-settlement/index.html.

53  plato.stanford.edu/entries/liberty-positive-negative/.

54  plato.stanford.edu/entries/liberty-positive-negative/.

55  https://edition.cnn.com/interactive/2021/06/business/asians-workplace-discrimination-covid/.

56  https://www.globalslaveryindex.org/.

57  www.lockheedmartin.com.au/.../corporate/.../ethics/code-of-conduct.pdf.

58  http://communicationtheory.org/management-by-objectives-drucker/.

59  Martin, G. & Pear, J. J. 2015. *Behavior Modification: What It Is and How to Do It* (10th ed.), New York: Psychology Press.

60  Raz, J. 1979. *The Authority of Law: Essays on Law and Morality*, Oxford: Clarendon Press; Head, M., Mann, S. & Matthews, I. 2016. *Law in Perspective: Ethics, Critical Thinking and Research*, Sydney: NewSouth Publishing.

61  Reich, R. 2016. The Majestic Inequality of the Law (www.the-american-interest.com, 19th January 2016, 5 pages).

62  Konrad, A. M. & Linnehan, F. 1995. Formalized HRM structures: coordinating equal employment opportunity or concealing organizational practices?, *Academy of Management Journal*, 38(3):787–820; Fox, C. 2017. *Stop Fixing Women: Why Building Fairer Workplaces Is Everybody's Business*, Sydney: NewSouth Publishing.

63 Doyle, A. 2020. Types of Discrimination in the Workplace (https://www.thebalancecareers.com/types-of-employment-discrimination-with-examples-2060914, updated June 23, 2020, accessed: 5th March 2021).

64 Thoroughgood, C. N. et al. 2020. Creating a trans-inclusive workforce, *Harvard Business Review*, 98(2):126–133.

65 Everly, B. A. & Schwarz, J. L. 2015. Predictors of the adoption of LGBT-friendly HR policies, *Human Resource Management*, 54(2):367–384; Sircar, O. & Jain, D. (eds.) 2016. *New Intimacies, Old Desires (LGBTI)*, Chicago, IL: Chicago University Press for Zubaan Books (Petrow, S. 2014. What is LGBTQ? https://www.washingtonpost.com, 23rd May 2014, accessed: 22nd January 2018).

66 www.bloomberg.com, 2nd March 2016, hsbc …unfair-dismissal).

67 Atzeni, M. 2016. Capitalism, workers organising and the shifting meanings of workplace democracy, *Labor History*, 57(3):374–389.

68 Johnstone, S. & Ackers, P. (eds.) 2015. *Finding a Voice at Work?: New Perspectives on Employment Relations*, Oxford: Oxford University Press; Harcourt, M. & Wood, G. E. 2004. *Trade Unions and Democracy: Strategies and Perspectives*, Manchester: Manchester University Press; Hodder, A. & Edwards, P. 2015. The essence of trade unions: understanding identity, ideology and purpose, *Work, Employment & Society*, 29(5):843–854.

69 Foley, J. R. & Polanyi, M. 2006. Workplace democracy: why bother?, *Economic and Industrial Democracy*, 27(1):173–191; Landemore, H. & Ferreras, I. 2016. In defense of workplace democracy: towards a justification of the firm-state analogy, *Political Theory*, 44(1):53–81.

70 Williamson, A. 2016. The bullock report on industrial democracy and the post-war consensus, *Contemporary British History*, 30(1):119–149; Emery, F. E. & Thorsrud, E. 2013. *Form and Content in Industrial Democracy: Some Experiences from Norway and Other European Countries*, London: Routledge; Blumberg, p. 1968; *Industrial Democracy: The Sociology of Participation*, London: Constable; Webb, S. & Webb, B. 1897. *Industrial Democracy*, London: Longmans, Green and Co.

71 Klikauer, T. 2014. *Seven Moralities of HRM*, Basingstoke: Palgrave, pp. 114–137.

72 Capaldi, N. 2005. Corporate social responsibility and the bottom line, *International Journal of Social Economics*, 32(5):408–423; DeGeorge, R. T. 2001. The myth of corporate social responsibility, in: Malachowski, A. R. (eds.) *Business Ethics – Critical Perspectives on Management Business and Management*, London: Routledge; DeGeorge, R. T. 2001. The myth of corporate social responsibility, in: Malachowski, A. R. (eds.), *Business Ethics – Critical Perspectives on Management Business and Management*, London: Routledge; IBM. 2013. *Corporate Responsibility* (http://www-07.ibm.com/ibm/au/responsibility/).

73 Cabanas, E. & Illouz, E. 2019. *Manufacturing Happy Citizens: How the Science and Industry of Happiness Control Our Lives*, Cambridge: Polity Press.

74 www.utilitarianism.com/mill2.htm; Windsor, D. 2016. Economic rationality and a moral science of business ethics, *Philosophy of Management*, 15(2):135–149.

75 https://www.careerbliss.com/facts-and-figures/careerbliss-50-happiest-companies-in-america-for-2020/.

76 Najeh, H. 2019. The function "chief happiness officer" and the double performance reality and perspectives in African countries case of B2S Morocco, *Journal of Behavior Studies in Organizations* (https://www.eurokd.com/Resources/Uploaded/Articles/0d6192ea8fea4c47a24be9d3ce9a6352/20200114224320BSO_Template_%200295.pdf).

77 www.corporatephilanthropyreport.com; https://hbr.org/2002/12/the-competitive-advantage-of-corporate-philanthropy; https://www.greenleft.org.au/content/big-charity-heist.

78 Clegg, S. et al. 2006. Business ethics as practice, *British Journal of Management*, 18(2):107–122.

79 Watson, D. 2003. *Death Sentence – The Decay of Public Language*, Sydney: Knopf, p. 48.

80 Greenberg, J. 1987. A taxonomy of organizational justice theories, *Academy of Management Review*, 12(1):9–22.

81 On 'seeking justice", Galloway (2018) noted, 'if you are seeking justice, you won't find it in the corporate world. You will be treated unfairly' (Galloway, S. 2018. *The Four: The Hidden DNA of Amazon, Apple, Facebook, and Google*, (eBook) New York: Portfolio, p. 432).

82 Rawls, J. 2001. *Justice as Fairness: A Restatement* (edited by Erin Kelly), London: Belknap Press.

83 Flick, G. A. 1984. *Natural Justice: Principles and Practical Application* (2nd ed.), Boston, MA: Butterworth Legal Publishers; Scutt, J. A. 2016. *Women and Magna Carta: A Treaty for Rights Or Wrongs?*, Basingstoke: Palgrave Macmillan.

84 Ceva, E. & Bocchiola, M. 2018. *Is Whistleblowing a Duty?*, London: Polity Press.

85 https://nader.org/; www.brockovich.com/.

86   Kramer, M. R. 2016. The ecosystem of shared value, *Harvard Business Review*, October Issue.

87   Keltner, D. 2016. Don't let power corrupt you, *Harvard Business Review*, October 2016; cf. https://www.transparency.org/cpi2015/.

88   Bishop, P. 2019. Kant and the categorical imperative, in: Bishop, P. (eds.) *German Political Thought and the Discourse of Platonism – Finding the Way Out of the Cave*, Cham: Springer, pp. 127–154.

89   Klikauer, T. 2015. HRM across the globe: a review essay, *Labour & Industry*, 25(3):250–256.

90   Höwing, T. 2016. (eds.) *The Highest Good in Kant's Philosophy*, Berlin: Walter de Gruyter Press; Paton, H. J. 1971. *The Categorical Imperative: A Study in Kant's Moral Philosophy*, Philadelphia: University of Pennsylvania Press.

91   Ellerman, D. 2015. On the renting of persons: the neo-abolitionist case against today's peculiar institution, *Economic Thought*, 4(1):1–20.

92   www.un.org/en/universal-declaration-human-rights/.

93   www.ilo.org/public/english/bureau/leg/declarations.htm; http://www.ilo.org/global/standards/introduction-to-international-labour-standards/conventions-and-recommendations/lang–en/index.htm; Klikauer, T. 2011. The ethics of the ILO, *Journal of Applied Ethics*, 1(2):33–56.

94   https://allthatsinteresting.com/lewis-hine-child-labor-photographs#15.

95   www.ilo.org/global/standards/lang–en/.

96   Llopis, G. 2011. Diversity Management Is the Key to Growth (www.forbes.com, 13th June 2011); de Anca, C. & Vazquez Vega, A. 2016. *Managing Diversity in the Global Organization: Creating New Business Values*, Heidelberg: Springer.

97   www.ohchr.org/Documents/Publications/GuideHRBusinessen.pdf.

98   Syed, J. & Ozbilgin, M. 2020. *Managing Diversity and Inclusion: An International Perspective*, London: Sage.

99   Klikauer, T. 2014. *Seven Moralities of HRM*, Basingstoke: Palgrave, pp. 185–209.

100  Hawken, P. 1993. *The Ecology of Commerce – A Declaration of Sustainability*, London: Phoenix; Iansiti, M. & Levien, R. 2004. Strategy as ecology, *Harvard Business Review*, 82(3):68–81; Winston, A. 2015. What business leaders need to know about the Paris climate conference, *Harvard Business Review*, 1st December 2015.

101  Gerdeman, D. 2014. What Do Chief Sustainability Officers Do? (www.forbes.com, 8th October 2014; http://www.elizabethwoyke.com/2016/05/23/rise-of-the-chief-sustainability-officer/; http://www.sustainabilityprofessionals/; Kiron, D., Kruschwitz, N., Haanaes, K. & Velken, I. V. S. 2012. Sustainability nears a tipping point, *Sloan Management Review*, 53(2):69.

102  Reinhardt, F. L. & Toffel, M. W. 2017. Managing climate change: lessons from the US navy, *Harvard Business Review*, July–August Issue; Renwick, D. W. S. 2018. *Contemporary Developments in Green HRM: Towards Sustainability in Action?*, London: Routledge; cf. https://ess-dive.lbl.gov/.

103  http://planetark.org/lowcarbon.cfm;   http://planetark.org/ourpartners/workplace-engagement.cfm; Cimadamore, A. D. et al. (eds.) 2016. *Development and Sustainability: The Challenge of Social Change*, London: Zed Books.

104  Bookchin, M. 1982. *The Ecology of Freedom: The Emergence and Dissolution of Hierarchy*, Palo Alto, CA: Cheshire Books; Bookchin, M. 1990. *The Philosophy of Social Ecology: Essays on Dialectical Naturalism*, Montréal: Black Rose Books; Iannone, A. P. 2016. *Practical Environmental Ethics*, New Brunswick: Transaction Publishers.

105  Mariappanadar, S. 2019. *Sustainable Human Resource Management*, London: Red Globe Press; Kalfagianni, A. 2020. *Routledge Handbook of Global Sustainability Governance*, London: Routledge; Rezaee, Z. 2019. *Business Sustainability in Asia*, Hoboken, NJ: Wiley & Sons; Malecki, C. 2018. *CSR Perspectives for Sustainable Corporate Governance*, Cheltenham: Edward Elgar; Molthan-Hill, P. 2017. *Business Student's Guide to Sustainable Management*, Saltaire: Greenleaf Publishing; Stringer, L. 2010. *The Green Workplace: Sustainable Strategies That Benefit Employees, the Environment, and the Bottom Line*, London: St. Martin's Publishing.

106  Mander, J. 2012. *The Capitalism Papers*, Berkeley, CA: Counter Point Press, p. 12.

107  Holland, P. 2019. *Contemporary HRM Issues in the 21st Century*, Bingley: Emerald Press, Chapter 11.

108  https://hrmi.org/green-hrm/.

109  https://sustainabledevelopment.un.org/post2015/transformingourworld.

110  https://www.nationalgeographic.com/environment/sustainable-earth/11-of-the-fastest-growing-green-jobs/.

111  Klikauer, T. 2013. Philosophy, business ethics and organisation theory: a review article, *Philosophy of Management*, 12(1):79–87; Klikauer, T. 2017. Business ethics as ideology?, *Critique*, 45(1–2):81–100; Hanlon, G. & Mandarini, M. 2015. On the impossibility of business ethics, in: Pullen, A. & Rhodes, C. (eds.) *Companion to Ethics, Politics and Organizations*, London: Routledge.

112  Mandalaki, E. & O'Sullivan, P. 2016. Organisational indulgences or abuse of indulgences: can good actions somehow wipe out corporate sins?, *M@n@gement*, 19(3):206 (http://www.management-aims.com/).

113  Elkington, J. 1998. *Cannibals with Forks: The Triple Bottom Line of 21st Century Business*, Gabriola Island: New Society Publishers; Gergen, C. & Vanourek, G. 2008. The triple bottom line, *Harvard Business Review*, 19th December 2008; Ralston, D. A., Egri, C. P., Karam, C. M., Naoumova, I., Srinivasan, N., Casado, T., Li, Y. & Alas, R. 2015. The triple-bottom-line of corporate responsibility: assessing the attitudes of present and future business professionals across the BRICs, *Asia Pacific Journal of Management*, 32(1):145–179; Kossek, E. E. 2016. Implementing organizational work–life interventions: toward a triple bottom line, *Community, Work & Family*, 19(2):242–256.

114  Deloitte. 2016. Business Ecosystems Come of Age (www2.deloitte.com).

115  Mander's eleven inherent rules of corporate behaviour (dieoff.org/page12).

116  Thiele, L. P. 2016. *Sustainability* (2nd ed.), Oxford: Polity Press.

117  http://www.un-documents.net/our-common-future.pdf.

118  Suzuki, D. & Hanington, I. 2017. *Just Cool It!: The Climate Crisis and What We Can Do*, Vancouver: Greystone Books.

119  McLaughlin, J. F., Hellmann, J. J., Boggs, C. L. & Ehrlich, P. R. 2002. Climate change hastens population extinctions, *Proceedings of the National Academy of Sciences*, 99(9):6070–6074; Wallace-Wells, D. 2017. *The Uninhabitable Earth* (http://nymag.com/, 9th July 2017, accessed: 5th January 2019); Attenborough, D. 2018. Climate Change 'Our Greatest Threat' (https://www.bbc.com/, 3rd December 2018, accessed: 5th January 2019); Jarvis, B. 2018. The Insect Apocalypse Is Here (https://www.nytimes.com/, 27th November 2018, accessed: 5th January 2019).

120  General Mills (generalmills.com with 43,000 employees, 2014) is "pledging to eliminate 28% of the greenhouse gas (GHG) emissions in its value chain by 2015" (wdi-publishing.com, 25th February 2016).

121  Climate model projections indicate that during the 21st century the global surface temperature is likely to rise a further 0.3 to 1.7C for their lowest emissions scenario using stringent mitigation and 2.6 to 4.8C for their highest.

122  Pennock, M., Poland, B. & Hancock, T. 2016. Resource depletion, peak oil, and public health: planning for a slow growth future, in: Kerr, R. B. (eds.), *Geographies of Health and Development*, Geographies of Health and Development, London: Routledge, p. 177; Hall, C. 2016. Predicting peak oil, *Science*, 352(6282):155–155; Reynes, S. J. O. F. & Hofkes, M. W. 2015. Modeling peak oil and the geological constraints on oil, *Review of Economics and Statistics*, (72):1–10; Tuck, R. & Mittelman, R. 2015. Say when: a theory of peak social benefit, *Academy of Management Proceedings*, (1):17122.

123  https://en.wikipedia.org/wiki/Climate_Change_Performance_Index; https://www.climate-change-performance-index.org/.

124  http://data.worldbank.org/indicator/EN.ATM.CO2E.PC.

125  globalcarbonatlas.org/?q=en/emissions; carbonfootprintofnations.com/.

126  https://www.wwf.org.au/get-involved/change-the-way-you-live/ecological-footprint-calculator.

127  Iannone, A. P. 2016. *Practical Environmental Ethics*, New Brunswick: Transaction Publishers; Pojman, L. P., Pojman, P. & McShane, K. 2016. *Environmental Ethics: Readings in Theory and Application* (7th ed.), Boston, MA: Cengage Learning.

128  www.deepecology.org/deepecology; Naess, A. 1973. The shallow and the deep, long-range ecology movement, *Inquiry*, (16):94–100; Naess, A. 1989. *Ecology, Community, Lifestyle* (trans. by Rothenberg), Cambridge: Cambridge University Press.

129  Crutzen, P. J. 2002. Geology of mankind, *Nature* (January 3), 415(6867):23; Gardiner, S. M. & Thompson, A. 2015. *Oxford Handbook of Environmental Ethics*, Oxford: Oxford University Press; Fassbinder, S. D. 2017. The literature of the anthropocene: four reviews, *Capitalism Nature Socialism*, 28(1):139–148.

130  Gardner, D. 2011. *GrowthBusters – Hooked on Growth* (DVD/video), Colorado Springs: Citizen-Powered Media. www.growthbusters.org/.

131   De Vos, A. & Van der Heijden, B. (eds.) 2015. *Handbook of Research on Sustainable Careers*, Northampton: Edward Elgar.
132   Gerdeman, D. 2014. What Do Chief Sustainability Officers Do? (www.forbes.com, 8th October 2014).
133   Colbert, B. A. & Kurucz, E. C. 2007. Three conceptions of triple bottom line business sustainability and the role for HRM, *People and Strategy*, 30(1):21; Gloet, M. 2006. Knowledge management and the links to HRM: developing leadership and management capabilities to support sustainability, *Management Research News*, 29(7):402–413; Dubois, C. L. & Dubois, D. A. 2012. Strategic HRM as social design for environmental sustainability in organizations, *Human Resource Management*, 51(6):799–826; Kramar, R. & Mariappanadar, S. 2015. Call for papers for a special issue: sustainable human resource management, *Asia Pacific Journal of Human Resources*, 53(3):389–392; Goswami, T. G. & Ranjan, S. K. 2015. Green HRM: approach to sustainability in current scenarios, *Journal for Studies in Management and Planning*, 1(4):250–259.
134   Burg, N. 2013. How to Become a Carbon Neutral Business (www.forbes.com, 18th June 2013).
135   www.greenrecruitmentcompany.com/; for example through "green recruitment" (paperless); Henderson, H. 2014. *Becoming a Green Building Professional: A Guide to Careers in Sustainable Architecture, Design, Engineering, Development, and Operations*, Hoboken, NJ: Wiley & Sons.

## Further Readings

Adler, P. 2015. The Environmental Crisis and Its Capitalist Roots, *ASQ*, 60(2):13–25.
Armstrong, A. 2013. *Ethics and Justice for the Environment*, Milton Park: Routledge.
Attfield, R. 2014. *Environmental Ethics* (2nd ed.), Oxford: Polity.
Banji, M. R., Baerman, M. H. & Chugh, D. (2011) How (Un)ethical Are You? HBR (eds.) *HBR's 10 Must Reads – On Managing People*, Cambridge: Harvard Business School Press.
Barak, G. (eds.) 2015. *Routledge Handbook of the Crimes of the Powerful*, London: Routledge.
Barendregt, B. & Jaffe, R. (eds.) 2014. *Green Consumption*, London: Bloomsbury.
Barker, B. et al. 2013. Employee Integration in CSR, *Labour & Industry*, 23(1):34–53.
Birsch, D. & Fielder, J. H. (eds.) 1994. *The Ford Pinto Case*, Albany: State University of New York Press.
Boylan, M. 2014. *Business Ethics* (2nd ed.), Chichester: John Wiley & Sons.
Chambers, N., Simmons, C. & Wackernagel, M. 2014. *Sharing Nature's Interest: Ecological Footprints as an Indicator of Sustainability*, London: Routledge.
Cohen, A. 2015. *Fairness in the Workplace*, New York: Palgrave.
Cooper, T. L. 2012. *The Responsible Administrator* (6th ed.), San Francisco, CA: Jossey-Bass.
Eiglad, E. 2015. *Social Ecology and Social Change*, Porsgrunn: New Compass Press.
Fehr, R. et al. 2015. Moralized Leadership, *Academy of Management Review*, 40(2):182–209.
Felber, C. 2015. *Change Everything: Creating an Economy for the Common Good*, London: Zed-Books
Fleming, P. & Jones, T. M. 2013. *The End of CSR*, London: Sage.
Fooks, G. et al. 2013. The Limits of CSR, *Journal of Business Ethics*, 112(2):283–299.
Garbie, I. 2016. *Sustainability in Manufacturing Enterprises*, Heidelberg: Springer.
Hannigan, J. 2014. *Environmental Sociology* (3rd ed.), London: Routledge.
Hawken, P. 2010. *The Ecology of Commerce: A Declaration of Sustainability*, New York: Harper.
HR. 2014. *Human Rights Watch Report 2014*, New York: Seven Stories Press.
Hulme, D. 2015. *Global Poverty: How Global Governance Is Failing the Poor*, Milton Park: Routledge.
Hurst, D. 2014. *New Ecology of Leadership*, New York: University Press.
Hutchinson, J. 2012. Rethinking Workplace Bullying as an ER Problem, *Journal of IR*, 54(5):637–652.
Jackall, R. 2010. *Moral Mazes: The World of Corporate Managers*, Oxford: Oxford University Press.
Jamali, D. et al. 2015. Exploring HRM's Roles in CSR, *Business Ethics*, 24(2):125–143.
James, S. P. 2015. *Environmental Philosophy*, Cambridge: Polity Press.
Jurkiewicz, C. L. 2015. *The Foundations of Organizational Evil*, London: Routledge.

Kemper, A. 2012. Saving the Planet, *Harvard Business Review*, 1st April.

Kirsch, S. 2014. Imagining Corporate Personhood, *Political & Legal Anthropology Review*, 37(2):207–217.

Klare, M. 2015. Is the Age of Renewable Energy Already Upon Us? (www.tomdispatch.com).

Klein, N. 2014. *This Changes Everything: Capitalism Vs. the Climate*, London: Penguin.

Klikauer, T. 2013. *Managerialism*, Basingstoke: Palgrave-Macmillan.

Loomis, E. 2015. *Out of Sight: The Long & Disturbing Story of Corp. Outsourcing Catastrophe*, London: New Press.

Lussier, R. N. & Sherman, H. 2014. *Business, Society, and Government Essentials*, New York: Routledge.

Macklin, R. 2007. The Morally Decent HR Manager, in: Pinnington, A. et al. (eds.) *Human Resource Management – Ethics and Employment*, Oxford: Oxford University Press.

Monahan, T. 2015. The Right to Hide, *Communication & Critical/Cultural Studies*, 12(2):159–178.

Myers, V. L. 2014. *Exploring Management Perspectives of Calling & Work Ethics*, London: Routledge.

Nicholson, S. & Wapner, P. (eds.) 2015. *Global Environmental Politics*, Boulder, CO: Paradigm Publishers.

Pedersen, E. R. G. 2015. *Corporate Social Responsibility*, London: Sage.

Porter, M. E. & Reinhardt, F. L. 2007. A Strategic Approach to Climate, *Harvard Business Review*, 85:22.

Radkau, J. 2014. *The Age of Ecology*, Oxford: Polity Press.

Rees W. & Porter C. 2015. *Skills of Management*, London: Palgrave, Chapter 13, Disciplinary Handling.

Romani, L. & Szkudlarek, B. 2014. The Struggles of the Interculturalists: Professional Ethical Identity and Early Stages of Codes of Ethics Development, *Journal of Business Ethics*, 119(2):173–191.

Root, T. (eds.) 2015. *Biodiversity in a Changing Climate*, Los Angeles: University of California Press.

Royce, E. 2015. *Classical Social Theory & Modern Society*, Lanham, MD: Rowman & Littlefield.

Sandoval, M. 2014. *From Corporate to Social Media: Critical Perspectives on CSR*, London: Routledge.

Scalet, S. 2014. *Markets, Ethics, and Business Ethics*, Boston, MA: Pearson.

Schneider, B. et al. 2014. *Oxford Handbook of Organizational Climate & Culture*, Oxford: Oxford University Press.

Siddiqui, S. 2015. Silicon Valley Stands Up to Anti-Gay Laws, *Guardian Weekly*, 192(18):10.

Silva, M. R. & Caetano, A. 2014. Organizational Justice: What Changes, What Remains the Same?, *Journal of Organizational Change Management*, 27(1): 3.

Singer, P. 2013. *A Companion to Ethics*, New York: Wiley.

Smith, H. et al. 2013. Discrimination in the Workplace, *Advances in Management*, 6(2):3–9.

Spinello, R. A. 2014. *Global Capitalism, Culture, and Ethics*, New York: Routledge.

Sweeney, S. 2015. Green Capitalism Won't Work, *New Labor Forum*, 24(2):12–17.

Thiele, L. P. 2013. *Sustainability*, Oxford: Polity Press.

Upchurch, M. 2014. The Internet, Social Media & Workplace, *International Journal of Socialism*, 141:119–138.

Utting, P. 2015. *Social and Solidarity Economy*, London: Zed Books.

Van der Graaf, S. 2015 Participatory Culture?, in: *Handbook of Digital Transformations*, London: Elgar.

Van Gramberg, B., Teicher, J. & O'Rourke, A. 2014. Managing Electronic Communications: A New Challenge for HR Managers, *International Journal of HRM*, 25(16):2234–2252.

Weisman, S. R. 2015. *The Great Trade Off: Confronting Moral Conflicts in the Age of Globalization*, Washington, DC: Peterson Institute.

WWF. 2014. World Living Planet Report (www.worldwildlife.org/pages/living-planet-report-2014).

# 11 Green HRM

## People, Planet, Performance

### Executive Summary

Green HRM focuses on the contribution of HRM at company level in directing firms towards sustainability. Based on several key reports by international agencies such as the United Nations and the Brundtland report issued during the past decades, companies have not just realised the impact of global warming but have also started to move towards sustainability. Supporting this, Green HRM focuses on the micro level (firms), the meso level (industry), and the macro level (national and international). Green HRM has been working in six areas of HRM. These are environmental or green recruitment; green industrial relations; green employees training and development; green performance management; green compensation; and green strategic HRM. Transitioning from non-sustainable business practices towards sustainability inextricably demands organisational change where Green HRM offers four models.

### Key Learning Objectives

1. Realise the importance of Green HRM for businesses;
2. Describe the key characteristics of sustainable people management;
3. Understand the ways in which GHRM contributes to sustainability;
4. Link core elements of HRM to sustainable people management;
5. Identify the impact of GHRM on an organisation;
6. Ascertain the influence of global sustainability on Green HRM;
7. Comprehend Green stakeholders in HRM;
8. Describe change management and its links to Green HRM; and
9. Develop a formal HR policy on Green HRM.

### Managing People Sustainably

HRM operates with two terms that signify HRM's move towards environmental sustainability.[1] One term is **Sustainable HRM** (SHRM), the other one Green HRM (GHRM). Since SHRM can easily be confused with **Strategic HRM** (SHRM), this book prefers the term GHRM in order to avoid a potential strategic vs. sustainability confusion.

Green HRM is still in its early stages. Despite this, Green HRM has become a pressing issue for HR managers, CEOs, boardroom, and corporate leaders[2] as well as employees.[3] In many cases, the drive to improve an organisation's **environmental**

DOI: 10.4324/9781003293637-11

**performance**[4] comes from *external* rather than *internal* stakeholders. Perhaps one of the clearest indications for an organisational need to become sustainable has been the United Nations' IPCC reports. The IPCC has recently issued its 6th report.[5]

Apart from the universal agreement among scientists on the issue of global warming,[6] there have also been numerous – and more popular – descriptions on what the world is facing under global warming.[7] Recently, the impact of human beings on our climate has been termed the **Anthropocene**[8] or **Capitalocene**.[9] Already in the year 2007, the *Harvard Business Review* demanded to "Take Responsibility for Climate Change".[10] Outside of business, the foremost expressions of the impact of global warming[11] on our world are:

- McKibben's *The End of Nature* (1990) as well as his *Falter* (2019)[12] and
- Wallace-Wells' *The Uninhabitable Earth*.[13]

Some of the harshest critiques on Green HRM are likely to argue that given the magnitude of what the world is facing under global warming,[14] Green HRM is nothing more than **Greenwashing**.[15] Greenwashing is a compound word modelled on whitewashing. It combines "green" and "washing". Greenwashing opponents argue that Green HRM is a mix of marketing spin, propaganda, and public relations (PR).[16] Under greenwashing, green PR, green values, and green marketing are deceptively used to persuade the public that a business organisation and its products, aims, and policies are sustainable and environmentally friendly and therefore *better*.[17] Evidence an organisation is greenwashing often comes from pointing out the spending differences. Significantly more money and time is spent on advertising being *green* than is actually spent on environmentally sound practices. Greenwashing therefore is a *mask* used to cover up unsustainable corporate agendas.

Despite accusations like these, various management initiatives like the 3P's – *people, planet, profits*[18] also known as the **triple bottom line**[19] (TBL[20] or 3BL – some say "crippled bottom line"[21]) have been developed and are in practice.[22] The TBL is an accounting framework emphasising on three parts: social, environmental (e.g. ecological) sustainability,[23] and financial performance.[24] Many organisations have adopted the TBL framework to evaluate their environmental performance, create greater business value, and improve their eco-friendly reputation.[25] In all of these initiatives, Green HRM plays a vital role.

## The Emergence of Green HRM

HRM has developed responses to global warming,[26] also called climate change.[27] Green HRM can be seen as organisational HR practices that enhance environmental sustainability. This, of course, means that Green HRM focuses on achieving an organisation's ecological goals based on long-term strategies. In that, the task of Green HRM can be seen as both proactive and reactionary. On the proactive side, it seeks to implement green HR strategies whilst on the reactionary side it seeks to prevent harm, e.g. harm reduction. One of the most common ways to identify HRM (without the Green) has been to contrast the Harvard (soft) with the Michigan (hard[28]) Model of HRM.[29] Doing this for Green HRM, the following picture emerges (Table 11.1)[30]:

*Table 11.1* The Harvard (Soft) vs. the Michigan (Hard) Model of GHRM

|   | *Harvard GHRM* | *Michigan GHRM* |
|---|---|---|
| 1 | Sustainable stakeholders | Shareholder |
| 2 | Socio-environmental system | Individual perspective |
| 3 | Environmental wellbeing | Organisational effectiveness |
| 4 | Sustainability perspective | Corporate perspective |

Overall, one might like to argue that the softer Harvard model of HRM is preordained for Green HRM because it has a longer-term and strategic focus while focusing on longer-range workforce planning; it favours strong, regular, and above all, two-way communication. It empowers employees – also called **green-collar workers**[31] – favours delegation, and encourages responsibility. Its appraisal system focuses on addressing training inside flatter organisational structures. Finally, its more democratic leadership style fits the demands of Green HRM as well as sustainability approaches.

The Harvard model also furnishes what is known as **environmental impact hypothesis** which denotes that the actual cost of implementing Green HRM is beneficial to an organisation. The **available funds hypothesis** suggests that good management relies on Green HRM to encourage environmental performance based on an organisation ⇔ stakeholder interface.[32] The task for Green HRM is to encourage employees to achieve **eco-efficiency indicators** that focus on the reduction of water usage, cutbacks in energy consumption, resource efficiency, and waste elimination.[33] The goal of Green HRM is to preserve the long term health of the earth's ecological system – a global moral goal that exists irrespective of monetary values.

This reaches well beyond the confinements of traditional HRM (companies and corporations). In this understanding, Green HRM contains a macro-, meso-, and micro level as shown in Table 11.2:

*Table 11.2* Three Levels of Green HRM

| *Level* | *Engagement of Green HRM* |
|---|---|
| Macro | Multilateral institutions, the United Nations, global NGOs, society, states |
| Meso | Industrial relations systems, trade unions, employer and industry associations, etc. |
| Micro | Organisational context, recruitment, performance management, operations management |

At the macro level, Green HRM might have originated in the Club of Rome's *Limits to Growth* report of 1972.[34] A second macro-environmental initiative came with the United Nation's *World Commission on Environment and Development* (WCED – known as the Brundtland Report, 1987).[35] This was followed by various UN summits like the *Rio Earth Summit* (1992), the Copenhagen summit (2009), etc.

Most specifically, the Brundtland report highlighted the accelerated deterioration of the global environment and our natural resources. It was flanked by numerous environmental disasters that have occurred, ranging from the infamous London Smog in 1952, followed by the Minamata Mercury Poisoning (Japan, 1956), Seveso (Italy, 1976), Three Miles Island (USA, 1979), Bhopal (India, 1984) to Chernobyl and BSE in Europe (both in 1986), Exxon Valdez (1989), Jilin (China, 2005), BP Oil (Gulf of Mexico, 2010), Fukushima (Japan, 2011), Samarco Dam Collapse (Brazil, 2016), etc.[36]

One of the macro outcomes was, for example, the **Global Reporting Initiative**[37] supporting Green HRM's development of HR policies (micro level) that focus on sustainability, specific organisational action plans for an eco-friendly organisation,[38] highlight data on potential impacts of organisational activities on the environment and list objectives that create corporate sustainability. In supporting these, Green HRM focuses on two key elements:

1.  **Green Stakeholders**: Green HRM's consultation with stakeholders via employee blogs and forums, community advisory panels, market research on reputational issues, scanning industry trends, etc.[39]
2.  **Green Practices**: The development of policies on corporate sustainability; creating specific organisational action plans; and the assessment of potentially positive and negative impacts on sustainability.

Today about 92% of the largest 250 global corporations issue sustainability reports and 73% of the largest 100 national companies in 45 countries issue such reports.[40] In 2019, the world's ten most sustainable firms were: Chr. Hansen Holding, Kering SA, Nestle, Orsted, GlaxoSmithKline, Prologis, Inc., Banco do Brasil, Shinhan Financial Group, and Taiwan Semiconductor.[41] Similar to this, the **Dow Jones Sustainability Index**[42] which evaluates the sustainability performance of thousands of companies trading publicly is the longest-running global sustainability benchmark worldwide. When Green HRM assists management in compiling sustainability reports, environmental HR managers focus on six key issues:

1.  Accuracy: information is sufficiently accurate;
2.  Balance: positives and negatives are highlighted;
3.  Clarity: the report is understandable and accessible;
4.  Comparability: the report allows to analyse environmental performance over time;
5.  Reliability: sound information gathering processes are used; and
6.  Timeliness: the environmental report is issued on a regular schedule

Beyond sustainable reporting, Green HRM has ten characteristics: long-term orientation, care for employees, care for the environment, employee participation,[43] employee development, external partnerships, flexibility, adherence to industrial relations and labour regulation, cooperation,[44] fairness, and equality. These Green characteristics assist organisations in achieving three goals: (1) supporting a precautionary approach to environmental challenges; (2) commencing environmental initiatives that promote environmental responsibility; and finally, (3) inspire the development and diffusion of eco-friendly technologies and workplace practices. Coming from external regulation, Green HRM adopts the **compliance approach** or the **deterrence approach**:

1.  Green HRM's **compliance approach** sees a positive role in civil environmental regulation because it highlights the role of stakeholders (NGOs, etc.) in building and maintaining our natural environment;
2.  Green HRM's **deterrence approach** relies on state initiated sanctions against companies and corporations for breaching environmental rules and laws.

## The Environmental Management System

In either case, Green HRM needs to be aligned with a company's **environmental management system** (EMS).[45] In a company's EMS, Green HRM supports the creation of competitive advantage through environmental developments, develops environmental sensitivities in management and employees, supports individual and altruistic motivation, lowers the potentials for environmental harm inside and outside a business organisation, creates a sustainable corporate assistance programme,[46] supports sustainability wellness, and advances a pro-environmental action programme to preserve the eco system. Next to instrumental, social, and political GHRM,[47] there are four versions of sustainable HRM[48]:

*Table 11.3* Four Types of Green HRM

| | Type of HRM | Key Features |
|---|---|---|
| ⇧ | Common Good HRM | Ecological-sustainable development; sustainable working conditions; economic democracy |
| ⇧ | 3P HRM | Focuses on people, planet, profits; sustainable economy; and workers' wellbeing |
| ⇧ | Sustainable HRM | Involving employees to reduce carbon footprint |
| ⇧ | Socially Responsible HRM | Sustainable values are used to enhance the social reputation and attractiveness of the company |

Table 11.3 shows four approaches to Green HRM ranked in order of their seriousness (1 → 4). At the lowest level (Table 11.3[4]), Green HRM is simply used to enhance the reputation of a company and to make companies and corporations look good externally. At the second lowest level (Table 11.3[3]), Green HRM is engaged with the reduction of a company's carbon footprint which is a vital activity of sustainability.[49] At the second highest level (Table 11.3[2]), Green or 3P HRM involves broader aspects of sustainability such as creating a sustainable economy while simultaneously improving the social, psychological, and environmental wellbeing of employees. At the highest level (Table 11.3[1]), Green HRM becomes **Common Good HR**. This is where Green HRM moves truly into sustainability seen as an eco-friendly development. Common Good GHRM also creates sustainable working conditions. At the highest level, Green HRM moves towards **economic democracy**, i.e. the thorough involvement of employees and trade unions inside a company. Table 11.3 shows a clear ascendency towards Common Good HRM (no. 1). To various degrees, Green HRM focuses on six key areas of sustainable human resource management.

## Six Key Areas of Sustainable People Management

Green HRM has identified six core areas in which it engages to create environmental sustainability. It starts at the very beginning of employment. The initial subject Green HRM engages in is (1) environmental recruitment and selection. The second area is (2) green industrial relations, followed by (3) green employee training and development, (4) green performance management, (5) green compensation, and finally (6) strategic green HRM.[50]

### 1. Green Recruitment

Attracting environmentally conscious staff is a key challenge for Green HRM. Many companies and corporations have begun to realise the fact that gaining a positive environmental reputation as a green employer is a successful way to attract young and new employees.[51] Companies like IKEA, Panasonic, Patagonia, Siemens, BASF, IBM, Bayer, Mannesmann, Unilever, etc. use corporate environmental activities and green initiatives to attract high-quality staff. Some companies and corporations make environmental accountabilities[52] and employee qualifications part of their new pro-environmental job profile.

Progressively, eco-friendly job descriptions with environmental elements have been included for employees within Green HRM's environmentally friendly recruitment agenda. Green HRM's environmental recruitment is based on a green HR policy (e.g. a statement of intent) that governs the **environmental recruitment and selection**[53] process, e.g. less paper and more online; virtual interviewing (Skype, Zoom, etc.); and digital portfolio presentation. This saves $CO_2$ emissions as, for example, a 630 km trip by car creates 380 kg of $CO_2$, by train 65 kg, and during a video interview: between 0.8 kg and 1.1 kg.[54] Green HRM's recruitment and selection is defined as the process of hiring employees with knowledge, skills, and behaviours conducive to a company's environmental management systems.

Green HRM's recruitment practices support effective environmental management by making sure that new entrants are familiar with the organisation's environmental culture, policies, initiatives, reputation, and are capable of maintaining the organisation's environmental values.[55] In turn, this also means that an organisation is sensitive towards the needs of a prospective employee in terms of, for example, a **green work–life balance**.[56]

Green HRM's environmental recruitment and selection system focuses on the significance and importance of an organisation's sustainable environment. New recruits become aware that this is a major element within the organisation. Green HRM seeks to select new recruits who are enthusiastic – and perhaps even passionate – about being employed by an organisation that supports environmental sustainability.

Recruiting candidates with an environmental awareness supports an organisational fit for firms reflecting on an environmental organisational culture also known as *green corporate culture*.[57] Green HRM selects professionals who depict an awareness of corporate sustainable processes and are, to some extent, familiar with eco-friendly initiatives like *re*-cycling and *up*-cycling[58] – known as the creative reuse of products to transform by-products, waste materials or useless, and unwanted products into new materials or products perceived to be of greater quality and environmental value. It also includes energy conservation and the design of a low-carbon workplace[59] with the goal of creating a more environmentally friendly world.[60]

Green recruitment and selection is keenly aware of the impact of local environmental standards for a company. Newly recruited employees with an environmental commitment to a company add to the eco-profile of a company.[61] Such newly recruited professionals are more concerned with respecting and working towards the environmental strategies of a company.

Green recruitment provides employers with opportunities to reach ahead of the business world. It increases a company's environmental reputation and its ability to attract environmentally conscious candidates as well as retain them after the completion of the company's induction programme. As a consequence, Green HRM's environmental recruitment and selection process has to be aligned with virtually all environmentally friendly aspects of a business organisation.

Green recruitment and selection is further enhanced by a company's passion for achieving environmental goals. In turn, Green recruitment and selection focuses on how potential job seekers perceive and rate a business organisation's sustainability. In the environmental recruitment and selection process, Green HRM focuses on green job descriptions,[62] eco-friendly locations of the firm, paperless interviewing processes, and adjacent practices in the recruitment portfolio. Potential recruits are made aware of the company's environmental policies and its commitment to eco-friendly goals.

### 2. Green Industrial Relations

Industrial relations remains a key issue for HRM. Green HRM continues to be committed to establishing a positive employer ⇔ trade union relationship. In this relationship, union "members want their unions to take a leading role".[63] Such a positive relationship facilitates individual as well as corporate motivation. It entices the environmental morale of employees and has been shown to lead to increased productivity. The concept of industrial relations involves trade unions as well as employee participation and empowerment activities. Together with trade unions, Green HRM can build what has been called **climate solidarity**.[64]

Good industrial relations prevent and resolve organisational problems that arise at the workplace. In fact, environmental industrial relations create intangible and enduring assets and sources directed towards competitive advantage for any organisation.[65] Trade union and employee participation[66] in Green initiatives – known as **Green EI** (employees' involvement[67]) – increases environmental management as it aligns employees' goals, capabilities, motivations, and perceptions with eco-friendly organisational practices and environmental management systems (EMS).

Involving trade unions and employees in EMS improves an organisation's efficient resource usage. It leads to reducing waste and pollution from companies and corporations. Beyond that, individual empowerment positively influences productivity and environmental performance and facilitates self-control, individual environmental initiatives, and environmental problem-solving skills.

The scope of Green IR extends beyond the confinements of companies and corporations. Green IR broadens eco-friendly initiatives as well as suggestion schemes directed towards environmental sustainability within an organisation. Under Green IR, each employee from top-management to the lowest level gets an opportunity to contribute to environmental schemes. Green HRM assists a practice that will help creating greater awareness on environmental issues. It will foster sustainable ideas for eco-friendly organisational practices. Green HRM is inextricably linked to **engagement theory**[68] that features four elements:

1. **psychological safety**: an organisational environment in which employees can develop trust to engage in environmental issues;
2. **psychological availability**: a positive influence on the development of self-esteem to find the confidence to make valuable suggestions towards sustainability;
3. **values**: to positively engage with the value of environmentalism[69]; and
4. **purpose**: to find positive rationale for the support of sustainability.

Other benefits of trade union and employee involvement are improvements in employee and organisational health and safety as well as the development of an eco-friendly organisational culture that can be promoted via sustainability brochures, mini-lectures, a green concierge, etc. Green HRM will keep sustainable policies in place and encourages long-term trust among the management, trade unions, and employees. Green IR will build opportunities for trade unions and employees to express eco-friendly ideas at the workplace and help create climate conducive green management practices and systems.

### 3. Green Training and Development

*Green Employee Training and Development* (GEDT) is a practice that focuses on the development of employees' environmental skills, sustainable knowledge, and eco-friendly attitudes. In this, what is known as the **Green Skills Manifesto**[70] focuses on eight areas: (1) government leadership, (2) consultations, (3) training the workforce, (4) green apprenticeships, (5) local authorities, (6) curriculum changes, (7) employers, and (8) building alliances. All of these assist the development of such knowledge, skills, abilities, and attitudes. GEDT can foster **Employees' Green Behaviours** (EGBs[71]) based on employees that carry positive green values. EGB demand an acute awareness in five key areas[72]:

1. **conserving's 4R's**: reusing, recycling, repurposing, and reducing;
2. **work sustainably**: positive environmental performance;
3. **avoid harm**: reduce negative environmental behaviours;
4. **influence others**: educate, engage, and motivate; and
5. **take initiative**: fostering an environmental entrepreneurial spirit.

Much of this demands green training and development that educates employees about the value of sustainability. For that, Green HRM often conducts a **needs analysis** (Chapter 4). This consists of three elements:

1. **organisational analysis**: does the organisation need people with environmental skills, knowledge, and abilities;
2. **personal analysis**: what kind of employees have the right environmental attitude and can be selected to be offered training on sustainability issues;
3. **task analysis**: what are the environmental tasks to be performed and what kind of training needs to be provided (external-vs.-internal, etc.).

GEDT trains employees in working methods that conserve energy, reduce wastage, and spread environmental awareness and an environmental culture within an organisation. It also provides opportunity to engage employees in environmental problem-solving. Green HRM's GEDT activities make employees aware of different aspects and values of environmental sustainability. It helps them embrace different organisational methods of conservation including waste management. Furthermore, GEDT sharpens the skill of an employee to deal with different environmental issues. When managers focus on best management practices, they are encouraged to include environmental training and education. Such best environmental HRM practices can be seen from three perspectives:

1. The **Best Practice Perspective**: it indicates the best environmental practices applied by Green HRM to facilitate environmental performance in organisations[73];
2. The **Contingency Perspective**: this approach highlights the effects of contingent variables such as industry size and types, etc. on an organisation's environmental performance; and,
3. The **Configuration Perspective**: it examines patterns of multiple interdependent HRM variables such as various HRM practices on the environmental performance of an organisation.

GEDT also establishes a favourable environmental organisational culture among employees. Under such an organisational environmental culture, employees feel that they are part of the environmental outcomes of a company. GEDT is one of the most important GHRM processes that facilitate the achievement of an organisation's environmental goals. Green HRM identifies five goals to ascertain GEDT:

1.  Raise the alertness and commitment of employees about sustainability;
2.  Equip employees with environmental skills and knowledge to make a positive contribution;
3.  Train employees in methods to conserve energy, reduce waste, etc.;
4.  Coach environmental problem-solving skills; and finally,
5.  Enable employees to shift a traditional to a sustainable organisational culture.

The role of GHRM's GEDT is to maintain a sustainable organisational culture. This suggests that an organisation's HR department also offers environmental leadership – **green leaders**[74] – training and workshops to help management develop environmental people skills and behavioural competencies. It also means that Green HRM moves itself towards sustainability by, for example, moving most HR functions online. Green HRM focuses on the development of environmentally supportive senior management furnished with competencies to facilitate strategic environmental planning.

GEDT fosters teamwork (e.g. green teams, recycling teams, etc.), diversity, and an organisational culture that fosters collaboration directed towards sustainability. Green organisations train their employees on best environmental business practices that are, in many cases, linked to external green initiatives.[75] Supported by sustainable training and education initiatives, employees will be adept to educate other stakeholders like suppliers, customers, etc. regarding the advantages of becoming more earth-friendly organisations.

### 4. Green Performance Management

Green performance management (GPM) is the process by which employees are prompted to enhance their environmental skills that help achieve sustainable organisational goals and objectives.[76] GPM can be seen as "a system of evaluating activities of employees" performance in the environmental management process.[77] Green HRM fosters an alignment of environmental business strategies with GPM. An overall business strategy needs to be linked to environmental performance management. This, in turn, will also influence green organisational initiatives in various aspects.

GPM consists of issues related to environmental concerns and policies of an organisation. Green performance management concentrates on the usage of environmental responsibilities. Green HRM deals with GPM by introducing company-wide environmental performance standards, Green information systems, and **environmental auditing**.[78] These allow an environmentally friendly organisation as well as Green HRM to gain and understand useful data on environmental performance – known as **eco-literacy**[79] – and, initiated by employees, this leads to the greening of the business performance matrix.[80] Green HRM knows that the environmental performance of an organisation depends largely on three aspects:

1.  Employee involvement and empowerment;
2.  A positive environmental organisational culture; and
3.  Classical HR issues such as recruitment, EDT, and trade unions.

Similar to traditional performance management, the most important aspect of GPM remains the performance appraisal. In addition to meeting the criteria of reliability, validity, and fairness, a green performance appraisal (GPA) provides useful feedback to employees and supports the continuous environmental improvement of companies and corporations.

The GPA concerns the need for managers to be held accountable for an organisation's environmental performance in addition to other performance objectives. Green HRM suggests that green performance appraisals focus on five key issues:

1. environmental incidents,
2. environmental responsibilities,
3. the communication of environmental policy,
4. green information systems, and
5. environmental auditing.

Green HRM will assure that job descriptions are aligned with the environmental tasks and goals of an organisation. It also assures that these environmental objectives are achieved. Green HRM relies on three broad motivational theories: the (A) **goal-setting theory** notes that people are motivated by specific environmental challenges on which they can receive feedback rather than a general "try your best" attitude. The (B) **self-determination theory** argues that employees are motivated by activities that they enjoy and find meaningful. Finally, the (C) **job characteristic theory** suggests that employees are motivated when performing work that is autonomous, significant, varied, complete, and provides feedback. Sustainability is an area in which Green HRM can focus on B and C rather than A. Aligned to these theories is the **AMO model** – ability, motivation, opportunity. Green HRM supports:

- A: ability and skills (EDT) for working on environmental tasks;
- M: motivation:
  - *intrinsic*, e.g. eco-pioneers, eco-awards, eco-volunteer programmes, etc. and
  - *extrinsic*, e.g. discounts for environmentally friendly products, etc.; and
- O: the opportunity to perform an environmental task inside a team, for example.

Green HRM will initiate an environmental performance appraisal rating system to include dimensions for rating people. These can include the following behavioural as well as technical competencies: teamwork, employee collaboration, organisational diversity, eco-friendly innovations, and **environmental stewardship**.[81] These environmental competencies reinforce a company's core values directed towards sustainability.

Overseen by Green HRM, individual managers will discuss the environmental performance of employees and give performance feedback not only during the scheduled time of appraisal, but also during the gaps between these meetings. Green HRM and line management will assist employees to enhance their environmental knowledge as well as their eco-friendly skills, abilities, and motivations.

### 5. *Green Compensation*

For Green HRM, reward management and compensation remain major HRM processes through which employees are rewarded for their performance. Such HR practices are one of the most powerful methods that link an employee's interests in sustainability to the organisation's overall sustainability. Such environmental incentives and rewards can influence employees' attention on sustainability by motivating employees to exert efforts directed towards achieving the environmental goals of their organisation.

Positive compensation and rewards will increase green initiatives inside organisations. Developing effective monetary incentives linked to an organisation's overall sustainability strategy can be challenging because of difficulties found in accurately and fairly evaluating environmental behaviours[82] and eco-friendly performance. By incorporating elements of sustainable management in a company's compensation programme, Green HRM promotes the environmental behaviour of employees which, in turn, can lead to the promotion of employees.

Furthermore, managers can ask employees to suggest specific environmental initiatives pertaining to their individual jobs which can enhance mutual decision-making processes at the organisation level. This includes long-term environmental objectives for the upcoming year, for example. Achieving such environmental objectives would be the basis of receiving incentives.

Green HRM will modify environmental employee compensation programmes to issue bonuses based in part on an employee's appraisal ratings and on behavioural and technical competencies as well as the level of environmental suggestions made to further the goal of corporate sustainability. In addition, Green HRM awards employees with bonuses for their work on organisational sustainability projects. Green rewards can include workplace and lifestyle benefits. These can range from carbon credit offsets to free bicycles and bicycle user groups, carpooling databases, support for public transport usage, and *travel-to-work-without-driving* days.

It can also include an increased use of home office or working from home,[83] flexible work arrangements to suit carpooling and public transport, etc. Improving sustainability might mean moving catering towards ecological produce, *fairtrade*[84] products, and meat-free days. It could include the move away from capsule coffee to avoid aluminium waste. These strategies engage people in an organisational green agenda while continuing to recognise an individual's contribution to an environmental business strategy.

Green HRM will give emphasis to environmentally effective approaches that will help to design and implement green compensation practices that lead to the achievement of corporate environmental goals.

### 6. Green HRM Strategies

One of the main functions of Green HRM's environmental strategies is to relate such strategies to an organisation's overall business strategy on sustainability. With this, strategic green HRM (SGHRM) facilitates management in sustaining an organisation's sustainability strategy. SGHRM focuses on attracting employee competencies and the development of an environmental culture that represents an organisation's core values. A capability approach to SGHRM focuses on HR strategies that emphasise on environmental competencies required to attract, train, and motivate employees to develop and support an organisational culture that maintains sustainability. In the aforementioned harm reduction model, SGHRM sustains organisational practices that reduce the negative impact of companies and corporations on the environment.

This is often measured as **carbon footprint**[85] which represents the total greenhouse gas emissions caused by an organisation, expressed as carbon dioxide equivalent.[86] Greenhouse gases, including the carbon-containing gases carbon dioxide and methane, can be emitted through the burning of fossil fuels, land clearance, and the production and consumption of food, manufactured goods, materials, wood, roads, buildings, transportation, and other services. Green HRM works towards lowering these emissions.

Green HRM might focus on the development of what became known as **sustainability champion**.[87] A sustainability champion is an advocate for the sustainable development of an organisation. A sustainability champion takes an active decision-making role which achieves tangible benefits for an organisation in terms of sustainability. Green HRM also develops **environmental stewardship**[88] which refers to the responsible use and protection of the natural environment established through conservation and organisational sustainable practices. Environmental stewardship was originally based on a land ethic dealing with people's relation to land, animals,[89] and plants which grow upon it.

Green HRM empowers such sustainability champions to facilitate ecological HRM policies and practices. These align an overall environmental business strategy to a company's environmental performance. Beyond that, strategic Green HRM moves traditional SHRM towards environmental SHRM outlined in Figure 11.1:

| Traditional Strategic HRM | | Sustainable Strategic HRM |
|---|---|---|
| economic rationality | | the environmental rationality of sustainability |
| organisation oriented strategies | → | environmental HR strategies |
| development of business oriented processes | | self-reflective and environmentally oriented processes |
| benefits business organisations | → | organisational and environmental benefits |
| organisational citizenship | | environmental championship |
| harm imposed on organisation and workers | → | achieving organisational and environmental wellbeing |
| organisational focus that includes stakeholders | | focuses on environmental stakeholders |

*Figure 11.1* From Traditional-Strategic to Environmental-Strategic HRM.

Perhaps the key difference between traditional-strategic HRM and environmental-strategic HRM is that the latter focuses on avoiding negative externalities. Sustainable HRM strategies no longer allow the off-loading of intended and unintended environmental consequences of environmentally harmful organisational actions onto others, i.e. the community, the environment, etc. Sustainable strategic HRM underscores the merit of a strategic organisational response to the complexities of external environmental pressures. To achieve that, environmentally sustainable HR strategies are geared towards preserving and maintaining the natural environmental life-support systems which include the atmosphere, water, and soil.[90] In this, Green HRM assumes four key roles[91]:

1. **GHRM as a Collaborator**: pools diversified capacities together for a win-win outcome; develops a framework of the realisation of the win-win condition and supports an organisation internally and externally.
2. **GHRM as an Inventor**: pushes a firm to develop a green learning culture, contributes special and unique approaches towards environmental concerns.
3. **GHRM as a Strategic Partner**: HR knowledge of employees and business system enhances pools of appropriate stakeholders and dialogue with management on the importance of managing sustainability.
4. **GHRM as a Change Agent**: GHRM oversees the execution of changes and procedures with consideration of a necessity transformation towards sustainability.

Unlike marketing, operations and supply chain[92] management, accounting, etc., GSHRM is in a unique position to deliver tangible moves towards environmental sustainability that positively impact on an organisation's longer term, i.e. planned environmental health and eco-reputation. Just as strategic management believes *planning can do no wrong*,[93] environmental SGHRM also relies on planning. For GSHRM, this involves a four-step process:

1.  SGHRM's environmental planning starts with organising a company's environmental resources to plan a future development and develop distinctive environmental strategies;
2.  in the implementation phase, GSHRM identifies environmental specialists with appropriate competencies who can raise environmental awareness, plan long-term compensation schemes, and publish environmental reports that enhance sustainability communication;
3.  Green HRM measures and evaluates environmental business practice using objective measures to ascertain a company's environmental performance over a given time period[94]; and finally,
4.  based on environmental audit reports, Green HRM works with management to review the human input on a company's environmental performance to facilitate continuous improvements.

Green HRM will link this to what became known as the European Union's **Eco-Management and Audit Scheme** (EMAS).[95] EMAS fosters employee engagement,[96] ensuring legal compliance or the publication of an environmental statement. Such EMAS (EU) and EMS (environmental management systems) are linked to ISO 14001,[97] and **SA 8000** (social accountability). For Green HRM, ISO 14001 specifies requirements for an environmental management system that an organisation can use to enhance its environmental performance.[98] The role of Green HRM is vital in this because EMS certification (e.g. ISO 14001) requires strong employee participation (e.g. Green industrial relations), environmental training programmes (Green EDT), and improving environmental awareness among employees on the prevention of negative impacts on the environment (harm reduction).

Inevitably, GSHRM will lead to organisational change as companies transition from non-sustainability towards sustainability. Commonly, four ways of organising such a change towards an eco-friendly company have been identified:

1.  **Top-Down** approach to change management (the boss orders the company to be eco-friendly and people change);
2.  **Piecemeal** change (a company slowly moves towards sustainability);
3.  **Bargaining** for change (trade unions and Green HRM settle on an agreement that converts a traditional company into a sustainable firm); and finally,
4.  **Systemic-Jointism** (employees and managers build teams to organise the move towards organisational sustainability.

To make matters even more complicated, three types of **change agents**[99] have emerged: (1) environmental activists who believe in sustainability; (2) those with ambivalent views (the straddlers); and (3) those who distance themselves from sustainability (the cynics).[100] Such change agents might also be in tune with **Deep Ecology** rather than shallow ecology.[101] Deep ecology is an environmental philosophy based in the belief that humans must radically change their relationship to nature from one that values nature solely for its usefulness to human beings to one that recognises that nature has an inherent value.

# Workbook

## III. Five Discussion Questions on Green HRM

### And One Report Question on Green HRM

### 1. Discussion Questions:

1. How can Green HRM contribute to the creation of a sustainable future?
2. What is the contribution of Green HRM within the corporate context?
3. Which of the above-outlined six key Green HRM areas is best suited to support the environmental programme of a company?
4. In changing from traditional HRM towards Green HRM, which of the above-outlined approaches to organisational change is best suited for the purpose of creating an eco-friendly organisation?
5. Given the magnitude of challenges that come with global warming,[102] can Green HRM make a difference or is it just greenwashing, i.e. a mere public relations exercise to make companies and corporations look good?

### 2. Report Question

### On GHRM as a Change Agent

Imagine you are an HR manager dedicated to the concept of "GHRM as a Change Agent"[103] (HR-manager oversees the execution of changes and procedures with consideration of a necessity transformation towards sustainability). Your company seeks to lower your carbon footprint. How can HRM contribute to the goal of sustainability? Develop four [4] recommendations on how to involve your workforce into this plan.

## IV. The "5-by-5" Exercise: Five Case Studies and Five Questions

### 11.1 Electric Mobility at Timbuktu Motors

In many companies with sales units to contact customers, a company car is standard equipment. In practice, it is not always entirely replaceable by alternative means of travel. Nevertheless, Timbuktu Motors seeks to take action with a view to more climate protection. Timbuktu Motors' Green HRM has set up a bonus system with regard to the environmental friendliness of the cars used. The company is seeking to replace environmentally harmful vehicle types. Harmful engines should, of course, be completely removed from the list of possible service vehicles.

The issue of company cars and cars in general at Timbuktu Motors has always been known to be highly emotional. This is all the more true since many commercial vehicles allocated at Timbuktu Motors are also approved for private use. The privately available company car is often regarded by Timbuktu Motors as a tax-attractive benefit within the framework of corporate branding. In addition, many top managers at Timbuktu Motors still consider their own lavishly equipped company car to be an important status symbol.

Without a role model function of Timbuktu Motors' members of the executive board, a holistic rethinking of the company towards Green HRM becomes very difficult. Timbuktu Motors' Green HR department is already leading by example. It uses exclusively electric cars.

A complete switch to alternative drives such as electric vehicles is equally practicable for all managers at Timbuktu Motors as realistic electro-mobility scenarios are conceivable in the case of Timbuktu Motors' urban travel needs. For example, Timbuktu Motors' sales personnel and its logistics department remain highly dependent on car travel. Timbuktu Motors' Green HRM department already gives e-cars parking priority coupled with a free connection to appropriate charging stations.

### Car-Sharing Pools as a New Company Car Fleet

Green HRM at Timbuktu Motors is planning to gradually replace privately used service cars in favour of their own car-sharing fleet for travelling to and from Timbuktu Motors' headquarter. Timbuktu Motors' Green HRM is planning the use of an external car-sharing service provider.

### Green HRM Means Rail Instead of Aircraft

In general, Timbuktu Motors has already moved away from many other companies' mobility practices. It is also experimenting with the use of a general mobility budget. This means that, although workers who rely on professional mobility do not receive a fixed vehicle, they can plan a budget for their own journeys.

Timbuktu Motors supports environmentally friendly rail journeys as a clear preference over corporate flights. So far, Green HRM has left it up to Timbuktu Motors' employees in the field to decide for themselves which climate-friendly means of transport they use. Timbuktu Motors is considering to provide a company subsidised rail ticket in the near future.

1.  Imagine you are an HR manager in a company that seeks to move from traditional travel arrangements towards sustainable travelling as outlined in the case study above. Your CEO has asked to assess Timbuktu Motors' current car fleet and make three suggestions on how Timbuktu Motors can move further towards sustainability.
2.  Timbuktu Motors is seeking to limit and possibly end unnecessary air travel. Green HRM is setting up a working group to make the necessary arrangements. As a green HR department, who should be on Timbuktu Motors' sustainability committee? How do you select the right people?
3.  As a Green HR manager at Timbuktu Motors, make five suggestions on how to avoid travelling?
4.  At Timbuktu Motors, top management is still using fuel inefficient, unsustainable corporate cars. Your new and eco-friendly CEO has asked you to move Timbuktu Motors' corporate board and its top-management team from unsustainable cars towards eco-friendly cars. Which of the four models of organisational change (I–IV) outlined above would you select to organise this change and why?

5.  Imagine you are responsible for green performance management and Green rewards, what would you suggest to encourage the five heads of Timbuktu Motors' five key departments (accounting, operations management, sales, logistics, and marketing) to conserve energy and become more sustainable?

## 11.2 *TikTik's Sustainability Programme*

As a global leader in ICT sustainability, TikTik short-form mobile videos has a long commitment to reducing the environmental impact of our operations. Here in Europe, our most significant impact is from our data centre operations and the consumption of electricity. However, our sustainability strategy is much broader than this and covers all aspects of our operations across Europe, including greenhouse gas emissions, water, and waste. While many organisations accept that they have a duty or moral obligation to be environmentally responsible, there are also other key drivers that should be acknowledged.

These can include legal requirements, customer or stakeholder demands and expectations from present and potential future employees. These drivers require organisations to not only pursue profit but seek to do so in a manner that is considerate, if not actively beneficial to the environment. While many organisations have acknowledged these drivers, the leading organisations have gone a step further and are harnessing the societal shift towards greater sustainability to deliver innovation and new forms of value.

*TikTik's Sustainability Team* is dedicated to the development and execution of the company's ambitious sustainability vision. As part of this transformation process, Green HRM needs to connect to all parts of the organisation and integrate them into all layers of the company, from the fundamental underpinning processes all the way through to the culture, company brand, and identity.

Any sustainability transformation programme is dependent on its integrity. The company must be genuine in its intentions and actions. It is fundamental to understand what impact the company's operations are having on the environment, what action is being taken to reduce these impacts, and how successful these actions are in their implementation. The Environmental Management System (EMS) underpins the company's objectives which in turn support our goals and ultimately our sustainability vision. The EMS is the framework to move from strategy to realisation.

TikTik has a global EMS certified under ISO 14001. However, as with other management systems, we opted to seek a local certification for our operations. Our primary reasons for doing this were to enable closer integration with the existing management systems such as ISO 9001; that the EMS would benefit from greater integrity from closer management attention and also from a higher audit frequency.

The TikTik EMS provides a framework for a systematic approach to meeting our environmental objectives. This enhances the likelihood of meeting them through a rigorous plan-do-check-act approach that is independently verified. TikTik's Noah Wooden (GHR Manager) said,

> In TikTik's EMS certification audits conducted during August 2019, we found evidence of an exceptional level of commitment, input and support from top

management and staff alike with a focus on sustainability. This has ensured that the EMS provides TikTik with the intended controls, prevention and reduction of pollution as well as customer focus and system improvement opportunities through effective implementation.

The health and performance of Green HRM's system is monitored via a comprehensive set of goals, "green KPIs"[104] and related targets along with a well-implemented internal audit programme. TikTik's operations include office locations, warehouses, and distribution centres, and of course, our data centres. Each of these types of locations has been included in our EMS. Of these facilities, it is our data centres which have the greatest environmental impact, so naturally these were the focus of our EMS roll out.

Today all of TikTik's data centres are managed under our local ISO 14001 certified Environmental Management System. This is something above and beyond our competition and is something that TikTik is rightfully proud of. Building a virtual team from across the organisation and working closely with our Business Management Systems team, we developed an extremely robust environmental management framework. We have clear and measureable objectives with associated measurements and controls.

As part of our EMS, Green HRM has trained more than 1,500 staff so that participation and understanding of our obligations and impacts are known and understood by our staff.

**The benefits:** At TikTik, we have reduced operating expenses and injected additional impetus into our path to sustainability. From a 2010 baseline, the emissions generated by our offices have been cut by more than 18%, travel-related GHG emissions have been reduced by more than 50%, and our data centre facilities have reduced their environmental impact by 12%.

1.  Which of the four approaches (I–IV) to change management did TikTik's Green HRM apply to move TikTik towards sustainability and why?
2.  Describe the key elements of TikTik's environmental management system and the support Green HRM supplied?
3.  What is ISO 14001, why was it important for the management of TikTik to get ISO 14001 certification and what was the role of Green HRM in this process?
4.  Conduct a quick "needs analysis" on TikTik to identify training needs. Develop an answer for all three areas of the needs analysis.
5.  Describe the overall role of Green HRM at TikTik and its assistance during the company's move towards sustainability. Develop two more suggestions on the further development of TikTik's sustainability programme.

### 11.3 Environmental Improvements at Sushi Corp.

*Eco-Efficiency in Our Operations*

Sushi Corp. aims to reduce the environmental footprint of our operations even as our business grows. Improving the eco-efficiency of our manufacturing sites and offices[105] helps us cut our environmental impact, reduce running costs, and enhance overall site performance.

*Driving Sustainable Improvements*

The Sushi Corp. Sustainable Plan (SCP) sets out our greenhouse gas, water, and waste reduction targets, and our ambition to play a leadership role in the transition to a zero-carbon economy. Our EMS system provides a framework for continual improvement at our manufacturing and office sites. It helps us work towards the ambitious environmental targets set out in the SCP. We also set annual global targets for each of our eco-efficiency performance indicators to drive progress; these are supported by site-specific targets set by our regions and divisions.

Each manufacturing site is different, so the best ways to drive efficiency depend on use, scale, location, and capacity. In terms of our operations, we focus on driving efficiencies in our manufacturing sites as they have a bigger footprint. To view our performance, please see our sustainability performance data. Our progress on eco-efficiency has also been recognised by numerous external benchmarks.

*Sushi Corp.'s Codes of Sustainability Principles*

Our *Code of Sustainability Principles* contains a specific principle on the environment:

> Sushi Corp. is committed to making continuous improvements in the management of our environmental impact and to the longer-term goal of developing a sustainable business. Sushi Corp. will work in partnership with others to promote environmental care, increase understanding of environmental issues and disseminate good practice.

Each organisation must identify and evaluate its products, operations, activities, or services to determine those which have (or could have) a significant impact on the environment. The evaluation must be reviewed periodically, taking into account any changes to our standards or external legislation.

Where the requirements are specific to a site or business risk, Sushi Corp. publishes specific standards and separate supporting guidance. Such specific standards include those for third-party manufacturing (including further standards for new factories), auditing, reporting, and verification of management systems, environmental performance reporting, notification and investigation, and reporting of SHE incidents. We have also developed standards for activities such as biomass sourcing and polychlorinated biphenyls in electrical equipment (where applicable).

*Our Environmental Care Framework Standard*

Based on the requirements of the international ISO 14001 standard for environmental management systems, our Environmental Care Framework Standard maintains the robustness of ISO 14001, while enabling us to tailor the framework specifically to our operations to drive improvements more effectively. The framework ensures a robust process by incorporating requirements for planning, implementation and operation, checking, corrective action, and management review.

Using our own framework allows us to quickly update the requirements of the standard when needed, for example, to reflect emerging best practices or in response to incidents that have occurred.

## *Our Framework*

Sushi Corp. believes ISO 14001 is a great mark of environmental compliance. However, the scale of our business means we need more flexibility. By basing our framework on ISO 14001, we are ensuring the robustness of our system while tailoring requirements to our own operations. This approach also enables us to audit 100% of our production output, using a combination of third-party assessments and internal verification.

When developing our standard, we mapped all requirements to ISO 14001 one by one to ensure close alignment. Therefore, sites certified using our standard should also be ISO 14001 compliant.

## *Internal and External Auditing*

Regular environmental audits support continuous improvement. All our manufacturing sites are audited regularly (e.g. annually) to assess the robustness of their implementation of our environmental sustainability standards. More than 25% of our sites are audited against this standard every year. In 2019, around 20% of them were also certified to the external ISO 14001 standard.

We also provide annual training to ensure all sites and their relevant OHS and environmental professionals are reminded about the standard's requirements and its alignment with ISO 14001.

In 2015, 50% of our manufacturing sites were covered by our sustainability framework, with the remaining ones being certified by ISO 14001. By 2019, this had increased to 71%, reinforcing the confidence we have in our sustainability standard. In total, 92% of our manufacturing sites were covered by either our Care Framework Standard or ISO 14001 in 2019. The remaining 8% had audits managed locally.

Audits are conducted either by a third-party auditor or by a trained employee who is independent of the site being audited. The process, similar to that used for ISO 14001 audits, sees auditors gathering evidence to demonstrate compliance against the standard through the collection of documentation or employee interviews. Where we have ISO 14001 certification, audits are completed annually by a relevant certifying body.

1. As outlined previously, HRM and Green HRM work with stakeholders. Sushi Corp.'s Codes of Sustainability Principles mentions that Sushi Corp. "will work in partnership with others". Who are the five most important sustainability stakeholders for Sushi Corp. and why?
2. Why has ISO 14001 certification been important for Sushi Corp.? Develop four reasons.
3. Why does Sushi Corp. provide employee training on sustainability? Find three reasons.
4. Compile a quick "sustainability report" on Sushi Corp. reflecting on its six elements as outlined above.

5. What is the relevance of environmental standards for Sushi Corp.? And, can Sushi Corp.'s sustainability programme be successful? Find two arguments that support your answer.

## 11.4 Sustainability and Engagement at Chaos Software Ltd.

### Fostering Sustainability Conversations at Chaos Software Ltd.

To better understand how Chaos Software Ltd. compares to others in our industry, we regularly benchmark our environmental performance with software and other global IT companies. To build a supportive policy environment for private sector leaders on global warming, Chaos Software Ltd. participates in environmental organisations. In addition, Chaos Software Ltd. works with the Green Building Council (www.usgbc.org). USGBC aims to expand the number of software manufacturers implementing green sustainable practices. Chaos Software Ltd. also places emphasis on employees' involvement.

### Employee Engagement

Chaos Software Ltd.'s engagement programme – founded in 2009 – aims to increase employee engagement by providing direct communication between employees and the company's sustainability leaders (SLs) and fosters a corporate-wide sustainability community. Initially a lunch discussion among four Chaos Software Ltd. employees, our engagement programme now reaches employees via teleconference. We attribute the success of the series to the active participation of Chaos Software Ltd.'s employees who voluntarily have organised discussions outside of their regular jobs. Chaos Software Ltd. recognises our employees' desire to learn about the company's sustainability pursuits.

### A Sustainability Leader's Report

My name is Rudy Rocker and I am a sustainability leader at Chaos Software Ltd. In celebration of *Earth Month*, we are highlighting employees who are champions of sustainability and help make every day Earth Day at Chaos Software Ltd. SLs and employees have a long-standing commitment to sustainability, an eco-friendly workplace, and environmental responsibility. This has made it possible to harness the power of people and technology.

Sustainability started long before I joined Chaos Software Ltd. I studied chemical engineering in college and had great teachers that taught both sustainability and environmental engineering. My professors shared the power of understanding these fields as well as their undeniable passion for the environment. My education, along with disastrous events like Deepwater Horizon, only grew my interest in sustainability.[106]

So when it was time to choose the direction of my career, I decided to join Chaos Software Ltd. I started as an Environmental Engineer in hazardous waste management and have since transitioned into supply chain management.

But my passion for sustainability isn't limited to what I do in my day job. I am busy bringing sustainability information to other employees at Chaos Software Ltd. I run Chaos Software Ltd.'s sustainability engagement programme which invites corporate leaders in sustainability from inside and outside our company to share their expertise with Chaos Software Ltd. employees. It gives all employees visibility to the work Chaos Software Ltd. is doing as well as other sustainability leaders.

The Chaos Software Ltd.'s engagement programme was founded by another contagiously passionate employee, José *Durruti*. But when the programme needed a new leader to manage it in 2016, José approached me. José knew his passion for the project and wanted to leave it in good hands. I was honoured, though slightly hesitant to accept. I knew the time and energy I would need to devote to make it successful would be a big commitment, but in the end, I took on the project. Why? Not only would I be able to continue to engage employees on sustainability topics, but also connect with new employees.

I work closely with Chaos Software Ltd.'s employee resource group and our trade union which supports the induction of new hires and interns. We wanted to make sure new employees and interns had an opportunity to see the authentic commitment Chaos Software Ltd. has to corporate sustainability and the environment. I hope that when this potential talent makes a decision in coming to or staying at Chaos Software Ltd., environmental responsibility takes an element of that.

1. Chaos Software Ltd. has a well-developed employees' engagement programme. Explain why employees' engagement is important for Chaos Software Ltd. Find four reasons?
2. Chaos Software Ltd.'s employees' engagement programme is based on volunteers. Outline three reasons why a volunteer programme is better suited than a compulsory programme?
3. Why did Rudy Rocker become a sustainability leader at Chaos Software Ltd.? Describe the private-corporate interface and Mr Rocker's pro-environmental attitudes that encouraged him?
4. Outline the role of Chaos Software Ltd.'s sustainability leader and Mr Rocker's involvement in Chaos Software Ltd.'s engagement programme?
5. Describe the role of Chaos Software Ltd.'s sustainability leaders and its engagement programme in training new recruits on environmental issues?

### 11.5 Testing a Carbon Footprint Calculator

A carbon footprint is the total of greenhouse gas emissions caused by an individual, event, organisation, service, or product, expressed as carbon dioxide equivalent. Greenhouse gases, including the carbon-containing gases carbon dioxide and methane, can be emitted through the burning of fossil fuels, land clearance, and the production and consumption of food, manufactured goods, materials, wood, roads, buildings, transportation, and other services.

In most cases, the total carbon footprint cannot be calculated exactly because of inadequate knowledge of and data about the complex interactions between contributing processes, including the influence of natural processes that store or release carbon dioxide.

A measure of the total amount of carbon dioxide ($CO_2$) and methane ($CH_4$) emissions of a defined population, system, or activity, considering all relevant sources, sinks, and storage within the spatial and temporal boundary of the population, system, or activity of interest, is calculated as carbon dioxide equivalent using the relevant 100-year global warming potential.

**Task 1:** Your task is to test one [1] or up to all five [5] online carbon footprint calculator(s) – outlined below. Make a note of your experience, discuss these within your group, tell others about the positives and negatives of the carbon footprint calculator.

**Task 2:** Develop five [5] recommendations on who in an organisation can reduce its carbon footprint based on what you have learned from the carbon footprint calculator.

Here is a list of five carbon footprint calculators that can be tested:

1. https://www.conservation.org/carbon-footprint-calculator#/
2. https://www.carbonfootprint.com/calculator.aspx
3. https://www.wwf.org.au/get-involved/change-the-way-you-live/ecological-footprint-calculator
4. https://www.footprintcalculator.org/
5. https://co2.myclimate.org/en/footprint_calculators/new

## V. A Suggestion for an Online Guest Lecture

The CEO of the world's biggest carpet manufacturer, Ray Anderson, talks about sustainability, the environment and what businesses can do to make a change.

**The Business Logic of Sustainability**

https://www.ted.com/talks/ray_anderson_the_business_logic_of_sustainability?language=en

[the online guest lecture above is merely a suggestion – www.ted.com/talks offers additional material to choose from]

## VI. List of Suggested Documentaries on Strategic HRM

The carefully selected documentary videos below are mere suggestions to be used during tutorials. Documentaries have been selected to achieve two things: (1) to explain key HRM themes and (2) to provide an insight into the reality of HRM. Typically, these short documentaries should be viewed in class followed by a class discussion on the content of the video. Alternatively, questions on documentaries can be prepared beforehand and small group discussions can follow up the video after viewing is concluded. Should any of the web-links no longer function, please conduct an internet search for other – alternative – documentaries related to your tutorial topic (e.g. filmsforaction.org):

Leonardo DiCaprio: https://www.youtube.com/watch?v=2Cc8E3BWOqA

DiCaprio II: http://ezproxy.uws.edu.au/login?qurl=https://edutv.informit.com.au/watch-screen.php?videoID=1522321

DiCaprio III: https://www.leonardodicaprio.org/leonardo-delivers-landmark-speech-at-the-united-nations-climate-summit/

Sustainability:     https://www.ted.com/talks/johan_rockstrom_5_transformational_policies_for_a_prosperous_and_sustainable_world

Al Gore I: https://www.ted.com/talks/al_gore_the_case_for_optimism_on_climate_change

Al Gore II: https://www.youtube.com/watch?v=w-inEu9T1m4

Al Gore III: https://www.youtube.com/watch?v=YsA3PK8bQd8

NASA-Resources: https://climate.nasa.gov/climate_resources/144/video-how-global-warming-stacks-up/

NASA-Hansen: https://www.ted.com/talks/james_hansen_why_i_must_speak_out_about_climate_change?referrer=playlist-the_big_picture

Geographic: https://video.nationalgeographic.com/video/101-videos/climate-101-causes-and-effects

Stoknes: https://www.ted.com/talks/per_espen_stoknes_how_to_transform_apoc-alypse_fatigue_into_action_on_global_warming

Manufacturing I: https://www.youtube.com/watch?v=KVybNCPzG7M

Manufacturing II: https://www.youtube.com/watch?v=U2Dd4k63-zM

Harrison Ford: https://www.youtube.com/watch?v=99AwWQ-M2_M

Greta Thunberg: https://www.youtube.com/watch?v=VFkQSGyeCWg&app=desktop

Waste: https://storyofstuff.org/movies/story-of-stuff/

## Notes

1 Cohen, M. J. 2020. *Sustainability*, Cambridge: Polity Books; Park, H. S. (eds.) 2020. *The Palgrave Handbook of Corporate Sustainability in the Digital Era*, London: Palgrave Macmillan.
2 HBR. 2018. Sustainability – green boardrooms, *Harvard Business Review*, July–August 2018, p. 27.
3 HBR. 2018. Green borad rooms, *Harvard Business Review*, 96(4):27.
4 Yusoff, Y. M., Nejati, M., Kee, D. M. H. & Amran, A. 2020. Linking green human resource management practices to environmental performance in hotel industry, *Global Business Review*, 21(3):663–680.
5 IPCC. 2021. Sixth Assessment Report (https://www.ipcc.ch/assessment-report/ar6/, accessed: 15th July 2021).
6 McLaughlin, J. F., Hellmann, J. J., Boggs, C. L. & Ehrlich, P. R. 2002. Climate change hastens population extinctions, *Proceedings of the National Academy of Sciences*, 99(9):6070–6074; Klikauer, T. & Simms, N. 2020. Falter, *Marx & Philosophy Review of Books*, 19th March 2020; Gerretsen, I. 2021. The State of the Climate in 2021 (https://www.bbc.com/future/article/20210108-where-we-are-on-climate-change-in-five-charts, accessed: 5th April 2021).
7 Climate Change Interview with Harvard Professor James G. Anderson (https://www.youtube.com/watch?v=Y12P76EYQJ8, cf. https://archive.org/details/BentonLectureFinal01082018/mode/2up, accessed: 25th August 2020); Hood, M. 2020. A world redrawn: worry about climate, not COVID, says James 'Gaia' Lovelock (https://phys.org/news/2020-06-world-redrawn-climate-covid-james.html, 16th June 2020, accessed: 25th August 2020); https://climatereanalyzer.org/.
8 Vince, G. 2014. *Adventures in the Anthropocene*, Minneapolis, MN: Milkweed Editions; Crutzen, P. J. 2002, November. The anthropocene, *Journal de Physique IV* (Proceedings), 12(10):1–5; Crutzen, P. J. 2006. The "anthropocene", in: Eckart Ehlers, E. & Kraff, T. (eds.) *Earth System Science in the Anthropocene*, Berlin: Springer; Thomas J. A. et al. 2020. *The Anthropocene*, Cambridge: Polity Books.
9 Sir Richard Attenborough (BBC. 2020. https://www.bbc.com/news/science-environment-54268038); Moore, J. W. 2017. The capitalocene, part I: on the nature and origins of

our ecological crisis, *Journal of Peasant Studies*, 44(3):594–630; Moore, J. W. 2014. The Capitalocene – *Part II: Abstract Social Nature and the Limits to Capital* (http://naturalezacien-ciaysociedad.org/wp-content/uploads/sites/3/2016/02/The-Capitalocene-Part-II-REVISIONS-July-2014.pdf, accessed: 5th October 2020).

10 Bernotat, W. H. 2007. Take responsibility for climate change, *Harvard Business Review*, 85(7/8):58–59; cf. Klikauer, T. 2019. Accelerating ecological genocide, *Counterpunch*, 7th June 2019.

11 HBR. 2008. Earth: the sequel, *Harvard Business Review*, April 2008, p. 30.

12 McKibben, B. 1990. *The End of Nature*, New York: Anchor Books; McKibben, B. 2019. *Falter – Has the Human Game Begun to Play Itself Out?*, New York: Henry Holt and Company; Klikauer, T. 2019. Accelerating ecological genocide, *Counterpunch*, 7th June 2019 (www.counterpunch.org, accessed: 15th July 2020); Klikauer, T. & Simms, N. 2020. Falter, *Marx & Philosophy Review of Books*, 19th March 2020 (accessed: 15th July 2020).

13 Wallace-Wells, D. 2019. *The Uninhabitable Earth: Life after Warming*, New York: Tim Duggan Books.

14 Klikauer, T. 2019. Accelerating ecological genocide, *Counterpunch*, 7th June 2019 (www.counterpunch.org, accessed: 15th July 2020); Klikauer, T. & Simms, N. 2020. Falter, *Marx & Philosophy Review of Books* (https://marxandphilosophy.org.uk, 19th July 2020).

15 Jones, E. 2019. Rethinking greenwashing: corporate discourse, unethical practice, and the unmet potential of ethical consumerism, *Sociological Perspectives*, 62(5):728–754.

16 https://www.youtube.com/watch?v=yzcfsq1_bt8.

17 Dianati, S. & Banfield, G. 2020. 'Business as Usual': Critical Management Studies and the Case of Environmental Sustainability (http://www.jceps.com/wp-content/uploads/2020/09/18-2-10.pdf, accessed: 15th September 2020).

18 Villena, V. H. & Gioia, D. A. 2020. A more sustainable supply chain companies tend to focus on their top-tier suppliers, but the real risks come lower down, *Harvard Business Review*, 98(2):92.

19 White, R. D. 2018. *Climate Change Criminology*, Bristol: Bristol University Press, p. 98; cf. Klikauer, T. & Campbell, N. 2020. The criminology of global warming, *Counterpunch*, 15th August, 4 pages.

20 Isaksson, R. B., Garvare, R. & Johnson, M. 2015. The crippled bottom line–measuring and managing sustainability, *International Journal of Productivity and Performance Management*, 64(3):334–355.

21 Isaksson, R. B., Garvare, R. & Johnson, M. 2015. The crippled bottom line–measuring and managing sustainability, *International Journal of Productivity and Performance Management*, 64(3):334–355.

22 Savitz, A. W. 2014. *The Triple Bottom Line*, San Francisco, CA: Jossey-Bass.

23 https://www.bmwgroup.com/content/dam/grpw/websites/bmwgroup_com/responsibil-ity/downloads/en/2020/2020-BMW-Group-SVR-2019-Englisch.pdf.

24 Matakanye, R. M. & van der Poll, H. M. 2021. Linking sustainability reporting to sustain-ability performance through regulation (https://doi.org/10.1504/JGBA.2021.114321, 16th April 2021, accessed: 25th April 2021).

25 Elkington, J. 2018. 25 years ago I coined the phrase "triple bottom line." Here's why it's time to rethink it, *Harvard Business Review*, 25th June 2018.

26 Attenborough, D. 2018. Climate Change 'Our Greatest Threat' (https://www.bbc.com/, 3rd December 2018, accessed: 15th July 2020).

27 MGI. 2020. Climate Risk and Response, McKinsdey Global Institute (https://www.mckin-sey.com/business-functions/sustainability/our-insights/climate-risk-and-response-physical-hazards-and-socioeconomic-impacts, accessed: 15th July 2020).

28 Rayner, J. & Morgan, D. 2018. An empirical study of green workplace behaviours: ability, moti-vation and opportunity, *Asia Pacific Journal of Human Resources*, 56(1):59; Aust, I., Matthews, B. & Muller-Camen, M. 2020. Common good HRM: a paradigm shift in Sustainable HRM?, *Human Resource Management Review*, 30(3):2.

29 Aust, I., Matthews, B. & Muller-Camen, M. 2020. Common good HRM: a paradigm shift in sustainable HRM?, *Human Resource Management Review*, 30(3).

30 Ehnert, I. 2009. *Sustainable HRM: A Conceptual and Exploratory Analysis from a Paradox Perspective*, Berlin: Physica-Verlag, p. 87.

31 Bozkurt, Ö. & Stowell, A. 2016. Skills in the green economy: recycling promises in the UK e-waste management sector, *New Technology, Work and Employment*, 31(2):147.

32  Waddock, S. A. & Graves, S. B. 1997. The corporate social performance–financial performance link, *Strategic Management Journal*, 18(4):303–319.

33  UN. 2009. Eco-Efficiency Indicators (United Nations Publication: ST/ESCAP/2561, p. 4; https://sustainabledevelopment.un.org/content/documents/785eco.pdf, accessed: 15th July 2020).

34  Meadows, D. H. 1972. *The Limits to Growth; A Report for the Club of Rome's Project on the Predicament of Mankind*, New York: Universe Books.

35  WCED. 1987. *Our Common Future – World Commission on Environment and Development*, Oxford: Oxford University Press.

36  Lenntech. 2020. Top 10 of Anthropogenic and Natural Environmental Disasters (https://www.lenntech.com/environmental-disasters.htm, accessed: 15th July 2020; cf. https://www.insider.com/worst-modern-manmade-disasters-world-environment-day-2019-5#chernobyl-disaster-1986-4).

37  GRI. 2020. Global Reporting Initiative (https://www.globalreporting.org/, accessed: 15th July 2020).

38  Jyoti, K. 2019. Green HRM–people management commitment to environmental sustainability, in: *Proceedings of 10th International Conference on Digital Strategies for Organizational Success* (https://papers.ssrn.com/sol3/papers.cfm?abstract_id=3323800, accessed: 15th July 2020).

39  Yu, W., Chavez, R., Feng, M., Wong, C.Y. & Fynes, B. 2020. Green HRM and environmental cooperation: an ability-motivation-opportunity and contingency perspective, *International Journal of Production Economics*, (219):227; (e.g. Greening of Industry Networks Studies on: https://www.springer.com).

40  KPMG. 2017. The KPMG Survey of Corporate Responsibility Reporting 2017 (https://assets.kpmg/content/dam/kpmg/xx/pdf/2017/10/kpmg-survey-of-corporate-responsibility-reporting-2017.pdf, accessed: 15th July 2020); cf. https://ccpi.org/.

41  https://www.forbes.com/sites/karstenstrauss/2019/01/22/the-most-sustainable-companies-in-2019/#1d11a27f6d7d.

42  https://www.spglobal.com/spdji/en/indices/equity/dow-jones-sustainability-world-index/#overview.

43  Markey, R., McIvor, J., O'Brien, M. & Wright, C. F. 2019. Reducing carbon emissions through employee participation: evidence from Australia, *International Journal of Human Resource Management*, 50(1):57–83.

44  Yu, W., Chavez, R., Feng, M., Wong, C. Y. & Fynes, B. 2020. Green HRM and environmental cooperation: an ability-motivation-opportunity and contingency perspective, *International Journal of Production Economics*, (219):224–235.

45  Salim, H. K., Padfield, R., Hansen, S. B., Mohamad, S. E., Yuzir, A., Syayuti, K., Tham, M. H. & Papargyropoulou, E. 2018. Global trends in environmental management system and ISO14001 research, *Journal of cleaner production*, (170):645–653.

46  Berridge, J. & Cooper, C. L. 1993. Stress and coping in US organizations: the role of the employee assistance programme, *Work & Stress*, 7(1):89–102.

47  Voegtlin, C. & Greenwood, M. 2016. Corporate social responsibility and human resource management: a systematic review and conceptual analysis, *HRM Review*, 26(3):181–197.

48  Aust, I., Matthews, B. & Muller-Camen, M. 2020. Common good HRM: a paradigm shift in sustainable HRM?, *Human Resource Management Review*, 30(3):3; cf. David Starr-Glass, D. 2020. Embedding corporate sustainability in HRM practice, in: Machado, J. & Davim, P. (eds.) *Sustainable Management for Managers and Engineers*, Hoboken, NJ: Wiley and Sons.

49  https://www.thebalancecareers.com/the-hr-role-in-promoting-corporate-social-responsibility-1917743.

50  Tang, G., Chen, Y., Jiang, Y., Paille, P. & Jia, J. 2018. Green human resource management practices: scale development and validity, *Asia Pacific Journal of Human Resources*, 56(1):31.

51  Ismail, I. & Hassan, R. 2020. Employee and top-management engagement in green HRM, *International Journal of Business and Economy*, 2(1):20–24.

52  https://climateaccountability.org/carbonmajors_dataset2020.html.

53  Jepsen, D. M. & Grob, S. 2015. Sustainability in recruitment and selection: building a framework of practices, *Journal of Education for Sustainable Development*, 9(2):160–178.

54  https://taz.de/Weniger-Dienstreisen-nach-der-Pandemie/!5747496/.

55  Shaban, S. 2019. Reviewing the concept of green HRM (GHRM) and its application practices (green staffing) with suggested research agenda: a review from literature background and testing construction perspective, *International Business Research*, 12(5):86–94.

56 Muster, V. & Schrader, U. 2011. Green work-life balance: a new perspective for green HRM, *German Journal of Human Resource Management*, 25(2):140–156; Bangwal, D., Tiwari, P. & Chamola, P. 2017. Green HRM, work-life and environment performance, *International Journal of Environment, Workplace and Employment*, 4(3):244–268.

57 Harris, L. C. & Crane, A. 2002. The greening of organizational culture, *Journal of Organizational Change Management*, 15(3):214–234.

58 Bridgens, B., Powell, M., Farmer, G., Walsh, C., Reed, E., Royapoor, M., Gosling, P., Hall, J. & Heidrich, O. 2018. Creative upcycling: reconnecting people, materials and place through making, *Journal of Cleaner Production*, (189):145–154.

59 Redlein, A. (eds.) 2020. *Modern Facility and Workplace Management – Processes, Implementation and Digitalisation*, Cham: Springer.

60 Harvey, G., Williams, K. & Probert, J. 2013. Greening the airline pilot: HRM and the green performance of airlines in the UK, *International Journal of Human Resource Management*, 24(1):152–166.

61 Singh, D. & Pandey, A. 2020. Green HRM: an organizational commitment, *Journal of Indian Management & Strategy*, 25(1):14–18.

62 https://osha.europa.eu/en/emerging-risks/green-jobs.

63 Douglas, J. & McGhee, P. 2021. Towards an understanding of New Zealand Union responses to climate change, *Labour & Industry*, p. 15 (https://doi.org/10.1080/10301763.2021. 1895483).

64 Hampton, P. 2015. *Workers and Trade Unions for Climate Solidarity: Tackling Climate Change in a Neoliberal World*, London: Routledge.

65 Weil, D. 2015. A Green Industrial Relations System for Construction: Challenges and Opportunities (file:///Users/thomas/Downloads/1847-2539-1-PB.pdf, accessed: 15th July 2020).

66 Haski-Leventhal, D. et al. 2020. *Employee Engagement in Corporate Social Responsibility*, London: Sage.

67 Rayner, J. & Morgan, D. 2018. An empirical study of green workplace behaviours: ability, motivation and opportunity, *Asia Pacific Journal of Human Resources*, 56(1):59.

68 Kearsley, G. & Shneiderman, B. 1998. Engagement theory: a framework for technology-based teaching and learning, *Educational Technology*, 38(5):20–23.

69 Alzgool, M. 2019. Nexus between green HRM and green management towards fostering green values, *Management Science Letters*, 9(12):2073–2082.

70 UCU. 2013. Green Skills Manifesto (free download: https://www.ucu.org.uk/media/4977/ Green-Skills-Manifesto/pdf/Green_skills_manifesto_2013_to_print_1_.pdf, accessed: 25th August 2020).

71 Saifulina, N., Carballo-Penela, A. & Ruzo-Sanmartín, E. 2020. Sustainable HRM and green HRM: the role of green HRM in influencing employee pro-environmental behavior at work, *Journal of Sustainability Research*, 2(3) (http://wap.hapres.com/UpLoad/PdfFile/JSR_1244. pdf, accessed: 15th July 2020); Iqbal, Q. 2020. The era of environmental sustainability: ensuring that sustainability stands on human resource management, *Global Business Review*, 21(2):377–391.

72 Iqbal, Q. 2020. The era of environmental sustainability: ensuring that sustainability stands on human resource management, *Global Business Review*, 21(2):381.

73 Lakhera, A. & Sharma, P. 2020. Green HRM: best HR practices within an organization for reducing employees' carbon footprint, *International Journal of Knowledge-Based Organizations*, 10(3):1–8.

74 Singh, S. K., Del Giudice, M., Chierici, R. & Graziano, D. 2020. Green innovation and environmental performance: the role of green transformational leadership and green HRM, *Technological Forecasting and Social Change*, 150 (online before pint January 2020).

75 Franchetti, M. J. & Apul, D. 2012. *Carbon Footprint Analysis: Concepts, Methods, Implementation, and Case Studies*, Boca Raton, FL: CRC Press.

76 Yusoff, Y. M., Nejati, M., Kee, D. M. H. & Amran, A. 2020. Linking green HRM practices to environmental performance in hotel industry, *Global Business Review*, 21(3):663–680.

77 Tang, G., Chen, Y., Jiang, Y., Paille, P. & Jia, J. 2018. Green human resource management practices: scale development and validity, *Asia Pacific Journal of Human Resources*, 56(1):36.

78 Cook, W., van Bommel, S. & Turnhout, E. 2016. Inside environmental auditing: effectiveness, objectivity, and transparency, *Current Opinion in Environmental Sustainability*, (18):33–39.

79    Roy, M. J. & Thérin, F. 2008. Knowledge acquisition and environmental commitment in SMEs, *Corporate Social Responsibility and Environmental Management*, 15(5):249–259; Fleming, P. & Jones, M. T. 2013. *The End of Corporate Social Responsibility: Crisis & Critique*, London: Sage.

80    Marcus, A. A. & Fremeth, R. F. 2009. Green management matters regardless, *Academy of Management Perspectives*, 23(3):17–26.

81    Bennett, N. J., Whitty, T. S., Finkbeiner, E., Pittman, J., Bassett, H., Gelcich, S. & Allison, E. H. 2018. Environmental stewardship: a conceptual review and analytical framework, *Environmental Management*, 61(4):597–614.

82    Saifulina, N., Carballo-Penela, A. & Ruzo-Sanmartín, E. 2020. Sustainable HRM and green HRM: the role of green HRM in influencing employee pro-environmental behavior at work, *Journal of Sustainability Research*, 2(3).

83    Olson, M. H. & Primps, S. B. 1984. Working at home with computers: work and non-work issues, *Journal of Social Issues*, 40(3):97–112; Gottlieb, C., Grobovšek, J. & Poschke, M. 2020. Working from home across countries, *Covid Economics*, 1(8):71–91 (https://www.techrepublic.com/article/going-green-10-ways-to-make-your-office-more-eco-friendly-and-efficient/).

84    https://www.fairtrade.net/.

85    Wiedmann, T. & Minx, J. 2008. A definition of 'carbon footprint', *Ecological Economics Research Trends*, (1):1–11.

86    https://www.statista.com/statistics/575829/coca-colas-carbon-dioxide-emissions-worldwide/.

87    May, B. 2017. *How to Make Your Company a Recognized Sustainability Champion*, London: Routledge.

88    Bennett, N. J., Whitty, T. S., Finkbeiner, E., Pittman, J., Bassett, H., Gelcich, S. & Allison, E. H. 2018. Environmental stewardship: a conceptual review and analytical framework, *Environmental Management*, 61(4):597–614.

89    Jarvis, B. 2018. The Insect Apocalypse Is Here (https://www.nytimes.com/, 27th November 2018, accessed: 15th July 2020).

90    Klikauer, T. & Campbell, N. 2020. Dark Water Rising, BraveNewEurope, 11th November 2020, 5 pages.

91    Staffelbach, B., Brugger, E. A. & Bäbler, S. 2012. The role of strategic context in environmental sustainability initiatives: three case studies, in: Jackson, S. E., Ones, D. S. & Dilchert, S. (eds.) *Managing Human Resources for Environmental Sustainability*. San Francisco, CA: Jossey-Bass/Wiley, pp. 36–60.

92    Villena, V. H. & Gioia, D. A. 2020. A more sustainable supply chain, *Harvard Business Review*, 98(2):84–93.

93    Kerzner, H. 2002. *Strategic Planning for Project Management Using a Project Management Maturity Model*, New York: John Wiley, p. 302.

94    Shah, M. 2019. Green human resource management: development of a valid measurement scale, *Business Strategy and the Environment*, 28(5):771–785.

95    EMAS. 2017. Eco-Management and Audit Scheme (https://ec.europa.eu/environment/emas/index_en.htm, accessed: 15th July 2020).

96    Ismail, I. & Hassan, R. 2020. Employee and top-management engagement in green HRM, *International Journal of Business and Economy*, 2(1):20–24.

97    ISO. 2015. *Environmental Management System* (https://www.iso.org/standard/60857.html, accessed: 15th July 2020).

98    Boiral, O. 2007. Corporate greening through ISO 14001: a rational myth?, *Organization Science*, 18(1):127–146; Hersey, K. 1998. A close look at ISO 14000, *Professional Safety*, 43(7):26.

99    Nicol, P. 2005. *Scenario Planning as an Organisational Change Agent* (PhD thesis: https://espace.curtin.edu.au/handle/20.500.11937/2127, accessed: 15th July 2020).

100   Costas, J. & Kärreman, D. 2013. Conscience as control–managing employees through CSR, *Organization*, 20(3):394–415.

101   Naess, A. 1973. The shallow and the deep, long-range ecology movement. A summary, *Inquiry*, 16(1–4):95–100.

102   CNN. 2021. Dalai Lama and 100 other Nobel Prize Laureates Call for Fossil Fuels to Be Phased Out (https://edition.cnn.com/2021/04/21/world/earth-day-dalai-lama-climate-letter-intl/index.html, accessed: 25th April 2021).

103   http://article.sciencepublishinggroup.com/html/10.11648.j.edu.20150405.15.html.

104  https://www.youtube.com/watch?v=b2GyejpwiE0; Greiwe, J. & Schönbohm, A. 2011. *A KPI Based Study on the Scope and Quality of Sustainability Reporting By the DAX30 Companies,* Working Paper no. 64 (https://www.econstor.eu/handle/10419/74313); Oshika, T. & Saka, C. 2017. Sustainability KPIs for integrated reporting, *Social Responsibility Journal,* 13(3):625–642; Isaksson, R. B., Garvare, R. & Johnson, M. 2015. The crippled bottom line–measuring and managing sustainability, *International Journal of Productivity and Performance Management,* 64(3):334–355.

105  https://www.energyhog.org/case-study/office/.

106  Red Cross. 2020. Come Hear Or High Water (https://www.redcross.org.au/getmedia/ 3b02a528-ae91-481d-bcbb-9b8ef3a70364/20201113-WorldDisasters-Full-FINAL_1.pdf. aspx, accessed: 25th November 2020).

## Further Readings

Aragon-Correa, J. A. & Sharma, S. 2003. A Contingent Resource-Based View of Proactive Corporate Environmental Strategy, *Academy of Management Review,* 28(1):71–88.

Aravamudhan, N. 2012. Green HR Getting into the Business of Green. *HRM Review,* (12):31–40.

Bangwal, D. & Tiwari, P. 2015. Green HRM–A Way to Greening the Environment, *IOSR Journal of Business and Management,* 17(12):45–53.

Behrend, T. S., Baker, B. A. & Thompson, L. F. 2009. Effects of Pro-environmental Recruiting Messages: The Role of Organizational Reputation, *Journal of Business and Psychology,* 24(3):341–350.

Bernotat, W. H. 2007. Take Responsibility for Climate Change, *Harvard Business Review,* 85(7/8):58–59.

Berry, M. A. & Rondinelli, D. A. 1998. Proactive Corporate Environmental Management: A New Industrial Revolution, *Academy of Management Perspectives,* 12(2):38–50.

Chenevert, D. & Tremblay, M. 2009. Fits in Strategic Human Resource Management and Methodological Challenge: Empirical Evidence of Influence of Empowerment and Compensation Practices on Human Resource Performance in Canadian Firms, *International Journal of Human Resource Management,* 20(4):738–770.

Daily, B. F., Bishop, J. W. & Govindarajulu, N. 2009. A Conceptual Model for Organizational Citizenship Behavior Directed toward the Environment, *Business & Society,* 48(2):243–256.

Daily, B. F., Bishop, J. W. & Steiner, R. 2007. The Mediating Role of EMS Teamwork as It Pertains to HR Factors and Perceived Environmental Performance, *Journal of Applied Business Research (JABR),* 23(1): 95–110.

Deshwal, P. 2015. Green HRM: An Organizational Strategy of Greening People, *International Journal of applied research,* 1(13):176–181.

Fernández, E., Junquera, B. & Ordiz, M. 2003. Organizational Culture and Human Resources in the Environmental Issue: A Review of the Literature, *International Journal of Human Resource Management,* 14(4):634–656.

Guerci, M., Longoni, A. & Luzzini, D. 2016. Translating Stakeholder Pressures into Environmental Performance – The Mediating Role of Green HRM Practices, *International Journal of Human Resource Management,* 27(2):262–289.

Haddock-Millar, J., Sanyal, C. & Müller-Camen, M. 2016. Green Human Resource Management: A Comparative Qualitative Case Study of a United States Multinational Corporation, *International Journal of Human Resource Management,* 27(2):192–211.

Harmon, J., Fairfield, K. D. & Wirtenberg, J. 2010. Missing an Opportunity: HR Leadership and Sustainability, *People and Strategy,* 33(1):16.

Hawken, P. 2010. *The Ecology of Commerce: A Declaration of Sustainability,* New York: Harper.

Jabbour, C. J. C. & Santos, F. C. A. 2006. The Evolution of Environmental Management within Organizations: Toward a Common Taxonomy, *Environmental Quality Management,* 16(2):43–59.

Jabbour, C. J. C. & Santos, F. C. A. 2008a. Relationships between Human Resource Dimensions and Environmental Management in Companies: Proposal of a Model, *Journal of Cleaner Production,* 16(1):51–58.

Jabbour, C. J. C. & Santos, F. C. A. 2008b. The Central Role of Human Resource Management in the Search for Sustainable Organizations, *International Journal of Human Resource Management*, 19(12):2133–2154.

Jackson, S. E. & Seo, J. 2010. The Greening of Strategic HRM Scholarship, *Organization Management Journal*, 7(4):278–290.

Jackson, S. E., Renwick, D. W., Jabbour, C. J. & Muller-Camen, M. 2011. State-of-the-Art and Future Directions for Green Human Resource Management, *German Journal of Human Resource Management*, 25(2):99–116.

Kalfagianni, A. 2020. *Routledge Handbook of Global Sustainability Governance*, London: Routledge.

Kim, Y. J., Kim, W. G., Choi, H. M. & Phetvaroon, K. 2019. The Effect of Green Human Resource Management on Hotel Employees' Eco-friendly Behavior and Environmental Performance, *International Journal of Hospitality Management*, (76):83–93.

Klein, N. 2014. *This Changes Everything: Capitalism Vs. the Climate*, London: Penguin.

Klikauer, T. 2014. *Seven Moralities of Human Resource Management*, Basingstoke: Palgrave (chapter on environmental ethics).

Luu, T. T. 2018. Employees' Green Recovery Performance: The Roles of Green HR Practices and Serving Culture, *Journal of Sustainable Tourism*, 26(8):1308–1324.

Machin, A. 2013. *Negotiating Climate Change*, London: Zed.

Malecki, C. 2018. *CSR Perspectives for Sustainable Corporate Governance*, Cheltenham: Edward Elgar.

Margaretha, M. & Saragih, S. R. 2012. Developing New Corporate Culture through Green Human Resource Practice (http://repository.maranatha.edu/4061/1/Developing%20New%20Corporate%20Culture.pdf, accessed: 15th July 2020).

Mariappanadar, S. 2019. *Sustainable HRM: Strategies, Practices and Challenges*, London: Red Globe Press.

Markey, R. et al. 2016. Employee Participation & Carbon Emissions Reduction, *International Journal of HRM*, 27(2):173–191.

Molthan-Hill, P. 2017. *Business Student's Guide to Sustainable Management*, Saltaire: Greenleaf Publishing.

Obaid, T. F. & Alias, R. B. 2015. The Impact of Green Recruitment, Green Training and Green Learning on the Firm Performance: Conceptual Paper, *International Journal of Applied Research*, 1(12):951–953.

Opatha, H. H. P. & Arulrajah, A. A. 2014. Green Human Resource Management: Simplified General Reflections, *International Business Research*, 7(8):101.

Paillé, P., Chen, Y., Boiral, O. & Jin, J. 2014. The Impact of Human Resource Management on Environmental Performance: An Employee-Level Study, *Journal of Business Ethics*, 121(3):451–466.

Peerzadah, S. A., Mufti, S. & Nazir, N. A. 2018. Green Human Resource Management: A Review, *International Journal of Enhanced Research in Management & Computer Applications*, 7(3):790–795.

Ramus, C. A. & Steger, U. 2000. The Roles of Supervisory Support Behaviors and Environmental Policy in Employee "Ecoinitiatives" at Leading-Edge European Companies, *Academy of Management Journal*, 43(4):605–626.

Ramus, C. A. 2002. Encouraging Innovative Environmental Actions: What Companies and Managers Must Do, *Journal of World Business*, 37(2):151–164.

Razab, M. F., Udin, Z. M. & Osman, W. N. 2015. Understanding the Role of GHRM towards Environmental Performance, *Journal of Global Business and Social Entrepreneurship*, 1(2):118–125.

Ren, S., Tang, G. & Jackson, S. E. 2018. Green Human Resource Management Research in Emergence: A Review and Future Directions, *Asia Pacific Journal of Management*, 35(3):769–803.

Renwick, D. (eds.) 2018. *Contemporary Developments in Green HRM*, London: Routledge.

Renwick, D. W., Redman, T. & Maguire, S. 2013. Green Human Resource Management: A Review and Research Agenda, *International Journal of Management Reviews*, 15(1):1–14.

Rezaee, Z. 2019. *Business Sustainability in Asia*, Hoboken, NJ: Wiley & Sons.

Robertson, J. L. & Barling, J. 2013. Greening Organizations through Leaders' Influence on Employees' Pro-environmental Behaviors, *Journal of Organizational Behavior*, 34(2):176–194.

Sathyapriya, J., Kanimozhi, R. & Adhilakshmi, V. 2013. Green HRM-Delivering High Performance HR Systems, *International Journal of Marketing and Human Resource Management*, 4(2):19–25.

Shah, M. 2019. Green Human Resource Management: Development of a Valid Measurement Scale, *Business Strategy and the Environment*, 28(5):771–785.

Shahriari, B., Hassanpoor, A., Navehebrahim, A. & Jafarinia, S. 2019. A Systematic Review of Green Human Resource1 Management, *Environmental Protection*, 6(2):177–189.

Sheopuri, A. & Sheopuri, A. 2015. Green HR Practices in the Changing Workplace, *Business Dimensions*, 2(1):13–26.

Stringer, L. 2010. *The Green Workplace: Sustainable Strategies That Benefit Employees, the Environment, and the Bottom Line*, London: St. Martin's Publishing.

Suzuki, D. & Hanington. I. 2017. *Just Cool It! The Climate Crisis and What We Can Do*, Vancouver: Greystone.

Tang, G., Chen, Y., Jiang, Y., Paille, P. & Jia, J. 2018. Green Human Resource Management Practices: Scale Development and Validity, *Asia Pacific Journal of Human Resources*, 56(1):31–55.

Tariq, S., Jan, F. A. & Ahmad, M. S. 2016. Green Employee Empowerment: A Systematic Literature Review on State-of-Art in Green Human Resource Management, *Quality & Quantity*, 50(1):237–269.

Teixeira, A. A. Jabbour, C. J. C., de Sousa Jabbour, A. B. L., Latan, H. & De Oliveira, J. H. C. 2016. Green Training and Green Supply Chain Management: Evidence from Brazilian Firms, *Journal of Cleaner Production*, (116):170–176.

Thiele, L. P. 2016. *Sustainability* (2nd ed.), Oxford: Polity Press.

Winston, A. 2015. What Business Leaders Need to Know about the Paris Climate, *Harvard Business Review*, 1st December (https://hbr.org/2015/12/what-business-leaders-need-to-know-about-the-paris-climate-conference, accessed: 15th July 2020).

Yong, J. Y., Yusliza, M. Y., Jabbour, C. J. C. & Ahmad, N. H. 2019. Exploratory Cases on the Interplay between Green Human Resource Management and Advanced Green Manufacturing in Light of the Ability-Motivation-Opportunity Theory, *Journal of Management Development*, 39(1):31–49.

Yu, W., Chavez, R., Feng, M., Wong, C.Y. & Fynes, B. 2020. Green Human Resource Management and Environmental Cooperation: An Ability-Motivation-Opportunity and Contingency Perspective, *International Journal of Production Economics*, 219:224–235.

# Glossary for Managing People in Organisations

| | |
|---|---|
| 360-degree appraisal | An employee feedback programme whereby an employee is rated by surveys distributed to his or her co-workers, customers, and managers. |
| Action learning | Action learning is a process that involves a small group working on real problems, taking action, and learning as individuals, as a team, or as an organisation. |
| Adam's equity theory | John Stacey Adams' equity theory helps explain why pay and conditions alone do not determine motivation. |
| Adventure learning | Adventure learning is defined as an approach to the design of online and hybrid education that provides employees with opportunities to explore real-world issues through authentic learning experiences within collaborative learning environments. |
| Affirmative action | Proactive policies aimed at increasing the employment opportunities of certain groups (typically, minority men and/or women of all racial groups). |
| Alienation | Alienation is the contention that in modern industrial production under capitalist conditions workers will inevitably lose control of their lives by losing control over their work. |
| Applicant | An applicant is a person who has formally applied for a specific job. |
| Apprenticeship | An apprenticeship is a system of training a new generation of practitioners of a trade or profession with on-the-job training and often some accompanying study (classroom work and reading). |
| Arbitration | Arbitration is a form of dispute resolution outside of labour courts. |
| Assessment | An assessment is a systematic method and procedure for ascertaining work-related knowledge, skills, abilities, or other characteristics of people or a group of people, or the performance of people or a group of people. |
| Assessment centres | This is a special selection centre that uses multiple methods of selection and multiple evaluators in a process that lasts between one, day or two days or several days. |

| | |
|---|---|
| Attribute methods | This type of evaluation lists traits required for the job and asks the source to rate the individual on each attribute. |
| Authority | Authority is a concept that can be used to justify and the right to exercise power given by a particular entity, for example, management. |
| Automation | Automation is defined as the technology by which a process or procedure is performed without human assistance. |
| Autonomy | The degree of independence and freedom a worker has. |
| Balanced scorecard | A strategic planning and management system that is used to tie business activities to the vision and strategy of the organisation, improve internal and external communications, and monitor performance against goals. |
| Base pay | Base pay is the initial rate of compensation an employee receives in exchange for services. It excludes extra lump sum compensation such as bonuses or overtime pay as well as benefits and pay rises. |
| Behaviour | The ways in which the employee acts in relation to the job. This includes particular activities carried out in performing the job. |
| Behavioural observation scales | BOS is a method of performance evaluation in which directly related job behaviours are put on five-point scales and the evaluator is to check on these scales how often the employee was actually observed engaging in the behaviours. |
| Behaviourally anchored rating scales | BARS is a method of performance evaluation in which behaviours directly related to the job are arranged on certain scales and job performance is rated by selecting behaviours relevant to the employee being considered. |
| Behaviourism | Behaviourism is the theory that human and animal behaviour can be explained in terms of conditioning, without appeal to thoughts or feelings, and that psychological disorders are best treated by altering behaviour patterns. |
| Benefits | An indirect reward paid by the organisation to the employee because he/she is a member of the organisation. |
| Bias | A bias is a particular tendency, trend, inclination, feeling, or opinion, especially that is preconceived or unreasoned. |
| Big Mac Index | The Big Mac Index is published by the Economist magazine as an informal way of measuring the purchasing power parity (PPP) between two currencies. It provides a test of the extent to which market exchange rates result in goods costing the same in different countries. |
| Biological hazard | Biological hazard or bio-hazard refers to an organic substance/s that pose a threat to the health of humans and other living organisms. Biological hazards include pathogenic micro-organisms, viruses, toxins (from biological sources), spores, fungi, and bio-active substances. |

| | |
|---|---|
| Blended learning | Blended learning is an education programme (formal or non-formal) that combines online digital media with traditional classroom methods. It requires the physical presence of both teacher and student, with some elements of student control over time, place, path, or pace. |
| Blue ocean strategy | Blue ocean strategy generally refers to a company's creation of a new, uncontested market space that makes competitors irrelevant and creates new consumer value, often while also decreasing costs. |
| Bonded labour | Debt bondage or bonded labour is a person's pledge of labour or services as security for the repayment for a debt or other obligation where there is no hope of actually repaying the debt. The services required to repay the debt and the services' duration may be undefined. |
| Bonus | One-time payment, usually per year to the employee as an additional income. |
| Boss-napping | Boss-napping is a form of lock-in where employees detain management in the workplace, often in protest against lay-offs and redundancies, and has especially been carried out in France. |
| Bullying | Bullying is the repeated, health-harming mistreatment, verbal abuse, or conduct which is threatening, humiliating, intimidating, or sabotage that interferes with work, or a combination of these. |
| Bureaucratic control | Bureaucratic control is the use of rules, policies, hierarchy of authority, written documentation, reward systems, and other formal mechanisms to influence employee behaviour and assess performance. |
| Burnout | Burnout is thought to result from long-term, unresolvable job stress. It is characterised by a set of symptoms that includes exhaustion resulting from work's excessive demands as well as physical symptoms such as headaches, sleeplessness, and closed thinking. |
| Capitalism | Capitalism is an economic system based upon private ownership of the means of production and their operation for profit. Characteristics central to capitalism include private property, capital accumulation, wage labour, exchange, a price system, and competitive markets. |
| Carbon footprint | Carbon footprint is the amount of carbon dioxide released into the atmosphere as a result of the activities of a particular individual, business, corporation, organisation, or community. |
| Carbon neutral business | A carbon neutral business means having a net zero carbon footprint. It refers to achieving net zero carbon emissions by balancing a measured amount of carbon released with an equivalent amount sequestered or offset, or buying enough carbon credits to make up the difference. |
| Carbon offsets | A carbon offset is a reduction in emissions of carbon dioxide or greenhouse gases made in order to compensate for or to offset an emission made elsewhere. |

| | |
|---|---|
| Career | A career is a pattern of work-related experiences that span a person's life. |
| Career management | The HRM function that plans and develops careers of employees for the benefits of employees and the organisation. |
| Career stage | A career stage is a distinct phase of a person's career including entry, establishment, advancement, maintenance, transition, and maturity stage. |
| Categorical imperative | This is philosopher Kant's improvement on the golden rule expressed, for example, in 'act as you would want all other people to act towards all other people. Act according to the maxim that you would wish all other rational people to follow, as if it were a universal law'. |
| Centralisation | Centralisation in the HR department involves concentration of HR decision-making authority within top management of the department. |
| Change management | Change management is a term used for all approaches to prepare and support individuals, teams, and organisations in making organisational change. |
| Chemical hazard | A chemical hazard is a type of occupational hazard caused by exposure to chemicals in the workplace that can cause acute or long-term detrimental health effects. |
| Chief sustainability officer | The chief sustainability officer (sometimes also known by other titles) is the corporate title of an executive position within a corporation that is in charge of the corporation's environmental programmes. |
| Class | Class is a division of a society based on social and economic status. |
| Coaching and mentoring | A training method in which a senior manager or an expert works as the coach and trains a trainee or a few trainees on the job. |
| Code of conduct | A common code of conduct, written for employees of a company, protects the business and informs the employees of the company's expectations. It is ideal for even the smallest of companies to form a document containing important information on expectations for employees. |
| Code of practice | A code of practice provides detailed information on how employees can achieve the standards required. Codes of practice do not replace laws. They can be issued to help make employees understand what you have to do. |
| Collective agreement | The collective agreement regulates the terms and conditions of employees in their workplace, their duties, and the duties of the employer. It is usually the result of a process of collective bargaining between an employer (or a number of employers) and a trade union representing workers. |
| Collective bargaining | A process in which employer's representatives/ managers and worker's representatives/ trade union meet, discuss and attempt to negotiate about working conditions and terms of employment. The purpose of collective bargaining is to reach a collective agreement. |

| | |
|---|---|
| Common law duties | In tort law, a duty of care is a legal obligation which is imposed on an individual requiring adherence to a standard of reasonable care while performing any acts that could foreseeably harm others. It is the first element that must be established to proceed with an action in negligence. |
| Compensation | Compensation is defined as the combined rewards earned by an employee in return for their labour. This includes direct financial compensation consisting of pay received in the form of wages, salaries, bonuses, and commissions provided at regular and consistent intervals. |
| Competence | Competence is the ability to apply knowledge and skills to achieve intended results. |
| Competency | An individual's capability or ability to perform a certain task, role, or job successfully. |
| Competency-based pay | Competency-based pay is a compensation system that recognises employees for the depth, breadth, and types of skills they obtain and apply in their work. Also known as skill-based or knowledge-based pay. |
| Competency-based training | Competency-based training and completion is an approach to vocational education and training that places emphasis on what a person can do in the workplace as a result of completing a training programme. |
| Competitive advantage | A condition or circumstance that puts a company in a favourable or superior business position with a relatively better market share or rate of return of investments to competitors. |
| Conciliation | Conciliation is a voluntary proceeding, where labour and management are free to agree and attempt to resolve their dispute. The process is flexible, allowing parties to define the time, structure and content of the conciliation proceedings. |
| Consequentialism | Consequentialism is the class of normative ethical theories holding that the consequences of one's conduct are the ultimate basis for any judgment about the rightness or wrongness of that conduct. |
| Constructive discharge | The process of the employer purposefully influencing the employee so that he/she leaves the organisation permanently. |
| Contingent workers | Contingent workers are people who are engaged as casual labour, flexible labour, independent contractor, independent professional, and consultant. |
| Corporate citizenship | Corporate citizenship involves the social responsibility of businesses and the extent to which they meet legal, ethical, and economic responsibilities as established by shareholders. |
| Corporate culture | Corporate culture refers to the beliefs and behaviours that determine how a company's employees and management interact and handle outside business transactions. Often, corporate culture is implied, not expressly defined, and develops organically over time from the cumulative traits of the people the company hires. |

| | |
|---|---|
| Corporate philanthropy | Corporate philanthropy is the act of a corporation or business promoting the welfare of others, generally through charitable donations of funds or time. |
| Corporate psychopath | Corporate psychopaths within organisations may be singled out for rapid promotion because of their refinement, charm, and cool decisiveness. They are also helped by their manipulative and bullying skills. They create confusion around employees (divide and rule etc.) using instrumental bullying to promote their own agenda. |
| Corporate social irresponsibility | Corporate social irresponsibility is an un-ethical framework suggesting that a business organisation has no obligations to act for the benefit of society. |
| Corporate social responsibility | Corporate social responsibility is an ethical framework and suggests that an entity, be it an organisation or individual, has an obligation to act for the benefit of society. |
| Corporate sustainability | Corporate sustainability is an approach that creates long-term stakeholder value by implementing a business strategy that considers every dimension of how a business operates in the ethical, social, environmental, cultural, and economic spheres. |
| Corporation | A corporation is a company or group of people authorised to act as a single entity (legally a person) and recognised as such in law. Early incorporated entities were established by charter (i.e. by an ad hoc act granted by a monarch or passed by a parliament or legislature). |
| Corporatism | Corporatism is the socio-political organisation of a society by major interest groups, known as corporate groups (as well as syndicates or guilds) such as agricultural, business, ethnic, labour, military, patronage, or scientific affiliations, on the basis of their common interests. |
| Cost leader strategy | A strategy in which an organisation gains a competitive advantage by providing the same services or goods as its competitors, but at a lower cost. |
| Crafting strategy | Crafting strategy captures the process of strategy development, and how strategies get made. It is essentially analytic in character. |
| Creative destruction | Creative destruction refers to the incessant product and process innovation mechanism by which new production units replace out-dated ones. It is an essential fact of capitalism. |
| Critical incidents | A managerial training method that gives training through a short description of a very important event that involves at least a problem needed to be solved. |
| Critical pedagogy | Critical pedagogy is a teaching approach inspired by critical theory and other radical philosophies, which attempts to help students question and challenge posited "domination", and assists them to undermine the beliefs and practices that are alleged to dominate. |

| | |
|---|---|
| CSR policies | Corporate social responsibility (CSR) policies encourage companies to make a positive impact on the environment and stakeholders including consumers, employees, investors, communities, and others. |
| Customer performance measurement | A customer performance measurement system (CPMS) is a CRM (customer relationship management) system used to analyse, evaluate, control, and communicate customer performance and customer strategies. |
| CV – curriculum vitae | A curriculum vitae is a written overview of a person's experience and other qualifications for a job opportunity. |
| Cyberbullying | Cyberbullying is the use of technology to bully a person or group by an individual or group with the intent to harm the other person or group. |
| Decentralisation | Decentralisation in the HR department involves distributing HR decision-making authority to managers who are at middle and first level management in the department. |
| Deep ecology | Deep ecology is an ecological and environmental philosophy promoting the inherent worth of living beings regardless of their instrumental utility to human needs, plus a radical restructuring of modern human societies in accordance with such ideas. |
| Deficient performance measures | Criterion deficiency implies that the measures used to assess job performance fail to assess one or more aspects of the criterion domain considered to be part of the conceptual criterion. For instance, deficiency would exist if a component of the job of secretary is word processing and there is no criterion measure which assesses competency in performing word-processing tasks. |
| Demotion | The appointment of an employee who is currently working in the organisation to a job that is lower than the job currently being performed by him/her. |
| Deontological theory | This theory is sometimes described as duty or obligation, or rule-based ethics, because rules bind people to their duty. Deontological ethics denotes that action is more important than the consequences. |
| Differentiation strategy | A differentiation strategy calls for creating a product or service with sufficiently distinctive attributes that sets a business apart from the competition. If the differentiation strategy works, the company may be able to charge their customers a premium for this product or service. |
| Direct applicants | A direct applicant is anyone who applies directly to a business organisation's vacancy without prompting from the organisation. |
| Disciplinary action | The term 'discipline' is used to cover any action by an employer in relation to an employee which is designed to correct the employee's behaviour – in response to a perceived misdemeanour or wrongdoing or refusal of duty by the employee. |

| | |
|---|---|
| Dismissal | The moving of an employee out of the organisation permanently on disciplinary grounds. |
| Distributive bargaining | Distributive bargaining is a competitive bargaining strategy in which one party gains only if the other party loses something. It is used as a negotiation strategy to distribute fixed resources such as money, resources, assets, etc. between both the parties. |
| Distributive fairness | Distributive fairness refers to the comparison an individual makes of his or her outcome (e.g. offered price) to another's outcome. |
| Distributive justice | Distributive justice concerns the nature of a social justice allocation of goods. A society in which inequalities in outcome do not arise would be considered a society guided by the principles of distributive justice. |
| Diversity | The collective mixture of differences and similarities that may include: individual and organisational characteristics, values, beliefs, experiences, backgrounds, preferences, and behaviours. |
| Diversity management | Diversity management is the formal or informal processes, including policies and practices developed and implemented by organisations to effectively manage diversity and to foster inclusion among all organisational stakeholders. |
| Division of labour | This element of job design refers to breaking works into their smallest parts and employing separate persons to do each part separately. |
| Divisional structure | The divisional structure is a type of organisational structure that groups each organisational function into a division. These divisions can correspond to either products or geographies. |
| Drug testing | Employers often seek the right to be able to randomly test employees in an attempt to reduce the incidence of drunkenness and drug-affected employees in the workplace as part of the occupational health and safety policy. |
| Duty of care | The duty of care is a legal obligation which is imposed on an organisation (e.g. HR management) requiring adherence to a standard of reasonable care while performing any acts that could foreseeably harm others. It is the first element that must be established to proceed with an action in negligence. |
| E-learning | E-learning is a method of education via the Internet or other computer related resources. It presents just-in-time information in a flexible learning plan. E-learning can be combined with face-to-face courses for a blended learning approach. |
| E-recruiting | E-recruitment, also known as online recruitment, is the practice of using technology and in particular Web-based resources for tasks involved with finding, attracting, assessing, interviewing, and hiring new personnel. |

| | |
|---|---|
| Electronic surveillance | Electronic surveillance is the monitoring of a business or individual using a variety of devices such as CCTV, legal wiretapping, cameras, digital video equipment, and other electronic, digital, and audio-visual means. |
| Emergency action plan | An emergency action plan is a written document required by particular OHS standards. The purpose of an EAP is to facilitate and organise employer and employee actions during workplace emergencies. |
| Emission inventory | An emissions inventory is a database that lists, by source, the amount of air pollutants discharged into the atmosphere during a year or other time period. |
| Emotional labour | Emotional labour is the process of managing feelings and expressions to fulfil the emotional requirements of a job. More specifically, workers are expected to regulate their emotions during interactions with customers, co-workers, and superiors. |
| Employability | Employability refers to your ability to gain initial employment, maintain it, and obtain new employment if required. In simple terms, employability is about being capable of getting and keeping work. Employability is having a set of skills, knowledge, understanding, and personal attributes. |
| Employee assistance programme | An employee assistance programme (EAP) is an employee benefit programme that assists employees with personal problems and/or work-related problems that may impact their job performance, health, mental, or emotional wellbeing. |
| Employee referral | An employee referral is a potential employee recommended by current employee(s) of the organisation. These recommendations can be compensated. |
| Employer brand | An employer brand is an organisation's reputation and differentiating characteristics as an employer within and outside the organisation. |
| Employer federation | Just like trade unions being represented by workers for promoting their economic and social interests, in the same manner employers join employers' organisations. An employers' organisation or association is a collective organisation of manufacturers, retailers, or other employers of wage labour. It acts in the interest of employers. |
| Employment relations | Employee relations refer to a company's efforts to manage relationships between employers and employees. An organisation with a good employee relations programme provides fair and consistent treatment to all employees so they will be committed to their jobs. |
| Enterprise bargaining | Enterprise bargaining refers to wage and working conditions being negotiated at the level of the individual organisations. Once established, they are legally binding for employers and employees. |

| | |
|---|---|
| Environmental audit | Environmental audit is a general term that can reflect various types of evaluations intended to identify environmental compliance and management system implementation gaps, along with related corrective actions. In this way, they perform an analogous (similar) function to financial audits. |
| Environmental compliance | Environmental compliance means conforming to environmental laws, regulations, standards, and other requirements such as site permits to operate. In recent years, environmental concerns have led to a significant increase in the number and scope of compliance imperatives across all global regulatory environments. |
| Environmental ethics | Environmental ethics is the part of environmental philosophy which considers extending the traditional boundaries of ethics from solely including humans to including the nonhuman world. There are many ethical decisions that human beings make with respect to the environment. |
| Equal employment opportunity | Equal employment opportunity is a government policy that requires that employers to not discriminate against employees and job applicants based upon certain characteristics, such as age, race, colour, creed, sex, religion, and disability. |
| ERG motivation | ERG is a theory in psychology that builds on Maslow's hierarchy of needs by categorising the hierarchy into ERG groups (existence, relatedness, and growth). The existence group is concerned with providing the basic material existence requirements of humans. The second group of needs is those of relatedness – the desire people have for maintaining important interpersonal relationships. Finally, growth needs are seen as an intrinsic desire for personal development. |
| Ergonomics | A job design technique that considers matching physical settings of work with physiological characteristics of the employees. |
| Ethical stewardship | Ethical stewardship is a concept that encourages fair, just, and equal treatment of employees and shareholders and a management style focused on policies that work for the good of the organisation as a whole. The concept comes up often in management, business, and other areas concerned with the experience of employees. |
| Ethics | Ethics or moral philosophy is a branch of philosophy that involves systematising, defending, and recommending concepts of right and wrong conduct. |
| Ethnocentric staffing | Ethnocentric staffing means hiring management with the same nationality as the parent company, while polycentric companies hire management employees from the host country. |

| | |
|---|---|
| Exchange value | In political economy and especially Marxian economics, exchange value refers to one of four major attributes of a commodity – an item or service produced for, and sold on a market. The exchange value of a commodity for Marx is not identical to its price but represents rather what (quantity of) other commodities it will exchange for, if traded. The other three aspects of a commodity are use value, economic value, and price. |
| Executive search | Executive search (informally called headhunting) is a specialised recruitment service which organisations pay to seek out and recruit highly qualified candidates for senior-level and executive jobs (e.g. President, Vice-president, CEO). |
| Exit interview | An interview between a member of staff of the organisation that an employee is leaving to ascertain the reasons for the employee leaving the organisation. |
| Exit, loyalty, voice | The basic concept is that members of a business organisation have essentially two possible responses when they perceive that the organisation is demonstrating a decrease in quality or benefit to the member. They can exit (withdraw) or they can voice (complaint, grievance, or proposal for change). Loyal members become especially devoted to the organisation's success when their voice will be heard and when they can help to reform it. |
| Expatriate management | It is the management of an expatriate who is an individual living in a country other than their country of citizenship, often temporarily and for work reasons. An expatriate can also be an individual who has relinquished citizenship in their home country to become a citizen of another. |
| External cost | An external cost is the expense incurred to external vendors or individuals during the course of recruiting. |
| External equity | External equity exists when employees in an organisation perceive that they are being rewarded fairly in relation to those who perform similar jobs in other organisations. External equity exists when an organisation's pay rates are at least equal to the average rates in the organisation's market or sector. |
| Externality | In economics, an externality is the cost or benefit that affects a party who did not choose to incur that cost or benefit. Economists often urge governments to adopt policies that internalise an externality, so that costs and benefits will affect mainly parties who choose to incur them. |
| Extrinsic rewards | Extrinsic rewards are usually financial. These are the tangible rewards given to employees by managers, such as pay rises, bonuses, and benefits. They are called extrinsic because they are external to the work itself and other people control their size and whether or not they are granted. |

| | |
|---|---|
| Five force analysis | Porter's five forces framework is a tool to analyse competition of a business. It draws from industrial organisation economics to derive five forces that determine the competitive intensity and, therefore, the attractiveness (or lack of it) of an industry in terms of its profitability. |
| Flat organisational structure | A flat organisation refers to an organisational structure with few or no levels of management between management and staff level employees. The flat organisation supervises employees less while promoting their increased involvement in the decision-making process. |
| Fleischman's job analysis | The Fleishman job analysis is a long established job analysis instrument that consists of seventy-three knowledge and skill scales for a variety of abilities from the cognitive, the psychomotor, and the sensory domain as well as interactive and social domains. |
| Forced distributions | A method of performance evaluation under which the evaluator is required to sort employees into different classifications (approximate grades such as best 10%, next 20%, middle 40%, next 20%, and lowest 10%). |
| Fordism | Fordism is the basis of modern economic and social systems in industrialised, standardised mass production and mass consumption. It is used in social, economic, and management theory about production, working conditions, consumption, and related phenomena, especially regarding the 20th century. |
| Forming, storming, norming, performing | The forming–storming–norming–performing model is about group development stating that these phases are all necessary and inevitable in order for a team to grow, face challenges, tackle problems, find solutions, plan work, and deliver results. |
| Functional flexibility | Functional flexibility reflects an organisation's ability to adapt to changing conditions and requirements, and is affected by issues such as training, management, and outsourcing. |
| Functional structure | A functional structure is one of the most common organisational structures. Under this structure, the organisation groups employees according to a specialised or similar set of roles or tasks. |
| Gender mainstreaming | Gender mainstreaming is the public policy concept of assessing the different implications for women and men of any planned policy action, including legislation and programmes, in all areas and levels. Mainstreaming essentially offers a pluralistic approach that values the diversity among both men and women. |
| Gender pay gap | The gender pay gap is the average difference between the remuneration for men and women who are working. There are two distinct numbers regarding the pay gap: unadjusted versus adjusted pay gap. The latter takes into account differences in hours worked, occupations chosen, as well as education and job experience. |

| | |
|---|---|
| General strike | A general strike or mass strike is a strike action in which a substantial proportion of the total labour force in a city, region, or country participates. General strikes are characterised by the participation of workers in a multitude of workplaces and tend to involve entire communities. |
| Geocentric approach | The geocentric approach is a method of international recruitment where an MNC (multinational corporation) hires the most suitable person for the job irrespective of their nationality. |
| Geographical structure | Geographic organisational structure is used for organisations that have offices or business units in different geographic locations. |
| Glass ceiling | A term used to describe the barriers – often unseen – that keep minorities and women from career advancement regardless of their qualifications. |
| Global warming | Global warming, also referred to as climate change, is the observed century-scale rise in the average temperature of the Earth's climate system and its related effects. |
| Globalisation | Globalisation is the process by which the world is becoming increasingly interconnected as a result of massively increased trade and cultural exchange. It is characterised by the interaction and integration of people, companies, and governments of different nations, driven by international trade and investment and aided by information technology. |
| Golden parachute | A golden parachute is an agreement between a company and an upper executive specifying that the employee will receive certain significant benefits if employment is terminated. |
| Greater happiness principle | Utilitarianism is based on of the greatest happiness principle which states that actions are considered moral when they promote utility and immoral when they promote the reverse. Utility itself is defined by Mill as happiness with the absence of pain. |
| Greenwashing | Greenwashing argues that Green HRM is a form of marketing spin, propaganda, and public relations (PR). |
| Grey ceiling | The grey ceiling is a business/societal phenomenon where the existing workforce of those born during the baby boom era prevents the slightly younger Generation Xers from advancing or being promoted in their jobs. |
| Grievance | Any discontent or dissatisfaction arising from a feeling or a belief of injustice felt by an employee or a group of employees in connection with the work environment. A grievance is a formal complaint that is raised by an employee towards an employer within the workplace. There are many reasons as to why a grievance can be raised, and also many ways to go about dealing with such a scenario. |

| | |
|---|---|
| Hands on method | Hands-on learning is an educational method that directly involves the learner by actively encouraging them to do something in order to learn about it. In short, it is learning by doing. First and foremost, there are certain situations in which hands-on learning is the only way to teach something. |
| Hard HRM | Hard HRM is a style of HRM in which workers are considered a resource that needs to be controlled in order to achieve the best possible profit and competitive advantage. |
| Hazards | Those aspects of the work environment which suddenly or slowly and cumulatively (and often irreversibly) lead to deteriorating health of an employee. |
| High commitment management | High-commitment management emphasises on personal responsibility, independence, and empowerment of employees across all levels instead of focusing on one higher power; it always intends to keep commitment at a high level. |
| High performance work systems | A high-performance work system is a set of management practices that attempt to create an environment within an organisation where the employee has greater involvement and responsibility. |
| Hire-cost-ratio | An HCR is a formula and methodology comparing the cost-per-hire against the total compensation of the newly hired people. |
| Hiring | The process of appointing the candidate selected to the post/job which is vacant. |
| Holo and horns | An evaluator error that occurs when an evaluator appraises an employee high or low on many or all criteria because of one criterion. |
| Honesty tests | An honesty test is an integrity test. It is a specific type of personality test designed to assess an applicant's tendency to be honest, trustworthy, and dependable. A lack of integrity is associated with such counterproductive behaviours as theft, violence, sabotage, disciplinary problems, and absenteeism. |
| HR department | A special section of an organisation established under the leadership of a manager specialised in HRM for ensuring that HRM is properly performed throughout the organisation. |
| HR information system | HRIS uses information technology that supports human resource management. It integrates compensation and benefits, payroll, recruiting, learning and development, workforce planning, analytics, performance management (ill), and others. |
| HR planning | Human resource planning is a process that identifies current and future human resources needs for an organisation to achieve its goals. Human resource planning should serve as a link between human resource management and the overall strategic plan of an organisation. |

| | |
|---|---|
| HR policies | Human resource policies are continuing guidelines on the approach an organisation intends to adopt in managing its people. A good HR policy provides generalised guidance on the approach adopted by the organisation and therefore its employees, concerning various aspects of employment. |
| HR-manager | A manager who is responsible for the human resource (HRM) function in an organisation. |
| Human resource management | The efficient and effective utilisation of human resources to achieve goals of an organisation. |
| Human resource planning | The process of determining future employee needs and deciding steps or strategies to achieve those needs for the purpose of accomplishing organisational goals and objectives. |
| Human resources development | Human resource development (HRD) is the framework for helping employees develop their personal and organisational skills, knowledge, and abilities. |
| ILO conventions | There are eight fundamental conventions (a prohibition of forced labour and child labour, the right to organise in a trade union, and suffer no discrimination etc.) which are binding upon every member country of the International Labour Organisation. |
| Imperialism | Imperialism is an action that involves a nation extending its power by the acquisition of inhabited territory. It may also include the exploitation of these territories, an action that is linked to colonialism. Both are examples of imperialism. |
| Individual incentive plan | An individual incentive plan is a category of incentive plans which focuses on individual job performance and where incentives are paid individually. |
| Induction programme | An induction programme is the process used within many businesses to welcome new employees to the company and prepare them for their new role. Induction training should include development of theoretical and practical skills, but also meet interaction needs that exist among the new employees. |
| Industrial democracy | Industrial democracy is an arrangement which involves workers making decisions, sharing responsibility, and authority in the workplace. |
| Industrial society | In sociology, industrial society refers to a society driven by the use of technology to enable mass production, supporting a large population with a high capacity for division of labour. |
| Industry wide agreement | Industry wide collective agreements are collective agreements and agreements negotiated between employees in groups (rather than as individuals) and their employer about pay and working conditions. |
| Injury management | It includes treatment of the injury, rehabilitation back to work, and management of the compensation claim. Injury management is based on the philosophy that many injured workers can safely perform productive work during their period of recovery and remaining connected to the workplace is a vital part of recovery. |

| | |
|---|---|
| Institutional power | Institutional power is the power of a government, a business or a corporation. Corporations in particular wield enormous power over our lives. They control how we spend our working day and even how we spend our leisure time. |
| Integrative bargaining | Integrative bargaining or win–win bargaining is a negotiation strategy in which parties collaborate to find a win–win solution to their dispute. This strategy focuses on developing mutually beneficial agreements based on the interests of the disputants. |
| Interest dispute | Labour disputes are classifiable into disputes on rights based on laws or agreements, and disputes on conflicting economic interests. Disputes on rights are adjudicable, with suitable quasi-judicial adjustment machinery, provided such disputes may be settled without any need for strikes or lockouts. |
| Internal cost | An internal cost is the expense related to the internal staff, capital, and organisational costs of the recruitment. |
| Internal equity | Internal equity is the comparison of positions within your business to ensure fair pay. You must pay employees fairly compared to co-workers. Employees must also perceive that they are paid fairly compared to their co-workers. |
| International HRM | IHRM can be defined as set of activities aimed at managing organisational human resources at international level to achieve organisational objectives and competitive advantage over competitors at national and international level. |
| International Labour Organisation | The International Labour Organisation (ILO) is a United Nations agency dealing with labour problems, particularly international labour standards, social protection, and work opportunities for all. The ILO has 187 member states. |
| Internet of Things | The Internet of Things is the network of physical devices, vehicles, home appliances and other items embedded with electronics, software, sensors, actuators, and connectivity which enables these objects to connect and exchange data. |
| Internet recruitment | Internet recruiting is the act of scouring the Internet to locate both actively searching job seekers and also individuals who are content in their current position (these are called "passive candidates"). |
| Interview | A face-to-face, oral, and observational evaluation method of appraising an applicant's acceptability with regard to a certain job. |
| Interview panel | An interview consisting of more than one interviewer. |
| Intrinsic motivation | Intrinsic motivation is an energising of behaviour that comes from within an individual, out of will and interest for the activity at hand. No external rewards are required to incite the intrinsically motivated person into action. The reward is the behaviour itself. |

| | |
|---|---|
| Invisible hand | The invisible hand is a term used by Adam Smith to describe the unintended social benefits of individual self-interested actions. |
| IQ-tests | An intelligence quotient (IQ) is a total score derived from several standardised tests designed to assess human intelligence. |
| Job analysis | A systematic investigation of jobs and job holder characteristics in order to create a collection of information that can be used to perform various HRM functions. |
| Job boards | An online location that provides an up-to-date listing of current job vacancies in various industries. Applicants are able to apply for employment through the job board itself. |
| Job description | A document that describes duties and responsibilities, working conditions, and other aspects of a particular job. |
| Job design | The function of arranging tasks, duties, and responsibilities into an organisational unit of work for the purpose of accomplishing the primary goal and objectives of the organisation. |
| Job enlargement | To increase the scope of a job by including a new related duty or duties in addition to the current duties. Horizontal loading is an alternative term. |
| Job enrichment | To increase the depth of a job by expanding authority and responsibility for planning and controlling the job. |
| Job evaluation | A systematic process of determining the relative worth of jobs which are available within an organisation. |
| Job satisfaction | The extent of enjoyment an employee feels towards his/her job. |
| Job sharing | A part-time employment arrangement whereby two or more part-time employees share one full-time job. |
| Job specification | A document that specifies the key qualifications an individual needs to perform a particular job. The job specification is a statement of the essential components of a job class including a summary of the work to be performed, primary duties and responsibilities, and the minimum qualifications and requirements necessary to perform the essential functions of the job. |
| Job-ranking methods | A job evaluation method under which jobs are ranked from the most important to the least important according to the degree of relative contributions given by each job to achieve the organisational success. |
| Joint consultation | A method of worker and trade union participation in which management and workers/unions get together to discuss problems of concern to both and, where appropriate, make decisions acceptable to both parties. |
| Justice as fairness | "Justice as Fairness: Political Not Metaphysical" is an essay by John Rawls, published in 1985. In it, he describes his conception of justice. It comprises two main principles of liberty and equality. |

| | |
|---|---|
| Kantian ethics | Kant's theory is an example of a deontological moral theory – according to these theories, the rightness or wrongness of actions does not depend on their consequences but on whether they fulfil our duty. Kant believed that there was a supreme principle of morality, and he referred to it as The Categorical Imperative. |
| Karoshi | Karōshi which can be translated literally as "overwork death" is occupational sudden mortality. The major medical causes of karōshi deaths are heart attack and stroke due to work stress. This phenomenon is widespread in Japan, South Korea, and China. |
| Key performance indicators | KPIs are tasks that are central to the success of a business and show, when measured, whether the business is advancing toward its strategic goals. |
| Knowledge creation | Knowledge creation according to Nonaka's SECI model is about continuous transfer, combination, and conversion of the different types of knowledge as users practice, interact, and learn. |
| Knowledge economy | The production and services based on knowledge-intensive activities that contribute to an accelerated pace of technical and scientific advance as well as rapid obsolescence. The key component of a knowledge economy is a greater reliance on intellectual capabilities than on physical inputs or natural resources. |
| Knowledge management | Knowledge management (KM) is the process of creating, sharing, using, and managing the knowledge and information of an organisation. It refers to a multidisciplinary approach to achieving organisational objectives by making the best use of knowledge. |
| Knowledge worker | Knowledge workers are workers whose main capital is knowledge. Examples include software engineers, physicians, pharmacists, architects, engineers, scientists, design thinkers, public accountants, lawyers, and academics, and any other white-collar workers whose line of work requires one to "think for a living". |
| Labour contract | An employment contract or contract of employment is a kind of contract used in labour law to attribute rights and responsibilities between parties to a bargain. The contract is between an "employee" and an "employer". It has arisen out of the old master-servant law, used before the 20th century. Generally, the contract of employment denotes a relationship of economic dependence and social subordination. |
| Labour demand | In economics, the labour demand of an employer is the number of labour hours that the employer is willing to hire based on the various exogenous (externally determined) variables it is faced with, such as the wage rate, the unit cost of capital, the market-determined selling price of its output, etc. |

Labour law — Labour law (also known as employment law) mediates the relationship between workers, employing entities, trade unions, and the government. Collective labour law relates to the tripartite relationship between employee, employer, and union. Individual labour law concerns employees' rights at work and through the contract for work. Employment standards are social norms (in some cases also technical standards) for the minimum socially acceptable conditions under which employees or contractors are allowed to work.

Labour market — A geographical region (local, regional, national, or international) in which labour transactions occur and employers find workers and workers find work.

Labour process theory — Labour process theory is particularly concerned with the social relations of production, and issues of workplace conflict, control, and regulation.

Labour relations — Labour relations involve all dealings between workers/unions and managers in an organisation. This can also involve the state when the three labour relations actors meet – trade unions, employers, and the state.

Labour supply — Human resources planning uses forecasts about product and service demand and insights about internal labour fluctuations to measure the appropriate supply of labour for a firm's operations. Labour supply, on the other hand, comes from internal movements as much as external factors.

Learning — The process of acquiring knowledge, skills, and attitudes so as to create a relatively permanent change in learner's behaviour.

LGBT — LGBT (or GLBT) stands for lesbian, gay, bisexual, and transgender. In use since the 1990s, the term is an adaptation of LGB that was used to replace the term gay in reference to LGBT communities.

Lifelong learning — Lifelong learning is the on-going, voluntary, and self-motivated pursuit of knowledge for either personal or professional reasons. It enhances social inclusion, active citizenship, personal development, self-sustainability, and competitiveness and employability.

Line manager — Manager who manages a line department which makes or distributes the organisation's goods or services.

Macho management — It is an aggressive management style characterised by very little consultation with employees, a distrust of and hostility towards trade unions, an emphasis on unitarism, and the assertion of the management prerogative.

Management — A process that deals with efficient and effective utilisation of resources in order to achieve goals of an organisation.

Management by fear — The term management by fear refers to managers operating with fear. Managers treat their employees badly and keep them in line with unnecessary rules, policies and punishments so that workers are in a constant state of fear.

| | |
|---|---|
| Management by objective | A process of defining objectives within an organisation so that management and employees agree on the overall goals and objectives for the organisation. |
| Marginal performance | When employees' performance deteriorates, they often perform at the marginal level for a time before dropping to unacceptable levels. Catching and addressing poor performance before it becomes unacceptable is an easier and more effective way of dealing with performance problems. |
| Mass production | Mass production is the manufacture of large quantities of standardised products, frequently using assembly line or automation technology. Mass production refers to the production of a large number of similar products efficiently. |
| McDonaldisation | McDonaldisation becomes manifested when a society adopts the characteristics of the fast-food restaurant (e.g. efficiency, calculability, standardisation, and control). McDonaldisation is a reconceptualisation of rationalisation and scientific management. |
| McJobs | McJob is slang for a low-paying, low-prestige dead-end job that require few skills and offer very little chance of intra-company advancement. |
| Mentor | Mentorship is a relationship in which a more experienced or more knowledgeable person helps to guide a less experienced or less knowledgeable person. The mentor may be older or younger than the person being mentored, but he or she must have a certain area of expertise. |
| Mergers and acquisitions | Mergers and acquisitions (M&A) is a general term that refers to the consolidation of companies or assets. M&A can include a number of different transactions, such as mergers, acquisitions, consolidations, tender offers, purchase of assets, and management acquisitions. In all cases, two companies are involved. |
| Merit pay | Performance-related pay which provides bonuses or base pay increases for workers who perform their jobs effectively, according to measurable criteria. |
| Middle class | The middle class is a class of people in the middle of a social hierarchy. In socio-economic terms, the middle class is the broad group of people in contemporary society who fall socio-economically between the working class and upper class. |
| Minimum wage | The lowest amount an employer can pay an hourly employee. This rate is set by a government. |
| Mission statements | A description of an organisation's purpose: what it does, what markets it serves and what direction it is going in. |
| Mobbing | Mobbing, as a sociological term, means bullying of an individual by a group, in any context, such as a family, peer group, school, workplace, neighbourhood, community, or online. |

| | |
|---|---|
| Mono-chronic people | Monochronic people and cultures like to do just one thing at a time. They value a certain orderliness and sense of there being an appropriate time and place for everything. They do not value interruptions. Polychronic people and cultures like to do multiple things at the same time. |
| Morality | Morality can be a body of standards or principles derived from a code of conduct from a particular philosophy, religion or culture, or it can derive from a standard that a person believes should be universal. Morality may also be specifically synonymous with goodness or rightness. |
| Multi-divisional company | In a multidivisional structure, there is one parent company that consists of a number of different divisions operating separate businesses. Legally, the parent company owns all of the divisions, but it gives these divisions significant autonomy, which allows them to act independently. |
| Natural Justice | Natural justice is technical terminology for the rule against bias and the right to a fair hearing. The term natural justice is often retained as a general concept. |
| Needs analysis | A systematic attempt to identify training needs at the level of the organisation. |
| Negotiation | Bargaining between two or more parties with the goal of reaching consensus or resolving a problem. |
| Non-governmental organisations (NGOs) | NGOs are private and not-for-profit organisations and they represent stakeholder perspectives and they play an important role to act as a counterweight to business and global capitalism. |
| No-harm principle | The no-harm principle states that a person can do whatever he wants as long as his actions do not harm others, and if they do harm others, society is able to prevent those actions. |
| Numerical flexibility | Numerical flexibility is the ability of a firm to adjust the quantity of labour to meet fluctuations in demand. Functional flexibility is the ability to deploy employees to the best effect. |
| Occupational health and safety | Occupational health and safety (OHS), occupational health, or workplace health and safety (WHS), is a multidisciplinary field concerned with the safety, health, and welfare of people at work. |
| Off-shoring | The act of moving work to an overseas location to take advantage of lower labour costs. Offshoring usually occurs in areas of manufacturing, information technology, and back-office services like call centres and bill processing. Companies can build their own work centres abroad, establish a foreign division, or create a subsidiary in remote locations. |
| Office romance | An office romances is a romantic relationship between two people employed by the same employer. |
| OHS | All the activities involved in protecting and promoting physical and mental health of the employees. |

| | |
|---|---|
| OHS management system | An occupational health and safety management system (OHSMS) is a coordinated and systematic approach to managing health and safety risks. OHSMSs help organisations to continually improve their safety performance and compliance to health and safety legislation and standards. |
| On-the-job training | A training method under which training is given by allowing the trainee to perform duties of the job. An alternative term is job instruction training. |
| Operations management | Operations management is an area of management concerned with designing and controlling the process of production and redesigning business operations in the production of goods or services. |
| Organisational behaviour manipulation | Organisational behaviour manipulation is a type of social influence that aims to change the behaviour and perceptions of workers through abusive, deceptive, or underhanded tactics. By advancing the interests of the manipulator, often at another's expense, such methods could be considered exploitative, abusive, devious, and deceptive. |
| Organisational chart | An organisational chart (often called organisation chart, org chart, organigram, or organogram) is a diagram that shows the structure of an organisation and the relationships and relative ranks of its parts and positions/jobs. |
| Organisational design | Organisational design is a step-by-step methodology which identifies dysfunctional aspects of work flow, procedures, structures and systems, realigns them to fit current business realities/goals and then develops plans to implement the new changes. |
| Organisational development | Organisational development is a planned, systematic approach to improving organisational effectiveness – one that aligns strategy, people, and processes. To achieve the desired goals of high performance and competitive advantage, organisations are often required to undergo significant change. |
| Organisational justice | Organisational justice refers to employee perceptions of fairness in the workplace. These perceptions can be classified into four categories: distributive, procedural, informational, and interactional. |
| Organisational psychologist | Organisational psychologists work with people and organisations. They are experts in areas such as leadership and talent management, recruitment, performance management, occupational health and safety, change management, and career development. |
| Organisational stress | Organisational stress is the psychological strain or distress resulting from exposure to unusual or demanding situations, known as stressors. Occupational stress, specifically, is the response to organisational stressors in the workplace environment that pose a perceived threat to an individual's wellbeing or safety. |

| | |
|---|---|
| Outsource | To outsource is to make an arrangement where an external organisation performs part of an organization's function or process. |
| Outsourcing | Contracting out non-core functions, such as payroll, benefits administration or manufacturing, to save money and focus on what the company does best. |
| Paired comparison | A method of performance evaluation under which the employees are evaluated in pairs taking an employee at a time and completing him/her against every other. |
| Pay | Major payment given by the employer to an employee for the contribution or service rendered by that employee. It may be called wage or salary. |
| Pay grades | A pay grade is a unit in systems of monetary compensation for employment. Pay grades facilitate the employment process by providing a fixed framework of salary ranges, as opposed to a free negotiation. |
| Pay structure | A pay scale (also known as a salary structure) is a system that determines how much an employee is to be paid as a wage or salary, based on one or more factors such as the employee's level, rank or status within the employer's organisation, the length of time that the employee has been employed, and the difficulty of the specific work performed. |
| Perceptual-motor technique | A job design technique that considers matching requirements (tasks and duties) of the job with mental abilities and characteristics of the employees. |
| Performance | A performance is a measurable result. Performance can relate either to quantitative or qualitative findings. |
| Performance appraisal | A periodic review and evaluation of an individual's job performance. |
| Performance coaching | Performance coaching is a process where one person facilitates the development and action planning of another, in order that the individual can bring about changes in their lives. Performance Coaching is not advice-giving and does not involve the coach sharing their experience or opinions. |
| Performance fairness | The extent to which clear information of results of the employee's efficiency and effectiveness is provided. |
| Performance feedback | Performance feedback is the ongoing process between employee and manager where information is exchanged concerning the performance expected and the performance exhibited. Constructive feedback can praise good performance or correct poor performance and should always be tied to the performance standards. |

| | |
|---|---|
| Performance improvement plan | A performance improvement plan is a tool that employers can use to help underperforming employees succeed in the organisation. The plan allows them to specify the company's expectations with respect to employee performance and behaviour and to define what success looks like going forward. |
| Performance-related pay | Performance-related pay or pay for performance, not to be confused with performance-related pay rise, is a salary or wage system based on positioning the individual, or team, on their pay band according to how well they perform. |
| Personality test | Personality testing refers to techniques that are used to accurately and consistently measure personality. Personality is something that we informally assess and describe every day. When we talk about ourselves and others, we frequently refer to different characteristics of an individual's personality. |
| Philosophy | Philosophy is the love of wisdom. It is the study of general and fundamental problems concerning matters such as existence, knowledge, values, reason, mind, and language. |
| Physical hazards | A physical hazard is an agent, factor, or circumstance that can cause harm with or without contact. They can be classified as types of occupational hazard or environmental hazard. Physical hazards include ergonomic hazards, radiation, heat and cold stress, vibration hazards, and noise hazards. |
| Piece work | Piece work (or piecework) is any type of employment in which a worker is paid a fixed piece rate for each unit produced or action performed regardless of time. |
| Poly-chronic people | Traditionally, people and cultures are divided into mono-chronic (where time is regarded as linear, people do one thing at a time and lateness and interruptions are not tolerated) and poly-chronic (where time is seen as cyclical, punctuality is unimportant and interruptions are acceptable). |
| Positioning school | The positioning school of thought considers the strategies that are generic in nature and have positions which are identifiable in the market place. The positioning school strategies are based on the result of calculations done by the analysts who are monitoring the market with respect to the goal of the organisation. |
| Positive OHS culture | A positive OHS culture of an organisation is the product of individual and group values, attitudes, perceptions, competencies, and patterns of behaviour that determine the commitment to, and the style and proficiency of, an organisation's health and safety management. |
| Positive reinforcement | In operant conditioning, positive reinforcement involves the addition of a reinforcing stimulus following a behaviour that makes it more likely that the behaviour will occur again in the future. When a favourable outcome, event, or reward occurs after an action, that particular response or behaviour will be strengthened. |

| | |
|---|---|
| Power | Power is the ability to influence or outright control the behaviour of people. |
| Power asymmetry | Power asymmetry is characterised by an imbalance in power between two parties (employer and employee). It is a state in which differences in status exist between individuals and groups of individuals within an organisational hierarchy and these differences result in differential ability to take action or cause action to be taken. |
| Precariat | The precariat is a social class formed by people suffering from precarity, which is a condition of existence without predictability or security, affecting material or psychological welfare. The term is a portmanteau obtained by merging precarious with proletariat. |
| Principled negotiations | Principled negotiation is an interest-based approach to negotiation that focuses primarily on conflict management and conflict resolution. Principled negotiation uses an integrative approach to finding a mutually shared outcome. |
| Probationary period | A specified period of time during which a new employee who was hired for a permanent post works for an organisation. During this period, the new employee will have to prove that he/she is capable of performing the job successfully in order to maintain employment. |
| Procedural fairness | Procedural fairness is concerned with the procedures used by a decision-maker, rather than the actual outcome reached. It requires a fair and proper procedure to be used when making a decision. A decision-maker who follows a fair procedure is more likely to reach a fair and correct decision. |
| Procedural justice | Procedural justice is the idea of fairness in the processes that resolve disputes and allocate resources. One aspect of procedural justice is related to discussions of the administration of justice and legal proceedings. |
| Profession | A profession is a disciplined group of individuals that positions itself as possessing special knowledge and skills in a widely recognised body of learning derived from research, education, and training at a high level, and is recognised by the public as such. |
| Project teams | A project team is a team whose members usually belong to different groups, functions, and are assigned to activities for the same project. A team can be divided into sub-teams according to need. Usually project teams are only used for a defined period of time and are disbanded after the project is deemed complete. |
| Promotion | The advancement of an employee in an organisation to a job that is higher/more advanced than the job being currently performed by him/her. |
| Psycho-terror | The concept of psycho-terror provides a bridge that enables the investigation of common causes and mutually furthering moments in workplace bullying and violence. |

| | |
|---|---|
| Psychological contract | Psychological contracts are a set of promises or expectations that are exchanged between the parties in an employment relationship. These parties include employers, managers, individual employees and their work colleagues. |
| Psychological hazard | A psychological hazard is any hazard that affects the mental wellbeing or mental health of a worker by overwhelming individual coping mechanisms and impacting the worker's ability to work in a healthy and safe manner. |
| Psychometric testing | Psychometric testing is a standard and scientific method used to measure individuals' mental capabilities and behavioural styles. Psychometric tests are designed to measure a candidates' suitability for a role based on the required personality characteristics and aptitude (or cognitive abilities). |
| Quality of working life | Quality of work life (QWL) refers to the favourableness or unfavourableness of a job environment for the people working in an organisation. |
| Recruiting events | Hosting a recruitment event is a valuable opportunity to grow your talent pool and make a lasting impression as an employer. |
| Recruitment | The process of finding and attracting suitably qualified people to apply for employment. |
| Recruitment agency | An employment or recruitment agency is a company that provides a service to both employers and job seekers. They place job seekers into specific jobs on a permanent basis. |
| Reference checking | A reference check is when an employer contacts a job applicant's previous employers, schools, colleges, and other sources to learn more about his or her employment history, educational background, and qualifications for a job. |
| Referrals | Employee referral is an internal recruitment method employed by organisations to identify potential candidates from their existing employees' social networks. |
| Regiocentric approach | The regiocentric approach is an international recruitment method wherein the managers are selected from different countries within the geographic region of business. |
| Relationship recruitment | Relationship recruiting is a strategy that involves capturing the ideal people for an organisation (whether they are employed or unemployed) and continually engaging them until the right position opens up at the company. |
| Relative rating system | A rater employing an absolute system describes a ratee without making direct reference to other ratees, usually in terms of a point on a rating scale. In a relative rating system, on the other hand, rating is carried out in terms of comparisons among a group of ratees. |
| Repetitive strain injury | RSI (or repetitive strain injury) is a descriptive term for an overuse injury. Occupational overuse syndrome (OOS) is another name used to describe RSI. Repeated use of the same movements causes inflammation and damage to the soft tissues (muscles, nerves, tendons and tendon sheaths, etc.). |

| | |
|---|---|
| Retention rate | A retention rate is ratio of the total workforce that is retained over a defined period. |
| Retirement | A form of employee separation that involves leaving an employee from the organisation after he/she has reached the age at which a pension can be obtained. |
| Return to work plan | A rehabilitation (or return to work) programme is based on the principle that an employer can allow a coordinated return to work. The programme is delivered according to medical advice and, where necessary, through the use of a rehabilitation provider. |
| Reward | A generic term to include wages and salaries, incentives, and welfare facilities and benefits. Compensation and remuneration are two alternative terms. |
| Reward fairness | Perceived fairness of employee rewards (or the lack thereof) is often at the root of why employees leave organisations. |
| Reward structures | Reward management consists of analysing and controlling employee remuneration, compensation, and all other benefits for employees. |
| Reward system | A reward system refers to programmes set up by a company to reward performance and motivate employees on individual and/or group levels. They are normally considered separate from salary but may be monetary in nature or otherwise incur a cost to the company. |
| Right to manage | Management's right to manage is the ideology of having a natural right that allows employers to manage their employees. The manager's right to manage is the legitimation in capitalism, or other industrial societies, of the disciplinary powers that managers claim. |
| Rights dispute | Labour disputes are classifiable into disputes on rights based on laws or agreements, and disputes on conflicting economic interests. Disputes on rights are adjudicable, with suitable quasi-judicial adjustment machinery, provided such disputes may be settled without any need for strikes or lockouts. |
| Risk assessment | Risk assessment is the determination of a quantitative or qualitative estimate of risk related to a well-defined situation and a recognised threat (also called hazard). |
| Robotics | Robotics is an interdisciplinary branch of engineering and science that includes mechanical engineering, electrical engineering, computer science, and others. |
| Rule compliance | Many rules are already in place in the form of HR policies, contracts, procedures, regulations, laws, etc. Rule compliance seeks conformity with existing policy, contracts, and laws. |
| Rule deviance | Rule deviance describes an action or behaviour that violates organisational norms, including formally enacted rules, as well as informal violations of organisational norms (e.g. rejecting managerial policies). |

| | |
|---|---|
| Rules | Official instructions in respect of what employees must and are allowed to do and what they are not allowed to do. |
| Ruling elites | The ruling class is the social class of a given society that decides upon and sets that society's political agenda. It argues that the ruling class differs from the power elite. The latter simply refers to the small group of people with the most political power. |
| Selection | The process of making the choice of the most appropriate person from the pool of job applicants recruited to fill the relevant job vacancy. |
| Self-managed teams | A self-organised, semiautonomous small group of employees whose members determine, plan, and manage their day-to-day activities and duties under reduced or no supervision. Also called self-directed team or self-managed natural work team. |
| Self-rating | Self-rating or assessment is a process of clarifying a person's own value through discovering the relationship between various occupations and his/her personality type and work style, interests, career values, and skills. |
| Seniority | The length of time an employee has served for the organisation. |
| Service industry | The service industries involve the provision of services to businesses as well as final consumers. Such services include accounting, tradesmanship (like mechanic or plumber services), computer services, restaurants, tourism, etc. |
| Sexting | Sexting is sending, receiving, or forwarding sexually explicit messages, photographs, or images, primarily between mobile phones. |
| Sexual harassment | Sexual harassment is any unwanted or unwelcome sexual behaviour, which makes a person feel offended, humiliated, or intimidated. |
| Shallow ecology | Shallow ecology describes the viewpoint that ecologies should be preserved only if it is in our direct interest to do so. |
| Shareholder value | Shareholder value is a business term, sometimes phrased as shareholder value maximisation or as the shareholder value model, which implies that the ultimate measure of a company's success is the extent to which it enriches shareholders. |
| Simple control | Simple control takes the form of personal relations between the entrepreneur and a small group of employees. |
| Simulations | A training simulation is a virtual medium through which various types of skills can be acquired. They are most commonly used in corporate situations to improve business awareness and management skills. |
| Situational factors | Situational factors influencing customers are external factors usually outside of the control of marketers, manufacturers, and, sometimes even retailers. In general, the situation affects how consumers encounter and interact with a product, informing their opinion at that moment in time. |

| | |
|---|---|
| Skill-based pay | Skill-based pay is a salary system that determines an employee's pay based on his or her knowledge, experience, education, or specialised training. |
| Slavery | Slavery is any system in which principles of property law are applied to people, allowing individuals to own, buy and sell other individuals, as a de jure form of property. A slave is unable to withdraw unilaterally from such an arrangement and works without remuneration. |
| Social mobility | Social mobility is defined as the movement of individuals, families, households, or other categories of people within or between layers or tiers in an open system of social stratification. |
| Soft HRM | Soft human resources management is an employee management system in which workers are considered an important resource for a company's growth, they are looked after, and their skills are developed. |
| Staffing | Staffing is a process of acquiring, deploying, and retaining people – both internal and external. |
| Stakeholders | Stakeholders can affect or be affected by the organisation's actions, objectives, and policies. Some examples of key stakeholders are creditors, directors, employees, government (and its agencies), owners (shareholders), suppliers, unions, and the community from which the business draws its resources. |
| Statutory rights | Statutory rights are an individual's legal rights, given to him or her by the local and national ruling government. These are generally designed to protect citizens. They are typically enforced by local law enforcement, and their violation usually carries a penalty of legal prosecution and punishment. |
| Statutory welfare | Welfare services to be given by the organisation according to legal requirements imposed by a government. |
| Strategic congruence | The integration of multiple goals, either within an organisation or between multiple groups. Congruence is a result of the alignment of goals to achieve an overarching mission. |
| Strategic HRM (SHRM) | Formulation and implementation of HR systems which generate appropriate competencies, appropriate behaviours and appropriate results of employees at all levels so that the organisation will be able to achieve vision, mission, and strategic goals. |
| Strategic HRP | SHRP is a process that identifies future human resource needs for an organisation to achieve its goals. It links HRP to the overall strategic plan of an organisation. |
| Strategic management | A systematic process of defining an organisation's long-term vision, mission, and objectives, and determining a strategy for achieving its vision, mission, and objectives. |
| Strategic recruitment | A strategic recruitment approach requires adopting staffing strategies in response to changes in the internal, external, or global environment. |

| | |
|---|---|
| Strategy | The organisation's long-term plan (strategic plan) for how it will match its internal strengths and weaknesses with its external opportunities and threats to achieve, maintain or enhance a competitive advantage. |
| Strategy metrics | Statistics used to measure the degree of success of accomplishment of the strategic goals and objectives of HRM. |
| Strikes | Strike action, also called labour strike or simply strike, is a work stoppage caused by the mass refusal of employees to work. |
| Structural change | A structural change is a shift or change in the basic ways a market or economy functions or operates. Such change can be caused by factors such as economic development, global shifts in capital and labour, changes in resource availability due to war or natural disaster or discovery or depletion of natural resources, or a change in the political system. |
| Structural violence | Structural violence refers to a form of violence wherein some social structure or social institution may harm people by preventing them from meeting their basic needs. |
| Structure follows strategy | Structure follows strategy means that a corporate structure is created in order to implement a given corporate strategy. |
| Structured interview | An interview that includes a predetermined set of questions that is addressed to each applicant. |
| Succession plan | A succession plan is a process for identifying and developing current employees with the potential to fill key positions in the organisation. |
| Succession planning | Succession planning is a process for identifying and developing new leaders who can replace old leaders when they leave, retire, or die. Succession planning increases the availability of experienced and capable employees that are prepared to assume these roles as they become available. |
| Surplus labour | Surplus labour means labour performed in excess of the labour necessary to produce the means of livelihood of the worker (necessary labour). The "surplus" in this context means the additional labour a worker has to do in his/her job, beyond earning his own keep. |
| Sustainability | Sustainability can be defined as the ability to maintain healthy environmental, social, and economic systems in balance, indefinitely, on a local and global scale. |
| Sustainable employability | Sustainable employability is the long-term capability to acquire or create and maintain work. |
| Sweatshop | Sweatshop is a pejorative term for a workplace that has very poor, socially unacceptable working conditions. Workers in sweatshops may work long hours with low pay, regardless of laws mandating overtime pay or a minimum wage; child labour laws may also be violated. |

| | |
|---|---|
| SWOT analysis | SWOT analysis is a strategic planning technique used to help an organisation identify the strengths, weaknesses, opportunities, and threats related to competition. |
| Symbolic analytical jobs | Symbolic-analytical workers identify and solve problems. They are strategic brokering people and typically compete on an international level for positions. They work in computer-mediated communication. |
| Termination | The complete end of service of an employee by the employer. |
| Theory X and theory Y | Theory X explains the importance of heightened supervision, external rewards, and penalties. Theory Y highlights the motivating role of job satisfaction and encourages workers to approach tasks without direct supervision. |
| Total compensation | Total compensation includes all direct or indirect compensation received within a specific time period. This can be salary, bonuses, perquisites, benefits, stock options, insurance, and others. |
| Trade union | A formal organisation of employees established with the primary purpose of protecting and enhancing the wellbeing of its members. |
| Training | The formal process of changing employee behaviour and motivation in the way that will enhance employee job performance and the organisational overall performance. |
| Trait appraisal instruments | A trait is a characteristic that an individual possesses. Traits include things such as appearance, attitude, initiative, work ethic, leadership ability, a sense of ethics, loyalty, adaptability, and judgment. Supervisors in the trait-focused system rate employees by indicating specific traits each employee exhibits. |
| Transferability | The ability of an employee to be moved within the same job/class/grade. Moving may be from one job to another job, from one place to another place, from one time to another time, or from office to field or vice versa. |
| Tripartism | Tripartism is economic corporatism based on tripartite contracts of business, labour, and state. Tripartite agreements are an important component in practical labour law. |
| Triple bottom line | Triple bottom line, TBL or 3BL is an accounting framework with three parts: social, environmental (or ecological) and financial. Some organisations have adopted the TBL framework to evaluate their performance in a broader perspective to create greater business value |
| Turnover | The number of employees lost and gained over a given time period. |
| Turnover rate | A turnover rate is the ratio of separations set against the total workforce during a defined period. |
| Unfair dismissal | Firing an employee in a way that the courts do not find justifiable (i.e. unfairly or in violation of the employment contract). |

| | |
|---|---|
| Unit labour costs | Unit labour costs measure the average cost of labour per unit of output and are calculated as the ratio of total labour costs to real output. In broad terms, unit labour costs show how much output an economy receives relative to wages, or labour cost per unit of output. |
| Use-value | The usefulness of a commodity vs. the exchange equivalent by which the commodity is compared to other objects on the market. It distinguishes between the use-value and the exchange value of the commodity. |
| Utilitarianism | Utilitarianism is an ethical theory that states that the best action is the one that maximises utility. Utility is defined in various ways, usually in terms of the wellbeing of sentient entities. |
| Virtue ethics | Virtue ethics are normative ethical theories that emphasise virtues of mind and character. Virtue ethicists discuss the nature and definition of virtues and other related problems. |
| Vocational training | Vocational education is education that prepares people to work in various jobs, such as a trade, a craft, or as a technician. Vocational education is sometimes referred to as career education or technical education. |
| Vroom's expectancy theory | Vroom's expectancy theory assumes that behaviour results from conscious choices among alternatives whose purpose it is to maximise pleasure and minimise pain. Vroom realised that an employee's performance is based on individual factors such as personality, skills, knowledge, experience, and abilities. |
| Wage claim | An employee or former employee may file an individual wage claim to recover unpaid wages including overtime, commissions, and bonuses or wages paid by cheque issued with insufficient funds. |
| Wage compression | Wage compression refers to the empirical regularity that firms, given their wage policies, prefer better workers over poorer workers for any given job. This causes them to offer higher wages to new workers than those that are given to existing workers. |
| Wage negotiations | Salary negotiation is a process where one party (usually the employee) negotiates the amount of their pay, income, earnings, commission, salary, wages, wage remuneration, annual review, or salary raise with another party (usually a representative of the employer, such as their manager). |
| Wage theft | Wage theft is the denial of wages or employee benefits that are rightfully owed to an employee. Wage theft can be conducted through various means such as: failure to pay overtime, minimum wage violations, employee misclassification, illegal deductions in pay, working off the clock, or not being paid at all. |
| Wellness programmes | These are programmes offered by an employer that are designed to promote health or prevent disease. |

| | |
|---|---|
| Whistle blowing | An employee who publicly reveals a perceived wrongdoing, misconduct or unethical activity within an organisation to the public or to those in positions of authority. |
| Work intensification | Work intensification is defined as more workload for each worker, and work extensification as less dead-time or work rest and more overtime. |
| Work life balance | The attempt to balance work and personal life in order to have a better quality of life. A person with a balanced life is considered an asset to a business as he or she experiences greater fulfilment at work and at home. |
| Work samples | Work samples are intended to provide employers with condensed examples of an employee's best work. They function both independently of each other and as a set, similar to a series of art prints. |
| Work stress | What an employee experiences internally in response to an event, a situation or a thing he/she finds difficult to deal with. It is the pressure or strain an employee feels in his work life. |
| Workers cooperative | A workers cooperative is a type of cooperative where the members are the employees of the business. Accordingly, a workers cooperative is a business entity that is owned and controlled by the people who work in it. It is important in such cooperatives that all workers own the business together (not just some). |
| Workforce productivity | Workforce productivity is a measurement of the productivity of the workforce. It includes quality and quantity |
| Workplace | A workplace is an area(s) in which the worker's activities are carried out. |
| Workplace hazard | Every workplace has hazards. A workplace hazard is anything that has the potential to cause harm to a person. |
| Workplace surveillance | There may be circumstances when the employer deems it necessary to conduct covert or overt surveillance to obtain evidence of dishonest behaviour by members of the workforce. |
| Wrongful dismissal | Wrongful dismissal, wrongful termination, or wrongful discharge is a situation in which an employee's contract of employment has been terminated by the employer but where the termination breaches one or more terms of the contract of employment, or a statute provision or rule in employment law. |
| Zero-sum bargaining | In this type of bargaining, the parties view the negotiations as a zero-sum game. If one person wins, the other loses. In other words, a gain by the employer is a loss to the employees and vice versa. |

# Index

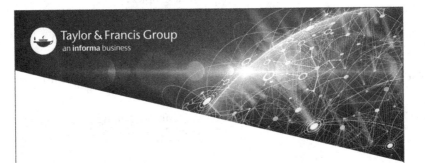